STRENGTHENING INTERNATIONAL FISHERIES LAW IN AN ERA OF CHANGING OCEANS

This collection addresses the central question of how the current international framework for the regulation of fisheries may be strengthened in order to meet the challenges posed by changing fisheries and ocean conditions, in particular climate change. International fisheries law has developed significantly since the 1990s, through the adoption and establishment of international instruments and bodies at the global and regional levels. Global fish stocks nevertheless remain in a troubling state, and fisheries management authorities face a wide array of internal and external challenges, including operational constraints, providing effective management advice in the face of scientific uncertainty and non-compliance by States with their international obligations. This book examines these challenges and identifies options and pathways to strengthen international fisheries law. While it has a primarily legal focus, it also features significant contributions from specialists drawn from other disciplines, notably fisheries science, economics, policy and international relations, in order to provide a fuller context to the legal, policy and management issues raised. Rigorous and comprehensive in scope, this will be essential reading for lawyers and nonlawyers interested in international fisheries regulation in the context of profoundly changing ocean conditions.

Strengthening International Fisheries Law in an Era of Changing Oceans

Edited by
Richard Caddell
and
Erik J Molenaar

•HART•
OXFORD • LONDON • NEW YORK • NEW DELHI • SYDNEY

HART PUBLISHING

Bloomsbury Publishing Plc

Kemp House, Chawley Park, Cumnor Hill, Oxford, OX2 9PH, UK

HART PUBLISHING, the Hart/Stag logo, BLOOMSBURY and the Diana logo are
trademarks of Bloomsbury Publishing Plc

First published in Great Britain 2019

Reprinted 2019

A catalogue record for this book is available from the British Library.

Library of Congress Cataloging-in-Publication data

Names: Caddell, Richard, editor. | Molenaar, Erik Jaap, editor.

Title: Strengthening international fisheries law in an era of changing oceans /
edited by Richard Caddell, Erik J Molenaar.

Description: Oxford, UK ; Portland, Oregon : Hart Publishing, 2019. | Includes bibliographical
references and index.

Identifiers: LCCN 2018052063 (print) | LCCN 2018056239 (ebook) |
ISBN 9781509923359 (EPub) | ISBN 9781509923342 (hardback)

Subjects: LCSH: Fishery management, International—Law and legislation. |
BISAC: LAW / International. | LAW / Environmental.

Classification: LCC K3895 (ebook) | LCC K3895 .S77 2019 (print) | DDC 343.07/6922—dc23

LC record available at https://lccn.loc.gov/2018052063

ISBN: HB: 978-1-50992-334-2
        ePDF: 978-1-50992-336-6
        ePub: 978-1-50992-335-9

Typeset by Compuscript Ltd, Shannon
Printed and bound in Great Britain by CPI Group (UK) Ltd, Croydon CR0 4YY

To find out more about our authors and books visit www.hartpublishing.co.uk.
Here you will find extracts, author information, details of forthcoming events
and the option to sign up for our newsletters.

Preface

THIS BOOK IS the outcome of an interdisciplinary project on the theme of strengthening international fisheries law in the context of changing fisheries and ocean conditions. The project was led by the Netherlands Institute for the Law of the Sea (NILOS) and the Utrecht Centre for Water, Oceans and Sustainability Law (UCWOSL) of Utrecht University, and was developed in the context of our involvement in the Nereus Program "Predicting Future Oceans"[1] and the project "Allocation, Participation and the Ecosystem Approach in Polar Fisheries", funded by the Netherlands Polar Programme administered by the Netherlands Organization for Scientific Research (NWO).[2]

The book features an array of contributions from specialists on aspects of international fisheries and their management, comprising a blend of senior and emerging researchers. While it has a primarily legal focus, it also features significant contributions from specialists drawn from other disciplines, notably fisheries science, economics, policy and international relations, in order to provide a fuller context to the legal, policy and management issues raised.

The book is divided into five Parts. Part I provides an introduction to the achievements, limitations and challenges of international fisheries law by the editors. Parts II-IV cover the three substantive themes of the book, namely "Identifying Future Regulatory Challenges: Science, Law and Management", "The Ecosystem Approach to Fisheries Management" and "Compliance and Enforcement". These three overarching themes canvas the main challenges and shortcomings of the domain of international fisheries law at present and in the foreseeable future.

Part II opens with Chapter 2: "Modelling Future Oceans: The Present and Emerging Future of Fish Stocks and Fisheries", (William WL Cheung, Vicky WY Lam, Yoshitaka Ota and Wilf Swartz) a multidisciplinary contribution providing an overview of the current state of affairs in global fisheries from noted specialists in fisheries science, fisheries economics and fisheries policy. This is followed by Chapter 3 – entitled "Alternative Histories and Futures of International Fisheries Law" (Richard Barnes) – which provides a more theoretical perspective upon the regulatory trajectory of international fisheries law, using the technique of counterfactual reconsideration of the broad trends and regulatory context for the regulation of fisheries. Chapter 4 – entitled "Management Options for High Seas Fisheries: Making Regime Complexes More Effective"

---

[1] For information see nereusprogram.org/.
[2] For information see www.nwo.nl/en/research-and-results/programmes/Netherlands+Polar+Programme.

(Olav Schram Stokke) – brings a political science perspective to the development of international commitments and the resilience of regional institutions.

The remaining two chapters in Part II focus on the regional element of international fisheries law, which is of paramount importance to the implementation and application of the global component. Chapter 5 – entitled "Key Challenges relating to the Governance of Regional Fisheries" (James Harrison) – provides an overview of the main challenges confronting regional fisheries governance, with particular attention to the international community's preferred vehicles in this regard, namely regional fisheries management organizations (RFMOs). One of these key challenges is further considered by Chapter 6 – entitled "Participation in Regional Fisheries Management Organizations" (Erik J Molenaar).

As is clarified in Part III, the ecosystem approach to fisheries management remains a fundamental guiding principle in international fisheries law, but has long remained a rather nebulous concept. To this end, this Part seeks to articulate the substantive elements of this principle and to evaluate how, and to what extent, they have been implemented in current practices. Chapter 7 – entitled "International Fisheries Law and Interactions with Global Regimes and Processes" (Richard Caddell) – considers the impact of other global regimes and processes upon the development of standards for international fisheries, including the current negotiations towards an international legally-binding instrument for the conservation and sustainable use of biodiversity in areas beyond national jurisdiction. Chapter 8 – entitled "Bycatch Mitigation and the Protection of Associated Species" (Karen N Scott) – advances an overview of the current international framework for the regulation of incidental catches of associated species, an issue that remains one of most troublesome aspects of improving fisheries governance. On an allied theme, Chapter 9 – entitled "Area-Based Fisheries Management" (Daniel C Dunn, Guillermo Ortuño Crespo and Richard Caddell) – focuses on fisheries closures, marine protected areas and other location-based tools in improving the ecological footprint of fisheries. Improving this footprint is also the focus of Chapter 10 – entitled "Environmental Assessment and International Fisheries Law" (Simon Marsden) – which considers the array of assessment-related tools and their prospective application to fisheries development. Part III concludes with Chapter 11 – entitled "Addressing Climate Change Impacts in Regional Fisheries Management Organizations" (Rosemary Rayfuse) – which examines the extent to which international fisheries law has responded to climate change and the emergence of mitigation and adaptation strategies.

Part IV considers the vexed issues of compliance and enforcement, which continue to dominate discourses on the further development of international fisheries law. It opens with Chapter 12 – entitled "An International Relations Perspective on Compliance and Enforcement" (Áslaug Ásgeirsdóttir) – which considers, *inter alia*, the factors that inhibit and promote international cooperation in this respect. This is complemented by Chapter 13 – entitled "Problems and Progress in Combating IUU Fishing" (Eva R van der Marel) – which provides an overview of the international community's response to illegal, unreported and unregulated (IUU) fishing so far, and offers a more in-depth analysis of the contribution of the European Union (EU) in this regard. Subsequently, Chapter 14 – entitled "International Trade Law Aspects of Measures to Combat IUU and Unsustainable Fishing" (Robin Churchill) – explores the interaction between the domains of international fisheries law and international trade law.

Chapters 15–17 deal with distinct actors in compliance and enforcement. Chapter 15 – entitled "Strengthening Flag State Performance in Compliance and Enforcement" (Natalie Klein) – considers the efforts of the international community to enhance the performance of the primary actor in high seas fisheries. In view of the persistent substandard performance of flag States in marine capture fisheries, however, the latter chapters explore alternative means of promoting compliance with these obligations. Chapter 16 – entitled "Ensuring Compliance with Fisheries Regulations by Private Actors" (Carmino Massarella) – examines the increasing role of private military contractors and environmental activists in enforcement activities. Meanwhile Chapter 17 – entitled "Emerging Regulatory Responses to IUU Fishing" (Richard Caddell, George Leloudas and Bariş Soyer) – explores the potential responsibility of those providing commercial and other services to fishing vessels and the prospective role of transnational criminal law in bolstering the response to fisheries infractions.

Finally, in Chapter 18 the editors draw together the lessons learned from the preceding contributions and identify options and pathways to strengthen international fisheries law in an era of changing oceans.

After extensive preparations and consultations with contributing authors, the project led to the convening of a workshop on 7–8 February 2017 at Utrecht University. At this workshop, authors presented the draft manuscripts that they had submitted beforehand, and designated commentators, the editors and other participants provided comments. The authors then finalized their manuscripts based on the discussions and comments at the workshop, and multiple rounds of review by the editors. In keeping with the obligations of cooperation promoted in many key instruments of international fisheries law, this volume thus represents a truly collaborative effort to re-examine fundamental issues in the regulation of fisheries resources.

The individual chapters of this volume do not specify the last date of access of websites. Links have been checked by the authors and are current as of 1 August 2018.

This project would not have been possible without financial support from the Nereus Program "Predicting Future Oceans" – funded by the Nippon Foundation – and the Netherlands Polar Programme, administered by the Netherlands Organization for Scientific Research (NWO) in the context of the project "Allocation, Participation and the Ecosystem Approach in Polar Fisheries". Moreover, we are deeply grateful for the support and assistance of our colleagues in convening the workshop and, especially, to our families during the editing and preparation of this volume. Richard Caddell is particularly appreciative of his wife Sasha, for facilitating and supporting his period of residence as a Senior Nereus Fellow at Utrecht University, where this project was substantively conducted.

Finally, our appreciation goes to Anne-Rose Stolk for her valuable editorial assistance, and to Sinéad Moloney, Savannah Rado and the team at Hart Publishing for their efforts towards the publication of this volume.

Richard Caddell
Erik J Molenaar
Cardiff and Utrecht, 1 August 2018

Table of Contents

PART IV
COMPLIANCE AND ENFORCEMENT

PART V
OPTIONS AND PATHWAYS TO STRENGTHEN INTERNATIONAL
FISHERIES LAW IN AN ERA OF CHANGING OCEANS

List of Contributors

Áslaug Ásgeirsdóttir is a Professor of Politics at Bates College in Lewiston, Maine. Her research focuses on cooperation and conflict among States around resource-sharing and the settlement of boundaries in the world's oceans. She is the author of *Who Gets What? Domestic Influences on International Negotiations Allocating Shared Resources*, published by SUNY Press in 2008. In addition, her work has appeared in the *Journal of Conflict Resolution*, *Global Environmental Politics*, *The Review of International Organizations* and *Marine Policy*. Her current research focuses on various aspects of ocean governance, including marine spatial planning, emerging negotiations on biodiversity in areas beyond national jurisdiction, and the use of dispute settlement mechanisms in the law of the sea. Full cv available at www.bates.edu/politics/faculty/aslaug-asgeirsdottir/.

Richard Barnes is Professor of Law and Associate Dean for Research in the Faculty of Business, Law and Politics at the University of Hull. He has published widely on law of the sea matters. He authored *Property Rights and Natural Resources* (2009) (winner of the SLS Prize for Outstanding Legal Scholarship) and his edited books include: *The United Nations Convention on the Law of the Sea: A Living Instrument* (with Barrett, 2016); *Beyond Responsibility to Protect* (with Tzevelekos, 2016); and *Law of the Sea: Progress and Prospects* (with Freestone and Ong, 2006). Recent publications include: "Environmental Rights in Marine Spaces" in Bogojevic and Rayfuse (eds.) *Environmental Rights in Europe and Beyond* (2018) and several contributions to Proelss (ed.) *The United Nations Convention on the Law of the Sea. A Commentary* (2017). He has advised a range of organizations, including the WWF, the European Parliament and Defra. His current research is focused on new governance mechanisms for fisheries in areas beyond national jurisdiction, and the legal implications of Brexit for marine fisheries, a topic on which he has been called as an expert witness before several UK Parliamentary committees.

Richard Caddell is a Lecturer in Law at Cardiff University, where he teaches a number of courses in Maritime Law and is Convenor of the LLM Programme in Shipping Law. Between 2014 and 2017 he was Senior Research Associate and the Nippon Foundation Senior Nereus Fellow in International Fisheries Law at the Netherlands Institute for the Law of the Sea, Utrecht University. He was educated at Cardiff University, completing his Ph.D. in 2009 on the international regulation of cetaceans. His primary research interests lie in the law of the sea, international environmental law and human rights, with a particular emphasis

on biodiversity conservation, marine environmental regulation, fisheries governance, energy law and polar law. He is the editor (with Rhidian Thomas) of
Shipping, Law and the Environment in the Twenty-First Century (2013). He
regularly acts as a legal advisor to national governments, intergovernmental
bodies and NGOs on environmental and marine issues and is an academic
member of Francis Taylor Building, the UK's foremost Planning and Environment Law set of barristers. He is also an Associate Editor of the *Review of
European, Comparative and International Environmental Law*, and serves on
the editorial boards of the *Journal of International Wildlife Law and Policy* and
Communications Law. Full biography available at www.cardiff.ac.uk/people/
view/478838-caddell-richard.

William Cheung is Associate Professor in the Institute for the Oceans and Fisheries at the University of British Columbia, and Director (Science) of the Nippon
Foundation-UBC Nereus Program. He is an internationally recognized expert
in the effects of climate change on marine ecosystems and fisheries, and is a
lead author for the *Fifth Assessment of the Intergovernmental Panel on Climate
Change* (IPCC) and coordinating lead author for the *IPCC Special Report on
the Ocean and Cryosphere in the Changing Climate*. He has published over
100 peer-reviewed articles, many in impactful journals such as *Nature, Science*
and *PNAS*, and is the 2017 laureate of the Prix'd Excellence Award of the
International Council for the Exploration of the Seas for his contributions to
marine sciences.

Robin Churchill is Emeritus Professor at the University of Dundee, UK, having
been Professor of International Law there from 2006 until his retirement in
2016. Before moving to Dundee, he was Professor of International Law at the
University of Cardiff. During his academic career he taught a variety of international law topics, including human rights, law of the sea and trade law, as
well as EU law. His main research interests are international environmental law,
human rights and law of the sea, on all of which he has published to a significant degree. He is the author (with Daniel Owen) of *The EC Common Fisheries
Policy* (Oxford University Press, 2010) and of a number of book chapters and
journal articles on international fisheries law. He has also acted as a consultant
on fisheries issues to the European Parliament, a number of governments and
various fisher organizations.

Daniel C Dunn is an Assistant Research Professor with the Marine Geospatial Ecology Lab in the Nicholas School of the Environment at Duke University.
As an interdisciplinary marine geospatial ecologist, his research focuses on
applying ecological theory to develop applied solutions to natural resource
management and conservation problems through area-based management
across a range of scales. He has authored over 35 peer-reviewed publications in
journals such as *Science*, the *Proceeding of the National Academy of Sciences*
and *Science Advances*. His work has been pivotal in developing the concept of

Dynamic Ocean Management and understanding the status, need and potential for conservation of areas beyond national jurisdiction. He co-chairs the Biology & Ecosystems Panel of the Global Ocean Observing System (GOOS), and sits on the Science Board of the Global Ocean Biodiversity Initiative (GOBI) and the Global Ocean Refuge System (GLORES). He also engages with the Convention on Biological Diversity's Ecologically or Biologically Significant Areas (EBSAs) process, the International Seabed Authority's efforts to develop regional environmental management plans and negotiations over a new international legally binding instrument for the conservation and sustainable use of biodiversity beyond national jurisdiction at the UN.

James Harrison has been a member of staff at Edinburgh Law School since 2007. He is now a senior lecturer in international law and he teaches and researches on a wide range of international law topics, specializing in international law of the sea, international environmental law and international dispute settlement. He has written broadly on these subjects, including two monographs: *Making the Law of the Sea: A Study in the Development of International Law*, published by Cambridge University Press in 2011, and *Saving the Oceans through Law: The International Legal Framework for the Protection of the Marine Environment*, published by Oxford University Press in 2017. Alongside his academic work, he has carried out a number of consultancies for governments, intergovernmental organizations and non-governmental organizations, as well as being involved in delivering lectures and training for the International Foundation for the Law of the Sea, the United Nations Division for Ocean Affairs and the Law of the Sea and the International Tribunal for the Law of the Sea. He was also legal assistant for the Government of Japan in the *Case concerning Whaling in the Antarctic* and legal advisor to the Government of São Tomé and Principé in the *Duzgit Integrity Arbitration*. Full biography available at www.law.ed.ac.uk/people/jamesharrison.

Natalie Klein is a Professor at UNSW Sydney's Faculty of Law, Australia. She was previously at Macquarie University where she served as Dean of Macquarie Law School between 2011 and 2017, as well as Acting Head of the Department for Policing, Intelligence and Counter-Terrorism at Macquarie in 2013–2014. Professor Klein teaches and researches in different areas of international law, with a focus on law of the sea and international dispute settlement. She has been a Visiting Fellow at the Lauterpacht Centre for International Law at Cambridge University and MacCormick Fellow at the University of Edinburgh. Professor Klein provides advice, undertakes consultancies and interacts with the media on law of the sea issues. Prior to joining Macquarie, Professor Klein worked in the international litigation and arbitration practice of Debevoise & Plimpton LLP, served as counsel to the Government of Eritrea (1998–2002) and was a consultant in the Office of Legal Affairs at the United Nations. Her masters and doctorate in law were earned at Yale Law School and she is a Fellow of the Australian Academy of Law.

Vicky WY Lam is a Fisheries Economist and Program Manager at the Nereus Program at the University of British Columbia (UBC) in Canada. She dedicates herself to a broad range of fisheries related researches. One of her research interests is to focus on understanding the socio-economic impacts of global change on marine resources, fisheries and human wellbeing. She has studied economic impacts of climate change on global fisheries in terms of change in economic variables; and the socio-economic implication of the impacts of projected climate change and ocean acidification on marine resources in some regions, which are highly vulnerable to the change in climate, such as West Africa and the Arctic region. She is experienced in studying the vulnerability and adaptation of coastal countries, communities and fishers to global change. She is interested in understanding the spatial dynamics of fishing effort and how the change in fishers' behaviour would affect the harvest under climate change by using a modelling approach. She has also studied and analyzed the potential policies and measures for mitigating and adapting to these global changes. Full publication list available at https://scholar.google.ca/citations?user=PRymv7YA AAAJ&hl=en.

George Leloudas is an Associate Professor at the Institute of International Shipping and Trade Law (IISTL) of Swansea University, which he joined in 2011. He is a graduate of the National and Kapodistrian University of Athens. He holds LLM degrees in Commercial Law from the University of Bristol (2002) and in Air and Space Law from the Institute of Air and Space Law of McGill University (Montreal, 2003). He also completed his Ph.D. degree in air law at Trinity Hall, Cambridge University in 2009. He has most recently published his second monograph together with Professor Malcolm Clarke of Cambridge University on air cargo insurance. Also, in 2018 he published (with Professor Baris Soyer) an article on the carriage of passengers by sea in *Michigan State University International Law Review* and an article on IUU fishing (with Professor Barış Soyer and Dr Dana Miller) in *Transnational Environmental Law*. He is also one of the editors of the preeminent air law publication, *Shawcross and Beaumont*, being responsible for the liability chapters of the publication. Full cv available at www.swansea.ac.uk/staff/law/georgeleloudas/.

Simon Marsden is a Professor and Chair in Energy Law at the University of Stirling, Scotland, appointed in 2016. He is also an Adjunct Professor at Flinders University in South Australia, his employer from 2010 to 2016. He specializes in environmental assessment and environmental law. His Ph.D., "Legislative Environmental Assessment: An Evaluation of Procedure and Context with Reference to Canada and the Netherlands" (1999, University of Tasmania), included researching as a visiting graduate student at the Institute for Resources and Environment, University of British Columbia (1997). He has since worked in both academia (University of Exeter, University of South Australia, and the Chinese University of Hong Kong – CUHK), and in legal practice (Environment Agency of England and Wales). At CUHK he was most recently a Senior Fellow at the Institute of Environment, Energy and Sustainability (2014–2015). He is the author or editor of seven books, including on strategic environmental assessment, transboundary environmental governance and environmental regimes, with a focus on Europe, Asia and the Poles. He has had over 100 other publications, which have also focused on protected areas, public participation and compliance.

Carmino Massarella is a solicitor (England and Wales) and lecturer in Law at the University of Hull in the UK, a position he has held since 2014. His Ph.D. was on the topic "Jurisdiction over Maritime Piracy in International Law". Since then his research has continued to focus on topics relating to the law of the sea, in particular, piracy, maritime security and issues related to jurisdiction and regulation at sea.

Eva R van der Marel started as a doctoral candidate at the KG Jebsen Centre for the Law of the Sea (JCLOS) at UiT The Arctic University of Norway at the end of 2014. Her research focuses on the role of unilateral market measures that aim to ensure legal and sustainable fishing abroad, with a focus on EU IUU. Eva holds an LLB (English and French law) from the University of Exeter (UK), a Maitrise in European law from the Université de Rennes 1 (France) and an LLM in Environmental Law and Policy from University College London (UK). In the two years before embarking on her Ph.D., she worked as a research assistant on the Carbon Capture Legal Programme at University College London and on the "Beyond 2020" EU renewable energy sources project at the University of Oxford (UK).

Erik J Molenaar has been with the Netherlands Institute for the Law of the Sea (NILOS) at Utrecht University since 1994 and currently holds the position of Deputy Director. In 2006, he was also employed by UiT The Arctic University of Norway – in Tromsø – where he is at present a Professor with the KG Jebsen Centre for the Law of the Sea (JCLOS). After having completed his Ph.D. on "Coastal State Jurisdiction over Vessel-Source Pollution" (1998), he broadened his research field with international fisheries law and the international law relating to the Antarctic and Arctic. He has a large number of publications (~90) – as author or editor – ; has participated in various diplomatic conferences and other intergovernmental meetings – including the annual meetings of several regional fisheries management organizations – on various delegations; and has been involved in international litigation as well as a large number of consultancies. Since late 2013 his research has had a specific focus on participation, allocation and the ecosystem approach to polar fisheries. Full cv available at www.uu.nl/staff/EJMolenaar.

Guillermo Ortuño Crespo is based at Duke University, where he is completing his Ph.D. at the Marine Geospatial Ecology Lab (MGEL). He is also a fellow with the Nippon Foundation Nereus Program. His background is in Marine Biology (B.A.) and Ecosystem-based Management of Marine Systems (M.Sc.)

from Rollins College and the University of St. Andrews, respectively. His current research intersects the spatial ecology of pelagic species and fisheries management, where he explores the use of predictive models of fishing efforts and species distribution to inform pelagic fisheries area-based management. He has also been engaged in the ongoing negotiations at the United Nations to draft a new international legally binding instrument on the conservation and sustainable use of marine biodiversity of areas beyond national jurisdiction under the UN Convention on the Law of the Sea. His contributions through MGEL have centred around the topics of transboundary ecological connectivity, dynamic oceanic systems and the impacts of fisheries on open-ocean ecosystems. As the negotiations proceed, he is interested in further exploring how the impacts of fishing on biological diversity in the high seas will be discussed and the role that area-based management can play.

Yoshitaka Ota is a social anthropologist, specializing in indigenous fisheries and global ocean governance, coastal management and research communication. He is a Research Assistant Professor for the School of Marine and Environmental Affairs at the University of Washington. He completed his B.Sc. (1995), M.Sc. (1998) and Ph.D. (2006) in Anthropology at the University College London. Since 2011, he has been Director (Policy) at the Nereus Program, an interdisciplinary ocean research initiative between the non-profit Nippon Foundation and the University of British Columbia. He led a study in 2016 on global seafood consumption by coastal indigenous peoples, which involved building a database of more than 1,900 indigenous communities and finding that coastal indigenous peoples consume nearly four times more seafood per capita than the global average.

Rosemary Rayfuse is Scientia Professor in International Law at UNSW Sydney, Australia. Since 2011 she has been a Conjoint Professor in the Faculty of Law, Lund University, Sweden and from 2014–2017 she was a Visiting Professor in Oceans Law and Governance at the University of Gothenburg. Prior to joining UNSW Sydney she was a Research Fellow at the Lauterpacht Research Centre for International Law and practiced law in Vancouver, Canada. Her research deals with public international law in general and the law of the sea in particular, focusing on issues of oceans governance, high seas fisheries, protection of the marine environment in areas beyond national jurisdiction and the normative effects of climate change on international law. She is the author or editor of 14 books and more than 300 other publications in these and other areas of international law including state responsibility, the law of treaties, international humanitarian law, use of force, international crimes and international dispute settlement. She is on the editorial or advisory boards of a number of international law journals, is a member of the IUCN Commission on Environmental Law, and Chair's Nominee on the International Law Association's Committee on International Law and Sea-Level Rise. Full cv available at www.law.unsw.edu.au/profile/rosemary-rayfuse.

Karen N Scott is a Professor of Law at the University of Canterbury in New Zealand, having previously been at the University of Nottingham in the UK. She was the Head of the School of Law between 2015 and 2018, Vice-President of the Australian and New Zealand Society of International Law (ANZSIL) from 2011–2016 and the General Editor of the *New Zealand Yearbook of International Law* from 2009 to 2012. She researches and teaches in the areas of public international law, law of the sea and international environmental law. Recent and current projects include the modern tools of ocean management including marine protected areas and spatial and integrated planning, geoengineering and the law, environmental treaties and treaty law and law in the polar regions. Full cv available at www.canterbury.ac.nz/business-and-law/contact-us/people/karen-scott.html.

Barış Soyer has been with the Institute of International Shipping and Trade Law (IISTL) at Swansea University since 2001 and currently holds the position of Director. He is a Visiting Professor in several universities including Lorraine University (France), Dalian Maritime University (PR China) and Shanghai Maritime University (PR China). He is the author of *Warranties in Marine Insurance* published by Cavendish Publishing (2001) and *Marine Insurance Fraud* published by Informa Law (2014). He has also published extensively in elite law journals such as *Lloyd's Maritime and Commercial Law Quarterly, Journal of Business Law, Cambridge Law Journal, Law Quarterly Review, Torts Law Journal* and *Journal of Contract Law*. His book on Marine Warranties was the joint winner of the Cavendish Book Prize 2001 and was awarded the British Insurance Law Association Charitable Trust Book Prize in 2002, for the best contribution to insurance literature. A third edition of this book was published in 2016. Similarly, his new book on *Marine Insurance Fraud* was awarded the same BILA Prize in 2015. He is an on the editorial board of *Shipping and Trade Law* and the *Journal of International Maritime Law*. Full cv available at www.swansea. ac.uk/staff/law/barissoyer/.

Olav Schram Stokke is a Professor of Political Science at the University of Oslo, the Director of the University's cross-disciplinary Bachelor Program on International Relations, and a Research Professor at the Fridtjof Nansen Institute (FNI), where he also served as Research Director for many years. Previous affiliations include the Centre for Advanced Study (CAS) at the Norwegian Academy of Science and Letters and the International Institute of Applied Systems Analysis (IIASA). His area of expertise is international relations with special emphasis on institutional analysis, resource and environmental management, and regional cooperation in the polar regions. Among his recent books are *Disaggregating International Regimes: A New Approach to Evaluation and Comparison* (MIT Press, 2012), *Managing Institutional Complexity: Regime Interplay and Global Environmental Change* (MIT Press 2011) and *International Cooperation and Arctic Governance* (Routledge 2007, pb. 2010, Chinese version by Ocean Press of China 2014). He publishes in leading international journals, including *Annals* *of the American Academy for Political and Social Science, Cooperation and Conflict, Global Environmental Politics, International Environmental Agreements, International Journal, Journal of Business Research, Marine Policy, Ocean and Coastal Management, Ocean Development and International Law* and *Strategic Analysis.*

Wilf Swartz is a resource economist at the University of British Columbia (Vancouver, Canada) and the Nippon Foundation Nereus Program. In 2011, he was a Research Officer at the World Trade Organization (Geneva, Switzerland) and from 2016 to 2018, he was the Director of Environmental Policies at the Ocean Policy Research Institute, Sasakawa Peace Foundation (Tokyo, Japan). After completing his Ph.D., which examined the role of international trade and subsidies in global fisheries, his recent work has focused on seafood supply chains, including the roles of private governance mechanisms such as market-based sustainability certification programs and corporate social responsibility policies of the large seafood firms.

List of Abbreviations[1]

ABMT	Area-Based Management Tools
ABNJ	Areas Beyond National Jurisdiction
AIS	Automatic Identification Systems
APEI	Area of Particular Environmental Interest
BBNJ	Biodiversity Beyond National Jurisdiction
BPA	Benthic Protected Area
CBS	Central Bering Sea
CCAMLR	Commission on the Conservation of Antarctic Marine Living Resources
CCSBT	Commission for the Conservation of Southern Bluefin Tuna
CDS	Catch Documentation Schemes
CFP	Common Fisheries Policy
CIA	Cumulative Impact Assessment
CMM	Conservation and Management Measures
CNM	Cooperating Non-Members
COFI	Committee on Fisheries
COLTO	Coalition of Legal Toothfish Operators
COP	Conference of the Parties
DML	Dolphin Mortality Limit
DSU	Dispute Settlement Understanding
EA	Environmental Assessment
EAF	Ecosystem Approach to Fisheries
EBSA	Ecologically or Biologically Significant Area
ECtHR	European Court of Human Rights

---

[1] This List does not include abbreviations used in relation to treaties, which are included in the Table of Treaties.

EEZ	Exclusive Economic Zone
EIA	Environmental Impact Assessment
EMP	Environmental Management Plan
EPO	Eastern Pacific Ocean
ETP	Eastern Tropical Pacific
EU	European Union
FAD	Fish Aggregation Devices
FAO	United Nations Food and Agriculture Organization
FFA	South Pacific Forum Fisheries Agency
FRA	Fisheries Restricted Area
GFCM	General Fisheries Commission for the Mediterranean
Global Record	Global Record of Fishing Vessels, Refrigerated Transport Vessels and Supply Vessels
HSI	Humane Society International
IATTC	Inter-American Tropical Tuna Commission
ICCAT	International Commission on the Conservation of Atlantic Tunas
ICES	International Council for the Exploration of the Sea
ICG	Intersessional Correspondence Group
ICJ	International Court of Justice
ICSP	Informal Consultations of the States Parties to the Fish Stocks Agreement
IGO	Intergovernmental Organization
ILBI	International Legally Binding Instrument
ILC	International Law Commission
ILO	International Labour Organization
IMO	International Maritime Organization
IOTC	Indian Ocean Tuna Commission
IPCC	Intergovernmental Panel on Climate Change
IPOA	International Plans of Action

IPOA-IUU	International Plan of Action on IUU fishing
ISA	International Seabed Authority
ISSF	International Seafood Sustainability Foundation
ITLOS	International Tribunal for the Law of the Sea
IUU	Illegal, Unreported and Unregulated fishing
IWC	International Whaling Commission
JNRFC	Joint Norwegian-Russian Fisheries Commission
LCA	Life Cycle Assessment
MEA	Multilateral Environmental Agreement
MINSA	Mackerel Industry Northern Sustainability Alliance
MGR	Marine Genetic Resources
MOP	Meeting of the Parties
MOU	Memorandum of Understanding
MPA	Marine Protected Area
MSC	Marine Stewardship Council
MSC system	Monitoring, Control and Surveillance system
MSP	Marine Spatial Planning
MSY	Maximum Sustainable Yield
NAFO	Northwest Atlantic Fisheries Organization
NASCO	North Atlantic Salmon Conservation Organisation
NEAFC	North-East Atlantic Fisheries Commission
NGO	Non-Governmental Organization
NPFC	North Pacific Fisheries Commission
OBIS	Ocean Biogeographic Information System
OECD	Organization for Economic Co-operation and Development
OECS	Organisation of Eastern Caribbean States
OSPAR Commission	Commission for the Protection of the Marine Environment of the North-East Atlantic
OUV	Outstanding Universal Value

P&I Club	Protection and Indemnity Club
PMSC	Private Maritime Security Company
PrepCom	Preparatory Committee
PSC	Pacific Salmon Commission
PSSA	Particularly Sensitive Sea Area
PTA	Preferential Trade Agreement
REIO	Regional Economic Integration Organization
RFB	Regional Fisheries Body
RFMO/As	Regional Fisheries Management Organizations or Arrangements
RSRMPA	Ross Sea region marine protected area
SAI	Significant Adverse Impact
SASS	Special Area for Scientific Study
SBSTTA	Subsidiary Body for Scientific, Technical, and Technological Advice
SBT	Southern Bluefin Tuna
SCRS	Standing Committee on Research and Statistics
SEA	Strategic Environmental Assessment
SEAFO	South-East Atlantic Fisheries Organization
SIA	Social Impact Assessment
SIDS	Pacific Small Island Developing Nations
SIODFA	Southern Indian Ocean Deep-Sea Fisheries Association
SIOF	Southern Indian Ocean Fisheries
SPAMI	Specially Protected Areas of Mediterranean Importance
SPLOS	Meeting of States Parties to the LOS Convention
SPREP	South Pacific Regional Environment Programme
SPRFMO	South Pacific Regional Fisheries Management Organization
SRFC	Sub-Regional Fisheries Commission
TAC	Total Allowable Catch

TDS	Trade Documentation/Information Schemes
TED	Turtle Excluder Devices
UK	United Kingdom
UN	United Nations
UNCED	UN Conference on Environment and Development
UNCLOS III	Third United Nations Conference on the Law of the Sea
UNECE	United Nations Economic Commission for Europe
UNEP	United Nations Environment Programme
UNESCO	United Nations Educational, Scientific and Cultural Organization
UNGA	United Nations General Assembly
UNICPOLOS	United Nations Open-Ended Informal Consultative Process on Oceans and the Law of the Sea
UNODC	United Nations Office on Drugs and Crime
UNSG	United Nations Secretary General
US	United States
UVI	Unique Vessel Identifier
VME	Vulnerable Marine Ecosystems
VMS	Vessel Monitoring Systems
WCPFC	Western and Central Pacific Fisheries Commission
WECAFC	Western Central Atlantic Fishery Commission
WTO	World Trade Organization

Table of Treaties

Part I

Introduction

1

International Fisheries Law: Achievements, Limitations and Challenges

ERIK J MOLENAAR AND RICHARD CADDELL

1. INTRODUCTION

I NTERNATIONAL FISHERIES LAW is the domain (or: 'rule-complex') of international law that relates specifically to the conservation, management and/or development of marine capture fisheries. It consists of substantive norms (e.g. rights, obligations and objectives), substantive fisheries standards (e.g. catch restrictions) as well as institutional rules and arrangements (e.g. mandates and decision-making procedures). International fisheries law is part of public international law and can also be seen as a branch or part of the domain of the international law of the sea. The origins of international fisheries law can be traced back to the end of the 19th century, when North Sea coastal States adopted multilateral rules on fisheries enforcement at sea, and the United States unsuccessfully asserted coastal State jurisdiction for the purpose of the conservation of fur seals in high seas areas adjacent to its territorial sea.[1]

The cornerstone in the current global jurisdictional framework for marine capture fisheries is provided by the LOS Convention,[2] which divides seas and oceans in maritime zones and specifies the basic rights and obligations of States therein. The LOS Convention regulates the exercise of entitlements to fishing that States have in their capacities as coastal or flag States through various key obligations. Whereas coastal States have exclusive access and jurisdiction over fisheries resources in essentially all their maritime zones,[3] the two main entitlements of flag States are their right to fish on the high seas, and access to the

[1] Y Takei *Filling Regulatory Gaps in High Seas Fisheries* (Brill, Leiden: 2013) 14–16.
[2] United Nations Convention on the Law of the Sea of 10 December 1982 (1833 UNTS 3).
[3] Arts. 2(1), 49(1), 56(1)(a) and 77(4) of the LOS Convention.

surplus of the total allowable catch (TAC) in exclusive economic zones (EEZs) of coastal States.[4]

The general obligations included in the LOS Convention have been built upon by a suite of global fisheries instruments, in particular the Fish Stocks Agreement,[5] legally binding and non-legally binding instruments adopted by the United Nations Food and Agriculture Organization (FAO) – for instance the Compliance Agreement,[6] the PSM Agreement,[7] the Code of Conduct[8] and the IPOA-IUU[9] – as well as certain (parts of) United Nations General Assembly (UNGA) Resolutions. As a result, these obligations have now developed into the following:

1. to avoid over-exploitation of target species by setting a science-based TAC, which strives for Maximum Sustainable Yield as qualified by the precautionary approach;
2. to strive for the optimum utilization of target species within the EEZ by providing other States with access to the surplus of the TAC;
3. to pursue an ecosystem approach to fisheries (EAF), which often focuses in particular on (a) predator-prey relationships; (b) impacts of fisheries on non-target species and the ecosystem as a whole; and (c) impacts of oceanographic or climate processes, or pollution, on fish stocks;
4. to cooperate in relation to transboundary fish stocks and fish stocks that occur exclusively on the high seas (further "discrete high seas fish stocks"); and
5. to exercise effective jurisdiction and control over a State's own vessels.

The LOS Convention, the Fish Stocks Agreement and FAO's fisheries instruments are predominantly concerned with establishing the jurisdictional framework. They do not contain substantive fisheries measures such as catch restrictions through TACs, allocations of fishing opportunities through national quotas, gear restrictions, or temporal/seasonal or area-based measures (e.g. closed areas). Actual fisheries regulation is conducted by States acting individually or collectively. The primary means for collective regulation is through regional fisheries management organizations or arrangements (RFMO/As), which have

---

[4] Arts. 62(2) and 116 of the LOS Convention.

[5] Agreement for the Implementation of the Provisions of the United Nations Convention on the Law of the Sea of 10 December 1982 relating to the Conservation and Management of Straddling Fish Stocks and Highly Migratory Fish Stocks of 4 August 1995 (2167 UNTS 3).

[6] Agreement to Promote Compliance with International Conservation and Management Measures by Fishing Vessels on the High Seas of 24 November 1993 (2221 UNTS 91).

[7] Agreement on Port State Measures to Prevent, Deter and Eliminate Illegal, Unreported and Unregulated Fishing of 22 November 2009 (available at www.fao.org/Legal).

[8] Code of Conduct for Responsible Fisheries of 31 October 1995 (available at www.fao.org/3/a-v9878e.pdf).

[9] International Plan of Action to Prevent, Deter and Eliminate Illegal, Unreported and Unregulated Fishing of 2 March 2001 (available at www.fao.org/fi).

the mandate to impose legally binding fisheries conservation and management measures on their members or participants.

RFMO/As are designated by the Fish Stocks Agreement as the preferred vehicles for the conservation and management of straddling fish stocks (i.e. stocks occurring within the maritime zones of one or more coastal States and on the high seas) and highly migratory fish stocks (e.g. tuna).[10] The adoption and entry into force of the Fish Stocks Agreement, in tandem with mounting concerns over the impacts of bottom-fishing on benthic habitats and deep-sea species since the late 1990s, have steadily led to the filling of geographical gaps in full high seas coverage with RFMO/As and the modernization of the constitutive instruments of existing RFMO/As. In addition, many existing RFMOs have conducted performance reviews. Some gaps in geographical coverage nevertheless remain and the performance of RFMO/As continues to be a concern.[11]

2. THE FRAGMENTED AND NON-HIERARCHICAL NATURE OF INTERNATIONAL FISHERIES LAW

As suggested above, international fisheries law is noticeably fragmented and non-hierarchical, in a similar manner to public international law more generally.[12] At the global level, both the UNGA and FAO – principally through its Committee on Fisheries (COFI) – have contributed to the development of international fisheries law. Neither the LOS Convention nor the Fish Stocks Agreement establish an overall decision-making body, but meetings of parties to these treaties have been held on a near-annual basis since their entry into force. Whereas the Meeting of States Parties to the LOS Convention (SPLOS) deals largely with issues that are essentially administrative in nature and not relevant to marine capture fisheries, the ICSP[13] were mainly intended to consider the regional, subregional and global implementation of the Agreement.[14] In addition, the (Resumed) Fish Stocks Agreement Review Conferences held in 2006, 2010 and 2016 pursuant to Article 36 of the Fish Stocks Agreement,

---

[10] See especially Arts. 8–14.

[11] See Chapter 5, Section 2 of this volume (Harrison). Note also that the 14th (2019) round of informal consultations of States Parties to the Fish Stocks Agreement (ICSP) will be devoted to performance reviews of RFMO/As (cf. the 2017 UNGA 'Sustainable Fisheries' Resolution (UNGA Res. 72/72 of 5 December 2017), para. 55).

[12] See the Report of the Study Group of the International Law Commission "Fragmentation of International Law: Difficulties Arising from the Diversification and Expansion of International Law" (doc. A/CN.4/L.702 of 18 July 2006).

[13] See note 11.

[14] See the Report of ICSP1 (2002; doc. ICSP/UNFSA/REP/INF.1 of 9 October 2002), para. 1. The 2016 Resumed Fish Stocks Agreement Review Conference recommended that the ICSP "be dedicated, on an annual basis, to the consideration of specific issues arising from the implementation of the Agreement, with a view to improving understanding, sharing experiences and identifying best practices for the consideration of States parties, as well as the General Assembly and the Review Conference" (Doc. A/CONF.210/2016/5 of 1 August 2016, para. 15 of the Outcome (Annex)).

have assessed the adequacy and effectiveness of the provisions of the Agreement and proposed means to strengthen the substance of and methods for their implementation.

A much larger and diverse group of fisheries bodies operates at the regional level. In addition to the distinctions between RFMOs and RFMAs,[15] and between tuna-RFMOs and non-tuna RFMO/As, there are also a considerable number of regional fisheries bodies that do not qualify as RFMO/As for lack of a mandate to impose legally binding conservation and management measures on their members or participants (e.g. the Western Central Atlantic Fishery Commission (WECAFC)). Furthermore, some regional fisheries bodies are established within the framework of FAO, and some have functions or characteristics that make them 'more than an RFMO'.[16]

Apart from the regional fisheries bodies established within the framework of the FAO (e.g. WECAFC and the Indian Ocean Tuna Commission (IOTC),[17]) and the Commission on the Conservation of Antarctic Marine Living Resources (CCAMLR) established in the context of the Antarctic Treaty System, regional fisheries bodies are entirely separate, autonomous bodies without formal hierarchical relationships with overarching bodies. Nevertheless, it can be assumed that any recommendations of the UNGA, COFI, ICSP or the (Resumed) Fish Stocks Agreement Review Conferences specifically directed at members or participants of RFMO/As will be given serious consideration by them. The UNGA's recommendations relating to high seas bottom-fishing were a case in point.[18] Moreover, members or participants of RFMO/As with competence over straddling or highly migratory fish stocks that are also parties to the Fish Stocks Agreement are bound not only by the objectives of the Agreement but also the features, functions and other guidance for RFMO/As set out in Articles 8–14 of the Agreement.

As noted at the outset of this section, public international law as a whole is also highly fragmented and generally non-hierarchical. It is therefore appropriate to assume there are no hierarchical relationships between the domain of international fisheries law and other distinct, specialized domains of international law. In case of an overlap in substantive and/or geographical competence, actual conflicts in the exercise of such competence can be avoided by

---

[15] See Chapter 5, Section 3 of this volume (Harrison).

[16] See R Billé, L Chabason, P Drankier, EJ Molenaar and J Rochette "Regional Oceans Governance. Making Regional Seas Programmes, Regional Fishery Bodies and Large Marine Ecosystem Mechanisms Work Better Together" (*UNEP Regional Seas Reports and Studies* No. 197: 2016; available at www.unenvironment.org/resources/report/regional-oceans-governance-making-regional-seas-programmes-regional-fishery-bodies), 29–34. See also Chapter 6, Section 2 of this volume (Molenaar).

[17] Based on respectively Arts. VI and XIV of the Constitution of the Food and Agriculture Organization of the United Nations of 16 October 1945 (available at www.fao.org/Legal).

[18] E.g. the proactive approach pursued by the North-East Atlantic Fisheries Commission described in EJ Molenaar "Addressing Regulatory Gaps in High Seas Fisheries" (2005) 20 *International Journal of Marine and Coastal Law* 533–570, at 538-539.

coordination – whether ad hoc or through dedicated mechanisms – or so-called 'primacy arrangements', as has increasingly framed the practices of multilateral environmental agreements in their dealings with each other. Primacy arrangements can be explicitly included in the constitutive instruments of relevant bodies[19] or in more informal arrangements agreed between them, for instance by means of a memorandum of understanding.

Specialized domains of international law are often in a constant state of flux due to a wide array of factors, including the evolving needs and views of the States involved, technological, economic or geopolitical developments, emerging new problems, deteriorating existing problems, or the desire to address existing problems by new regulatory tools or approaches. The potential for duplication or working at cross-purposes in such a fragmented and dynamic system is therefore quite high. States also use this system for so-called 'forum shopping' in order to achieve their desired result. Well-known examples in the context of marine capture fisheries are attempts to list commercially exploited fish species on the Annexes of CITES.[20] The primary motivation of the initiating States was their view that the balance of interests in RFMO/As was overly weighted towards utilization, and that progress in conservation could only be achieved by recourse to the more conservation-oriented balance of interests in CITES.

While interaction and conflicts between the domains of international fisheries law on the one hand, and international trade law and international environmental law on the other hand have existed for some time, new domains such as the international law on merchant shipping, maritime labour standards, human rights and transnational organized crime have entered into the fold more recently.[21]

3. ACHIEVEMENTS, LIMITATIONS AND CHALLENGES

The pace at which international fisheries law has developed since the 1990s is quite remarkable; a trend apparent not only at the global level but also at the

---

[19] E.g. the recognition of the primacy of the International Whaling Commission in Art. VI of the CAMLR Convention (Convention on the Conservation of Antarctic Marine Living Resources of 20 May 1980 (1329 UNTS 47; also available at www.ccamlr.org)) or the acknowledgement that the OSPAR Commission does not have competence to regulate marine capture fisheries (Art. 4(1) of Annex IV to the OSPAR Convention (Convention for the Protection of the Marine Environment of the North-East Atlantic of 22 September 1992 (2345 UNTS 67, as amended); consolidated text available at www.ospar.org)).

[20] Convention on International Trade in Endangered Species of Wild Fauna and Flora of 3 March 1973 (993 UNTS 243). For instance, Atlantic bluefin tuna (*Thunnus thynnus*) and Patagonian and Antarctic toothfish (*Dissostichus* spp.). See S Guggisberg *The Use of CITES for Commercially-exploited Fish Species – A Solution to Overexploitation and Illegal, Unreported and Unregulated Fishing?* (Springer, Heidelberg: 2016) and MA Young *Trading Fish, Saving Fish: The Interaction between Regimes in International Law* (Cambridge University Press, Cambridge: 2011) 134–188.

[21] See Chapters 4 (Stokke), 7 (Caddell), 8 (Scott), 14 (Churchill) and 17 (Caddell, Leloudas and Soyer) of this volume. See also the 2017 UNGA Sustainable Fisheries Resolution, note 11.

regional level. Since the adoption of the Fish Stocks Agreement in 1995, FAO has undeniably been the main source of new global international fisheries instruments. In addition to those mentioned in Section 1, the following are of key importance to this book:

- the Guidelines to Reduce Sea Turtle Mortality in Fishing Operations (2009);
- the International Plans of Action (IPOAs) on reducing incidental catch of seabirds in longline fisheries (1999) and on management and conservation of sharks (1999);
- the International Guidelines on Deep-sea Fisheries in the High Seas (2008);
- the Recommendations on a Global Record of Fishing Vessels, Refrigerated Transport Vessels and Supply Vessels (2010);
- International Guidelines on Bycatch Management and Reduction of Discards (2010);
- the Voluntary Guidelines for Flag State Performance (2013); and
- the Voluntary Guidelines for Catch Documentation Schemes (2017).[22]

Notwithstanding these achievements, the current state of global marine fishery resources leaves much to be desired.[23] The many challenges faced by the domain of international fisheries law are both internal and external. The former are well known and include over-exploitation, overcapacity, subsidies, illegal, unreported and unregulated (IUU) fishing, bycatch and discards of target and non-target species, impacts on benthic ecosystems, other unsustainable fishing practices (e.g. large-scale pelagic drift-net fishing and dynamite fishing) and abandoned, lost or discarded fishing gear.[24] External challenges are not as widely known, but this may well change once their seriousness becomes more broadly acknowledged. They include the various impacts of climate change – in particular, poleward shifts in the distributional range of fish stocks, and ocean acidification – other forms of marine pollution (e.g. microplastics) and alien invasive species.[25] Many of these internal and external factors are examined in detail in this volume.

Fortunately, despite the lack of improvement in – or even deterioration of – global marine fishery resources, there are also examples of States and regions

---

[22] All these are available at www.fao.org/fishery/en.

[23] See *The State of World Fisheries and Aquaculture 2018 – Meeting the Sustainable Development Goals* (FAO, Rome: 2018) at 6, which notes that the "state of marine fishery resources, based on FAO's monitoring of assessed marine fish stocks, has continued to decline".

[24] See the many references to these in the 2017 UNGA Sustainable Fisheries Resolution, note 11 and SOFIA 2018, note 23.

[25] See the references in the 2017 UNGA Sustainable Fisheries Resolution, note 11 and SOFIA 2018, note 23, in particular at 131–138 and 156–157. See also Chapter 2, Section 2 of this volume (Cheung, Lam, Ota and Swartz); and the 18th (2017) Meeting of the United Nations Open-ended Informal Consultative Process on Oceans and the Law of the Sea (ICP; see doc. A/72/95 of 16 June 2017).

that have been quite successful in rebuilding fish stocks. These include Australia, the United States and the North-East Atlantic and adjacent seas.[26] Progress in rebuilding fish stocks in many other parts of the globe is therefore likely to depend to a considerable extent on capacity-building in developing States.

In addition to States that are unable to comply with their international obligations, there are also many others that are unwilling to do so and/or are hesitant to strengthen the compliance-component of international fisheries law. This paramount limitation of international fisheries law is no different from that of public international law in general, and derives directly from the sovereign equality of States, the consensual nature of international law and the principle of *pacta tertiis*. While some States may be opposed to strengthening the compliance-component of international fisheries law more generally, others may be motivated by the short-term benefits offered by a weak fisheries regime. Opposition from the former States may also be part of an overarching resistance to the strengthening of public international law as a whole. Reference should be made in that context to the non-participation by China and the Russian Federation in recent dispute settlement procedures instituted under the LOS Convention.[27] At least as troubling is the decision of the United States not to participate in the merits phase of the *Nicaragua case* before the International Court of the Justice (ICJ),[28] its subsequent withdrawal from the ICJ's compulsory jurisdiction, its continued non-participation in the LOS Convention,[29] as well as the Trump administration's withdrawal from various multilateral regimes, including the climate change regime. This isolationist stance is likely to provoke further unilateralism and thereby lead to an overall weakening of multilateral regimes.

Other States may be further concerned that international fisheries bodies may turn their newly acquired teeth against them or apply these powers in a discriminatory manner. While distant water and high seas fishing States and entities are often blamed for over-exploitation, failed fisheries management and conservation, or slow progress in the development of international fisheries law more generally, this often completely ignores or downplays the role and responsibility of coastal States with respect to fisheries management and conservation in their own maritime zones, including in relation to transboundary fish stocks.

---

[26] SOFIA 2018, note 23 at 6.

[27] *South China Sea* arbitration (*The Republic of Philippines v. The People's Republic of China (Philippines v. China)*), Award on the Merits of 12 July 2016; PCA Case No. 2013-19; available at www.pcacases.com/web; and *Arctic Sunrise* arbitration (*Netherlands v. Russia*), Award on the Merits of 14 August 2015; PCA Case No. 2014-02; available at www.pcacases.com/web/.

[28] *Case concerning Military and Paramilitary Activities in and against Nicaragua* (Nicaragua v. United States of America), Merits, Judgment of 27 June 1986, ICJ Reports 1986.

[29] Even though the United States is a party to the Fish Stocks Agreement, and thereby its system of compulsory third-party dispute settlement entailing binding decisions.

As unwilling or non-complying States are by no means a new phenomenon confined to the domain of international fisheries law, 'willing' States are accustomed to relying on an array of jurisdictional grounds in order to exert pressure on unwilling or non-complying States. This so-called "comprehensive and integrated approach" is included among the principles and strategies of the IPOA-IUU that States are encouraged to use.[30] Examples include jurisdiction in a State's capacity as a port or market State[31] or with respect to natural and juridical persons bearing its nationality.[32] Complementary action has been increasingly pursued by various non-State actors, such as fishing industry associations and environmental non-governmental organizations.[33]

---

[30] Para. 9.3.
[31] See Chapters 13 (van der Marel) and 14 (Churchill) of this volume.
[32] E.g. insurers (see Chapter 17 of this volume (Caddell, Leloudas and Soyer).
[33] See Chapters 4 (Stokke) and 16 (Massarella) of this volume.

Part II

Identifying Future Regulatory Challenges: Science, Law and Management

2

Modelling Future Oceans: The Present and Emerging Future of Fish Stocks and Fisheries

WILLIAM WL CHEUNG, VICKY WY LAM,
YOSHITAKA OTA AND WILF SWARTZ*

1. INTRODUCTION

MARINE FISHERIES ARE important to the wellbeing of many people who are dependent on fish for food, livelihood and culture. Globally, fisheries catches from the oceans in the 2000s are estimated to amount over 120 million tonnes annually[1] (Figure 1), generating over USD 100 billion per year.[2] Fisheries and their dependent industries, such as fish processing, directly or indirectly support the livelihoods of approximately 10 per cent – 12 per cent of the world's population. Furthermore, fisheries catches provide around 2.9 billion people with over 20 per cent of their animal protein needs[3] and many coastal communities are dependent on fish as a major source of micro-nutrients such as omega-3-fatty acid and zinc.[4]

The sustainability of fisheries production from capture fisheries to support these important ecosystem services has become increasingly uncertain due to the influence of climate change. Global fisheries production peaked in the 1990s,

* The authors gratefully acknowledge the support of the Nereus Program (www.nereusprogram. org) in facilitating the writing of this Chapter.

[1] D Pauly and D Zeller "Catch Reconstructions Reveal That Global Marine Fisheries Catches Are Higher than Reported and Declining" (2016) 7 *Nature Communications* 7:10244.
[2] UR Sumaila et al. "Benefits of Rebuilding Global Marine Fisheries Outweigh Costs" (2012) 7 *PloS One* e40542.
[3] See further UT Srinivasan et al. "Food Security Implications of Global Marine Catch Losses due to Overfishing" (2010) 12 *Journal of Bioeconomics* 183–200; and LCL Teh and UR Sumaila "Contribution of Marine Fisheries to Worldwide Employment" (2013) 14 *Fish and Fisheries* 77–88.
[4] CD Golden et al. "Fall in Fish Catch Threatens Human Health" (2016) 534 *Nature* 317–320.

Figure 1 Global fisheries catches based on the official landings records of the Food and Agriculture Organization statistics and catch reconstruction by Pauly and Zeller (note 1). CO_2-related impacts on marine ecosystems render the future sustainability of catches more uncertain

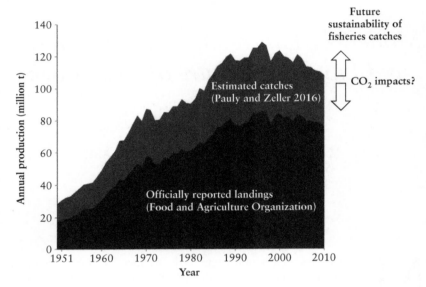

with most exploited fish stocks being fully- or over-exploited.[5] On the other hand, effective fishing effort has increased exponentially,[6] while fishing has now expanded to almost all parts of the global oceans.[7] Average production from global fisheries – at least regarding those fish stocks that are currently exploited – has reached or exceeded its capacity, hence scope to further increase catches is limited. Fisheries production may continue to decrease further if fish stocks are not properly managed. On the other hand, climate change is altering the distributions and productivity of fish stocks, and challenging the effectiveness of fisheries management in unprecedented ways.[8] Thus, a vicious cycle

[5] See especially C Costello et al. "Status and Solutions for the World's Unassessed Fisheries" (2012) 338 *Science* 517–520; R Froese et al. "What Catch Data Can Tell us about the Status of Global Fisheries?" (2012) 159 *Marine Biology* 1283–1292; and TJ Pitcher and WWL Cheung "Fisheries: Hope or Despair?" (2013) 74 *Marine Pollution Bulletin* 506–516.

[6] RA Watson et al. "Global Marine Yield Halved as Fishing Intensity Redoubles" (2013) 14 *Fish and Fisheries* 493–503.

[7] W Swartz et al. "The Spatial Expansion and Ecological Footprint of Fisheries (1950 to Present)" (2010) 5 *PLoS ONE* e15143.

[8] See further WWL Cheung, R Watson and D Pauly "Signature of Ocean Warming in Global Fisheries Catch" (2013) 497 *Nature* 365–368; HO Pörtner et al. IPCC *Fifth Assessment Report Working Group II: Ocean Systems* (2014); WWL Cheung and D Pauly "Impacts and Effects of Ocean Warming on Marine Fishes" in D Laffoley and JM Baxter (eds.) *Explaining Ocean Warming: Causes, Scale, Effects and Consequences* (IUCN, Gland: 2016) 239–253; and M Pinsky et al. "Preparing Ocean Governance for Species on the Move" (2018) 360 *Science* 1189–1191.

perpetuates whereby the future sustainability of fisheries catches becomes ever more uncertain.

In this chapter, we provide an overview of the effects of climate change on marine fisheries, the implications for their management and potential adaptation measures to reduce climate risk on fisheries. We first summarize the major impacts of climate change (including ocean acidification) on marine ecosystems and fisheries (Section 2). In Section 3 we then discuss how these impacts can affect fisheries management. Section 4 explores the ways in which fisheries management may need to change in order to adapt to these impacts, and the scope to which these impacts can be avoided, while Section 5 concludes.

2. IMPACTS OF CLIMATE CHANGE ON MARINE ECOSYSTEMS AND FISHERIES

Climate change alters ocean conditions, including seawater temperature, ocean acidity and oxygen levels that affects the biology and ecology of marine fish and invertebrates.[9] Sea surface temperature has increased at an average rate of 0.11 °C per decade over the period 1971 to 2010, while the pH of ocean surface water has decreased by 0.1 (thus representing a 26 per cent increase in acidity) since the Industrial Revolution.[10] Many parts of the oceans are also becoming less oxygenated.[11] Marine fish and invertebrates undergo shifts in distribution in response to changing environmental factors, moving to areas in which environmental conditions are more suitable for them to live. In response to global warming in the 20th century, shifts in distribution have been most commonly observed towards higher latitudes and deeper waters[12] at rates of tens to hundreds of kilometres per decade.[13] Areas wherein environmental conditions alter beyond the boundaries of the biological limits of the species in question accordingly experience decreases in abundance, or local extinction in severe cases.[14] Moreover, changes in ocean primary productivity as a result of changing ocean conditions affect the capacity of the ecosystem to support fish stocks and their production.[15] In addition, shellfishes and important biological

---

[9] Pörtner et al., note 8; Cheung and Pauly, note 8.

[10] R Pachuari et al. (eds.) *Climate Change 2014: Synthesis Report. Contribution of Working Groups I, II and III to the Fifth Assessment Report of the Intergovernmental Panel on Climate Change* (IPCC, Geneva: 2014).

[11] L Stramma et al. "Ocean Oxygen Minima Expansions and Their Biological Impacts" (2010) 57 *Deep Sea Research Part I: Oceanographic Research Papers* 587–595.

[12] ML Pinsky et al. "Marine Taxa Track Local Climate Velocities" (2013) 341 *Science* 1239–1242.

[13] Ibid.; see also ES Poloczanska "Responses of Marine Organisms to Climate Change across Oceans" (2016) 3 *Frontiers in Marine Science* 62–83.

[14] MC Jones and WWL Cheung "Multi-Model Ensemble Projections of Climate Change Effects on Global Marine Biodiversity" (2015) 72 *ICES Journal of Marine Science* 741–752.

[15] See further WWL Cheung et al. "Application of Macroecological Theory to Predict Effects of Climate Change on Global Fisheries Potential" (2008) 365 *Marine Ecology Progress Series* 187–197; and

habitats such as coral reefs are particularly sensitive to impacts from ocean acidification, as this affects their growth, reproduction and prospects for survival.[16]

Climate change-induced impacts on marine ecosystems are affecting capture fisheries. From 1970 to 2006, global catches demonstrated an increase in the dominance of warmer water species in sub-tropical and higher latitude regions, concurrent with a reduction in the dominance of sub-tropical species catches in equatorial waters.[17] Recruitment of many fish stocks globally also decreased during this period.[18] These changes are partly attributed to ocean warming.

If climate change continues under a business-as-usual model in the 21st century, global fisheries will be substantially impacted by changes in fish distributions, as well as their productivity and, ultimately, economic revenues (Figure 2). Recent studies project global fisheries catch to decrease by 3.4 million tonnes per degree Celsius of atmospheric surface warming relative to pre-industrial level.[19] To put this in context, the goal under the Paris Agreement is to limit warming to 1.5 °C–2.0 °C. Concurrently, fisheries will be challenged by changes in species composition through species turnover (i.e. species gains and local extinctions caused by distribution shifts). The effects of decreasing catch potential, combined with changes in species composition, are projected to impact the revenue of global fisheries by approximately USD 10 billion per year if greenhouse gas emissions are not mitigated,[20] while hundreds of millions of people will face an increased risk of malnutrition through the loss of nutrients that they would otherwise have obtained from fish.[21] Tropical developing countries (e.g. in the Indo-Pacific and West Africa) are demonstrated to be even more vulnerable, as impacts in these regions are projected to be among the most severe since they are heavily dependent on fish for food and livelihoods, but their capacity to mitigate these impacts is comparatively lower.[22] In addition, the Arctic is also projected to be highly vulnerable to climate change as a result of a rapid rate of warming and the loss of sea ice that may ultimately cause an elevated

CA Stock et al. "Reconciling Fisheries Catch and Ocean Productivity" (2017) 114 *Proceedings of the National Academy of Sciences* E1441–E1449.

[16] KJ Kroeker et al. "Impacts of Ocean Acidification on Marine Organisms: Quantifying Sensitivities and Interaction with Warming" (2013) 19 *Global Change Biology* 1884–1896.

[17] Cheung et al., note 8.

[18] GL Britten, M Dowd and B Worm "Changing Recruitment Capacity in Global Fish Stocks" (2016) 113 *Proceedings of the National Academy of Sciences* 134–139.

[19] WWL Cheung, G Reygondeau and TL Frölicher "Large Benefits to Marine Fisheries of Meeting the 1.5 C Global Warming Target" (2016) 354 *Science* 1591–1594.

[20] VWY Lam et al. "Projected Change in Global Fisheries Revenues under Climate Change" (2016) 6 *Scientific Reports* 32607.

[21] Golden, note 4.

[22] See especially EH Allison et al. "Vulnerability of National Economies to the Impacts of Climate Change on Fisheries" (2009) 10 *Fish and Fisheries* 173–196; VWY Lam et al. "Climate Change Impacts on Fisheries in West Africa: Implications for Economic, Food and Nutritional Security" (2012) 34 *African Journal of Marine Science* 103–117; and M Barange et al. "Impacts of Climate Change on Marine Ecosystem Production in Societies Dependent on Fisheries" (2014) 4 *Nature Climate Change* 211–216.

rate of species invasion, even if intensive ocean acidification may further render impacts on future fisheries in the region more uncertain.[23]

Figure 2 Projected changes in maximum catch potential (MCP, a proxy of Maximum Sustainable Yield) and maximum economic rent (MRP) under the 'business-as-usual' Representative Concentration Pathway (RCP) 8.5 scenario relative to the 'strong mitigation' RCP 2.6 scenario (redrawn from Lam et al., note 20)

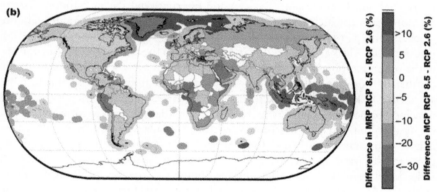

3. CHALLENGES TO FISHERIES MANAGEMENT

The impacts of climate change on fish stocks will prove challenging for future fisheries management in four main ways: (1) disturbing the management of transboundary stocks; (2) diminishing the accuracy of scientific management advice; (3) reducing the effectiveness of management strategies; and (4) increasing the potential social and economic inequity between fishing sectors. Each of these challenges is discussed separately in the following sections.

3.1. Transboundary Stock Management

The effectiveness of international fisheries agreements in managing transboundary fish stocks is partly determined by the stability of the distribution of the resources and the conduct of those States that share the stocks in question.[24]

---

[23] VWY Lam, WWL Cheung and UR Sumaila "Marine Capture Fisheries in the Arctic: Winners or Losers under Climate Change and Ocean Acidification?" (2016) 17 *Fish and Fisheries* 335–357.

[24] Pinsky et al., note 8; see also G Ishimura, S Herrick and UR Sumaila "Stability of Cooperative Management of the Pacific Sardine Fishery under Climate Variability" (2013) 39 *Marine Policy* 333–340; and KA Miller et al. "Governing Marine Fisheries in a Changing Climate: A Game-Theoretic Perspective" (2013) 61 *Canadian Journal of Agricultural Economics* 309–334.

A fundamental challenge to international fisheries governance is the management of resources shared between different States.[25] Specifically, economic theory predicts that the success of any purported joint management of shared resources will decrease as the number of States seeking to exploit that resource increases, while uncertainty in the potential availability of resources to each State further serves to destabilize these arrangements. For example, the Pacific Salmon Commission (PSC, or the International Pacific Salmon Fisheries Commission which until 1985 preceded this body) manages Pacific salmon stocks shared between Canada (British Columbia) and the United States (US) (the States of Alaska, Washington and Oregon). In the late 1970s, major changes in the oceanographic conditions of the North Pacific Ocean resulted in a shift in the distribution of salmon, resulting in an increased abundance of some salmon stocks in Alaska and a decrease in Canadian waters. Correspondingly, the abundance of some salmon stocks increased in Canada but decreased in the States of Washington and Oregon. In view of this, Canada and the US attempted to negotiate to maximize their individual benefits, thereby complicating the prospects for securing an effective and agreeable arrangements for these stocks.[26] Indeed, between 1993 and 1998, the PSC failed to agree on a full set of cooperative management regimes, leaving each State largely free to institute its own management measures. The historical example of the management of Pacific salmon under oceanic changes provides an analogy to future climate change impacts on transboundary stock management at the meta-level.

A more recent example that highlights the impacts of climate change on the effectiveness of fisheries management is the case of Atlantic mackerel (*Scomber scombrus*). Atlantic mackerel is a commercially important species with a distribution throughout the North Atlantic Ocean. In the 2000s, partly as a result of the warming of the North Atlantic Ocean, the distribution of Atlantic mackerel shifted poleward.[27] This has resulted in an increase in the abundance of Atlantic mackerel located in the exclusive economic zone (EEZ) of Iceland. However the various interested States disagreed over appropriate allocations, thereby triggering a major dispute over the sharing of quota between countries fishing this species.[28] The destabilization of the management of fish stocks in this manner clearly illustrates the prospective challenges confronting the performance of existing and future fisheries management.

---

[25] See further Chapter 1 of this volume (Molenaar and Caddell).

[26] Miller et al., note 24.

[27] KM Hughes, L Dransfeld and MP Johnson "Climate and Stock Influences on the Spread and Locations of Catches in the Northeast Atlantic Mackerel Fishery" (2015) 24 *Fisheries Oceanography* 540–552. On the management challenges generated in this region, see Chapter 12 of this volume (Ásgeirsdóttir).

[28] See J Spijkers and WJ Boonstra "Environmental Change and Social Conflict: The Northeast Atlantic Mackerel Dispute" (2017) 17 *Regional Environmental Change* 1835–1851. This affair also raised the spectre of a trade dispute: on the trade dimensions of fishing conflicts, see Chapter 14 of this volume (Churchill).

The projected decrease in fisheries catches in the EEZs of tropical coastal States (e.g. in West Africa and the Indo-Pacific region as illustrated starkly in Figure 2) may further increase the demand for fish drawn from stocks that straddle national waters and the high seas. The development of fishing industries for pelagic resources such as tunas and mackerels within the EEZs of some tropical developing countries has been promoted partly to supplement catches from coastal fisheries for economic, food and livelihood purposes[29] but more specifically to compensate for the expected decreases in catches that will be generated by the effects of climate change.[30] Computer simulation modelling exercises suggest that improving the management of straddling fisheries stocks in the high seas can help to compensate for some of the losses in the potential catch of coastal States under climate change.[31]

Finally, an emerging area of conflicts over transboundary stocks may arise over the issue of national sovereignty. The legitimacy of operational rights for fishing and access to stocks can be questioned not only in respect of food security, but also in the light of social responsibility requirements. As climate change continues to affect distributions of transboundary stocks and increases the need to consider the prospective impact of climate change on fisheries management, it is a prerequisite for management authorities to adequately address the interests of different stakeholders, including coastal communities, to meet the different ecological, social and economic goals of sustainable development.[32]

3.2. Accuracy of Management Advice and Effectiveness of Management Strategies

Shifts in the baseline oceanographic conditions affect the accuracy of scientific advice concerning fisheries management. In many fisheries, management decisions are based on information from stock assessments, such as the setting of total allowable catches, limiting fishing mortalities and instituting spatial or temporal fisheries closures. Conventional stock assessment models assume that the baseline oceanographic conditions and their relationship with population dynamics are constant (i.e. the assumption of stationarity). However, in reality, environmental conditions and the key attributes determining the abundance and productivity of fish stocks are closely related. Thus, while ocean conditions are changing, continuing to dogmatically apply the assumption of stationarity

---

[29] GM Okemwa et al. "Managing Coastal Pelagic Fisheries: A Case Study of the Small-scale Purse Seine Fishery in Kenya" (2017) *Ocean and Coastal Management* 31–39.

[30] J Bell et al. "Impacts and Effects of Ocean Warming on the Contributions of Fisheries and Aquaculture to Food Security" in "Explaining Ocean Warming: Causes, Scale, Effects and Consequences" (IUCN, Gland: 2016).

[31] WWL Cheung et al. "Transform High Seas Management to Build Climate Resilience in Marine Seafood Supply" (2017) *Fish and Fisheries* 254–263.

[32] JN Kittinger et al. "Committing to Socially Responsible Seafood" (2017) 356 *Science* 912–913.

results in biases in the estimation of management reference points, such as Maximum Sustainable Yield or sustainable fishing mortality, which are then used to (mis)inform stock management. If a fisheries assessment fails to detect a decrease in the productivity of fish stocks under changing ocean conditions, the unpalatable result may be a scientific recommendation for a level of fishing that is higher than that which can be sustained by the stocks. As a result, the performance of fisheries management will be adversely impacted, resulting in a decrease in catches and/or the over-exploitation of the resource.

The case of the Gulf of Maine cod (*Gadus morhua*) fisheries vividly illustrates the implications of ocean warming for the accuracy of stock assessment, and the consequential impacts upon management performance. The cod stock in the Gulf of Maine has been historically overfished, and a fisheries management plan has been put in place that aims to rebuild the stock. However, despite a substantial cut in catch quota since the early 2000s, the abundance of the stock has continued to decrease. The Gulf of Maine is at the southern boundary of cod distribution and empirical evidence suggests that cod are shifting their distribution poleward due to ocean warming.[33] In particular, the rapid rise in summer temperatures in the region has been linked to a decrease in recruitment and an increased mortality of juvenile cod.[34] However, the stock assessment model that was used to inform the management of the cod stock did not account for such environmental effects. Thus, the model would indicate that cod could sustain a higher level of fishing. In reality, however, there was an elevated mortality rate of cod due to the impacts of warming in addition to fishing. Consequently, rather than providing meaningful and accurate projections, the quota recommendations based on the results yielded from this model have led to a continual decrease in cod populations.

A common sustainable fisheries target, and an obligation that is ubiquitous in international fisheries law, is to reduce the level of bycatches.[35] Nevertheless, climate change-induced shifts in species distribution may increase the likelihood of bycatch in fisheries. Changes in the distribution of the species or alterations to important habitats may also displace targeted populations into existing fishing closures.[36] For example, in the North Sea, the poleward shift in the distribution of hake (*Merluccius merluccius*) – a warmer water species – has resulted in an increased spatial overlap between hake distribution and the fishing grounds for cod fishing. As a result, the catch of hake by cod fishermen has increased substantially in recent years. However, both hake and cod fishing are subject to specific catch quotas, with hake considered to be a bycatch product in cod fisheries. Cod fishermen have increasingly found themselves swiftly filling

---

[33] Pinsky et al., note 12.

[34] AJ Pershing et al. "Slow Adaptation in the Face of Rapid Warming Leads to Collapse of the Gulf of Maine Cod Fishery" (2015) 350 *Science* 809–812.

[35] For further discussion of this issue, see Chapter 8 of this volume (Scott).

[36] On potential strategies to mitigate overlaps between associated species and targeted fish stocks under area-based management, see Chapter 9 of this volume (Dunn, Ortuño Crespo and Caddell).

up their hake quota before they can catch sufficient volumes of cod, hence the incidental catch of hake is currently 'choking' the target fishery for cod.[37] This may incentivize the discard of hake by fishermen, perversely resulting in increased mortalities within the hake stock as well as the wastage of marine living resources.

Moreover, the protection of critical fish habitat is now considered a fisheries management tool to ensure the sustainability of exploited fish stocks. However, beyond the realm of anthropogenic interventions, extreme events such as typhoons and other unpredictable weather systems can also severely damage coral reefs and other areas of critical habitat, reducing the effectiveness of the protection granted to such areas in order to enhance production from surrounding locations. As a case in point, the Philippines is currently considering relocating the famous Apo Island Marine Protected Area because the coral reef within the current designation was destroyed by Typhoon Haiyan.[38] Accordingly, there is a need to consider not only the impacts of fishing and other industrial activities in the vicinity of the area, but also the vulnerability of stocks and fishing grounds to natural phenomena.

It is virtually axiomatic that the management of international fish stocks, such as that undertaken by regional fisheries management organisations (RFMOs) will increasingly need to operate under uncertainty in a changing climate. Strategies and approaches are available to manage fisheries under such uncertainties. A combination of optimal control, adaptive management and scenario planning should therefore inform an effective portfolio of approaches towards managing fisheries in the light of global and localized changes to the climate. Although there are significant gaps in the scientific knowledge concerning changing ocean conditions and their prospective impacts upon fish stocks and fisheries, proactive adaptation strategies and new approaches to fisheries management in the light of elevated uncertainty may be advanced through further cooperation between States.[39]

3.3. Increasing Potential Social and Economic Inequities between Fishing Sectors/States

When the impacts of climate change affect the abundance, productivity and distribution of fish stocks, fisheries managers must adapt their strategies and tactics to reflect these new ecological and socio-economic dynamics and conditions. However, the sensitivity and adaptive capacity to these climate-induced

---

[37] JK Pinnegar and P Buckley *Climate Change and UK Fisheries – Perceptions of Risk and Possible Adaptation Options; Document ICES CM 2015/G:06*.

[38] Personal communication with J Antacamara (on file with the authors).

[39] Pinsky et al., note 8; Miller et al., note 24; see also Chapters 9 (Dunn, Ortuño Crespo and Caddell) and 11 (Rayfuse) of this volume on how such strategies could be developed further.

changes can vary substantially between different fishing sectors within and between States. Thus, the different level of climate impacts that may be experienced by different sectors can further increase the social and economic inequities between States, as well as between different fishing industries within the same State. For example, climate change-induced shifts in the distribution and abundance of fish stocks can result in a disproportionate allocation of the economic benefits and conservation burdens between fisheries in developed and developing fisheries. Such inequity cannot be swiftly resolved by simply improving the state of scientific knowledge as to the rate and impacts of climate change. Instead, there needs to be further consideration of strategies by which to rearrange the distribution of responsibilities for the management and conservation of fish stocks between countries, while also accounting for the fact that this inherent uncertainty can be amplified by issues that are politically complex.[40] Furthermore, the disparity may widen between States that have the capacity to monitor and protect their waters and those that do not. As fish stocks increasingly disperse into areas in which fisheries management is less effective, it is likely to become even more difficult to secure the effective and rational management of many fisheries and thereby a consistent food supply for particular communities and constituencies.

4. PATHWAYS TO SUSTAINABLE FISHERIES UNDER CLIMATE CHANGE

Climate change is undeniably affecting marine ecosystems and fisheries. Environmental changes in the ocean that are caused, influenced or exacerbated by climate change and ocean acidification – as well as other human drivers – have led to an array of ecological responses, ranging from shifts in the distributions of fish stocks to changes in their potential catches and to the prospects of new fisheries for previously un(der)fished species.[41] Given the current trajectory of greenhouse gas emissions and climate change, the oceans in the past will not be the same as the oceans in the future. They are expected to change at a rate and magnitude that are unprecedented in human history. Accordingly, the empirical relationships and experience aggregated between oceans, fishes and fisheries, alongside the management strategies that have been observed and deployed in the past, may no longer be applicable in the future. It is thus essential to improve our ability to anticipate and respond to future ocean changes by exploring the evolving nature of both ecological and socio-economic systems.

---

[40] See further Q Hanich and Y Ota "Moving beyond Rights-Based Management: A Transparent Approach to Distributing the Conservation Burden and Benefit in Tuna Fisheries" (2013) 28 *International Journal of Marine and Coastal Law* 135–170.

[41] See further R Caddell "Precautionary Management and the Development of Future Fishing Opportunities: The International Regulation of New and Exploratory Fisheries" (2018) 33 *International Journal of Marine and Coastal Law* 199–260, at 200–204.

A range of strategies can be applied to address immediate challenges to the sustainability of marine living resources, with a particular emphasis on fisheries. These strategies will also require further research to fully appreciate their importance and influence in contributing to the sustainability of the future oceans. First, based on our current understanding of the oceans and available technology, emission reductions will be the most effective method for mitigating the risks associated with climate change and ocean acidification. However, due to historical CO_2 emissions, the effects of climate change on the oceans will continue to be visible across the course of the coming decades, particularly in sensitive regions and ecosystems. Therefore, adaptation measures for both natural and social systems are needed.

Marine ecosystems have some intrinsic ability to absorb stressors. Through improved management and the reduction of non-climatic stressors – such as fishing and habitat modification – the intrinsic adaptive capacity of marine ecosystems can be enhanced and preserved. However, there are still limits on how much ecosystems can endure, and thus mitigation is still a necessary pre-condition. Specifically, ecosystem-based ocean management recognizes a full array of interactions within an ecosystem, including human impacts and environmental changes. Accordingly, the risks posed by climate change can be reduced by narrowing the gaps in ocean governance through the application and implementation of ecosystem-based management in fisheries. However, such an approach needs to be paired with local strategies that consider regional impacts. Finally, risk reduction through adaptation can also be fostered by providing economic opportunities and food security, especially for those politically and economically marginalized coastal communities in both developed and developing countries, including indigenous communities and communities in extreme poverty.

5. CONCLUSION

Fisheries management will have to operate under increasing uncertainty in the changing climate. Strategies and approaches are available to manage fisheries under such uncertainties. However, the scope for effective fisheries management to achieve goals and targets of sustainable ocean development is likely to be limited by unabated climate change. This highlights the importance of undertaking both climate mitigation as well as implementing interventions in fisheries management to reduce climate risks. In addition, proactive exploration of the potential impacts on transboundary fisheries management through the use of scenarios will need to be taken by RFMOs, while cooperative actions will also be necessary to develop adaptive governance responses in order to ensure the continued pursuit of sustainable fisheries in an era of changing oceans.

3

Alternative Histories and Futures of International Fisheries Law

RICHARD A BARNES

1. INTRODUCTION

WHAT IF WE were to apply counterfactual thinking to the international regulation of fisheries? Would it help improve our understanding of fisheries law? Possibly. Counterfactual thinking is used to analyze historical events or the effectiveness of political regimes.[1] It is also used to show the contingency of events. The approach is sometimes used in law, where it is inherent to questions of causation.[2] In one of the few papers on counterfactuals by an international lawyer, Venzke suggests that counterfactual thinking is useful in three ways.[3] First, to help free analysis from the bias of necessity; of seeing law as somehow pre-determined by historical events. Second, it allows us to explain the workings of law without recourse to abstract theories. Counterfactuals allow us think about how events might have been different with calibrated changes to real world events, thus allowing us to remain true to how law operates in practice. Third, it stimulates imaginative thinking. If law is not inevitable, but in part the result of historical contingencies, then by foregrounding these contingencies we can strengthen calls for change to address any shortcomings that are the product of those past, less relevant, contingencies.

---

[1] JD Fearon "Counterfactuals and Hypothesis Testing in Political Science" (1991) 43 *World Politics* 169–195.

[2] Having surveyed the extent to which it features explicitly in legal analysis, Mushkat argues for its use as an additional tool of empirical enquiry: R Mushkat "Counterfactual Reasoning: An Effective Component of the International Law Methodological Armor?" (2017) 18 *German Law Journal* 59–98.

[3] I Venzke "What If? Counterfactual (Hi)stories of International Law" *Amsterdam Law School Research Paper* No. 2016-66; available at https://papers.ssrn.com/sol3/papers.cfm?abstract_id=2881226. See further K Raustiala "Compliance & Effectiveness in Regulatory Cooperation" (2000) 32 *Case Western Reserve Journal of International Law* 387–440.

These are important ambitions, but they must be weighed against the challenges. The principal challenge is to cope with the potential complexities of real and imagined multi-causal scenarios, and so to retain the coherence and analytical merit of any comparison between these scenarios.[4] Invariably, events are the result of complex processes and to describe the counterfactual approach as challenging is perhaps an understatement. Consider for a moment: what if the tribunal in the *Bering Fur Seals* case[5] had found in favour of the United States? What if the Stockholm Declaration[6] had emerged decades earlier, prompting the consolidation of international environmental law before the LOS Convention[7] had been negotiated? These are important questions because fishing is one of the main adverse effects on marine biodiversity and many lawful fishing practices are environmentally unsound. It is therefore justified to think about how differently we should conduct them.

Such creative thinking is not so far-fetched. Indeed, many aspects of fisheries management are based upon scientific models about stock conditions, and so entail some form of counterfactual thinking.[8] As anyone familiar with environmental impact assessment (EIA) knows, a key element of the EIA process is to present to a decision-maker some form of scenario analysis enabling her or him to make a decision, in part based upon a comparison of two situations: one with and one without a development. In the future, oceans governance will increasingly involve some form of impact assessment, whether through the extension of domestic EIA processes to fisheries, or through the adoption of international agreements requiring some form of EIA as part of the international regulation of fisheries.[9] Counterfactual thinking will be increasingly used in fisheries and oceans governance, so it is instructive to understand how such thinking can be used now.

This chapter breaks new ground in using counterfactual thinking to analyse international fisheries law. In Section 2, I outline the relationship between

---

[4] M Glennon "Remarks. Does International Law Matter?" (2004) 98 *ASIL Proceedings* 311–317, at 315. Also, RB Mitchell "Evaluating the Performance of Environmental Institutions: What to Evaluate and How to Evaluate It?" in OR Young, LA King and H Schroeder (eds.) *Institutions and Environmental Change: Principal Findings, Applications and Research Frontiers* (MIT Press, Cambridge, MA: 2008) 79–114.

[5] Award between the United States and the United Kingdom relating to the rights of jurisdiction of United States in Bering's Sea and the preservation of fur seals of 15 August 1893 (*28 Reports of International Arbitral Awards* 263).

[6] Declaration of the United Nations Conference on the Human Environment of 16 June 1972 (11 ILM 1416).

[7] United Nations Convention on the Law of the Sea of 10 December 1982 (1833 UNTS 3).

[8] See e.g. TK Davies, CC Mees and EJ Milner-Gulland "Use of a Counterfactual Approach to Evaluate the Effect of Area Closures on Fishing Location in a Tropical Tuna Fishery" (2017) 12(3) *PLoS One* e0174758. See also Chapter 2 of this volume (Cheung, Lam, Ota and Swartz).

[9] See the development of the third implementation agreement to the LOS Convention on "the conservation and sustainable use of marine biological diversity of areas beyond national jurisdiction" (further: BBNJ Implementation Agreement) envisaged by United Nations General Assembly (UNGA) Res. 72/249 of 24 December 2017. See also Chapter 10 of this volume (Marsden).

international fisheries law and international environmental law so that we have a point of comparison for the counterfactual analysis. In Section 3, I set out the main approaches to counterfactual analysis. Given the novelty of a counterfactual approach, it is important to identify and assess its modes of application as far as possible. In Section 4, I provide some short case studies to show how counterfactual analysis can help evaluate international fisheries regulation. The tentative conclusions are that the systemic complexity of international fisheries and environmental law make it difficult to posit clear and instructive counterfactuals. As such we have to be very cautious about the lessons that we draw. For example, one should not assume that fisheries management would be more sensitive to environmental concerns. Whilst this is not as positive as we would like, one encouraging lesson is that it is precisely the systemic complexity that inhibits counterfactual thinking that might actually serve us well in developing a stronger environmental dimension to fisheries management in the longer term.

2. CONTEXT: FISHERIES AND ENVIRONMENTAL LAW

If we are to understand the lessons of history and the alternative futures, then we need a clear picture of the current position and how we arrived there. There needs to be a point of comparison for the counterfactual analysis. What follows is a schematic outline of international fisheries law, which seeks to identify some of the key institutions, processes, content and variables in fisheries law, in order to provide points of reference for testing our counterfactual thinking.

International fisheries law is part of the law of the sea and a branch of international law more generally, sharing the same structural attributes of international law (i.e. actors, sources, jurisdiction, State responsibility, dispute settlement and cross-cutting institutions like the United Nations (UN)). It is a State-centric, horizontal system of law that places primacy on consent for law-making. Such features can be regarded as fundamental structural constraints that must be accounted for in any counterfactual analysis. These shared structural attributes do not necessarily entail the integration of substantive norms, either externally or internally. Thus, many aspects of general international law or specific fields of international law – such as international human rights law – have not permeated law of the sea to any significant extent. And, within the law of the sea, there remains a strong disaggregation of regulation along sectoral lines. Although the idea that international law is a systemic body of law, with coherence and mutual influence of related norms, is compelling and can be witnessed in some areas,[10] it remains a work in progress. Despite the ambition of the LOS Convention to establish an integrated framework to address the problems of oceans space as a whole, in reality it falls considerably short

---

[10] C McLachlan "The Principle of Systemic Integration and Article 31(3)(c) of the Vienna Convention" (2005) 54 *International and Comparative Law Quarterly* 279–319.

of integrating sectoral activities, and in particular fisheries and environmental concerns.[11] Only with the start of the BBNJ process in 2006,[12] some 24 years after the conclusion of the third United Nations Conference on the Law of the Sea (UNCLOS III), did a stronger integrative agenda emerge. And even here, the extent to which fisheries should form part of a new LOS Convention Implementation Agreement remains contested.[13]

Whilst fisheries regulation has long been a concern of the law of the sea, marine environmental protection is a relative newcomer. The same is true of domestic fisheries management, with the dominance of sectoral approaches to marine regulation. Only recently have these areas of regulation begun to merge. As such, much of international fisheries law has evolved separately from international environmental law. This is unfortunate because fishing is one of the most significant threats to marine biodiversity and the health of marine environments more generally.[14]

Fisheries regulation is invariably framed in terms of 'conservation and management'. Whilst this may be indicative of environmental concerns, the environment and, indeed, conservation were simply incidental consequences of regulating access.[15] Historically, fisheries were subject to limited protection. Prior to the 20th century, international fisheries law was principally concerned with managing local conflicts, rather than conservation and management in general.[16] The idea that stocks were inexhaustible dominated management approaches into the late 19th century.[17] Exceptional claims to apply conservation restrictions were generally resisted, as was shown in the *Bering Fur Seals* case. Advances in our understanding of the state of fish stocks improved in the 20th century. With it came a realization that unrestricted access to resources was contributing to overfishing. The International Council for the Exploration of the Sea met for the first time in 1902, seeking to put fisheries management

[11] R Barnes "The Law of the Sea Convention and the Integrated Regulation of the Oceans" (2012) 27 *International Journal of Marine and Coastal Law* 859–866.

[12] See note 9.

[13] R Barnes "The Proposed LOSC Implementation Agreement on Areas Beyond National Jurisdiction and its Impact on International Fisheries Law" (2016) 31 *International Journal of Marine and Coastal Law* 583–619.

[14] R Barnes "Fisheries and Biodiversity" in M Fitzmaurice, D Ong and P Merkouris (eds.) *Research Handbook on International Environmental Law* (Edward Elgar, Cheltenham: 2010) 542–563.

[15] P Birnie, A Boyle and C Redgwell *International Law and the Environment* 3rd ed. (Oxford University Press, Oxford: 2009) 712.

[16] Typical of this was the International Convention for the Purpose of Regulating the Police of the Fisheries in the North Sea Outside Territorial Waters of 6 May 1882 (160 CTS 219), which focused on rules for fishing gear, as well as reciprocal inspection measures, beyond territorial waters. See further K Bangert "The Effective Enforcement of High Seas Fishing Regimes: The Case of the Convention for the Regulation of the Policing of the North Sea Fisheries of 6 May 1882" in G Goodwin Gill and S Talmon (eds.) *The Reality of International Law: Essays in Honour of Ian Brownlie* (Oxford University Press, Oxford: 1999) 1–20.

[17] T Smith *Scaling Fisheries: The Science of Measuring the Effects* (Cambridge University Press, Cambridge: 1994) ch. 2.

decisions on a scientific footing. In the early 20th century, a number of stock-specific agreements applied the principle of abstention, and the need to limit or stabilize fishing effort to ensure stocks were not overfished.[18] However, conservation really only gained traction in the years after World War II, as States sought to justify and secure claims to preferential fishing rights in coastal waters. This paved the way for the exclusive economic zone (EEZ) and the possibility of more sophisticated conservation and management systems within domestic law, and via regional fisheries bodies. Throughout this period we have moved steadily away from the oceans as a hunting ground to a space in which economic activities are structured – spatially and legally – and where many activities operate on an industrial scale.

It is important to stress that the LOS Convention is a product of its time, negotiated before environmental norms gained traction in international law more generally. This means few of its provisions on EEZ or high seas fisheries directly address the protection of the marine environment. The main focus of the LOS Convention is to prevent over-exploitation of stocks, whilst targeting their optimum utilization.[19] Article 56(1)(b)(iii) grants coastal States jurisdiction to protect and preserve the marine environment. This acknowledges regulatory authority, but without any linkage to fisheries management. The main direction to an integration of rights and duties is found in Article 56(2), which requires coastal States to have due regard to the rights and interests of other States.[20] At best, Article 60(3) provides that, in adopting conservation measures, States shall seek to maintain or restore populations of harvested species at levels that "can produce the maximum sustainable yield, as qualified by relevant *environmental* and economic factors" (emphasis added).[21] In summary, the door is open for consideration of environmental issues, but States do not have to address these in any particular way. This stands in marked contrast to instruments adopted after the LOS Convention, where the influence of environmental considerations is more noticeable.

International environmental law is usually traced to the 1972 Stockholm Conference on the Human Environment. Too early to really influence negotiations at UNCLOS III, this later had an influence on some aspects of international fisheries law. Apart from producing the CBD,[22] the 1992 Rio Conference on Environment and Development, and Agenda 21 in particular, served to initiate developments in fisheries law by calling for the convening of a conference to

---

[18] E.g. the Convention on Preservation and Protection of Fur Seals of 7 July 1911 (37 Stat. 1542); the Convention between the United States of America and Canada for the Preservation of the Halibut Fisheries of the Northern Pacific Ocean of 2 March 1923 (32 LNTS 93); and the Convention for the Protection, Preservation and Extension of the Sockeye Salmon Fisheries of the Fraser River System of 26 May 1930 (184 LNTS 305).

[19] Arts. 61–62 of the LOS Convention.

[20] On the high seas, the equivalent provision is Art. 87(2).

[21] See also Art. 119(1)(a) in respect of the high seas.

[22] Convention on Biological Diversity of 22 May 1992 (1760 UNTS 143).

deal with the regulation of straddling and highly migratory fish stocks.[23] This eventually resulted in the Fish Stocks Agreement.[24] The influence of international environmental law can also be traced through the various instruments adopted by the United Nations Food and Agriculture Organization (FAO), including the Code of Conduct[25] and the Compliance Agreement.[26] The explicit reference to environmental law and distinctive environmental components of such instruments adds credence to the hypothesis that fisheries law could have taken a different pathway – or at least made quicker progress on environmental protection – if international environmental law had consolidated sooner.

The Code of Conduct is explicit in addressing the environmental impact of fishing. Article 6.6 provides, for instance, that:

> Selective and environmentally safe fishing gear and practices should be further developed and applied, to the extent practicable, in order to maintain biodiversity and to conserve the population structure and aquatic ecosystems and protect fish quality. Where proper selective and environmentally safe fishing gear and practices exist, they should be recognized and accorded a priority in establishing conservation and management measures for fisheries [...]

The Fish Stocks Agreement has yet stronger environmental credentials. It requires the application of the precautionary approach (Article 6), the adoption of measures to prevent pollution and use of environmentally safe gear (Article 5(f)), the use of integrated and ecosystem-based approaches (Article 5(d) and (e)), the protection of marine biodiversity (Article 5(g)) and conducting impact assessments (Article 5(d)). These provisions have since influenced the practice of regional fisheries management organizations (RFMOs), although the extent to which environmental principles have permeated such institutions is inconsistent and sometimes quite deficient.[27] Not all RFMO constitutive instruments include a commitment to protect and preserve the marine environment, with even fewer requiring the protection of marine biodiversity, the adoption of an ecosystem-based approach to fisheries management or the conduct of rigorous EIAs. Indeed, the limited remit of RFMOs generally precludes the adoption of environmental measures other than as incidental to controls on the conduct of fishing activities. The gap in integrated fisheries

---

[23] Report of the United Nations Conference on Environment and Development, UN Doc. A/CONF.151/26 vol. II of 13 August 1992 (available at www.un.org/documents/ga/conf151/aconf15126-2.htm), para. 17.49.

[24] Agreement for the Implementation of the Provisions of the United Nations Convention on the Law of the Sea of 10 December 1982 relating to the Conservation and Management of Straddling Fish Stocks and Highly Migratory Fish Stocks of 4 August 1995 (2167 UNTS 3).

[25] Code of Conduct for Responsible Fisheries of 31 October 1995 (available at www.fao.org/fishery/en), preface, para. 4.

[26] Agreement to Promote Compliance with International Conservation and Management Measures by Fishing Vessels on the High Seas of 24 November 1993 (33 ILM 969), preambular paras. 4 and 6.

[27] See Barnes, note 13 at 601 and Table 1.

and environmental regulation is compounded by the fact that regional marine environmental bodies lack the authority to manage fisheries. Only exceptionally is there cooperation between fisheries and environmental bodies.[28] In 2008, a Memorandum of Understanding (MOU) between the North-East Atlantic Fisheries Commission (NEAFC) and the Commission for the Protection of the Marine Environment of the North-East Atlantic (OSPAR Commission) was adopted, recognizing their respective competences and areas of shared concern, and establishing mechanisms for sharing of information, joint discussions and common approaches to the application of precautionary approaches and area-based management measures.[29] However, this is a somewhat recent development and it falls someway short a systemic practice.[30] It is interesting to note that the fusion of fisheries and environmental objectives has been very much a concern in the preparatory meetings for the BBNJ Implementation Agreement.[31]

Other environmental agreements have become relevant to fisheries management, but they do not comprise an integral aspect of fisheries management. They operate alongside or in parallel to fisheries management, but do not form a fundamental part of fisheries management obligations. Thus the CBD requires States to plan for the conservation and sustainable use of biodiversity, and to take in situ and ex situ measures to conserve it.[32] Although the Ramsar Convention[33] predates the LOS Convention, it applies to wetlands and, potentially, adjacent waters, so it only marginally impacts on commercial fishing when conducted in wider ocean areas.[34]

As a generalization, it might be concluded that it took around 20 years for environmental principals to permeate into international fisheries law. It has taken another 15 years for some degree of institutional coordination of fisheries and environmental matters to emerge. Even now, this cross-cutting governance of issues remains ad hoc and under development. This indicates a slow process of cross-fertilization of ideas and practices.

3. COUNTERFACTUAL METHODOLOGIES

We cannot change the past, but we can learn its lessons. Counterfactual thinking is not merely wishful thinking.[35] It is an established analytical technique in political and historiographical research, as well other social sciences, where it

---

[28] Ibid., 602.

[29] Available at www.ospar.org/about/international-cooperation/memoranda-of-understanding.

[30] Barnes, note 13 at 602.

[31] Ibid., 592–596.

[32] Arts. 6, 8 and 9.

[33] Convention on Wetlands of International Importance especially as Waterfowl Habitat of 2 February 1971 (996 UNTS 245).

[34] See Arts. 1(1) and 2(1).

[35] Cf. EH Carr *What is History?* (Macmillan, London: 1961) 127–128.

is used to test arguments about the importance of historical events.[36] It enables the construction of different points of comparison and thereby facilitates the evaluation of events. It is a common, although often under-acknowledged, facet of legal thinking,[37] one Strassfield describes as pervasive.[38] Counterfactual analysis provides an important tool for thinking creatively and critically about international fisheries law. However, before using this tool, we must present a methodology because of its novelty, and because it is not free of weaknesses.[39]

3.1. A Short Account of Counterfactual Thinking

Let us begin with a basic definition: "A counterfactual is a statement, typically in the subjunctive mood, in which a false or 'counter to fact' premise is followed by some assertion about what would have happened if the premise were true".[40] For example, if international environmental law had existed prior to international fisheries law, this would have resulted in a higher degree of environmental protection within fisheries management regimes.

There are three key elements in the process of counterfactual reasoning: the use of a false antecedent, a reliance on causal reasoning, and the assertion of contingencies. In the present example, the false premise is the prior existence of a body of international environmental law. It is constructed in order to help evaluate the significance of environmental law on fisheries law. However, since this state of affairs did not occur in the real world, there is no empirical evidence upon which we can evaluate the counterfactual. In order to get round this problem, it is typical to consider the premise as if it were true in the closest possible world. This in turn requires one to evaluate other variables sufficiently closely connected to the false antecedent, otherwise the purpose of the exercise would be defeated as only one thing, ie the false antecedent, would have changed. This means we must evaluate the effect of other variables, either in the event itself (i.e. what were the particular contents of this earlier constructed body of law, or changes to the dates of adoption) or from other events (i.e. could other regulatory changes have prevented or precipitated some of the consequences for fisheries law).

---

[36] M Weber *Kritische Studien auf dem Gebiet kulturwissenschaftlicher Logik* (Archiv für Sozialwissenschaft und Sozialpolitik: 1904; reprinted as "Critical Studies in the Logic of the Cultural Sciences" in *The Methodology of the Social Sciences* (transl and ed, EA Shils and HA Finch; Free Press, New York: 1949)) 113–188, at 171–188.

[37] Venzke, note 3 at 3.

[38] RN Strassfield "Counterfactuals in the Law" (1992) 60 *George Washington Law Review* 339–416, at 345.

[39] RJ Evans *Altered Pasts: Counterfactuals in History* (Brandeis University Press, Lebanon NE: 2014). More stridently, EP Thompson described it as "*geschichtswissenschlopff*" (unhistorical shit) *The Poverty of Theory: or an Orrery of Errors* (Merlin Press, London: 1995) 144–145.

[40] HE Brady "Causation and Explanation in Social Science" in RE Goodwin (ed.) *The Oxford Handbook of Political Science* (Oxford University Press, Oxford: 2011) 1054–1107, at 1057.

The latter point directly concerns the second element of counterfactual thinking: causation. This commits us to identifying plausible and similar cause/effect scenarios in the real and counterfactual worlds. This is challenging because the fundamental nature of causation and causal relationships is evasive. Even Hume had to settle for the somewhat loosely constructed observation that events are causally related when they are contiguous in time and place, that one precedes the other and they occur with regularity.[41] Causality entails identifying and weighing up events and their relationship. Some events may have more causative potency than others. Also, some may be more fragile than others (meaning that the event could easily not have occurred) and so we need to think carefully about the how, whether and when of the event.[42]

This leads us to the contingency of events. When we describe something as contingent, we mean that something is not certain or preordained. Its form is shaped by conditioning factors (determinants). These determinants are not unlimited because some are more probable than others, so we need to be able to indicate and explain these. To return to the point above: the LOS Convention was a product of its time; its content and structure was determined by the number and diversity of States, the negotiating venue and process, the state of knowledge, the resources of the delegates, the state of play of international law in general and law of the sea in particular. These contingencies need to be considered.

3.2. The Benefits of Counterfactual Thinking

Whilst counterfactual thinking has its critics, some, like Weber, have argued forcefully for its value: "If history is to be raised above the level of a mere chronicle of notable events and personalities, it has no alternative but to pose such questions".[43] It moves us beyond narrating events and opens up possibilities in analytical critique. Drawing upon Venzke, three benefits from counterfactual thinking are considered next, to contextualize the later discussion of fisheries and environmental counterfactuals.

The first benefit is freedom from the necessity bias. Law is often fixated on the past. Precedent appears to predetermine the future, by requiring that legal disputes are resolved consistently with past decisions.[44] This is not to say that we are always in the grip of the past. The role of lawyers is to mediate the past

---

[41] D Hume *A Treatise of Human Nature* (1739), edited by LA Selby-Bigge and PH Nidditch (Clarendon Press, Oxford: 1978) 155.

[42] See D Lewis "Causation as Influence" in J Collins, E Hall and L Paul (eds.) *Causation and Counterfactuals* (Cambridge, Mass, MIT Press: 2004) 75–106.

[43] Weber, note 36 at 164.

[44] As Anne Orford observes: "The past, in other words, may be a source of present obligations" (A Orford "The Past as Law or History? The Relevance of Imperialism for Modern International Law" *Institute for International Law and Justice (IILJ)* Working Paper 2012/2, 2).

for use in the present under conditions of free will. Nothing is inevitable unless it has already happened, but in using history we must guard against the use of false assumptions: that because something has happened, it was somehow inevitable. When we know that things have happened, we tend to load our evidence of circumstances in favour of those outcomes. We elevate the inevitable and ignore or marginalize the contingency of things.[45] This is reinforced by insights from social psychology, which show that we suffer from hindsight bias: that we see the probability of an outcome happening as higher once we know that outcome has in fact happened.[46]

The second benefit is that it forces us to explain how law works free of recourse to abstract theories. It focuses the mind on actual events and so foregrounds the authentic over the ideal. In order to maintain coherence, theories carve out regularities from the world and overlook the way in which concrete events influence what happens.[47] We must be careful not to ignore the importance and influence of actual events. Since counterfactual thinking is explicitly concerned with context, it provides better accounts of how legal practices work. It exposes the contingency of events and so is closer to how law works in practice. If we can provide more exact accounts of how events unfold, then we can think about how to utilize or respond to such contingencies when charting the course of future regulation.

The third benefit is that it stimulates imaginative thinking and regulatory possibility. Much legal thinking is concerned with the consequences. For a judge, the legal and behavioural consequences of his ruling.[48] For a law-maker, the regulatory impacts, costs and benefits of proposed legislation.[49] The same holds true, and more, for a researcher, who is less bound by the institutional demands of his/her office. Counterfactual thinking forces us to consider possible consequences – real and imagined – in detail. It can improve the rigor of consequentialist analysis. More than this, it can inspire thoughts of what may yet be. This creativity is deeply rooted in our approaches to legal thinking. Rawls' veil of ignorance is just one such device used to provoke reflection upon alternative possibilities.[50] By thinking about how fisheries regulation might be, for better or worse, we can choose to imagine or follow different regulatory pathways.[51] In this way, the act of counterfactual thinking can facilitate behavioural change.

---

[45] Venzke, note 3 at 7 citing RM Unger *False Necessity* (Verso, London: 2001).

[46] Ibid., 9, referring to NJ Roese and KD Vohs "Hindsight Bias" (2012) 7 *Perspectives on Psychological Science* 411–426.

[47] Ibid., 10.

[48] B Rudden "Consequences" (1979) 24 *Juridical Review* 193–201. See also K Mathis "Consequentialism in Law" in K Mathis (ed.) *Efficiency, Sustainability, and Justice to Future Generations* (Springer, Dordrecht: 2012) 3–29.

[49] See CA Dunlop and CM Radaelli (eds.) *Research Handbook of Regulatory Impact Assessment* (Edward Elgar, Cheltenham: 2016).

[50] J Rawls *A Theory of Justice* (Oxford University Press, Oxford: 1973) 136–142.

[51] The analogy from literature is the fate of Ebenezer Scrooge in Charles Dickens' *A Christmas Carol*.

3.3. Some Limitations of Counterfactual Thinking

There are four broad challenges with the use of counterfactual thinking: evidence, complexity and two related issues of causation. First, since counterfactuals depend on hypotheticals – rather than empirical cause and effect – it is impossible to provide actual evidence to 'prove' the outcome of the thought experiment. The absence of proof means outcomes are more readily open to challenge. Accordingly, the effectiveness of our analysis depends upon the counterfactual's proximity to real world situations. Accordingly, smaller and more proximate false antecedents are likely to generate stronger case studies than more general or radical scenarios. However, this may limit the potential for counterfactual thinking.

Second, how do we handle complexity? It is difficult enough to make sense of the past, but this pales into comparison when trying to predict the future.[52] This is usually done with some form of scientific model, simulation or scenario testing.[53] These techniques often entail assumptions, generalizations or simplifications of the variables, and so science can be more easily contested. Counterfactual thinking requires one to contextualize an antecedent (and so have some sense of a past situation), and then effectively predict what will follow from this changed variable. As such, there is an element of real and imagined predictive thinking inherent in counterfactual analysis. This is no small task since reality is so rich in detail and meaning.

Third, one must reconstruct causal relationships in an alternative world in light of a changed antecedent. As such one needs a clear and reliable account of causation. As noted above, counterfactual thinking is most effective in simple cause and effect scenarios. For example, if I had not dropped the glass, it would not have smashed. However, when the phenomenon under analysis is complex, one has to account for a greater array of variables. Fisheries regulation is one such complex scenario, and so one must be very careful in how one explains causal relationships between antecedents and consequences.[54] Potentially, there is scope to draw upon other legal approaches to inform this, such as tort law with its notions of multiple causation and necessary and sufficient conditions.

Finally, it should be acknowledged that counterfactual thinking often suffers from extrapolating a general lesson from a single event into a generalized causal explanation.[55] Lawyers are drawn to make policy recommendations, but it is

---

[52] PE Tetlock "Theory-Driven Reasoning About Plausible Pasts and Probable Futures in World Politics: Are We Prisoners of Our Preconceptions?" (1999) 43 *American Journal of Political Science* 335–336.

[53] M Haddon *Modelling and Quantitative Methods in Fisheries* 2nd ed. (CRC Press, Boca Raton: 2011).

[54] See further HLA Hart and T Honoré *Causation in the Law* 2nd ed. (Clarendon Press, Oxford: 2002).

[55] G Mitchell "Case Studies, Counterfactuals, and Causal Explanations" (2004) 152 *University of Pennsylvania Law Review* 1517–1608, at 1540.

important not to make sweeping inductive leaps from limited premises. For example, taking the *Estai* case[56] scenario as a counterfactual, if we allowed Canada to enforce multilaterally-agreed catch restrictions on all — foreign and Canadian — vessels fishing on the entirety of the Grand Banks, then this would have averted the collapse of the cod stock.[57] The conclusion might be that coastal State enforcement of catch limits on the high seas is a necessary restriction on fishing. However, this analysis might be contested for a number of reasons, but specifically on the grounds that it assumes that the specific lessons from the *Estai* case are generalizable to all other situations where straddling fish stocks are overfished. That said, there seems to be little disagreement that poor flag State monitoring and compliance has undermined effective fisheries regulation, and this must be addressed going forward.[58]

These limitations demand that we posit a robust counterfactual methodology.

3.4. Making Counterfactual Thinking More Robust

Mitchell has broken important ground by developing some responses to the main criticism of counterfactual analysis, and, in particular, the claim that counterfactual approaches can only draw inferences from single case studies.[59] He provides six normative criteria for use in strengthening counterfactual narratives: (1) transparency; (2) counterfactuality of the proposed antecedent; (3) consideration of competing hypotheses; (4) theoretical and statistical reasonableness of the proposed causal chain; (5) co-tenability and counterfactual minimalism; and (6) projectability.

Transparency entails being explicit and precise in stating the terms of the counterfactual, including the selection of evidence, causal inferences and generalizations that flow from this.[60] The more particular the detail, then the more testable the hypothesis. In the cases studies advanced in the next section, this entails: (1) precision about what elements of environmental law (the antecedents) could have precipitated changes in fisheries law; (2) drawing a clear link between the antecedents and the consequences; and (3) providing details about the alternative regime of fisheries that would result from this.

The second requirement is that the antecedent is actually a counterfactual; something that does not exist in the real world.[61] It may be difficult to

---

[56] *Fisheries Jurisdiction (Spain v. Canada)*, Judgment of 4 December 1998; ICJ Reports 1998, p. 432.

[57] PGG Davies "The EC/Canadian Fisheries Dispute in the Northwest Atlantic" (1995) 44 *International and Comparative Law Quarterly* 927–939.

[58] See further Chapter 15 of this volume (Klein). Also, R Barnes "Flag States" in DR Rothwell, AG Oude Elferink, KN Scott and T Stephens (eds.) *The Oxford Handbook on the Law of the Sea* (Oxford University Press, Oxford: 2015) 304–324.

[59] Mitchell, note 55 at 1587–1602.

[60] Ibid., 1589–1591.

[61] Ibid., 1591.

separate out real from imagined events because the antecedent may change just one dimension of reality, for example the point in time of an event. In most cases this normative check serves to reinforce the importance of precision in the selection of the antecedent. In our case, some elements of environmental law predated some fisheries law (e.g. the *sic utere* principle), whilst others did not (e.g. the precautionary principle). Thus we should be specific in identifying those elements of environmental law that have emerged after international fisheries law had matured.

Third, competing hypotheses must be considered. Mitchell notes that single observation case studies (i.e. use of singular antecedents) are vulnerable to challenge because there may be multiple causative antecedents.[62] It is only when competing explanations are discounted that the remaining hypothesis is strengthened. This is important because counterfactuals are easily controvertible given their imagined status. Here we can discount patent absurdity or logical failures, but this may still leave scope for debating alternative causal factors. Even if these cannot be fully discounted, a failure to address them leaves one open to the criticism of over-determination or outcome bias.

Fourth, it is necessary to consider the robustness of the causal link between the antecedent and the consequences. As Mitchell states: "The more theoretically or statistically justifiable the propositions in a thought experiment, the more defensible the conclusions drawn from the experiment".[63] It seems unlikely in the following scenarios, that one can provide a high – let alone absolute – probability of cause and effect. Of course, most social science approaches tend to rely upon probability-based causation. As such, we settle for weaker statistical thresholds, such as 'more likely than not', or 'on the balance of probabilities'. What is critical in this context is to identify and explain the probabilities on the basis of identifiable patterns of behaviour and real world constraints on action. For example, we understand how international law deals with conflicts of norms, and we also have experience of how States have handled the emergence of environmental norms subsequent to the development of international fisheries law. These insights can inform how our scenario might work, with fisheries law emerging post-environmental law. To quote Marks: "[...] possibilities are framed by circumstances. While current arrangements can indeed be changed, change unfolds within a context that includes systematic constraints and pressures".[64] These constraints (as outlined in Section 2 above) may provide reasonable proxies for explaining how States would have handled matters in our counterfactual.

Fifth, co-tenability requires us to consider "whether the features of the alternative world are logically and historically consistent".[65] As far as possible the

[62] Ibid., 1592.
[63] Ibid., 1594.
[64] S Marks "False Contingency" (2009) 62 *Current Legal Problems* 1–21, at 2.
[65] Mitchell, note 55 at 1595–1596.

counterfactual world must resemble the real world, so the logic, structure and operation of that world should be retained. Arguably, this is the most difficult criterion to satisfy because it entails consideration of the systemic context and consequences of one's proposed antecedent. For example, it would be less tenable to assert the emergence of much environmental law preceding the emergence of the UN, given its pivotal role in facilitating the advance of environmental issues. On the other hand, a decision in favour of the United States in the *Bering Fur Seals* case might have turned on the quality of the litigants' arguments. This points towards a minimization of change in the antecedent. The greater the change, the greater the risk of systemic inconsistency. Compensating for this entails more and more explanation. These explanations become more difficult to articulate and so the greater likelihood of ignoring some variables that would impact upon the predicted consequences. Indeed, this requirement must inform how we approach the task of constructing an antecedent around the pre-existence of international environmental law to international fisheries law. International environmental law comprises a complex system of values, rules, standards, processes, institutions and actors. To explain and map the implications of these is a Sisyphean task. A more tenable counterfactual would therefore be to focus on a specific rule or process.

Finally, a strong counterfactual will 'project' valid predictions for other cases.[66] This should follow from the requirement that the counterfactual is co-tenable and plausible. It further allows the hypothesis to be tested in other contexts and identify any limits in its potential application. Space precludes multiple scenario testing, but if counterfactual analysis can illuminate historical contingencies that no longer matter, and which have resulted in unsatisfactory or out-dated regulatory arrangements, then exposing these contingencies helps strengthen the case for reform in those areas.

4. "WHAT IF INTERNATIONAL ENVIRONMENTAL LAW PREDATED INTERNATIONAL FISHERIES LAW ...?"

Would international fisheries law be any different if it had been preceded by a body of rules of international environmental law? If we want to imagine how international fisheries law might be different, then we need to reimagine history at some point prior to the preparatory work of the International Law Commission (ILC) on the four Geneva Conventions on the law of the sea of 1958. In examining how some of the key rules and principles of international environmental law could have influenced international fisheries law, an effort is made to ensure that the six normative criteria in subsection 3.4 are considered.

---

[66] Ibid., 1600–1601.

There are good reasons for this choice of scenario. First, it uses a self-evidently false antecedent. Second, it allows us to reconstruct international fisheries law at a critical juncture in time, when treaty law was becoming the preferred modus operandi of law-making. This allows us to generalize not just about specific rules, but also about processes. Much of modern international fisheries law can be traced back to the 1958 Geneva Conventions, which codified and structured the main features of the law of the sea. Many of the Geneva rules (e.g. zonal allocations of authority, freedom of the high seas and primacy of flag State jurisdiction on the high seas) found their way into the LOS Convention with little change, and so became more firmly established as core elements of the law of the sea. Much of international environmental law became established by 1992, as signified by the Rio Conference. It is accepted that these statements are rough generalizations, and that they gloss over the full legal heritage of both areas of law. However, this makes it possible to draw out from the Rio Declaration and related agreements both general points of evaluation and specific analysis of novel environmental principles and rules that are fundamentally relevant to fishing activities. We can assume that any changes to the 1958 Geneva Conventions would permeate through to the LOS Convention in similar fashion. In a sense we are advancing the progress of legal development. The timeframe also allows us to draw upon insights as to how international fisheries law has developed in the 25 years or so since Rio. This is important as these insights can help ensure the tenability and robustness of some of the analytical lessons drawn from the counterfactual.

By way of transparency, some caveats are required about the following scenario analysis. In setting out the provisions of law and providing some indication of the outcomes, it is quite clear that we are often proceeding from one set of generalities to another as regards the principles canvassed. The LOS Convention is a framework instrument. One of its most observed features is the open-textured language and structure which admits of a variety of different principles and approaches to be accommodated within its framework, including environmental norms. In our counterfactual, clear and strong norms on environmental protection could have been integrated into the 1958 Geneva Conventions. Over time these would have consolidated and more directly influenced the text of the LOS Convention and later agreements. Paradoxically, this could have a counter-productive effect of rendering the LOS Convention's text more fixed and less open to flexible development. A second paradox relates to the specific principles of international environmental law. As one moves to greater levels of specificity, it becomes increasingly difficult to isolate precise normative developments and their consequences. Many principles or approaches such as precaution, polluter pays and ecosystem-based management are deeply rooted in complex processes and so cannot be surgically isolated and introduced into a counterfactual. For example, due diligence to prevent environmental harm (e.g. through licensing of fishing vessels) is not a novel, discrete principle, but something that originated in and developed since the *Trail Smelter* case.[67]

4.1. The "Rio Conference 1952: What if ..."

Imagine the following:[68]

> *The Earth Summit took place between 3 and 14 June 1952, and became known as 'Rio 1952'. It marked a turning point in the development of measures to protect the global environment. Attended by representatives from nearly 100 nations, the conference resulted in three major international conventions (the '1952 United Nations Framework Convention on Climate Change', the '1952 Convention on Biological Diversity' (1952 CBD), and the '1952 United Nations Convention to Combat Desertification') and the 1952 Rio Declaration, which set forth 27 core principles of international environmental law. It also spurred on the development of regional seas environmental agreements, such as the '1962 OSPAR Convention'. The ILC had already begun work on codifying the law of the sea in 1949. However, it was sensitive to the wider developments in international law and so these formed part of the existing legal structure into which the law of the sea and fisheries law would need to fit.*

Before looking at how some specific principles of international environmental law would have impacted upon international fisheries law, some general observations can be made. First, the make-up of international society was quite different in 1952, with many present-day States still part of colonial empires. If nothing else, this points to the contingency of law-creation upon the number and identity of members of the legal order. Here, the particular interests and aims of developing States would have had less profile in negotiations and the outcomes of the alternative Rio 1952.

Second, treaties are drafted with sensitivity to existing legal frameworks. This is generally reflected in preambular statements of context, as well as specific conflict clauses.[69] In the 1958 Geneva Conventions, there were no such references to relevant or overlapping treaties. This would need to be accounted for in the counterfactual. The mere existence of potentially overlapping agreements would force States to address the question of priority as

---

[67] *Trail Smelter* case (United States of America, Canada) Award of 16 April 1938 and 11 March 1941, 3 *Reports of International Arbitral Awards* 1905–1982.

[68] To ensure narrative clarity, accounts of the counterfactual are italicized. Comment and analysis thereof is left in regular text format. In the counterfactuals, alternative versions of real environmental instruments are used. These are self-evident given the false dates. The counterfactual law of the sea conventions remain fixed in time at 1958 and 1982 to facilitate the analysis. To ensure alternative instruments are distinguished from the real instruments in the analysis, the counterfactual versions are specifically designated as alternative conventions or placed in quotes.

[69] See e.g. Art. 311 of the LOS Convention, Art. 4 of the Fish Stocks Agreement, and Art. 4 of the Agreement on Port State Measures to Prevent, Deter and Eliminate Illegal, Unreported and Unregulated Fishing of 22 November 2009 (available at www.fao.org/Legal).

a political matter, and to structure the relationship between different agreements within a conflict clause. As a general rule, compatible agreements or terms are often preserved, and later agreements usually take priority over older agreements.[70] However, specific terms can be included in the later treaty to preserve the rules of earlier agreements deemed more foundational or constitutive of the general legal order.[71] The key point is that once this is done, it secures and structures treaty relationships at a given point of time. This may make it difficult to restructure legal relationships or normative priorities between treaties at a later date. This is a particular concern with the constituent agreements of RFMOs predating the Fish Stocks Agreement, and which do not accommodate modern principles of international fisheries law. This highlights the contingency of agreements, and the need to ensure conflict clauses (or means of amending agreements) are capable of adapting to changes in wider legal frameworks. Both environmental and fisheries agreements deal with dynamic systems and regulatory agendas, so caution must be taken in trying to embed certain rules and regimes too strongly in the international legal framework.

> *Rio 1952 resulted in a number of important outcomes, both symbolically and substantively. The former included its role in raising collective awareness about the magnitude of environmental issues and the need to address them.[72] Indeed, its partner instrument, Agenda 20, carried with it a strong "moral obligation to ensure its fulfilment" by the end of the century. This clear signal from so many States exerted a sway over contemporary law-making agendas. The latter included a range of techniques and principles relevant to fisheries: Principle 3 (intergenerational equity); Principle 7 (ecosystem approach); Principle 10 (participatory decision-making); Principle 15 (precaution); Principle 17 (environmental impact assessment); and Principle 27 (cooperation).*

Before looking at the influence of the substantive rules of international environmental law in our counterfactual, a brief comment is offered on the symbolism and agenda-setting influence of Rio 1992.[73] Whilst not strictly normative, Rio 1992 and related instruments are regularly emphasized within the preamble of modern fisheries agreements (and other environmental agreements). They are part of the context for purposes of treaty interpretation.[74] It may be observed that the term 'environment' does not appear in any of the real

---

[70] See Art. 30 of the Vienna Convention on the Law of Treaties of 23 May 1969 (1155 UNTS 331).

[71] This is done in Art. 4 of the Fish Stocks Agreement, which states it to be without prejudice to the LOS Convention. See also Art. 103 of the United Nations Charter.

[72] For this argument in our real history, see DC Esty "Beyond Rio: Trade and the Environment" (1993) 23 *Environmental Law* 387–396, at 388.

[73] A counterfactual around Principle 1 of Rio 1952 and a right to a healthy environment could have been included. However, it was omitted on the basis that such a right remains contested, and so difficult to evaluate on the basis of co-tenability. At best it would serve to reinforce the significance attached to State concerns rather than individual concerns in international fisheries law.

[74] See e.g. paras. 5 and 7 of the Preamble to the Fish Stocks Agreement, and paras. 4 and 6 of the Compliance Agreement.

1958 Geneva Conventions, and there is only limited reference to pollution.[75] In contrast, the language and terminology of the '1952 Rio instruments' (e.g. sustainable use, ecosystem) would likely permeate later agreements. The use of shared language and conceptualization of issues invariably shapes the understanding of what particular rules mean. We know this already occurs in the sense that the LOS Convention is a 'living instrument'. The evolution of treaties is indirect in that it utilizes a flexible approach to the interpretation of treaties, something that can be contested. A direct embedding of rules, concepts and institutions into earlier fisheries agreements could have removed much of the uncertainty about how these rules relate to environmental activities. Of course, this risks the prized flexibility of some fisheries agreements as noted above.

> *Principle 3 of the 1952 Rio Declaration emphasized the importance of meeting the developmental and environmental needs of present and future generations. This foregrounding of inter-generational concerns directed attention to the need to limit or restrict fishing effort. Accordingly, Article 2 of the alternative 1958 High Seas Fishing Convention stated the objective of fishing to be to secure "a long term supply of food for human consumption". This general commitment proved to be uncontentious since 'long term' was not defined. The ILC drew upon and attached greater weight to the abstention doctrine in its draft articles. This doctrine sought to limit fishing when a stock was fully exploited. Ultimately, a duty to abstain from fisheries was framed in hortative terms, or made subject to specific agreements between interested fishing States. Debates at the ILC demonstrated that it was difficult to secure agreement on the precise operation of the abstention doctrine, and many feared that it could be cynically used to appropriate resources.[76] Following the adoption of the 1958 Geneva Conventions, the virtue of limiting access to depleted stocks was hampered by difficulties in securing 'abstention' in specific agreements. Whilst abstention worked well within a bilateral fishery, it remained difficult to sustain as a general rule of international fisheries law.[77] As a result, it served mainly to precipitate unilateral claims to exclusive control over important coastal fisheries at risk of overfishing.*

In reality, the abstention doctrine gained limited traction in United States fisheries after World War II, and took longer to feed into international debates about fisheries.[78] It remained on the periphery of debates, although, indirectly, it focused attention on the notion of the Maximum Sustainable Yield (MSY). The impact on the alternative 1958 Geneva Conventions was limited to strengthening sustainability with an intra-generational focus. Even now, fisheries regulation remains strongly focused on intra-generational equity, as indicated in the Preamble of the LOS Convention.[79] Also, Article 59 – concerning conflicts between

---

[75] See Arts. 24–25 of the Convention on the High Seas of 29 April 1958 (450 UNTS 11).

[76] This resonates with the actual debates in the ILC: See Summary Records of the Eighth Session, [1956] 1 *Yearbook of the International Law Commission* 123; UN Doc. A/CN.4/SR.357, 43–49.

[77] H Scheiber "Origins of the Abstention Doctrine in Ocean Law: Japanese-US Relations and Pacific Fisheries. 1937–1958" (1989) 16 *Ecology Law Quarterly* 23–99, at 94.

[78] Ibid., 91.

[79] "[T]he achievement of these goals will contribute to the realization of a just and equitable international economic order which takes into account the interests and needs of mankind as a

States in the EEZ – and Article 69 – concerning land-locked States – both possess an intra-generational focus. Inter-generational equity is indirectly addressed through Articles 61 and 119, which articulate the notion of the MSY. However, this is more narrowly concerned with conserving resources than advancing broader environmental interests.

It might be possible that some concern for future needs could have appeared in the preamble to an alternative LOS Convention, and might have suffused other provisions with a stronger concern for inter-generational concerns. However, the scenario indicates that despite our awareness of inter-generational concerns it is difficult to accommodate such interests within a system of law that lacks representative standing for future generations. And that meeting the current needs of their populace represents a more immediate political concern for States.

The term 'ecosystem' first appeared as a concept in 1937.[80] Principle 7 of the 1952 Rio Declaration provides that "States shall cooperate in a spirit of global partnership to conserve, protect and restore the health and integrity of the Earth's ecosystem". This was developed in more detail in Chapter 17 of Agenda 20. By the time that the alternative 1958 Geneva Conventions were being drafted, it had gained sufficient credibility in science, and traction in policy debates, to merit inclusion. Thus, Article 2 of the alternative 1958 High Seas Fishing Convention required States to assess the impacts of fishing on associated species within the same ecosystem. By the time the alternative LOS Convention had developed, the obligation had strengthened into a duty to take steps to maintain the integrity of marine ecosystems. This was factored into a more complex institutional process for assessing the impacts of fishing, and designating marine protected areas. More significantly, the unexpected collapse of several major commercial fisheries and scientific appreciation of the way in which ecosystems operated – both locally and at larger scales – provided a compelling reason to adopt more nuanced forms of spatial management that correlated to the natural boundaries of ecosystems. As a result, exclusive coastal State jurisdiction was limited to a "security zone of 12 nautical miles (nm)". Beyond this, regional seas arrangements under the shared management coastal States became responsible for adopting fisheries conservation and management measures, as well as measures to protect and preserve the marine environment.

We operate a regime of maritime zones that have little connection to the function of ecosystems. An explicit ecosystem-based approach is absent from the LOS Convention in our reality. The term 'ecosystem' is used in the Fish Stocks Agreement (Articles 5(d) and (e)), but only as a factor linking species/stocks, and not as way of managing in light of how ecosystems function. Whilst the LOS Convention considers the issues of oceans space as closely related and to be considered as a whole, this arguably refers to different sectoral activities, rather than nuanced concepts of ecosystem functioning. The LOS Convention's

---

whole and, in particular, the special interests and needs of developing countries, whether coastal or land-locked".

[80] AJ Willis "The Ecosystem: An Evolving Concept Viewed Historically" (1997) 11 *Functional Ecology* 268–271.

framework for managing fisheries is tied to the rather crude and ecologically meaningless maximum outer limit set for the EEZ.[81] It also possesses a sectoral structure that divides resource matters from marine environmental protection.

Post LOS Convention, this has been a key focus of regulatory developments. One of the objectives of Chapter 17 of Agenda 21 was to "integrate protection of the marine environment into relevant general environmental, social and economic development policies".[82] However, international fisheries law remains wedded to jurisdictional arrangements that simply do not match ecological needs, or indeed, the dependent resource activities.[83] At a regional level, the European Union (EU) Marine Strategy Framework Directive operates on the basis of regional seas and sub-regions.[84] Although this is contingent upon underlying jurisdiction over EEZs, the actual management measures operate across jurisdictions. It establishes 11 descriptors (targets) of good environmental status – which includes fisheries – and so represents a significant improvement in the alignment of regulatory measures with natural systems. This element of the scenario highlights the contingency of legal developments upon the state and influence of scientific information. It also flags up the possibilities for change in how we designate spatial management zones.

Principle 17 of the 1952 Rio Declaration provides that "Environmental impact assessment (EIA), as a national instrument, shall be undertaken for proposed activities that are likely to have a significant adverse impact on the environment and are subject to a decision of a competent national authority". The 1952 Rio Declaration does not articulate how this is to be done, leaving such matters to individual States.

This complemented Principle 10, which called for participatory decision-making, appropriate access to information about the environment, and opportunities for involvement in decision-making and access to effective judicial and administrative remedies. This provision was strongly influenced by the wider recognition afforded to human rights at the time. Both these provisions were recognized in the alternative 1958 High Seas Fishing Convention, although to a lesser extent. It required States to adopt processes to assess the impact of fishing and ensure that information concerning such decision-making process be publicly available. Within domestic environmental and fisheries regimes, more sophisticated marine impact assessment processes emerged. These established more specific criteria concerning the threshold for assessments, the factors to be assessed, and any mitigation or adaptation measures to be taken if a development was to proceed despite the potential for harm.

---

[81] RR Churchill and AV Lowe *The Law of the Sea* 3rd ed. (Manchester University Press, Manchester: 1999) 163.

[82] Agenda 21, para. 17.22.

[83] Less radically, Árnadóttir suggests changing ecological circumstances could justify changing some parts of an agreed maritime boundary, when the boundary no longer suits the underlying fishing or resource activities that helped determine its course (S Árnadóttir "Ecological Changes Justifying Termination or Revision of EEZ and EFZ Boundaries" (2017) 84 *Marine Policy* 287–292).

[84] Art. 4 of Directive 2008/56/EC of the European Parliament and of the Council of 17 June 2008 establishing a framework for community action in the field of marine environmental policy. OJ L 164, 25.6.2008, pp. 19–40.

Initially focused on physical developments at sea, these were extended to fish farms, new fisheries and fisheries that had been closed to facilitate stock recovery. Significantly, the data and understanding derived from such assessments was used to inform a wider range of marine planning initiatives. The use of EIA helped facilitate the integration of fisheries and environmental matters. By the time UNCLOS III had convened, States recognized the value of accommodating such assessments, and facilitating the conduct of project- and programme-based assessments between States. As a result the alternative LOS Convention embodied detailed provisions on EIA. This was complemented by a broader commitment by States to conduct strategic assessments at a regional level.

In our world, Article 206 of the LOS Convention contains only general requirements to assess the potential effects of activities. This falls short of the standard of environmental assessment anticipated by the 1992 Rio Declaration. Whilst some States require EIAs for marine projects, this usually excludes fisheries because such systems are designed to apply to new activities rather than continuing activities.[85] Fisheries are part of the background noise of environmental harm.

The LOS Convention merely contains general provisions on publication of information, or the provision of information to other States, particularly in the context of marine scientific research.[86] It does not countenance individual engagement in, for example, decision-making in fisheries management or marine environmental protection. A low level of participatory decision-making has undermined confidence in some fisheries management regimes, such as the EU Common Fisheries Policy.[87]

This element of the scenario again highlights the contingency of legal developments upon the state and influence of scientific information. It also demonstrates the adverse impacts of path dependency in legal developments. As most commercial fishing activities have existed prior to the legal requirement to conduct full EIAs, they tend to be excluded from this process. Although we recognize the adverse impact of fishing on marine ecosystems, it is difficult to retrofit fisheries management regimes with more rigorous assessment processes.

Arguably the most important but challenging contribution of Rio 1952 was the precautionary principle: "Where there are threats of serious or irreversible damage, lack of full scientific certainty shall not be used as a reason for postponing cost-effective measures to prevent environmental degradation". This had no analogue in other instruments adopted at the time, although it has similarities with the

---

[85] F Guerra, C Grilo, NM Pedroso and H Cabral "Environmental Impact Assessment in the Marine Environment: A Comparison of Legal Frameworks" (2015) 55 *Environmental Impact Assessment Review* 182–194.

[86] Arts. 200, 244, 248 and 302 of the LOS Convention.

[87] J Hatchard and T Gray "Stakeholders and the Reform of the European Unions' Common Fisheries Policy" (2003) 2 *Maritime Studies (MAST)* 5–20; C Pita, GJ Pierce and I Theodossiou "Stakeholders' Participation in the Fisheries Management Decision-making Process: Fishers' Perceptions of Participation" (2010) 34 *Marine Policy* 1093–1102.

abstention doctrine.[88] *Fishing would not then resume until sufficient scientific evidence was provided showing the stocks were capable of supporting fishing effort. Following intense debates within the ILC, precaution was included in the draft text. Article 2(2) of the alternative 1958 High Seas Fishing Convention provided that: "States shall apply the precautionary approach to conservation, management and exploitation of fish stocks in order to protect the living marine resources and preserve the marine environment". Implementation remained sporadic in the early years, largely due to disputed data on stock conditions. However, following the collapse of some major commercial fisheries, States began to establish precautionary reference points for fish stocks. By focusing attention on risk assessment, scientific evidence came more strongly to the fore in decision-making processes. By the mid-1960s, over-exploitation of some fisheries was reducing, but at some social and political cost. Excess capacity remained in the industry, and so more radical steps were taken to try and remove this capacity, including decommissioning payments. In some cases excess capacity moved into unregulated fisheries, either on the high seas, or in coastal waters of developing States.*

It is relatively easy to claim that the precautionary principle (or approach) would have permeated a wider range of legal instruments sooner. This is evident from how modern fisheries agreements developed post-Rio 1992.[89] The challenge with counterfactual thinking about the precautionary principle is that it really demands some assessment of the behavioural or problem-solving impacts of the principle. For example, what would be the state of global fish stocks if we had used precautionary measures 30 years earlier? FAO data indicates that production from capture fisheries more than trebled between 1950 and 1980, but has remained relatively static since then.[90] Stocks have not improved. The proportion of fish stocks within biologically sustainable levels decreased from 90 per cent in 1974 to 68.6 per cent in 2013. The number of under-exploited stocks decreased in the same period.[91] This might indicate that precautionary measures in fisheries have not had any impact. However, the response to this is that they might be in even worse shape had not some precautionary measures been introduced. It is not unreasonable to assume that the earlier introduction of precautionary measures may have helped restrict major fleet expansion post-World War II and so mitigate over-exploitation. We simply do not know.

In our reality, the precautionary principle found its way into international fisheries and environmental instruments during the late 1980s and 1990s.[92]

---

[88] Exceptionally, one might note the International Convention for High Seas Fisheries of the North Pacific Ocean of 9 May 1952 (205 UNTS 80), which used adopted conservation measures on grounds including the *abstention* principle. See note 77 and the accompanying discussion.

[89] D Freestone "International Fisheries Law since Rio: The Continued Rise of the Precautionary Principle" in A Boyle and D Freestone (eds.) *International Law and Sustainable Development: Past Achievements and Future Challenges* (Oxford University Press, Oxford: 1999) 135–164.

[90] *The State of World Fisheries and Aquaculture 2016* (FAO, Rome: 2016) 2–3.

[91] Ibid., 5–6.

[92] D Freestone and E Hey "Origins and Development of the Precautionary Principle" in D Freestone and E Hey (eds.) *The Precautionary Principle and International Law: The Challenge*

This indicates that the strength and influence of the precautionary principle is rooted in the numerous instruments within which it is found.[93] Posited alone in the Rio instruments, the precautionary principle would have had far weaker normative standing. As such one might question and doubt how a principle rooted only in a soft-law instrument would have been factored into early fisheries agreements. This points to the importance of systemic relationships within the law-creation process, rather than singular cause and effect relationships. Our counterfactual cannot escape the complexity of such contingent relationships. On a positive note, the precautionary principle serves to inform everyday fisheries management with a counterfactual method: it demands that future scenarios (i.e. limited or unconstrained fishing levels) be evaluated and optioned. As such we may become better equipped to engage in counterfactual analyses within fisheries going forward.

It is opportune to make some general remarks on the counterfactual in light of the criteria for counterfactual analysis noted above. The first relates to the theoretical and statistical reasonableness of the proposed causal chain. On the balance of probabilities, the 1958 Geneva Conventions would have been suffused with some important, but rather general changes owing to the existence of earlier environmental norms. These in turn would have evolved further and penetrated the LOS Convention to a greater extent. The precise outcome of this is hard to map. However, the existence of such changes can be readily assumed because treaties are not negotiated in a vacuum. Drafters are careful to ensure a degree of coherence between new and existing treaties. As post-LOS Convention developments in our real world indicate, jurists have sought to reconcile subsequent developments with the LOS Convention. Our desire to ensure system coherence requires us to mediate potential conflicts. Given the generality of the LOS Convention and also of the 1992 Rio Principles, there is little reason to suspect that drafters of the LOS Convention in a counterfactual world would have sought to detach the LOS Convention from contemporary and potential compatible environmental norms. It is highly probable that this integration would have extended to cooperation between different sectoral bodies, or that cross-cutting regional arrangements could have evolved. In recent years, semi-formalized cooperative approaches to fisheries and marine environmental issues have been developed.[94] This is not an isolated phenomenon, but is part of a broader trend of cooperation within and between multilateral environmental agreements (MEAs).[95] This has grown

of Implementation (Kluwer, The Hague: 1996) 3–15; G Hewison "The Precautionary Approach to Fisheries Management: An Environmental Perspective" (1996) 11 *International Journal of Marine and Coastal Law* 301–332.

[93] P Cameron and J Abouchar "The Status of the Precautionary Principle" in Freestone and Hey, note 92, 29–52, at 30.

[94] E.g. between the OSPAR Commission and NEAFC (see note 29 and accompanying text).

[95] Strengthened links between MEAs were recommended in the Report of the United Nations Task Force on Environment and Human Settlements (Annex to UN Doc. A/53/463 of 6 October 1998, para. 30).

naturally out of institutional practices, by virtue of express or implied powers, and the growth of institutional capacity per se.[96]

To shore up some of the above analysis, lessons can be drawn from a comparison between fisheries regimes and the development of the deep-seabed mining regime, and how the latter demonstrates the traction and impact that environmental principles have had. The deep-seabed mining regime emerged after the LOS Convention through the Deep-Seabed Mining Agreement[97] and has continued to develop through the International Seabed Authority (ISA)'s Mining Code[98] since 2000. As such, it was negotiated and drafted in light of a stronger body of international environmental rules and principles, which, in turn, advance both inter- and intra-generational concerns.[99] Here the ISA acts as a quasi-legislator and administrator for activities in the Area. The ISA's environmental mandate was partially structured within the LOS Convention: with Article 165(2)(d) requiring its Legal and Technical Commission to "prepare assessments of the environmental implications of activities in the Area". This does not quite correspond to a detailed EIA process, but indicates the importance of having facilitative provisions built into the basic structure of agreements, which can be built upon by later agreements or institutional developments.

Perhaps the greatest weakness is to establish co-tenability. This is because law is the product of complex and diffuse processes. Agreements are highly contingent upon preceding events, the state of knowledge and wider political agendas. Whilst aspects of international fisheries law and the 1992 Rio instruments might be complementary,[100] they are also distinctive in terms of nature and scope. The careful observer might note that our 'Rio 1952' was not preceded by an equivalent 'Stockholm 1932', and so lacked that intellectual and policy heritage. To rectify this we are required to revisit and restructure another major event in order to account for this, locating an international conference in the inter-war years. Alternatively, we could simply assert that Stockholm 1972 produced the same outcomes as Rio 1992. However, this ignores the progressive development of principles between the two. It also ignores the fact that these developments are not singular events in history, but rather the apex of more complex processes of negotiation and preparatory events. Important way stations included the work of the Brundtland Commission (1982–1987) and its development of the core principle of sustainable development. More challenging is the fact that the influence of many of the principles and approaches advanced at Rio 1992

---

[96] See RR Churchill and G Ulfstein "Autonomous Institutional Arrangements in Multilateral Environmental Agreements: A Little-Noticed Phenomenon in International Law" (2000) 94 *American Journal of International Law* 623–659, at 654–655.

[97] Agreement relating to the Implementation of Part XI of the United Nations Convention on the Law of the Sea of 10 December 1982 of 28 July 1994 (1836 UNTS 42).

[98] Available at https://www.isa.org.jm/mining-code.

[99] A Jaeckel, KM Gjerde and JA Ardron "Conserving the Common Heritage of Humankind – Options for the Deep-seabed Mining Regime" (2017) 78 *Marine Policy* 150–157, at 151–152.

[100] A Yankov "The Law of the Sea and Agenda 21: Marine Environmental Implications" in Boyle and Freestone, note 89 at 271–96.

cannot be viewed apart from the complex structure of agreements and practices within which it is located. As such it is difficult to understand Rio 1992 apart from these; hence undermining the tenability of the counterfactual. Paradoxically, Agenda 21 assumes the existence of the LOS Convention and built upon its general framework. For that reason we would have to reimagine Agenda 21 without the LOS Convention and this might present quite different outcomes for our analysis. Of course, the briefly sketched picture of deep-seabed mining serves to strengthen our conclusion that international fisheries law would have been imbued with stronger environmental law norms.

5. COUNTERFACTUAL LESSONS

The following tentative conclusions are suggested from our counterfactual exercise. First, at best, cross-cutting integrative approaches would be more deeply rooted in international fisheries law, and we could have seen the evolution of institutional practices and mechanisms at an earlier stage. One of the most important – but general – consequences of international environmental law is that is encourages systemic thinking. This is not inconsistent with a LOS Convention in either the real or an alternative world, and so one could foresee that an alternative LOS Convention negotiated against a background of greater environmental awareness and putative environmental norms would have been imbued with stronger systemic linkages between different sectors. However, whilst we can claim with some degree of confidence that the content of the law would be different, it is far more challenging to assess the behaviour and problem-solving impacts this would have had on fisheries. This is because the wider technological, economic and social changes within which such rules operate are complex and have changed quite significantly over the past six decades since 'Rio 52'.

Second, international environmental law has developed in a systematic, progressive fashion, with a gradual evolution and building of norms. This shows that there are quite strong constraints built into international law, and implies that counterfactual thinking may be limited or at least should focus on how discreet events could induce different outcomes. Counterfactual scenarios focusing on broad systemic changes, such as the earlier consolidation of international environmental law, have limits as analytical tools. Sharper insights can be drawn from examining specific principles or events and tracing their alternative pathways. Even at a general level these flag up some of the contingencies that have driven legal developments. Given that many of these historical contingencies have less significance now, this can be used to strengthen calls for reform of current legal instruments. In other words, we should refuse to be tied to outdated historical contingencies. This represents something of a departure from the dominant mode of thinking in international fisheries law, which is often quite cautious and sensitive to past events.

Finally, another challenge is that some principles of modern international environmental law require the existence of particular institutional capacities to maximize how information is gathered, held, verified, used, monitored and evaluated. For example, our ability to conduct EIAs requires a certain quality of information and expertise (within decision-making structures). Given the limitations in some States to support this, it is quite probable that the LOS Convention would not have established rigorous commitments to conduct EIAs. However, if these EIA processes had gained traction within domestic law earlier, there is the chance that States would have been more comfortable with their inclusion in the LOS Convention or RFMOs. Alongside the International Tribunal for the Law of the Sea, the ISA and the Commission for the Limits of the Continental Shelf, it is possible there would have been other institutional structures to handle such assessments. Returning to our initial proposition, law is not inevitable, it is the product of historical contingencies. Many of those contingencies that kept environmental factors out of fisheries law are much less relevant today than they were in 1958 or indeed 1982. Having worked through our counterfactual analysis to expose these contingencies, we should be saying not "what if ...", but "now that environmental principles are strongly grounded in international law, how best can we properly realize them in international fisheries law."

4

Management Options for High Seas Fisheries: Making Regime Complexes More Effective

OLAV SCHRAM STOKKE

1. INTRODUCTION

WHAT ARE THE most promising options for improving the management of the world's high seas fisheries? Here, a 'management option' refers to any institutional measure that States or other actors may take to improve the balance between the use and the conservation of marine living resources. High seas fisheries management involves all the challenges that any common property poses for States seeking to coordinate their actions to achieve such a balance, with the additional challenge that only the flag State has extensive jurisdiction over the vessels that engage in fishing or fishing-related activities, such as provisioning of fuel, water etc., and transshipment of catch.

This near-monopoly of the flag State on regulatory and enforcement action is one important reason why effective high seas fisheries management generally requires coherent operation of several public/State institutions as well as private ones, at the national, regional and global levels of governance. Each component institution in such regime complexes has distinctive capacities relevant to one or more of three tasks that governance systems for resource management must attend to. One task is cognitional: building a shared, well-founded understanding of what measures will best balance use and conservation. Another is regulatory: translating this shared understanding of means-ends relationships into agreed commitments. The third governance task is to ensure that actual fisher behaviour complies with those commitments. Each task poses distinctive challenges which must be overcome if high seas fisheries management is to succeed over an extended period of time. The performance of the regime complex for managing high seas fisheries depends crucially upon institutional coherence; namely, the extent to which component institutions are well aligned, providing complementary or synergistic capacities for each of these tasks and promoting the same governance policy objectives.

This chapter first briefly examines the nature of the problem posed by the availability of commercially lucrative fish stocks on the high seas. That problem is defined primarily by the configurations of interests among governmental players such as flag States, coastal States and port States, but also by the goals and strategies of transnational industry and environmental organizations active in the policy area. The chapter then outlines the institutional complex that has evolved for managing this problem, highlighting not only national fisheries agencies and regional fisheries regimes but also global institutions specializing in areas other than resource management, such as international trade or the combat of trafficking in persons or drugs, or money laundering, as well as private governance initiatives like fisheries certification schemes. The substantive core of the chapter examines the coherence of these various contributions to solving the cognitional, regulatory and behavioural tasks of fisheries management, including whether such coherence requires explicit coordination among the component institutions. Empirically, the chapter focuses on several regional regime complexes, including those aiming to govern high seas fisheries in the Barents Sea, the Norwegian Sea and the Southern Ocean.

2. THE PROBLEM OF HIGH SEAS FISHERIES MANAGEMENT

Stocks available in commercially lucrative amounts in high seas waters pose a particularly malign management problem. They entail several challenges associated with any scarce common property resource, plus two others: international coordination, and the limited jurisdiction and leverage for regulation and enforcement by actors other than the flag State.

In general, resource management involves making and implementing authoritative decisions on use and conservation. 'Use' refers here to resource exploitation and allocation of benefits among harvesters, whereas 'conservation' is about ensuring future availability.[1] The root problem of common property resources is that they generate individual incentives that, if unchecked, are likely to prove collectively disruptive. That is because some of the costs associated with resource use disappear from the user's cost-benefit calculus, and such 'externalities' tend to generate more extensive use than is collectively desirable.[2] Whereas each fisher enjoys the full benefit from the catch hauled on board, the costs associated with reduced future availability must be shared by many. Conversely, if some fishers exercise restraint, that will only leave more for the others to catch.

---

[1] OS Stokke "Fisheries and Whaling" in *Encyclopedia of Global Environmental Governance and Politics* (Cheltenham, Edward Elgar: 2015) 364–373.
[2] A Underdal "International Cooperation: Transforming 'Needs' into 'Deeds'" (1987) 24 *Journal of Peace Research* 167–183.

So, unless also those others are prepared to join the programme, the sensible course of action would seem to be to take as much fish as possible. For hundreds or even thousands of years, breaking this tragedy-of-the-commons link between individual rationality and collective ruin is precisely what national institutions for fisheries management have sought to achieve.[3]

When a common property resource is shared by two or more States, additional problems arise; notably that international management institutions tend to be much weaker than those at domestic levels. Inside their maritime zones, coastal States can require all vessels – their own as well as foreign – to submit detailed fisher reports and adhere to whatever management rule they see fit, and may take any enforcement action deemed necessary for ensuring compliance. By contrast, their means for influencing foreign vessels operating beyond their maritime zones are far more limited, despite the regional management commissions that have been established, especially after World War II. Such international fisheries regimes provide indirect means for influencing foreign vessels, working through the regulatory competence of the flag State Members of the regime. The inability of these institutions to prevent the collapse of several major commercial fish stocks was one of the drivers of extended coastal State fisheries jurisdiction in the 1970s, codified in the LOS Convention.[4] Although the emergence of exclusive economic zones (EEZs) served to reduce transboundary fish stocks in terms of numbers, such stocks remain commonplace in world fisheries. International cooperation therefore continues to be required for solving the common property problem.

Among the transboundary fish stocks, shared ones remain within the jurisdictional waters of two or more coastal States and pose a somewhat less malign cooperation problem than straddling stocks, i.e. those occurring both in high seas waters and in coastal State maritime zones.[5] That is in part because management of shared stocks requires agreement among fewer States: the set of coastal States only. Effective management of straddling stocks, in contrast, typically involves more distant user States as well, frequently with the additional complication that some are non-Members of the relevant regional fisheries management organization or arrangement (RFMO/A). Under such circumstances, the near-monopoly on regulation and enforcement that flag States retain on the high seas considerably narrows the range of measures available for inducing compliance with national and international regulations.

---

[3] G Hardin "The Tragedy of the Commons" (1968) 162 *Science* 1243–1248.

[4] United Nations Convention on the Law of the Sea of 10 December 1982 (1833 UNTS 3). See OS Stokke "International Fisheries Politics: From Sustainability to Precaution" in EL Boasson, G Hønneland and S Andresen (eds.) *International Environmental Agreements: An Introduction* (Routledge, London: 2012) 97–116.

[5] On the malignancy of governance problems, see A Underdal "One Question, Two Answers" in A Underdal, EL Miles, S Andresen, J Wettestad, JB Skjærseth and EM Carlin (eds.) *Environmental Regime Effectiveness: Confronting Theory with Evidence* (MIT Press, Cambridge, MA: 2002) 3–45.

The problem faced in high seas fisheries management, therefore, is the generic common property problem, plus that of achieving international coordination with a potentially large number of participants, some of which are not Members of the relevant RFMO/A. Such narrow jurisdictional basis for regulation and enforcement is a major reason why the institutional complex for managing high seas fisheries has expanded considerably during the past two decades. That is the subject of the next section.

3. INSTITUTIONAL COMPLEXES, VALUE CHAINS AND HIGH SEAS FISHERIES

Alongside the rising density of institutional arrangements in global governance, scholars have deepened our understanding of how separate institutional arrangements interact, overlap, complement, or interfere with each other in various ways. Frequently, governance of specific issue-areas, such as fisheries, derives from the interplay within a complex of institutions. This section explains why the concept of 'institutional complexes' is particularly helpful when examining high seas fisheries management, and how the number of institutions capable of influencing such management has grown in recent years.

3.1. Complexity, Coherence and Institutional Effectiveness

Institutional interplay involves interactions among institutions that are distinct in terms of membership and decision-making, but deal with the same activity, or aspects of the same activity, usually in a non-hierarchical manner.[6] Taking an aggregate view of institutional interplay can direct attention to the distinctive capacities of each institution and to the ways in which several may complement one another in the overall governance of an issue-area.[7]

In high seas fisheries management, the institution best placed to generate scientific knowledge about the effects of various management programmes may not be the one empowered to establish such programmes or enforce their regulations. For instance, as elaborated below, two distinctive institutional properties render the International Council for the Exploration of the Sea (ICES) particularly well suited to providing scientific advice on the management of high seas

---

[6] This formulation is compatible with Raustiala and Victor's often-cited definition of a regime complex as a set of "partially overlapping and nonhierarchical institutions governing a particular issue-area", but it does not preclude normative hierarchy (K Raustiala and DG Victor "The Regime Complex for Plant Genetic Resources" (2004) 58 *International Organization* 277–309, at 279).

[7] OS Stokke and OR Young "Integrating Earth Observation Systems and International Environmental Regimes" in M Onoda and OR Young (eds.) *Satellite Earth Observations and Their Impact on Society and Policy* (Springer, Singapore: 2017) 179–203.

fisheries in the North-East Atlantic. Those properties are its membership – comprising the national marine science organizations of regional coastal States – and certain procedures that insulate its operations from political pressure without diminishing its relevance for sustainable use and conservation. In contrast, the actual regulation of high seas fisheries in the region generally rests with narrower bodies whose membership typically reflects the pattern of historic fishing as well as the zonal attachment of the stocks in question.[8] Typically, such regional bodies are reticent to admit new entrants, which may impinge on their ability to respond to changes in the availability of fish stocks on the high seas.[9] Effective compliance control may require yet another institution, for instance because catches taken on the high seas are landed in States that are non-Members of the regulatory body. Each of the institutions involved in this institutional complex retains its operational autonomy, but interactions are managed in ways that enhance the combined contributions to overall fisheries governance.

The 'effectiveness' of any international regime is straightforwardly defined as the extent to which it contributes significantly to solving the problem it was set up to address.[10] When an individual regime is examined as part of an institutional complex, this definition still applies, but it invites additional analysis of how the regime contributes to the operation of other regimes. An important part of that analysis involves clarifying which institutions in the larger complex have distinctive contributions to offer each of the governance tasks examined in this chapter: the cognitional, the regulatory and the behavioural.

'Coherence' here means that the activities conducted under each institution in the relevant governance complex align well.[11] A minimum requirement for coherence is that the institutions active in a given government task do not disrupt the positive contributions that other institutions make to each of the governance tasks. High-level coherence applies if the institutions clearly support each other's effectiveness; and full coherence implies that they do so by reaping any synergies derivable from complementary institutional capabilities.

3.2. Value Chains and Profitability

Institutional complexity is increasingly relevant to high seas fisheries because States and other actors have sought to circumvent the narrow jurisdictional basis in international fisheries law for regulating high seas fisheries, and for enforcing

---

[8] OS Stokke "Trade Measures and the Combat of IUU Fishing: Institutional Interplay and Effective Governance in the Northeast Atlantic" (2009) 33 *Marine Policy* 339–349.

[9] See Chapter 6 of this volume (Molenaar).

[10] A Underdal "The Concept of Regime 'Effectiveness'" (1992) 27 *Cooperation and Conflict* 227–240.

[11] See also Chapter 5 of this volume (Harrison).

agreed regulations. They have done so by developing supplementary measures, targeting links in the seafood value chain that occur either prior or subsequent to the harvesting at sea. As this section shows, fisheries management institutions have important roles to play in the implementation of such measures, but so do several other institutions.

Some vessels operating on the high seas do so with licences granted by Members of RFMO/As; others have no such licences. Some licensed vessels report all their catches to national authorities, whereas others do so only for part of their catch or not at all. Quite a few vessels fly flags of convenience – implying that their State of registry has not assumed any commitment to constrain harvesting operations – and lacks the inclination as well as the capacity to exercise meaningful control over fishing and fishing-related activities by its vessels.[12] Among the things this diverse set of actors have in common, however, is their placement in a chain of economic transactions – at arm's-length or otherwise – involving suppliers of various goods and services as well as recipients of catches.

The actual harvesting of fish is only one link in a chain of actions, each contributing to the value of the seafood product acquired by the final consumer, and each offering a potential target for influencing harvesting. Efforts to manage fisheries by targeting either the inputs to harvesting operations or the subsequent transshipment, landing, processing or distribution, serve to broaden the set of institutions that could potentially contribute to problem-solving.

Links prior to harvesting include those involving vessel or crew brokerage, liability insurance, fisheries gear and equipment, as well as bunkering.[13] Companies providing such inputs to the harvesting operations are subject to the jurisdiction of the States where they are based, which makes them answerable to national legislation that may constrain commercial ties with actors found to be involved in undesirable activities on the high seas. Seeking to reduce the profitability of harvesting operations in the high seas area known as the Barents Sea Loophole, for instance, Norway enacted a legal ban on the supply of services to vessels that had engaged in high seas activities contrary to international rules or to the desired harvesting pattern.[14] Private sanctions may also affect the availability of necessary inputs to unwanted harvesting activities. In the Loophole case, several private boycott actions were introduced prior to the implementation of the legal ban, aimed at removing at least the Norwegian flow of supply of provisions, fuels and services to vessels operating in the Loophole, as well as

---

[12] For a recent overview of fisheries-relevant varieties, see DD Miller and UR Sumaila "Flag Use Behavior and IUU Activity within the International Fishing Fleet: Refining Definitions and Identifying Areas of Concern" (2014) 44 *Marine Policy* 204–211. On means to deal with the flag of convenience problem in fisheries, see Chapter 15 of this volume (Klein).

[13] On the potential role of liability insurance in combating illegal fishing on the high seas, see Chapter 17 of this volume (Caddell, Leloudas and Soyer).

[14] Norway, Legal Order No. 802 of 8 June 1993, paras. 6–9, available at https://lovdata.no/dokument/SF/forskrift/1993-08-06-802.

punishing domestic companies that failed to adhere to such boycotts.[15] Mobilizing actors with legal or market-based influence on the companies that provide services to high seas fishing vessels is one way to reduce the lucrativeness of undesired high seas fisheries.

Similar comments apply to value-chain links subsequent to harvesting, including transshipment, port services provided in connection with the landing of fish, one or more rounds of wholesaling and processing, as well as retailing to the final consumer. A prominent example of national legislation that constrains transactions further down the distribution chain is the Lacey Act of the United States[16] (US) – adopted more than a century ago – which makes it unlawful for any person subject to US jurisdiction to import, export, transport, sell, receive, acquire, possess or purchase fish caught in violation of national or international rules. Private initiatives that may impinge on the profitability of high seas harvesting include ecolabelling and certification schemes, aiming especially at large retailers with corporate-responsibility commitments or general brand-name concerns that place a premium on products deriving from sustainable fisheries.[17]

The remainder of this chapter elaborates on the recent broadening of the institutional complex relevant to the governance of high seas fisheries, highlighting the distinctive capacities each of them can bring to bear on the various tasks of governance, and examining the extent of coordination needed for obtaining coherence among them.

4. BROADENING OF FISHERIES MANAGEMENT COMPLEXES

An increasing number of institutions weigh heavily in efforts to govern high seas fisheries. RFMO/As remain central, but they have been joined by several other types of institutions, public as well as private. Among the public institutions outside the fisheries sector that merit attention are those regulating international trade or economic policies, as well as certain United Nations (UN) bodies that coordinate their Members' law enforcement in areas such as terrorism, drugs and other criminal activities. Private institutions gaining in significance include partnerships among business and environmental non-governmental organizations (NGOs) that make access to market-rewarded ecolabels dependent on commitment to management standards that build on, or even go beyond, those agreed among States.

---

[15] OS Stokke "Managing Fisheries in the Barents Sea Loophole: Interplay with the UN Fish Stocks Agreement" (2001) 32 *Ocean Development and International Law* 241–262, at 245.

[16] 16 U.S.C. §§3371–3378. On the prospective application and utility of the Lacey Act, see further Chapter 17 of this volume (Caddell, Leloudas and Soyer).

[17] LH Auld, G Gulbrandsen and CL McDermott "Certification Schemes and the Impacts on Forests and Forestry" (2008) 33 *Annual Review of Environment and Resources* 187–211.

4.1. Fisheries Institutions

RFMO/As remain central among the institutions States use for dealing with high seas fisheries, but effectiveness increasingly requires conducive interplay with other international institutions. Around 16 RFMO/As regulate harvesting activities on the high seas today;[18] in addition, numerous bilateral agreements frame the management of stocks shared by two States only. Their hub position in each of the regional complexes of institutions relevant to high seas fisheries derives from their core assignment: to integrate all three tasks of governance, regularly bringing together national agencies with knowledge-building capacity or regulatory competence over much of the harvesting capacity employed in the fishery in question – on the high seas as well as within coastal State maritime zones. These multilateral or bilateral regimes allow Members to coordinate their management measures towards own fishers, often providing transparency by means of reporting or reciprocal inspection procedures that serve to reduce fears of being exploited in the cooperative relationship. In dealing with high seas fisheries, those operating regional fisheries regimes have found it helpful to relate in various ways to a rising number of other types of institutions, both within and outside the fisheries branch of government.

Within the fisheries sector, the interplay of regional management bodies with global institutions centred on the UN has been important for developing and diffusing management principles and measures for high seas fisheries. Consider for instance how the Fish Stocks Agreement[19] negotiated in the mid-1990s was instrumental in promoting and standardizing approaches such as the precautionary and the ecosystem-based approaches to fisheries management, building on the practices that had been pioneered by ICES and the Commission for the Conservation of Antarctic Marine Living Resources (CCAMLR) respectively.[20] Similarly, those elaborating on, and strengthening the concept of, flag State responsibility over vessels engaged in high seas fisheries during the negotiations of the Compliance Agreement,[21] subsequently brought into the Fish Stocks Agreement, could draw upon innovative provisions developed in tuna-management regimes in the South Pacific.[22] Although not aspiring to result in new global instruments, the (Resumed) Fish Stocks Agreement Review Conferences – initiated in 2006 and resumed in 2010 and 2016 – similarly

---

[18] See Chapter 6 of this volume (Molenaar).

[19] Agreement for the implementation of the Provisions of the United Nations Convention on the Law of the Sea of 10 December 1982 relating to the Conservation and Management of Straddling Fish Stocks and Highly Migratory Fish Stocks of 4 August 1995 (2167 UNTS 3).

[20] OS Stokke (ed.) *Governing High Seas Fisheries: The Interplay of Global and Regional Regimes* (Oxford University Press, Oxford: 2001).

[21] Agreement to Promote Compliance with International Conservation and Management Measures by Fishing Vessels on the High Seas of 24 November 1993 (33 ILM 969).

[22] B Vukas and D Vidas "Flags of Convenience and High Seas Fishing: The Emergence of a Legal Framework" in Stokke, note 20 at 53–90.

provide a global arena for presenting and debating regional cutting-edge practices in high seas management, covering the full range of governance tasks from knowledge-building to compliance inducement.[23] The distinctive edge that global institutions bring to high seas fisheries governance is the combination of universal membership and a mandate to promote the diffusion of best practices.

4.2. Other Sectors of Governance

Among the management principles diffused by means of such global processes, the ecosystem-based approach to fisheries management has promoted cross-issue interplay with regional environmental regimes. Governments are expected to manage stocks under a comprehensive plan that links the larger food webs of micro-organisms and complex predator-prey relationships to the broader environmental conditions in a given sea-area. The institutional implications of this approach are illustrated by the interplay between the North-East Atlantic Fisheries Commission (NEAFC) and Commission for the Protection of the Marine Environment of the North-East Atlantic (OSPAR Commission).[24] While initially reluctant to engage with the OSPAR Commission on matters related to fisheries, the NEAFC gradually warmed to the idea of taking into consideration wider environmental concerns, such as protection of cold-water coral reefs. Partly because both institutions base their decisions on scientific inputs from ICES, NEAFC adapted its 2009 closure of certain high seas areas for bottom trawling to the spatial boundaries of the OSPAR Commission's emerging network of marine protected areas (MPAs).[25] The distinctive edge that international environmental bodies can offer regarding problem-solving efforts derives from their expertise in identifying ecologically and biologically significant areas, the societal legitimacy associated with ecosystem-based management, and their partial regulatory competence over various marine activities other than fisheries.

Important as such greater interaction among fisheries and environmental regimes is, the most prominent cross-issue institutional interplay in high seas fisheries management concerns the 'chilling effect' expected from imposition of trade restrictions set forth in international trade agreements, notably those administered by the World Trade Organization (WTO).[26] These agreements generally prohibit discrimination in trade among the 164 WTO Members,

---

[23] See Report of the 2016 Resumed Fish Stocks Agreement Review Conference, doc. A/CONF.210/2016/5 of 1 August 2016.

[24] See also Chapter 5 of this volume (Harrison).

[25] I Kvalvik "Managing Institutional Overlap in the Protection of Marine Ecosystems on the High Seas. The Case of the North East Atlantic" (2012) 56 *Ocean & Coastal Management* 35–43, at 40.

[26] E.g. R Eckersley "The Big Chill: The WTO and Multilateral Environmental Agreements" (2004) 4 *Global Environmental Politics* 24–50. See also Chapter 14 of this volume (Churchill).

so compatibility depends on designing trade restrictions that fit the WTO 'environmental window', a set of exceptions defined first in Article XX of GATT 1947 and reproduced in subsequent agreements.[27] Subject to the *chapeau* requirement that trade restrictions "are not applied in a manner which would constitute a means of arbitrary or unjustifiable discrimination [....] or a disguised restriction on international trade", such measures may be compatible with the global trade regime if they are "necessary to protect human, animal or plant life or health" (paragraph b) or "relating to the conservation of exhaustible natural resources if such measures are made effective in conjunction with restrictions on domestic production and consumption" (paragraph g). Subsequent decisions by dispute settlement bodies have clarified and developed the ramifications of these exceptions, which were accorded even higher prominence by the inclusion of the words "sustainable development" in the Preamble to the WTO's constitutive instrument.[28]

As elaborated below, the distinctive institutional capacity provided by trade regimes is the authority States have given them to define generally accepted criteria for restrictions that are compatible with trade rules, allowing those operating regional fisheries regimes to adapt their trade-related compliance measures to fit the specifications of this environmental window.

A more recent cross-issue interplay involves law enforcement activities in areas that differ from fisheries management but impinge on it, especially those set up to combat drugs, money laundering and terrorism. The overlaps between illegal fishing activities and other kinds of maritime crime, such as drug smuggling, trafficking in persons and piracy, have caught the attention of the UN Office on Drugs and Crime (UNODC), the International Organization for Migration, the International Labour Organization, as well as INTERPOL.[29] The distinctive institutional capacities these organizations bring to bear on high seas fisheries management revolve around their expertise in preventing and investigating transnational criminal action, as well as their roles in legal prosecution.

4.3. Private Governance

Yet another category of institutions interacting with regional fisheries regimes on matters pertaining to high seas fisheries are market-based instruments operated by private organizations, typically partnerships involving industry as well

---

[27] General Agreement on Tariff and Trade 1947, superseded by GATT 1994, available at www.wto. org. See e.g. OS Stokke "Trade Measures and Climate Compliance: Interplay between WTO and the Marrakesh Accords" (2004) 4 *International Environmental Agreements* 339–357.

[28] Marrakesh Agreement Establishing the World Trade Organization of 15 April 1994, available at www.wto.org. See TJ Schoenbaum "International Trade and Protection of the Environment: The Continuing Search for Reconciliation" (1997) 91 *American Journal of International Law* 268–313.

[29] *Transnational Organized Crime in the Fishing Industry* (UNODC, Vienna: 2011). See also Chapter 17 of this volume (Caddell, Leloudas and Soyer).

as civil society organizations.[30] Early examples of such instruments targeted single species whose stocks were threatened by depletion or were harvested using techniques with insufficient regard for bycatches of charismatic (and thus well-suited for fund-raising efforts) fauna such as dolphins or sea turtles.[31] Today's leading certification scheme for capture fisheries – the Marine Stewardship Council (MSC) – has a much broader orientation. This private governance institution is open to applications from any industry groupings engaged in the fishery of a specific stock, applying one or several gear types, and prepared to set up a chain-of-custody system that separates production and distribution chains based on a certified fishery from those that are not.[32] Obtaining and retaining the right to apply the MSC label on seafood products requires a stamp of approval from an accredited third-party certifying company, stating that the fishery in question is conducted and managed in accordance with three basic principles involving the health of the fish stock, the harvesting pressure and the management system.[33] By 2017, the MSC had certified some 300 fisheries in 34 States – mostly in the Northern Hemisphere but recently including China as well – taking as much as 9.5 million tonnes or more than 12 per cent of global seafood catch.[34] The distinctive institutional capacity that this type of institution brings to bear on the high seas fisheries problem is its growing ability to transform corporate environmental responsibility – whether idealistically or opportunistically derived – among leading retail chains in Western Europe and North America, into fishing-industry incentives that contribute actively to developing better harvesting practices.

4.4. An Aggregate Perspective

Examining options for high seas fisheries management from an aggregate perspective, therefore, brings out how the set of relevant institutions has broadened in recent years. To be sure, regional fisheries regimes have remained central elements in this complex due to their integrative role for all three governance tasks, bringing together the national agencies with knowledge-building and regulatory competence in all or most user States. However, other institutions also have distinctive capacities that can support complementary efforts, often in tandem with regional fisheries bodies. The broad participation that marks

---

[30] See also the broader discussion in Chapter 16 of this volume (Massarella).

[31] On national (US) legislation defining requirements for labelling tuna as 'dolphin-safe', see Chapter 14 of this volume (Churchill).

[32] LH Gulbrandsen "The Emergence and Effectiveness of the Marine Stewardship Council" (2009) 33 *Marine Policy* 654–660.

[33] LH Gulbrandsen and G Auld "Contested Accountability Logics in Evolving Nonstate Certification for Fisheries Sustainability" (2016) 16 *Global Environmental Politics* 42–60.

[34] See the MSC Annual Report 2016–2017 available at msc.org/global-impacts/msc-annual-report.

many UN-based fisheries conferences has been crucial for their ability to help in diffusing advanced principles or management measures from one regional regime to another. The distinctive capacity provided by trade regimes is their competence to define the general parameters for trade-law-compatible environmentally motivated trade restrictions. Broad-spectrum economic cooperation organizations such as the Organization for Economic Co-operation and Development (OECD) are well placed to identify means for information-sharing among Members concerning the operations of private companies that provide goods or services to those engaging in undesirable high seas fisheries. International law enforcement bodies set up to fight societal problems other than illegal, unreported or unregulated (IUU) fishing (such as drugs, trafficking, and money laundering) can provide intelligence data otherwise unavailable to fisheries management authorities. And partnerships among industrial, environmental and social interests such as the MSC are uniquely placed to incentivize fishing companies and their associations to play constructive roles whenever re-certification requires reduced harvesting pressure or specific improvements in the management system.

5. INTERPLAY MANAGEMENT, COHERENCE AND EFFECTIVE GOVERNANCE

This broadening complex of institutions engaged in high seas fisheries management, each bringing distinctive capacities to bear on one or more of the governance tasks, gives rise to questions of the coherence among them. Central here is whether institutional coherence requires interplay management: deliberate efforts by States or other actors to improve the interplay of the institutions involved.[35] Such interplay management may involve overarching principles of international law or explicit cross-institutional coordination of regulatory or programmatic activities, but often takes the less ambitious form of unilateral or mutual adaptation to the objectives or measures of other institutions.[36]

In examining the extent of coherence among the many institutions now relevant to high seas fisheries management, and the degree of coordination needed for obtaining it, we may usefully consider each governance task separately; that is: provision of scientific advice, adoption of adequate regulations, and inducement of behavioural compliance with agreed-upon rules.

---

[35] OS Stokke *The Interplay of International Regimes: Putting Effectiveness Theory to Work*, FNI Report 10/2001 (The Fridtjof Nansen Institute, Lysaker: 2001). See also S Oberthür "Interplay Management: Enhancing Environmental Policy Integration among International Institutions" (2009) 9 *International Environmental Agreements* 371–391.

[36] OS Stokke and S Oberthür "Introduction: Institutional Interaction in Global Environmental Change" in S Oberthür and OS Stokke (eds.) *Managing Institutional Complexity: Regime Interplay and Global Environmental Change* (MIT Press, Cambridge, MA: 2011) 1–24, at 9–10.

5.1. Providing Scientific Advice

The cognitional problem facing States and other stakeholders in fisheries management is to build a shared, well-founded understanding of how best to balance use and conservation.[37] Solving this problem requires generating research-based advice that can differentiate convincingly among alternative management programmes in terms of the impacts on the state of targeted and related stocks. Three closely related aspects of that task are particularly relevant to high seas fisheries, each requiring distinctive institutional capacities: maintaining high credibility among decision-makers, ensuring adequate funding for the underlying research activities, and nurturing the perception that management decisions not compatible with scientific advice are likely to prove costly in the longer term. Of the governance tasks examined here, provision of scientific advice relies least on institutions other than the regional fisheries regimes. Yet here too, new institutions are becoming more important, notably private governance initiatives.

The central role of regional fisheries management regimes in cognitional problem-solving is not surprising, since their distinctive feature is the mandate to provide venues for coordination among the national fisheries bureaucracies of user States. These bureaucracies practically monopolize the aggregate willingness to pay for the costly fisheries survey operations needed for providing research-based advice on the state of a stock and how it is likely to be affected by specific harvesting-pressure patterns. Accordingly, participants in regional fisheries regimes tend to be dominant funding agencies for the marine research institutions that conduct those surveys and interpret the evidence in light of catch reports and other information used in developing the advice.

At first sight, the role of ICES in providing scientific advice to various national and international fisheries management authorities with respect to most North-East Atlantic fisheries might seem to contradict the claim that regional fisheries regimes have a practical monopoly on this particular management task. After all, this venerable international institution – founded back in 1902 – is clearly separate from each of the fisheries management bodies – whether organizations or arrangements – that recommend or make decisions on regional fisheries measures. But that observation only serves to illustrate that a 'regime' may be something different from an 'organization' or 'arrangement'. An international regime is a set of "explicit rules, agreed upon by governments, that pertain to particular sets of issues in international relations [.... and] prescribe behavioural roles, constrain activity, and shape expectations".[38] Accordingly,

---

[37] OS Stokke *Disaggregating International Regimes: A New Approach to Evaluation and Comparison* (MIT Press, Cambridge, MA: 2012).

[38] RO Keohane "Neoliberal Institutionalism: A Persepective on World Politics" in RO Keohane (ed.) *International Institutions and State Power. Essays in International Relations Theory* (Westview Press, Boulder, CO: 1989) 1–12, at 3–4.

ICES is better seen as a key component of several regional fisheries management regimes, each centred on an organization or an arrangement that has incorporated written advice from ICES into its decision-making procedure. Examples include the Joint Norwegian-Russian Fisheries Commission (JNRFC), NEAFC and the European Union (EU)'s Common Fisheries Policy.[39]

As noted above, the institutional features that make ICES particularly well suited to solving the cognitional problem in North-East Atlantic fisheries management are its membership, comprising national fisheries research institutions in all coastal States, and a set of procedures aimed at balancing relevance to the governments that fund the research (often referred to as the 'saliency' of the advice), with insulation from political pressure that may be exercised by industry or governments.[40] On the relevance side, ICES receives annual requests for advice from the management bodies or their Members, specifying stocks in various regions and often identifying particular issues in need of scientific elucidation.[41] In responding to such requests, ICES first calls upon a working group typically dominated by experts from the Members involved in the fisheries, and therefore with incentives for financing research activities. This working group compiles available data and conducts the necessary analyses. Subsequently, a review group or process involving experts from Members without any stakes in this particular fishery examines the analysis against the benchmark of 'best available science', and develops draft advice. Finally, the ICES Advisory Committee reviews that draft, modifies it as appropriate and adopts the final advice.[42] Thus, the generation and provision of scientific advice takes place in a multilateral setting with third-party peer review, but the substantive basis is typically provided by researchers from the main harvesting States.

Adding to the relevance or saliency of the advice, the ICES has a long tradition of 'dialogue meetings' with stakeholders, initially focusing on the participants in the management bodies that receive the advice. Responding to input from those users, ICES has gradually adapted its form of advice, most notably with the shift during the 1980s to providing a range of options (with impact statements for each) for stocks not in imminent danger – and the subsequent specification of the precautionary approach to fisheries advice.[43] The high level of coherence that marks the institutional interplay between ICES and each of the regional fisheries management bodies is therefore supported by recurrent

---

[39] OS Stokke and C Coffey "Precaution, ICES and the Common Fisheries Policy: A Study of Regime Interplay" (2004) 28 *Marine Policy* 117–126.

[40] On this balance, see WC Clark, RB Mitchell and DW Cash "Evaluating the Influence of Global Environmental Assessments" in WC Clark, RB Mitchell, DW Cash and NM Dickson (eds.) *Global Environmental Assessments: Information and Influence* (MIT Press, Cambridge, MA: 2006) 1–28.

[41] On ICES' advisory procedure, see www.ices.dk/sites/pub/Publication%20Reports/Advice/2016/2016/Introduction_to_advice_2016.pdf.

[42] Stokke, note 37 at 93.

[43] P Gullestad "The Scope for Research in Practical Fishery Management" (1998) 37 *Fisheries Research* 251–258.

and formalized coordination, as with the regimes that have placed their advisory component within the same organizational boundaries as the decision-making component.[44]

While these regional fisheries management bodies remain the natural targets for most initiatives aimed at improving the basis and provision of scientific advice on high seas fisheries, private governance institutions have now begun to carve out their own niche in this area.[45] They do so partly by incentivizing industries to contribute resources to fisheries research, and partly by enhancing the persuasiveness of the advice provided to regional fisheries management bodies.

As to financial resources, high seas areas pose special challenges to achieving funding for costly scientific research, because the returns in terms of better management are less certain than for stocks that occur wholly or mostly in coastal State maritime zones. This follows from the generic externality problem examined above; such challenges multiply if spatial remoteness raises the costs of research, as in the case of krill stocks in the Southern Ocean. Norwegian companies engaged in harvesting krill for production of omega-3-rich krill oil for high-end nutritional markets in North America and Europe, soon discovered that MSC certification would be required for access to the most lucrative distribution chains. Such certification was achieved in 2010 and 2015, respectively. The companies' interest in retaining this label can explain why they maintain an observer coverage twice as high as required by CCAMLR, which manages the fishery at the intergovernmental level.[46] Similarly, industry incentives aimed at impressing certifying bodies that apply assessment standards stricter than those agreed under the relevant regional fisheries regime, provide the most convincing explanation for the preparedness of one major company – Aker BioMarine – to make its vessels available free of charge for regular survey operations in the Southern Ocean by the Norwegian Institute for Marine Research.[47] The rise of private governance institutions in fisheries therefore nudges private industries to contribute more actively than before to the costs of scientific research.

Specific criteria in the MSC assessment procedure can also enhance the persuasiveness of scientific advice, depending primarily on the practices and the reputation of the scientific body itself. Among the advantages of conducting marine-science investigations under the framework of an international

---

[44] Examples of the latter include the Northwest Atlantic Fisheries Organization (NAFO), CCAMLR and the International Commission on the Conservation of Atlantic Tunas (ICCAT).

[45] On institutional niches, see H Aldrich *Organizations Evolving* (SAGE, London: 1999).

[46] See G Hønneland "Fisheries Certification in the Southern Ocean", paper presented at the international workshop *Law and Governance: Emerging Issues of the Polar Regions*, 20–21 June 2017, Shanghai Jiao Tong University, Shanghai, China. On the certifications in question, see www.msc.org/newsroom/news/aker-biomarine-krill-fishery-gains-msc-certification for Aker BioMarine (2010) and www.msc.org/newsroom/news/antarctic-krill-fishery-achieves-msc-certification for Olympic (2015). Since then, Olympic has gone bankrupt.

[47] Hønneland, note 46.

institution – whether CCAMLR in the Southern Ocean or ICES in the North-East Atlantic – are the greater credibility and legitimacy that derive from substantial involvement of experts from States other than those engaged in the specific fishery. The persuasiveness of scientific advice from ICES is mainly due to the reputation this organization has developed for high-quality, impartial input, but other institutions in the larger complex can also contribute. For instance, the MSC assessment team that evaluated a Russian trawl fishery in the Barents Sea gave a much higher score in 2012 than it had two years earlier, because in the meantime ICES had accepted a revised harvest control rule by the JNRFC as being compatible with the precautionary approach.[48] The fact that compatibility of regulatory measures with ICES advice weighs heavily in the assessment score of a private governance body whose ecolabel is increasingly seen as necessary for gaining access to the most lucrative distribution channels, undoubtedly adds to the persuasiveness of such scientific advice among political decision-makers.

In summary, the institutional complexes relevant to providing scientific inputs to high seas fisheries management are centred on their respective regional fisheries management regime, but private governance institutions like the MSC are becoming more important. That is so because these partnerships make access to lucrative ecolabels conditional on industry practices that support fisheries research and on management practices that are compatible with scientific advice. Relationships among the institutions involved are coherent, as they clearly support each other. In the dominant part of this complex – involving governmental research institutions and international decision-making bodies – such coherence is upheld by regular, formalized coordination. In contrast, the coherence that marks relationships among the public and the private parts of the complex has been obtained without explicit coordination. Instead, the main mechanism delivering coherence is that the private body in question – the MSC – has specified standards for the government-orchestrated management of the fishery in question that are even higher than those agreed among States.

5.2. Obtaining Adequate Regulation

The general regulatory problem for States facing a collective action situation is to establish a set of agreed behavioural rules that covers all major users and reflects the best available knowledge on how to achieve the social purpose of the regime.[49] In fisheries management, that purpose is to obtain the maximum

---

[48] LH Gulbrandsen and G Hønneland "Fisheries Certification in Russia: The Emergence of Nonstate Authority in a Postcommunist Economy" (2014) 45 *Ocean Development & International Law* 341–359, at 350.
[49] Stokke, note 37 at 18.

sustainable yield (MSY) from the resource, as qualified by the precautionary approach, aiming to safeguard its ability to replenish. As discussed above, a challenge specific to the high seas variant has been the inadequate participation in existing national or international regulatory arrangements – often referred to as the 'outsider' problem. Estimates (necessarily rough) indicate that up to 20 per cent of the vessels fishing on the high seas fly flags of non-Members to the relevant regional fisheries management body.[50]

Related to this outsider problem is the regulatory lenience problem, deriving from the unwillingness of members of a regional fisheries regime to commit themselves to very strict rules if they have reason to fear that non-Members will not cooperate. Whereas regional fisheries regimes provide certain means for combating each of those two problems, interplay with other institutions is gaining in significance; even more so than for the provision of persuasive scientific advice.

An often-powerful option available under a regional management regime for dealing with the outsider problem is coordinated use of the coastal State quota card – typically, the trading of access to fishing in waters under coastal State jurisdiction in return for flag State promises to keep out of high seas areas. Consider, for instance, the role of the JNRFC in coordinating the playing of the quota card to dissuade newcomers from entering the North-East Arctic cod fishery in the Barents Sea Loophole; a high seas enclave surrounded by the maritime zones of Norway and Russia.[51] Coordinated allocation of parts of the total allowable catch (TAC) to third parties is provided for in the annual bilateral protocols drawn up under the JNRFC. After bilateral negotiations with Norway in 1991–1992, Greenland and the then European Economic Community decided to limit their fishing activities in the Loophole and keep total harvests in the Barents Sea within the overall quotas allotted under reciprocal access agreements. The Faroe Islands similarly agreed in 1996 to prohibit landings of fish that had been taken without quotas in the Loophole. Finally, three years later, following a decline in the availability of cod in the Loophole, Iceland – the last remaining participant without any licence from any of the coastal States – agreed to cease operations in exchange for a small but permanent share of the stock to be taken inside the coastal States' EEZs.[52]

More recently, institutional interplay *among* distinctive regional fisheries regimes has come to the fore. Such cross-regional interplay has gained in significance partly because certain management tasks can be conducted more effectively if coordinated among adjacent regimes, and partly because certain stocks have changed their migratory pattern, reducing the spatial fit between institutional boundaries and those of the activity system they aim to govern.

---

[50] E DeSombre *Global Environmental Institutions* (Routledge, London: 2006) 92.

[51] Stokke, note 15 at 244.

[52] RR Churchill "The Barents Sea Loophole Agreement: A 'Coastal State' Solution to a Straddling Stock Problem" (1999) 14 *International Journal of Marine and Coastal Law* 467–483, at 472.

For several years, NEAFC has cooperated with the Northwest Atlantic Fisheries Organization (NAFO) in the management of North Atlantic redfish, a stock that shifted westward during the late 1990s and became available also in the NAFO area. The joint management option chosen was that NEAFC determines the TAC, setting aside a part that NAFO may allocate among its Members.[53] Those two Atlantic fisheries commission cooperate closely on many other high seas management issues of a regulatory nature, as illustrated by the establishment in 2014 of a joint NEAFC-NAFO advisory group on data management, aimed at harmonizing reporting procedures.[54]

Global-level running orders serve to stimulate such cross-regional collaboration. The 2010 Resumed Fish Stocks Agreement Review Conference encouraged RFMOs to set up joint working groups on matters of mutual interest.[55] This call has been heeded not only by the spatially defined fisheries regimes in the North Atlantic but also by the five tuna RFMOs that coordinate some of their work through the so-called 'Kobe Process', including by establishing a joint global register of active tuna vessels, common criteria for performance review, and joint work on fish aggregating devices in tuna harvesting.[56] Such alignment of measures taken across several regimes requires active coordination, in the form of regular meetings among participants in decision-making bodies – as in the case of the Kobe Process – or through joint working groups.

The need for active coordination might be expected to be even greater when alignment is sought among measures taken under regimes in different issue-areas, as in the NEAFC-OSPAR Commission case. Environmental regimes are typically based on components of national bureaucracies that are distinct from those participating in fisheries regimes, and are therefore not exposed to the same harmonizing global processes as are participants in regional fisheries regimes (e.g. the Fish Stocks Agreement Review Conference), nor are they likely to benefit much from personal overlaps among the delegations attending the respective meetings.[57]

However, one should not jump to the conclusion that conducive institutional interplay across sectors is best achieved through *explicit* coordination. As Kvalvik's analysis[58] brings out, the alignment of NEAFC's closed-area measures to the OSPAR Commission's planned network of MPAs derived not from joint

---

[53] A Thomson "The Management of Redfish *(Sebastes Mentella)* in the North Atlantic: A Stock in Movement" in *Papers Presented at the Norway-FAO Expert Consultation on the Management of Shared Fish Stocks (FAO Fisheries Report* No. 695, Supplement: 2003).

[54] See UN doc. A/CONF.210/2016/1 of 1 March 2016, para. 175.

[55] Ibid., para. 169.

[56] See e.g. www.tuna-org.org/; also Chapter 5 of this volume (Harrison).

[57] See, however, R Billé, L Chabason, P Drankier, EJ Molenaar and J Rochette "Regional Oceans Governance. Making Regional Seas Programmes, Regional Fishery Bodies and Large Marine Ecosystem Mechanisms Work Better Together" *(UNEP Regional Seas Reports and Studies* No. 197: 2016), 43.

[58] Kvalvik, note 25 at 39.

decision-making but from adaptation on the part of the international fisheries body to concerns as well as measures in progress under the environmental regime. Indeed, the initial reluctance to engage with the OSPAR Commission, on grounds that the interface between environmental and fisheries concerns are national rather than international issues, highlights the inclination among those operating institutions to safeguard their formal role and competence in decision-making.[59] From this point of view, exchange of information and cooperation on technical issues, combined with readiness to take into consideration the concerns and the management measures of the other institution, may provide a sufficient vehicle for coherence, and one less prone to trigger institutional jealousy. One-sided or mutual adaptation is probably more easily achieved than institutional coordination across issue-areas.

Similarly, the contributions made by the MSC certification procedure in supporting regulatory work under regional fisheries management do not seem to rely on coordination: rather, the private governance body places considerable emphasis on internal accountability; on assessment criteria that align well with the governmental management system surrounding the fishery seeking certification. Among the concerns expressed by several MSC assessment teams evaluating applicants in the Russian fisheries industry were inadequate implementation of the precautionary approach – required by the Fish Stocks Agreement – in the domestic legislation of the Russian Federation, as well as inadequate involvement of civil society organizations in regulatory work.[60] Faced with the risk of losing the certification, an umbrella organization covering nearly 40 per cent of the North-West Russian harvesting capacity participated in, and contributed to, seminars and conferences arranged by the national fisheries authorities, arguing for explicit inclusion of the precautionary approach in Russian legislation.[61] Another applicant for MSC certification responded to the complaint regarding civil society participation by actively involving environmental NGOs in its meetings with governmental agencies.[62] As in cognitional problem-solving, coherence among private and public governance efforts has been achieved in these cases not through overarching institutions or cross-institutional coordination, but by a private certification criterion that sets the standard higher than the governmentally defined level; and an industry that perceives it as being in its own interest to obtain certification.

A further illustration of how private governance schemes can mobilize politically influential segments of the fishing industry in support of more sustainable public fisheries management can be found with the North-East Atlantic mackerel fishery. This fishery lost its MSC certification in 2012, following the

---

[59] Ibid., 39. See also the observations Harrison makes on the relationship between NEAFC and the OSPAR Commission in Chapter 5 of this volume.
[60] Gulbrandsen and Hønneland, note 48 at 352.
[61] Ibid., 353.
[62] Ibid., 355.

breakdown of coastal State cooperation on this stock two years before, which had yielded several unilateral quotas and total harvesting pressure well in excess of the ICES advice. In response, industry groups controlling more than 700 vessels from all regional user States except Iceland and the Faroe Islands, joined in the Mackerel Industry Northern Sustainability Alliance (MINSA). In 2016, the companies succeeded in regaining MSC certification, on grounds that they had played an important and productive role in negotiations that had brought most of the user States back into a cooperative arrangement on mackerel.[63]

To sum up, institutional interplay relevant to the outsider and the regulatory lenience problems facing high seas fisheries management centres on regional fisheries management regimes, but it also involves national fisheries agencies, global processes under the UN, spatially adjacent regional regimes, institutions with mandates in other issue-areas such as environmental protection, as well as private certification schemes. One important measure facilitated by a regional regime is the coordinated use of the quota card for inducing non-Members of such a regime to adhere to its regulations. Achieving coherence across institutional boundaries can be facilitated by explicit coordination of decision-making among the institutions involved, as illustrated in the NEAFC-NAFO case, although such coordination is generally easier to obtain among regimes that operate in the same issue-area and involve the same sectors of government. Less ambitious modes of obtaining such coherence include one-sided or mutual adaptation, which is especially relevant when one or both regimes have formal decision-making roles their operators would like to protect; as is often the case for institutional interplay across issue-areas. Similarly, achieving coherence of efforts under private governance schemes with governmental management regimes has proven fairly simple as regards coordination. The main mechanism is the unilateral requirement enshrined in the MSC principles: that a well-functioning public management regime must be in place *before* access can be granted to its market-rewarded ecolabel. Separately or jointly, these types of institutional interplay can reward participation in international cooperation, raise the costs of non-participation or sub-standard regulatory practices, and facilitate the diffusion of substantively ambitious conservation and management measures.

5.3. Inducing Compliance

Among the three high seas governance tasks examined here, enhancing behavioural compliance with international commitment is the one that has benefited

---

[63] See MSC, "Mackerel wins back its certified-sustainable status" 11 May 2016, www.msc.org/newsroom/news/mackerel-wins-back-its-certified-sustainable-status. On the North-East Atlantic mackerel dispute, see e.g. J Spijkers and WJ Boonstra "Environmental Change and Social Conflict: The Northeast Atlantic Mackerel Dispute" (2017) 17 *Regional Environmental Change* 1835–1851.

the most from deliberate management of institutional interplay. Processes of demonstration and learning, partly through global bodies like the Food and Agriculture Organization of the United Nations (FAO), have helped to diffuse innovative compliance measures and practices among regional management regimes. Such efforts have also received support from private certification schemes as well as initiatives primarily targeting criminal activities outside the fisheries sector, and from features of international trade regimes that provide fisheries regimes sufficient leeway to put in place environmentally motivated trade restrictions. Consolidating and further improving this compliance-oriented interplay will require somewhat deeper cross-institutional coordination than may seem necessary with respect to science and regulation.

Advances in compliance measures for curbing undesirable fishing on the high seas derive in part from conducive interplay among regional fisheries regimes and global fisheries institutions. The period following the 1992 UN Conference on Environment and Development (UNCED) was particularly dynamic.[64] Interplay management of the global-regional variety was provided by the UN, through the Agenda 21 programme of action adopted at UNCED, as well as initiatives under the FAO's Committee on Fisheries, triggering negotiation of the Fish Stocks Agreement and a string of FAO instruments, notably the Compliance Agreement, the Code of Conduct[65] and its IPOA-IUU,[66] and the PSM Agreement.[67] Major compliance-inducing advances include stricter flag State responsibilities, procedures allowing non-flag States to inspect and, in certain cases, detain fishing vessels on the high seas, and increasingly coordinated port State measures, often linked to satellite-based vessel monitoring systems (VMS). Cross-regional interplay management has also been important, as illustrated by the mutual endorsement of IUU vessel lists under NAFO and NEAFC; the latter body also endorses the lists maintained by CCAMLR and the South-East Atlantic Fisheries Organisation (SEAFO), implying restrictions on access to ports, transshipment and fishing licences in any Member.[68]

The high degree of coherence that marks the interplay among these many fisheries institutions mobilized in a large-scale and long-term offensive to combat unsustainable pressures on high seas stocks has been achieved by intensive interplay management, as evident in a series of deliberately linked international conferences, global agreements, soft-law instruments and inter-agency working groups.

---

[64] DA Balton "Strengthening the Law of the Sea: The New Agreement on Straddling Fish Stocks and Highly Migratory Fish Stocks" (1996) 27 *Ocean Development and International Law* 125–151.

[65] Code of Conduct for Responsible Fisheries of 31 October 1995, available at www.fao.org/fishery/en.

[66] International Plan of Action to Prevent, Deter and Eliminate Illegal, Unreported and Unregulated Fishing of 2 March 2001, available at www.fao.org/fishery/en.

[67] Agreement on Port State Measures to Prevent, Deter and Eliminate Illegal, Unreported and Unregulated Fishing of 22 November 2009, available at www.fao.org/Legal.

[68] See OS Stokke "Barents Sea Fisheries: the IUU Struggle" (2010) 1 *Arctic Review on Law and Politics* 207–224. See also Chapter 5 of this volume (Harrison).

Lower-order interplay management, involving adaptation rather than coordination, has proven sufficient for obtaining high coherence among trade and fisheries institutions with respect to compliance-oriented restrictions on access to ports and markets. Such coherence is a two-sided achievement. From a resource-management perspective, the adoption of trade-law compatible compliance measures implies successful avoidance of the 'chilling effect' of imposing international trade restrictions that conservationists have warned against. For the free trade community, coherence has made it possible to pursue legitimate conservation and management objectives, without jeopardizing the non-discrimination norm that has been enshrined in international trade regimes for more than seven decades. Those fisheries regimes have tailored their trade-restrictive compliance measures to the 'environmental window' of the global trade regime, accepting guidance from that regime's *general* compatibility criteria while claiming competence to hammer out *specific* measures that can serve to raise the costs of non-compliance.

On the fisheries side of this relationship, interplay management began in the early 1990s with various tuna RFMOs implementing import bans on States whose vessels had been found to engage in unregulated fishing.[69] Key standards of WTO compatibility are whether States have exhausted less restrictive measures, have minimized and justified any remaining discrimination, and have developed criteria for avoiding trade restrictions that are transparent, non-discriminatory and not excessively intrusive on the jurisdictional autonomy of the target State.[70]

Regional fisheries management regimes have proven to be conducive platforms for developing trade-restrictive compliance measures that meet those standards, even without significant cross-institutional coordination. First, concerning exhaustion of less trade-restrictive measures, the introduction of stringent requirements to document that landed fish derives from a licensed vessel, and other port State measures was agreed only after a string of less- or non-trade restrictive measures based on international ocean law had proven ineffective. Secondly, with a view to minimizing discrimination, advanced documentation schemes like the one implemented by NEAFC refrained from employing significantly trade-restrictive measures used by certain other RFMOs, including 'positive lists' whereby only listed vessels may land or transship their catches in Member ports or restrictions imposed on the flag State and not only the individual vessel. Cooperation with non-Members is yet another feature that enhances the WTO-compatibility of advanced fisheries compliance schemes: the NEAFC variant allows non-Members to apply for a status as 'cooperating non-Contracting Party' in order to avoid trade restrictions, provided they agree to play by the same rules as the Members do. The idea of non-Members

---

[69] See also Chapter 14 of this volume (Churchill).
[70] See e.g. Stokke, note 8.

'cooperating' with an RFMO's documentation system emerged within CCAMLR and was aimed precisely at minimizing tension with WTO rules.[71]

Finally, regional fisheries regimes are generally better placed to avoid charges of opportunistic design or excessive intrusiveness than are States operating unilaterally, as the multilateral framework makes it more difficult to tailor provisions in ways that hit foreigners harder than domestic players. The coherence among trade- and fisheries regimes relevant to compliance has resulted not from cross-institutional coordination but rather from a long-standing adaptation of specific compliance measures to the environmental window of the global trade regime. Such adaptation was conducted by those operating the fisheries management regimes that pioneered these measures, subsequently emulated by others.

Increasing attention to the high seas fisheries problem has also prompted the engagement of international bodies tasked with crime prevention and criminal justice more generally. The OECD's Committee for Fisheries set out in the early 2000s to identify new strategies for combating undesirable fishing on the high seas, focusing on value-chain interventions that might affect the cost-benefit ratio of non-adherence to international rules.[72] A core idea with that initiative was to explore ways of expanding the enforcement network beyond actors with competence over fisheries or ports, taking cues from how States deal with other types of transnational crime such as tax evasion, financial fraud, or trafficking in narcotics, arms or human beings.[73] The subsequent engagement of UNODC in the fisheries sector has triggered several awareness-raising studies of overlaps between IUU fisheries operations and high-priority criminal activities, as well as a series of fish-crime conferences aimed at identifying ways of strengthening operational contacts among relevant national, intergovernmental and transnational institutions.[74] A clear message deriving from these studies and expert meetings is that achieving coherence in this new but expanding segment of the fisheries-compliance complex will require radically deeper inter-agency coordination of investigation and prosecution, nationally as well as internationally.[75] Among the most advanced instances of such coordination

---

[71] DJ Agnew "The Illegal and Unregulated Fishery for Toothfish in the Southern Ocean, and the CCAMLR Catch Documentation Scheme" (2000) 24 *Marine Policy* 361–374, at 370.

[72] C-C Schmidt "Economic Drivers of Illegal, Unreported and Unregulated (IUU) Fishing" (2005) 20 *International Journal of Marine and Coastal Law* 479–507, at 480.

[73] The OECD initiative fed into the High Seas Task Force, an international mission hosted by the OECD Round Table on Sustainable Development; see High Seas Task Force *Closing the net: Stopping Illegal Fishing on the High Seas* (available at www.oecd.org/sd-roundtable/aboutus/stoppingillegalfishingonthehighseas.htm). On enforcer networks, see OS Stokke "Actor Configurations and Compliance Tasks in International Environmental Governance" in N Kanie, S Andresen and PM Haas (eds.) *Improving Global Environmental Governance. Best Practices for Architecture and Agency* (Routledge, London: 2014) 83–107.

[74] *Stretching the Fishnet: Identifying Opportunities to Address Fisheries Crime* (Vienna, UNODC: 2017).

[75] Outcome of the UNODC/WWF Fisheries Crime Expert Group Meeting, 24–26 February 2016, doc. E/CN.15/2016/CRP.2 of 11 May 2016.

is the North Atlantic Fisheries Intelligence Group. By working closely with INTERPOL's Fisheries Crime Working Group, it enables customs, tax and fisheries-enforcement authorities in 11 European States and territories as well as Canada and the US to share data and intelligence on fisheries and related industries.[76] The mobilization for fisheries purposes of international collaborative structures for combating higher-priority crimes is still in a relatively early stage, and delivering on the objectives will require sustained coordination of activities under a broad set of institutions.

Private governance bodies have also carved out niches in the institutional complex dealing with high seas fisheries compliance, involving both industry associations and environmental NGOs. The private certification scheme examined above is highly relevant for compliance as well, as the management-system requirement for MSC certification may incentivize industries and States to promote or accept more intrusive or stringent enforcement measures. Among other compliance-relevant measures employed by NGOs are information-gathering, including VMS of fishing vessels on the high seas, as well as naming and praising/shaming of companies involved in the high seas fisheries value chain.[77]

Satellite-based tracking of individual fishing vessels as part of systems for monitoring compliance is a well-established practice in many regional fisheries management regimes, and one that can be reinforced by complementary private action. Thus far, governmental VMS have required specially devised on-board transponders typically linked to flag State enforcement agencies. However, that has made them relevant only for vessels registered with a regime Member, which is an unfortunate limitation, given the frequency of regime outsiders participating in high seas fisheries operations. The Global Fishing Watch initiative by Google, a growing player in the provision of earth observation data, in partnership with environmental NGOs interested in countering unsustainable fishing operations, seeks to overcome that limitation by using the Automatic Identification System (AIS) that is mandatory under the International Maritime Organization (IMO)'s SOLAS 74.[78]

The Global Fishing Watch initiative is coherent with the intergovernmental regime in supporting the same objective, but it cannot make a substantial difference without complementary action under global and regional institutions responsible for maritime safety or resource management.[79] That is because

---

[76] See respectively nafig.org/ and www.interpol.int/News-and-media/News/2017/N2017-123.

[77] Chapter 16 of this volume (Massarella) examines two other, more adversarial, types of measures: litigation, and various protest actions such as physical impediment of harvesting operations.

[78] International Convention for the Safety of Life at Sea of 1 November 1974 (1184 UNTS 277; with protocols and regularly amended). See W Ouellette and W Getinet "Remote Sensing for Marine Spatial Planning and Integrated Coastal Areas Management: Achievements, Challenges, Opportunities and Future Prospects" (2016) 4 *Remote Sensing Applications: Society and Environment* 138–157. For details of the Global Fishing Watch initiative, see globalfishingwatch.org.

[79] DJ McCauley et al. "Ending Hide and Seek at Sea" (2016) 351 *Science* 1148–1150.

SOLAS 74 requires AIS only for vessels larger than 300 gross tonnes and engaged in international voyages, which means that application to most fishing vessels is discretionary for the flag States; implying that such application is unlikely whenever high seas fishing vessels fly a 'flag of convenience'. The adaptation of other institutions that would raise coherence is not necessarily forthcoming. A 2015 submission by two environmental NGOs encouraging a joint FAO/IMO working group on IUU fishing to advocate stricter AIS regulations met with only a lukewarm response.[80] Among the counter-arguments is the expectation that use of AIS for compliance purposes will encourage tampering or even disabling transponders, thereby undermining the safety-at-sea objectives that motivated the creation of AIS. Raising the coherence of this private initiative and intergovernmental efforts to strengthen high seas fisheries compliance will require involving potential users of these data with sufficiently high stakes in the outcome to mobilize political energy for creating an effective institutional environment.[81]

Private organizations have also engaged in naming and shaming of firms and vessels engaged in IUU fishing. This has been done most systematically by the Coalition of Legal Toothfish Operators (COLTO), which is currently composed of 41 companies active in the value chain of toothfish species taken largely in the Southern Ocean.[82] Despite its routine use of controversial and undiplomatic language in web postings and televised films explicitly targeting named fishing companies and service providers, COLTO has for 15 years remained one of very few NGOs that receive a standing invitation to attend the annual CCAMLR meetings as observers.[83] Its attention-grabbing strategies have included a 'Rogues Gallery' of 'poacher' and 'plunderer' vessels and their associated company structures, as well as a 'wanted campaign' of posters in 18 languages offering up to USD 100,000 in reward for information leading to the capture or conviction of those responsible for illegal harvesting of Patagonian toothfish.[84]

More recently, COLTO has added naming and *praising* to its portfolio of compliance measures, by sponsoring CCAMLR's annual 'tag-return lottery' among reports on recaptured toothfish, encouraging adherence to CCAMLR's

---

[80] Report of the Third Session of the Joint FAO/IMO Ad Hoc Working Group on Illegal, Unreported and Unregulated (IUU) Fishing and Related Matters (*FAO Fisheries and Aquaculture Report*, no. 1152 (2015)).

[81] Stokke and Young, note 7 at 191.

[82] On COLTO's membership and mission, see www.colto.org. This organization has conducted further activities pioneered by the International Southern Oceans Longline Fisheries Information Clearing House (ISOFISH), a partnership of industries and environmental NGOs; see LD Fallon and LK Kriwoken "International Influence of an Australian Nongovernment Organization in the Protection of Patagonian Toothfish" (2004) 35 *Ocean Development & International Law* 221–266.

[83] The other two are the Antarctic and Southern Ocean Coalition (ASOC), an umbrella environmental NGO; and the Association of Responsible Krill harvesting companies (ARK). See www.ccamlr.org/en/organisation/cooperation-others.

[84] H Österblom and UR Sumaila "Toothfish Crises, Actor Diversity and the Emergence of Compliance Mechanisms in the Southern Ocean" (2011) 21 *Global Environmental Change* 972–982, at 977.

compulsory tagging and release programme for exploratory fisheries.[85] Although its *de facto* observer status under CCAMLR certainly adds to the prestige and saliency of this private organization, and thereby also to the coherence of this part of the institutional complex, it is clearly possible to compile and disseminate company-specific information relevant to shaming or praising without extensive coordination with the regional regime.

For all three governance tasks, therefore, the trend is towards broadening of the complex of institutions relevant in countering undesirable harvesting on the high seas. Such broadening is particularly notable on the compliance side of governance. Here we can note the increasing involvement of more actors other than the flag State, capable of influencing the costs or gains associated with non-adherence to international fisheries regulations.

6. CONCLUSIONS

The most promising options for improving high seas fisheries management are those that serve to enhance the coherence of problem-solving efforts under a steadily broader set of institutions, with each bringing distinctive capacities to bear on the advisory, regulatory or compliance tasks of governance.

Regional fisheries regimes have traditionally been the core arenas for pursuing such coherence, as their *raison d'être* is to bring together, on a regular basis, the fisheries bureaucracies of the major harvesting States in order to integrate those three tasks. Today, however, more and more institutions inside as well as outside the fisheries sector have roles to play, due to the interconnectedness of measures taken for fisheries purposes and those targeting other governance issues such as environmental protection, labour standards and international trade. Among the drivers of this interplay is the rising interest in fisheries compliance measures that target other links in the seafood value chain besides harvesting, such as vessel registration and insurance, crewing and bunkering, transshipment and various port State measures on landings and subsequent distribution that build on the jurisdiction of port States over any vessel on voluntary call. Several UN-based institutions have helped to sharpen and broaden the use of such measures, which have typically evolved within a small number of particularly advanced regional fisheries regimes.

Achieving coherence among this expanding range of management contributions requires interplay management: deliberate efforts among those operating the institutions to maintain or improve the synergies among them. Such interplay management sometimes takes the demanding form of sustained or recurrent

---

[85] See   www.ccamlr.org/en/news/2017/ccamlr-tag-return-lottery-2017-%E2%80%93-winners-announced. By 2017, more than 200,000 toothfish had been tagged and released under this programme.

cross-regime coordination. That has been the case for the institutionalized provision of science-based advice to decision-making when advice is generated outside the fisheries bodies, and for the ongoing attempts to make better use of criminal justice capacities for investigation and prosecution of fisheries crime. However, the interplay management needed is usually far more modest. Diffusion of best practices among regional fisheries regimes is enhanced by overlaps in the delegations who represent governments in various regulatory bodies and in global soft-law processes. Achieving adaptation of fisheries measures to area-protection instruments under regional environmental regimes can be easier in the absence of joint decision-making, as each institution involved will typically be reluctant to renounce any of its regulatory competence. Similarly, in several cases coherence has been obtained among compliance-motivated trade restrictions and the non-discrimination rule in international trade regimes by adapting those measures to the general exceptions articulated in agreements under the WTO. And, finally, private governance institutions have achieved coherence with intergovernmental institutions largely through one-sided adaptation; typically by incorporating the intergovernmental standard among their own requirements for avoiding shaming, or obtaining either praise or access to a lucrative ecolabel.

This chapter has brought out the merits of examining international resource management at the aggregate level, highlighting the interplay among several institutions with distinctive capacities relevant to various governance tasks. The findings reported here indicate that reasonable levels of coherence can be achieved within such institutional complexes even without a clear-cut hierarchy among the institutions involved, and without ambitious means of cross-institutional coordination.

5

Key Challenges Relating to the Governance of Regional Fisheries

JAMES HARRISON

1. INTRODUCTION

INTERNATIONAL LAW CALLS for cooperation in the conservation and management of fish stocks, although it does not specify the precise form that such cooperation must take.[1] Generally speaking, States have chosen to pursue cooperation at the regional level, in order to allow them to respond to the varying ecological, geographical and political particularities of each individual fishery. Most regional fisheries cooperation takes place through some type of international institution, generically referred to as a regional fisheries body (RFB).[2] Yet, the functions of RFBs vary from the collection and dissemination of data to the adoption of legally binding conservation and management measures (CMMs). It is this latter form of cooperation that is of particular interest in the present chapter, as it offers the best chances of ensuring the effective management of the world's fish stocks.

The purpose of this chapter is to explore the key trends in regional fisheries management and the extent to which a comprehensive, coherent and effective system of regional fisheries governance has emerged since the entry into force of the LOS Convention.[3] The focus of the chapter is on the regulation of high seas fisheries, including straddling and highly migratory stocks. The chapter will question the extent to which common trends have emerged in relation to such governance arrangements. It will address five key issues that are critical to the effective functioning of regional fisheries regulation, namely: drivers of regional

---

[1] United Nations Convention on the Law of the Sea of 10 December 1982 (LOS Convention; 1833 UNTS 3), Arts. 63, 64 and 118.

[2] This is an umbrella term used by the Food and Agriculture Organization of the United Nations; see www.fao.org/fishery/topic/16800/en.

[3] See note 1. The LOS Convention entered into force on 16 November 1994.

fisheries cooperation (Section 2); institutional form (Section 3); decision-making procedures (Section 4); dispute settlement (Section 5); and inter-institutional cooperation (Section 6).[4] The conclusions in Section 7 will draw together the overall trends in this field and will suggest that there are signs of increasing systematization evident through emerging principles by which all RFBs are judged, as well as increasing collaboration between RFBs in order to promote shared goals.

2. KEY DRIVERS OF REGIONAL FISHERIES REFORM

Whilst fisheries cooperation can be traced back to the late 19th and early 20th centuries,[5] there is little doubt that cooperation in this field has intensified since the 1990s when broader considerations of sustainability emerged as an international priority.[6] The political impetus generated by events such as the 1992 Rio Conference on Environment and Development led to further developments in the global legal framework for international fisheries management, as well as to reform of regional fisheries regimes.

One of the most important developments in international fisheries law following the Rio Conference was the adoption of the Fish Stocks Agreement.[7] Much of the Agreement is concerned with improving the governance of fisheries at the regional or subregional level, in order to ensure transparent, timely and effective decision-making.[8] The Fish Stocks Agreement itself explicitly calls for the establishment of new subregional and regional fisheries management organizations or arrangements where none exist[9] and the strengthening of existing organizations and arrangements in order to improve their effectiveness.[10] The principles and policy goals in this Agreement, as reinforced by subsequent international instruments,[11] declarations[12] and meetings,[13] not only provide a

---

[4] See also Chapter 6 of this volume (Molenaar).

[5] See e.g. K Bangert "Fisheries Agreements" in *Max Planck Encyclopedia of Public International Law On-line Edition* (Oxford University Press, Oxford: 2008).

[6] See discussion in e.g. Y Takei *Filling Regulatory Gaps in High Seas Fisheries* (Martinus Nijhoff, Leiden: 2013) 88–111.

[7] Agreement for the Implementation of the Provisions of the United Nations Convention on the Law of the Sea of 10 December 1982 relating to the Conservation and Management of Straddling Fish Stocks and Highly Migratory Fish Stocks of 4 August 1995 (2167 UNTS 3).

[8] Ibid., Arts. 10(j) and 12.

[9] Ibid., Art. 8(5).

[10] Ibid., Art. 13.

[11] See e.g. Code of Conduct for Responsible Fisheries of 31 October 1995, para. 6.12; International Plan of Action to Prevent, Deter and Eliminate Illegal, Unreported and Unregulated Fishing of 2 March 2001, paras. 78–83.

[12] 2001 Reykjavik Declaration on Responsible Fisheries in the Marine Environment, para. 3; 2005 St John's Declaration on the Governance of High Seas Fisheries, paras. 1, 4; 2005 Rome Declaration on IUU Fishing, para. 5.

[13] See e.g. Report of the Meeting of FAO and Non-FAO Regional Fishery Bodies or Arrangements (*FAO Fisheries Report* No. 597: 1999), para. 41(v).

checklist for evaluating the functioning of fisheries cooperation, but they also provide an important baseline for States when negotiating the establishment of new cooperative mechanisms, whether they apply to straddling and highly migratory stocks or discrete high seas stocks.[14]

In practice, the follow-up to the Rio Conference and the Fish Stocks Agreement has seen both reform of existing regional fisheries treaties to reflect modern governance principles, as well as the establishment of new fisheries treaties to cover new and emerging fisheries. All of these developments have confirmed RFBs as the main vehicle for managing high seas fisheries. In particular, a key shift in this post-Rio period has been a trend towards the establishment of mechanisms to agree upon legally binding CMMs for high seas fish stocks, largely through the establishment of regional fisheries management organizations or arrangements (RFMO/As).[15]

Significant steps have been taken to fill gaps in the regulatory framework for high seas fisheries, although some gaps remain.[16] In part, gaps arise because existing RFMO/As may not necessarily cover all of the relevant species that are fished in the region. The United Nations General Assembly (UNGA) has particularly highlighted the need to ensure the mandates of RFMO/As cover bottom fisheries.[17] In other areas, the relevant RFBs may not have a mandate to adopt legally binding CMMs for the fish stocks under their purview. For example, in the Central and South-West Atlantic and the Central Eastern Atlantic, the two existing regional fisheries institutions do not possess the power to adopt legally binding management measures, although discussions are ongoing about upgrading these bodies to address this shortcoming.[18] In some areas, there is simply a lack of institutions. Whilst coverage is generally considered to be good for tuna and tuna-like species, the situation for other fish stocks is patchier. One gap relates to certain parts of the Central Pacific, in areas that fall between the mandates of the North Pacific Fisheries Commission (NPFC) and the South Pacific Regional Fisheries Management Organization (SPRFMO). The situation is more complex in the South-West Atlantic, where proposals have been made for

---

[14] See e.g. R Barnes and C Massarella "High Seas Fisheries" in E Morgera and K Kulovesi (eds.) *Research Handbook on International Law and Natural Resources* (Edward Elgar, Cheltenham: 2016) 369–389, at 374; Takei, note 6 at 152–153.

[15] J Swan "Decision-Making in Regional Fisheries Bodies or Arrangements: The Evolving Role of RFBs and International Agreement on Decision-Making Processes" (*FAO Fisheries Circular* No. 995: 2004) 10; Takei, note 6 at 205–272. See below for discussion of the differences between RFMOs and RFMAs.

[16] United Nations General Assembly (UNGA) Res. 71/123 of 7 December 2016, para. 140; Report of the 2016 Resumed Fish Stocks Agreement Review Conference (doc. A/CONF.210/2016/5 of 1 August 2016), Outcomes, para. A18.

[17] UNGA Res. 59/25 of 17 November 2004, para. 68. See also Chapter 7 of this volume (Caddell).

[18] For discussion, see Fishery Committee for the Eastern Central Atlantic (CECAF) Performance Review (2012) para. 21; K Hoydal "Findings of the Independent Cost-Benefit Assessment of the Options for Strategic Re-Orientation of WECAFC" (*FAO Fisheries and Aquaculture Circular* No. 1117: 2016).

the establishment of an RFMO to fill a gap in fisheries regulation, but they have been resisted by coastal States in the region, in part due to ongoing territorial disputes.[19] Finally, there is a gap for all fish species in the central Arctic Ocean, where the ice is retreating and opening up new fishing grounds. Although there is not yet any commercial fishing in these areas, there are ongoing negotiations on how to address this situation in a pre-emptive manner.[20]

Alongside the drive towards comprehensive regulatory coverage, the international community has also stressed the need to ensure that institutions are effective in fulfilling the mandate that they have been given. Momentum for performance reviews of RFBs began in 2005, when the 26th Session of the United Nations Food and Agriculture Organization (FAO)'s Committee on Fisheries agreed to "extend an invitation to RFMO members and other interested parties encouraging them to participate in the development of parameters for any such review process".[21] These discussions were followed up in the 2005 UNGA Fisheries Resolution, which "[e]ncourage[d] States, through their participation in regional fisheries management organizations and arrangements, to initiate processes for their performance review"[22]

The North-East Atlantic Fisheries Commission (NEAFC) was amongst the first RFMOs to undertake a performance review[23] using criteria developed by its Working Group on the Future of NEAFC.[24] In particular, the review took into account the manner in which NEAFC had performed in several core areas with reference to relevant international treaties and other instruments, including the LOS Convention and the Fish Stocks Agreement. Most RFMO/As have now carried out at least one performance review, many following a similar model to NEAFC.[25] Yet, there are key differences between the processes, particularly when it comes to the composition of the review panel. Whilst

---

[19] See A Bensch et al. "Worldwide Review of Bottom Fisheries in the High Seas" (*FAO Fisheries and Aquaculture Technical Paper* No. 522/Rev.1: 2009) 62.

[20] An agreement to prevent unregulated high seas fishing in the central Arctic Ocean was signed in October 2018; see https://www.state.gov/r/pa/prs/ps/2018/10/286348.htm. For a discussion of this process, see EJ Molenaar "International Regulation of Central Arctic Ocean Fisheries" in MH Nordquist, J Moore and R Long (eds.) *Challenges of the Changing Arctic. Continental Shelf, Navigation, and Fisheries* (Brill, Leiden: 2016) 429–463.

[21] Report of the Twenty-Sixth Meeting of the Committee on Fisheries (*FAO Fisheries Report* R780: 2005), para. 112.

[22] UNGA Res. 60/31 of 29 November 2005, paras. 60. See also UNGA Res. 61/105 of 8 December 2006, para. 73 and the Report of the 2006 Fish Stocks Agreement Review Conference (doc. A/CONF.210/2006/15 of 5 July 2006), Outcome, para. 32(j).

[23] The North Atlantic Salmon Conservation Organization (NASCO) had undertaken a performance review in 2004–2005, although this was an internal exercise linked to reform of the organization.

[24] Report of the 2006 NEAFC Performance Review.

[25] See M Ceo et al. "Performance Reviews by Regional Fisheries Bodies: Introduction, Summaries, Synthesis and Best Practices" (*FAO Fisheries and Aquaculture Circular* No. 1072: 2012) 43; PD Szigeti and G Lugten "The Implementation of Performance Reviews Reports by Regional Fisheries Bodies, 2004–2014" (*FAO Fisheries and Aquaculture Circular* No. 1108: 2013) 6.

some RFMO/As involve a mixture of internal and external experts,[26] others have opted for the appointment of a completely independent panel composed of experts in fisheries management, fisheries science and the law of the sea.[27] This latter approach arguably increases the rigor of the assessment process by minimizing any influence that the organization may have upon the findings. Nevertheless, many RFMO/As continue to stress the benefit of including representatives of the organization in order to provide some internal knowledge and guidance as to how cooperation works within the region.[28] The reviews also differ in the manner in which they engage with external stakeholders and civil society. Many RFMO/As have chosen to actively consult stakeholders as part of the review process and some have gone as far as including a representative from a non-governmental organization (NGO) on the review panel.[29]

These periodic reviews, which have become a legal requirement for the most recently established RFMOs,[30] are not only an important tool for assessing the effectiveness of fisheries measures adopted within a particular region, but they are also a way of considering best practices from other regional settings, thus contributing to the systematization of regional fisheries governance.

3. INSTITUTIONAL STATUS OF REGIONAL FISHERY BODIES

The Fish Stocks Agreement makes a distinction between cooperation that is carried out "directly or through appropriate subregional or regional fisheries management organizations and arrangements".[31] Whilst it reserves the option for direct cooperation, the Agreement goes on to specify that States are under an obligation to "cooperate to establish such an organization or enter

---

[26] This was the case for the first NEAFC Performance Review in 2006. This model was followed by, *inter alia*, the Commission for the Conservation of Antarctic Marine Living Resources (CCAMLR), the Western and Central Pacific Fisheries Commission (WCPFC), the South-East Atlantic Fisheries Organization (SEAFO), the Indian Ocean Tuna Commission (IOTC) and the Northwest Atlantic Fisheries Organization (NAFO).

[27] The International Commission on the Conservation of Atlantic Tunas (ICCAT) was the first body to establish a completely independent review panel in 2008 and it has been followed by, *inter alia*, NEAFC in its second review, the General Fisheries Commission for the Mediterranean (GFCM), and (to some extent) the Commission on the Conservation of Southern Bluefin Tuna (CCSBT). The Inter-American Tropical Tuna Commission (IATTC) employed an independent consultancy to conduct its review.

[28] See Report of the NAFO Performance Review virtual Working Group (doc. NAFO/GC Doc.16/02 of 2016), 3.

[29] See e.g. Terms of Reference and Criteria to Conduct the Performance Review of the Indian Ocean Tuna Commission (2014); Report of the Thirty-Fifth Meeting of CCAMLR (2016) Annex 8.

[30] Convention on the Conservation and Management of High Seas Fishery Resources in the South Pacific Ocean of 14 November 2009 (SPRFMO Convention; available at www.sprfmo.int), Art. 30; 2012 Convention on the Conservation and Management of High Seas Fisheries Resources in the North Pacific Ocean of 24 February 2012 (NPFC Convention; available at https://www.npfc.int/), Art. 22.

[31] Art. 8(1).

into other appropriate arrangements" where one does not already exist.[32] Such a duty to cooperate can only practically operate as an obligation of conduct, not an obligation of result,[33] but it nevertheless sets a clear preference for more institutionalized forms of cooperation. This preference is also reflected in subsequent international fisheries policy documents.[34] Yet, these instruments still leave a choice for States between cooperation through an RFMO or an RFMA and it is therefore pertinent to consider the key differences between these institutional forms.

The Fish Stocks Agreement does not expressly define an RFMO, but there are three key features that are at the core of any international organization. First, the establishment of an organization implies a minimum degree of institutionalization, including distinct legal personality.[35] An organization will thus be subject to the rules of international law, including principles of international institutional law, which define the scope of powers that may be exercised by an organization. In particular, this branch of international law can be used to determine whether or not an international organization is able to regulate matters that are incidental to its main functions,[36] as well as the existence of implied powers that may be necessary to the achievement of its objectives.[37] Secondly, all RFMOs will also have some form of permanent organ that exercises decision-making powers on behalf of its Members.[38] In practice, it is common for RFMOs to have a complex structure of organs and sub-organs, each exercising different functions. Finally, an organization will have a secretariat that arranges meetings and oversees the day-to-day operation of the organization on behalf of the membership. In this regard, modern international relations scholarship posits that the establishment of a secretariat, separate from the individual Members, has significant effects on the dynamics of international law-making by providing "relatively unbiased information to all",[39] thereby "influencing how problems are framed and discussed".[40] Indeed, the secretariat may also be ascribed certain functions in relation to implementation and oversight of agreed CMMs, including bringing instances of infractions to the attention of the relevant organs of the RFMO. This is a possibility that is often neglected in the context of regional fisheries

---

[32] Ibid., Art. 8(5). See also UNGA Res.71/123, note 16, para. 140.

[33] See e.g. *Railway Traffic between Lithuania and Poland* (1931) PCIJ Reports, Series A/B, 108, 116.

[34] See e.g. Code of Conduct, note 11, para. 7.1.3.

[35] See e.g. International Law Commission, Draft Articles on the Responsibility of International Organizations, Art. 2(a).

[36] See e.g. *Advisory Opinion on the Competence of the International Labour Organization to Regulate, Incidentally, the Personal Work of the Employer* (1926) PCIJ Reports, Series B, No. 13, 6.

[37] See e.g. *Advisory Opinion on Reparations for Injuries Suffered in the Service of the United Nations* (1949) ICJ Reports 174.

[38] See e.g. HG Schermers and NM Blokkers *International Institutional Law* 3rd ed. (Brill, Leiden: 1995) 23.

[39] J Alvarez *International Organizations as Law-Makers* (Oxford University Press, Oxford: 2005) 341.

[40] EM Hafner-Burton, DG Victor and Y Lupu "Political Science Research on International Law: The State of the Field" (2012) 106 *American Journal of International Law* 47–97, at 57.

management, however, and performance reviews have sometimes recommended that certain aspects of the secretariat should be strengthened in order to provide better support to reviewing compliance with CMMs.[41]

The concept of an RFMA implies a lesser degree of institutionalization. The Fish Stocks Agreement defines such an arrangement as:

> a cooperative mechanism established in accordance with the Convention and this Agreement by two or more States for the purpose, inter alia, of establishing [CMMs] in a subregion or region for one or more straddling fish stocks or highly migratory fish stocks.[42]

This concept is a broad one and it potentially covers a range of different forms of cooperation. On the one hand, it would cover non-binding mechanisms agreed between relevant fishing States. This form of arrangement is most common as a means of promulgating interim measures, either pending the conclusion of a treaty or pending its entry into force. For example, the States and entities negotiating the NPFC Convention[43] agreed in February 2007 to the adoption of (non-legally binding) interim measures for the North-East Pacific and the North-West Pacific, pending the conclusion of a treaty for this region. These interim measures were revised a number of times during their lifetime, demonstrating that such arrangements can evolve over time to reflect new developments. Nevertheless, this sort of arrangement can clearly be distinguished from an RFMO because there is no permanent body with legal personality responsible for overseeing the development of the measures.

At the same time, the term 'arrangement' could also include a legally binding agreement on applicable decision-making procedures that falls short of establishing a formal international organization. The CBS Convention[44] provides an example of such an arrangement in practice. This treaty aims to "establish an international regime for conservation, management and optimum utilization of Pollock resources in the Convention Area",[45] which operates through an "Annual Conference of the Parties"[46] held in rotation among the Parties.[47] The conference is also supported by a Scientific and Technical Committee, demonstrating that even an RFMA can encompass a more complex institutional structure. One reason for choosing this model was to reduce cost for the Parties, as there is no need for a permanent headquarters or a secretariat.[48]

---

[41] Report of the 2014 NEAFC Performance Review, 99.

[42] Art. 1(1)(d).

[43] Note 30.

[44] Convention on the Conservation and Management of Pollock Resources in the Central Bering Sea of 16 June 1994 (34 ILM 67).

[45] Ibid., Art. II(1).

[46] Ibid., Art. III(1)(a).

[47] Ibid,. Art. VI(1). Indeed, since 2010, the Parties have held a virtual conference; see www.afsc.noaa.gov/refm/cbs/.

[48] See DA Balton "The Bering Sea Doughnut Hole Convention: Regional Solution, Global Implications" in OS Stokke (ed.) *Governing High Seas Fisheries* (Oxford University Press, Oxford: 2001)

Yet, it is possible for such an arrangement to make provision for an independent secretariat, as one sees in the SIOFA.[49] Indeed, it has been argued elsewhere that this type of autonomous institutional arrangement should be treated as an international organization, subject to the rules of international institutional law,[50] thus blurring the distinction with a formal international organization. This observation means that it is more important to consider the detailed functioning of an organization or arrangement, rather than its formal designation or status.[51]

4. RFMO/A DECISION-MAKING PROCEDURES

RFMO/As are established with the primary aim of conferring the power to make decisions relating to the conservation and management of fish stocks, including decisions relating to fishing levels, catch allocation and other CMMs. Decision-making procedures are a key aspect of negotiations related to the establishment of a regional fisheries treaty, as the precise parameters of these procedures will determine how much control States give up over fishing opportunities and how much influence States have over the decision-making process within the institution.

The Fish Stocks Agreement has emphasized the importance of transparent, timely and effective decision-making procedures within RFMO/As.[52] These requirements have been reiterated by the 2016 Resumed Fish Stocks Agreement Review Conference, which encouraged RFMO/As to review their decision-making procedures in order to facilitate the adoption of CMMs in a timely and effective manner.[53] The importance of timeliness in the context of fisheries management is self-explanatory. The pursuit of effectiveness is more complex and there is a balance to be achieved between the ambition of adopting decisions on the one hand, and their widespread acceptance on the other hand. In practice, decision-making procedures are the product of political compromises between the States involved in the negotiations. It follows that there is no single model of decision-making.[54] Indeed, decision-making procedures often contain

---

143–178, at 158. See also EJ Molenaar, "Addressing Regulatory Gaps in High Seas Fisheries" (2005) 20 *International Journal of Marine and Coastal Law* 533–570, at 545.

[49] Southern Indian Ocean Fisheries Agreement of 7 July 2006 (available at www.fao.org/legal), Art. 9.

[50] See R Churchill and G Ulfstein "Autonomous Institutional Arrangements in Multilateral Environmental Agreements" (2000) 94 *American Journal of International Law* 623–659, at 633.

[51] See further Section 2 of Chapter 6 of this volume (Molenaar).

[52] Fish Stocks Agreement, Arts. 10(j) and 12. See also Art. 28.

[53] Report of the 2016 Resumed Fish Stocks Agreement Review Conference, note 16 at para. B5(d).

[54] See TL McDorman "Implementing Existing Tools: Turning Words into Actions – Decision-making processes of Regional Fisheries Management Organizations (RFMOs)" (2005) 20 *International Journal of Marine and Coastal Law* 423–457, at 427.

a number of elements, which must be considered side-by-side in order to understand the degree to which Members are constrained.

At one end of the spectrum lie those organizations that operate on the basis of unanimity or consensus, such as the Inter-American Tropical Tuna Commission (IATTC). The IATTC Convention[55] provides that, unless otherwise agreed,[56] decisions of the IATTC shall be made by consensus,[57] which is defined as "the adoption of a decision without voting and without the expression of any stated objection".[58] Whilst consensus is ordinarily to be distinguished from unanimity, the lack of an alternative voting procedure means that consensus in this context is very close to unanimity. Indeed, the Convention even provides an opportunity for States that were not able to attend the meeting to block the consensus within a certain time-period.[59] Other treaties are more explicit in requiring unanimity prior to a decision being adopted.[60] The two main RFMAs also operate by consensus.[61]

It has been recognized that consensus decision-making has advantages and disadvantages. Thus, it has been argued that "decisions reached by consensus were preferable as they enjoyed greater levels of support and compliance when implemented".[62] Furthermore, as noted by the performance review of the IATTC, "consensus is the most egalitarian, collaborative decision-making model", but it also has drawbacks, as it "tends to support the status quo and impede change".[63] From this perspective, consensus has been criticized as coming at the cost of "lowest common denominator outcomes and, in some cases, only after prolonged debate leading to non-timeliness of adoption of management measures".[64] Ultimately, this form of decision-making means that all States must consent to a new measure and thus any single State can veto a decision. This can lead to delays in decision-making, but evidence on this point

---

[55] Convention for the Strengthening of the Inter-American Tropical Tuna Commission Established by the 1949 Convention Between the United States of America and the Republic of Costa Rica of 14 November 2003 (commonly known as the 'Antigua Convention'; available at www.iattc.org).

[56] The Convention further specifies those issues where consensus is always required.

[57] Ibid., Art. IX(1).

[58] Ibid., Art. I(5).

[59] Ibid., Art. IX(4) and (5).

[60] Convention for the Conservation of Southern Bluefin Tuna of 10 May 1993 (CCSBT Convention; 1819 UNTS 359), Art. 7. This treaty only requires unanimity of Members present at the meeting. See also the Convention on the Conservation and Management of Fishery Resources in the South East Atlantic Ocean of 10 April 2001 (SEAFO Convention; 2221 UNTS 189), Art. 17(1), and the Convention on the Conservation of Antarctic Marine Living Resources of 20 May 1980 (CAMLR Convention; 1329 UNTS 47), Art. XII(1).

[61] CBS Convention, note 44, Art. V. Balton, note 48 at 158–159 suggests that other decision-making procedures were discussed in the course of the negotiations. See also the SIOFA, note 49, Art. 8.

[62] Report of the Meeting of FAO and Non-FAO Regional Fishery Bodies or Arrangements, note 13 at para. 36.

[63] Report of the 2016 IATTC Performance Review, 9.

[64] McDorman, note 54 at 429.

is mixed. In the 2008 performance review of the Commission for the Conservation of Antarctic Marine Living Resources (CCAMLR), the panel noted that:

> Consensus has worked for CCAMLR over a long period of time [...] The need for consensus on matters of substance has not prevented CCAMLR from addressing any important issues.[65]

However, the operation of consensus decision-making procedures will in practice depend on the number of Members and their diversity of interests.[66]

At the other end of the spectrum lie those organizations that make provision for qualified majority voting. Required majorities vary from two-thirds of Members present and voting[67] to three-quarters of Members casting an affirmative or negative vote.[68] When a vote is taken, such decisions are often also subject to a quorum.[69]

An even more complex decision-making procedure is found in the constitutive instrument of the Western and Central Pacific Fisheries Commission (WCPFC), which distinguishes between decisions relating to allocation and decisions relating to CMMs. The former must be adopted by consensus,[70] whereas the latter require a three-quarters majority including three-quarters of the Members of the South Pacific Forum Fisheries Agency (FFA) and three-quarters of non-Members of the FFA.[71] This qualified majority demonstrates how decision-making procedures are often tailored to the particular circumstances of a region.

Many agreements seek to reconcile these two positions and adopt a middle ground, by demanding that an effort is made to seek consensus prior to the casting of a vote.[72] The decision as to when a vote is possible is often granted to the chairperson. In the case of the WCPFC, the chair is granted the power to appoint a conciliator for the purpose of reconciling the differences between

---

[65] Report of the 2008 CCAMLR Performance Review, 81. See also the comments in the Report of the 2010 SEAFO Performance Review, 40 noting that while the "consensus approach to decision-making may effectively weaken the final outcome in some cases, this has not been apparent in SEAFO practice".

[66] See discussion in the Report of the 2016 ICCAT Performance Review, 50.

[67] International Convention for the Conservation of Atlantic Tunas of 14 May 1966 (ICCAT Convention; 673 UNTS 63, as amended; consolidated version available at www.iccat.int), Art. VIII(1)(b); Convention on Future Multilateral Cooperation in North-East Atlantic Fisheries (NEAFC Convention; 1285 UNTS 129, as amended; consolidated version available at www.neafc.org), Art. 3(9); and Agreement for the Establishment of the General Fisheries Council for the Mediterranean (GFCM Agreement; 126 UNTS 239, as amended; consolidated version available at www.fao.org/legal/treaties/treaties-under-article-xiv/en/), Art. XIII(1).

[68] SPRFMO Convention, note 30, Art. 16(2); NPFC Convention, note 30, Art. 8(2).

[69] E.g. NPFC Convention, note 30, Art. 8(4).

[70] Convention on the Conservation and Management of Highly Migratory Fish Stocks in the Western and Central Pacific Ocean of 5 September 2000 (WCPFC Convention; 2275 UNTS 43), Art. 10(4).

[71] Ibid., Art. 20(2).

[72] E.g. ibid., Art. 20(3), whereby the chair "shall fix a time during that session of the Commission for taking the decision by a vote" but the Parties may by a simple majority decide to defer the question to a later time.

Members that may be blocking consensus.[73] Consensus may also be adopted as a decision-making practice, even if it is not formally recognized in the constituent instrument of an RFMO. Thus, the International Commission on the Conservation of Atlantic Tunas (ICCAT) has a practice of deferring decisions until consensus can be achieved, even though its constituent instrument allows for majority voting.[74] Similarly, NEAFC Members have agreed through their rules of procedure that "the Commission shall endeavor to make decisions on the basis of consensus".[75] However, it is less clear in these circumstances when recourse can be had to a vote. Given that the constituent instrument provides for a vote without the requirement to exhaust efforts to reach consensus, it would seem that any Party may demand a vote at any time.[76] As a result, the dynamics of negotiations may be subtly different from those organizations in which the limits of consensus decision-making are pre-defined.

Whilst those treaties containing provisions for voting may seem to suggest a move away from traditional consensual law-making, it must also be understood that most treaties grant States the option to object to decisions within a certain time period after they have been adopted in accordance with the applicable decision-making requirements, which prevents that decision from becoming binding on that State.[77] These procedures thus retain some element of consent in the decision-making process. Such opt-out procedures may even apply if a measure has been adopted by consensus.[78] An important feature of the opt-out procedures is that States must object within a specific timeframe, which varies from 50 days[79] to six months.[80] However, an objection by one State can trigger a new period for other States to reconsider their options and make their own objection. Moreover, the constituent instruments of some RFMOs allow a Member to terminate its acceptance of a recommendation after a fixed period of time, usually one year.[81]

In practice, objection procedures are widely used[82] and they have been criticized for undermining the effectiveness of measures adopted by RFMOs.[83]

---

[73] Ibid., Art. 20(2).

[74] The delay caused by postponing decision-making in an effort to achieve consensus was criticized in the Report of the 2016 ICCAT Performance Review, 2.

[75] NEAFC Rules of Procedure, para. 22.

[76] See the Report of the 2014 NEAFC Performance Review, 105 where the Panel recommends a provision specifying that decisions by voting would only be taken after all efforts to reach consensus have been exhausted. See also the Report of the 2011 GFCM Performance Review, 78–79.

[77] See e.g. NEAFC Convention, note 67, Art. 12(2).

[78] SEAFO Convention, note 60, Arts. 17(1) and 23; CAMLR Convention, note 60, Art. 9(6).

[79] See NEAFC Convention, note 67, Art. 12(a).

[80] See ICCAT Convention, note 67, Art. VIII(3).

[81] NEAFC Convention, note 67, Art. 13(1).

[82] Although their use varies from organization to organization it has been noted that the objection procedure in CCAMLR has only been used twice in 28 years (Report of the 2008 CCAMLR Performance Review, 82). See also the comments in the Report of the 2010 SEAFO Performance Review, 40 noting that the objection procedure had not been invoked at the time of writing.

[83] See discussion in D Diz Pereira Pinto *Fisheries Management in Areas beyond National Jurisdiction: The Impact of Ecosystem Based Law-Making* (Martinus Nijhoff, Leiden: 2013) 128.

The inclusion of such procedures must be understood against the backdrop of the international legal framework for the regulation of fisheries and the historical freedom to fish on the high seas. Thus, as noted by Fitzmaurice

> arguably, opt-out procedures have encouraged States to sign up to conventions which they might otherwise have been reluctant to join because of the possibility of finding themselves bound by onerous provisions on the basis of majority decisions in the convention's organs.[84]

From this perspective, failure to accommodate diverse views within the decision-making procedure could lead some States to withdraw from the organization completely; most RFMOs allow withdrawal after a notice period has been served.[85] Whether such arguments continue to provide strong grounds to support the inclusion of the opt-out procedure can be debated, however, in light of further developments in international fisheries law. For Parties to the Fish Stocks Agreement in particular, the situation would appear to have changed, as the Agreement explicitly stipulates:

> Only those States which are members of such an organization or participants in such an arrangement, or which agree to apply the [CMMs] established by such an organization or arrangement, shall have access to the fishery resources to which those measures apply.[86]

It follows that the right of RFMO Members to opt out of CMMs is no longer about ensuring that such States would not be worse off within the organization than outside the organization. Rather, as noted by McDorman:

> the curiosity of this provision is that [a Party to the Fish Stocks Agreement] may be in a better position to avoid the application of an RFMO decision (e.g. by use of an objection procedure) as a member of the RFMO, than as a non-member of the RFMO.[87]

More recent regional fisheries treaties have sought to counter the perceived problem of overuse of objection procedures by introducing limits on the ability of a State to make objections to CMMs. To this end, the 2016 Resumed Fish Stocks Agreement Review Conference encouraged RFMOs to

> ensure that post opt out behavior is constrained by rules to prevent opting-out parties from undermining conservation, by establishing clear processes for dispute

---

[84] M Fitzmaurice *Whaling and International Law* (Cambridge University Press, Cambridge: 2015) 64.

[85] E.g. SPRFMO Convention, note 30, Art. 41 requires one year's notice; NPFC Convention, note 30, Art. 31 requires six months' notice.

[86] Art. 8(4). Whether or not this reflects customary international law is controversial.

[87] McDorman, note 54 at 426, fn. 8. McDorman also suggests that "implicitly the obligation on UNFSA parties not to undermine RFMO measures can be seen as possibly providing a constraint on an UNFSA party using an RFMO objection procedure" (430) but this interpretation is not supported by practice. See e.g. the discussion below on Russia's objection under the SPRFMO Convention, despite it being a Party to the Fish Stocks Agreement.

settlement and for the adoption of alternative measures with equivalent effect that would be implemented in the interim.[88]

In response to this pressure, some RFMOs have done away with objection procedures altogether. Thus, the WCPFC Convention replaces the ability to opt out with a power to "seek a review of the decision by a review panel".[89] If the panel finds that the decision is discriminatory or incompatible with the WCPFC Convention, the LOS Convention or the Fish Stocks Agreement, it may recommend to the Commission that the decision is modified, amended or revoked and the Commission is obliged to take action thereon.[90]

Alternatively, regional fisheries treaties have sought to control the exercise of objections. A leading example is the SPRFMO Convention, which provides that

> the only admissible grounds for an objection are that the decision unjustifiably discriminates in form or in fact against the member of the Commission, or is inconsistent with the provisions of this Convention or other relevant international law as reflected in [the LOS Convention or the Fish Stocks Agreement].[91]

This provision thus limits the discretion of a Member as to the reasons for making an objection. In addition, the Convention requires an objecting State to advise the Executive Secretary of "alternative measures that are equivalent in effect to the decision to which it has objectives and have the same date of application".[92] In other words, Members cannot escape regulation completely. Indeed, the SPRFMO Convention goes further by providing that any objection is automatically considered by an independent review panel with a mandate to decide whether the objection is permissible and, if so, whether the proposed alternative measures are equivalent.[93] This procedure thus further limits the possibility of abuse of the objection procedure by introducing an element of independent scrutiny.

This innovative procedure was invoked for the first time in 2013[94] in order to address an objection presented by the Russian Federation to SPRFMO's CMM 1.01 relating to *Trachurus murphyi*. Ultimately, the Review Panel upheld the permissibility of the objection, but went on to find that the alternative measure proposed by Russia was not equivalent because it could affect the allocations

---

[88] Report of the 2016 Resumed Fish Stocks Agreement Review Conference, note 16 at para. B5(b).

[89] WCPFC Convention, note 70, Art. 20(6)

[90] Ibid., Art. 20(9). As noted by McDorman, note 54 at 432: "the modification of the decision could include non-application of the decision to the state as an alternative to revocation of the decision and, in this way, an 'opt-out' equivalent to the results of an objection procedure may arise".

[91] SPRFMO Convention, note 30, Art. 17(2)(c).

[92] Ibid., Art. 17(2)(b)(ii).

[93] Ibid., Art. 17(5) and Annex II.

[94] Findings and Recommendations of the Review Panel, 5 July 2013 (available at https://pcacases.com/web/sendAttach/2082).

given to other Members.[95] The Panel therefore recommended a different alternative measure, which would allow Russia to authorize its vessels to fish in the Convention Area only after Russia had determined that the total catch in 2013 will not reach the overall TAC and only until this limit is reached.[96] The Review Panel's report reads largely like a legal decision, turning on legal concepts of discrimination and compatibility with the relevant treaties. Indeed, the process itself resembles in some respects arbitration, and two of the nominated panelists were in fact taken from the list of arbitrators held by FAO under Article 2 of Annex VIII to the LOS Convention, with the chair being an expert in the law of the sea. Moreover, despite being designated as 'recommendations', it would appear that States must comply or choose to initiate dispute settlement proceedings under the SPRFMO Convention.[97]

The SPRFMO Convention is the only regional fisheries treaty to automatically trigger an independent review of objections, but other regions have introduced similar restraints on the use of objections that would allow questions of compatibility to be submitted to either an ad hoc expert panel[98] or to international dispute settlement.[99] Some of the older treaties have similarly adopted amendments to treaties[100] or to the applicable rules of procedure[101] in order to increase oversight of objection procedures. Given the specific circumstances of each regional fishery, it is unlikely that a single model will be appropriate for all of them. Nevertheless, the quasi-judicial nature of these emerging procedures could raise expectations of the development of a jurisprudence concerning the interpretation of the common terms related to the validity of objections, as well as the concept of equivalence, which may be applicable across the various new regimes. If this were to happen, it would be a further indicator of an emergent system of RFMOs, all subject to similar principles of operation.

---

[95] For a more detailed discussion, see A Serdy "Implementing Article 28 of the UN Fish Stocks Agreement: The First Review of a Conservation Measure in the South Pacific Regional Fisheries Management Organisation" (2016) 47 *Ocean Development and International Law* 1–28.

[96] In reality, the decision was a chimeric victory for the Russian Federation as it ended up with zero catch in 2013, although it has since been allocated a share of the TAC (SPRFMO CMM 4.01 (2016)).

[97] SPRFMO Convention, note 30, Annex II, para. 10.

[98] SEAFO Convention, note 60, Art. 23(g) – such a request is made pending a review by the Commission. See discussion in HS Schiffman *Marine Conservation Agreements: The Law and Policy of Reservations and Vetoes* (Martinus Nijhoff, Leiden: 2008) 201–202.

[99] NPFC Convention, note 30, Art. 9(c).

[100] See e.g. NAFO Convention (Convention on Cooperation in the Northwest Atlantic Fisheries – originally named "Convention on Future Multilateral Cooperation in the Northwest Atlantic Fisheries" – of 24 October 1978 (1135 UNTS 369, as amended; consolidated version available at www.nafo.int)), Art. XIV.

[101] NEAFC Rules of Procedure, para. 41 (not in force at the time of writing). The legal status of this new arrangement is not clear. See also the discussion in the Report of the 2016 ICCAT Performance Review, 57.

5. DISPUTE SETTLEMENT

Another feature of the increasing institutionalization of regional fisheries coop-eration is the inclusion of ever more complex and varied third-party dispute settlement mechanisms. Fishing has traditionally been a subject that has provoked litigation between States.[102] Nevertheless, many early regional fisher-ies treaties did not provide for the compulsory settlement of disputes.[103] For example, neither the NAFO Convention nor the NEAFC Convention originally contained a dispute settlement clause. Some of the other earlier regional trea-ties do contain dispute settlement clauses but they condition the submission of a dispute upon the consent of both of the interested parties and only after attempts at conciliation have failed.[104] Such procedures have been described as "weak" and "unsatisfactory".[105]

Nevertheless, attitudes towards compulsory settlement for high seas fisheries disputes have strengthened since the conclusion and entry into force of the LOS Convention, which allows such disputes, at least as they relate to the high seas portion of a fishery,[106] to be submitted to one of the compulsory procedures contained in Part XV of the Convention. The LOS Convention emphasizes freedom of choice concerning the forum for dispute settlement,[107] but if States cannot agree on a mechanism, it provides for arbitration of disputes by default.[108] The Fish Stocks Agreement further encourages this trend by requiring parties to "promote the peaceful settlement of disputes".[109] The Agreement provides for the consensual submission of technical disputes to an ad hoc panel of experts.[110] Otherwise, disputes concerning the interpretation and application of the Agree-ment may be submitted to the compulsory dispute settlement procedures in the LOS Convention.[111] Indeed, the Fish Stocks Agreement goes further and allows

---

[102] See e.g. *Anglo-Norwegian Fisheries Case* (1951) ICJ Reports 116; *Icelandic Fisheries Case* (1974) ICJ Reports 175; and *Canada-Spain Fisheries Case* (1998) ICJ Reports 432.

[103] The Convention on Fishing and Conservation of the Living Resources of the High Seas of 29 April 1958 (559 UNTS 285) did provide for the settlement of disputes by an expert commission, although the treaty was not widely accepted, with only 37 ratifications.

[104] GFCM Agreement, note 67, Art. 19; CAMLR Convention, note 60, Art. XXV.

[105] Report of the 2008 CCAMLR Performance Review, 84. See also the criticism in the Report of the 2011 GFCM Performance Review, 79–80.

[106] Exclusive economic zone (EEZ) fisheries disputes are excluded from compulsory dispute settle-ment (see LOS Convention, Art. 297). According to AE Boyle "Problems of Compulsory Jurisdiction and the Settlement of Disputes relating to Straddling Fish Stocks" in OS Stokke (ed.) *Governing High Seas Fisheries* (Oxford University Press, Oxford: 2001) 91–120, at 100 and 113, however, the exception should be construed narrowly to cover fisheries issues that exclusively relate to the EEZ. But, as he himself notes, this is not the natural meaning of the language.

[107] LOS Convention, Art. 280.

[108] Ibid., Art. 287 and Annex VII.

[109] Fish Stocks Agreement, Art. 10(k).

[110] Ibid., Art. 29.

[111] Ibid., Art. 30.

"disputes between States Parties to [the] Agreement concerning the interpretation and application of a subregional, regional or global fisheries agreement relating to straddling fish stocks or highly migratory fish stocks to which they are parties" to be submitted to the procedures set out in Part XV of the LOS Convention.[112] This innovative clause would compensate for the lack of dispute settlement provisions in some regional fisheries treaties, if the disputants are Parties to the Fish Stocks Agreement.[113] Nevertheless, limited participation in the Agreement means that it does not fully address this issue.[114] It is particularly unclear whether the dispute settlement provisions under the Fish Stocks Agreement can be utilized to challenge a measure adopted by an RFMO with Members who are not Party to the Fish Stocks Agreement.[115] If not, this would be very limiting indeed.

In practice, it is increasingly common to find compulsory dispute settlement in modern regional fisheries treaties. Amendments to this end have been adopted for many existing RFMOs, including for NEAFC in 2004 and for NAFO in 2007, although entry into force of these provisions has been slow and the NEAFC amendments remain pending. Most other treaties negotiated after the adoption of the Fish Stocks Agreement have dispute settlement clauses within them, whether they establish an RFMO or an RFMA.[116] As with the global instruments, the regional treaties reflect the principle of freedom of choice,[117] followed by reference to two main types of dispute settlement procedures, mirroring the relevant provisions of the Fish Stocks Agreement.[118]

First, these treaties often provide for the use of expert panels for technical disputes. For example, the SEAFO Convention provides:

> In cases where a dispute between two or more Contracting Parties is of a technical nature, and the Contracting Parties are unable to resolve the dispute amongst themselves, they may refer the dispute to an *ad hoc* expert panel established in accordance with the procedures adopted by the Commission at its first meeting.[119]

There are several features of this procedure which merit further comment. First, the procedure would appear to require the consent of both parties. This

---

[112] Ibid., Art. 30.

[113] See the discussion of various interpretations of this provision in Boyle, note 106 at 111. He concludes that "the [better view is] that, as between parties to the Fish Stocks Agreement, Article 30(2) amends existing fishery treaties and incorporates into them the disputes settlement provisions of part XV of the 1982 UNCLOS".

[114] For a discussion of the reasons for non-participation, see EJ Molenaar "Non-Participation in the Fish Stocks Agreement: Status and Reasons" (2011) 26 *International Journal of Marine and Coastal Law* 195–234.

[115] McDorman, note 54 at 440.

[116] In the latter context, see SIOFA, note 49, Art. 20.

[117] See e.g. SPRMO Convention, note 30, Art. 34(1).

[118] Indeed, several agreements simply incorporate in toto Part VIII of the Fish Stocks Agreement; see NPFC Convention, note 30, Art. 19; SPRMO Convention, note 30, Art. 34(2).

[119] SEAFO Convention, note 60, Art. 24(3). See also www.seafo.org/SEAFO-Bodies/The-Commission/Dispute-Settlement.

is confirmed by the more detailed procedure agreed by the Commission, which makes clear that "[t]he other Contracting Party shall communicate whether it accepts or not [the proposal to submit a dispute to an ad hoc expert panel]". In this respect, this procedure is distinct from the role of ad hoc expert panels under the objection procedures, where any Party can unilaterally initiate panel proceedings. Secondly, the outcome of the process is non-binding. There are no known examples of these procedures being used in practice and it has been pointed out that one of their weaknesses is that the scope of what is a 'technical dispute' is highly obscure.[120] Nevertheless, such informal procedures could be quicker and less costly than the pursuit of litigation.[121]

Most modern regional fisheries treaties also provide for compulsory adjudication of disputes. In this respect, the SEAFO Convention,[122] the SPRFMO Convention,[123] the NPFC Convention[124] and the WCPFC Convention[125] all provide for disputes to be submitted to the compulsory procedures set out in the Fish Stocks Agreement, including compulsory arbitration in situations where States do not agree to an alternative forum for settlement. The continuing choice of ad hoc arbitration as the residual forum for the settlement of such disputes suggests that States prefer to retain flexibility in who should be appointed to decide such disputes.

The procedures discussed above both concern the settlement of a dispute between two of the Parties concerning the interpretation and application of a relevant treaty. For a dispute to exist, there must be "a disagreement on a point of law or fact, a conflict of legal views or of interests between two persons".[126] There must also be a State that is willing to bring a claim, and an identifiable respondent. However, not all legal disagreements in the regional fisheries context will necessarily have these characteristics. An alternative option would be to submit legal questions to an advisory process. Advisory opinions can provide useful clarifications on the state or meaning of the law, without the need for a formal dispute to arise. Such an approach would make use of the ability of the International Tribunal for the Law of the Sea (ITLOS) under Article 138 of its Rules of Procedure to "give an advisory opinion on a legal question if any international agreement related to the purposes of the Convention specifically provides for the submission to the Tribunal of a request for such an opinion". ITLOS confirmed its ability to grant advisory opinions in 2015[127] when it

---

[120] See the Report of the 2014 NEAFC Performance Review, 110.
[121] See comments of Boyle, note 107 at 109.
[122] SEAFO Convention, note 60, Art. 24.
[123] SPRFMO Convention, note 30, Art. 34.
[124] NPFC Convention, note 30, Art. 19.
[125] WCPFC Convention, note 70, Art. 31.
[126] *Mavromattis Palestine Concessions* (1924) PCIJ Reports, Series A, No. 2, 11.
[127] *Fisheries Advisory Opinion* (2015) ITLOS Case No. 21, para. 56. For a critical discussion of this decision, see T Ruys and A Soete "Creeping Advisory Jurisdiction of International Courts and Tribunals?" (2016) 29 *Leiden Journal of International Law* 155–176.

received a request from the Sub-Regional Fisheries Commission, one of the few bodies to possess such a competence. ITLOS went on to say that "a request for an advisory opinion should not in principle be refused except for compelling reasons".[128] It remains to be seen whether other RFMOs will be given such a power through continuing reforms of these bodies.

6. INTER-INSTITUTIONAL COOPERATION AND COORDINATION

Most RFMO/As are established as autonomous institutions and they are designed in order to reflect the particularities of the region and the interests of the States concerned. Nevertheless, there is little doubt that lessons can be learned between regional regimes. Moreover, in some instances, the effective and efficient management of fish stocks may require the involvement of more than one RFMO/A, where they are responsible for overlapping or adjacent areas.

The power to enter into cooperative arrangements is recognized in the constituent instruments of most RFMO/As,[129] although it can be argued that this ability could be exercised as an implied power in the case of those RFMO/As without an express power. In some regional fisheries treaties, specific organizations are expressly identified as suitable partners for cooperation,[130] whilst leaving open the possibility for cooperation with other organizations. Most treaties, however, do not specify the modalities for cooperation, simply referring to the need for "suitable arrangements".[131] In practice, cooperation operates at two levels.

First, individual RFMO/As have entered into 'bilateral' arrangements with a view to ensuring that they adopt consistent rules in cases where their competence may to some extent overlap or where vessels may fish in areas falling under the competence of more than one RFMO/A. These practices have become even more important following the proliferation of RFMO/As in the past decade.[132]

An example is provided by the relationship between the WCPFC and the IATTC, whose areas of competence overlap in the Southern-Central Pacific. The constituent instruments of both of these institutions call for cooperation with other relevant organizations in order to reach agreement on a consistent set of CMMs.[133] The two RFMOs concluded a Memorandum of Understanding

---

[128] Fisheries Advisory Opinion, note 127 at para. 71.

[129] See e.g. NAFO Convention, note 100, Art. XVII(c); GFCM Agreement, note 67, Art. 17(1). See also SPRFMO Convention, note 30, Art. 31(1); NPFC Convention, note 30, Art. 21(1).

[130] See e.g. CAMLR Convention, note 60, Art. XXIII; WCPFC Convention, note 70, Art. 22.

[131] NPFC Convention, note 30, Art. 21(4).

[132] This will be a consideration in the negotiation of a new agreement for the Central Arctic Ocean, discussed above, which may include areas that are already under the competence of NEAFC.

[133] WCPFC Convention, note 70, Art. 22; Antigua Convention, note 55, Art. 24.

(MOU) in 2006 setting out the basic framework for further cooperation, identifying both the areas and modalities of cooperation. The MOU calls for information-sharing, as well as reciprocal participation in relevant meetings.[134] The MOU also establishes a consultative meeting between the secretariats of the two organizations in order to "review and enhance cooperation".[135] Further practical arrangements were agreed in subsequent instruments. The 2009 Memorandum of Cooperation on the Exchange and Release of Data agreed to the exchange of data relating to fishing effort and catch (including bycatch); observer reports; monitoring, control and surveillance; and unloading, transshipment and port inspections. A further step towards greater coordination of measures was taken in 2011 with the conclusion of the Memorandum of Cooperation on the Cross-endorsement of Observers, which aims to facilitate the operation of vessels that fish in areas falling under the mandate of both organizations on the same fishing trip. Most importantly, however, the two organizations have reached an agreement on how to deal with vessels that fish in the area that falls under both of their competence. Based upon a document jointly prepared by the secretariats of the two organizations, the WCPFC and the IATTC each adopted a recommendation, whereby they agreed that vessels listed on the WCPFC register will apply WCPFC measures, vessels listed on the IATTC register will apply IATTC measures, and vessels that appear on both registers will have the option to notify the commissions of which set of measures it will follow.[136] The organizations also agreed to continue working towards a longer-term solution, which could feasibly include designating a single organization to regulate fisheries in the area, thus removing the overlap.[137] Similar cooperation arrangements have been established between other RFMOs in order to harmonize their regimes.[138]

Another area that has seen cooperation taking place is the establishment of joint measures to prevent and deter illegal, unreported and unregulated (IUU) fishing. Such a step was taken by NAFO and NEAFC when they agreed to transmit information concerning vessels on their individual IUU vessel lists and this cooperation has since been extended to CCAMLR and SEAFO.[139] However, such an arrangement does not guarantee harmonization of the respective lists. Under the NEAFC Scheme of Control and Enforcement, notifications lead to

---

[134] The WCPFC has also entered into similar framework arrangements with the North Pacific Anadromous Fish Commission (NPAFC), CCAMLR, CCSBT and IOTC.

[135] 2006 MOU, para. 2.2.

[136] IATTC Recommendation on IATTC-WCPFC Overlap Area (2012); WCPFC9 Decision on the WCPFC-IATTC Overlap Area (2012).

[137] See IATTC-WCPFC Overlap Area, doc. IATTC-83 INF-B of 2012, 5. Alternatively, regulation in the overlap area could be divided depending upon the gear type.

[138] See e.g. 2015 MOU between the CCSBT and IOTC for Monitoring Transshipment at Sea by Large-Scale Tuna Longline Fishing Vessels; 2016 Arrangement between SPRFMO and CCAMLR. See also the Report of the 2016 ICCAT Performance Review, 62.

[139] See e.g. NEAFC Scheme of Control and Enforcement (2016), Art. 44(5).

automatic listing of vessels identified by other organizations and the relevant rules provide that

> [v]essels placed on the [IUU list] in accordance with [this procedure] may only be removed if the RFMO which originally identified the vessels as having engaged in IUU fishing activity has notified the NEAFC Secretary of their removal of the list.[140]

In contrast, under the equivalent rules adopted by NAFO, a Member has the right to object to the inclusion of a vessel proposed by NEAFC on certain grounds, thus preventing it from being listed.[141] Indeed, not all RFMOs have even accepted the policy of cross-listing; CCAMLR simply circulates its IUU vessel list to other RFMOs but it does not include vessels listed by other RFMOs on its own IUU vessel list.[142] These examples illustrate the challenges of cooperation between organizations with different memberships and internal political dynamics.

Secondly, cooperation between RFMOs also takes place at the global level. In this context, the FAO has provided an important forum for discussing best practice amongst RFMOs. One particular initiative for promoting cooperation between RFMOs is the Coordinating Working Party on Fisheries Statistics, which was first established in the late 1950s as a body for agreeing on common definitions on fisheries statistics in the North Atlantic[143] and was later expanded to cover the entire globe.[144] Representatives of RFMOs also participate in discussions in the Committee on Fisheries (COFI), although as observers. A step to improve direct cooperation between RFMOs was taken in the late 1990s by establishing a forum for these organizations to meet and discuss common challenges. The first meeting of RFMOs took place at FAO headquarters in February 1999 and it was agreed that further meetings should be held in conjunction with meetings of the COFI.[145] In 2005, the name of the arrangement was changed to 'Regional Fishery Body Secretariats' Network' in order to better reflect the informal nature of the meetings, as well as the fact that cooperation continued between meetings.[146] The Network has adopted rules of procedure,[147] although it has been emphasized that it is limited to

---

[140] Ibid., Art. 44(6).

[141] NAFO Conservation and Enforcement Measures (2017), Art. 53(4)(d). See also SEAFO System of Observation, Inspection, Compliance and Enforcement (2016), Art. 28.

[142] CCAMLR Conservation Measure 10–07 (2016), para. 23.

[143] FAO Conference Res. 23/59 (1959).

[144] See "FAO, The Coordinating Working Party on Fishery Statistics: Its Origin, Role and Structure" (*FAO Fisheries Circular* No. 903: 1995).

[145] Report of the Meeting of FAO and Non-FAO Regional Fishery Bodies or Arrangements, note 13 at para. 41(i).

[146] See Report of the Fourth Meeting of RFMOs (*FAO Fisheries Report* No. 778: 2005), para. 7.

[147] Albeit on an ad interim basis; see Report of the Sixth Meeting of the Regional Fishery Body Secretariats' Network (*FAO Fisheries and Aquaculture Report* No. 1175: 2014) App. 13, fn. 1.

pursuing administrative coordination, as the RFB secretariats are not able to agree upon policy on behalf of their Members.[148] This feature of the meetings, as well as the heterogeneity of its membership, limits the utility of this arrangement.[149]

A more focused approach to cooperation can be seen through the so-called Kobe Process of Cooperation between Tuna RFMOs, which began in January 2007. Unlike the RFB Secretariats' Network, the Kobe Process is open to Members and co-operating non-Members of RFMOs, as well as other relevant intergovernmental organizations (IGOs) and NGOs. The first meeting agreed upon key areas to be addressed through closer cooperation. One decision of particular interest for present purposes was agreement on a common set of criteria for performance reviews, which have been implemented by all tuna RFMOs.[150] In addition, participants identified four areas of technical cooperation that they would actively pursue, namely harmonization and improvement of trade-tracking programmes, including catch documentation schemes; creation of a harmonized list of tuna fishing vessels and a global list of IUU vessels;[151] harmonization of transshipment control measures; and standardization of the presentation form of stock assessment results. Intersessional work has been carried out on each of these topics and the tuna RFMOs have since met on two further occasions in order to review progress. Participants have also established a website in order to communicate the results of the cooperation.[152] Certainly, cooperation between the tuna RFMOs has become more focused, even if progress has not been as rapid as some may have wished, and there have been calls to promote greater cooperation of other 'sectoral' RFMO/As through similar joint meetings to share experiences and good practices.[153]

It is not only cooperation between RFMO/As that is on the international agenda today. The 2016 Resumed Fish Stocks Agreement Review Conference also called for States to "strengthen cooperation and coordination between [RFMO/As] and Regional Seas Conventions and Action Plans".[154] Such

---

[148] In discussion of the rules of procedure for the Network, concerns were raised about having a rule relating to decision-making, even though it did expressly say that decisions were non-binding. Ultimately, this rule was deleted.

[149] Suggestions to strengthen the Network were not widely supported at the most recent meeting; see Report of the Sixth Meeting of the Regional Fishery Body Secretariats' Network, note 146 at paras. 62–78.

[150] See report of the first meeting of the Tuna RFMOs (2007) App. 14.

[151] See www.tuna-org.org/GlobalTVR.htm.

[152] See www.tuna-org.org/.

[153] See UNGA Res. 71/123, note 16, paras. 155 (relating to RFMO/As with competence to manage straddling stocks) and 156 (relating to RFMO/As with competence to manage deep-sea fisheries). In the latter context, see the Record of the meeting of the deep-sea fisheries secretariats contact group (2016), attended by representatives of CCAMLR, NAFO, GFCM, NEAFC, NPFC, SEAFO and SPRFMO.

[154] Report of the Resumed Fish Stocks Agreement Review Conference, note 16 at para. B3(b).

cross-sectoral cooperation is becoming increasingly important, particularly as the mandate of RFMOs is extending to address the effect of fisheries on marine biological diversity, meaning that their work overlaps with the work of environmental bodies.[155] Some RFMOs have already taken steps in this direction, particularly NEAFC, which has established a close working relationship with the OSPAR Commission[156] under the so-called Collective Arrangement between Competent International Organizations on Cooperation and Coordination regarding Selected Areas in Areas beyond National Jurisdiction in the North-East Atlantic,[157] and the General Fisheries Commission for the Mediterranean (GFCM), which has worked closely with the Meetings of Parties to the Barcelona Convention in pursuing an ecosystem approach in the Mediterranean.[158] Such arrangements have been identified as a potential model that could be used in other regions to build inter-sectoral cooperation,[159] even though regional differences will dictate that adaptations may have to be made.[160]

A more radical solution would be the establishment of Integrated Regional Oceans Management Organizations, which combine the functions of regional seas bodies and regional fishery bodies.[161] However, many authors believe that this is a step too far given the heterogeneity of geographical scopes and participation, as well as the different constituencies that would need to be brought together.[162] The time and effort that would be necessary to promote such an agenda could be better spent on making more effective use of existing tools.

---

[155] See e.g. JA Ardron et al. "The Sustainable Use and Conservation of Biodiversity in ABNJ: What can be Achieved Using Existing International Agreements?" (2014) 49 *Marine Policy* 98–108, at 103. The current negotiations towards a new legally binding instrument on the conservation of biological diversity in areas beyond national jurisdiction is also intended to address this issue. See further Chapter 7 of this volume (Caddell).

[156] The OSPAR Commission was established by the Convention for the Protection of the Marine Environment of the North-East Atlantic of 22 September 1992 (2354 UNTS 67, as amended; available at www.ospar.org/).

[157] See discussion in S Asmundsson and E Corcoran "The Process of Forming a Cooperative Mechanism between NEAFC and OSPAR" (*UNEP Regional Seas Reports and Studies* No. 196: 2015) 16; D Johnson "Can Competent Authorities Cooperate for the Common Good: Towards a Collective Arrangement for the North-East Atlantic" in PA Beckman and AN Vylegzhanin (eds.) *Environmental Security in the Arctic Ocean* (Springer, New York: 2013) 333–343, at 341.

[158] MOU between the UNEP MAP-Barcelona Convention and FAO-GFCM (2012); *Draft Elements of a Common Strategy among RAC/SPA, GFCM, ACCOBAMS and IUCN-Med, with collaboration of MedPAN*, doc. UNEP(DEPI)/MED WG.408/17 (2015).

[159] See Johnson, note 157 at 341; D Freestone et al. "Can Existing Institutions Protect Biodiversity in Areas Beyond National Jurisdiction? Experiences from Two Ongoing Processes" (2014) 49 *Marine Policy* 167–175, at 171.

[160] Asmundsson and Corcoran, note 157 at 30. See further Chapter 7 of this volume (Caddell).

[161] See Global Ocean Commission, *From Decline to Recovery: A Rescue Package for the Oceans*, Report Summary (2016) 16.

[162] See e.g. J. Rochette et al. "Regional Oceans Governance Mechanisms: A Review" (2015) 60 *Marine Policy* 9–19, at 17, concluding that "trying to fully integrate the governance system formally rather than functionally is but a pipe dream".

7. CONCLUSIONS

The past decades have seen considerable effort put into strengthening regional fisheries management in order to meet the challenges of promoting sustainable fishing. New RFMO/As have been established in order to fill regulatory gaps and existing institutions have been modernized to reflect emerging governance principles. Change has sometimes been slow, particularly when it relies upon treaty amendment or it has been opposed by key States. Nevertheless, the report by the UN Secretary-General to the 2016 Resumed Fish Stocks Agreement Review Conference reflected significant developments in relation to the issues examined in this chapter, including "steady progress [...] in strengthening the mandates and measures of the organizations and arrangements"[163] and "some progress [...] in constraining opt-out behavior".[164]

Not only has there been a clear push for reform within individual RFMO/As, but overall developments would also appear to support the emergence of a system of regional fisheries governance, composed of autonomous yet interconnected institutions. Practice suggests that RFMO/As do not operate in clinical isolation, but they are increasingly subject to a framework of common principles and shared values. Moreover, developments in one region can influence regulatory arrangements elsewhere.

This trend is evident in part through the practices that inform performance reviews of RFMO/As. In its most concrete form, this is illustrated by the agreement amongst tuna RFMOs to apply the same performance criteria in their reviews. However, even when organizations have adopted their own review criteria, panels have made references to global fisheries instruments and the best practices of other RFMOs to support their findings and recommendations.[165] In some cases, the need to take into account best practices has been codified in the constituent instrument of the RFMO itself.[166] Similarly, in recent consultations aimed at addressing high seas fishing in the central Arctic Ocean, participating States agreed to only allow fishing "pursuant to one or more regional or subregional fisheries management organizations or arrangements that are or may be established to manage such fishing in accordance with recognized international standards".[167]

The trend towards systematization is also illustrated by the growing cooperation between RFMOs. Overlaps are being addressed and adjacent regimes have worked towards the harmonization of measures. Yet, practice in this regard

---

[163] Report of the Secretary-General to the 2016 Resumed Fish Stocks Agreement Review Conference, doc. A/CONF.210/2016/1 of 1 March 2016, para. 157.

[164] Ibid., para. 198.

[165] See e.g. Report of the 2014 NEAFC Performance Review; Report of the 2016 ICCAT Performance Review.

[166] SPRFMO Convention, note 30, Art. 30(2); see also NPFC Convention, note 30, Art. 22.

[167] 2015 Oslo Declaration concerning the Prevention of Unregulated High Seas Fishing in the Central Arctic Ocean. See also www.state.gov/e/oes/ocns/opa/rls/269126.htm.

demonstrates that successful cooperation is largely the result of horizontal engagement, rather than top-down imposition. There has been some resistance to the development of a formal hierarchy, with particular opposition to the idea that the independent RFMOs could be reviewed by the FAO or any other global institution.[168] Indeed, it is still true that many States are keen to stress the independence of RFMOs[169] and it is unlikely that any formal hierarchy will emerge in the near future. Moreover, entrenched political and geographical differences between regions also mean that, despite the obvious convergence in regional fisheries management, complete harmonization is unlikely to occur.

---

[168] Report of the Fourth Meeting of RFMOs, note 145 at para. 11, where it was underlined that "FAO is free to review the work of the FAO RFMOs. However, a review of the non-FAO RFMOs could only be initiated by the governing councils of the organizations concerned, although FAO may be able to provide assistance in this regard".

[169] See e.g. the comments reported in Report of the Secretary-General to the 2016 Resumed Fish Stocks Agreement Review Conference, note 163 at para. 250.

6

Participation in Regional Fisheries Management Organizations

ERIK J MOLENAAR*

1. INTRODUCTION

THE ISSUE OF participation in regional fisheries management organizations (RFMOs) is of crucial importance for the performance, credibility and legitimacy of international fisheries law. Concerns over the rules and practices of RFMOs on participation have frequently been raised in global fora, followed by recommendations to address these concerns.[1] While States and 'entities' (see explanation below) may have several reasons for participating in RFMOs or for desiring to obtain a participatory status, they are often predominantly motivated by the socio-economic benefits derived from engaging in fishing or fishing-related activities (e.g. provisioning of fuel, water etc., and transhipment of catch) under the auspices of an RFMO. Criticism by an unsuccessful applicant concerning RFMOs that have restrictive rules and practices on participation – or: 'closed' RFMOs – will therefore be primarily based on inequitable distribution of resources.

There are nevertheless also instances in which participation is predominantly motivated by the desire to participate in an RFMO's decision-making process, and thereby influence the substance of individual decisions as well as the wider

* Writing this chapter was made possible by funding from the Netherlands Polar Programme. The author is very grateful for assistance and/or comments received from Richard Barnes, Richard Caddell, Nicola Ferri, Solène Guggisberg, Johanne Fisher, Luis Molledo, Alex Oude Elferink and François Ziegler on an earlier version.
[1] E.g. the 2017 United Nations General Assembly (UNGA) 'Fisheries' Resolution (UNGA Res. 72/92 of 5 December 2017), para. 142; Report of the 2006 Fish Stocks Agreement Review Conference (Doc. A/CONF.210/2006/15 of 5 July 2006), paras. 72 and 80 of the discussion, and para. 30 of the Outcome (Annex); Report of the 2010 Resumed Fish Stocks Agreement Review Conference (Doc. A/CONF.210/2010/7 of 27 July 2010), paras. 82–83 of the discussion; and Report of the 2016 Resumed Fish Stocks Agreement Review Conference (Doc. A/CONF.210/2016/5 of 1 August 2016), para. 109 of the discussion, and paras. B(4)(a) and (c) and D(2)(a) of the Outcome (Annex).

evolution of the RFMO and its constitutive instrument. Participants could, for instance, be mainly concerned with strengthening an RFMO's performance on conservation in general or minimizing the impacts of fishing on (iconic) non-target species or ecosystems in particular. This chapter refers to this group of participants as 'non-user States'. Moreover, a State or entity could cherish a participatory status within a particular RFMO due to the prestige associated with that status – in particular for RFMOs that are relatively 'closed' – or the evidence it provides of that State or entity's commitment to, and efforts towards, responsible fishing. The latter can be of crucial importance for avoiding restrictions on access to important market States or entities (e.g. the United States (US) or the European Union (EU)) and other measures taken against States and entities whose vessels and nationals are involved in illegal, unreported and unregulated (IUU) fishing.

The rules and practices of RFMOs on participation, allocation and combating IUU fishing are closely linked. As a general rule, allocations of fishing opportunities and other benefits are only available to formal participants in RFMOs. Many RFMOs have two main formal participatory categories for States and entities, namely (full) membership and cooperating status.[2] RFMOs commonly treat engagement in fishing or fishing-related activities by vessels flying the flag of States or entities that do not have either of these two participatory categories as IUU fishing, thereby triggering a range of measures to combat IUU fishing.[3] Such measures can only be avoided by not engaging in fishing or fishing-related activities (abstention) or by obtaining membership or cooperating status. The reality, however, is that membership or cooperating status commonly does not automatically entitle a participant to an allocation.[4]

This chapter only examines participation by States and entities and not by (other) non-State actors (e.g. (other) intergovernmental organizations and non-governmental organizations). For the purpose of this chapter, the term 'entity' relates exclusively to the EU and Taiwan (Chinese Taipei).[5] In the domain of international fisheries law, these entities are the two exceptions to the general rule that the status of full participant in intergovernmental fisheries bodies is reserved exclusively for States. The international community's recognition of the EU and its predecessors as a full participant in international fisheries law – as well as the international law of the sea more generally – materialized during the third United Nations Conference on the Law of the Sea (UNCLOS III) and was laid down in the LOS Convention.[6] At present, many international fisheries instruments allow regional economic integration organizations (REIOs) to

---

[2] Some RFMOs use another designation (see Subsection 5.4).
[3] See in particular Chapter 13 of this volume (van der Marel).
[4] See note 82 and accompanying text.
[5] See also note 48.
[6] United Nations Convention on the Law of the Sea of 10 December 1982 (1833 UNTS 3). See Art. 305(1)(f) and Annex IX.

become Parties, and Members of their bodies.[7] So far, the EU has been the only REIO to have exercised this option.[8]

Once Taiwan's significant role in international marine capture fisheries became generally accepted, the international community's recognition of its status was enshrined in the Fish Stocks Agreement.[9] Many RFMOs now have arrangements to ensure the applicability of their constitutive instruments to Taiwan – rather than entitling Taiwan to become a Party – and/or allow Taiwan's involvement in the bodies established by those instruments. The participation of the EU, EU Member States and Taiwan in selected RFMOs is examined further in Subsection 5.3.

The remainder of this chapter consists of four sections. Section 2 is aimed at clarifying the selection of the RFMOs whose rules and practices on participation are examined in this chapter. Subsequently, Section 3 contains some general observations on participation in intergovernmental instruments and bodies. The provisions in global framework conventions that are relevant to participation in RFMOs – i.e. the LOS Convention and the Fish Stocks Agreement – are examined in Section 4. The analysis of the rules and practices of selected RFMOs on participation is carried out in Section 5. The chapter ends with conclusions in Section 6.

In order to ensure conciseness and avoid consistent cross-references, this chapter refers to individual RFMOs and their constitutive instruments by means of acronyms and abbreviations. Their full titles and details are included in Table 1, further below.

2. SELECTED RFMOS

Chapter 5 of this volume (Harrison) examines the differences between the concepts of an RFMO and a regional fisheries management arrangement (RFMA), and notes that there are at present no generally accepted definitions for either concept. Whereas the Fish Stocks Agreement defines an RFMA in Article 1(1)(d), it is clear that the concepts of an RFMO and an RFMA are not exclusively used in relation to straddling and highly migratory fish stocks, but also for other categories of fish stocks, such as anadromous, shared and discrete high seas fish stocks. Illustrative in this regard is the broad concept of a regional fishery body (RFB) used by the United Nations Food and Agriculture Organization (FAO), to denote a mechanism through which States and entities cooperate

---

[7] E.g. Arts. 1(g) and 35(2) of the WCPF Convention, note 28.

[8] Interestingly, Arts. 9–11 of the CAOF Agreement, note 36, mention the EU explicitly, rather than the generic notion of REIOs.

[9] Agreement for the Implementation of the Provisions of the United Nations Convention on the Law of the Sea of 10 December 1982 relating to the Conservation and Management of Straddling Fish Stocks and Highly Migratory Fish Stocks of 4 August 1995 (2167 UNTS 3), Arts. 1(3) and 17(3).

for the conservation and management of marine living resources – fish as well as marine mammals – and/or the development of marine capture fisheries.[10]

This chapter focuses exclusively on RFMOs and RFMAs. These are a subset of RFBs that can ultimately be distinguished from other RFBs on account of the fact that (1) they relate to marine fisheries, rather than inland fisheries; and (2) they have a mandate to impose legally binding conservation and management measures on their members or participants, rather than merely exercising an 'advisory' mandate (whether primarily science-oriented or management-oriented). Furthermore, in view of this chapter's focus on participation, attention is only devoted to RFMOs and RFMAs whose regulatory areas include areas of high seas or consist entirely of high seas.[11] At the time of writing, these are the five 'tuna RFMOs' and the 11 'non-tuna RFMOs and RFMAs' listed in Table 1.[12]

Four of the latter 11 are regarded as RFMAs and listed separately in Table 1. One of these has a Conference of the Parties (COP), and two a Meeting of the Parties (MOP) as the main decision-making body. The fourth – the Joint Norwegian Russian Fisheries Commission (JNRFC) – seems to be regarded as an RFMA by its two Members, even though they named it a 'Commission'.[13] As became evident during the negotiations on the CAOF Agreement,[14] however, several delegations question the JNRFC's status as an RFMA.[15] Furthermore, while these delegations have so far not exchanged views or positions as to whether the CAOF Agreement qualifies as an RFMA within the meaning of the Fish Stocks Agreement, it is submitted that there are arguments in support of such a qualification.[16]

---

[10] See the information at www.fao.org/fishery/topic/16800/en. It should be noted that while this page distinguishes a 'regional fishery arrangement' from an RFB, FAO's list of RFBs on www.fao.org/fishery/rfb/search/en does not use this distinction. It is important to note that inclusion of a body in FAO's list of RFBs cannot be regarded as a form of multilateral recognition of the status of these bodies under international law. Unless explicitly provided otherwise, the competence to make such determinations lies with States and entities, whether individually or collectively.

[11] The North Atlantic Salmon Conservation Organization (NASCO) and the North Pacific Anadromous Fish Commission (NPAFC) are excluded due to their prohibitions on high seas fishing. Participation in RFMOs and RFMAs whose regulatory areas consist entirely of coastal State maritime zones will logically be limited to coastal States.

[12] The Western Central Atlantic Fishery Commission (WECAFC) is currently engaged in a process to re-constitute itself as an RFMO (Report of the 2016 WECAFC Meeting, para. 55).

[13] EJ Molenaar "International Regulation of Central Arctic Ocean Fisheries" in MH Nordquist, JN Moore and R Long (eds.) *Challenges of the Changing Arctic. Continental Shelf, Navigation, and Fisheries* (Brill/Nijhoff, Leiden/Boston: 2016) 429–463, at 443.

[14] See note 36.

[15] EJ Molenaar "Participation in the Central Arctic Ocean Fisheries Agreement" in A Shibata et al. (eds.) *Emerging Legal Orders in the Arctic: The Role of Non-Arctic Actors* (Routledge: forthcoming in 2019).

[16] The restrictions imposed on exploratory fishing included in Arts. 3(3) and 5(1)(d) of the CAOF Agreement, note 36, seem to qualify as "conservation and management measures" pursuant to the definition in Art. 1(1)(b) of the Fish Stocks Agreement. More importantly, in light of, *inter alia*, its Objective (Art. 2), its qualified and temporary abstention from commercial high seas fishing

Whether or not the Commission for the Conservation of Antarctic Marine Living Resources (CCAMLR) is an RFMO has been debated repeatedly among its Members. One of the principal arguments against such qualification is that CCAMLR is a component of the Antarctic Treaty System (ATS) rather than an RFMO.[17] In 2002, however, there was broad agreement among the Members that CCAMLR has "the attributes of an RFMO within the context of the UN and its subsidiary bodies".[18] Or – in other words – CCAMLR is 'more than an RFMO'. A similar argument could be made with regard to the General Fisheries Commission for the Mediterranean (GFCM), on account of its competence relating to aquaculture.[19]

In recent years, debates over CCAMLR's status as an RFMO resurfaced in the context of proposals for the establishment of marine protected areas (MPAs). Advocates for the establishment of MPAs highlighted features of CCAMLR that arguably distinguish it from 'most RFMOs', thereby triggering a discussion on the (alleged) supremacy of conservation over rationale use.[20] Finally, it is interesting that CCAMLR is not only included in FAO's list of RFBs but is also treated by the United Nations Environment Programme (UNEP) as an independent regional seas programme.[21] Listing CCAMLR among RFBs is more convincing, as its competence is in principle limited to fishing, fishing-related activities and research, but does not extend to any other human activity.[22] Conversely, the mandates of the principal decision-making bodies under regional seas programmes extend in principle to all human activities, while accepting the primacy of relevant sectoral organizations such as RFMOs.[23]

For the remainder of this chapter, references to RFMOs are meant to include RFMAs, unless indicated otherwise.

(Art. 3(1)) and the establishment of a Joint Program of Scientific Research and Monitoring to inform future fisheries management (Art. 4), the CAOF Agreement qualifies as a "cautious conservation and management measure" in the context of the obligations on new and exploratory fisheries included in Art. 6(6) of the Fish Stocks Agreement.

[17] Report of the 14th (1995) Annual CCAMLR Meeting at 70, para. 15.2.

[18] Report of the 21st (2002) Annual CCAMLR Meeting at 88, para. 15.2.

[19] Art. 2(2) of the GFCM Agreement.

[20] Report of the 35th (2016) Annual CCAMLR Meeting, 60–61, paras. 9.12–9.21.

[21] See web.unep.org/regionalseas/.

[22] Art. II(1) of the CAMLR Convention stipulates that its objective is "the conservation of Antarctic marine living resources", while Art. II(2) clarifies that "the term 'conservation' includes rational use". The Preamble and many provisions indicate that CCAMLR's competence is in principle limited to fishing, fishing-related activities and research (e.g. Arts. II(3), V, VI, IX and XXIX(1)). Moreover, CCAMLR has taken measures to prevent impacts by fishing vessels and scientific research vessels on Antarctic marine living resources by adopting measures relating to maritime safety, vessel-source pollution and the introduction of alien species (see e.g. CCAMLR Conservation Measures 26-01 (2015) and 91-04 (2011), para. 6, and CCAMLR Resolutions 20/XXII (2003), 23/XXIII (2004), 28/XXVII (2008), 29/XXVIII (2009), 33/XXX (2011) and 34/XXXI (2012)).

[23] E.g. the mandate of the OSPAR Commission established under the OSPAR Convention (Convention for the Protection of the Marine Environment of the North-East Atlantic of 22 September 1992 (2345 UNTS 67, as amended; consolidated version available at www.ospar.org vis-à-vis fisheries and maritime transport pursuant to Art. 4 of Annex V.

Table 1 Selected RFMOs and RFMAs

Acronym	Name in full	Constitutive instrument
Tuna RFMOs		
CCSBT	Commission for the Conservation of Southern Bluefin Tuna	CCSBT Convention[24]
IATTC	Inter-American Tropical Tuna Commission	IATTC Convention[25]
ICCAT	International Commission on the Conservation of Atlantic Tunas	ICCAT Convention[26]
IOTC	Indian Ocean Tuna Commission	IOTC Agreement[27]
WCPFC	Western and Central Pacific Fisheries Commission	WCPF Convention[28]
Non-Tuna RFMOs		
CCAMLR	Commission for the Conservation of Antarctic Marine Living Resources	CAMLR Convention[29]
GFCM	General Fisheries Commission for the Mediterranean	GFCM Agreement[30]
NAFO	Northwest Atlantic Fisheries Organization	NAFO Convention[31]
NEAFC	North-East Atlantic Fisheries Commission	NEAFC Convention[32]

(continued)

[24] Convention for the Conservation of Southern Bluefin Tuna, Canberra of 10 May 1993 (1819 UNTS 360; also available at www.ccsbt.org).

[25] Convention for the Strengthening of the Inter-American Tropical Tuna Commission Established by the 1949 Convention Between the United States of America and the Republic of Costa Rica of 14 November 2003 (also known as the 'Antigua Convention'; available at www.iattc.org).

[26] International Convention for the Conservation of Atlantic Tunas of 14 May 1966 (673 UNTS 63, as amended; consolidated version available at www.iccat.int). At the time of writing, the ICCAT Working Group (WG) on Convention Amendment had essentially concluded its work on 'modernizing' the ICCAT Convention (see Docs No. CONV_03C/2018 and CONV_08C/2018). ICCAT will have to resolve the remaining procedural issues at its 2018 Annual Meeting. See also J Spencer, JJ Maguire and EJ Molenaar *Report of the Second Independent Performance Review of ICCAT* (ICCAT: 2016, available at www.iccat.int/en/pubs_spec.htm), *inter alia* at 9-10, 57-58, 60 and 65.

[27] Agreement for the Establishment of the Indian Ocean Tuna Commission of 25 November 1993 (available at www.iotc.org).

[28] Convention on the Conservation and Management of Highly Migratory Fish Stocks in the Western and Central Pacific Ocean of 5 September 2000 (2275 UNTS 43; also available at www.wcpfc.int).

[29] Convention on the Conservation of Antarctic Marine Living Resources of 20 May 1980 (1329 UNTS 47; also available at www.ccamlr.org).

[30] Agreement for the Establishment of a General Fisheries Council for the Mediterranean of 24 September 1949 (126 UNTS 239, as amended; consolidated version available at www.fao.org/legal/treaties/treaties-under-article-xiv/en/).

[31] Convention on Cooperation in the Northwest Atlantic Fisheries – originally named 'Convention on Future Multilateral Cooperation in the Northwest Atlantic Fisheries' – of 24 October 1978 (1135 UNTS 369, as amended; consolidated version available at www.nafo.int).

[32] Convention on Future Multilateral Cooperation in the North-East Atlantic Fisheries of 18 November 1980 (1285 UNTS 129, as amended; consolidated version available at www.neafc.org).

Table 1 (*Continued*)

Acronym	Name in full	Constitutive instrument
NPFC	North Pacific Fisheries Commission	NPFC Convention[33]
SEAFO	South East Atlantic Fisheries Organisation	SEAFO Convention[34]
SPRFMO	South Pacific Regional Fisheries Management Organisation	SPRFMO Convention[35]
Non-Tuna RFMAs		
CAOF Agreement	Agreement to Prevent Unregulated High Seas Fisheries in the Central Arctic Ocean (MOP)	CAOF Agreement[36]
CBS Convention	Convention on the Conservation and Management of Pollock Resources in the Central Bering Sea (COP)	CBS Convention[37]
JNRFC	Joint Norwegian Russian Fisheries Commission	JNRFC Agreement[38]
SIOFA	Southern Indian Ocean Fisheries Agreement (MOP)	SIOFA[39]

3. PARTICIPATION IN INTERGOVERNMENTAL
INSTRUMENTS AND BODIES

3.1. The Formation of Grounds and Requirements for Participation

The formation of the grounds (or: bases) and requirements for participation in intergovernmental instruments and bodies depends above all on whether or not the envisaged instrument or body will be negotiated under the auspices of an existing (overarching) intergovernmental body and its constitutive instrument, and whether or not there are other overarching frameworks or rules in place that must be taken into account. In circumstances in which neither are in

---

[33] Convention on the Conservation and Management of High Seas Fisheries Resources in the North Pacific Ocean of 24 February 2012 (available at www.npfc.int).

[34] Convention on the Conservation and Management of Fishery Resources in the South East Atlantic Ocean of 10 April 2001 (2221 UNTS 189; also available at www.seafo.org).

[35] Convention on the Conservation and Management of High Seas Fishery Resources in the South Pacific Ocean of 14 November 2009 (available at www.sprfmo.int).

[36] Agreement to Prevent Unregulated High Seas Fisheries in the Central Arctic Ocean of 3 October 2018; text included in the Annex to doc. COM(2018) 453 final, of 12 June 2018.

[37] Convention on the Conservation and Management of Pollock Resources in the Central Bering Sea of 16 June 1994 (34 ILM 67; also available at www.afsc.noaa.gov/REFM/CBS).

[38] Agreement between the Government of the Kingdom of Norway and the Government of the Union of Soviet Socialist Republics on Co-operation in the Fishing Industry of 11 April 1975 (983 UNTS 7).

[39] Southern Indian Ocean Fisheries Agreement of 7 July 2006 (available at www.siofa.org).

place, States sharing certain characteristics, interests and/or concerns can form an initiating group – often referred to as the 'founding fathers' or '(original) signatory States' (further: Founding Fathers) – and determine the grounds and requirements of participation largely as they see fit. It goes without saying that the grounds and requirements for participation will as a minimum incorporate the characteristics, interests and/or concerns which the initiating States have in common. In some instances, they may even claim a special participatory status, special rights or (implicitly) exclude other States and entities.

The negotiation of the Charter of the United Nations (UN)[40] is a useful example in this regard. As the League of Nations had neither been able to prevent aggression by the Axis powers in the 1930s nor the outbreak of World War II, the main Allied States – China (Republic of), the Soviet Union, the United Kingdom (UK) and the US; also known as the 'Big Four' – decided towards the end of 1943 that the League of Nations had to be replaced by a new intergovernmental body. Subsequently, the Big Four developed an advanced de facto 'draft UN Charter' during the 1944 Dumbarton Oaks Conference, which was further developed and adopted by around 50 States during the 1945 'United Nations Conference on International Organization'. The 'draft UN Charter' already envisaged that the Big Four "and, in due course, France" would be permanent members of the UN Security Council and have a right of veto.[41]

3.2. Issues of Statehood

In addition to the special arrangements relating to Taiwan discussed above, reference should be made to Palestine's accession to the LOS Convention in 2015.[42] This occurred after the UNGA[43] accorded Palestine the status of non-member observer State with the UN in 2012,[44] thereby comprising Palestine within the 'all States' formula contained in Article 305(1)(a) of the LOS Convention.[45] The only RFMO in which Palestine seems to have participated so far is GFCM, as an observer.[46]

Article 305(1)(c) and (d) of the LOS Convention allows 'Associated States' to sign the LOS Convention and thereby become a Party to it. So far, only the Cook Islands and Niue – both in free association with New Zealand – have made use of this entitlement.[47]

---

[40] Charter of the United Nations of 26 June 1945 (1 UNTS xvi).

[41] Proposals for the Establishment of a General International Organization at Ch. 6, Sec. A.

[42] For the status of participation in the LOS Convention, see www.un.org/depts/los/convention_agreements/convention_agreements.htm.

[43] Note 1.

[44] UNGA Res. 67/19 of 29 November 2012.

[45] See S Rosenne and LB Sohn (vol. eds) and MH Nordquist (ed-in-chief) *United Nations Convention on the Law of the Sea 1982, A Commentary, Volume V* (Martinus Nijhoff Publishers, Dordrecht/Boston/London: 1989) 181.

[46] Report of the 40th (2016) GFCM Session at 41.

[47] The status of participation is available at www.un.org/depts/los. For a recent analysis of Art. 305 of the LOS Convention, see A Proelß (ed.) *United Nations Convention on the Law of the Sea.*

Non-self-governing territories are also able to sign, and thereby become a Party to the LOS Convention, pursuant to the somewhat unclear specifications of Article 305(1)(e) of the LOS Convention. While none have done so far, some have argued that Western Sahara would be entitled to do so.[48]

All this notwithstanding, a uniform practice exists within RFMOs relating to 'non-metropolitan' components of (federal) States. So far, none have become members in their own right, without formal involvement of the (federal) States in parallel. The Kingdom of Denmark, for instance, is a Member of NEAFC in respect of Greenland and the Faroe Islands, but not mainland Denmark, in view of the latter's EU membership. The only exception to this uniform practice which could arise relates to Associate Members of FAO, who are entitled to become Members of GFCM and IOTC in their own right.[49] At the time of writing, neither of the two existing Associate Members – the Faroe Islands and Tokelau[50] – had made use of this entitlement. SPRFMO and WCPFC have a distinct participatory status for territories, without the right to vote.[51] While the CAOF Agreement recognizes the entitlement of Arctic indigenous peoples to participate in subsidiary bodies established by the MOP, they can only do so as part of the delegations of Parties and not in their own right.[52]

3.3. The EU and EU Member States

As was already observed above, the EU is generally regarded as qualifying as a REIO in the domain of international fisheries law. The need for the EU and its predecessors to participate in their own right in this arose from the transfer, from EU Member States to the EU and its predecessors, of exclusive competence over "the conservation of marine biological resources under the common fisheries policy".[53] As a general rule, this transfer of exclusive competence implied that the EU and its predecessors would replace EU Member States in

---

A Commentary (C.H. Beck/Hart/Nomos: 2017). At present, both Niue and the Cook Islands are Members of WCPFC, and the Cook Islands is also an Acceding State to the CAMLR Convention, a Party of SIOFA and a Member of SPRFMO (see Table 2 in Subsection 5.1).

[48] JJ Smith *From the Desert to the Sea: The Maritime Jurisdiction of an Independent Western Sahara* (LLM Thesis, The Fletcher School, Tufts University: 2010; available at no0ilcanarias.files. wordpress.com/2012/10/westernsahara-doc.pdf) 171–173. Note that the words "no Fishing Entity other than Chinese Taipei" in the 'Draft Resolution by ICCAT Regarding Participation by Fishing Entities under the Amended ICCAT Convention' (Doc. No. CONV_08C/2018; see note 26) is aimed at ensuring that it does not apply to Western Sahara.

[49] This entitlement is based on Art. II(11) of the FAO Constitution (Constitution of the Food and Agriculture Organization of the United Nations of 16 October 1945 (as amended; consolidated version available at www.fao.org/Legal) in conjunction with Arts. 4(1) and 23(1) of the GFCM Agreement, and Arts. IV(1) and XXII(1) of the IOTC Agreement.

[50] The status of membership is available at /www.fao.org/legal/home/membership-of-fao/en/.

[51] See Table 2 in Subsection 5.1 and note 79 and accompanying text.

[52] Art. 5(2) of the CAOF Agreement.

[53] Art. 3(1)(d) of the Treaty on the Functioning of the European Union (TFEU; consolidated version available at eur-lex.europa.eu/collection/eu-law/treaties.html).

intergovernmental bodies relating to marine capture fisheries. Several exceptions to this general rule nevertheless exist, for instance in relation to parts of
EU Member States that are not subject to the EU's Common Fisheries Policy,
whether as flag States, coastal States or both.[54] As noted in the previous subsection, this allows the Kingdom of Denmark to participate in several RFMOs in
respect of Greenland and/or the Faroe Islands. This, and other exceptions, are
reflected in the overview of participation by the EU and EU Member States in
the selected RFMOs in Subsection 5.3.

3.4. Evolving Participation due to State Succession, Continuation, Dissolution or Transfer of Competence

Broader geopolitical events such as the end of the Cold War and the progressive cooperation among European States within the European Economic
Community (EEC) and its successors, as well as the gradual expansion in the
membership of these European institutions, each had significant impacts on
participation in RFMOs. NEAFC is again a good example in this regard. Upon
its original establishment pursuant to the 1959 NEAFC Convention,[55] membership still comprised all the European coastal States to the North Sea and the
North-East Atlantic. Many of these States had joined the EEC upon the entry
into force of the current NEAFC Convention, and several other States discontinued NEAFC membership due to accession to the EU or its predecessors since
then. The UK's withdrawal from the EU will lead the UK to formally apply for
NEAFC membership. While such an application is only successful if it meets the
approval of three-fourths of the existing NEAFC Members,[56] such approval is
highly unlikely to be withheld for various reasons. This includes considerations
that are largely similar to those that arise in the context of State succession, as
the UK has been a Member of NEAFC or represented within NEAFC since its
establishment.

4. RELEVANT PROVISIONS IN GLOBAL FRAMEWORK INSTRUMENTS

Even though the first RFMOs[57] were already operating at the start of the first
United Nations Conference on the Law of the Sea (UNCLOS I), the 1958
High Seas Fishing Convention[58] did not accord regional fisheries bodies or

---

[54] Cf. Art. 355 and Annex II of the TFEU. See also R Churchill and D Owen *The EC Common Fisheries Policy* (Oxford University Press, Oxford: 2010) 359–360.
[55] North-East Atlantic Fisheries Convention of 24 January 1959 (486 UNTS 157).
[56] NEAFC Convention, Art. 20(4).
[57] E.g. IATTC and GFCM.
[58] Convention on Fishing and Conservation of the Living Resources of the High Seas of 29 April 1958 (559 UNTS 285).

comparable mechanisms a prominent role. Rather, the Convention relied above all on the special interests of coastal States in "the maintenance of the productivity of the living resources in any area of the high seas adjacent to [their] territorial sea", as well as compulsory arbitration.[59] The only implicit reference to fisheries bodies is included in Article 6(2), which reads:

> A coastal State is entitled to take part on an equal footing in any system of research and regulation for purposes of conservation of the living resources of the high seas in that area, even though its nationals do not carry on fishing there.

The phrase "any system of research and regulation" would have certainly comprised the then existing RFMOs, but was presumably also broad enough to encompass other regional and global bodies. The prominent role of the coastal State is reflected in the fact that its entitlement to participate in such bodies even existed when its nationals were not engaged in high seas fishing. It is notable that Article 6(2) only creates a right, but not an obligation, to participate.[60] Reference must also be made to Article 8(1), which acknowledges the "special interest in conservation" of a State "in an area of the high seas not adjacent to its coast". However, these are not necessarily exclusively non-user State interests[61] and – in contrast with Article 6(2) – no reference is made to "any system of research and regulation" or an entitlement to participate therein. Attempts by the US at UNCLOS I and during its preparatory phase to garner support for the doctrine of abstention – which aimed to restrict participation in fisheries bodies in case fishing opportunities were fully utilized or allocated – proved fruitless.[62]

The LOS Convention does not explicitly mention a right of States – whether in their capacity as coastal States, States fishing on the high seas, or otherwise – to participate in existing regional fisheries bodies either. To some extent, however, such a right can be inferred from the phrase "with participation by all States concerned" that is included in Articles 61(5) and 119(2), in the context of the obligation to contribute and exchange scientific information, catch and fishing effort statistics and other data through competent international organizations. Furthermore, a participatory right could be construed based on the entitlements to marine living resources of coastal States

---

[59] Ibid., Arts. 6(1) and 9. See, however, Resolution III 'International fishery conservation conventions' of 25 April 1958; and the International Law Commission (ILC)'s "Commentary to the articles concerning the law of the sea" (*Yearbook of the International Law Commission*, 1956, vol. II) 286–288, containing its Commentary on Art. 49 (which eventually became Art. 1(1) of the 1958 High Seas Fishing Convention), in particular paras. 4, 9 and 19, which refer to earlier proposals involving international fisheries bodies. See A Serdy *The New Entrants Problem in International Fisheries Law* (Cambridge University Press, Cambridge: 2015) 11–13 for a fuller account.

[60] Such an obligation formed part of the earlier proposals discussed by the ILC (see note 59).

[61] The ILC, in its Commentary on Art. 55, note 59 at 291 – which eventually became Art. 8 of the 1958 High Seas Fishing Convention – gives the following example: "if the exhaustion of the resources of the sea in the area would affect the results of fishing in another area where the nationals of the State concerned do engage in fishing".

[62] See the discussion by Serdy, note 59 at 68–72.

(i.e. sovereignty and sovereign rights) and flag States (i.e. their right for their nationals to fish on the high seas, and their entitlement to access to the surplus of the total allowable catch in third States' EEZs) in conjunction with their obligations to cooperate with each other in relation to straddling and highly migratory fish stocks, as well as high seas fisheries in general. As regards highly migratory fish stocks and high seas fisheries, this obligation to cooperate includes the establishment of regional fisheries bodies.[63]

Article 8(3) of the Fish Stocks Agreement contains an explicit right for "States having a real interest in the fisheries concerned" to become Members of an existing RFMO. As this right is preceded in the same paragraph by an obligation for "States fishing for the stocks on the high seas and relevant coastal States" to become Members of such RFMOs, these States can be presumed to have a real interest. It seems reasonable to assume that the decision to include the requirement of a real interest must have been motivated by a desire to exclude States without it. This might have been inspired by the lack of any substantive restrictions on membership of the International Whaling Commission (IWC),[64] which has resulted in a situation where whaling States are often outnumbered by non-user States.[65] Another category of States that existing Members of RFMOs can be expected to be inclined to exclude are so-called 'new entrants', namely States that are not presently fishing but would like to do so.[66]

Whereas Article 8(3) applies to existing RFMOs, Articles 8(5) and 9(2) apply to the establishment of new RFMOs. In case of a "particular straddling fish stock or highly migratory fish stock" for which no existing RFMO has the mandate to establish conservation and management measures, Article 8(5) requires "relevant coastal States and States fishing on the high seas" to cooperate to establish such an RFMO. Once these States have commenced such cooperation, Article 9(2) requires them to "inform other States which they are aware have a real interest in the work of the proposed [RFMO] of such cooperation". While this could denote non-user States or new entrants, it may also relate to coastal States and States fishing on the high seas that are not yet involved in the negotiations. Attention should finally be drawn to the words 'inform' and 'in the work of', which were apparently preferred over an invitation to participate in the (negotiation of) the establishment of the RFMO.[67]

As inclusion of the requirement of a real interest within the Fish Stocks Agreement constrains the freedom of high seas fishing, this raises the question as to whether this is consistent with the LOS Convention, as required by

---

[63] Arts. 64 and 118 of the LOS Convention.

[64] Arts. III(1) and X(2) of the International Convention for the Regulation of Whaling of 2 December 1946 (161 UNTS 72, as amended; consolidated version available at iwc.int).

[65] EJ Molenaar "The Concept of 'Real Interest' and Other Aspects of Co-operation through Regional Fisheries Management Mechanisms" (2000) 15 *International Journal of Marine and Coastal Law* 475–531, at 496.

[66] Ibid. On new entrants more generally, see Serdy, note 59.

[67] See also Molenaar, note 65 at 495–496, 513 and 522.

Article 4 of the Fish Stocks Agreement. Moreover, even though the Fish Stocks Agreement does not explicitly give RFMOs competence to determine whether or not an applicant for membership meets the requirement of real interest,[68] the constitutive instruments of several RFMOs that were already in existence during the negotiation of the Fish Stocks Agreement contained restrictions on membership and gave these RFMOs competence to approve or reject (further: approval role) applications for accession and/or membership.[69] It would therefore not have been difficult to imagine that new RFMOs would follow in their footsteps – if only due to overlaps in participation – and impose similar restrictions on membership and/or claim such an approval role. Furthermore, as the Fish Stocks Agreement lacks a definition of the requirement of real interest and any guidance as to how it should be applied, it is unable to ensure some level of inter-regional uniformity. So far, the (Resumed) Fish Stocks Agreement Review Conferences have not been used for this purpose either.[70]

5. RULES AND PRACTICES OF SELECTED RFMOS

5.1. Introduction

This section contains an analysis of the rules and practices of selected RFMOs concerning participation. Whereas the rules and practices on the substantive requirements and procedures of these RFMOs are examined in Subsection 5.2, the participation of the EU, EU Member States and Taiwan is examined in further detail in Subsection 5.3. Subsection 5.4 then focuses on the various categories of cooperative status used in selected RFMOs.

Table 2 provides an overview of current participation in these RFMOs, revealing significant differences. In terms of the number of participants, for instance, ICCAT is by far the largest. Moreover, the average number of participants in the tuna RFMOs is larger than the average number of participants in the non-tuna RFMOs. Whereas the membership of most RFMOs is a mix of coastal States and high seas fishing States, four RFMOs solely or predominantly have coastal States as Members: namely GFCM, JNRFC, NEAFC and NPFC. While GFCM only has one non-coastal State Member (Japan), this should be

---

[68] Art. 11 of the Fish Stocks Agreement does not deal with membership of RFMOs as such, but rather with the "nature and extent of participatory rights".

[69] E.g. Art. 20(4) of the NEAFC Convention. Pursuant to the preceding version of the current NAFO Convention – namely the Convention on Future Multilateral Cooperation in the Northwest Atlantic Fisheries of 24 October 1978 (1135 UNTS 369) – any State could accede (cf. Art. XXII(4)) but membership of the Fisheries Commission – then also the main management body under the NAFO Convention – was reserved for Parties already participating in the fisheries or those that had provided satisfactory evidence that they expect to participate in the fisheries within a certain time (Art. XIII(1)).

[70] See note 1.

seen in light of the fact that if all coastal States were to exercise fisheries jurisdiction up to 200 nautical miles, no high seas pockets would remain. Finally, China, the EU, Japan, Korea and the US participate in most of the selected RFMOs.

Table 2 Current Participation in Selected RFMO/As[71]

RFMO/A	Members[72]	Other Participatory Status[73]
CAOF Agreement	Current: 0 Upon entry into force (10): Canada, China, Denmark, EU, Iceland, Japan, Korea, Russian Federation and US	None
CBS Convention	6: China, Japan, Korea, Poland, Russian Federation and US	None
CCAMLR	25: Australia, Argentina, Belgium, Brazil, Chile, China, EU, France, Germany, India, Italy, Japan, Korea, Namibia, New Zealand, Norway, Poland, Russian Federation, South Africa, Spain, Sweden, Ukraine, UK, US and Uruguay	Acceding States (11): Bulgaria, Canada, Cook Islands, Finland, Greece, Mauritius, Netherlands, Pakistan, Panama, Peru and Vanuatu CNCPs-CDS[d] for 2018 (2): Ecuador and Singapore
CCSBT	6: Australia, Indonesia, Japan, Korea, New Zealand, South Africa	Members of the Extended Commission (2): EU and Taiwan CNMs[b] for 2018: 0
GFCM	24: Albania, Algeria, Bulgaria, Croatia, Cyprus, Egypt, EU, France, Greece, Israel, Italy, Japan, Lebanon, Libya, Malta, Monaco, Montenegro, Morocco, Romania, Slovenia, Spain, Syria, Tunisia and Turkey	CPCs[a] for 2018 (4):[74] Bosnia and Herzegovina, Georgia, Moldova and Ukraine
IATTC	21: Belize, Canada, China, Colombia, Costa Rica, Ecuador, El Salvador, EU, France, Guatemala, Japan, Kiribati, Korea, Mexico, Nicaragua, Panama, Peru, Taiwan, US, Vanuatu and Venezuela	CNMs[b] for 2017–2018 (5): Bolivia, Chile, Honduras, Indonesia and Liberia

(continued)

[71] Accurate as at 7 June 2018.
[72] As regards EU Member States, see Subsection 5.3
[73] Other than 'observer' status.
[74] The Reports of the 2014–2017 Annual GFCM Meetings also list participation by the Russian Federation in different ways. The 2016 and 2017 Reports list the Russian Federation under the heading 'Non-Contracting Party', even though that status is not used in the GFCM's Rules of Procedure.

Table 2 (*Continued*)

RFMO/A	Members	Other Participatory Status
ICCAT	**52:** Albania, Algeria, Angola, Barbados, Belize, Brazil, Canada, Cabo Verde, China, Côte d'Ivoire, Egypt, El Salvador, Equatorial Guinea, the EU, France, Gabon, Ghana, Grenada, Guatemala, Guinea, Guinea-Bissau, Honduras, Iceland, Japan, Korea, Liberia, Libya, Mauritania, Mexico, Morocco, Namibia, Netherlands,[75] Nicaragua, Nigeria, Norway, Panama, Philippines, Russian Federation, St. Vincent & the Grenadines, Sao Tome and Principe, Senegal, Sierra Leone, South Africa, Syria, Trinidad and Tobago, Tunisia, Turkey, UK, US, Uruguay, Vanuatu and Venezuela	Cooperating Status[c] for 2018 (5): Bolivia, Costa Rica, Guyana, Suriname and Taiwan
IOTC	**31:** Australia, Bangladesh, China, Comoros, Eritrea, EU, France, India, Indonesia, Iran, Japan, Kenya, Korea, Madagascar, Malaysia, Maldives, Mauritius, Mozambique, Oman, Pakistan, Philippines, Seychelles, Sierra Leone, Somalia, Sri Lanka, South Africa, Sudan, Tanzania, Thailand, UK and Yemen	CNCPs[a] for 2017–2018 (2):Liberia and Senegal Invited experts and consultants (1): Taiwan
JNRFC	**2:** Norway and Russian Federation	None
NAFO	**12:** Canada, Cuba, Denmark, EU, France, Iceland, Japan, Norway, Korea, Russian Federation, Ukraine and US	None
NEAFC	**5:** Denmark, EU, Iceland, Norway and Russian Federation	CNCPs[a] for 2018 (5): Bahamas, Canada, Liberia, New Zealand and St. Kitts and Nevis
NPFC	**8:** Canada, China, Japan, Korea, Russian Federation, Taiwan, US and Vanuatu	CNCPs[a] for 2018: None
SEAFO	**7:** Angola, EU, Japan, Korea, Namibia, Norway and South Africa	None
SIOFA	**9:** Australia, Cook Islands, EU, France, Japan, Korea, Mauritius, Seychelles and Thailand	None

(continued)

[75] See note 96.

Table 2 (*Continued*)

RFMO/A	Members	Other Participatory Status
SPRFMO	15: Australia, Chile, China, Cook Islands, Cuba, Denmark, Ecuador, EU, Korea, New Zealand, Peru, Russian Federation, Taiwan, US and Vanuatu	CNCPs[a] for 2018 (4): Colombia, Curaçao,[76] Liberia and Panama Participating territories (1): Tokelau
WCPFC	26: Australia, China, Canada, Cook Islands, EU, Federated States of Micronesia, Fiji, France, Indonesia, Japan, Kiribati, Korea, Marshall Islands, Nauru, New Zealand, Niue, Palau, Papua New Guinea, Philippines, Samoa, Solomon Islands, Taiwan, Tonga, Tuvalu, US and Vanuatu	CNMs[b] for 2018 (7): Ecuador, El Salvador, Liberia, Mexico, Panama, Thailand, and Vietnam Participating territories (7): American Samoa, French Polynesia, Guam, New Caledonia, the Northern Mariana Islands, Tokelau, and Wallis and Futuna

[a] Cooperating Non-Contracting Parties.
[b] Cooperating Non-Members.
[c] Cooperating Non-Contracting Party, Entity or Fishing Entity.
[d] Cooperating Non-Contracting Party re the Catch Documentation Scheme for *Dissostichus* spp.

5.2. Rules and Practices on Eligibility Requirements and Criteria, and Procedures

A distinction must first of all be made between the formal rules on eligibility requirements and criteria, and procedures laid down in the constitutive instruments of the selected RFMOs on the one hand, and the subsequent practice on the application of those rules and procedures on the other hand. As regards the formal rules, Table 3 below provides an overview of specific eligibility criteria and procedures. Due to spatial constraints, however, this chapter only considers the most pertinent examples of practice rather than providing an exhaustive overview.

   In addition to the specific eligibility criteria on accession listed in Table 3, the constitutive instruments of the selected RFMOs also contain other categories of requirements or criteria on eligibility. The first category relates to statehood. Accession to – and thereby membership of[77] – most of the selected RFMOs is in principle reserved for States. As examined further in Subsection 5.3, however, the EU and Taiwan have become members of several RFMOs. In addition, while membership of GFCM and IOTC is also open to Associate Members to FAO,

---

[76] See note 107 and accompanying text.
[77] See note 81.

this entitlement has so far not been exercised.[78] The constitutive instruments of NAFO, SPRFMO and WCPFC refer to Article 305(1)(c), (d) and (e) of the LOS Convention – which do not seem to have been used so far – and the latter two instruments also allow participation by territories – which has in fact been used in both cases.[79]

The second category consists of requirements relating to participation in intergovernmental organizations. Only three of the selected RFMOs use these: GFCM, ICCAT and IOTC. As regards GFCM and IOTC, however, States that are not Members of FAO can still accede if their applications secure a two-thirds majority of the votes of the Members of these RFMOs (see Table 3).

The third category consists of criteria relating to Founding Fathers, which provide full participants at the final session of the negotiations on the establishment of an RFMO, or Members of an RFMO's precursor, with a right to accede that is not subject to approval. The constitutive instruments of four RFMOs do not contain such criteria: GFCM, ICCAT, IOTC and JNRFC. The latter is a striking exception to the other selected RFMOs, because it does not provide criteria for accession at all. As regards GFCM and IOTC, the absence of a Founding Father criterion can be explained by the fact that they have been established under FAO, and are therefore at any rate open to Members and Associate Members of FAO. As ICCAT has no specific eligibility criteria or procedure for accession – other than involving a depositary – and is therefore almost entirely 'open', it was perhaps felt that there was no pressing need for a Founding Father criterion. As is evident from Table 3, however, the negotiators of other RFMOs decided differently. In some of these cases, they may perhaps have wished to avoid or minimize unanticipated or undesirable interpretations of the provisions on accession and membership by the depositary and members. Finally, Founding Father-criteria are by no means always fully utilized; not even for RFMOs that are relatively 'closed', as evidenced by the unused entitlements of, for example, Cuba in relation to NEAFC, and the UK in relation to WCPFC.[80] The costs of membership must apparently outweigh the benefits.

Table 3 Specific Eligibility Criteria and Procedures on Accession[81] in the Constitutive Instruments of Selected RFMOs

Eligibility criteria	
None	ICCAT Convention (Art. XIV(1))
	NAFO Convention (Art. XXIII)
	NEAFC Convention (Art. 20(4))

(continued)

---

[78] See notes 49 and 50 and accompanying text.

[79] NAFO Convention (Art. I(d)(2)); SPRFMO Convention (Art. 1(2)(b) and 40); and WCPF Convention (Arts. 35(1) and 43). See also Table 2 in Subsection 5.1.

[80] As regards the UK, see also the discussion on CCSBT, GFCM, ICCAT, SEAFO, SIOFA (MOP) and SPRFMO in Subsection 5.3.

[81] Except for the CAMLR Convention, accession also implies membership.

Table 3 (*Continued*)

Specific	CAOF Agreement: real interest (Art. 10(2))
	CBS Convention: wish to conduct fishing (Art. 16(4))
	CAMLR Convention
	Accession: interest in research or harvesting activities (Art. XXIX(1))
	Membership: engagement in research or harvesting activities (Art. VII(2)(d))
	CCSBT Convention: coastal States, and flag States engaged in fishing (Art. 18)
	GFCM Agreement: coastal States, and flag States engaged in fishing, or that wish to conduct fishing (Art. 4)
	IATTC Agreement: coastal States, and flag States engaged in fishing, following consultations with the Parties (Art. XXX)
	IOTC Agreement: coastal States, and flag States engaged in fishing (Art. IV(1)(a))
	NPFC Convention: coastal States, and REIOs or flag States that wish to conduct fishing activities (Art. 24(2))
	SEAFO Convention: coastal States, and flag States and REIOs engaged in fishing (Art. 26(2))
	SIOFA: coastal States, any other State or REIO interested in fishing activities (Art. 23(1))
	SPRFMO: State or entity having an interest in fishery resources (Art. 37(1))
	WCPFC: flag States and REIOs that wish to engage in fishing (Art. 35(2))
Procedures on accession other than involving a depositary	
None	CAMLR Convention: except for accession by REIOs, for which approval by consensus is required (Art. XXIX(2))
	CCSBT Convention (Art. 18)
	ICCAT Convention (Art. XIV(1))
	NAFO Convention (Art. XXIII)
	SEAFO Convention: except for accession by REIOs other than the EU (Art. 26(2))
	SIOFA (Art. 23)
	SPRFMO Convention (Art. 37)
Specific	CAOF Agreement: invitation by consensus (Art. 10(2))
	CBS Convention: invitation by unanimity (Art. XVI(4))
	CAMLR Convention: approval role on membership for all applicants, by consensus (Art. VII(2)(d))
	CCSBT Convention: approval role on membership of the Extended Commission by REIOs, entities and fishing entities ('Resolution to Establish an Extended Commission and an Extended Scientific Committee' of April 2001, as replaced in October 2013)
	GFCM Agreement: approval role on non-FAO Members, by a 2/3 majority (Art. 23(2))

(continued)

Table 3 (*Continued*)

IATTC Agreement: approval role in residual cases, by consensus (Art. XXX)
IOTC Agreement: approval role on non-FAO Members, by a 2/3 majority (Arts. IV(2) and XVII(2))
NEAFC Convention: approval role, by 3/4 majority (Art. 20(4))
NPFC Convention: invitation by consensus (Art. 24(2)), provided that a Party that does not join the consensus must present NPFC in writing its reasons for this (Art. 24(3))
WCPFC Convention: invitation by consensus (Art. 35(2))

Table 3 deals separately with eligibility criteria and procedures on accession other than involving a depositary. As regards both, the constitutive instruments of RFMOs are either grouped together as having no such eligibility criteria and procedures ('None') or specific criteria and procedures. The constitutive instruments listed among 'None' in both can be presumed to be the most open. As noted earlier, however, membership does not automatically entitle a participant to an allocation. For example, NAFO has indicated that its fish stocks are "fully allocated".[82] The relative openness of some RFMOs is also explained by their low level of fishing effort (e.g. SEAFO) or the absence of fishing at present (e.g. SIOFA).

A closer look at their eligibility criteria sheds further light on the openness of RFMOs. Of the constitutive instruments specifying eligibility criteria, almost all either explicitly mention coastal States, have eligibility criteria wide enough to also cover coastal States (e.g. SPRFMO Convention) or have Founding Father criteria that cover all relevant coastal States (e.g. the CAOF Agreement and the CBS Convention). The only exception in this regard is the WCPF Convention, which is explained by the failure to agree on a northern and a western boundary to the WCPF Convention Area, which was largely caused by the various disputes relating to the South China Sea. As regards Vietnam this means that, even though there is no consensus among WCPFC Members that Vietnam is a coastal State to the WCPF Convention Area, Vietnamese vessels fishing in Vietnam's own maritime zones catch tuna species managed by WCPFC whose distributional range includes waters that are indisputably part of the WCPFC Convention Area. According to the LOS Convention, therefore, Vietnam is a coastal State with respect to those tuna species managed by WCPFC.

Apart from coastal States, several of the constitutive instruments mention flag States engaged in fishing. This raises the dilemma highlighted in the introduction to this chapter, namely that many RFMOs categorize fishing

---

[82] NAFO Resolution 1/99 'to guide the expectations of future new members with regard to fishing opportunities in the NAFO Regulatory Area'. For a detailed account on ICCAT, and in particular its reliance on historic catch as the principal allocation criterion, see Serdy, note 59 at 80–89.

by non-Members as IUU fishing, which thereby triggers measures aimed at combating IUU fishing. The experience of the Cook Islands with regard to CCAMLR described below is a case in point. The eligibility criterion "wish to conduct/engage in fishing" avoids this dilemma, but not the potential conflict between the requirement of real interest and the freedom of high seas fishing. Finally, it is noteworthy that membership of three RFMOs is explicitly open to non-user States (CCAMLR, SIOFA and SPRFMO), implicitly so in three other RFMOs (ICCAT, NAFO and NEAFC), and possibly in one other RFMO (CAOF Agreement). This entitlement has been exercised in particular within CCAMLR.

While Table 3 shows there are differences among the procedures on accession involving an approval role, it seems fair to conclude that about half of the selected RFMOs have such a procedure. This is either by qualified majority, consensus or unanimity, with four using the 'invitation by consensus/unanimity' approach: CAOF Agreement, CBS Convention, NPFC and WCPFC. Among these are the two newest RFMOs: CAOF Agreement and NPFC. The establishment of SPRFMO – one of the most open RFMOs – in 2013 therefore did not set a new trend.

The extent to which RFMOs are closed or open depends of course on their practices. For academics, however, a thorough and comprehensive analysis of these practices is nearly impossible, since much of the relevant information is not in the public domain. It is nevertheless safe to assume that there are considerable divergences in these practices. While CCAMLR has an approval role by consensus for membership – but not accession (except for REIOs) – it has only once rejected an application. This concerned the application by the Cook Islands in 2007, which was apparently rejected on the ground that the Cook Islands was not engaged in research or harvesting, even though harvesting by Acceding States would at that time have been treated as IUU fishing and have triggered various measures aimed at combating IUU fishing.[83] During the negotiations of the CAMLR Convention, requests by Korea and the Netherlands to participate – which, if accepted, would have made them Founding Fathers – and Taiwan, were rejected.[84]

The fact that NPFC, which was only established in 2015, admitted Vanuatu in 2017 as its first 'non-Founding Father Member'[85] despite the NPFC's 'invitation by consensus' procedure, can be interpreted as a sign of its openness. This is also true for the innovative requirement for a Party to the NPFC Convention that opposes an invitation for membership to present its reasons in writing to NPFC (Article 24(3)).[86] The dismissal of the EU's request for an invitation to accede at

---

[83] Cf. Report of the 26th (2007) Annual CCAMLR Meeting, paras. 4.37–4.48 and 13.10–13.22; files held by the author; and notes made by the author during Annual CCAMLR Meetings.

[84] See the references to Barnes in notes 94 and 95.

[85] Report of the 3rd (2017) Annual NPFC Meeting, 1.

[86] Art. 24(3) of the NPFC Convention.

the NPFC's subsequent Annual Meeting in 2018 casts doubts on the openness of NPFC, however.[87]

A similarly open start was made by WCPFC, which invited the then European Community (EC) to accede to the WCPF Convention at its first Session in 2004.[88] During the negotiations on the WCPF Convention, the EC's repeated requests to be accepted as a full participant – and thereby become a Founding Father – were all rejected.[89] For almost a decade, however, several States have expressed an interest in becoming Members or have made explicit requests to be invited to accede. Attempts by these States – notably Ecuador and El Salvador – to raise this issue during plenary at Annual WCPFC Meetings proved largely fruitless until 2017.[90] Facilitated by a US discussion paper, the opponents of broadening membership then highlighted in particular the special nature of WCPFC and the benefits offered by CNM status.[91] This opposition implies that the prospects for Ecuador, El Salvador and others to become WCPFC Members in the near future are not promising.

5.3. The EU, EU Member States and Taiwan

CAOF Agreement

The EU and Denmark – in respect of its territories – are among the ten Founding Fathers. The CAOF Agreement contains no arrangements for the participation of Taiwan.

CBS Convention

Only Poland – one of the six Founding Fathers – is a Party but, uniquely, not the EU. Once Poland acceded to the EU in 2004, it should in principle have been replaced by the EU. Proposals by Poland (and the EU) to amend the CBS Convention to provide for this have not secured the necessary support, mainly because there has been no high seas fishing since the Convention's adoption, and there have been no indications that this will change in the near term.[92]

---

[87] Report of the 4th (2018) Annual NPFC Meeting, 2.

[88] Report of the 1st (2004) Annual WCPFC Meeting, 1.

[89] See Molenaar, note 65 at 509–514.

[90] See e.g. Report of the 12th (2015) Annual WCPFC Meeting, paras. 761–762; Report of the 13th (2016) Annual WCPFC Meeting, paras. 41–46.

[91] Report of the 14th (2017) Annual WCPFC Meeting, paras. 72–87. It is submitted that the analysis of the rules and practices of other RFMOs contained in the US discussion paper (Doc. WCPFC14-2017-DP18 of 3 November 2017) is insufficiently balanced due to its selection of RFMOs and its exclusion of allocation issues, and thereby incorrectly concludes "that WCPFC stands apart [as] most other RFMOs are relatively open to new members, or at least have a process for, or experience with, inviting new members to join the organization" (at 3). In view of the complexity of the issues – as for instance highlighted by the length of this chapter – putting together a paper that is not only concise but also comprehensive and balanced, is not that easy.

[92] Report of the 20th (2015) COP to the CBS Convention, para. 8.1.

Reports of the COPs commonly refer to Poland in conjunction with the EU (e.g. Poland/EU, or Poland on behalf of the EU). The CBS Convention also contains no arrangements for the participation of Taiwan.

CCAMLR

The EU, Belgium, France, Germany, Italy, Poland, Spain, Sweden and the UK are Members. Some EU Member States also participate in respect of some of their territories – namely France and the UK – others only on account of CCAMLR's special status.[93] Bulgaria, Finland, Greece and the Netherlands[94] have acceded to the CAMLR Convention and participate as 'Acceding States'. The CAMLR Convention contains no arrangements for the participation of Taiwan, and CCAMLR also has not provided Taiwan with any participatory status, even though Taiwan sought to cooperate with CCAMLR.[95]

CCSBT

The EU and Taiwan are Members of the 'Extended Commission'. For the EU, this is the only RFMO in which it participates as a full Member without being a Party to the RFMO's constitutive instrument. France and the UK are not Members, even though they have territories and associated maritime zones in which southern bluefin tuna potentially occur.

GFCM

The EU, Bulgaria, Croatia, Cyprus, France, Greece, Italy, Malta, Romania, Slovenia and Spain are Members. The UK was a Member until it withdrew in 1968, even though it remains a coastal State in respect of Gibraltar. This parallel membership is based on, *inter alia*, the GFCM's competence relating to aquaculture and its broad geographical mandate, which includes the territorial sea and

---

[93] See note 17 and accompanying text.

[94] Also in respect of its territories. While the Netherlands intended to apply for full membership in 2018 (Report of the 36th (2017) Annual CCAMLR Meeting, paras. 2.4 and 12.15), this may not happen until 2019. During the final stages of the negotiations of the CAMLR Convention, a request by the Netherlands (and Korea) to participate was declined (cf. JN Barnes "The Emerging Convention on the Conservation of Antarctic Marine Living Resources: An Attempt to Meet the New Realities of Resource Exploitation in the Southern Ocean" in JI Charney (ed.) *The New Nationalism and the Use of Common Spaces* (Osmun Publishers, Allanheld: 1982) 239–286, at 246 (fn 39) and 258.

[95] Among other things by requesting Taiwan to participate voluntarily in the CDS (see Table 2) in 2004, and to attend the 24th (2005) Annual CCAMLR Meeting as an observer (based on files held by the author). In 2000 and 2001, CCAMLR had in fact asked Taiwan to cooperate in the implementation of the CDS (cf. Report of the 19th (2000) Annual CCAMLR Meeting, para. 2.44; Report of the 20th (2001) Annual CCAMLR Meeting, paras. 5.27 and 2.31–2.32). Arguably, China's accession to the CAMLR Convention in 2006 and application for membership in 2007 was to a considerable extent aimed at ensuring that Taiwan would not obtain any formal participatory status with CCAMLR, and thereby the ATS. Barnes observes, note 94 at 239 (fn 3), 241 (fn 12), 245 (fn 37), 258 (fn 76) and 272 that Taiwan had expressed an interest in participating in the negotiations on the CAMLR Convention, but was not invited due to political reasons.

marine internal waters. The GFCM Agreement contains no arrangements for the participation of Taiwan.

IATTC

The EU, France – in respect of some of its territories – and Taiwan are Members.

ICCAT

The EU and France, the Netherlands[96] and the UK[97] – in respect of some of their territories – are Members. Taiwan has been granted Cooperating Status[98] since 2008. In the still ongoing negotiations on the amendment of the ICCAT Convention, the issues of the participation of Taiwan as a Member, and the depositary(ies) are inherently linked.[99]

IOTC

The EU and France and the UK – on account of some of their territories – are Members. Taiwan participates as an observer, in the category 'Invited consultants and experts'.[100] The many years of discussions on amending or replacing the IOTC Agreement to enhance participation of Taiwan have not led to a solution that is acceptable to all Members.[101]

JNRFC

The only Members are Norway and the Russian Federation, and the JNRFC Agreement does not provide for accession at all.

NAFO

The EU and Denmark and France – in respect of some of their territories – are Members. The NAFO Convention contains no arrangements for the participation of Taiwan.

---

[96] The Netherlands Antilles and one of its successors – Curaçao – have in the past been granted Cooperating Status by ICCAT. At the time of writing, the ICCAT website and ICCAT documents treated Curaçao as a Party to the ICCAT Convention and a member of ICCAT (e.g. Report of the 2016 Annual ICCAT Meeting, para. 3, and other information at www.iccat.int). This is incorrect, as the Kingdom of the Netherlands acceded to the ICCAT Convention on 6 February 2014 on behalf of Curaçao (*Tractatenblad* 2014, Nr. 76; verdragenbank.overheid.nl/nl/Verdrag/Details/003671) rather than facilitating the accession of Curaçao in its own right. In light of the words 'any State' in Art. XIV(1) of the ICCAT Convention, this would also not have been possible. The depositary's overview of the status of the ICCAT Convention (see www.fao.org/legal/treaties/treaties-outside-fao-framework/en/) also listed the Netherlands, rather than Curaçao, as a 'participant'. The practice of ICCAT is all the more surprising as both France and the UK have been members in respect of some of their territories since 1 January 1998. See also note 107 and accompanying text on the status of Curaçao within SPRFMO.
[97] But not in relation to Gibraltar, even though a fishery for Atlantic bluefin tuna occurs there (see Spencer, Maguire and Molenaar, note 26 at 11 and 66–68.
[98] See also note 96.
[99] See Spencer, Maguire and Molenaar, note 26 at 9.
[100] E.g. Report of the 21st (2017) IOTC Session, para. 6(d).
[101] See Report of the 20th (2016) IOTC Session, 23 and 109.

NEAFC

The EU and Denmark – in respect of its territories – are Members. The NEAFC Convention contains no arrangements for the participation of Taiwan.

NPFC

Taiwan is a Member, but the EU is not. The NPFC Convention nevertheless provides for accession by REIOs, and steps towards making use of this were taken within the EU in February 2018.[102] While Denmark – in respect of the Faroe Islands – participated in the eighth and ninth Sessions of the negotiations on the NPFC Convention and claimed a right to become a Member soon thereafter,[103] it no longer seemed interested in membership at the time of writing.

SEAFO

The EU is a Member, but there are no EU Member States among the SEAFO Members, even though the UK – in respect of some of its territories – is a coastal State to the SEAFO Convention Area, and one of the Founding Fathers.[104] This situation is probably caused mainly by the low level of fishing effort in recent years. It is likely that the other States that participated in the negotiations on the SEAFO Convention but have not become Members so far,[105] have done so for similar reasons. The SEAFO Convention contains no arrangements for the participation of Taiwan.

SIOFA

The EU and France – in respect of some of its territories – are Parties, but not the UK – in respect of some of its territories – even though it is a coastal State to the SIOFA Area. Article 15 of SIOFA contains an arrangement for the participation of Taiwan, even though Taiwan did not participate in the negotiations on the SIOFA.[106]

---

[102] Note 87.

[103] See the Record of the 10th (2011) Session of the Negotiations, 1–2.

[104] The UK participated as an observer in the 2nd (2005) and 14th (2017) Annual SEAFO Meetings. Para. 5.4 of the Report of the 4th (2007) Annual SEAFO Meeting reads: "The United Kingdom had communicated to SEAFO that its overseas territories are not in position to implement the Convention and UK can not [sic] join the Organisation on their behalf".

[105] Iceland and the US signed (information based on www.fao.org/legal/treaties/treaties-outside-fao-framework/en/), and Poland, the Russian Federation and Ukraine participated but did not sign (cf. "Final Minute of the Conference on the South East Atlantic Fisheries Organization and of the Meetings of Coastal States and other Interested Parties on a Regional Fisheries Management Organisation for the South East Atlantic", at 3; on file with author).

[106] Cf. "Final Act of the Conference on the Southern Indian Ocean Fisheries Agreement" (available at www.siofa.org/). Taiwan nevertheless participated in the 4th (2017) MOP to SIOFA and indicated that it aspired to make use of the arrangement in Art. 15 prior to the 5th MOP (cf. para. 6 of the Report of the 4th (2017) MOP to SIOFA).

SPRFMO

The EU and Denmark – in respect of some of its territories – and Taiwan are Members, but not France and the UK – in respect of some of their territories – even though they are coastal States to the SPRFMO Convention Area. Curaçao – one of the four countries of the Kingdom of the Netherlands – was granted CNCP status for 2018.[107]

WCPFC

The EU and France – in respect of some of its territories – and Taiwan are Members, but not the UK – in respect of some of its territories – even though it is a coastal State to the WCPFC Convention Area and one of the Founding Fathers.

In summary, the EU does not participate in three of the 16 selected RFMOs (CBS Convention, JNRFC and NPFC), one of which – at least so far – is by choice (NPFC). Of the 13 RFMOs of which the EU is a Member, there are only two in which the EU does not participate alongside one or more EU Member States (CCSBT and SEAFO). Taiwan's participation is less extensive than that of the EU, and includes all of the five tuna RFMOs – but as regards ICCAT and IOTC not as Members – as well as two non-tuna RFMOs (NPFC and SPRFMO). So far, Taiwan has not made use of the arrangement for the participation of Taiwan included in the SIOFA. None of the other non-tuna RFMOs contain such arrangements.

5.4. Cooperating Status

As shown in Table 2 in Subsection 5.1, a majority of the selected RFMOs have one or more participatory categories for States and entities other than membership. Most of these categories are based on Article 8(3) and (4) of the Fish Stocks Agreement, which acknowledges that the duty to cooperate with an RFMO can be met and operationalized in different ways. Apart from the status of Acceding States within CCAMLR, cooperating status is commonly granted or renewed at annual meetings and laid down in the reports of these meetings. Arguably, such granting or renewal does not create rights or obligations governed by international law.

Cooperating status can provide limited fishing opportunities or engagement in activities associated with fishing (e.g. provisioning and transshipment), but does not allow for participation in decision-making. In return for participatory rights, status holders are expected to comply with the RFMO's conservation and

---

[107] Report of the 6th (2018) Annual SPRFMO Meeting, 2.

management measures and other specific conditions, with some RFMOs also expecting them to make 'voluntary' financial contributions.[108]

A significant disadvantage of cooperating status – from the perspective of status holders – is the considerable lack of stability and predictability that ensues from the RFMO's competence to revoke or not to renew cooperating status on an annual basis. While the exercise of this competence is legitimate and understandable where a status holder does not comply with the conditions attached to its cooperating status, there is always a risk of abuse of competence.[109] Non-members will therefore often conduct a comparative analysis of the costs and benefits of full membership and other participatory categories. However, as the discussion in Subsection 5.2 has shown, such a comparative analysis is of limited use for quite a few RFMOs, as full membership is simply not attainable for new applicants.

6. CONCLUSIONS

As shown in this chapter, the current participation in the selected RFMOs underscores their uniqueness. The only common denominators that are easily discernable are that participation commonly includes all coastal States as well as some or all of a small group of developed distant water fishing States and entities (China, the EU, Japan, Korea and the US).

The analysis of the rules and practices on participation in RFMOs highlights that a considerable number of the selected RFMOs are essentially 'closed' to all or certain new participants, despite their rights concerning high seas fishing and participation in RFMOs enshrined in the LOS Convention and the Fish Stocks Agreement. As the two newest RFMOs – NPFC and the CAOF Agreement – are part of the group of closed RFMOs, there is certainly no indication of a trend towards openness. This, however, needs to be confirmed or rebutted by practice concerning the application of the formal rules on accession. It should also be acknowledged that the preferential position of existing participants is likely to be even more pronounced when account is also taken of the (very) limited fishing opportunities that seem to be available to new participants of many RFMOs that are essentially 'open'; an issue that is beyond the scope of this chapter.

A crucial question is whether, and, if so, to what extent, the rules and practices of RFMOs on participation that create preferential treatment for existing participants are in conflict with the current global component of international fisheries law. While an explicit right to participate in RFMOs was first recognized

---

[108] SPRFMO Decision 2–2016, para. 3(g); WCPFC Conservation and Management Measure 2009–11, para. 2(g); and Rule 10.5 of the NPFC Rules of Procedure. For a discussion on Cooperating Status with ICCAT, see Spencer, Maguire and Molenaar, note 26 at 64–66.

[109] E.g. the difficulties experienced by Vietnam in renewal of CNM status by WCPFC in 2012–2015 due to the construction of large-scale tuna fishing vessels in Vietnam (e.g. Report of the 12th (2015) Annual WCPFC Session, paras. 65–66).

in Article 8(3) of the Fish Stocks Agreement, this right is reserved for States with a 'real interest'. The absence of a definition for this requirement, or any guidance as to how it should be applied, is already problematic due to the lack of inter-regional uniformity which it was bound to generate. Perhaps even more troublesome, however, is that no specific arrangements were included to guide and restrain RFMOs that assert competence to determine whether or not the real interest requirement is met. The dispute settlement procedures in the domain of international fisheries law can offer little or no help in this regard, as they are insufficiently tailored to the scenarios that arise in relation to participation in RFMOs, for instance because the dispute would have to be brought against all or most Members of the relevant RFMO.[110] No such dispute settlement proceedings on participation in RFMOs have at any rate been instituted so far.

As there seems at present to be insufficient support to address the inability of many States to exercise their right to fish on the high seas in the context of the Resumed Fish Stocks Agreement Review Conferences, the impending negotiations on the BBNJ Implementation Agreement[111] or other global fora within the domain of international fisheries law, change could perhaps come from the regional level. It will be interesting to see if checks and balances, such as the requirement for a Party to the NPFC Convention that opposes an invitation for membership to present its reasons in writing to NPFC,[112] will gradually be accepted as best practice among RFMOs. Pressure for change could also come from outside the domain of international fisheries law. This could for instance arise within the domain of international trade law, whether in the context of a complaint against a Member's implementation of an RFMO's trade measure(s),[113] or perhaps even more directly against an RFMO's rules and practices on participation.

When considering options for change, the utmost care should be taken to avoid outcomes that are ultimately less desirable than the status quo, for instance in terms of over-exploitation. It is therefore also likely that the dilemma on participation in RFMOs cannot be resolved without first addressing the dilemma on the allocation of fishing opportunities for new entrants.[114] Judging by the very slow progress within the IOTC's negotiations towards a quota allocation system, this is no easy hurdle indeed.[115]

[110] See further Serdy, note 59 at 66–67 – in the context of allocation – and EJ Molenaar "Participation, Allocation and Unregulated Fishing: The Practice of Regional Fisheries Management Organizations" (2003) 18 *International Journal of Marine and Coastal Law* 457–480, at 477–479.

[111] The implementation agreement to the LOS Convention on 'the conservation and sustainable use of marine biological diversity of areas beyond national jurisdiction' envisaged by UNGA Res. 72/249 of 24 December 2017.

[112] See note 86 and accompanying text.

[113] As contemplated by N Ferri *Conflicts over the Conservation of Marine Living Resources. Third States, Governance, Fragmentation and Other Recurring Issues in International Law* (G. Giappichelli Editore, Turin: 2015) 234 and Ch III. See also Chapter 14 of this volume (Churchill).

[114] See in this regard Serdy, note 59 at Ch. 5 on quota trading in RFMOs.

[115] The Technical Committee on Allocation Criteria (TCAC) began its work in 2011 and held its fourth meeting in February 2018, but had not yet secured a breakthrough at the time of writing.

Part III

The Ecosystem Approach to Fisheries Management

7

International Fisheries Law and Interactions with Global Regimes and Processes

RICHARD CADDELL*

1. INTRODUCTION

L IKE THE LAW of the sea more generally, international fisheries law is the cumulative product of multiple sources, processes, actors and institutions. Modern international obligations concerning fisheries are derived in the first instance from the LOS Convention,[1] popularly dubbed the 'Constitution for the Oceans'. As with all purported constitutions, however, the LOS Convention requires supplementation and periodic development in order to retain its practical relevance, adapt to changing circumstances and oversee the exercise of its central entitlements. In a fisheries context, the LOS Convention prescribes a general framework wherein States enjoy extensive rights to fish on the high seas[2] and within their respective exclusive economic zones (EEZs),[3] subject to broad obligations concerning the conservation of the stocks in question.[4] As observed in Chapter 1, this framework has evolved further through a suite of instruments developed in the 1990s – namely the Fish Stocks Agreement,[5] the Code of Conduct[6] and the Compliance Agreement[7] – alongside the myriad

* The author gratefully acknowledges the support of the Nereus Program (www.nereusprogram. org) in facilitating the writing of this Chapter.
[1] United Nations Convention on the Law of the Sea of 10 December 1982 (1833 UNTS 3).
[2] Ibid., Arts. 87(1)(a) and 116.
[3] Ibid., Art. 62.
[4] Ibid., Arts. 61 (EEZ) and 117–119 (high seas).
[5] Agreement for the implementation of the Provisions of the United Nations Convention on the Law of the Sea of 10 December 1982 relating to the Conservation and Management of Straddling Fish Stocks and Highly Migratory Fish Stocks of 4 August 1995 (2167 UNTS 3).
[6] Code of Conduct for Responsible Fisheries of 31 October 1995 (1995 WTS 3).
[7] Agreement to Promote Compliance with International Conservation and Management Measures by Fishing Vessels on the High Seas of 24 November 1993 (2221 UNTS 91).

conservation and management measures (CMMs) adopted by regional fisheries management organizations (RFMOs) concerning the various areas and species over which they exercise regulatory competence.

Beyond these cornerstone provisions, a growing number of disparate regimes and processes also exert an under-appreciated influence over the trajectory of international fisheries law. Non-binding aspirations, albeit expressed through the global authority of the United Nations (UN), may establish a clear basis for action against unsustainable and destructive fishing practices. The LOS Convention itself has been periodically re-oriented to address elements that were under-considered at the UNCLOS III negotiations, exemplified by the Fish Stocks Agreement and emerging arrangements for areas beyond national jurisdiction (ABNJ), which has further implications for international fisheries management. Moreover, an array of multilateral instruments concerned with the protection of the marine environment have also sought to mitigate the negative impacts of fisheries upon the ecosystems and species protected under their purviews. Meanwhile, RFMOs may lack the mandate, resources, expertise or inclination to address important matters ancillary to the conduct of fishing, notably labour rights, vessel safety and the welfare of fishers, which are necessarily displaced almost exclusively to the agenda of other actors. The international governance of fisheries may therefore be considerably strengthened by an array of external initiatives beyond the specialized regimes for fisheries management. Thus far, however, there has been relatively little exploration of the extent to which other global regimes and processes have interacted with and impacted upon international fisheries law.

Accordingly, this chapter considers four distinct points of intersection between international fisheries law and other international regimes and processes. Section 2 evaluates the role of the UN General Assembly (UNGA) in formulating regulatory priorities and inspiring further action to regulate elements of fishing in ABNJ. Section 3 outlines the role of Implementation Agreements in the further development of the LOS Convention and their implications for fisheries, including the impending negotiations towards a new International Legally-Binding Instrument (ILBI) for the conservation and sustainable use of biodiversity in ABNJ.[8] Section 4 examines the broadly complementary role of multilateral environmental agreements (MEAs), whereby the development of tactical partnerships with fisheries regulators may further advance the ecosystem approach to fisheries. Section 5 reviews the contribution of the International Labour Organization (ILO) and International Maritime Organization (IMO), with particular reference to labour and vessel management considerations, which have developed largely outside the framework of international fisheries law, while Section 6 concludes.

---

[8] UNGA Resolution 69/292 of 6 July 2015.

2. STRENGTHENING INTERNATIONAL FISHERIES LAW THROUGH GLOBAL REGULATORY OBJECTIVES: THE UN GENERAL ASSEMBLY

The UNGA plays an understated, yet vitally important role in the coordination of the law of the sea and the further development of the LOS Convention,[9] an influence that accordingly extends to the ongoing regulation of international fisheries. Although no specific organizational responsibilities were assigned to the UNGA under the LOS Convention,[10] its quasi-universal membership means that it has nevertheless assumed the mantle of the most convenient forum through which to review the implementation of the Convention and other instruments pertaining to the oceans,[11] in a manner that Oude Elferink argues "under most treaties would be fulfilled by a conference of the parties".[12] Treves attributes this development to a desire among many delegations energized by the UNCLOS III negotiations to retain a globalized platform for the regular discussion of marine issues.[13] Beyond the mere expediency of providing a readily available forum for the consideration of such matters, Boyle observes that formal amendment of the LOS Convention is fraught with practical and procedural difficulty, hence the (re)interpretive value of UNGA Resolutions may be quietly significant in the evolution of this regime.[14]

Aside from internal organizational matters, the eclectic collection of Resolutions adopted annually by the UNGA are not legally binding. However, this does not divest them of broader regulatory importance. Indeed, UNGA Resolutions exert a significant influence over the subsequent activities of States and regional and global bodies and are thus "negotiated as seriously as international agreements".[15] Accordingly, UNGA Resolutions are not orthodox law-making tools,

---

[9] See L de la Fayette "The Role of the United Nations in International Oceans Governance" in D Freestone, R Barnes and D Ong (eds.) *The Law of the Sea: Progress and Prospects* (Oxford University Press, Oxford: 2006) 63–74, 69 and J Harrison *Making the Law of the Sea: A Study in the Development of International Law* (Cambridge University Press, Cambridge: 2013) 250–252.

[10] Under Art. 319, depositary functions and other administrative tasks are assigned to the UN Secretary-General. In a fisheries context, the Secretary-General plays a vital role in reporting on the implementation of UNGA commitments.

[11] J Harrison "The Law of the Sea Convention Institutions" in DR Rothwell, AG Oude Elferink, KN Scott and T Stephens (eds.) *The Oxford Handbook of the Law of the Sea* (Oxford University Press, Oxford: 2015) 373–393, 389.

[12] AG Oude Elferink "Reviewing the Implementation of the LOS Convention: The Role of the United Nations General Assembly and the Meeting of States Parties" in AG Oude Elferink and DR Rothwell (eds.) *Oceans Management in the 21st Century: Institutional Frameworks and Responses* (Martinus Nijhoff, Leiden/Boston: 2004) 295–312, at 304.

[13] T Treves "The General Assembly and the Meeting of the States Parties in the Implementation of the LOS Convention" in AG Oude Elferink (ed.) *Stability and Change in the Law of the Sea: The Role of the LOS Convention* (Martinus Nijhoff, Leiden/Boston: 2005) 55–74, at 61.

[14] A Boyle "Further Development of the Law of the Sea Convention: Mechanisms for Change" (2005) 54 *International and Comparative Law Quarterly* 563–584, at 572–574.

[15] de la Fayette, note 9 at 69. In response to concerns over time constraints, since 2006 the annual UNGA discussions on the two core marine Resolutions have been capped at a maximum of four weeks to ensure focus and to avoid overlaps with other meetings: Resolution 60/30 of 8 March 2006 (para. 111).

but from a fisheries standpoint they exert a more nuanced influence on state practice by "drawing attention to the current threats to fish stocks and encouraging international efforts taking place in other institutions to address them".[16] Moreover, unlike the resolutions and recommendations of the executive bodies of treaties, a significant operational advantage of the UNGA is its ability to direct particular issues to the attention of other specialized bodies of the UN.[17] For example, UNGA Resolutions have proved valuable in directing the IMO to cooperate fully with the United Nations Food and Agriculture Organization (FAO) on illegal, unreported and unregulated (IUU) fishing,[18] and the ILO to focus further on improving labour standards for fishing vessels.[19]

In any given year, the UNGA adopts two standing Resolutions of particular relevance to fisheries, namely the 'Sustainable Fisheries' Resolution and its more general Resolution on 'Oceans and the Law of the Sea' ('Oceans'). The former is self-evidently oriented towards addressing deficiencies in the development and implementation of international fisheries law, especially concerning the high seas, while the latter addresses fisheries matters through the broader lens of oceans governance. The Oceans Resolution is considered to provide an opportunity to contemplate particular issues that were not foreseen at the time of the UNCLOS III negotiations.[20] It thus constitutes an important tool to facilitate the progressive development of a treaty that was always intended to mature organically to adapt to changing circumstances. As both Resolutions have expanded considerably, many of the fisheries-related issues raised in previous Oceans Resolutions have steadily migrated into the text of successive Sustainable Fisheries Resolutions. Nevertheless, particular items of relevance to the strengthening of international fisheries law have remained as consistent themes within the Oceans Resolutions, including recognition of the scientific value of fisheries data, the need for universal participation in the Fish Stocks Agreement, concerns over labour issues and the protection of seafarers and the need for further institutional cooperation.[21]

The Sustainable Fisheries Resolution has evolved from a specific pronouncement made in 1989 on the threats posed by proliferating driftnet fisheries (considered further below), subsequently incorporating the review of these initiatives and two separate Resolutions on unauthorized fishing in zones of national jurisdiction[22] and bycatches and discards,[23] before being repackaged in its current format in 2003 to include consideration of the Fish Stocks Agreement.[24]

---

[16] Harrison, note 9 at 204.
[17] Oude Elferink, note 12 at 305–306.
[18] Resolution 55/8 of 2 March 2001, para. 16.
[19] Resolution 58/240 of 5 March 2004, para. 31.
[20] D Diz Pereira Pinto *Fisheries Management in Areas Beyond National Jurisdiction: The Impact of Ecosystem-Based Law-Making* (Martinus Nijhoff, Leiden/Boston: 2013) 65; Treves, note 13 at 58.
[21] See most recently Resolution 72/73 of 4 January 2018.
[22] Resolution 49/116 of 19 December 1994.
[23] Resolution 49/118 of 19 December 1994.
[24] Resolution 57/141 of 21 February 2003.

In recent years, the Sustainable Fisheries Resolution has provided a general forum to focus political attention upon the ecological impact of global fisheries and IUU activities, as well as reviewing progress towards specific commitments established in earlier Resolutions, exemplified in Subsection 2.2 below. While the review function of the Sustainable Fisheries Resolution is non-contentious, as are the general exhortations towards the ratification of international fisheries instruments, hard-fought discussions underpin the commitments established in the Resolution and the manner in which they are expressed.[25] Moreover, concerns have been raised in some quarters over the perceived endorsement by these Resolutions for RFMOs to exercise authority over non-Members and States that have not consented to such measures.[26]

Beyond these general considerations, the Sustainable Fisheries Resolution and its early predecessors have provided a valuable impetus to address destructive fishing practices, with tangible regulatory outcomes apparent in two key instances. Respectively, these involve curtailing the use of large-scale pelagic driftnets on the high seas and protecting vulnerable marine ecosystems (VMEs), especially those located in ABNJ in deep-water locations that have been threatened by the poorly regulated spread of bottom fishing.

2.1. The Regulation of Large-scale Pelagic Driftnet Fishing

An intriguing precedent was set for strengthening international fisheries law through the UNGA in the early 1990s in response to strong concerns over the proliferation of driftnets. Due to their propensity to take large numbers of juvenile fish and non-target species as bycatch, modern driftnets remain a controversial form of fishing gear.[27] Driftnets were historically ubiquitous in many coastal fisheries and were long viewed as highly sustainable, since they were usually small and primarily constructed from biodegradable materials. However, subsequent technological developments allowed for the manufacture of synthetic netting on an immense scale. Although largely concentrated in particular locations, by the mid-1980s high seas driftnetting capacity had proliferated far beyond its initial in-shore application, with nets extending for up to 60km in some instances, generating opprobrium over wholesale bycatches and pervasive nautical obstruction.[28]

---

[25] E.g. there is considerable disagreement over the desirability of recognizing IUU fishing as a form of transnational organized crime within these Resolutions: see Chapter 17 of this volume (Caddell, Leloudas and Soyer).

[26] See e.g. the views expressed in UN Doc. A/65/PV.59.

[27] A Wright and DJ Doulman "Driftnet Fishing in the South Pacific: From Controversy to Management" (1991) 15 *Marine Policy* 303–329, at 313–314.

[28] MR Islam "The Proposed 'Driftnet-Free' Zone in the South Pacific and the Law of the Sea Convention" (1991) 40 *International and Comparative Law Quarterly* 184–198, at 184.

International opposition to driftnet fishing first emerged in the South Pacific[29] through the adoption of the 1989 Tarawa Declaration,[30] which sought to curtail large-scale driftnets in the region. Following the breakdown of regional negotiations towards voluntary restrictions, the 1989 Wellington Convention[31] limited the maximum length of driftnets in the South Pacific to 2.5km.[32] Parallel concerns were expressed in other regions and concurrent with the adoption of the Wellington Convention, the Organisation of Eastern Caribbean States (OECS) issued the Castries Declaration[33] advocating similar restrictions. These initiatives placed large-scale driftnet fishing firmly on the international agenda and a number of influential coastal States began to advocate a global moratorium on large-scale driftnet fishing.

The process by which large-scale driftnet fishing was ultimately curtailed through the UNGA is an illuminating saga of environmental politics and the development of legal norms. In December 1989 two very different motions on driftnet fishing were tabled in the UNGA by the United States (US) and Japan.[34] The US proposal called for a three-year phase out of driftnet fishing vessels culminating in a global moratorium from June 1992, while the Japanese initiative advocated a comparatively limited series of restraints. A compromise was eventually reached, loosely contemplating a future global moratorium on large-scale driftnet fishing,[35] which was to be discontinued in the South Pacific forthwith.[36] The specific recognition of the South Pacific was significant, since despite the political agitation from within this region, driftnet fishing activities were more heavily concentrated in the North Pacific, hence this consensus was largely the product of shrewd political bargaining. Nevertheless, it prompted the swift cessation of large-scale driftnet fishing in the South Pacific in the manner envisaged by the Wellington Convention by those States that had steadfastly refused to engage with these earlier regional provisions. A global moratorium was subsequently imposed on such netting on the high seas effective from 31 December 1992.[37]

---

[29] See further GJ Hewison "High Seas Driftnet Fishing in the South Pacific and the Law of the Sea" (1993) 5 *Georgetown International Environmental Law Review* 313–374, at 316–22 and B Miller "Combating Drift-Net Fishing in the Pacific" in J Crawford and DR Rothwell (eds.) *The Law of the Sea in the Asian Pacific Region: Developments and Prospects* (Martinus Nijhoff, Leiden/Boston: 1995) 155–174, at 161.

[30] (1990) 14 *LOSB* 29.

[31] Convention for the Prohibition of Fishing with Long Driftnets in the South Pacific of 24 November 1989 (1899 UNTS 3).

[32] Art. 1(b).

[33] (1990) 14 *LOSB* 28.

[34] See DR Rothwell "The General Assembly Ban on Driftnet Fishing" in D Shelton (ed.) *Commitment and Compliance: The Role of Non-Binding Norms in the International Legal System* (Oxford University Press, Oxford: 2003) 121–146, at 126–131.

[35] This concept was not defined in Resolution 44/225, but has subsequently been widely interpreted as netting above 2.5km in length as specified in the Wellington Convention, which is in turn attributed to the earlier equivalent US restrictions introduced in the 1987 Driftnet Impact Monitoring, Assessment and Control Act: 16 U.S.C. §1822.

[36] Resolution 44/225 of 22 December 1989, para. 4.

[37] Resolution 46/215 of 20 December 1991.

While non-binding in nature, a striking number of RFMOs and other regulatory actors swiftly adopted measures to give effect to the tenor of the UNGA driftnet Resolutions in the high seas.[38] These standards were also enshrined within the domestic legislation of numerous States,[39] whereby the responses of the main driftnet fishing States are particularly noteworthy. Japan, the chief opponent of these restrictions, nevertheless considered the overwhelming support for the UNGA Resolutions as representing the institutionalization of a norm against driftnet fishing, which as a member of the international community it felt compelled to follow.[40] South Korea and Taiwan also followed suit, although unlike Japan, neither State was a Member of the UN at the material time. Instead, South Korea, which subsequently joined the UN in 1991, initially accepted these restrictions through its practice within the International Whaling Commission (IWC), which had adopted a Resolution to further its own adherence to the UNGA Resolutions.[41] Meanwhile Taiwan, which has remained unable to obtain UN membership, unilaterally deregistered all domestic driftnet vessels, although these subsequently stateless craft continued to operate as a rogue fleet for a period of months.[42] Given the near-universal adherence to these standards, the UNGA driftnet restrictions have arguably exerted "a greater impact on the actual behaviour of states than many ostensible legal norms"[43] and have been considered in some quarters to represent customary international law.[44]

While the UNGA driftnet Resolutions are rightly lauded as a prominent example of their utility in influencing regulatory trends, these provisions have not proved unproblematic. Indeed, commentators have raised concerns that the "bully pulpit"[45] of the UNGA is an unsuitable forum for the development

[38] See further Chapter 8 of this volume (Scott) and GJ Hewison "The Legally Binding Nature of the Moratorium on Large-Scale High Seas Driftnet Fishing" (1994) 25 *Journal of Maritime Law and Commerce* 557–580.

[39] Rothwell, note 34 at 142–143. Indeed, where divergent approaches to these standards have been adopted, it has been to adopt more, rather than less, stringent requirements. Notably, the European Union (EU) has fully banned the use of driftnets in particular fisheries: see R Caddell "The Prohibition of Driftnet Fishing in European Community Waters: Problems, Progress and Prospects" (2007) 13 *Journal of International Maritime Law* 265–288, at 271–278.

[40] I Miyaoka *Legitimacy in International Society: Japan's Response to Global Wildlife Preservation* (Palgrave, Basingstoke: 2004) 65.

[41] IWC Resolution 1990–6: Resolution in Support of the United Nations General Assembly Initiative Regarding Large-Scale Pelagic Driftnet Fishing and Its Impact on the Living Marine Resources of the World's Oceans and Seas; see further Miller, note 29 at 166.

[42] TL McDorman "Stateless Fishing Vessels, International Law and the UN High Seas Fisheries Conference" (1994) 25 *Journal of Maritime Law and Commerce* 531–555, at 533.

[43] D Bodansky *The Art and Craft of International Environmental Law* (Harvard University Press, Cambridge, Massachusetts: 2010) 15.

[44] Hewison, note 38 at 578–580.

[45] WT Burke, M Freeberg and EL Miles "United Nations Resolutions on Driftnet Fishing: An Unsustainable Precedent for High Seas and Coastal Fisheries Management" (1994) 25 *Ocean Development and International Law* 127–186, at 137.

of technical fisheries standards. Moreover, certain coastal States, while ostensibly accepting the driftnet fishing restrictions, have sought to undermine these provisions through definitional semantics in national legislation, allowing for the continued deployment of driftnets with largely cosmetic modifications. This practice, which was largely confined to the Mediterranean region, required the stern judicial intervention of the EU, although the slow operation of its enforcement machinery meant that such nets were still widely used for a number of years.[46] More significantly, the role of the US in bolstering these restrictions should not be overlooked. Indeed, through the extraterritorial application of its fisheries legislation, which prescribes considerable scope to act against foreign vessels,[47] the US has maintained the spectre of trade measures against States that continue to use driftnets in contravention of the UNGA standards.[48] The US has ultimately stopped short of imposing such sanctions, but has previously contemplated their application against Japan and Italy.[49] Accordingly, and certainly in the years immediately following its institution, the UNGA moratorium on large-scale pelagic driftnet fishing on the high seas has in practice maintained an under-appreciated reliance upon the latent threat of trade sanctions to secure its transformative effect upon state practice.

2.2. Bottom Fishing and the Protection of Vulnerable Marine Ecosystems

In a similar vein, standards to address the impacts of bottom fishing upon VMEs in areas beyond national jurisdiction (ABNJ) have also emerged from a clear mandate established through UNGA Resolutions. Since the 1960s, fisheries have steadily progressed into offshore areas and deeper waters, as shallow-water stocks have become increasingly depleted and fishers have been accordingly forced to pursue alternative opportunities.[50] Acute regulatory tensions have subsequently arisen over the continued expansion of bottom fishing[51] into ABNJ and at unprecedented depths. The proliferation of these fisheries continued

---

[46] R Caddell "Caught in the Net: Driftnet Fishing Restrictions and the European Court of Justice" (2010) 22 *Journal of Environmental Law* 301–314, at 307–312.

[47] See especially Driftnet Impact Monitoring, Assessment and Control Act 1987, 16 U.S.C. §1822; Driftnet Act Amendments 1990, 16 U.S.C. §1826; and High Seas Driftnet Fishing Moratorium Protection Act 1995, 16 U.S.C. §1826g.

[48] On the concerns raised by this approach see Chapters 13 (van der Marel) and 14 (Churchill) of this volume.

[49] Rothwell, note 34 at 142–144. There has been deep official reluctance to do so however, and the extensive standing accorded to environmental NGOs under the legislation to trigger executive action has led to diplomatic wrangling to avert the threat of sanctions for continued driftnet fishing: see further Chapter 16 of this volume (Massarella).

[50] T Morato et al. "Fishing Down The Deep" (2006) 7 *Fish and Fisheries* 24–34, at 31.

[51] Bottom fishing is generally defined as the use of gear "that either contact or are likely to contact the sea floor during the course of the fishing operation": A Bensch et al. *Worldwide Review of Bottom Fisheries in the High Seas* (FAO, Rome: 2009) 2.

largely unchecked until the late 20th century, when opposition began to mobilize against the use of an array of destructive fishing gear. By the late 1990s, bottom fisheries – especially those using heavy trawl nets dragged along the seabed itself, or across seamounts and other fragile benthic features known to entice sizeable aggregations of fish – had attracted international notoriety. Nevertheless, by the turn of the 21st century, although a number of bodies had expressed strong concerns over these practices, there appeared to be little obvious forum through which regulatory standards might be further developed.[52]

The UNGA driftnet Resolutions provided a helpful regulatory template with which to address the growing international concerns over the impacts of deep-sea bottom fishing. Following a series of discussions in other fora, in 2004 the UNGA duly adopted its first major Resolution addressing elements of the deep-sea environment.[53] In four core paragraphs, Resolution 59/25 lamented a general lack of regulatory competence for the regulation of particular marine ecosystems and called upon a variety of actors to seek to rectify these governance challenges as a matter of priority, calling upon States to apply the precautionary approach to prohibit "destructive fishing practices, including bottom trawling that has adverse impacts on vulnerable marine ecosystems", until appropriate conservation and management measures have been adopted.[54]

This represents the inaugural (and undefined) use of the term "vulnerable marine ecosystem", which has subsequently become a notable and ubiquitous addition to the lexicon of global marine governance. The commitment to seek the interim prohibition of destructive fishing practices on a case-by-case basis nonetheless fell short of the moratorium on particular fisheries in ABNJ that had been strongly advocated by activists – and had indeed been initially present in earlier drafts of the Resolution.[55] Resolution 59/25 called upon those RFMOs with competence over bottom fisheries to "urgently" adopt conservation and management measures in accordance with international law to address destructive fishing practices, including bottom fishing that has adverse impacts on VMEs and to ensure compliance with such measures. Prospectively, the Members of RFMOs that lacked these competences at the time were requested to extend these pre-existing mandates to regulate bottom fisheries,[56] while the

---

[52] On these difficulties, see further LA Kimball "Deep-Sea Fisheries of the High Seas: The Management Impasse" (2004) 19 *International Journal of Marine and Coastal Law* 259–287; EJ Molenaar "Addressing Regulatory Gaps in High Seas Fisheries" (2005) 20 *International Journal of Marine and Coastal Law* 533–570; and R Caddell "International Environmental Governance and the Final Frontier: The Protection of Vulnerable Marine Ecosystems in Deep-Sea Areas beyond National Jurisdiction" (2018) 29 *Yearbook of International Environmental Law* 1–36.

[53] Resolution 59/25 of 17 November 2004.

[54] Ibid., para. 66.

[55] Y Takei *Filling Regulatory Gaps in High Seas Fisheries: Discrete High Seas Fish Stocks, Deep-Sea Fisheries and Vulnerable Marine Ecosystems* (Martinus Nijhoff, Leiden/Boston: 2013) 113.

[56] Resolution 59/25, para. 68. These operative paragraphs are not entirely coherent and consistent, with para. 67 referencing bottom fisheries with regard to addressing all types of destructive fishing, while paras. 68 and 69 refer only to bottom fishing and VMEs. The repetitive and poorly-edited

international community was urged to cooperate in the creation of new RFMOs for unregulated areas of the global oceans, which would be endowed with these powers *ab initio* and thereby be able to address deep-sea fishing as an immediate operative priority upon their inception.

In 2006, a further and arguably more influential Resolution was adopted by the UNGA, expressing dissatisfaction with the rate of progress since 2004 and calling for steps to be taken "immediately" to sustainably manage deep-sea fish stocks and VMEs.[57] Significantly, paragraph 83 of Resolution 61/105 listed for the first time a series of targeted action points for RFMOs to complete, notably the assessment of whether individual bottom fishing activities have significant adverse impacts on vulnerable marine ecosystems, and to ensure that if so they are managed to prevent such impacts, or not authorized to proceed; to identify vulnerable marine ecosystems and determine whether bottom fishing activities would cause significant adverse impacts to such ecosystems; to close such areas to bottom fishing and ensure that such activities do not proceed unless conservation and management measures have been established to prevent significant adverse impacts; and to require RFMOs to cease bottom fishing where VMEs are encountered.[58]

Resolution 61/105 therefore represents a more nuanced series of restrictions upon bottom fisheries, whereby such commitments are triggered only where there is a threat of a significant adverse impact (SAI) on VMEs. The regulatory onus is therefore placed upon identifying locations within which VMEs are present and in establishing a precautionary requirement for vessels to cease fishing upon encountering such features, or that these areas are pre-emptively closed to bottom fishing until it may be established that no such encounters are likely to result from either commercial or exploratory fishing activities. In principle, this allows for the co-existence of fisheries and environmental restrictions in ABNJ identified as susceptible to the adverse impacts of deep-sea bottom fishing if not managed proactively.

Nevertheless, Resolution 61/105 raised a series of immediate interpretive difficulties, since the threshold by which a marine ecosystem may be considered 'vulnerable' and an adverse impact deemed 'significant' – and, indeed, the precise circumstances under which an 'encounter' may be considered to have occurred in the first place – was not defined further, hence the FAO was called upon to elaborate detailed practical guidance on these issues.[59] Resolution 61/105

---

wording afflicting these key paragraphs of Resolution 59/25 is attributed to "its compromise nature and the fact that it does not contain the clear-cut prohibition on bottom fishing in areas beyond national jurisdiction that some UN Member States and NGOs had sought": R Churchill and D Owen *The EC Common Fisheries Policy* (Oxford University Press, Oxford: 2010) 121.

[57] UNGA Resolution 61/105 of 8 December 2006, para. 80.

[58] On the area-based management of VMEs, see further Chapter 9 of this volume (Dunn, Ortuño Crespo and Caddell).

[59] Resolution 61/105, para. 89.

also recommended the expedited development of interim measures to address locations without operational RFMO coverage[60] and, for the first time, directed specific action points to States in areas for which no competent authority was in existence, whereby flag States were requested to cease the national authorization of fishing vessels in ABNJ without a competent RFMO or to unilaterally introduce measures applicable to nationally-registered ships to implement the broad commitments advanced therein.[61]

In 2008, following an extensive technical consultation process, the FAO adopted an influential set of international Guidelines to frame the practical implementation of the relevant UNGA Resolutions for fisheries exploiting deep-sea species "in a targeted or incidental manner".[62] The Guidelines expressly address ABNJ – although States are also encouraged to adopt these approaches where appropriate within their national waters[63] – and are applicable to fisheries for which the total catch includes species that can only sustain low exploitation rates and the fishing gear used in this process is likely to contact the seafloor during the course of fishing operations.[64] The overarching objectives of the Guidelines are therefore to ensure the long-term and sustainable use of marine living resources in the deep-sea and to prevent significant adverse impacts upon VMEs in the process.[65] States and RFMOs are requested to adopt and implement measures consistent with the precautionary and ecosystem approaches to fisheries management to identify areas in which VMEs are known or likely to occur and to take action using the best available information.[66]

The Guidelines were swiftly endorsed by the UNGA, which called upon States to act to secure their implementation "immediately, individually and through regional fisheries management organizations and arrangements".[67] Nevertheless it was observed that the operative paragraphs of the previous UNGA Resolutions had "not been sufficiently implemented in all cases".[68] Accordingly, Resolution 64/72 reiterated the action points called for in Resolution 61/105, adding a further commitment to promote the adoption of conservation and management measures to ensure the long-term sustainability of deep-sea stocks

---

[60] Ibid., para. 85.

[61] Ibid., para. 86.

[62] *International Guidelines for the Management of Deep-Sea Fisheries in the High Seas* (FAO, Rome: 2008) para. 5.

[63] Indeed, approximately 58 per cent of the Australian EEZ has been subsequently closed to bottom trawling in response to these developments: TK Mazor et al. "Trawl Exposure and Protection of Seabed Fauna at Large Spatial Scales" (2017) 23 *Diversity and Distributions* 1280–1291, at 1288.

[64] *International Guidelines for the Management of Deep-Sea Fisheries in the High Seas*, para. 8. The total catch is defined herein as "everything brought up by the gear", reinforcing the notion that the Guidelines ought to be applied even where deep-sea species are taken incidentally.

[65] Ibid., para. 11.

[66] Ibid., para. 12.

[67] Resolution 64/72 of 4 December 2009, para. 113.

[68] Ibid., para. 118.

and associated species, particularly through setting appropriate levels for fishing effort, capacity and catch limits.[69] This was reinforced in 2011, wherein the UNGA observed that "despite the progress made, the urgent actions called for in the relevant paragraphs of resolutions 61/105 and 64/72 have not been fully implemented in all cases".[70] In a notable departure from the previous instruments, Resolution 66/68 further called for the strengthening of assessment procedures so as "to take into account individual, collective and cumulative impacts, and for making the assessments publicly available, recognizing that doing so can support transparency and capacity-building globally".[71]

In this manner, an evolving suite of priority activities has thus been established across a series of UNGA Resolutions, which have been implemented by the expanding cohort of RFMOs exercising competence over deep-sea fisheries. These requirements have prompted many RFMOs to restrict bottom trawling to areas of historical activity and to insist upon proposed extensions to these national footprints to be subject to prior approval and to be conducted under exploratory conditions, with commitments to observer coverage and the submission of agreed volumes of data.[72] Many RFMOs have also instituted a series of area closures to protect VMEs in line with the UNGA Resolutions,[73] although criticism remains that such measures have required an onerous amount of scientific data to become operational and have been prioritized in areas within which little or no fishing is undertaken.[74] Similarly, with the exception of the Commission for the Conservation of Atlantic Marine Living Resources (CCAMLR) and the South Pacific Regional Fisheries Management Organization (SPRFMO), the environmental assessments called for under the UNGA Resolutions have left much to be desired, especially with regard to consideration of cumulative impacts.[75]

These operational deficiencies notwithstanding, the UNGA VME Resolutions can be considered to have strengthened international fisheries law markedly by providing guiding principles where regulatory efforts had largely

[69] Ibid., para. 119(d).

[70] Resolution 66/68 of 6 December 2011, para. 129.

[71] Ibid., para. 129(a).

[72] For a full accounting of RFMO practices in this respect, see R Caddell "Precautionary Management and the Development of Future Fishing Opportunities: The International Regulation of New and Exploratory Fisheries" (2018) 33 *International Journal of Marine and Coastal Law* 199–260, at 253–258.

[73] See further Chapter 9 of this volume (Dunn, Ortuño Crespo and Caddell) and Caddell, note 52 at 28–30.

[74] G Wright et al. "Advancing Marine Biodiversity Protection through Regional Fisheries Management: A Review of Bottom Fisheries Closures in Areas beyond National Jurisdiction" (2015) 61 *Marine Policy* 134–148, at 146.

[75] Actions taken by States and regional fisheries management organizations and arrangements in response to paragraphs 80 and 83 to 87 of General Assembly resolution 61/105 and paragraphs 113 to 117 and 119 to 127 of General Assembly resolution 64/72 on sustainable fisheries, addressing the impacts of bottom fishing on vulnerable marine ecosystems and the long-term sustainability of deep-sea fish stocks: Report of the Secretary-General, UN Doc. A/66/307, para. 158.

stagnated due to limitations in the mandates of RFMOs and the lack of an obvious forum for the development of such commitments. In particular, they have proved instrumental in closing significant governance gaps in high seas fisheries, with the RFMOs established in the present century having expressly included consideration of VMEs within their respective mandates as a result. This is clearly illustrated by the North Pacific Fisheries Commission (NPFC), whereby the Preamble to its constituent treaty expressly references the relevant UNGA Resolutions, while the prevention of significant adverse impacts from fisheries upon VMEs is established as a 'general principle' for this body.[76] Similarly, consideration of VMEs is established as a specific aspect of the mandate of the scientific fora of SPRFMO.[77] More significantly, perhaps, the conclusion of these instruments was preceded by a series of interim arrangements focused on the regulation of bottom fishing in these areas. Likewise, flag States have also used the UNGA commitments as a basis for unilaterally addressing bottom fishing by nationally-registered vessels in areas in which no such protection has been instituted multilaterally. This is strikingly exemplified by the EU, which has adopted a Regulation specifically addressing the actions of its Member States in ABNJ for which no RFMO has been established or where interim measures have not yet been agreed for the protection of VMEs.[78]

3. STRENGTHENING INTERNATIONAL FISHERIES LAW BY DEVELOPING THE LOS CONVENTION: THE ROLE OF IMPLEMENTATION AGREEMENTS

While the UNGA Oceans and Sustainable Fisheries Resolutions provide a regular opportunity to consider particular issues that were overlooked or emerged subsequent to the UNCLOS III negotiations, alternative avenues exist to further develop the LOS Convention in a manner that may also strengthen international fisheries law. One particularly valuable mechanism in this respect is the use of implementation agreements, which provides a means of amending and/or clarifying key elements of these provisions. Thus far, two such instruments

---

[76] Convention on the Conservation and Management of High Seas Fisheries Resources in the North Pacific Ocean of 1 April 2012 (www.npfc.int/about_npfc/convention_and_npfc_area_of_application), Preamble and Art. 3(e).

[77] Convention on the Conservation and Management of High Seas Fishery Resources in the South Pacific Ocean of 14 November 2009 (2012 ATS 28), Art. 11.

[78] Council Regulation (EC) No. 735/2008 of 15 July 2008 on the protection of vulnerable marine ecosystems in the high seas from the adverse impacts of bottom fishing gears [2008] OJ L201/8. This was introduced primarily to address fishing in the South-East Atlantic, where political complications have stymied efforts to establish an RFMO. Spain, as the Member State most active in these waters, has subsequently closed nine separate areas to bottom fishing by its vessels on this basis. Nevertheless, further unilateral regulation by the EU in the North-East Atlantic has raised concerns that such measures could unduly influence VME regulation through the North-East Atlantic Fisheries Commission (NEAFC): GA Oanta "International Organizations and Deep-Sea Fisheries: Current Status and Future Prospects" (2018) 87 *Marine Policy* 51–59, at 57.

have been adopted: the Deep-Seabed Mining Agreement[79] and the Fish Stocks Agreement. Negotiations towards a third implementation agreement, concerning the conservation and sustainable management of marine biological diversity beyond areas of national jurisdiction (BBNJ Process), will commence in September 2018.[80]

As observed in Chapter 1 of this volume (Molenaar and Caddell), while the LOS Convention establishes a basic framework to elucidate rights and duties over fishing, this has required considerable supplementation by a suite of global fisheries instruments. This is particularly true in the case of straddling and highly migratory fish stocks, the legal status of which generated considerable discord at the UNCLOS III negotiations. A compromise was eventually brokered through the rather nebulous phrasing of Article 63, which requires States to "seek, either directly or through appropriate sub-regional or regional organisations to agree on the measures necessary" for the conservation of such stocks. Following further discussions within the UNGA, a mandate was established to convene a Conference to address the regulation of these stocks in a manner "fully consistent with the United Nations Convention on the Law of the Sea".[81] The Conference was open to all States, following which the Fish Stocks Agreement was adopted by consensus in August 1995 and entered into force on 11 December 2011.

This mandate has ensured that the Fish Stocks Agreement remains a very different legal animal to the preceding Deep-Seabed Mining Agreement. In the first place, unlike the Deep-Seabed Mining Agreement, the Fish Stocks Agreement is a free-standing treaty, open to participation by all States,[82] irrespective of ratification of the LOS Convention. Moreover, the legal relationship between the LOS Convention and Fish Stocks Agreement is also distinct. Unlike the Deep-Seabed Mining Agreement, which is to be "interpreted and applied together as a single instrument"[83] with the LOS Convention, the Fish Stocks Agreement "shall be interpreted and applied in the context of and in a manner consistent with" the 1982 Convention.[84] In many respects, the term 'implementation agreement' is a misnomer in the context of the Deep-Seabed Mining Agreement, its titular designation essentially representing a political fig-leaf for a document that expressly amended key elements of the LOS Convention to secure its palatability to key coastal States, rather than facilitating the implementation of particular provisions as is the purpose of the Fish Stocks Agreement.[85] The UNFSA is

---

[79] Agreement Relating to the Implementation of Part XI of the LOS Convention of 10 December 1982 of 28 July (1836 UNTS 42).

[80] UNGA Resolution 72/249 of 24 December 2017, para. 3.

[81] UNGA Resolution 47/192 of 22 December 1992, para. 3.

[82] FSA Agreement, Art. 1(2).

[83] Art. 2 of the Deep-Seabed Mining Agreement.

[84] Fish Stock Agreement, Art. 4.

[85] RR Churchill "The 1982 United Nations Convention on the Law of the Sea" in Rothwell, Oude Elferink, Scott and Stephens, note 11, 24–45 at 27.

instead generally considered by commentators to have developed these provisions in the light of subsequent developments in international environmental law.[86] This is not, however, a view shared by all constituents. Indeed, some States, notably those of South America, consider that certain elements of the Fish Stocks Agreement serve to amend rather than interpret the LOS Convention and are therefore inconsistent with the latter treaty, accordingly precluding their ratification of the 1995 instrument.[87]

The Fish Stocks Agreement does not elaborate substantive measures for the conduct of fishing; rather, it lays down the jurisdictional framework for the regulation of such stocks. In this respect, notable provisions include the establishment of an ecosystem approach to fishing, based *inter alia* on considering the inter-dependence of stocks and the surrounding environment, using the best scientific evidence to promote the long-term sustainability of the stocks, minimizing pollution, bycatch, waste and discards, protecting marine biodiversity, instituting measures to eliminate overfishing and overcapacity and considering the interests of artisanal and subsistence fishers.[88] Article 6 also establishes a precautionary approach to the conservation, management and exploitation of straddling and highly migratory stocks, inspired largely by its provenance in Agenda 21.[89] This provision also incorporated burgeoning elements of best practice from other regulatory regimes, notably the requirement to proceed with particular care in the context of new and exploratory fisheries, which was inspired by contemporaneous developments within CCAMLR.[90] Significantly, the Fish Stocks Agreement elaborates the primary functions of RFMOs, which are the intended vehicle through which the instrument is to be implemented, thereby casting particular light on the previously cryptic intent of Article 63.[91]

In addition to further expanding the broad principles for fisheries management under the LOS Convention, the Fish Stocks Agreement has had a dramatic effect upon the emergence of new RFMOs and the strength of the environmental obligations advanced by their respective mandates. At the material time, there were significant lacunae in the governance of international fisheries, with many pre-existing RFMOs addressing only single species, such as tuna or salmon, while large swathes of the ocean were otherwise devoid of RFMO oversight. In this respect, the entry into effect of the Fish Stocks Agreement has inspired the emergence of an array of new RFMOs, often preceded by interim arrangements, which have advanced the ecosystem approach more centrally within their constituent treaties.

---

[86] Harrison, note 9 at 104; Churchill, ibid., 43.
[87] EJ Molenaar "Non-Participation in the Fish Stocks Agreement: Status and Reasons" (2011) 26 *International Journal of Marine and Coastal Law* 195–234, 201.
[88] Fish Stocks Agreement, Art. 5.
[89] Harrison, note 9 at 105.
[90] Fish Stocks Agreement, Art. 6(6). On the development of this provision see Caddell, note 72 at 208–213.
[91] Ibid., Arts. 8–14.

One striking example in this regard is SPRFMO where, at a preliminary stage in the negotiations, it was determined that this emergent regime would transcend the basic principles of the Fish Stocks Agreement, which was seen as a useful regulatory template but representative only of minimum requirements for fisheries management.[92] The resulting formulation of the SPRFMO Convention has been duly lauded as having "raised the legal standard for international fisheries management".[93] Equally significant has been the response of older structures, some of which have expressly sought to retro-fit these principles into their pre-1995 mandates. A prominent example of this approach is the Northwest Atlantic Fisheries Organization (NAFO), which adopted a series of extensive textual revisions to its constituent treaty in 2007 to promote an ecosystem approach to fisheries management, which eventually entered into effect on 18 May 2017.[94] Moreover, throughout this interim period, many of these obligations had been applied provisionally,[95] which enabled NAFO to institute proactive regulation for VMEs in the light of the UNGA Resolutions, as outlined above. A similar approach has been adopted by the International Commission on the Conservation of Atlantic Tunas (ICCAT), again to incorporate a more central recognition of the principles enunciated in the Fish Stocks Agreement and to pursue a protective regime for VMEs as promoted through the relevant UNGA commitments.[96]

A further practical benefit of the Fish Stocks Agreement is derived from Article 36, which makes provision for a conference to review the implementation of the Agreement. Three such instalments have been convened to date, in 2006, 2010 and 2016 respectively, with a further session scheduled for 2021. The resumed Review Conference provides a forum to identify operational priorities and to signal areas of success and failure in the application of the Agreement. These sessions are also supported by rounds of Informal Consultations of the States Parties (ICSP), which have proved to be quietly influential in progressing the work of the Agreement. Indeed, in 2016, following discussions in this forum, the resumed Review Conference considered for the first time the labour rights

---

[92] Takei, note 55 at 210–211.

[93] Report of the resumed Review Conference on the Agreement for the Implementation of the Provisions of the United Nations Convention on the Law of the Sea of 10 December 1982 relating to the Conservation and Management of Straddling Fish Stocks and Highly Migratory Fish Stocks, Doc. A/CONF/210/2010/7, para. 37.

[94] Convention on Cooperation in the Northwest Atlantic fisheries of 24 October 1978 (1135 UNTS 369); consolidated version available at www.nafo.int/Portals/0/PDFs/key-publications/NAFOConvention-2017.pdf.

[95] Indeed, the 2007 amendments were expressly intended to be applied "in accordance with Article 6 of the 1995 [UN Fish Stocks] Agreement": Resolution 1/08 of 26 September 2008 on the Interpretation and Implementation of the Convention on Future Multilateral Cooperation in the Northwest Atlantic Fisheries.

[96] See further Z Scanlon "The Art of 'Not Undermining': Possibilities within Existing Architecture to Improve Environmental Protections in Areas beyond National Jurisdiction" (2018) 75 *ICES Journal of Marine Science* 405–416, at 410.

of fishers and the notion of disproportionate burdens of conservation measures, thereby further advancing the thematic concerns of the Agreement.[97]

Given the influence of the Fish Stocks Agreement on the trajectory of international fisheries law, the prospective development of a third implementation agreement is now brought into sharper focus. This initiative pertains to the consideration of biodiversity located in ABNJ, for which the LOS Convention also provides a broad, if relatively incomplete, framework to address activities in the high seas and within the Area. A mandate for the consideration of this issue was first established in 2004 through the UNGA, leading to an extensive series of meetings convened between 2006 and 2015 by the Ad-Hoc Open-Ended Informal Group to study issues related to the conservation and sustainable management of marine biological diversity beyond areas of national jurisdiction (BBNJ Working Group).[98] In 2015 a further UNGA Resolution[99] confirmed an intent to develop an International Legally-Binding Instrument (ILBI) under the framework of the LOS Convention, centred around four thematic priorities – marine genetic resources, area-based management tools (ABMTs), environmental assessment and capacity-building and technology-transfer. Pursuant to Resolution 69/292, a Preparatory Committee (PrepCom) held four individual meetings between 2016 and 2017 to identify points of convergence and divergence between the participants,[100] to facilitate a clearer direction for the elaboration of the ILBI when negotiations commence in earnest in late 2018.

The elaboration of a clearer position on the use of ocean space in ABNJ raises searching questions as to the position of fisheries management in any future arrangements. Indeed, the prospective inclusion of fisheries has provoked strong divisions between the various negotiating parties within the BBNJ process. At the outset, certain States considered that a new implementation agreement could mitigate some of the wider problems encountered in the international governance of fisheries; this view was nevertheless opposed by other delegations, which insisted that fisheries are already comprehensively addressed through a variety of instruments – including a distinct implementation agreement of their own – while others contended that RFMOs generally lack the competence or capacity to meaningfully address threats to marine biodiversity.[101]

---

[97] Report of the resumed Review Conference on the Agreement for the Implementation of the Provisions of the United Nations Convention on the Law of the Sea of 10 December 1982 relating to the Conservation and Management of Straddling Fish Stocks and Highly Migratory Fish Stocks, Doc. A/CONF.210/2016/5, para. 18.

[98] UNGA Resolution 59/24 of 17 September 2004. The extensive reports of the BBNJ Working Group are available at: www.un.org/Depts/los/biodiversityworkinggroup/biodiversityworkinggroup.htm.

[99] UNGA Resolution 69/212 of 6 July 2015, para. 1.

[100] The documentation and reports pertaining to the PrepCom meetings are available at www.un.org/depts/los/biodiversity/prepcom.htm.

[101] Report of the Ad Hoc Open-Ended Informal Working Group to Study Issues relating to the Conservation and Sustainable Use of Marine Biological Diversity beyond Areas of National Jurisdiction; Co-Chairpersons' Summary of Discussions, UN Doc. A/61/65, paras. 24–25.

These divisions continued throughout the PrepCom process,[102] notwithstanding broad consensus over the specific themes to be addressed in the developing ILBI. Nevertheless, fisheries considerations will still cast a significant shadow, not least since they continue to represent a leading global threat to marine biodiversity. Moreover, fisheries are highly relevant to the four key themes of the ILBI and will thus have a lurking presence in these deliberations, if not necessarily a central role. Instead, the participants are broadly aligned in the recognition that RFMOs constitute an important aspect of the regulatory puzzle contemplated by the ILBI and, insofar as their respective mandates allow, should therefore be harnessed in the pursuit of the wider objectives of the nascent instrument.

With this in mind, in the rather stilted vernacular of the BBNJ process, the prospective third implementation agreement is to operate in a manner that does "not undermine" the work of an array of pre-existing regimes and sectoral initiatives operating within ABNJ,[103] a formulation motivated to a large extent to avoid conflicts with RFMOs.[104] At the time of writing the negotiations had yet to commence, hence consideration of the prospective ILBI remains firmly in the realm of speculation. In principle, there would at this juncture appear to be opportunities for the oversight of certain issues related to fisheries management to be enhanced through this process. This is particularly true of environmental assessment, which is addressed among the more ambiguous provisions of the LOS Convention and lacks unified requirements and methodologies on a multilateral level, for which further standardization could have beneficial consequences for fisheries regulation.[105] Likewise, promoting greater coherence in the creation of and interaction between ABMTs established by numerous sectoral regulators (including RFMOs) could also have ecosystem benefits for areas that are significant for fisheries and fish production.[106] This is, however, likely to be a formidable task in practice, as illustrated by the experience of RFMOs to date in this regard, to which this chapter now turns.

4. STRENGTHENING INTERNATIONAL FISHERIES LAW THROUGH INSTITUTIONAL COLLABORATIONS: THE ROLE OF MULTILATERAL ENVIRONMENTAL AGREEMENTS

In keeping with the collaborative aspirations of the prospective ILBI, considerable scope exists for international fisheries law to be influenced and strengthened

---

[102] See further R Barnes "The Proposed LOSC Implementation Agreement on Areas beyond National Jurisdiction and its Impact on International Fisheries Law" (2016) 31 *International Journal of Marine and Coastal Law* 583–616, at 594–95, and KJ Marciniak "New Implementing Agreement under UNCLOS: A Threat or an Opportunity for Fisheries Governance?" (2017) 84 *Marine Policy* 320–326, at 320–21.

[103] UNGA Resolution 69/292 of 6 July 2015, para. 3.

[104] Marciniak, note 102 at 321.

[105] See further Chapter 10 of this volume (Marsden).

[106] See further Chapter 9 of this volume (Dunn, Ortuño Crespo and Caddell).

through strategic partnerships with other multilateral and sectoral regulators. To date, this has been most pronounced in the context of multilateral environmental agreements (MEAs), which exercise competence over an eclectic and extensive array of species and habitats that may be adversely affected by the conduct of commercial fishing activities. The sprawling mandates of MEAs often generate thematic overlaps with numerous other regulators, hence the pursuit of strategic alignments and coordinated working partnerships has long been a central aspiration of interactions among treaties with a clear degree of commonality between their respective mandates.[107]

On a global level, a number of MEAs exercise competence to implement policies for marine space that could directly impinge upon the management of fisheries. Of particular relevance is the CBD,[108] which boasts near-universal participation and applies to areas within and beyond national jurisdiction, for which it has developed a series of policies to promote the spatial management of biodiversity. Moreover, the CBD has adopted specific global objectives to inform the national biodiversity strategies of its parties through its Aichi Targets, which includes a pledge that

> [b]y 2020 all fish and invertebrate stocks and aquatic plants are managed and harvested sustainably, legally and applying ecosystem based approaches, so that overfishing is avoided, recovery plans and measures are in place for all depleted species, fisheries have no significant adverse impacts on threatened species and vulnerable ecosystems and the impacts of fisheries on stocks, species and ecosystems are within safe ecological limits[109]

This pledge sits alongside commitments for at least 10 per cent of coastal and marine areas to be conserved through *inter alia* protected areas.[110] Despite these stated objectives, the CBD has thus far placed little emphasis on the development of collaborative partnerships with individual RFMOs. The CBD routinely concludes Memoranda of Understanding (MOUs) with prospective partners to frame future cooperation. Strikingly, however, despite having formulated over 200 such arrangements, none have yet been concluded with RFMOs. The CBD has also initiated an influential process describing Ecologically or Biologically Significant Areas (EBSAs) across the world's oceans and seas.[111] Although this

---

[107] On the format of and legal basis for these approaches, see KN Scott "International Environmental Governance: Managing Fragmentation through Institutional Connection" (2011) 12 *Melbourne Journal of International Law* 177–207; R Caddell "The Integration of Multilateral Environmental Agreements: Lessons from the Biodiversity-Related Conventions" (2012) 22 *Yearbook of International Environmental Law* 37–75; and R Caddell "'Only Connect'? Regime Interaction and Global Biodiversity Conservation" in M Bowman, P Davies and E Goodwin (eds.) *Research Handbook on Biodiversity and Law* (Edward Elgar, Cheltenham: 2016) 437–471.

[108] Convention on Biological Diversity of 5 June 1992 (1760 UNTS 79).

[109] Aichi Target 6; available at www.cbd.int/sp/targets/.

[110] Aichi Target 11.

[111] For a full history of this process, see DC Dunn et al. "The Convention on Biological Diversity's Ecologically or Biologically Significant Areas: Origins, Development, and Current Status" (2014) 49 *Marine Policy* 137–145, at 138–140.

process does not engender formal legal obligations, such descriptions have nevertheless guided the designation of fisheries closures in both ABNJ and national waters, while particular RFMOs have also been directly involved in these exercises.[112]

Similarly, the CMS,[113] has adopted a plethora of Resolutions on bycatch through its Conference of the Parties (COP), calling for *inter alia* the development of collaborative partnerships with RFMOs. Moreover, bycatch mitigation remains the primary operational priority for those subsidiary agreements of the CMS addressing seabirds, marine mammals, turtles and sharks.[114] Likewise, in recent years certain Parties to CITES[115] have controversially (and unsuccessfully) sought to extend the application of this regime to include a number of commercially significant fish species, raising concerns over mandate creep and potential impediments to the work of RFMOs.[116]

Given the specific spatial focus of individual RFMOs, operative synergies have emerged on a predominantly regional basis. In this respect, partnership arrangements have been developed in two particularly valuable contexts, namely to promote bycatch mitigation policies in tandem with regionally-based MEAs, and to prospectively align area-based management approaches in a manner broadly considered by the nascent ILBI.

4.1. Bycatch Mitigation Strategies

The establishment of collaborative working practices in the context of bycatch mitigation is arguably the most evident and significant point of intersection between MEAs and RFMOs. As outlined fully in Chapter 8 of this volume (Scott), the reduction of bycatch remains key priority for both organizations, generating a series of obligations and mitigation strategies, albeit elaborated from different regulatory standpoints. Nevertheless, effective bycatch mitigation strategies require a high volume of both fisheries-dependent and fisheries-independent data. There is accordingly considerable merit in pooling the complementary data sets held by RFMOs and MEAs and making provision for cooperative input

---

[112] See further Chapter 9 of this volume (Dunn, Ortuño Crespo and Caddell).

[113] Convention on the Conservation of Migratory Species of Wild Animals of 23 June 1979 (1651 UNTS 333).

[114] For a full accounting of these policies, see Chapter 8 of this volume (Scott).

[115] Convention on International Trade in Endangered Species of Wild Fauna and Flora of 3 March 1973 (993 UNTS 243).

[116] See Chapter 14 of this volume (Churchill); see also MA Young *Trading Fish, Saving Fish: The Interaction between Regimes in International Law* (Cambridge University Press, Cambridge: 2011) 134–188; and S Guggisberg *The Use of CITES for Commercially-Exploited Fish Species: A Solution to Illegal, Unreported and Unregulated Fishing?* (Springer, Heidelberg: 2016) 215–316.

into the development of the particular bycatch mitigation strategies elaborated by these respective institutions.

A series of collaborative activities have emerged in this respect, for which interactions between RFMOs and subsidiary agreements of the CMS illustrate both the utility of and broad modus operandi for such arrangements. One key example is the long-standing relationship between the General Fisheries Commission for the Mediterranean (GFCM) and ACCOBAMS,[117] involving overlapping regulation of an area for which fisheries interactions have been repeatedly identified as a significant factor militating against the recovery of populations of cetaceans. From a rather complicated start – relations between these two bodies were considered "somewhat difficult initially"[118] – in 2007 ACCOBAMS recognized that "ecosystem-based fishery management ... can only be addressed by close collaboration between relevant regional fisheries and conservation bodies"[119] and prioritized cooperation with the GFCM. In 2006, ACCOBAMS and the GFCM initiated the ByCABMS initiative to collect data on cetacean bycatch, while in 2007, the GFCM established a transversal Working Group on bycatch under the auspices of its Sub-Committee on Marine Environment and Ecosystems and the Sub-Committee on Stock Assessment. Most recently, in 2015–2017 ACCOBAMS and the GFCM undertook an extensive joint project to identify interactions between endangered marine species and fishing activities, extending beyond cetacean mortalities to also include consideration of turtles and seabirds.[120]

In a similar vein, significant collaborative activities have been also undertaken by ACAP,[121] which applies to Southern Hemisphere seabirds, with an extensive series of RFMOs. The activities of ACAP largely exemplify the MOU-led approach favoured by many MEAs. In May 2009, at its Third Meeting of the Parties (MOP), a specific template to frame interactions with RFMOs was developed under the auspices of ACAP. This has subsequently been used to foster collaboration with CCAMLR, SPRFMO, ICCAT, the Commission for the Conservation of Southern Bluefin Tuna (CCSBT), the Inter-American Tropical Tuna Commission (IATTC), the Indian Ocean Tuna Commission (IOTC), the Western and Central Pacific Fisheries Commission (WCPFC) and, prospectively, the South-East Atlantic Fisheries Organization (SEAFO) and the Southern

---

[117] Agreement on the Conservation of Cetaceans of the Black Sea, Mediterranean Sea and Contiguous Atlantic Area of 24 November 1996 (2183 UNTS 303). Indeed, ACCOBAMS is a rare example of a multilateral instrument that has made specific provision for institutional sub-units to cooperate directly with the pertinent Regional Seas Organizations in the discharge of its mandate: Art. V(1).

[118] Report of the Third Meeting of the Parties to ACCOBAMS (ACCOBAMS, Monaco: 2007) 25.

[119] Resolution 3.8: Strengthening Collaboration with the GFCM.

[120] www.fao.org/gfcm/activities/technical-assistance-and-cooperation/mava-project/en/.

[121] Agreement on the Conservation of Albatrosses and Petrels of 19 June 2001 (2258 UNTS 257). Art. X of the ACAP Agreement specifically mandates liaison between the various ACAP institutions and other pertinent bodies.

Indian Ocean Fisheries Agreement (SIOFA). These MOUs are primarily serviced through the work of ACAP's Seabird Bycatch Working Group, which has established a distinct RFMO Engagement Strategy, through which it promotes participation in reviews of seabird bycatches and the effectiveness of CMMs, strengthening seabird bycatch mitigation measures by RFMOs and strengthening bycatch collection and reporting requirements, advancing tailored priorities in this regard for each of the RFMOs in question.[122]

4.2. Inter-sectoral Area-based Management

Sectoral regulators – both multilateral and domestic – are frequently criticized for adopting a perceived 'silo' approach towards policy-making, the forbidding industrial metaphor suggesting that such governance structures are monolithic, solitary and impervious to the influence of external elements. As observed further in Chapter 9 of this volume (Dunn, Ortuño Crespo and Caddell), RFMOs cohabit with an increasing number of sectoral regulators, each of which exercise (or may prospectively attain) competence to approve or restrict the pursuit of certain activities within particular locations. As Freestone observes, "[e]ach of these approaches has value, but each is developed and assessed by its own epistemic community; it is not developed with any reference to the work of other sectoral bodies".[123] Accordingly, in the absence of meaningful coordination, RFMOs could in theory approve intensive fishing activities in locations that have been set aside for ecological purposes by other organizations, which could in turn endorse industrial activities within areas closed by RFMOs to promote fisheries production. Concurrently, there has been strong encouragement during the BBNJ process for areas subject to sectoral restrictions to be more closely integrated with other forms of protected areas, such as those developed by regional institutions and the initiatives of other sectoral regulators.[124]

Potential sectoral interactions are most plausible with regard to international shipping, seabed mining and environmental regulation. On a global level the IMO, through its Particularly Sensitive Sea Area (PSSA) concept, may identify locations that require special attention due to their inherent ecological, socio-economic or scientific attributes and could be adversely affected by the impacts of shipping. Moreover, the IMO considers that PSSAs are most appropriately established in areas for which there is a degree of pre-existing environmental

---

[122] *Review of ACAP RFMO Engagement Strategy*; Doc. SBWG.Doc13 (2017), 4–14.

[123] D Freestone "Governance of Areas beyond National Jurisdiction: An Unfinished Agenda?" in J Barrett and R Barnes (eds.) *Law of the Sea: UNCLOS as a Living Instrument* (BIICL, London: 2016) 231–265, at 264.

[124] Report of the Ad Hoc Open-Ended Informal Working Group to Study Issues relating to the Conservation and Sustainable Use of Marine Biological Diversity beyond Areas of National Jurisdiction; Co-Chairpersons' Summary of Discussions, UN Doc. A/61/65, para. 58.

protection,[125] thereby providing further impetus to develop a more cohesive relationship with protected areas established by other actors. Thus far, no such areas have been identified within ABNJ, although the global legitimacy of the IMO would nevertheless provide a clear regulatory basis to do so in the future. Similarly, the International Seabed Authority (ISA) may preclude seabed mining in certain locations and establish MPA-like protected areas,[126] for which a series of Areas of Particular Environmental Interest (APEIs) have been deployed throughout the Clarion-Clipperton Zone. As with the area closures adopted by RFMOs, sectoral restrictions instituted by the IMO or ISA apply solely to the particular activity in question. Thus, while they provide protection to a marine area, they are not formal MPAs. Conversely, regional environmental regulators, notably the global suite of Regional Seas Organizations, often have the capacity to establish MPAs, but lack the corresponding competence to regulate specific sectoral activities in these locations.[127]

To date, purported synergies between RFMOs and other sectoral regulators concerning area-based management have generated rather mixed results. This is vividly exemplified by the pioneering relationship forged between North-East Atlantic Fisheries Commission (NEAFC) and the Convention for the Protection of the Marine Environment of the North-East Atlantic (OSPAR),[128] whose respective jurisdictional purviews intersect within the North-East Atlantic region and include a significant portion of ABNJ. The legal mandate of NEAFC is confined to fisheries management, while OSPAR's competence to address "non-polluting human activities" strictly excludes any consideration of fisheries.[129] In discharging this mandate, OSPAR has placed considerable emphasis upon establishing a network of MPAs and has a comparatively lengthy history of promoting interactions with other organizations in this capacity.[130] With both organizations exercising complementary competences, there is clear scope for OSPAR and NEAFC to work collaboratively towards a more coherent pursuit of area-based management for these waters.

In 2008, a MOU was concluded between NEAFC and OSPAR[131] to explore areas of mutual interest and formalize a basis for potential future collaboration,

---

[125] B Sage-Fuller, *The Precautionary Principle in Marine Environmental Law with Special Reference to High Risk Vessels* (Routledge Abingdon: 2013) 233.

[126] See A Jaeckel "An Environmental Management Strategy for the International Seabed Authority? The Legal Basis" (2015) 30 *International Journal of Marine and Coastal Law* 93–119, at 106–09.

[127] The notable exception in this regard is CCAMLR, whose unique mandate has allowed for the institution of formal MPAs as well as fisheries closures in ABNJ that lie within its geographical purview: see further Chapter 9 of this volume (Dunn, Ortuño Crespo and Caddell).

[128] Convention for the Protection of the Marine Environment of the North-East Atlantic of 22 September 1992 (2354 UNTS 67).

[129] Art. 4 of Annex V to the OSPAR Convention, added in 1998.

[130] See further EJ Molenaar and AG Oude Elferink "Marine Protected Areas in Areas beyond National Jurisdiction: The Pioneering Efforts under the OSPAR Convention" (2009) 5 *Utrecht Law Review* 5–20, at 16.

[131] Reproduced at www.ospar.org/about/international-cooperation/memoranda-of-understanding.

for which the most significant outcome was the conclusion in 2014 of a Collective Arrangement between competent international organisations on cooperation and coordination regarding selected areas in ABNJ in the North-East Atlantic. In 2009, NEAFC had closed a series of areas to bottom fishing that broadly corresponded to the designations within the OSPAR MPA network, notably within the Charlie Gibbs and Mid-Atlantic Ridge MPAs. The Collective Arrangement therefore addresses specific locations of mutual interest within the region, which are outlined in Annex I and are jointly maintained by both organizations. While not exclusively focused on area-based management – promising lines of cooperation have also emerged for marine litter and shark conservation – the Collective Arrangement provides a platform for data exchange and updates on amendments to the respective restricted areas, with annual meetings having been convened since 2015 to promote these objectives further.

The OSPAR/NEAFC arrangements illustrate both the opportunities and the complexities facing purported collaborative exchanges of this nature. The Collective Arrangement seeks to include other pertinent global and regional actors to minimize potential interference with Annex I areas.[132] OSPAR and NEAFC have thus encouraged the IMO and ISA to join this process, albeit with little success. As with many synergistic endeavours between multilateral bodies, incompatible meeting schedules have inhibited interactions with the IMO.[133] More significantly, however, such initiatives have met with internal resistance from IMO participants that are geographically and economically removed from shipping activities in the region opposed to devoting time and resources on matters of more localized concern.[134] Meanwhile, the ISA has considered its participation to be "premature" in the absence of a clearly defined project-based role in the region.[135] Wariness about open-ended collaborative demands has also been expressed internally within the OSPAR Commission, with some participants concerned that cross-sectoral management represents a significant but small aspect of an extensive portfolio of activities that could impede the pursuit of more central regulatory priorities.[136]

Tellingly, few parallel initiatives have emerged in other regions to promote inter-sectoral management. This may be largely attributed to the absence of comparable regulatory conditions elsewhere, namely two well-resourced bodies with complementary legal and geographical mandates. Attempts have been

---

[132] The International Commission for the Conservation of Atlantic Tunas (ICCAT) is also identified as a potential partner, given its application to tuna fisheries in the region. Similarly, OSPAR has developed a rather more concise MOU with the North Atlantic Salmon Conservation Organisation (NASCO), although it is more ambiguous and prescribes few direct action points.

[133] *Aide Memoire and Key Actions Resulting from the First Meeting under the Collective Agreement*, para. 2.7.

[134] *Aide Memoire and Key Actions Resulting from the Second Meeting under the Collective Agreement*, para. 3.6.

[135] Ibid.

[136] D Freestone et al. "Can Existing Institutions Protect Biodiversity in Areas beyond National Jurisdiction? Experiences from Two On-Going Processes" (2014) 49 *Marine Policy* 167–175, at 173.

made within the Mediterranean region by the General Fisheries Commission for the Mediterranean (GFCM) to promote a greater degree of coherence with the network of Specially Protected Areas of Mediterranean Importance (SPAMIs) established under the Convention for the Protection of the Marine Environment and the Coastal Region of the Mediterranean.[137] Although the small number of area closures instituted by the GFCM provides a similar basis of conjoined management, this has not yet emerged in practice. Nevertheless, unsuccessful moves towards this objective have, as noted above, resulted in the development of clearer bycatch policies for marine mammals instead, suggesting that such endeavours may at least have beneficial spin-off effects for the management of marine resources in ABNJ.

5. STRENGTHENING INTERNATIONAL FISHERIES LAW THROUGH SPECIALIZED REGULATION: THE CONTRIBUTION OF THE ILO AND IMO

A further point of external influence lies in the respective activities of the ILO and IMO, which may serve to markedly strengthen the operational elements of international fisheries law. This is especially pertinent in the context of labour standards and vessel safety requirements, both of which have been largely deferred to specialist regulators and have thus received little attention within RFMOs or the core instruments regulating fisheries.

Due to the nature of the work, labour conditions are inherently challenging even on well-managed vessels, hence fishing remains one of the most dangerous professions in terms of workplace injuries and fatalities. A chronic lack of data militates against reliable global estimates of fishing casualties, but in virtually all cases in which national reports exist, death rates in the fishing industry are disproportionately higher than those in terrestrial occupations.[138] Compounding this problem, strong concerns have also arisen over egregious breaches of human rights on particular vessels, including instances of slavery, forced labour, child labour, human trafficking, seafarer abuse and enforced participation in at-sea criminality.[139] There is also a clear link between the lack of a safety

---

[137] Convention for the Protection of the Marine Environment and the Coastal Region of the Mediterranean of 16 February 1976 (1242 UNTS 174). See Resolution GFCM/37/2013/1 on area-based management of fisheries, including through the establishment of Fisheries Restricted Areas (FRAs) in the GFCM convention area and coordination with the UNEP-MAP initiatives on the establishment of SPAMIs.

[138] A Jaleel and D Grewal "A Perspective on Safety and Governance Issues of Fishing Vessels" (2017) 31 *Ocean Yearbook* 472–501, at 475–476.

[139] For a recent accounting of worldwide incidents, see A Couper, HD Smith and B Ciceri *Fishers and Plunderers: Theft, Slavery and Violence at Sea* (Pluto Press, London: 2015) 121–162; on the role of international law enforcement institutions in combating such practices, see further Chapters 4 (Stokke) and 17 (Caddell, Leloudas and Soyer) of this volume.

culture – including long hours, poor training, inadequate accommodation and vessels of dubious seaworthiness – and an amplified risk of personal injury.[140] These factors are often associated with and exacerbated by IUU fishing, hence addressing labour and safety concerns may further strengthen responses to combating illicit fishing activities.

Labour conditions on fishing vessels are addressed rather tangentially in the LOS Convention. Under Article 94(3), responsibility for the seaworthiness, crewing, training and labour conditions of vessels is vested in the flag State. There is accordingly some circularity between improving flag State performance in adhering to international fisheries commitments[141] and promoting enhanced labour and safety standards since, as observed by the UN Secretary-General, "ineffective flag State implementation can affect labour conditions aboard fishing vessels".[142] Meanwhile, the Fish Stocks Agreement is silent on labour issues, although these matters were considered for the first time in 2016 at the third instalment of the resumed Review Conference, at which point the preceding ICSP deemed this an important addition to the work of this forum.[143] Nevertheless, labour standards ultimately received a rather mixed reception at the Review Conference itself, as a number of delegations considered it an unsuitable arena for such deliberations, arguing that these matters are more appropriately addressed through the ILO.[144] Also notable was the couching of this issue in the language of sustainability, with other delegations viewing poor labour standards on vessels as an IUU fishing or environmental problem, rather than a social concern.[145] Instead, within the framework of core fisheries instruments, labour standards are most directly (albeit fleetingly) raised in the non-binding Code of Conduct, wherein States are called upon to ensure that "fisheries activities allow for safe, healthy and fair working and living conditions and meet international agreed standards adopted by relevant international organizations".[146] As noted above, these issues have also received prominence in both the UNGA Sustainable Fisheries and Oceans Resolutions, which has helped to maintain their political visibility and to promote these as discrete themes to be addressed by the relevant UN Specialized Agencies.

---

[140] Jaleel and Grewal, note 138 at 476–479.

[141] See further Chapter 15 of this volume (Klein).

[142] Report submitted to the resumed Review Conference in accordance with paragraph 41 of General Assembly resolution 69/109 to assist it in discharging its mandate under Article 36(2) of the Agreement, Doc. A/CONF.210/2016/1, para. 209.

[143] Report of the Twelfth Round of Informal Consultations of States Parties to the Agreement for the Implementation of the Provisions of the United Nations Convention on the Law of the Sea of 10 December 1982 relating to the Conservation and Management of Straddling Fish Stocks and Highly Migratory Fish Stocks, Doc. ICSP12/UNFSA/ INF.3, para. 44.

[144] Doc. A/CONF.210/2016/5, note 97 at para. 177.

[145] Ibid., paras. 176–177.

[146] Code of Conduct, para. 6.17.

The development of labour standards for vessels is complicated somewhat by the overlapping remits of the ILO and IMO. The ILO was established in 1919 to improve global labour conditions and was subsequently incorporated into the UN family in 1946 as the first of its Specialized Agencies. Since its inception, it has adopted an array of Conventions and non-binding Recommendations on the protection of seafarers. Meanwhile, the IMO, which was inaugurated in 1948, has focused more centrally on the 'human element' of its mandate since 1997.[147] The protection of seafarers therefore represents an obvious point of intersection in the work of both Agencies. Conversely, however, it also raises possibilities for operational conflict since these bodies "may approach these issues from different perspectives and without knowledge of what the other organization has done".[148] This has been mitigated through the adoption of a Relationship Agreement between the two organizations,[149] although labour standards for fishing vessels have remained largely the preserve of the ILO, with essentially supporting contributions from the IMO.

Since the turn of the present century, concerted efforts have been made under the auspices of the ILO to consolidate the sprawling array of instruments, implementation guidelines and grievance mechanisms pertaining to the rights of seafarers. In 2006, the Maritime Labour Convention (MLC)[150] was adopted to streamline international recognized standards for seafarers, although this instrument expressly excluded "ships engaged in fishing or in similar pursuits" from its scope of application.[151] Instead, labour standards on fishing vessels are now primarily addressed through the ILO's Work in Fishing Convention (No. 188), which was adopted in 2007. In a similar manner to the MLC, the Convention revised and codified a series of pre-existing – and poorly ratified – ILO instruments pertaining to the fishing industry. Regrettably, this instrument has received a lukewarm reception from the international community, inching its way into force in November 2017 having gradually acquired the necessary ten ratifications over the course of the preceding decade.[152] Nevertheless, the Convention boasts a number of significant features and, if global enthusiasm towards its ratification were to increase, it presents considerable scope to promote an improved culture of vigilance towards labour conditions on board fishing vessels. Under the Convention, the vessel owner bears overall

---

[147] D Fitzpatrick and M Anderson *Seafarers' Rights* (Oxford University Press, Oxford: 2005) 47–48.

[148] Harrison, note 9 at 242.

[149] Agreement between the International Labour Organisation and the Intergovernmental Maritime Consultative Organization (www.ilo.org/public/english/bureau/leg/agreements/imo.htm).

[150] Maritime Labour Convention of 23 February 2006 (2952 UNTS 51299).

[151] Ibid., Art. II(4). The concept of 'similar pursuits' raises questions as to the potential status of transhipment vessels and supply vessels: in the case of doubt, a party may determine whether a particular category of vessel is caught by the MLC "after consultation with the shipowners' and seafarers' organizations concerned": Art. II(5).

[152] The current adherents are Angola, Argentina, Bosnia and Herzegovina, Congo, Estonia, France, Lithuania, Morocco, Norway and South Africa.

responsibility for ensuring that the vessel has the necessary resources and facilities to comply with these obligations.[153] Thereafter, the competent authorities of States Party to the Convention are to adopt legislation to *inter alia* establish a minimum age for service,[154] standards for crewing and rest periods,[155] work agreements,[156] regulate employment agencies[157] and address medical care, health protection and social security.[158]

Although primary responsibility for compliance is vested in the vessel owner and flag State,[159] the Convention's teeth are drawn from its mechanisms on port State control, whereby the principle of 'no more favourable treatment' is applied to all fishing vessels.[160] Accordingly, a Party may investigate complaints from any vessel that enters its ports, irrespective of nationality and of whether the flag State is a Party to the Convention, and may take "measures necessary to rectify any conditions on board which are clearly hazardous to safety or health".[161] Broad standing is given for the submission of complaints, which may be made by individual seafarers, professional bodies or trade unions on their behalf, or indeed by "any person with an interest in the safety of the vessel".[162] The enforcement potential of these provisions was illustrated for the first time in July 2018, when the South African authorities detained a Taiwanese-flagged vessel that had docked at Cape Town, in response to complaints made to them by the crew.[163] The vessel was deemed to be unstable and unseaworthy, with considerable alarm expressed about the state of its lifesaving equipment, accommodation and provisions for the crew. The (as yet unnamed) vessel was eventually released once it had undertaken repairs to the satisfaction of the authorities, addressed concerns over its seaworthiness and capacity for long-term human habitation and paid a detention fee.

The Work in Fishing Convention establishes particular requirements concerning working and living conditions during the conduct of fishing activities. These tailored obligations also serve alongside the general entitlements accorded to all workers under the array of current global and regional human rights instruments, which include injunctions against slavery, forced labour, human trafficking and other abusive treatment, enshrine protections for freedom of speech and association and recognize particular socio-economic entitlements.

---

[153] Work in Fishing Convention, Art. 8(1).

[154] Ibid., Art. 9.

[155] Ibid., Arts. 13 and 14.

[156] Ibid., Arts. 16–20.

[157] Ibid., Art. 22.

[158] Ibid., Arts. 29–37.

[159] Ibid., Art. 40.

[160] GP Politakis "From Tankers to Trawlers: The International Labour Organization's New Work in Fishing Convention" (2008) 39 *Ocean Development and International Law* 119–128, 121.

[161] Work in Fishing Convention, Art. 43(2).

[162] Ibid., Art. 43(4). This could accordingly include the port authorities themselves.

[163] ILO "First Vessel Detained under ILO Fishing Convention"; available at www.ilo.org/global/about-the-ilo/newsroom/news/WCMS_634680/lang--en/index.htm.

Although consideration of the limits of human rights law at sea is beyond the scope of this chapter,[164] it is nevertheless striking that few interactions with these standards have been apparent in promoting enhanced labour conditions at sea. Indeed, human rights treaties "have simply not been used in any strategic way by those seeking to protect the rights of those on board vessels".[165] This is primarily attributed to ignorance of individual entitlements and/or a lack of support to uphold them, jurisdictional uncertainties and legislative deficiencies on the part of port and flag States and the fact that the systems for individual petition established under many such treaties are optional in nature and have not been accepted by States in which these concerns are most prevalent.[166]

Alternatively, other entities have sought to leverage market access to incentivize improvements to labour conditions in the fishing industries of particular States. Indeed, such concerns were represented in the 'yellow card' – a precursor to trade sanctions if rapid adjustments are not made to national fisheries practices – issued by the EU in 2015 under its IUU Regulation[167] to Thailand, which has attracted global notoriety for the plight of migrant workers in its domestic fishing industries. Nevertheless, such approaches have not generally inspired meaningful improvements to working conditions or national legislation. Indeed, the IUU Regulation does not explicitly require adherence to particular labour standards, hence such demands must be repackaged (as in this instance) as concerns over illegal fishing, further entrenching human welfare as an IUU fishing problem rather than an issue requiring holistic and targeted solutions on its own merit. Moreover, as exemplified by the experience of other recipients of subsequently rescinded yellow cards, IUU fishing can be addressed to the satisfaction of the EU without the need to entertain the reform of national labour practices.[168]

Meanwhile, seaworthiness and safety standards for fishing vessels are set through the IMO. The safety of merchant vessels is addressed through SOLAS 74,[169] although fishing vessels are expressly excluded from a number of key provisions of this instrument. Instead, a series of non-mandatory standards for fishing vessels has been adopted by the IMO, in conjunction with the ILO and FAO, to address design, construction and safety on board fishing vessels,

---

[164] See further I Papanicolopoulou *International Law and the Protection of People at Sea* (Oxford University Press, Oxford: 2018) 61–110.

[165] U Khaliq "Jurisdiction, Ships and Human Rights Treaties" in H Ringbom (ed.) *Jurisdiction over Ships: Post-UNCLOS Developments in the Law of the Sea* (Martinus Nijhoff, Leiden/Boston: 2015) 324–361, at 359.

[166] Ibid.

[167] Regulation (EC) No. 1005/2008 establishing a Community system to prevent, deter and eliminate illegal, unreported and unregulated fishing [2008] OJ L286/1; see further Chapter 13 of this volume (van der Marel).

[168] M Marschke and P Vandergeest "Slavery Scandals: Unpacking Labour Challenges and Policy Responses within the Off-shore Fisheries Sector" (2016) 68 *Marine Policy* 39–46, at 43 (citing the examples of the Philippines and South Korea).

[169] International Convention for the Safety of Life at Sea of 1 November 1974 (1184 UNTS 278).

supported by a Code of Safety for Fishermen and Fishing Vessels introduced in 2005. Moreover, the IMO has promoted separate standards for fishing vessels, albeit with limited endorsement from the international community. In 1977 the Torremolinos Convention[170] was adopted by the IMO, subsequently amended by a Protocol,[171] although neither instrument entered into force. In 2012, the IMO reconstituted these provisions within a further Agreement,[172] but this too has failed to attract a sufficient corpus of tonnage and participants to yet enter into effect. In the meantime, elements of SOLAS 74 (notably Chapter V on Safety of Navigation) continue to apply to all vessels at sea, while further measures are being considered by the IMO's Maritime Safety Committee to apply the provisions of the Polar Code to non-SOLAS vessels, including fishing vessels in these waters.

Beyond its primary functions of addressing shipping safety, combating IUU fishing is also a relatively unheralded element of the mandate of the IMO, which has developed a number of quietly significant initiatives to facilitate the tracing of vessels and their equipment. One particularly fruitful synergy has been formed with the FAO through the establishment of a joint working group on IUU fishing, which will expand to include the ILO at its next meeting in 2019. In this regard, the IMO is likely to posit its main contribution through its work on gear-marking initiatives, which could assist greatly in identifying the provenance of confiscated netting to aid in civil and criminal enforcement of fisheries standards. Moreover, this could have particular value in bycatch mitigation strategies, with the IMO's gear-marking policies identified as "a critical tool" for reducing abandoned, lost or otherwise abandoned fishing gear.[173]

6. CONCLUSIONS

As is the case with many distinct subjects of international regulation, principles for the management of international fisheries have been increasingly inspired by interactions with global regimes and processes. This chapter has accordingly considered the more significant contexts in which international fisheries law may be catalysed through external intervention. On a political level, it can be seen that the UNGA has played a notable role in shaping regulatory priorities with regard to particular fishing practices, which has directly informed the practice of States, RFMOs and other multilateral bodies exercising competence

---

[170] International Convention on the Safety of Fishing Vessels of 2 April 1977.

[171] Protocol of 2 April 1993 relating to the 1977 Torremolinos International Convention on the Safety of Fishing Vessels.

[172] Agreement of 11 October 2012 on the Implementation of the Provisions of the Torremolinos Protocol relating to the 1977 Torremolinos International Convention on the Safety of Fishing Vessels.

[173] FAO, *Report of the Thirty-Second Session of the Committee on Fisheries* (FAO, Rome: 2016) para. 148. Discarded fishing gear is also addressed under MARPOL: see further Chapter 8 of this volume (Scott).

over marine ecosystems. The restrictions on large-scale high seas driftnet fishing represent a striking example of the influence of global regulatory opinion, expressed through the UNGA, upon the activities of States, including those that were initially staunchly opposed to these measures. More recently, and arguably more dramatically, the UNGA VME Resolutions have inspired significant regulatory developments within a relatively short timeframe towards area-based management, the elaboration of precautionary procedures to frame the expansion of future fishing effort and the closure of long-standing gaps in the governance of high seas fisheries, with particular reference to the deep-sea environment.

A more pessimistic interpretation of these developments is that the increasing reliance upon other globalized bodies to influence standard-setting of this nature exposes the limitations of LOS Convention in addressing depleted fisheries and ecosystem concerns effectively.[174] This is not to suggest that this framework has been unable to promote landmark improvements to the governance of fisheries, however. Indeed, the Fish Stocks Agreement has served to substantively strengthen international fisheries law by elaborating clearer requirements for RFMOs, as well as instituting a central recognition of the (admittedly vaguely-defined) precautionary and ecosystem-based approaches to fisheries. This has been reflected in the greater ecological focus of the post-1995 RFMOs, as well as the retro-fitting of such principles within the mandates of pre-existing fisheries governance structures. The prospective elaboration of a third implementation agreement to the LOS Convention provides a timely opportunity to promote greater coherence in the regulation of ABNJ, for which international fisheries management could benefit further, if residually, from unified methodologies for environmental assessment and area-based management.

Nevertheless, the ILBI faces significant practical challenges in its pursuit of greater institutional symbiosis. While valuable operational partnerships have been brokered with environmental regulators, particularly in the context of bycatch mitigation, the purported alignment of sectoral regulation has exposed considerable difficulties in synergizing the policies of competing industrial interests in ABNJ. Moreover, as Barnes observes, the ILBI will be no panacea to the broader concerns facing RFMOs,[175] such as serial non-compliance, increasing demands upon dwindling and finite natural resources and the paradigm-shifting impacts of climate change on fish stocks and marine ecosystems. The answers to some of these challenges inevitably lie predominantly or exclusively outside the specific confines of international fisheries law. However, as exemplified in the context of labour and welfare considerations in particular, attempts to strengthen international fisheries law through alternative global regimes and processes frequently encounter familiar problems in mobilizing political will and securing adequate participation in and adherence to these requirements.

---

[174] KM Gjerde "High Seas Fisheries Management under the Convention on the Law of the Sea" in Freestone, Barnes and Ong, note 9, 281–307, at 295.

[175] Barnes, note 102 at 616.

8

Bycatch Mitigation and the Protection of Associated Species

KAREN N SCOTT

1. INTRODUCTION

B YCATCH AND DISCARDS present a significant threat to fish stocks[1] and the health of ecosystems, and have implications for food security while also raising ethical questions associated with waste.[2] The most recent assessment of bycatch and discards was conducted in 2005 and estimated that about 7.3 million tonnes or 8 per cent of global catch was discarded, a decrease on the estimated 27 million tonnes or 25 per cent of global catch, which was discarded in 1994.[3] Bycatch regularly impacts on species with a vulnerable conservation status, with birds, sharks, turtles and marine mammals particularly vulnerable. More insidiously, so-called 'ghost fishing' through abandoned fishing gear is estimated to catch fish up to the equivalent of 30 per cent of landed catches within Europe and North America,[4] while raising concerns over animal welfare, invasive species and even navigational safety.[5]

The regulatory framework for managing bycatch and discards is complex, involving multiple actors and organizations. The global framework comprises an amalgam of hard- and soft-law commitments developed under the LOS

---

[1] G Morandeau et al. "Why Do Fisherman Discard? Distribution and Quantification of the Causes of Discards in the Southern Bay of Biscay Passive Gear Fisheries" (2014) 48 *Marine Policy* 30, at 30.

[2] RWD Davies et al. "Defining and Estimating Global Marine Fisheries Bycatch" (2009) 33 *Marine Policy* 661, at 661.

[3] FAO *The State of the World Fisheries and Aquaculture 2016* (FAO, Rome: 216) 121. The decrease represents some progress on this issue but different methodologies in data-gathering mean that comparisons between years are not straightforward.

[4] E Gilman "Status of International Monitoring and Management of Abandoned, Lost and Discarded Fishing Gear and Ghost Fishing" (2015) 60 *Marine Policy* 225, at 227.

[5] Ibid., 226–227.

Convention,[6] the Fish Stocks Agreement,[7] the Code of Conduct[8] and Guidelines and International Plans of Action (IPOAs) issued by the United Nations Food and Agriculture Organization (FAO) on bycatch and discards generally,[9] and for birds,[10] sharks[11] and marine turtles[12] specifically. This combination of binding and non-binding commitments is also the approach adopted by most regional fisheries management organizations/arrangements (RFMO/As) in their management of bycatch and discards, and the extent to which States must require their vessels to adopt mandatory mitigation measures varies considerably between RFMOs.[13]

With respect to particularly vulnerable non-target species, bycatch measures have been developed by a number of treaties with a mandate for the conservation of wildlife more generally, including the CMS[14] and its subsidiary instruments on cetaceans, seabirds and sharks, CITES[15] and the ICRW.[16] In the case of both turtles and cetaceans, regional treaties have been adopted with a specific mandate to address bycatch. These include the Inter-American Turtle Convention[17] and the AIDCP,[18] the latter being closely affiliated with the Inter-American Tropical Tuna Commission (IATTC). Finally, a number of Regional Seas Agreements, notably those which operate in the North-East Atlantic and the Mediterranean, have begun to address bycatch within a suite of management measures which focus on the protection of the ecosystem as a whole or seek to protect vulnerable species. This multifarious approach to discards and, particularly, bycatch management requires a significant level of coordination

[6] United Nations Convention on the Law of the Sea of 10 December 1982 (1833 UNTS 3).

[7] Agreement for the Implementation of the Provisions of the United Nations Convention on the Law of the Sea of 10 December 1982 Relating to the Conservation and Management of Straddling Fish Stocks an Highly Migratory Fish Stocks of 4 August 1995 (2167 UNTS 3).

[8] Code of Conduct for Responsible Fisheries of 31 October 1995. All FAO Codes, Guidelines and International Plans of Action are available at www.fao.org.

[9] International Guidelines on Bycatch Management and Reduction of Discards, 2001 (Bycatch Guidelines).

[10] International Plan of Action for Reducing Incidental Catch of Seabirds in Longline Fisheries, 1998 (IPOA–SEABIRDS).

[11] International Plan of Action for the Conservation and Management of Sharks, 1998 (IPOA–SHARKS).

[12] Guidelines to Reduce Sea Turtle Mortality in Fishing Operations (Turtle Guidelines).

[13] RFMOs are not the sole organization with a mandate to manage fisheries at the regional level. The European Union (EU) for example, effectively carries out RFMO functions for its Member States in EU waters through the Common Fisheries Policy.

[14] Convention on the Conservation of Migratory Species of Wild Animals of 23 June 1979 (1651 UNTS 333). All CMS MOUs cited in this chapter are available at www.cms.int/.

[15] Convention on International Trade in Endangered Species of Wild Fauna and Flora of 3 March 1973 (933 UNTS 243).

[16] International Convention for the Regulation of Whaling of 10 November 1948 (161 UNTS 72).

[17] Inter-American Convention for the Protection and Conservation of Sea Turtles of 12 January 1996 (Reprinted in (2002) 5 *Journal of International Wildlife Law and Policy* 157–163).

[18] Agreement on the International Dolphin Conservation Program of 15 May 1998 ((1998) 37 ILM 1246).

and collaboration between these institutions and the creation of formal institutional links between RFMOs, CMS Agreements and, to a lesser extent, regional seas conventions, is an important feature of the regional fisheries regulatory framework.

This chapter will examine international and regional regulation as it relates to discards and bycatch. It will begin by exploring the nature of bycatch and discards, noting that the absence of an agreed definition for both terms creates challenges in developing a consistent regulatory approach at all levels of management. The range of potential mitigation measures will be highlighted, noting that many (such as area closures) intersect with other aspects of fisheries and marine ecosystem management, hence regulating bycatch and discards is an integral component of an ecosystem-based approach to fisheries management. The global and regional approach to discards and bycatch management will be explored in Sections 3 and 4 of this chapter, with specific measures addressing the conservation of associated species, namely seabirds, sharks, turtles and marine mammals being addressed in Section 5. Finally, this chapter will conclude with selected recommendations for improving the management of discards and bycatch.

2. BYCATCH, DISCARDS AND MITIGATION STRATEGY

Globally there is no universally agreed definition of bycatch or discards. The Bycatch Guidelines provide a basic definition of discards as "that portion of the total catch which is thrown away or slipped"[19] but does not define bycatch owing to excessive regional variation.[20] Davies et al. describe bycatch as non-target organisms which may be sold or which may be unusable for economic or regulatory reasons, and discards as a subset of bycatch where the organisms are thrown back into the sea.[21] Gilman expands this further, including "unobserved mortalities" by referring to ghost fishing and discarded live catch that subsequently dies in the definition of discarded catch.[22] A particular challenge in developing an overarching definition lies in the differing perceptions of non-target catch, especially where fisheries have changed over time and what was previously viewed as bycatch is now a targeted but potentially unregulated catch.[23] Accordingly, Davies et al. offer a broad definition of bycatch as "catch that is either unused or unmanaged".[24] To the extent that this definition

---

[19] Bycatch Guidelines, note 9, para. 2.5.
[20] Ibid., para. 2.4.4.
[21] Davies et al., note 2 at 661.
[22] EL Gilman "Bycatch Governance and Best Practice Mitigation Technology in Global Tuna Fisheries" (2011) 35 *Marine Policy* 590, at 590.
[23] Davies et al, note 2 at 661.
[24] Ibid., 662.

encompasses targeted but unmanaged fisheries there is a clear overlap with measures addressing the 'unregulated' component of illegal, unregulated and unreported (IUU) fishing.[25] It is however, agreed that environmental damage more generally associated with fishing such as the destruction of coral reefs or the impacts of bottom trawling (considered in Chapter 9 of this volume) does not fall within the definition of bycatch and discards. Nevertheless, the absence of an agreed definition of bycatch may lead "to a failure to fully appreciate the impact this often unmanaged, undocumented, biomass removal is having on the marine environment",[26] creating both regulatory and enforcement challenges.

Measures designed to address bycatch and discards are integral to an ecosystem-based approach to fisheries management. Although the notion of the ecosystem as a tool of objective environmental management was developed in the 1960s, it is only more recently that it has begun to be integrated into fisheries management.[27] The Commission for the Conservation of Antarctic Marine Living Resources (CCAMLR) pioneered the ecosystem approach, pursuant to its mandate under Article II(3)(b) of the CAMLR Convention[28] to maintain the ecological relationships between harvested, dependent and related populations of Antarctic marine living resources. The need to consider non-target species belonging to the same ecosystem and the impact of fishing effort on ecosystems more generally is a principle highlighted in the Fish Stocks Agreement[29] and the Code of Conduct.[30] High level guidance on the scope and application of the ecosystem approach to fisheries management was provided in the 2002 Reykjavik Declaration on Responsible Fisheries in the Marine Ecosystem, alongside more detailed Guidelines issued by the FAO in 2003.[31]

Given that bycatch is all-pervasive, spanning all fisheries, it is unsurprising that mitigation measures are diverse, involving the application of a wide range of tools of fisheries management. The modification of fishing gear constitutes arguably the most well-known mitigation measure. Examples include: using circle hooks;[32] weighting lines and/or delivering baited hooks under water to reduce access to longlines by seabirds and turtles;[33] removal of 'tickler chains'

---

[25] Ibid., 662.

[26] Ibid., 661.

[27] RD Long, A Charles and RL Stephenson "Key Principles of Marine Ecosystem-based Management" (2015) 57 *Marine Policy* 53, at 54.

[28] Convention on the Conservation of Antarctic Marine Living Resources of 20 May 1980 (1329 UNTS 47).

[29] Fish Stocks Agreement, Art. 5(d), (e), (f) and (g).

[30] Code of Conduct, Art. 6.6.

[31] SM Garcia et al. "The Ecosystem Approach to Fisheries. Issues, Terminology, Principles, Institutional Foundations, Implementation and Outlook" (FAO Fisheries Technical Paper 443: 2003).

[32] H Huang et al. "Influence of Hook Type on Catch of Commercial and Bycatch Species in an Atlantic Tuna Fishery" (2016) 65 *Marine Policy* 68–75.

[33] FAO "Bycatch in Longline Fisheries for Tuna and Tuna-like Species. A Global Review of Status and Mitigation Measures" (FAO Technical Paper 588: 2014) 113–119.

fitted to the front of a trawl net which are associated in particular with the bycatch of elasmobranchs;[34] modification of mesh sizes in gillnets;[35] and the utilization of turtle excluder devices (TEDs).[36] Other measures address operational matters and examples include: using fish instead of squid bait;[37] use of blue-dyed bait to reduce its visibility;[38] setting longlines at night with minimum lighting; setting longlines from the side as opposed to the back of the vessel reducing access to the bait by seabirds;[39] restricting the use of driftnets and fish aggregation devices (FADs);[40] utilization of deterrent devices such as tori poles designed to scare birds;[41] restricting or prohibiting the discharge of offal during the setting and hauling of longlines;[42] and requiring release and safe handling of species.[43]

In respect of marine mammal bycatch in particular, vessels are prohibited from targeting dolphins in the purse-seine tuna industry and in some areas must carry marine mammal observers and cease fishing effort where marine mammals are located in the targeted area.[44] Some actors have adopted bycatch quotas and caps[45] or require that all catch be landed (in effect a discard ban) or that no part of a particular species, such as shark, be retained on board (in order to eliminate the bycatch entering the market).[46] In respect of sharks, where the most important market is for fins rather than the fish itself, controls have been introduced to ban finning or limit the amount of fins that can be carried on board a vessel.[47] In some regions areas are closed altogether for fishing in order to protect associated species.[48] Finally, industry- and market-based efforts have

---

[34] RJ Kynoch, RJ Freyer and FC Neat "A Simple Technical Measure to Reduce Bycatch and Discard of Skates and Sharks in Missed-species Bottom-trawl Fisheries" (2015) 72 *ICES Journal of Marine Science* 1861–1868.

[35] See e.g. TL Catchpole and AS Revill "Gear Technology in *Nephrops* Trawl Fisheries" (2008) 18 *Reviews in Fish Biology and Fisheries* 17–31.

[36] D Brewer et al. "The Impact of Turtle Excluder Devices and Bycatch Reduction Devices on Diverse Tropical Marine Communities in Australia's Northern Prawn Trawl Fishery" (2006) 83 *Fisheries Research* 176–188.

[37] FAO, note 33 at 106–114.

[38] Ibid.

[39] Ibid.

[40] L Dagorn, KN Holland and V Restrepo "Is it Good or Bad to Fish with FADs? What are the Real Impacts of the Use of Drifting FADs on Pelagic Marine Ecosystems?" (2013) 14 *Fish and Fisheries* 391–415.

[41] FAO, note 33 at 106–114.

[42] Ibid.

[43] Typically measures require vessels to carry equipment to cut turtles and birds free of longlines and to follow guidelines for safe handling.

[44] See SL Brown, D Reid and E Rogan "Spatial and Temporal Assessment of Potential Risk to Cetaceans from Static Fishing Gears" (2015) 51 *Marine Policy* 267–280.

[45] E.g. CCAMLR.

[46] E.g. the EU.

[47] EJ Techera "Fishing, Finning and Tourism: Trends in Pacific Shark Conservation and Management" (2012) 27 *International Journal of Marine and Coastal Law* 597–621.

[48] AS Little et al. "Real-time Spatial Management Approaches to Reduce Bycatch and Discards: Experiences from Europe and the United States" (2015) 16 *Fish and Fisheries* 576–602.

been used such as fleet communication whereby vessels collaborate in identify-ing and avoiding areas with high levels of bycatch[49] or markets are created for fish that would otherwise be discarded. All of these measures impact on fishing operators, often negatively, as costs rise as a consequence of their implementa-tion and they may also affect the broader ecosystem as fishing effort is displaced from one area to another.[50]

3. THE GLOBAL FRAMEWORK FOR MANAGING BYCATCH AND DISCARDS

The regulation of bycatch dates back at least 1000 years with legislation prohib-iting the sale of undersize fish being enacted in England in 966.[51] From the nineteenth century onwards, bycatch regulation became an increasing focus of fisheries management as the fishing industry developed new technologies[52] and several early fisheries treaties began to apply what would be described today as limited ecosystem-based management.[53]

Today, the overarching global framework for all marine activities including fishing is the LOS Convention. Bycatch, and indeed fishing more generally, is not subject to detailed regulation under the Convention, and the global regulatory framework for fisheries management has been developed in subsequent instru-ments. Nevertheless, Article 61(4) of the LOS Convention requires coastal States in managing their exclusive economic zones (EEZs) to

> take into consideration the effects on species associated with or dependent upon harvested species with a view to maintaining or restoring populations of such asso-ciated or dependent species above levels at which their reproduction may become seriously threatened.

This obligation is reiterated in Part VII of the LOS Convention in respect of States' obligations to conserve marine resources on the high seas.[54] The empha-sis on addressing non-target species and managing bycatch and discards has, as noted above, provided a crucial foundation of the ecosystem-based approach to fisheries management as developed by the UN, through the FAO and the UN General Assembly (UNGA), and at the regional level, during the 1990s.

---

[49] KE O'Keefe, SX Cadrin and KDE Stokesbury "Evaluating the Effectiveness of Time/Area Closures, Quotas/Caps, and Fleet Communications to Reduce Fisheries Bycatch" (2015) 71 *ICES Journal of Marine Science* 1286–1297.

[50] See S Copello et al. "Exporting the Problem: Issues with Fishing Closures in Seabird Conserva-tion" (2016) 74 *Marine Policy* 120–127.

[51] A Gillespie, "Wasting the Oceans: Searching for Principles to Control Bycatch in International Law" (2002) 17 *International Journal of Marine and Coastal Law* 161–193, at 163.

[52] Ibid., 171.

[53] Ibid., 171 – 175.

[54] Art. 119(1)(b).

Bycatch was specifically addressed in Agenda 21, adopted in 1992,[55] and highlighted in the Cancun Declaration adopted in the same year.[56]

In 1995 the Fish Stocks Agreement and the Code of Conduct were both adopted, forming the foundation of the global fisheries regulatory regime. Both instruments highlighted the importance of the marine ecosystem and, in particular, identified the regulation of bycatch and discards as a significant component of fisheries management. The Fish Stocks Agreement obliges Parties to assess the impact of fishing on species associated with target stocks,[57] adopt conservation and management measures for those species "with a view to maintaining or restoring populations of such species above levels at which their reproduction may become seriously threatened"[58] and "minimize pollution, waste, discards, catch by lost or abandoned gear catch of non-target species" and develop to the extent practicable "selective, environmentally safe and cost-effective fishing gear and techniques".[59] Flag States are specifically required to regulate fishing activities carried out by their vessels so that they comply with regional and global measures including those "aimed at minimizing catches of non-target species".[60] The function of RFMOs to assess the impact of fishing on non-target species and to obtain and evaluate scientific advice in relation thereto is specifically highlighted under the Fish Stocks Agreement.[61] These obligations are supported by the non-binding Code of Conduct. The importance of the ecosystem, including non-target species, is identified as a key principle of the Code,[62] and States are encouraged to develop and use selective and environmentally safe fishing gear in order to minimize waste and the catch of non-target species.[63] The Code reiterates Article 5(f) of the Fish Stocks Agreement as a key management measure, encouraging States to address pollution, waste, discards and to develop environmentally safe fishing techniques,[64] and Parties are specifically encouraged to apply a precautionary approach to managing discards and bycatch.[65]

The FAO has taken the lead in addressing bycatch and discards in the context of ecosystem-based fisheries management and issued the overarching non-binding Bycatch Guidelines in 2011. The Guidelines encourage States and

---

[55] Agenda 21. Program of Action for Sustainable Development, paras. 17.46(c), 17.50, 17.74 and 17.87.

[56] Cancun Declaration of the International Conference on Responsible Fishing (reproduced at http://www.fao.org/docrep/003/V5321E/V5321E11.htm), para. 8.

[57] Fish Stocks Agreement, Art. 5(d).

[58] Ibid., Art. 5(e).

[59] Ibid., Art. 5(f).

[60] Ibid., Art. 18(i). See further Chapter 15 of this volume (Klein).

[61] Ibid., Art. 10(d).

[62] Code of Conduct, Art. 6.2.

[63] Ibid., Art. 6.6.

[64] Ibid., Arts. 7.2.2(g) and 7.6.9 and 8.5.

[65] Ibid., Art. 7.5.2.

RFMOs to adopt a precautionary approach in managing bycatch[66] and urge RFMOs to strengthen their capacity to regulate bycatch and discards.[67] States are encouraged to support measures to reduce bycatch and discards that have been adopted by global and regional institutions including RFMOs,[68] and the Guidelines set out a range of measures to mitigate bycatch[69] as well as principles relating to data collection.[70] More specifically, the FAO has adopted non-binding IPOAs for seabirds and sharks, as well as Guidelines to reduce bycatch of marine turtles. These are discussed in Section 5 below, but it is worth noting that despite their soft law status they have been largely adopted by RFMOs and integrated into regional bycatch measures, a number of which are binding on RFMO Member States.

The most important global instrument outside the field of fisheries management in relation to bycatch mitigation is the CMS, which obliges Parties to take action to prevent migratory species becoming endangered and, individually or in cooperation, to take steps to conserve species and their habitat.[71] Although bycatch is not specifically highlighted in the text of the CMS, it is a topic that has been brought to the attention of the 126 States Parties through regular Conference of Parties (COP) Resolutions.[72] More importantly, pursuant to Articles IV and V the range States of migratory species with an unfavourable conservation status may enter into binding Agreements or non-binding Memoranda of Understanding (MOUs) setting out specific obligations to restore those species to a more favourable conservation status. To date, two binding Agreements have been adopted in respect of cetaceans (ASCOBANS and ACCOBAMS)[73] and one in respect of albatrosses and petrels (ACAP).[74] Two non-binding MOUs have been adopted relating to marine turtles,[75] one in relation to sharks[76] and two in respect of marine mammals, of the Pacific[77] and Western Africa respectively.[78]

---

[66] Bycatch Guidelines, note 9, para. 3.2.2(i).

[67] Ibid., paras. 3.2.5 and 4.1.1–4.1.3.

[68] Ibid., para. 3.1.1.

[69] Ibid., paras. 4.1.4 and 7.3.

[70] Ibid., para. 5.1.1.

[71] CMS, Art. II(1) and (2).

[72] See e.g. CMS Resolution 6.2 Bycatch (1999); CMS Resolution 8.14 Bycatch (2005); CMS Resolution 9.18 Bycatch (2008); CMS Resolution 10.14 Bycatch of CMS-Listed Species in Gillnet Fisheries (2011); CMS Resolution 12.22 Bycatch (2017).

[73] Agreement on the Conservation of Small Cetaceans of the Baltic, North East Atlantic, Irish and North Seas of 17 March 1992 (1772 UNTS 217) and Agreement on the Conservation of Cetaceans of the Black Sea, Mediterranean Sea and Contiguous Atlantic Area of 24 November 1996 (2183 UNTS 303).

[74] Agreement on the Conservation of Albatrosses and Petrels of 19 June 2001 (2258 UNTS 257).

[75] MOU Concerning Conservation Measures for Marine Turtles off the Atlantic Coast of Africa 1999; MOU on the Conservation and Management of Marine Turtles and their Habitats of the Indian Ocean and South East Asia 2001 (amended 2009).

[76] MOU on the Conservation of Migratory Sharks 2010 (amended in 2016).

[77] MOU for the Conservation of Cetaceans and Their Habitats in the Pacific Islands Region 2006.

[78] MOU concerning the Conservation of the Manatee and Small Cetaceans of Western Africa and Macaronesia 2008. Additionally a MOU on the Conservation and Management of Dugongs and their Habitats throughout their Range was concluded in 2007.

Moreover, Article III of the CMS encourages Parties to take action to protect endangered migratory species listed in Appendix I of the Convention, and a recent example of such action was the adoption of a single species action plan for the Logger Head Turtle in the South Pacific Ocean in 2014.[79] All of these instruments address issues of bycatch and urge Parties to work through relevant RFMOs to mitigate the impact of fishing operations on these migratory species. Moreover, some – particularly ACAP – have established productive institutional relationships with RFMOs collaborating on bycatch mitigation.

Other global instruments not directly involved in fisheries management per se but with mandates of some relevance to bycatch is the ICRW and CITES. The International Whaling Commission (IWC) has in the past taken an interest in cetacean bycatch, working closely with ASCOBANS and ACCOBAMS,[80] and CITES lists a number of migratory species of marine turtles, cetaceans and sharks in its appendices restricting their trade for commercial purposes where they are caught outside of national jurisdiction. This provides indirect support for bycatch regulation in that it creates a disincentive to retain and attempt to profit from bycatch although it is limited to fishing taking place in international waters.[81] Of indirect application is the MARPOL 73/78,[82] which in Annex V regulates the discharge of garbage, including plastics from vessels and discarded fishing gear.

Finally, UNGA Resolutions also contribute to the global framework for managing bycatch and discards. Of particular importance are Resolutions adopted in 1989,[83] 1991[84] and 1998[85] calling for a moratorium on large-scale pelagic driftnet fishing supporting or leading to the adoption of binding measures prohibiting or restricting driftnet fishing in the South Pacific,[86] the Southern Ocean[87] and European waters.[88] The moratorium on driftnet fishing has been endorsed in more recent Resolutions and, furthermore, the issue of by-catch and discards has been subject to considered discussion with States urged to

---

[79] CMS Resolution 11.21 Single Species Action Plan for the Logger Head Turtle (Caretta Caretta) in the South Pacific Ocean (2014).

[80] Note 73. See especially IWC Resolution 1993-11 on Harbour Porpoise in the North Atlantic and Baltic Sea (1993). Other pertinent measures include IWC Resolution on the Conservation of Freshwater Cetaceans 2000-9 (2001) and IWC Resolution on Western North Atlantic Right Whales 2000-8 (2001). The competence of the IWC to regulate small cetaceans nevertheless remains controversial among certain Parties.

[81] CITES, Art. 1(e); CITES CONF. Resolution 14.6 (Rev. CoP16).

[82] International Convention for the Prevention of Pollution from Ships of 2 November 1973, as modified by the Protocol of 1978 1340 UNTS 62.

[83] Resolution. 44/225 of 22 December 1989.

[84] Resolution 46/215 of 20 December 1991.

[85] Resolution 53/33 of 24 November 1998.

[86] Convention for the Prohibition of Fishing with Long Driftnets in the South Pacific of 24 November 1989 (1899 UNTS 3).

[87] CCAMLR Resolution 7/IX Driftnet Fishing in the Convention Area.

[88] Council Regulation (EC) No. 894/79 of 29 April 1997 amended by Council Regulation (EC) 1239/98 and Council Regulation (EC) 809/2007 prohibit driftnet fishing when targeting highly migratory species and large and medium sized pelagic species.

comply with FAO Guidelines as well as measures adopted by RFMOs and other organizations.[89] Moreover, the Sustainable Development Goals adopted by the UNGA in 2015[90] urge States to effectively regulate harvesting and end overfishing, illegal, unreported and unregulated fishing and destructive fishing practices by 2020[91] and, by 2030, halve per capital global food waste at the retail and consumer levels and reduce food losses along production and supply chains,[92] requiring States to address discards as well as bycatch.

4. MITIGATING BYCATCH AND DISCARDS THROUGH REGIONAL FISHERIES MANAGEMENT ORGANIZATIONS AND THE EU

All RFMOs now address discards and/or bycatch albeit with significant regional and institutional variation in the nature and extent of the measures adopted. An exhaustive survey is beyond the scope of this chapter, but a number of examples of good practice will be noted.

Unsurprisingly, older RFMOs generally omit specific references to bycatch or discards or even to the ecosystem approach more generally within their principal treaty text.[93] In contrast, the constitutive instruments of modern RFMOs, such as the SPRFMO Convention explicitly endorse a precautionary and ecosystem-approach to fisheries management[94] and expressly require Members to address bycatch and discards.[95] The exception to this generalization is the CAMLR Convention, which as an older quasi-RFMO, pioneered the application of the ecosystem-approach to fisheries management in the Southern Ocean in the 1980s. Commission Members are obliged to maintain "ecological relationships between harvested, dependent and related populations of Antarctic marine living resources",[96] providing a mandate to address bycatch and discards.

At the most basic level, the majority of RFMOs require Parties to collect and collate data on bycatch and discards as a minimum requirement. Several RFMOs, including the South Pacific Regional Fisheries Management Organization (SPRFMO) and the Western and Central Pacific Fisheries Commission (WCPFC), prohibit the use of large-scale driftnets and others,

---

[89] See e.g. Resolution 64/72 of 4 December 2009.

[90] Resolution 70/1 of 25 September 2015.

[91] Ibid., Goal 14.4.

[92] Ibid., Goal 12.3.

[93] See e.g. the Agreement for the Establishment of the Indian Ocean Tuna Commission of 25 November 1993 (available at www.iotc.org) and the International Convention for the Conservation of Atlantic Tunas of 14 May 1966 (673 UNTS 63, as amended; consolidated version available at www.iccat.int).

[94] Convention on the Conservation and Management of High Seas Fishery Resources in the South Pacific Ocean of 1 January 2010 ([2012] ATS 28), Art. 2.

[95] SPRFMO Convention, Art. 3(1)(x). See also the Convention on the Conservation and Management of Highly Migratory Fish Stocks of the Western and Central Pacific of 5 September 2000 (2275 UNTS 43). Arts. 5(c), (d) and (e).

[96] CAMLR Convention, Art. II(3)(b).

including WCPFC, IATTC, the Indian Ocean Tuna Commission (IOTC) and the International Commission on the Conservation of Atlantic Tunas (ICCAT) limit the use of, or close areas to, FADs. The requirement to retain all targeted catch (and in some cases, bycatch) unless unfit for human consumption is an increasingly common requirement and the leader in this area is arguably the Northwest Atlantic Fisheries Organization (NAFO), which sets bycatch limits for individual species[97] and requires a vessel to leave its original fishing position for a period of at least 60 hours if the bycatch limit is exceeded.[98]

A particularly robust approach to discards is being developed by the EU under the auspices of the Marine Strategy Framework Directive (MSFD),[99] which specifically requires the Common Fisheries Policy (CFP) to take account of the environmental impacts of fishing and the objectives of the MSFD.[100] Ecosystem-based management and precaution are core principles underpinning the CFP, which was substantially revised in 2013.[101] The revised CFP directly addresses unwanted catches and discards and creates an obligation to land all catches ('the landing obligation') of species which are subject to catch limits and, in the Mediterranean Sea, also catches of species which are subject to minimum sizes and to count those catches against existing quotas.[102] Where there are no management plans in respect of individual fisheries the Commission may adopt a discard plan setting out quotas.[103] The landing obligation has been implemented on a fishery-by-fishery basis from 1 January 2015, with a view to all species being covered by 1 January 2019.[104]

Arguably the most comprehensive approach to bycatch adopted to date has been implemented by CCAMLR in the Southern Ocean. Pursuant to the ecosystem-based approach to fisheries management noted above, CCAMLR has adopted measures limiting the percentage of bycatch-to-catch ratio in certain areas[105] as well as restricting the bycatch of specific species, such as marbled rock-cod.[106] Bycatch limits are also set with respect to species such as skates and

---

[97] NAFO Conservation and Enforcement Measures (2017), Art. 6.3.

[98] Ibid., Art. 6.6.

[99] Directive 2008/56/EC of the European Parliament and of the Council of 17 June 2008 establishing a framework for community action in the field of marine environmental policy [2008] OJ L164/19 [8].

[100] Ibid., [40].

[101] Regulation (EU) No. 1380/2013 of the European Parliament and of the Council of 11 December 2013 on the Common Fisheries Policy, amending Council Regulations (EC) No. 1954/2003 and (EC) No. 1224/2009 and repealing Council Regulations (EC) No. 639/2004 and Council Decision 2004/585/EC [2013] OJ L354/22 [10] and [13] and Art. 2(2) and (3).

[102] Ibid., Art. 2(5)(a), Art. 15. Consequent amendments to other EU Regulations to ensure compatibility between those regulations and the landing obligation were adopted in Regulation (EU) 2015/812 of the European Parliament and of the Council of 20 May 2015, [2015] OJ L133/1.

[103] Ibid., Art. 15(6).

[104] Ibid., Art. 15(1).

[105] CM 33-02 (2016) Limitation of By-catch in Statistical Division 58.5.2 in the 2016–2017 season.

[106] CM 33-01 (1995) Limitation of the By-catch of Gobionotothen gibberifrons, Chaenocephalus aceratus, Pseudochaenichthys georgianus, Notothenia rossi and Lepidonotothen squamifrons in Statistical Subarea 48.3.

rays in new and exploratory fisheries.[107] In relation to fishing gear, CCAMLR has endorsed UNGA Resolution 44/225 and recommends there be no expansion of large-scale driftnet fishing in the Convention area.[108] Responding to the issue of ghost fishing, CCAMLR has introduced a temporary prohibition on gillnets for purposes other than scientific research and requires vessels transiting the Convention area carrying gillnets covering a cumulative area greater than 100 m² to give advance notice of their intent.[109] More generally, CCAMLR has adopted rules relating to the use and discard of plastic packaging as well as banning the dumping of offal and discards south of 60° South.[110]

A significant weakness in the application of these measures is that not all measures apply to the entire CCAMLR area; the waters adjacent to the Kerguelen and Crozet Islands as well as the Prince Edward Islands are, for example, commonly excluded from CCAMLR conservation measures. These geographical lacunae result from a compromise reached between France and the Commission set out in the so-called Chairman's Statement appended to the Convention on its adoption, permitting France to decide whether the scope of any conservation measure would apply to the waters surrounding Kerguelen and Crozet. The principles within the Statement have since been applied to the waters under the jurisdiction of any State within the Convention area. These States may choose to apply the standards set out in CCAMLR conservation measures to waters under their jurisdiction or indeed impose higher standards. However, there is obvious scope for inferior protection and this has occurred on occasion.[111]

5. MITIGATING BYCATCH OF SEABIRDS, SHARKS, MARINE TURTLES AND MARINE MAMMALS

As noted above, seabirds, sharks, marine turtles and marine mammals are all at particular risk from bycatch as well as other threats such as habitat destruction. It is unsurprising therefore that bycatch regulation is most extensive in relation to each of these species and conservation obligations can be found across a range of instruments beyond the specific action taken by RFMOs.

---

[107] CM 33-03 (2016) Limitation of By-catch in New and Exploratory Fisheries in the 2016/17 Season.

[108] Resolution 7/IX Driftnet Fishing in the Convention Area.

[109] CM 22-04 (2010) Interim Prohibition of Deep-sea Gillnetting.

[110] CM 36-01 (2015) General Environmental Protection during Fishing.

[111] E.g. in 2011 CCAMLR highlighted "the Scientific Committee's general advice on incidental mortality of seabirds and marine mammals (SC-CAMLR-XXX, paras. 4.6 and 4.7), in particular noting that the total extrapolated mortalities of seabirds within the French EEZ in Subarea 58.6 and Division 58.5.1 was estimated to be 220 and that incidental mortalities elsewhere in the Convention Area were similar to the near-zero levels of recent years". See Report of the 30th Meeting of the Commission (CCAMLR-XXX), [6.2].

5.1. Seabirds

Seabirds, especially albatrosses and petrels, are at particular risk from a range of fishing activities. It is estimated that some species of albatross have suffered a 90 per cent decline in their population with longline fishing posing the most significant threat.[112] Unsurprisingly, extensive bycatch mitigation techniques and strategies have been developed which, as outlined in Section 2 above, range from the modification of fishing gear, changes in operational practices and area closures.[113]

The global framework is provided by the voluntary IPOA-SEABIRDS adopted by the FAO in 1998. The IPOA-SEABIRDS sets out a range of mitigation strategies which should be adopted by vessels, as well as technical requirements such as hook modification, line weighting and bird scaring. It urges States to carry out an assessment to identify whether seabird bycatch is an issue for fisheries within which their vessels are operating and, if so, encourages States to develop a National Plan of Action for seabirds. Although a voluntary measure, several RFMOs, including ICCAT,[114] IATTC[115] and WCPFC[116] have each adopted measures within the areas under their control to be implemented by the Parties. CCAMLR similarly encourages Parties to implement the IPOA-SEABIRDS in respect of their vessels but goes further by inviting ten other RFMOs to do likewise.[117] CCAMLR also encourages Members that are also Members of other RFMOs to put the topic of seabird bycatch on the agenda of those RFMOs and to develop and evaluate mitigation measures within these auspices.[118] IPOA-SEABIRDS is also implemented through ACAP, which covers 31 species and has 13 Parties. Addressing bycatch is a core objective of this Agreement and detailed guidance is developed within its Action Plan, which is supported by a clear obligation to cooperate with CCAMLR and other RFMOs.[119]

All five tuna RFMOs (IOTC, ICCAT, IATTC, the Commission for the Conservation of Bluefin Tuna (CCSBT) and WCPFC), as well as SPRFMO, have adopted measures to mitigate seabird bycatch including reporting and

---

[112] A Bergin "Albatross and Longlining – Managing Seabird Bycatch" (1997) 21 *Marine Policy* 63–72 at 65.

[113] See also LS Bull "Reducing Seabird Bycatch in Longline, Trawl and Gillnet Fisheries" (2007) 8 *Fish and Fisheries* 31–56.

[114] Resolution 02-14 Incidental Mortality of Seabirds.

[115] Resolution C-05-01 on Incidental Mortality of Seabirds (2005).

[116] WCPFC Resolution 2005-01 on the Incidental Catch of Seabirds and WCPFC Conservation Measure 2015-03 to Mitigate the Impact of Fishing for Highly Migratory Fish Stocks on Seabirds.

[117] Resolution 22/XXV International Actions to Reduce the Incidental Mortality of Seabirds arising from Fishing.

[118] Ibid.

[119] ACAP, Art. XIII. ACAP has entered into collaborative arrangements with CCAMLR, IATTC, ICCAT, CCSBT, IOTC, SPRFMO and WCPFC.

the use of tori poles (bird-scaring devices). Other measures including night-setting, restrictions relating to the discharge of offal, line weighting and gear specification (such as the use of hooks) are either optional or comprise measures from which one or two must be selected by the vessel operator. Most RFMOs require measures to be deployed in selected areas rather than in the whole convention area.

More stringent and geographically comprehensive measures have been adopted by CCAMLR. The Commission has established binding requirements relating to the weighting of longlines and the use of lighting when fishing at night,[120] in particular, that the location and level of light minimizes illumination directed out from the vessel.[121] The dumping of offal and discards is prohibited during line setting the haul[122] and where vessels cannot retain or process offal on board or discharge it from the opposite side of the haul they should not be authorized to fish in the CCAMLR area.[123] Moreover, nets must be cleaned to remove items to attract birds and maintenance must not be carried out in the water.[124] Vessels must employ bird-scaring devices (such as a streamer or tori pole), and in areas of average to high level of bycatch, bird exclusion devices should be used in order to discourage birds from accessing the bait whilst the line is being hauled.[125] Finally, every effort must be made to release any caught seabirds.[126] In addition to these specific mitigation measures, CCAMLR also requires a risk assessment of seabird bycatch in all proposals for new and exploratory fisheries.[127] The geographical lacunae noted above applies in respect of the Kerguelen and Crozet Islands and, to a lesser extent Prince Edward Islands, but France and South Africa have been encouraged to adopt and, have in fact adopted, comparable measures within waters under their jurisdiction.

5.2. Sharks

Sharks are a particularly challenging species to manage in this context as there is a significant market for shark fins, hence they occupy an unusual position on

---

[120] CM 25-02 (2015) Minimisation of the Incidental Mortality of Seabirds in the Course of Longline Fishing or Longline Fishing Research in the Convention Area.
[121] CM 25-03 (2016) Minimisation of the Incidental Mortality of Seabirds and Marine Mammals in the course of Trawl Fishing in the Convention Area.
[122] Ibid.
[123] CM 25-02 (2015).
[124] CM 25-03 (2016).
[125] CM 25-02 (2015). This requirement may be modified or abandoned where weather does not permit the deployment of bird exclusion devices.
[126] Ibid.
[127] CM 21-02 (2017) Exploratory Fisheries.

the continuum between bycatch and target species.[128] It is estimated that half of all shark production comprises incidental catch[129] and of the annual 224,000 tonne global trade in shark fins, 207,000 tonnes are landed as bycatch resulting in 94 per cent of the shark fin trade being classed as essentially unregulated.[130] Moreover, as trade in sharks and elasmobranchs is generally unreported, the unregulated catch of shark fins could be as high as 1.7 million tonnes.[131] In 2014, the International Union for the Conservation of Nature (IUCN) published an assessment concluding that one-quarter of all shark species are threatened with extinction, while only one-third of species are of low conservation concern.[132]

At the global level the FAO adopted a non-binding IPOA-SHARKS in 1998. The IPOA urges States to adopt a national plan of action if their vessels target sharks or if sharks are regularly caught as bycatch, to ensure that both directed and non-directed shark catches are sustainable with the minimization of waste and discards. The IPOA encourages the full use of dead sharks. States are also encouraged to cooperate, particularly in relation to straddling or migratory species. These principles are supported and expanded in the MOU on the Conservation of Migratory Sharks, adopted in 2010 under the auspices of the CMS. The MOU (as amended in 2016) has been signed by 48 States and 11 cooperating Parties and, in its Conservation Plan, urges States to take measures to reduce bycatch and to consider enacting legislation to require that sharks be stored and landed with their fins naturally attached.[133] Similar principles are expressed in CMS Resolution 11.20 adopted in 2014 and addressed to all 126 CMS Parties.[134] Furthermore, trade controls on 17 species of shark and elasmobranchs are provided for under CITES. More generally, CITES has called upon its Parties to implement the IPOA-SHARKS and to cooperate with relevant RFMOs and other States in managing the trade in sharks.[135]

Regionally, most RFMOs have adopted measures designed to reduce the bycatch of sharks and to manage trade in shark fins. Most RFMOs require their Members to implement the IPOA-SHARKS and develop national plans of

---

[128] KC James et al. "Drivers of Retention and Discards of Elasmobranch Non-target Catch" (2016) 43 *Environmental Conservation* 3–12, at 3.

[129] Techera, note 47 at 601.

[130] S Oliver et al., "Global Patterns in the Bycatch of Sharks and Rays" (2015) 54 *Marine Policy* 86–97, at 87.

[131] Ibid.

[132] NK Dulvy et al. "Extinction Risk and Conservation of the World's Sharks and Rays" (2014) *eLife3:* e00590. DOI: 10.7554/eLife.00590.

[133] Annex 3. See J Kraska and L Gaskins "Can Sharks be Saved? A Global Plan of Action for Shark Conservation in the Regime of the Convention on Migratory Species" (2015) 5 *Seattle Journal of Environmental Law* 415–439.

[134] CMS Resolution 11.20 Conservation of Migratory Species of Sharks and Rays (2014). The CMS also seeks to explore "future avenues of cooperation" with CITES and the FAO Committee on Fisheries: CMS Resolution 8.16 Migratory Sharks (amended 2017).

[135] Conf.12.6 (Rev. CoP17) Conservation and Management of Sharks. See also CITES Resolution 17.209 Sharks and Rays (Elasmobranchii spp.).

action, including undertaking research into gear to minimize bycatch, identifying nursery areas and making regular reports on levels of shark bycatch. ICCAT,[136] IOTC,[137] IATTC[138] and WCPFC[139] all require vessels to fully utilize their entire catch of sharks (apart from the head, guts and skins) and to retain shark fins on board constituting no more than 5 per cent of the weight of sharks. Designed to deter shark finning, this requirement has been criticized as being ambiguous as it does not address differences in the sizes of fins relative to shark species or differences in finning techniques.[140] NAFO has adopted the more straight-forward requirement of prohibiting the removal of shark fins onboard vessels and prohibiting the retention, transhipment and landing of fins separate to the carcass.[141] The General Fisheries Commission for the Mediterranean (GFCM) has banned shark finning altogether[142] and CCAMLR more generally prohibits the directed fishing of sharks, requiring that as far as possible bycatch is to be released alive.[143] Other RFMOs prohibit the retention, transhipment, landing or offering for sale of selected vulnerable species in order to prevent bycatch entering the market,[144] although such measures have been criticized for failing to encourage fishers to reduce their incidental capture of sharks, which are simply discarded dead or dying.[145]

Domestically, a number of States have introduced measures to reduce shark bycatch or ban shark finning.[146] For example bycatch quotas have been established for 11 species of shark in New Zealand,[147] with quotas set for individual species in Argentina, Australia, Canada, the EU, Korea, Malaysia, Mexico, Papua New Guinea, Samoa, Tonga, Thailand and the UK.[148] During the last decade shark sanctuaries have been established in Palau, the Federated States of Micronesia, the Republic of the Marshall Islands, the US territories of

---

[136] Rec 04-10 Recommendation by ICCAT Concerning the Conservation of Sharks Caught in Association with Fisheries Managed by ICCAT.

[137] Resolution 05/05 Concerning the Conservation of Sharks Caught in Association with Fisheries Managed by IOTC.

[138] Resolution C-05-03 on the Conservation of Sharks Caught in Association with Fisheries in the Eastern Pacific Ocean (June 2005).

[139] WCPFC Conservation and Management Measure 2010-07 for Sharks.

[140] Techera, note 47 at 605.

[141] NAFO, Conservation and Enforcement Measures (2017), Art. 12.

[142] Recommendation GFCM/36/2012/3 on Fisheries Management Measures for Conservation of Sharks and Rays in the GFCM Area.

[143] CM 32-18 (2006) Conservation of Sharks.

[144] See e.g. Rec 10-07, Recommendation by ICCAT on the Conservation of Oceanic Whitetip Shark Caught in Association with Fisheries in the ICCAT Convention Area and Resolution 12/09 on the Conservation of Thresher Sharks (Family Alopiidae) Caught in Association with Fisheries in the IOTC Area of Competence.

[145] MT Tolotti et al. "Banning is Not Enough: The Complexities of Oceanic Shark Management by Tuna Regional Fisheries Management Organizations" (2015) 4 *Global Ecology and Conservation* 1–7, at 3.

[146] See further Techera, note 47 at 609–612.

[147] FAO, note 33 at 40.

[148] Ibid., 40–41.

Guam and the commonwealth of the Northern Mariana Islands, Tokelau, the Bahamas, Honduras and the Maldives.[149]

Nevertheless, despite these measures the global conservation regime for sharks remains fragmented[150] with RFMO practice varying significantly between organizations ranging from strong directives under CCAMLR, to much narrower and weaker measures under IOTC. Only the oceanic whitetip shark is managed across all oceans.[151] Moreover, only one third of the 143 States that report shark catches to the FAO have developed national plans pursuant to the IPOA-SHARKS,[152] while many of those adopted many fall short of the appropriate conservation standard.[153]

5.3. Marine Turtles

All seven species of marine turtles interact with longline fisheries[154] with high rates of capture recorded in the Atlantic Ocean, Pacific Ocean and Mediterranean.[155] Particular risks are also posed by shrimp fisheries[156] and driftnets and trammel nets more generally.[157] Detailed voluntary guidelines to reduce sea turtle mortality in fishing operations were issued by the FAO in 2004 and re-issued in 2009.[158] The Guidelines set out standards relating to gear and operational matters designed to mitigate bycatch. These include the use of circle hooks and fish bait, replacing 'J' hooks and squid bait in longline fisheries, and turtle excluder devices in trawl fisheries as well as operational standards to release captured turtles from longlines and in purse seine fisheries.

In contrast to seabirds and sharks, conservation measures adopted in respect of sea turtles by RFMOs tend to be voluntary in nature. The exception is WCPFC, which requires purse seine vessels to avoid encircling sea turtles and releasing those accidentally entangled,[159] and longline vessels fishing for swordfish in a shallow manner to employ at least one of three mitigation

---

[149] Techera, note 47 at 607–609.

[150] See EJ Techera and N Klein "Fragmented Governance: Reconciling Legal Strategies for Shark Conservation and Management" (2011) 35 *Marine Policy* 73–78.

[151] Tolotti et al., note 145 at 2.

[152] FAO, note 11 at 4.

[153] See B Davis and B Worm "The International Plan of Action for Sharks: How Does National Implementation Measure Up?" (2013) 38 *Marine Policy* 312–320.

[154] FAO, note 33 at 53.

[155] Huang et al., note 32 at 69.

[156] PH Dutton and D Squires "Reconciling Biodiversity with Fishing: A Holistic Strategy for Pacific Sea Turtle Recovery" (2008) 39 *Ocean Development and International Law* 200–222, at 205.

[157] I Álvarez de Quevedo et al. "Sources of Bycatch of Loggerhead Sea Turtles in the Western Mediterranean other than Drifting Longlines" (2010) 67 *ICES Journal of Marine Science* 677–685.

[158] Turtle Guidelines, note 12; re-issued 2009.

[159] Resolution 2005-04 to Mitigate the Impact of Fishing for Highly Migratory Fish Species on Sea Turtles.

measures, namely, circle hooks, whole finfish for bait or any other mitigation plan that has been approved by the Commission.[160] IATTC also requires purse seine vessels in the Eastern Pacific Ocean to comply with Article VI of the AIDCP and release and report all turtles entangled.[161] Mitigation requirements relating to purse seine fisheries are also set out by GFCM, which prohibits sea turtles being taken on board any vessel in the Mediterranean area unless they are being rescued.[162] Typically, other RFMOs require turtle interactions to be reported, that equipment such as cutters and de-hookers are carried on board, that turtles should be released where possible using safe handling methods and recommend (rather than require) the research into, trial and adoption of bycatch mitigation practices.[163]

Bycatch of sea turtles is also addressed by the CMS, under which regional MOUs have been adopted in respect of turtles in the Indian Ocean and South East Asia (IOSEA)[164] and the Atlantic coast of Africa.[165] A single species action plan for the Logger Head Turtle in the South Pacific Ocean was also adopted by the CMS in 2014.[166] IOSEA has adopted a conservation and management plan which, as with the Logger Head Turtle Action plan, prescribes a series of bycatch mitigation measures. Moreover, within the framework of both initiatives signatories are urged to cooperate with relevant RFMOs[167] and other instruments including, in the case of the Logger Head turtle action plan, the Inter-American Turtle Convention. Nevertheless, both IOSEA and the African Turtle MOU are non-binding and, in the case of the latter instrument, no conservation or action plan has been adopted addressing bycatch or indeed any other conservation issue.

---

[160] CMM 2008-03 on Sea Turtles. The requirements relating to swordfish longline fisheries do not apply where a Member can prove minimal interaction with sea turtles over a three-year period and where there is a minimum 10 per cent observer coverage across the fishery.

[161] Resolution on Bycatch (10 October 1999).

[162] Recommendation GFCM/35/2011/4 on the incidental bycatch of sea turtles in the GFCM competence area.

[163] IOTC Resolution 12/04 on the Conservation of Marine Turtles; Resolution 03-11 by ICCAT on Sea Turtles; Recommendation 10-09 by ICCAT on the By-Catch of Sea Turtles in ICCAT Fisheries; Recommendation 13-11 by ICCAT Amending Recommendation 10-09 on the By-Catch of Sea Turtles in ICCAT Fisheries; Res 05-08 Resolution by ICCAT on Circle Hooks; IATTC Resolution C-03-10 Recommendation on Sea Turtles (June 2003); IATTC Resolution C-07-0 Resolution to Mitigate the Impact of Tuna Fishing Vessels on Sea Turtles (June 2007); IATTC Resolutions on Bycatch (2002, 2003 and 2006); WCPFC Resolution 2005-04 to Mitigate the Impact of Fishing for Highly Migratory Fish Species on Sea Turtles; WCPFC 2006 Sea Turtles Data Collection and Research Programme; WCPFC CMM 2008-03 on Sea Turtles.

[164] Note 75.

[165] Ibid.

[166] CMS Resolution 11.21 Single Species Action Plan for the Logger Head Turtle (Caretta Caretta) in the South Pacific Ocean (2014).

[167] Resolution 3.1 Urging the Indian Ocean Tuna Commission (IOTC) and its Member States to Address Marine Turtle bycatch Issues within the IOSEA Region (2005); Resolution to Promote the Use of Marine Turtle Bycatch Reduction Measures by IOSEA Signatory States (2008).

In contrast, more robust measures are required in respect of the five species of marine turtles listed in Annex II of the SPA Procotol.[168] Parties are required to develop cooperative management measures for listed species and, in the case of marine turtles, have adopted an Action Plan for the Conservation of Marine Turtles 2014–2019 which addresses, among other threats, bycatch.[169] Similarly, in the Atlantic, Pacific and Caribbean the Inter-American Turtle Convention requires its 15 Parties to reduce, to the greatest extent practicable, incidental mortality of turtles in fishing operations using appropriate gear modifications including, in particular, turtle excluder devices according to the standards set out in Annex III of the Convention.[170] Finally, support for these regional measures is provided by CITES, which lists all seven species of marine turtles in Appendix I of the Convention and therefore prohibits commercial trade in marine turtles or any part thereof where they have been caught in international waters.

5.4. Marine Mammals

The earliest measures addressing bycatch focused on marine mammals, particularly dolphins, which were often deliberately targeted as part of the tuna purse seine fishery.[171] It has been estimated that in the Eastern Pacific Ocean alone dolphin bycatch within the tuna fishery affected between 200,000 and 500,000 individuals in the 1960s and 1970s.[172] Responding to this, the United States adopted unilateral bycatch mitigation measures directed at US vessels and, subsequently, at foreign vessels that ultimately led to significant diplomatic and trade disputes.[173] Ultimately, States involved in the tuna fishery in the region adopted, in 1992, the La Jolla Agreement,[174] which was re-affirmed in 1995[175] and ultimately made binding under the AIDCP (amended in 2014). This initiative exemplifies a trend for marine mammal bycatch in that regulation is

---

[168] Protocol Concerning Specially Protected Areas and Biological Diversity in the Mediterranean adopted on 10 June 1995 ((1995) 6 *Yearbook of International Environmental Law*).

[169] Available at www.rac-spa.org/sites/default/files/doc_turtles/turtles_timeplan.pdf.

[170] Inter-American Turtle Convention, Art. IV(h).

[171] On bycatches in other fisheries, see A Proelss et al. "Protection of Cetaceans in European Waters – A Case Study on Bottom-Set Gillnet Fisheries within Marine Protected Areas" (2011) 26 *International Journal of Marine and Coastal Law* 5–46.

[172] C Hedley "The 1998 Agreement on the International Dolphin Conservation Program: Recent Developments in the Tuna-Dolphin Controversy in the Eastern Pacific Ocean" (2001) 32 *Ocean Development and International Law* 71–92, at 71–72.

[173] 1972 Marine Mammals Protection Act; see CKA Geijer and AJ Read "Mitigation of Marine Mammal Bycatch in US Fisheries since 1994" (2013) 159 *Biological Conservation* 54–60.

[174] Agreement for the Reduction of Dolphin Mortality in the Eastern Pacific Ocean of 23 April 1992 ((1994) 33 *ILM* 936).

[175] 1995 Panama Declaration.

largely dependent upon binding regional stand-alone agreements with no over-arching guidelines issued by the FAO and relatively few resolutions adopted by RFMOs.

The AIDCP operates within the framework of IATTC[176] and has been ratified by 13 States in the Americas plus the EU and is provisionally applied by Bolivia and Vanuatu. Its overall objective is to "progressively reduce inciden-tal dolphin mortalities in the tuna purse-seine fishery in the Agreement area to levels approaching zero, through the setting of annual limits"[177] as well as avoid-ing, reducing and minimizing bycatch and discards of juvenile tunas and other non-target species.[178] The Agreement establishes the International Dolphin Conservation Program, under which it is agreed to limit incidental dolphin mortality in the purse seine tuna fishery in the Agreement area to no more than 5,000 annually, with the aim of eliminating dolphin mortality.[179] Article V requires the establishment of "an equitable system for the assignment of dolphin mortality limits (DMLs) consistent with the per-year dolphin mortality caps"[180] with further details being set out in Annexes III and IV of the Agreement. Article V also establishes the range of measures designed to achieve this, includ-ing gear modification, operational matters, incentives, tracking and verification and an on-board observer programme.[181] In 2013, 90 vessels were allocated full-year DMLs with an average of 54.4 dolphins allocated per vessel.[182] The average mortality was 10.1 dolphins per vessels with 801 dolphins being killed in 10,736 intentional tuna sets. Although this does not meet the target of zero mortality, overall, 95.4 per cent of sets in 2013 caused no mortality or serious injury.[183]

Unsurprisingly purse seine fishing is the focus of bycatch measures adopted by a small number of RFMOs in addition to IATTC. IOTC[184] and WCPFC[185] have both adopted measures prohibiting intentionally setting a purse seine around cetaceans if the animal is sighted prior to the commencement of the set, and requiring vessels to release animals unintentionally entangled. In the case of WCPFC the measure applies to both the high seas and to EEZs located within the Convention area.[186] In the Mediterranean, Parties to GFCM must take measures to reduce the incidental taking of cetaceans and must prohibit gillnet fisheries using monofilament greater than 0.5mm as well as drift nets for

---

[176] AIDCP, Art. IV. IATTC also provides secretarial support for the Agreement under Art. XIV.
[177] AIDCP, Art. II(1).
[178] Ibid., Art. II(3).
[179] Ibid., Art. V(1) and (1)(a).
[180] Ibid., Art. V(1)(d).
[181] See further AIDCP Technical Guidelines to Prevent High Mortality During Sets on Large Dolphin Herds (2002).
[182] AIDCP Executive Report on the Functioning of the AIDCP in 2013, p. 1.
[183] Ibid.
[184] IOTC Resolution 13/04 on the Conservation of Cetaceans.
[185] WCPFC CMM 2011-03 for Protection of Cetaceans from Purse Seine Fishing Operations.
[186] Ibid.

large pelagic species.[187] Additional measures are in place to mitigate bycatch of the Mediterranean monk seal, including a prohibition on retaining monk seals on board or landing them unless for the purpose of rescue.[188]

The Mediterranean provides a good example of the intersection of and deliberate development of synergies between several regimes which have developed a mandate to manage or otherwise address bycatch of marine mammals. Measures adopted under the GFCM support broader-based conservation measures adopted under the SPA Protocol, which lists 19 species of marine mammals in Annex II and requires Parties to support their conservation status. More specifically, 90,000 km² of the North-Western Mediterranean has been designated a marine mammal sanctuary[189] in addition to being listed in the Barcelona List of Specially Protected Areas of Mediterranean Importance (SPAMIs) under Article 5 of the SPA Protocol. The Mediterranean, along with the Black Sea and part of the Atlantic, is also regulated under ACCOBAMS, which addresses bycatch through restricting the use of driftnets, acoustic harassment devices and promoting observers and training. Finally, under the Habitats Directive, EU Member States are obliged to take measures to monitor the incidental capture of marine mammals listed in Annex IV and to ensure that incidental capture does not have a significant negative effect on the species concerned.[190]

A similar network of regulatory instruments exists in the Baltic and North-East Atlantic. In addition to EU regulation, bycatch is addressed briefly in the joint OSPAR-HELCOM Statement on the Ecosystem Approach to the Management of Human Activities[191] but neither regional seas convention directly manages bycatch generally. The instrument of most importance in this area is ASCOBANS. In the conservation and management plan adopted pursuant to ASCOBANS, the 17 Parties have agreed to establish an efficient system for reporting and retrieving bycatches. In subsequent resolutions, States have agreed to restrict anthropogenic removal to below the threshold of 'unacceptable interactions' with the precautionary objective of reducing bycatch to less than 1 per cent of the best available abundance estimate, with a view to reducing it to zero.[192] Notably however, there is no target date to provide the parameters for

---

[187] Recommendation GFCM/36/2012/2 on the Mitigation of Incidental Catches of Cetaceans in the GFCM Area; Recommendation GFCM/37/2013/2 on the Establishment of a Set of Minimum Standards for Bottom-set Gillnet Fisheries for Turbot and Conservation of Cetaceans in the Black Sea.

[188] Recommendation GFCM/35/2011/5 on Fisheries Measures for the Conservation of the Mediterranean Monk Seal (*Monachus monachus*) in the GFCM Competence Area. The Mediterranean Monk Seal is also subject to a distinct CMS MOU.

[189] Pelagos Sanctuary Agreement for Mediterranean Marine Mammals.

[190] EU Directive 92/43/EEC on the conservation of natural habitats and of wild fauna and flora [1992] OJ L206/7, Art. 12.

[191] Available at www.ospar.org/site/assets/files/1232/jmm_annex05_ecosystem_approach_statement.pdf.

[192] MOP 2: Resolution on Incidental Take of Small Cetaceans (Bonn 1997); MOP 5: Resolution No. 5 Incidental Take of Small Cetaceans (2006); MOP 8: Resolution No. 5 Monitoring and Mitigation of Small Cetacean Bycatch (2009).

these bycatch reduction objectives, although ASCOBANS has adopted conservation and recovery plans for certain areas and species which address, in part, bycatch.

6. CONCLUDING REMARKS

Managing bycatch and discards takes place within the "twilight zone where international fisheries regimes and international nature conservation regimes meet".[193] This necessitates a high level of coordination between regimes, always a challenge at the international level, but particularly difficult where a coincidence in mandate does not necessarily reflect commensurate aims and objectives. It is perhaps unsurprising that the most successful bycatch measures, in respect of seabirds and marine mammals, apply to species that are not commercially targeted. In contrast, measures relating to discards, and the bycatch of sharks and turtles, are largely non-binding at the international level and highly variable in application at the regional level. Although measures adopted under conservation regimes such as the CMS provide a vital layer to the regulatory regime, it is apparent that bycatch cannot be addressed in isolation of the fishing industry, and measures must be adopted as part of broader fisheries ecosystem management subject to RFMO monitoring and compliance mechanisms.[194]

Bycatch and discards are a global challenge. While there are inevitable regional variations – in terms of the problem and potential solutions – what is required is the creation of binding global minimum standards that apply to and extend across regional organizations. The PSM Agreement[195] provides a potential model for such an instrument. The PSM Agreement develops globally applicable minimum standards for ports designed to address IUU fishing. These global measures are implemented on a regional and local basis, and the Agreement also provides for coordination and cooperation between interested bodies. One option to address bycatch and discards would be the negotiation of an international instrument setting out minimum standards as well as requirements relating to reporting designed to be implemented through RFMOs – using the model of the Fish Stocks Agreement – as well as by individual States. In contrast to the Fish Stocks Agreement, it is suggested that such an instrument provide a clear mechanism for the coordination of RFMOs and indeed other organizations, and a means of global oversight, perhaps through

---

[193] A Trouwborst "Seabird Bycatch – Deathbed Conservation or a Precautionary and Holistic Approach" (2009) 11 *Journal of International Wildlife Law and Policy* 293–333, at 293.

[194] TM Cox et al. "Comparing Effectiveness of Experimental and Implemented Bycatch Reduction Measures: The Ideal and the Real" (2007) 21 *Conservation Biology* 1155–1164, at 1161.

[195] Agreement on Port State Measures to Prevent, Deter and Eliminate Illegal, Unreported and Unregulated Fishing of 22 November 2009: [2010] ATNIF 41. See Chapter 13 of this volume (van der Marel).

the FAO. Processes for coordination and oversight should also provide opportunities to share best practice, knowledge and technologies. Such an instrument
would be able to bring together current practice as global standards, as well as
developing new standards in respect of species such as sharks, or addressing
issues that have not thus far been consistently addressed at the regional level.
Ultimately, any new mechanism must find a way to coordinate and implement
action at the regional and local levels in order to address what is undeniably one
of the greatest challenges to global fish stocks and their accompanying marine
ecosystems.

9

Area-based Fisheries Management

DANIEL C DUNN, GUILLERMO ORTUÑO CRESPO
AND RICHARD CADDELL*

1. INTRODUCTION

CONTEMPORARY FISHERIES MANAGEMENT aspires to an ecosystem approach to fisheries (EAF), which aims to "balance diverse societal objectives, by taking account of the knowledge and uncertainties about biotic, abiotic and human components of ecosystems and their interactions and applying an integrated approach to fisheries within ecologically meaningful boundaries".[1] Advocates of EAF have long sought to achieve particular ecological, economic and social objectives while addressing multiple environmental stressors.[2] Attempts to define this rather amorphous concept invariably include requirements to preserve ecosystem dynamics, stock structure and trophic interactions.[3] Fisheries managers have an array of regulatory tools to achieve these objectives, which are broadly categorized into input controls (e.g. gear, effort or area restrictions) and output controls (e.g. bag limits, annual catch limits and individual transferable quotas). Area restrictions, or area-based management tools (ABMTs), are commonly established by States within their national waters. However, due to jurisdictional constraints, such initiatives have had limited application in areas beyond national jurisdiction (ABNJ). In this chapter we consider the utility of ABMTs in advancing EAF and the challenges and opportunities raised by their prospective expansion into ABNJ.

---

* The authors gratefully acknowledge the support of the Nereus Program (www.nereusprogram. org) in facilitating the writing of this chapter.
[1] SM Garcia et al. "The Ecosystem Approach to Fisheries. Issues, Terminology, Principles, Institutional Foundations, Implementation and Outlook" (FAO Fisheries Technical Paper 443: 2003) 2.
[2] See J Brodziak and J Link (2002) "Ecosystem-based Fisheries Management: What is it and How Can We Do It?" (2002) 70 *Bulletin of Marine Science* 589–611; JS Link "What Does Ecosystem-Based Fisheries Management Mean?" (2002) 27 *Fisheries* 18–21; and E Pikitch et al. "Ecosystem-based Fishery Management" (2004) 305 *Science* 346–347.
[3] L Wenzel *Framework for the National System of Marine Protected Areas of the United States of America* (NOAA, Silver Spring, MD: 2015) 27.

To this end, this chapter commences by outlining the rationale for ABMTs and the legal considerations underpinning their establishment (Section 2), before examining the current application of ABMTs in ABNJ. Accordingly, Section 3 considers the deep-sea environment, for which a series of commitments derived from Resolutions of the United Nations General Assembly (UNGA) has facilitated the development of a unique regime for the regulation of Vulnerable Marine Ecosystems (VMEs), which have been primarily threatened by bottom-fishing activities. Section 4 reviews the ABMT practices of selected regional fisheries management organizations (RFMOs) in those areas of high seas under their regulatory purviews. Section 5 then addresses the prospective development of further ABMTs in ABNJ and their implications for fisheries management, notably through sectoral regulation, efforts under the CBD,[4] and the potential value of a new International Legally-Binding Instrument (ILBI) for the conservation and sustainable use of marine biodiversity in ABNJ. Section 6 evaluates the current and future challenges facing ABMTs in ABNJ and considers how such mechanisms could be strengthened in design and application, while Section 7 concludes.

2. FISHERIES GOVERNANCE AND THE ROLE OF AREA-BASED MANAGEMENT TOOLS

ABMTs include marine spatial planning (MSP), networks of marine protected areas (MPAs), sectoral closures (e.g. areas closed to fishing, shipping or mining), dynamic ocean management and, as articulated in the CBD's Aichi Target 11, "other effective area-based conservation measures" (e.g. indigenous, community and privately managed areas). While no universally accepted definition exists, ABMTs generally involve planning or implementing spatially explicit measures to facilitate enhanced protection of a particular site through the application of more stringent regulation of one or more human activities in comparison to the surrounding area. Area-based management is thus not a management objective itself, but a tool to address the ecological, social or cultural impacts generated by anthropogenic activities. Of the measures associated with ABMTs in a marine context, MPAs are the most well known and widely applied. MPAs vary greatly in size and stringency, ranging from strictly protected marine reserves to zoned areas wherein anthropogenic uses compatible with the objectives of the MPA objectives are permitted. ABMT objectives tend to reflect the broader motivations of the actor that has instituted these initiatives. Enumerating the objectives of MPAs should, therefore, provide some context for the overall scope of objectives of area-based management. Notably, fisheries objectives are only one component of MPA practices; the overall governance framework of ABMTs on a

---

[4] Convention on Biological Diversity of 5 June 1992 (1760 UNTS 79).

national and international basis is therefore guided by a cross-sectoral approach that also includes other ocean uses as well as biodiversity conservation for its own intrinsic value.

In order to understand the utility of MPAs (and ABMTs more broadly) to sustainable fisheries production, it is important to gauge the potential ecological impacts of fisheries upon marine ecosystems. Comprehensive assessments of these impacts have emerged over the last two decades[5] and can be broadly categorized into three groups, namely: species-, community- and ecosystem-level impacts.

Species-level impacts of fisheries primarily arise from excessive or asymmetric harvesting of marine populations. Harvesting a population below a certain biological threshold can lead to reduced productivity, or even the local, ecological or economic extinction of the population.[6] The current status of oceanic fish stocks provides cause for concern in ABNJ, where estimates by the United Nations Food and Agriculture Organization (FAO) indicate that straddling and highly migratory stocks are overfished or experiencing overfishing at more than twice the rate of fish stocks found within national waters (64.0 per cent v. 28.8 per cent respectively).[7] The conservation status of non-target species, especially sharks, seabirds, sea turtles and marine mammals, is also a concern.[8] In addition to changes in abundance,[9] overfishing and asymmetric fishing can lead to reductions in the range of species,[10] changes to average body size[11] and the population age structure,[12] as well as dilution of the genetic diversity of populations, which reduces their adaptability and, for overfished stocks, their potential rate of recovery.[13]

As the abundance and structure of marine species and populations deteriorates, so do the interlinkages that glue the biological communities in which they

---

[5] See especially PK Dayton et al. "Environmental Effects of Marine Fishing" (1995) 5 *Aquatic Conservation: Marine and Freshwater Ecosystems* 205–232; S Jennings and MJ Kaiser "The Effects of Fishing on Marine Ecosystems" (1998) 34 *Advances in Marine Biology* 201–352; MR Clark et al. "The Impacts of Deep-sea Fisheries on Benthic Communities: A Review" (2016) 73 *ICES Journal of Marine Science* i51–i69; and GO Crespo and DC Dunn "A Review of the Impacts of Fisheries on Open-Ocean Ecosystems" (2017) 74 *ICES Journal of Marine Science* 2283–2297.

[6] Clark et al., ibid.

[7] FAO, *The State of World Fisheries and Aquaculture 2018* (FAO, Rome: 2018) 40; see also S Cullis-Suzuki and D Pauly "Failing the High Seas: A Global Evaluation of Regional Fisheries Management Organizations" (2010) 34 *Marine Policy* 1036–1042 (noting that 67 per cent of RFMO-managed stocks are overfished or depleted).

[8] See further Chapter 8 of this volume (Scott).

[9] See further Chapter 2 of this volume (Cheung, Lam, Ota and Swartz).

[10] B Worm and DP Tittensor "Range Contraction in Large Pelagic Predators" (2011) 108 *PNAS* 11942–11947.

[11] P Ward and RA Myers "Shifts in Open-Ocean Fish Communities Coinciding with the Commencement of Commercial Fishing" (2005) 86 *Ecology* 835–847.

[12] ISC Pacific Bluefin Tuna Working Group "Executive Summary of the 2016 Pacific Bluefin Tuna Stock Assessment".

[13] MR Walsh et al. "Maladaptive Changes in Multiple Traits Caused by Fishing: Impediments to Population Recovery" (2006) 9 *Ecology Letters* 142–148.

exist. Bycatch and overfishing have reduced population abundance of target and non-target species, which in turn alters the ecological roles of the species within their community, modifying the food web dynamics throughout the ecosystem.[14] For instance, between the 1950s and 1990s, the abundance of several oceanic predatory species in the Eastern and Central North Pacific was reduced by a factor of ten, leading to an increase in abundance and body size of various intermediate trophic level species.[15]

Ecosystem-level impacts originate from deep changes in the dynamics and functioning of the communities and surrounding environment and can trigger changes in the stable state of the ecosystem, which is known as a regime shift. Stressors such as overfishing and climate change are known to contribute to regime shifts.[16] A second type of ecosystem-level impact affects the physical habitat of marine ecosystems. Physical impacts to habitat are primarily the result of fishing practices which involve the use of bottom-set gear that is in direct contact with the structures of the seafloor, which have long-lasting adverse impacts on deep-sea habitats such as seamounts.[17]

There are various approaches to mitigating negative impacts of fisheries on marine ecosystems and increasing productivity, including modifying fishing gear, instituting fisheries quotas, establishing fishing seasons and observer programmes, limiting fishing effort and utilising ABMTs. While fishing seasons have both a spatial and temporal component, they differ from ABMTs, which tend to affect only a small part of the species range. ABMTs reduce the spatiotemporal overlap between a stressor (e.g. fishing) and the distribution of vulnerable species or habitats, and are a widespread form of management in many marine systems, especially coastal areas. To help ensure sustainable and productive fisheries, managers employ ABMTs to conserve and manage reproduction areas, including larval sources and nursery grounds; areas for maintaining natural age/sex structure of important harvestable species; foraging grounds; areas that may help reduce the rate of bycatch; and areas that provide compatible opportunities for education and research.[18]

Assessments of marine reserves closed to fishing have revealed increases in the fish density, biomass, average body size and biological diversity inside these closures.[19] ABMTs can therefore play an important role in accomplishing

---

[14] These changes in the structure and composition of marine communities are defined as trophic cascades: ML Pace et al. "Trophic Cascades Revealed in Diverse Ecosystems" (1999) 14 *Trends in Ecology and Evolution* 483–488.

[15] JJ Polovina and P Woodworth-Jefcoats "Fishery-Induced Changes in the Subtropical Pacific Pelagic Ecosystem Size Structure: Observations and Theory" (2013) 8 *PLoS ONE* e62341.

[16] G Beaugrand et al. "Synchronous Marine Pelagic Regime Shifts in the Northern Hemisphere" (2014) 370 *Philosophical Transactions of the Royal Society B: Biological Sciences* 20130272.

[17] Clark et al., note 5.

[18] Wenzel, note 3.

[19] BS Halpern and RR Warner "Marine Reserves have Rapid and Lasting Effects" (2002) 5 *Ecology Letters* 361–366.

the conservation objectives of ecosystem-based management.[20] However, their establishment must be accommodated within a framework that accounts for trade-offs across stakeholder interests and ecosystem services. The benefits of MPAs are also highly dependent on funding, management and enforcement capacity.[21] ABMTs must therefore be targeted, scientifically-robust measures embedded in a wider governance framework that generates the necessary capacity to provide effective monitoring, control and surveillance of the site and to adapt to changing conditions or objectives.

Notwithstanding the prospective contribution of such tools in promoting ecosystem-based management, little obvious provision was made for ABMTs within the LOS Convention.[22] While the power to establish MPAs and similar designations may be broadly considered to fall under the exclusive sovereignty of the coastal State over its internal waters and territorial sea,[23] the position of the exclusive economic zone (EEZ) is more cryptic. Article 56(1)(b)(iii) prescribes jurisdiction over the protection and preservation of the marine environment, which might at first blush indicate a broad discretion to elaborate ABMTs. Nevertheless, this provision must be read in conjunction with the entitlement of foreign States to freedom of navigation in these waters,[24] hence objections could be legitimately raised against ABMTs that served to unreasonably impede the exercise of these rights. Instead, the clearest indication that ABMTs lies within the contemplation of the EEZ regime is Article 194(5), which requires States to take measures to prevent, reduce and control pollution of the marine environment, including "those necessary to protect and preserve rare or fragile ecosystems as well as the habitat of depleted, threatened or endangered species and other forms of marine life". To date, this provision appears to have been the primary basis for MPA designations within these waters.[25] States have also taken an expansive view of their entitlements to establish ABMTs upon their continental shelves, including areas beyond 200 nautical miles wherein the water column is composed of high seas.[26]

---

[20] BS Halpern, SE Lester and KL McLeod "Placing Marine Protected Areas onto the Ecosystem-based Management Seascape" (2010) 107 *PNAS* 18312–18317.

[21] DA Gill et al. "Capacity Shortfalls Hinder the Performance of Marine Protected Areas Globally" (2017) 543 *Nature* 665–669.

[22] United Nations Convention on the Law of the Sea of 10 December 1982 (1833 UNTS 3).

[23] Under Art. 21(1), in the territorial sea the coastal State may adopt laws and regulations for the conservation of the living resources of the sea and for the prevention of infringement of fisheries laws.

[24] Art. 58.

[25] See further A Proelß (ed.) *United Nations Convention on the Law of the Sea. A Commentary* (C.H. Beck/Hart/Nomos: 2017) 1313–1314.

[26] See MC Ribeiro "The 'Rainbow': The First National Marine Protected Area Proposed Under the High Seas" (2010) 25 *International Journal of Marine and Coastal Law* 183, at 191–92; and J Mossop *The Continental Shelf Beyond 200 Nautical Miles: Rights and Responsibilities* (Oxford University Press, Oxford: 2016) 217–221.

However, complications are more apparent with respect to the purported establishment of ABMTs on the high seas. Under Article 89 of the LOS Convention, "no State may validly purport to subject any part of the high seas to its sovereignty". While intended to deter creeping jurisdiction and the national appropriation of further maritime territory, this provision complicates the ability of States to altruistically (if unilaterally) designate MPAs in ABNJ. Although this is not unprecedented – indeed, in 1999 France, Monaco and Italy established the Pelagos Sanctuary for the protection of marine mammals, over half of which comprises areas of the Mediterranean high seas[27] – such examples remain isolated. Tellingly, the Pelagos sanctuary was swiftly incorporated into the network of Specially Protected Areas of Mediterranean Importance (SPAMIs) operated under the Barcelona Convention,[28] thereby acquiring the further legitimacy of multilateral oversight. Indeed, the greatest jurisdictional challenge confronting the use of ABMTs on the high seas is the need to establish such areas under multilateral authority. This chapter now considers the current bases for achieving this, using the examples of VMEs, for which regulatory authority is derived from the UNGA (Section 3) and pelagic fisheries restrictions adopted under the mandate of selected RFMOs (Section 4). Thereafter, this chapter examines how RFMOs may have to contend with an increasingly busy ocean space by cooperating with those other entities that are actively developing ABMTs in ABNJ (e.g. the International Seabed Authority (ISA), the International Maritime Organization (IMO) and Regional Seas Organizations (RSOs)), those that can inform their development (e.g. the CBD), and the prospective negotiation of a clearer framework for ABMT designations through the biodiversity beyond national jurisdiction (BBNJ) process (Section 5).

3. AREA-BASED FISHERIES MANAGEMENT IN THE DEEP-SEA

The context of the deep-sea environment provides a particularly striking example of the application of ABMTs in ABNJ. As outlined in Chapter 7, since 2004 the UNGA has adopted a series of Resolutions to mitigate the ecological problems associated with poorly-regulated bottom trawling.[29] Bottom trawling has raised concerns over the scraping of vulnerable benthic sediments,[30] damage

---

[27] See further G Notarbatolo-di-Sciarra "The Pelagos Sanctuary for Mediterranean Marine Mammals" (2008) 18 *Aquatic Conservation: Marine and Freshwater Ecosystems* 367–391.

[28] Convention for the Protection of the Marine Environment and the Coastal Region of the Mediterranean of 16 February 1976 (1242 UNTS 174).

[29] See further R Caddell "International Environmental Governance and the Final Frontier: The Protection of Vulnerable Marine Ecosystems in Areas Beyond National Jurisdiction" (2018) 29 *Yearbook of Environmental Law* 1–36, at 16–22.

[30] FG O'Neill and A Ivanović "The Physical Impact of Towed Demersal Fishing Gears on Soft Sediments" (2016) 73 *ICES Journal of Marine Science* i5–i14, at 12.

to fragile seabed features,[31] removal of habitat-forming species[32] and impacts upon fish productivity.[33] As bottom trawling is typically conducted around benthic locations known to attract significant aggregations of fish, area-based management could be a particularly appropriate form of regulation. To this end, ABMT responses to bottom trawling have primarily focused upon identifying areas of particular environmental sensitivity within which fishing is to be largely precluded, alongside mapping the footprint of current fishing activities and restricting trawls to these areas, and enforcing 'move-on' rules where protected ecosystems are encountered.

Since bottom fishing restrictions were first contemplated by the UNGA in 2004, eight RFMOs have established competence over deep-sea fisheries, each of which has developed particular policies to address the impacts of bottom fisheries. These institutions are the North-East Atlantic Fisheries Commission (NEAFC), the Northwest Atlantic Fisheries Organization (NAFO), the South-East Atlantic Fisheries Organization (SEAFO), the Southern Indian Ocean Fisheries Agreement (SIOFA), the North Pacific Fisheries Commission (NPFC), the General Fisheries Commission for the Mediterranean (GFCM), the South Pacific Regional Fisheries Management Organization (SPRFMO) and the Commission for the Conservation of Atlantic Marine Living Resources (CCAMLR). The ecological conditions of each of the regions managed by these entities precludes a neat comparative analysis. Instead, this section considers the primary area-based approaches taken by RFMOs toward VMEs in ABNJ required under the various UNGA Resolutions, namely the need to identify such ecosystems and regulate fishing effort accordingly and the closure of areas of particular ecological sensitivity to deep-sea bottom fishing.

A prominent commitment established across the suite of UNGA Resolutions is the need to identify VMEs and to institute appropriate precautionary management measures in order to protect such areas from significant adverse impacts of bottom fishing. Accordingly, considerable importance was vested in the elaboration of universal Guidelines by the FAO[34] to provide practical guidance for RFMOs in framing conservation and management measures for VMEs within their respective areas of oversight. The Guidelines elaborate a series of representative characteristics that should be used as criteria in identifying VMEs, namely the uniqueness or rarity of an area or ecosystem; the functional significance of the habitat; the fragility of the area; the life history traits of component

---

[31] MR Clark et al. "Effects of Fishing on the Benthic Biodiversity of Seamounts of the 'Graveyard' Complex, Northern Chatham Rise" (2010) 46 *New Zealand Aquatic Environment and Biodiversity Report* 1–40.

[32] SF Thrush, KE Ellingsen and K Davis "Implications of Fisheries Impacts to Seabed Biodiversity and Ecosystem-Based Management" (2016) 73 *ICES Journal of Marine Science* i44–i50, at 45.

[33] J Collie et al., "Indirect Effects of Bottom Fishing on the Productivity of Marine Fish" (2017) 18 *Fish and Fisheries* 619–637, at 634.

[34] *International Guidelines for the Management of Deep-Sea Fisheries in the High Seas* (FAO, Rome: 2008).

species that would make recovery difficult; and the structural complexity of an ecosystem.[35] Although a further, non-exhaustive, series of examples are listed in an Annex to the Guidelines, the individual biogeological conditions of each region mean that the ultimate decision as to whether a particular site or ecosystem constitutes a VME is made by the RFMO in question. The practice of RFMOs has been to develop extensive individual lists of indicator species and ecosystems and regulate the spatial footprint of fishing activities accordingly.

The capacity of Parties to RFMOs to monitor such ecosystems, even within areas in which significant research activities have been conducted, remains variable. Assessing whether an area might be sufficiently resilient to prospectively support a degree of fishing is also an exceptionally difficult undertaking. Consequently, the utilization of potential VMEs would appear to exemplify precisely the type of situation wherein the precautionary approach to fisheries management ought to be taken, which has prompted calls for institutional restraint, and continued demands for a moratorium on such activities in ABNJ.[36] Nevertheless, this initially proved to be problematic, with concerns having been expressed that support tools were limited[37] alongside few opportunities for institutional learning between RFMOs.[38] This has subsequently improved markedly, particularly through the development of a VME database[39] maintained by the FAO, which allows for a further degree of cross-reference and comparison.

Where VMEs have been identified, the Guidelines outline the context in which a significant adverse impact (SAI) is deemed to have occurred, thus prompting further mitigation strategies. A SAI occurs where ecosystem integrity is compromised in a manner that

> (i) impairs the ability of affected populations to replace themselves; (ii) degrades the long-term natural productivity of habitats; or (iii) causes, on more than a temporary basis, significant loss of species richness, habitat or community types. Impacts should be evaluated individually, in combination and cumulatively.[40]

---

[35] Ibid., para. 42.

[36] EA Norse et al. "Sustainability of Deep-Sea Fisheries" (2012) 36 *Marine Policy* 307–320, at 317.

[37] Actions taken by States and regional fisheries management organizations and arrangements to give effect to paragraphs 83 to 90 of General Assembly resolution 61/105 on sustainable fisheries, including through the 1995 Agreement for the Implementation of the Provisions of the United Nations Convention on the Law of the Sea of 10 December 1982 relating to the Conservation and Management of Straddling Fish Stocks and Highly Migratory Fish Stocks, and related instruments: Report of the Secretary-General, UN Doc. A/64/305, para. 202.

[38] Actions taken by States and regional fisheries management organizations and arrangements in response to paragraphs 80 and 83 to 87 of General Assembly resolution 61/105 and paragraphs 113 to 117 and 119 to 127 of General Assembly resolution 64/72 on sustainable fisheries, addressing the impacts of bottom fishing on vulnerable marine ecosystems and the long-term sustainability of deep-sea fish stocks: Report of the Secretary-General, UN Doc. A/66/307, para. 207.

[39] www.fao.org/in-action/vulnerable-marine-ecosystems/vme-database/en/vme.html.

[40] Guidelines, para. 16.

A SAI usually triggers a 'move-on' rule, requiring a vessel to move a particular distance away from the VME, for which numerous RFMOs have developed encounter protocols, which are predominantly based upon the incidental catch of indicator species above threshold levels.[41]

Nevertheless, concerns have been raised that these thresholds are contingent upon a certain volume of live bycatch. This, for instance, has been the approach of NAFO, NEAFC and SEAFO, although it is considered a poor tool to identify an encounter since the equipment used is designed exclusively to catch fish and is therefore not conducive to the effective sampling of benthic areas.[42] Moreover, the move-on rule – which has been traditionally applied to mobile fish species – may be ill-suited for essentially non-regenerative static habitats.[43] Operationally, given that cold-water reefs (which represent a substantial proportion of current VMEs) habitually comprise a framework of primarily dead coral, significant damage may be legitimately inflicted upon a VME without triggering the move-on rule.[44] There is also a risk that evidence of an encounter may be lost during the retrieval of a net, hence otherwise responsible fishers may be oblivious to an impact. Further, a fundamental objection to the application of this approach remains the tacit toleration of the destruction of habitat incumbent in the process.

Allied to the need to identify VMEs and advance appropriate encounter protocols and mitigation strategies, a primary commitment established within the multiple UNGA Resolutions is to prevent fishing activities where they may have a SAI upon such sites. In this respect, a two-pronged approach has been adopted by RFMOs, encompassing restrictions on both current and prospective fisheries.

In the first instance, RFMOs have required participants to identify their existing fishing footprints – i.e. those locations in which some fishing activity has previously been conducted – with controls and procedures subsequently imposed where a State wishes to extend this footprint by conducting exploratory fishing. For example, in 2008, NEAFC adopted an Interim Exploratory Bottom Fishing Protocol for New Bottom Fishing Areas.[45] Under these arrangements NEAFC, in consultation with the International Council on Exploration of the Sea (ICES), maintains a full accounting of such areas maintained in an Annex to the Recommendation which establishes a definitive, yet adjustable, list of existing fishing footprints. These footprints can be extended, but

---

[41] SEAFO, CM 30/5 and CCAMLR, CM 22-07.

[42] PJ Auster et al. "Definition and Detection of Vulnerable Marine Ecosystems on the High Seas: Problems with the 'Move-On' Rule" (2011) 68 *ICES Journal of Marine Science* 254–264, at 258.

[43] On the motivation for and implementation of move-on rules generally, see note 126 below and accompanying text.

[44] UN Doc. A/66/307, note 38 at para. 46.

[45] Recommendation XVI:2008.

any activities conducted therein are classed as 'exploratory' and subject to prior approval, based on the submission of a Notice of Intent to fish, alongside a harvesting plan, mitigation plan and a 'sufficient system' to record data.[46] Similar systems have been established by SEAFO,[47] the NPFC,[48] SPRFMO[49] and, especially, CCAMLR,[50] on whose pioneering system of exploratory fisheries such procedures have been largely modelled. This represents a regulatory trade-off, involving approval for a limited degree of fishing in exchange for returning an agreed volume of ecosystem data. Nevertheless, concerns have been raised as to whether such approaches are truly precautionary, since they can facilitate the perpetuation of exploratory fisheries that are operational for considerable timeframes without yielding meaningful information.[51]

The second main strategy has been the designation of restricted areas for bottom fishing. In this respect, a significant volume of area closures have been instituted by NEAFC, NAFO, SEAFO and CCAMLR. Moreover, the GFCM has established three separate Fisheries Restricted Areas (FRAs) for a more modest volume of territory – representative of the rather abbreviated pockets of ABNJ in these waters – but has also imposed a long-standing prohibition on bottom trawling in any area below 1000 metres.[52] Formal closures have not yet been instituted by the most recently created RFMOs, SPRFMO and the NPFC, although this consideration of VMEs – including the prospective designation of geographical restrictions – remain a significant operational priority. Meanwhile, perhaps most intriguingly, a series of Benthic Protected Areas (BPAs) have been established within the Southern Indian Ocean. While SIOFA has not yet implemented formal area closures, a mosaic of 13 voluntary BPAs has been instituted by the Southern Indian Ocean Deep-Sea Fisheries Association (SIODFA), with such moves therefore driven by the industry itself in these waters.[53]

---

[46] Recommendation 19:2014 on Protection of VMEs in NEAFC Regulatory Areas, as amended by Recommendation 09:2015 and Recommendation 10:2018; Arts. 6 and 7.

[47] CM 30/15.

[48] CMM 2016-05: Bottom Fisheries and Protection of Vulnerable Marine Ecosystems in the Northeast Pacific Ocean and CMM 2016-06: Bottom Fisheries and Protection of Vulnerable Marine Ecosystems in the North-western Pacific Ocean.

[49] CMM 03-2014 (Management of Bottom Fishing in the SPRFMO Convention Area).

[50] CM 22-06: Bottom Fishing in the Convention Area.

[51] See R Caddell "Precautionary Management and the Development of Future Fishing Opportunities: The International Regulation of New and Exploratory Fisheries" (2018) 33 *International Journal of Marine and Coastal Law* 199–260, at 232–233; and PA Abrams et al. "Necessary Elements of Precautionary Management: Implications for Antarctic Toothfish" (2016) 17 *Fish and Fisheries* 1152–1174, at 1156–1159.

[52] REC29/2005/1.

[53] See further G Wright and J Rochette "Regional Management of Areas beyond National Jurisdiction in the Western Indian Ocean: State of Play and Possible Ways Forward" (2017) 32 *International Journal of Marine and Coastal Law* 765–796, at 788–790.

4. PELAGIC AREA-BASED FISHERIES MANAGEMENT ON THE HIGH SEAS

While there is broad consensus on the potential conservation and management benefits of ABMTs for species and ecosystems in nearshore waters and deep-sea benthic habitats, the role of such tools in the protection of more dynamic, pelagic, offshore species and ecosystems is still being debated.[54] There is, however, a growing body of knowledge highlighting the importance and efficacy of pelagic ABMTs.[55] For example, the National Marine Fisheries Service successfully implemented a time-area closure within the national waters of the South-East United States (US) to reduce the incidental mortality of juvenile swordfish and other non-target species,[56] abating impacts at the population level, specifically on stock structure.

The siting of pelagic ABMTs is more complex than for similar measures in coastal or benthic ecosystems due to the differences in oceanographic dynamics of the pelagic realm. Suitable habitat in pelagic systems is rarely defined by physical features. Instead, favourable conditions are typically characterized by the biophysical and chemical properties of the water column, which change over space (horizontally and vertically) and time. As oceanographic conditions in pelagic systems change on daily, monthly, annual and decadal cycles, so does the habitat suitability for different pelagic species, which generates different configurations in community composition and distributions that must be accounted for.[57] The designation of pelagic ABMTs to protect species or ecosystems 'on the move' thus requires a change in tactics, from retrospective, static closures to predictive, adaptive or dynamic closures.[58] This paradigm shift will require advancements in our understanding of the drivers of distribution of not only target and non-target pelagic biodiversity, but also of human activities, such as fisheries.[59] Adopting this approach will require further (fisheries-dependent and fisheries-independent) data on the distribution and movement patterns of

---

[54] ET Game et al. "Pelagic Protected Areas: The Missing Dimension in Ocean Conservation" (2009) 24 *Trends in Ecology and Evolution* 360–369; DM Kaplan et al. "Pelagic MPAs: The Devil Is in the Details" (2010) 25 *Trends in Ecology and Evolution* 62–3; ET Game et al. "Pelagic MPAs: The Devil You Know" (2010) 25 *Trends in Ecology and Evolution* 63–64.

[55] See further H Grantham, S Petersen and H Possingham "Reducing Bycatch in the South African Pelagic Longline Fishery: The Utility of Different Approaches to Fisheries Closures" (2008) 5 *Endangered Species Research* 291–299; and AJ Hobday et al. "Seasonal Forecasting of Tuna Habitat for Dynamic Spatial Management" (2011) 68 *Canadian Journal of Fisheries and Aquatic Sciences* 898–911.

[56] M Dunphy-Daly *A Meta-Analysis of the Value of Marine Protected Areas for Pelagic Apex Predators* (Dissertation, Duke University: 2015; available at http://hdl.handle.net/10161/9961.

[57] Grantham, Petersen and Possingham, note 55.

[58] DC Dunn et al. "Dynamic Ocean Management Increases the Efficiency and Efficacy of Fisheries Management" (2016) 113 *PNAS* 668–676.

[59] GO Crespo et al. "The Environmental Niche of the Global High Seas Pelagic Longline Fleet" (2018) 4 *Science Advances* eaat3681.

pelagic biodiversity,[60] as well as access to data on static and dynamic oceano-graphic features. The use of satellite remote sensing,[61] bio-logging[62] and habitat modelling to support fisheries management is allowing these new forms of spatial management to emerge. The primary aim of these approaches – and pelagic ABMTs in general – is to reduce bycatches, particularly of juveniles or threatened species.[63]

Although the ecological benefits of establishing pelagic ABMTs are broadly similar between national and international waters, the political frameworks for the designation of such measures are very different. Responsibility for designating sectoral or cross-sectoral ABMTs within national waters is primarily vested in the domestic authorities. However, the establishment of sectoral ABMTs on the high seas falls under the purview of numerous interna-tional bodies. There are currently no internationally-recognized mechanisms to establish cross-sectoral ABMTs in ABNJ, although as noted elsewhere, some tentative developments in this respect have emerged on a regional basis.[64] As in the deep-sea, RFMOs are the competent authorities for implementing ABMTs for fisheries management in ABNJ. While some RFMOs have responsibility for both pelagic species and deep-sea species, the major entities governing fisheries for large pelagic species are the tuna RFMOs. Unlike RFMOs with compe-tence over deep-sea fisheries, the tuna RFMOs have been more hesitant to apply ABMTs. The establishment of the few existing closures instituted to date has been motivated by diverse factors, including the preservation of ecosystem services, the conservation of biodiversity and the pursuit of specific scientific objectives.

Many of these closures have species-specific objectives. For instance, the Western and Central Pacific Fisheries Commission (WCPFC) has instituted high seas closures primarily to reduce regional fishing pressure on the yellowfin tuna (*Thunnus albacares*) and bigeye tuna (*Thunnus obesus*),[65] representing one of the few examples of annual pelagic closures in ABMT (Figure 1). Other closures have sought to address particular types of fishing gear, such as the Indian Ocean

[60] DC Dunn et al. "Global Ocean Governance Requires Actionable Knowledge on Migratory Connectivity" (under review).

[61] E Chassot et al. "Satellite Remote Sensing for an Ecosystem Approach to Fisheries Manage-ment" (2011) 68 *ICES Journal of Marine Science* 651–666; D Kacev and RL Lewison "Satellite Remote Sensing in Support of Fisheries Management in Global Oceans" in F Hossein (ed.) *Earth Science Satellite Applications: Current and Future Prospects* (Heidelberg, Springer: 2016) 207–222.

[62] BA Block et al., "Tracking Apex Marine Predator Movements in a Dynamic Ocean" (2011) 475 *Nature* 86–90.

[63] EA Howell et al. "TurtleWatch: A Tool to Aid in the Bycatch Reduction of Loggerhead Turtles Caretta Caretta in the Hawaii-Based Pelagic Longline Fishery" (2008) 5 *Endangered Species Research* 267–278; AJ Hobday and K Hartmann "Near Real-Time Spatial Management Based on Habitat Predictions for a Longline Bycatch Species" (2006) 13 *Fisheries Management and Ecology* 365–380; and Hobday et al, note 55.

[64] See further Section 5 below and Chapter 7 of this volume (Caddell).

[65] CMM 2008-01: Bigeye and Yellowfin Tuna in the Western and Central Pacific Ocean.

Tuna Commission (IOTC) which, since 2010, has implemented a gear-specific spatiotemporal closure in the high seas, affecting purse seiners (Figure 1).[66] While this initiative clearly reduces regional fishing effort, the specific ecological objectives of the closure are nevertheless unclear. Similar closures were introduced by the Inter-American Tropical Tuna Commission (IATTC) in 2011, which are still in place, to reduce the use of longlines (Figure 1). Meanwhile, the International Commission for the Conservation of Atlantic Tunas (ICCAT) has, since 2012, closed an area of the Eastern tropical Atlantic to fishing with any form of fish aggregation device (FAD) (Figure 1).[67] These closures were introduced to support the long-standing regulation of FADs and surface gears in the ICCAT Area. However, while the primary objective of reducing the mortality of juvenile fish has been met, these ABMTs had the unpredicted side-effect of increasing fishing effort outside the closure. This generated compliance challenges, with some Members using flags of convenience to circumvent these restrictions, which duly eroded the willingness of other Members to voluntarily adhere to the closure.[68]

Beyond the tuna RFMOs, the fisheries regulator most closely associated with far-sighted high seas ABMTs is the Commission for the Conservation of Antarctic Marine Living Resources (CCAMLR), whose competence lies exclusively in ABNJ. While CCAMLR's status as an RFMO is debated, it nevertheless performs fisheries functions within its geographical purview and thus "qualifies as an RFMO in the sense of the 1995 Fish Stocks Agreement".[69] Under Article II of its constituent treaty,[70] CCAMLR is charged with promoting "the conservation of Antarctic marine living resources", hence its fisheries mandate is discharged in this unique context. As 'more than' an RFMO,[71] CCAMLR is empowered to institute MPAs in a manner that is beyond the competence of other multilateral fisheries regulators. In this respect, CCAMLR has established two high seas MPAs closed to commercial fishing – the South Orkney Islands southern shelf MPA (2009) and the Ross Sea region (2016) – notwithstanding concerns that areas of elevated conservation value were omitted from the process due to pressure from fishing States.[72] CCAMLR also advances the

---

[66] IOTC "Estimates of the Catch Reductions that might have been achieved historically through the application of the Time/Area Closures proposed in IOTC Resolution 10/01. IOTC-SC-2010-14" (2010) available at http://222.iotc.org/files/proceedings/2011/sc/IOTC-2011-SC14-R%5BE%5D.pdf.

[67] ICCAT "Circular Number: 5058/2011: recommendations and resolutions adopted at the 2011 Commission meeting, Madrid, 7 December 2011" (2011).

[68] R Hilborn et al. "When Can Marine Reserves Improve Fisheries Management?" (2004) 47 *Ocean and Coastal Management* 197–205.

[69] EJ Molenaar "CCAMLR and Southern Ocean Fisheries" (2001) 16 *International Journal of Marine and Coastal Law* 465–499, at 496.

[70] Convention for the Conservation of Antarctic Marine Living Resources of 20 May 1980 (1329 UNTS 47).

[71] See further Chapter 6 of this volume (Molenaar).

[72] See CM Brooks "Competing Values on the Antarctic High Seas: CCAMLR and the Challenge of Marine Protected Areas" (2013) 3 *Polar Journal* 277–300.

spatial management of seasonal exploratory fisheries, instituting closures once allocations have been fully prosecuted and promoting move-on practices in locations of elevated fishing concentration.[73] Additionally, CCAMLR has addressed sectoral activities (including the designation of fisheries closures) within other classifications of areas that are protected under its auspices, but are not formal MPAs, such as the recently-developed concept of 'newly-exposed marine areas' generated from collapsed portions of the Larsen ice-shelf.[74]

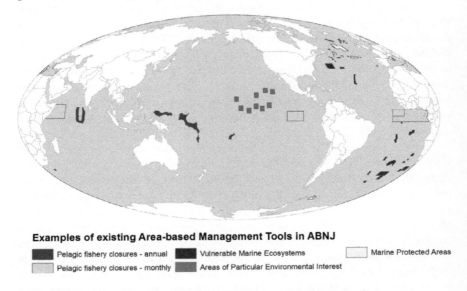

Examples of existing Area-based Management Tools in ABNJ

■ Pelagic fishery closures - annual	■ Vulnerable Marine Ecosystems	Marine Protected Areas
☐ Pelagic fishery closures - monthly	■ Areas of Particular Environmental Interest	

Figure 1 Examples of existing ABMTs in ABNJ across benthic and pelagic environments

5. CROSS-SECTORAL COOPERATION AND THE DEVELOPMENT OF ABMTs IN ABNJ

The establishment of areas in which fishing is restricted temporally and/or spatially (or precluded altogether) for the purpose of sustainable production is by no means the sole application of ABMTs, both within and beyond national jurisdiction. In the US for instance, Wenzel observes that two other significant motivations are represented within the national network of MPAs, namely natural heritage and cultural heritage objectives.[75] Therefore, ABMTs may

---

[73] Caddell, note 51, at 231–240.
[74] See further Chapter 11 of this volume (Rayfuse).
[75] Wenzel, note 3 at 13.

have numerous objectives that are unrelated to sustainable fisheries production. Moreover, no single objective holds a monopoly on how and when ABMTs ought to be used. As considered further in Chapter 7 of this volume (Caddell), fisheries closures, VMEs and other fisheries-specific ABMTs do not exist in a vacuum and must contend with an increasingly busy physical space on the high seas,[76] hence the use of ABMTs in fisheries management will have to be reconciled with the overall use of ABNJ. Indeed, due to fragmentation and lacunae between current and emerging ABNJ governance structures, the success of high seas ABMTs will depend upon strong inter-sectoral cooperation in key locations. Accordingly, this section considers the emergence of other bases for ABMTs in ABNJ and their potential implications for fisheries management.

5.1. Fishing in a Sea of Sectoral ABMTs

Area-based fisheries management in ABNJ will necessarily co-exist with broadly similar designations by other regulators. At present, an array of multilateral bodies exercise competence to establish ABMTs to advance sectoral regulation, although such initiatives are binding only on the sector in question and have been largely characterized by limited cooperation with other supervisory bodies.[77] Many such initiatives have also been predominantly established within national jurisdiction. Alternative high seas ABMTs are more nascent, while some bodies are still contemplating their mandates and considering whether to expand their area-based competences into ABNJ.

To date, beyond the activities of the RFMOs outlined above, the leading sectoral authority that has developed ABMTs in ABNJ is the ISA, which governs the mineral resources of the seabed in the Area and by definition operates exclusively beyond national jurisdiction.[78] The ISA currently manages mining interests in three mineral resources that are generally found in three unique environments: seafloor massive sulfides on mid-ocean ridges, polymetallic nodules on abyssal plains, and ferromanganese crusts on seamounts. To address potential impacts from deep-sea mining, the ISA has and continues to develop regional Environmental Management Plans (EMPs).[79] The first EMP for deep-sea mining was adopted in 2012 for the Clarion-Clipperton Zone (CCZ) of the central

---

[76] A Merrie et al. "An Ocean of Surprises – Trends in Human Use, Unexpected Dynamics and Governance Challenges in Areas beyond National Jurisdiction" (2014) 27 *Global Environmental Change* 19–31.

[77] D Freestone "Governance of Areas beyond National Jurisdiction: An Unfinished Agenda?" in J Barrett and R Barnes (eds.) *Law of the Sea: UNCLOS as a Living Instrument* (BIICL, London: 2016) 231–265, at 264; see also Chapter 7 of this volume (Caddell).

[78] LOS Convention, Art. (1)(1).

[79] DC Dunn et al. "A Strategy for the Conservation of Biodiversity on Mid-Ocean Ridges from Deep-Sea Mining" (2018) 4 *Science Advances* eaar4313.

Pacific Ocean.[80] Although there is general agreement that EMPs should take a broad view and describe requirements for, *inter alia*, environmental impact assessments, site-based conservation, transparent monitoring and mitigation measures, the main characteristic of the CCZ-EMP is a network of no-mining areas (referred to by the ISA, and herein, as 'Areas of Particular Environmental Interest' or APEIs).[81] APEIs cannot fulfil the environmental protection objectives of the ISA on their own. There is accordingly a need for additional deep-sea mining ABMTs that consider both benthic and pelagic ecosystems, including Impact Reference Zones and Preservation Reference Zones, which will have to be taken into account by RFMOs and other competent authorities when developing ABMTs in ABNJ.

Beyond the ISA, other significant multilateral organizations are competent to develop sectoral ABMTs in ABNJ or are considering extending their mandate to these waters. The IMO governs international shipping and maritime pollution and has the ability to designate areas as Particularly Sensitive Sea Areas (PSSAs) due to their "significance for recognized ecological, socio-economic, or scientific attributes where such attributes may be vulnerable to damage by international shipping activities".[82] A PSSA designation has no legal effect in and of itself, but the protective measures associated with such a move provide clearer normative content for the management of shipping in that location.[83] PSSAs require associated protective measures which can include the "designation of an area as a Special Area under MARPOL Annexes I, II or V, or a SO_x emission control area under MARPOL Annex VI, or application of special discharge restrictions to vessels operating in a PSSA".[84] While no PSSAs have yet been adopted that include areas of high seas, there have been discussions around the topic for over a decade.[85] Alternatively, the IMO can adopt vessel routing and reporting systems within the PSSA and/or designate it an area to be avoided. Nevertheless, the IMO has no direct mandate to manage natural resources and the fulfilment of those objectives through PSSAs accordingly remains limited and residual. Moreover, in a fisheries context, as noted in Chapter 7 of this volume (Caddell), the IMO has generally exhibited little enthusiasm for pursuing synergies with RFMOs.

---

[80] International Seabed Authority, "Environmental Management Plan for the Clarion-Clipperton Zone", Doc. ISBA/17/LTC/7: available at https://www.isa.org.jm/sites/default/files/files/documents/isba-17ltc-7_0.pdf.

[81] A Jaeckel "An Environmental Management Strategy for the International Seabed Authority? The Legal Basis" (2015) 30 *International Journal of Marine and Coastal Law* 93–119, at 106–09.

[82] See further J Roberts, A Chircop and S Prior "Area-Based Management on the High Seas: The Application of the IMO's Particularly Sensitive Sea Area Concept" (2010) 25 *International Journal of Marine and Coastal Law* 483–522.

[83] R Churchill "The Growing Establishment of High Seas Marine Protected Areas: Implications for Shipping" in R Caddell and R Thomas (eds.) *Shipping, Law and the Marine Environment in the Twenty-First Century* (Lawtext, Witney: 2013) 53–88, at 81.

[84] IMO Resolution A.982(24): Revised Guidelines for the Identification and Designation of Particularly Sensitive Sea Areas; UN Doc. IMO/A24/Res.982.

[85] CBD "Options for Cooperation for the Establishment of Marine Protected Areas in Marine Areas beyond the Limits of National Jurisdiction"; UN Doc. UNEP/CBD/WG-PA/1/2, para. 10.

More prospectively, a greater role for ABMT in ABNJ has been recently advocated for the WHC,[86] administered under the auspices of the UN Educational, Scientific and Cultural Organization (UNESCO). The WHC does not currently apply to ABNJ, but there have been strong calls for its mandate to be expanded to facilitate the designation and protection of World Heritage Sites in these waters and thus close a significant loophole in its application.[87] Given the virtually universal adherence to the WHC, such a development could have significant implications for the protection of sites recognized in ABNJ for their Outstanding Universal Value (OUV), including the feasibility of continued fishing activities in these areas. Nevertheless, such a move would require either prior revision of the Convention, the negotiation of an implementation agreement in a manner similar to the LOS Convention, or clear consensus on an ambitious evolutionary interpretation of the WHC itself.[88] None of these approaches is a straightforward – or swiftly attainable – undertaking in practice.

On a regional level, many of the natural heritage objectives of ABMTs fall under the purview of the RSOs. However, of the 18 current RSOs, only four have expressly extended their mandate to ABNJ, namely the Commission for the Protection of the Marine Environment of the North-East Atlantic (OSPAR Commission), the Barcelona Convention (in respect of small pockets of high seas within the Mediterranean region), the South Pacific Regional Environment Programme (SPREP) and CCAMLR. Of those, three have designated MPAs on the high seas. OSPAR has declared a network of MPAs in ABNJ,[89] but its constituent convention[90] does not prescribe authority to prevent fishing in those areas. Instead, complementary ABMTs have been coordinated through a non-binding Collective Arrangement[91] with the North-East Atlantic Fisheries Commission (NEAFC), which has closed areas to bottom trawling that broadly overlap with the OSPAR MPAs.[92] As noted above, the Pelagos sanctuary has been incorporated under the Barcelona Convention while CCAMLR, as 'more than' an RFMO, has also instituted a series of MPAs and additional

---

[86] UNESCO Convention Concerning the Protection of the World Cultural and Natural Heritage of 16 November 1972 (1037 UNTS 151).

[87] D Laffoley and D Freestone "A World of Difference – Opportunities for Applying the 1972 World Heritage Convention to the High Seas" (2017) 27 *Aquatic Conservation: Marine and Freshwater Ecosystems* 78–88, at 79.

[88] Ibid., 84–86.

[89] B O'Leary et al. "The First Network of Marine Protected Areas (MPAs) in the High Seas: The Process, the Challenges and Where Next" (2012) 36 *Marine Policy* 598–605.

[90] Convention for the Protection of the Marine Environment of the North-East Atlantic of 22 September 1992 (2354 UNTS 67).

[91] Collective Arrangement between Competent International Organisations on Cooperation and Coordination regarding Selected Areas in Areas beyond National Jurisdiction in the North-East Atlantic, OSPAR Agreement 2014–09; available at www.ospar.org/documents?v=33030.

[92] See further Chapter 7 of this volume (Caddell).

ABMTs to manage fishing activities under its unique regulatory mandate. Meanwhile, SPREP has not yet designated formal MPAs, but has implemented measures to restrict access to the areas of high seas enclosed by the EEZs of various nations.

5.2. Informing Area-based Planning in ABNJ: Ecologically or Biologically Significant Areas

A further basis for promoting ABMTs in ABNJ is forthcoming through the work of the CBD. Under Article 4(b), processes and activities conducted under the mandate of the CBD may apply to areas "beyond the limits of national jurisdiction". In 2002, the Plan of Implementation of the World Summit on Sustainability called inter *alia* for the establishment of a global network of MPAs,[93] a call heeded by the CBD since its seventh Conference of the Parties (COP) in 2006, which has sought to advance this objective by elaborating a process for describing Ecologically or Biologically Significant Areas (EBSAs) across the world's oceans and seas.[94]

In 2008, the CBD adopted seven criteria to describe EBSAs, distilled from reviews of existing biodiversity criteria suites, and specifically chosen for thematic breadth, so as to facilitate the CBD's role in providing scientific and, as appropriate, technical information and advice relating to marine biological diversity in ABNJ. These criteria include:

1. Uniqueness or rarity.
2. Special importance for life history of species.
3. Importance for threatened, endangered or declining species and/or habitats.
4. Vulnerability, fragility, sensitivity, slow recovery.
5. Biological productivity.
6. Biological diversity.
7. Naturalness.

While the EBSA process was originally focused on filling the gap in the protection of ABNJ, its scope has since been expanded to include informing the development of ABMTs including MSP both within and beyond national jurisdiction.[95]

---

[93] Plan of Implementation of the World Summit on Sustainability, para. 32; available at www.un.org/esa/sustdev/documents/WSSD_POI_PD/English/WSSD_PlanImpl.pdf.

[94] For a full history of this process, see DC Dunn et al. "The Convention on Biological Diversity's Ecologically or Biologically Significant Areas: Origins, Development, and Current Status" (2014) 49 *Marine Policy* 137–145, at 138–140.

[95] Ibid.

Set against the backdrop of the Aichi Biodiversity Targets adopted at COP10, the Parties also favoured a regional, State-based approach to the description of EBSAs through an array of Expert Workshops in which nominated experts proposed candidate EBSAs. Between 2011 and 2017, the CBD organized 13 regional Expert Workshops covering the vast majority of the ocean, with the notable exceptions of the Southern Ocean and South-West Atlantic, while this process in the Northeast Atlantic was instituted under the aegis of the ongoing collaboration between OSPAR and NEAFC. After having attained the consensus of all Parties involved in the workshop (agreed during a plenary) the outcomes are reviewed by the Subsidiary Body for Scientific, Technical, and Technological Advice (SBSTTA) then articulated in COP recommendations and communicated to the UNGA and other relevant bodies.[96] Eleven of the thirteen workshops have completed the review process to date, resulting in the description of some 279 individual EBSAs (Figure 2).

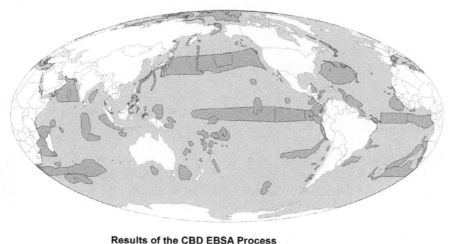

Results of the CBD EBSA Process

◻ Described EBSAs

◻ Post CoP 13 Workshops regions (Baltic, Caspian & Black Seas)

Figure 2 Results of the CBD process to describe Ecologically or Biologically Significant Areas: 279 sites distributed across 11 regions with more sites in two further regions remaining to be reviewed by CBD CoP 14

The technical description of an EBSA has no formal legal effect, as the designation is solely intended to inform States and pertinent sectoral bodies of the distribution and characteristics of these areas. Indeed, "the description of EBSAs is a scientific exercise that should not be conflated with any potential

---

[96] See NJ Bax et al. "Results and Implications of the First Global Effort to Identify Ecologically or Biologically Significant Marine Areas" (2016) 30 *Conservation Biology* 571–581; and DE Johnson et al. "Reviewing the EBSA Process: Improving on Success" (2018) 88 *Marine Policy* 75–85.

management requirements, and describing EBSAs does not come with any obligation to turn them into MPAs or other management commitments".[97] However, concerns have been raised in some quarters that EBSAs could be treated as a preliminary step towards the establishment of MPAs, even though the CBD currently lacks the power to establish such areas in ABNJ.[98] Nevertheless, the scientific and technical information generated through the EBSA process has already informed the development of ABMTs both within and beyond national jurisdiction. For example, the Western Central Atlantic Fishery Commission (WECAFC) recommended the designation of a VME on the Mid-Atlantic Ridge to protect hydrothermal vents whose boundaries and intent exactly matched the Hydrothermal Vent Fields EBSA, noting further that EBSAs provide a useful scientific basis for the establishment of closed areas.[99] EBSA information also reinforced current calls to expand the mandate of the WHC to better identify sites with OUV.[100] Similarly, information garnered from the EBSA process, and the criteria underpinning the process itself, have informed current negotiations over a new ILBI for the conservation and sustainable use of marine biological diversity beyond national jurisdiction (BBNJ),[101] as well as the work of the UN Ad Hoc Working Group of the Whole in considering Regular Process for Global Reporting and Assessment of the State of the Marine Environment.[102]

5.3. Developing a Holistic Approach to Biodiversity Beyond National Jurisdiction (BBNJ)

Finally, notwithstanding particular examples of comprehensive, joined-up regional area-based governance, efforts to promote ABMTs in ABNJ have been impeded by the absence of a global regulatory authority and widely-accepted designation methodologies. In this regard, considerable importance is attached to the BBNJ process as it reaches a critical point with the commencement in September 2018 of formal negotiations towards a new ILBI for the conservation and sustainable use of marine biodiversity in ABNJ, which will be eventually concluded as a third Implementation Agreement to the LOS Convention.

---

[97] Dunn et al, note 94 at 143.

[98] Ibid. Similarly, the potential influence of the CBD on navigational freedoms in ABNJ remains a vexed question; see further A Boyle "Further Development of the Law of the Sea Convention: Mechanisms for Change" (2005) 54 *International and Comparative Law Quarterly* 563–584, at 578–582.

[99] Report of the Sixteenth Session of the Western Central Atlantic Fishery Commission, para. 44; see also Recommendation WECAFC/16/2016/4 on the Management of Deep-Sea Fisheries in the High Seas.

[100] Laffoley and Freestone, note 87 at 82.

[101] KM Gjerde et al. "Protecting Earth's Last Conservation Frontier: Scientific, Management and Legal Priorities for MPAs beyond National Boundaries" (2016) 26 *Aquatic Conservation: Marine and Freshwater Ecosystems* 45–60, at 54.

[102] See further UNGA Resolution 70/235 of 23 December 2015, para. 282.

As outlined in Chapter 7 of this volume, the BBNJ process seeks to address a governance loophole that threatens the sustainability of biodiversity in the high seas, as environmental conditions change and human impacts on the marine realm multiply. The application of ABMTs, including MPAs, was identified as one of the four thematic priorities to be considered in the development of the ILBI.[103] Moreover, the negotiations will also provide overarching governance principles for ABNJ, the lack of which has to date resulted in different actors having very different interpretations of how ABNJ (and any ABMTs therein) should be used.

Significantly, the new instrument "should not undermine existing legal instruments and frameworks and relevant global, regional and sectoral bodies",[104] a rather inelegant phrasing that continues to shroud the process with a degree of ambiguity.[105] While this exhortation is intended to avoid institutional redundancies and conflicts, it offers little indication as to how cross-sectoral ABMTs might be developed and managed in ABNJ. This is not a moot consideration, with evidence mounting in recent years of an urgent need to establish a cross-sectoral approach to marine management.[106] Indeed, as discussed above, the fragmented institutional framework for managing resources in ABNJ limits the ability and potential effectiveness of ABMTs. For example, in a fisheries context, areas of ABNJ that have been identified as VMEs may nevertheless also be leased for exploration for deep-sea mining. A lack of coherence between management measures clearly undermines the utility of sectoral ABMTs, inevitably resulting in prioritization and trade-offs between ocean uses, features and processes.[107] The BBNJ process therefore faces a formidable task in seeking to establish a means of reconciling these disparate processes and establishing unified methodologies and further global legitimacy for the designation of ABMTs in the high seas.

6. FUTURE CHALLENGES AND CONSIDERATIONS FOR AREA-BASED FISHERIES MANAGEMENT

6.1. Knowledge Gaps

Implementing ABMTs on the high seas will require extensive data on the biodiversity and ecology of the open-ocean and deep-sea, and the suite of natural

---

[103] UNGA Resolution 69/292 of 6 July 2015, para. 2; see also UNGA Resolution 72/249 of 24 December 2017, para. 2.

[104] Resolution 69/292, para. 3.

[105] See further Z Scanlon "The Art of 'Not Undermining': Possibilities within Existing Architecture to Improve Environmental Protection in Areas beyond National Jurisdiction" (2018) 75 *ICES Journal of Marine Science* 405–416, at 406–409.

[106] See especially BS Halpern et al. "A Global Map of Human Impact on Marine Ecosystems" (2008) 319 *Science* 948–952; and BS Halpern et al. "Spatial and Temporal Changes in Cumulative Human Impacts on the World's Ocean" (2015) 6 *Nature Communications* 6:7615.

[107] NC Ban et al. "Better Integration of Sectoral Planning and Management Approaches for the Interlinked Ecology of the Open Oceans" (2014) 49 *Marine Policy* 127–136.

and anthropogenic stressors that may influence the dynamics of the ecosystems therein. However, the availability of data is known to decrease drastically (even exponentially) with distance from shore and depth,[108] undermining the knowledge base to support ABMTs in ABNJ. Nevertheless, there have been significant recent advancements in our ability to track and record many of the oceanographic, biological and human layers of information concerning the high seas. While this subsection cannot provide an exhaustive assessment of the existing knowledge gaps on the high seas, we identify the main elements that affect the implementation of fisheries ABMTs within a wider EAF framework, as well as existing systems and frameworks which are or could be used to collect such information.

Two fundamental pieces of information are required to inform decision-making regarding fisheries ABMTs, namely where fishing is occurring and what biodiversity is at risk from those activities. Without information on the location of fishing effort, potential ecological impacts cannot be localized and the place-based approach that underpins EAF is lost. As with most fisheries in national waters, information on the spatiotemporal distribution of fishing on the high seas is often limited due to confidentiality rules. While RFMOs provide some data about where fisheries operate – either directly to the public or through reporting to the FAO – this is aggregated spatially (1⁰x1⁰ or 5⁰x5⁰) and temporally (monthly or quarterly) at resolutions that impede any assessment of impacts upon oceanic features, such as specific seamounts. Emerging technologies, such as automatic identification systems (AIS) or vessel monitoring systems (VMS), are helping track the spatiotemporal footprint of oceanic fisheries at high resolutions.[109] Unfortunately, the implementation and regulation of these systems is highly variable (e.g. with regard to the size of boats required to carry transponders, or requirements to keep the systems on 24 hours per day) and these systems do not provide information about catch or bycatch. A more holistic monitoring, control and surveillance system for fisheries in ABNJ that can support cooperation among RFMOs with highly different capacities is therefore necessary.[110] Understanding the distribution of distant water fleets in the high seas is important, *inter alia*, to determine the extent of overlap and impacts on areas of ecological or biological importance.

The second piece of necessary information is the distribution and abundance of biodiversity within the area in question. Currently, there are various international data warehouses and systems that seek to record, standardize and distribute biotic and abiotic data in the open-ocean. The Ocean Biogeographic

---

[108] TJ Webb, E Vanden Berghe and R O'Dor "Biodiversity's Big Wet Secret: The Global Distribution of Marine Biological Records Reveals Chronic Under-Exploration of the Deep Pelagic Ocean" (2010) 5 *PloS One* e10223.

[109] See F Natale et al. "Mapping Fishing Effort through AIS Data" (2015) 10 *PLoS One* e0130746; and DA Kroodsma et al. "Tracking the Global Footprint of Fisheries" (2018) 359 *Science* 904–908.

[110] DC Dunn et al. "Empowering High Seas Governance with Satellite Vessel Tracking Data" (2018) 19 *Fish and Fisheries* 729–739.

Information System (OBIS), which is the most comprehensive source of spatially-explicit data on marine biodiversity globally, contains records for 20,355 individual species in ABNJ. While the distribution and intensity of biological sampling in the open-ocean under OBIS is highly heterogenous, it represents a fundamental source of knowledge for the international community to fulfil their mandates under different international governance frameworks for the conservation of the marine environment and marine life, including Article 117 of the LOS Convention on the conservation of the living resources of the high seas, and Articles 5 and 6 of the Fish Stocks Agreement[111] on the protection of biodiversity in the marine environment and the conservation of associated or dependent species of target stocks. Of these species, 4,052 belong to the Superclass *Pisces*. Of the known biodiversity in the high seas, fish represent the taxonomic group with the highest number of recorded species; however, 1,992 of these species have only one record in the OBIS system. This represents a substantial ecological knowledge gap that must be bridged if the international community, through RFMOs, intends to implement EAF. Information about the composition, abundance and distribution of biodiversity is an essential pillar of such an approach. Fisheries-independent monitoring programmes for ABNJ are expensive and logistically complex. Information from fisheries-independent sources, including research cruises, have to be complemented with fisheries-dependent forms of sampling. This will require a paradigm shift regarding how fishing operations are viewed, from simply extractive events to highly monitored sampling transects that serve harvesting and biological sampling purposes. The spatiotemporal extent of the global fishing fleet provides almost year-round coverage of the open-ocean. However, the existing coverage of fishing through scientific observer programmes is patchy and underfunded. A study assessing the observer coverage rates across 60 fisheries in 13 RFMOs found a wide range in coverage rates, from 0 per cent (n=47) to 100 per cent (n=11).[112] The poor performance of most RFMOs in terms of observer coverage or data quality and data collection protocols severely limits most assessments of catch, bycatch and community or ecosystem health. This is further exacerbated by data confidentiality rules that restrict access for external or independent analysis.

Clearly current levels of monitoring and coordination among RFMOs are insufficient to monitor non-target species, community and ecosystem level indicators. Increased cooperation between organizations with competency over ABNJ and large-scale biodiversity monitoring programmes like the Global Ocean Observing Systems (GOOS) is needed to improve ecosystem monitoring and incorporate those data into management processes. Similarly, the

---

[111] Agreement for the Implementation of the Provisions of the United Nations Convention on the Law of the Sea of 10 December 1982 relating to the Conservation and Management of Straddling Fish Stocks and Highly Migratory Fish Stocks of 4 August 1995 (2167 UNTS 3).

[112] E Gilman, K Passfield and K Nakamura "Performance of Regional Fisheries Management Organizations: Ecosystem-Based Governance of Bycatch and Discards" (2014) 15 *Fish and Fisheries* 327–351.

incorporation of data on species, community and ecosystem status into fisheries management requires an analytical and budgetary capacity that goes beyond that of present RFMOs. Assistance in meeting these challenges could be forthcoming through collaborations with industry and academic institutions.[113]

6.2. ABMTs in a Changing Climate

Marine ecosystems are non-static in space or time: the composition and distribution of biological communities are heavily influenced by changes in environmental conditions, many of which change in cyclical and predictable ways (e.g. diurnal or seasonal cycles). While natural, these cyclical patterns can have profound effects on the abundance, distribution and trophic dynamics of marine biological communities. For instance, as climatic conditions fluctuate in the Japanese, Californian, Humboldt and Benguela systems, so does the abundance of lower trophic level species such as sardine (*Sardinops sagax* and *Sardina pilchardus*) and anchovy (*Engraulis spp.*).[114] While profound, these changes in biophysical and ecological conditions tend to fluctuate between alternate stable states, which are well studied. It is not these natural oscillations that threaten the future sustainability of marine resource management, but rather the disruption of natural cycles due to changing atmospheric and oceanographic conditions. Given the close evolutionary link between the timing and intensity of environmental conditions to the phenology and physiological tolerances of marine life, changes in either of these conditions may profoundly impact the functional dynamics of marine ecosystems.[115] There is growing evidence that climate change is altering the physical and biochemical properties of marine systems, which in turn are impacting the phenology,[116] body size,[117] distribution[118] and productivity[119] of marine species and ecosystems.

---

[113] Crespo and Dunn, note 5. Similar calls have been made concerning data from marine environmental assessment procedures: R Caddell, "Uncharted Waters: SEA in the UK Offshore Area" in G Jones and E Scotford (eds.) *The Strategic Environmental Assessment Directive: A Plan for Success?* (Hart, Oxford: 2017) 283–309, at 303–304.

[114] D Lluch-Belda et al. "Sardine and Anchovy Regime Fluctuations of Abundance in Four Regions of the World Oceans: A Workshop Report" (1992) 1 *Fisheries Oceanography* 339–347.

[115] M Edwards and AJ Richardson "Impact of Climate Change on Marine Pelagic Phenology and Trophic Mismatch" (2004) 430 *Nature* 881–884.

[116] MJ Genner et al. "Temperature-Driven Phenological Changes within a Marine Larval Fish Assemblage" (2009) 32 *Journal of Plankton Research* 699–708.

[117] WWL Cheung et al. "Shrinking of Fishes Exacerbates Impacts of Global Ocean Changes on Marine Ecosystems" (2013) 3 *Nature Climate Change* 254–258.

[118] See AL Perry et al. "Climate Change and Distribution Shifts in Marine Fishes" (2005) 308 *Science* 1912–1915; NK Dulvy et al. "Climate Change and Deepening of the North Sea Fish Assemblage: A Biotic Indicator of Warming Seas" (2008) 45 *Journal of Applied Ecology* 1029–1039; WWL Cheung et al. "Projecting Global Marine Biodiversity Impacts under Climate Change Scenarios" (2009) 10 *Fish and Fisheries* 235–251.

[119] WWL Cheung et al. "Large-Scale Redistribution of Maximum Fisheries Catch Potential in the Global Ocean under Climate Change" (2010) 16 *Global Change Biology* 24–35.

Marine resource managers must be able to account for these changes in conditions, whether they are induced by natural multi-decadal oscillations or anthropogenically-driven climate change. This is particularly exigent for spatially-explicit management measures, given the changes in species abundance and distribution that are projected to occur with climate change. For example, climate change is projected to undermine the effectiveness of most existing ABMTs in the North Atlantic Ocean basin within the next 20 to 50 years.[120] Future-proofing ABMTs will thus require improved oceanographic data at higher spatiotemporal resolutions to more accurately identify possible refugia, alongside a precautionary approach, such as establishing larger ABMTs.[121] Moreover, changes in species, community and ecosystem dynamics will have to be monitored closely in space and time to ensure the continued appropriateness of management actions.

6.3. Dynamic Management

One potential strategy in addressing ABMTs in a changing environment may be the use of real-time closures through what has become known as 'dynamic management'. The delineation of the vast majority of ABMTs involves drawing fixed lines around species, habitats or resource users that are frequently highly vagile. While static delineations may successfully address benthic habitats and demersal species which are obligate to those habitats, the effective and efficient management of dynamic pelagic systems requires measures that can match the fluidity in space and time of the resources and users.[122] Dynamic ocean management – i.e. "management that rapidly changes in space and time in response to changes in the ocean and its users through the integration of near real-time biological, oceanographic, social and/or economic data"[123] – has been proposed as a mechanism that may afford managers the means to address rapidly changing conditions, attributable either to climactic shifts or shifts in abundance or distribution of resources or resource users.

Advancements in our ability to monitor ocean conditions and resources on finer spatial and temporal scales as a result of technological improvements have enabled higher resolution data collection of both fish and fisheries (e.g. electronic logbooks, vessel monitoring systems, smartphone technology, remote sensing and animal tracking).[124] Specifically, improvements in the temporal

---

[120] D Johnson, MA Ferreira and E Kenchington "Climate Change Is Likely to Severely Limit the Effectiveness of Deep-Sea ABMTs in the North Atlantic" (2018) 87 *Marine Policy* 111–122.

[121] Ibid., 120.

[122] Dunn et al, note 58.

[123] SM Maxwell et al. "Dynamic Ocean Management: Defining and Conceptualizing Real-Time Management of the Ocean" (2015) 58 *Marine Policy* 42–50, at 42.

[124] AJ Hobday et al. "Dynamic Ocean Management: Integrating Scientific and Technological Capacity with Law, Policy and Management" (2014) 33 *Stanford Environmental Law Journal* 125–165.

coverage of monitoring and the speed at which data are being transmitted allow for the refinement of the temporal and spatial scale of managed areas. The faster the data are communicated from the resource user or sampling station to the manager and back to the resource user, the quicker a particular problem (e.g. bycatch) may be addressed.

In contrast to traditional monthly or seasonal spatial closures of part of the fishery (and seasonal full-fishery closures), dynamic management has largely focused on three types of measures: grid-based hotspot closures, move-on rules and oceanographic closures. Grid-based closures are primarily used to address incidental catches and involve overlaying a static grid over all or part of a fishery and closing individual grid cells where bycatch has exceeded a threshold level.[125] Move-on rules also employ a threshold (e.g. number of juvenile fish caught per hour), although instead of using grids, they adopt a set distance in time and space wherein the fishers must move away before recommencing fishing.[126] Meanwhile, oceanographic closures are delineated by using environmental variables as thresholds.[127] For example, the Eastern Australia pelagic longline fishery has used sea surface temperature to delineate fishing zones to reduce bycatch of southern bluefin tuna (*Thunnus maccoyii*) that have an affinity for the colder temperatures in that region.[128]

While dynamic management has been successfully instituted in particular cases, its wider implementation will require a clearer legal framework, while also incorporating bio-economic models (rather than the purely ecological ones that have been used to date), as well as extending it to a broader range of resource users and identifying how it can complement MSP approaches. This new toolkit should be extremely valuable to RFMOs with competence to manage pelagic species and may be more palatable to States than simply imposing fixed fishery closures or MPAs. However, it is critical to recognize that an array of ABMT objectives have been described in this chapter, not all of which can be achieved solely through dynamic management.

6.4. Three-dimensional Spatiotemporal Closures

While the world's oceans cover 71 per cent of the surface area of the planet, its vastness can only truly be captured by considering the vertical dimension.

---

[125] CE O'Keefe and GR DeCelles "Forming a Partnership to Avoid Bycatch" (2013) 38 *Fisheries* 434–444.

[126] DC Dunn et al. "Empirical Move-on Rules to Inform Fishing Strategies: A New England Case Study" (2014) 15 *Fish and Fisheries* 359–375; CL Needle and R Catarino "Evaluating the Effect of Real-Time Closures on Cod Targeting" (2011) 68 *ICES Journal of Marine Science* 1647–1655; SA Little et al. "Real-Time Spatial Management Approaches to Reduce Bycatch and Discards: Experiences from Europe and the United States" (2015) 16 *Fish and Fisheries* 576–602.

[127] Howell et al, note 63.

[128] AJ Hobday et al. "Dynamic Spatial Zoning to Manage Southern Bluefin Tuna (Thunnus Maccoyii) Capture in a Multi-Species Longline Fishery" (2010) 19 *Fisheries Oceanography* 243–253.

The global ocean accounts for 99 per cent of the global biogenic habitat available to life and biodiversity has evolved to partition both the horizontal and vertical dimensions of this space. The average depth of the marine realm is ~3.6 kilometers, which is stratified into various zones with differing physical, chemical and biological properties. These zones are not static and are continuously changing their properties and distribution. Differences in light, oxygen and temperature directly affect the physiology of marine life and help shape its biogeography.[129]

Advancements in ocean monitoring and bio-logging of marine species in recent decades have helped researchers and managers to better understand the spatial ecology of marine biota.[130] This information is of particular relevance to fisheries management, especially in reducing conflicts between fishing operations and non-target species and habitats through ABMTs. Various studies have demonstrated how different pelagic species occupy different strata of the water column and there is evidence that this differentiation in vertical habitat could be applied to target and non-target species that have distinctive vertical mobility patterns.[131] For instance, studies on the vertical distribution of the five most bycaught shark species in central Pacific longline fisheries demonstrated that they partition the vertical water column in distinctive ways, allowing for the identification of areas of overlap with target tuna and billfish species.[132] Understanding these differences in spatial overlap in the vertical dimension can assist the development of more advanced forms of three-dimensional spatial management, which could be more targeted than the current two-dimensional closures that apply to the entire water column. For instance, based on studies of the vertical distribution of sea turtles,[133] mitigation measures have been introduced in particular pelagic longline fisheries to modify the depth of the fished area, thus reducing the probability of overlap with non-target species.[134]

As our ability to monitor horizontal and vertical oceanographic conditions in the global ocean advances,[135] our understanding of how pelagic species use their three-dimensional environment will continue to improve, thus allowing for novel forms of management to emerge. Indeed, increasing the spatiotemporal

[129] See AZ Horodysky et al. "Fisheries Conservation on the High Seas: Linking Conservation Physiology and Fisheries Ecology for the Management of Large Pelagic Fishes" (2016) 4 *Conservation Physiology* cov059; and AB Carlisle et al. "Influence of Temperature and Oxygen on the Distribution of Blue Marlin (Makaira Nigricans) in the Central Pacific" (2017) 26 *Fisheries Oceanography* 34–48.
[130] Block et al, note 62.
[131] Horodysky et al., note 129.
[132] MK Musyl et al. "Postrelease Survival, Vertical and Horizontal Movements, and Thermal Habitats of Five Species of Pelagic Sharks in the Central Pacific Ocean" (2011) 109 *Fishery Bulletin* 341–368.
[133] E Torres-Irineo et al. "Effects of Time-Area Closure on Tropical Tuna Purse-Seine Fleet Dynamics through Some Fishery Indicators" (2011) 24 *Aquatic Living Resources* 337–350.
[134] D Smith and J Jabour "MPAs in ABNJ: Lessons from Two High Seas Regimes" (2017) 75 *ICES Journal of Marine Science* 417–425.
[135] SC Riser et al. "Fifteen Years of Ocean Observations with the Global Argo Array" (2016) 6 *Nature Climate Change* 145–153.

resolution of ABMTs is known to increase their efficiency and reduce monitoring and implementation costs.[136] As the knowledge base develops further, the efficiency of ABMTs will therefore be increasingly refined through a greater consideration of the third spatial dimension to provide more targeted interspecies management in these areas.

7. CONCLUSIONS

The effective deployment of ABMTs represents a significant component of the successful application of ecosystem-based fisheries management. Such mechanisms are ubiquitous in the national waters of States, where in numerous instances they have provided an important tool to reconcile a host of growing and competing interests concerning the use of marine space, including socioeconomic imperatives, the protection of natural and cultural heritage, fisheries production and marine conservation objectives. Attempts to apply this approach to the high seas have, however, proved to be rather more circumspect. Beyond the burgeoning establishment of protected sites to preserve VMEs, in tandem with spatiotemporal closures instituted by particular RFMOs – and unique bodies such as CCAMLR – relatively little scope currently exists to advance area-based fisheries management in ABNJ. Acute jurisdictional challenges are inherent in attempts by States to impose area-based restrictions on foreign shipping in ABNJ, hence such approaches are best facilitated through multilateral activity. Nevertheless, at present there is no global authority under whose auspices such an initiative may be advanced, nor are there universally recognized methodologies to frame the establishment of a network of MPAs in the high seas. While ABMTs may be advanced on a sectoral level, including through the activities of RFMOs, such designations have generally occurred in regulatory isolation. Notwithstanding a small number of promising collaborations between largely regional organizations to more closely align their respective ABMTs, such examples remain the exception rather than the rule. There is accordingly considerable scope for sectoral closures adopted for fisheries management purposes to be undermined by industrial activities endorsed by alternative regulatory bodies, and *vice versa*.

The impending negotiation of the ILBI for the conservation and sustainable use of BBNJ provides a tantalizing opportunity to strengthen international fisheries law by addressing this regulatory lacuna and establishing clearer global principles and authority for the development of ABMTs in these waters. Nevertheless, it faces a formidable task in reconciling disparate ABMTs between sectoral regulators, while 'not undermining' pre-existing and future regimes. Moreover, the ILBI will be negotiated against a backdrop in which difficult

---

[136] Dunn et al., note 110.

political compromises will be required in order to deliver an end product that is sufficiently palatable to attract widespread support, while considerable points of divergence remain between the negotiating Parties as to the form and application of ABMTs under any future treaty.

Meanwhile, concerns remain over the ability of current ABMTs to adapt effectively to changing oceanic circumstances. Chronic gaps remain in the knowledge base of both target and non-target species, which undermines the ability of fisheries managers to respond proactively to current and emerging threats to fisheries production and the health of the surrounding ecosystem. Even well-managed ABMTs remain essentially static in nature, while many marine species are exhibiting unprecedented shifts in distribution. Data-collection remains a perennial challenge to efficient ABMTs, while new and far-sighted approaches – such as dynamic and three-dimensional ocean management – remain nascent. In an era of profoundly changing oceans, the adaptive capacity of management principles will thus be as important to the future of area-based fisheries management as it will to the ecosystems addressed under these auspices.

10

Environmental Assessment and International Fisheries Law

SIMON MARSDEN

1. INTRODUCTION

E NVIRONMENTAL ASSESSMENT (EA) is an established decision-aiding tool of global significance which operates in domestic, regional and global contexts and is required by law.[1] From its inception under the domestic law of the United States (US) – the federal National Environmental Policy Act (NEPA) 1969 – it has spawned 'mini-NEPAs' across the US,[2] and subsequently been incorporated in the law and policies of numerous States, regional and global treaties,[3] and the lending policies of multilateral development banks.[4] The Rio Declaration,[5] and the United Nations Environment Programme (UNEP) Goals and Principles of Environmental Impact Assessment (EIA),[6] established a soft-law basis for international EA generally.

---

[1] N Craik *The International Law of Environmental Impact Assessment: Process, Substance and Integration* (Cambridge University Press, Cambridge: 2008); K Bastmeijer and T Koivurova (eds.) *Theory and Practice of Transboundary Environmental Impact Assessment* (Martinus Nijhoff, Leiden: 2008).

[2] See R Clark et al. "SEA in the USA" in B Sadler et al. (eds.) *Handbook of Strategic Environmental Assessment* (Earthscan, London: 2011) 74–88.

[3] Notably the Convention on Environmental Impact Assessment in a Transboundary Context of 25 February 1991 (1989 UNTS 309) ('Espoo Convention').

[4] See e.g. European Bank for Reconstruction and Development (2014) *Environmental and Social Policy*, 7 May.

[5] Rio Declaration on Environment and Development, concluded 14 June 1992, Rio de Janeiro, Brazil, particularly Principles 17 (EIA) and 19 (notification and consultation). See JE Viñuales (ed.) *The Rio Declaration on Environment and Development: A Commentary* (Oxford University Press, Oxford: 2015) chs. 21 and 23.

[6] UNEP, Goals and Principles of Environmental Impact Assessment, Preliminary Note, 16 January 1987.

In relation to international fisheries, the CBD[7] and the LOS Convention[8] lead efforts, with the Conferences of the Parties (COPs) and United Nations General Assembly (UNGA) playing significant roles respectively. They have developed guidance (2009–2012),[9] and following Rio+20, taken steps to establish a new international legally binding instrument (ILBI) for the conservation and sustainable development of biodiversity beyond national jurisdiction (BBNJ) (2012-date), which includes EA as one of several areas of priority focus.[10] Both the guidelines and ILBI apply to international fisheries where these impact upon marine biodiversity, as voluntary guidelines must be supported by a legal framework if implementation and compliance are to be effectively managed. The 2015 BBNJ Resolution of the UNGA,[11] and activities of the Biodiversity Beyond National Jurisdiction (BBNJ) Working Group,[12] are a key part of the development of international marine EA.[13] Together these constitute the 'BBNJ Process'. This chapter will analyze these initiatives alongside the trio of the Compliance Agreement,[14] Fish Stocks Agreement[15] and Code of Conduct.[16] Both the BBNJ Process and these three instruments for regional fisheries management organization (RFMO)[17] governance are of key significance in developing and applying EA to international fisheries.

The chapter recognizes the limitations of the fishery-specific and other arrangements for effective environmental protection of the marine environment, highlighting the need for EA reform. It will additionally consider the

---

[7] Convention on Biological Diversity of 5 June 1992 (1760 UNTS 79), particularly Art. 14.

[8] United Nations Convention on the Law of the Sea of 10 December 1982 (1833 UNTS 3). See in particular Part XII, Section 4, Arts. 205 and 206.

[9] Convention on Biological Diversity, Conference of the Parties to the Convention on Biological Diversity. 11th meeting, Hyderabad, India, Item 10.2 of the provisional agenda, *Marine and Coastal Biodiversity: Revised Voluntary Guidelines for the Consideration of Biodiversity in Environmental Impact Assessments and Strategic Environmental Assessments in Marine and Coastal Areas*, note by the Executive Secretary, UNEP/CBD/COP/11/23 21 August 2012.

[10] R Warner "Assessing Environmental Impacts of Activities in Areas Beyond National Jurisdiction" in R Rayfuse (ed.) *Research Handbook on International Marine Environmental Law* (Edward Elgar, Cheltenham: 2015); E Druel and KM Gjerde "Sustaining Marine Life Beyond Boundaries: Options for an Implementing Agreement for Marine Biodiversity Beyond National Jurisdiction under the United Nations Convention on the Law of the Sea" (2014) 49 *Marine Policy* 90. See further Chapter 7 of this Volume (Caddell).

[11] UNGA Resolution 69/292 of 19 June 2015.

[12] Recommendations of the Ad Hoc Open-ended Informal Working Group to study issues relating to the conservation and sustainable use of marine biological diversity beyond areas of national jurisdiction and Co-Chairs' summary of discussions. UN doc. A/66/119 of 30 June 2011.

[13] See F Guerra et al. "Environmental Impact Assessment in the Marine Environment: A Comparison of Legal Frameworks" (2015) 55 *Environmental Impact Assessment Review* 182–194.

[14] Agreement to Promote Compliance with International Conservation and Management Measures by Fishing Vessels on the High Seas of 24 November 1993 (2221 UNTS 91).

[15] Agreement for the Implementation of the Provisions of the United Nations Convention on the Law of the Sea of 10 December 1982 relating to the Conservation and Management of Straddling Fish Stocks and Highly Migratory Fish Stocks of 4 December 1995 (2167 UNTS 3).

[16] Code of Conduct for Responsible Fisheries of 31 October 1995; FAO Doc. 95/20/Rev/1.

[17] International fisheries law refers to both 'subregional' and 'regional' fisheries management organizations. Use of the acronym RFMO is intended to cover both.

inadequacies of customary international law,[18] and the limitations of the Espoo Convention,[19] the primary international legal instrument for EIA. It will furthermore highlight specific regional initiatives, the role of the UNGA and the current direction of travel of the BBNJ Process, recognizing the absence of general EA practice as applied to international fisheries.

The chapter is structured as follows. Section 2 outlines the current obligations concerning EA in relation to fisheries, while Section 3 examines the different types of EA and their prospective value to international fisheries management. Section 4 considers the significance of EA in the context of precautionary and ecosystem approaches to fisheries management. Section 5 examines the classification of fisheries research and data collection in the context of EA. Section 6 outlines other relevant international instruments and obligations, while the conclusions in Section 7 highlight the significance of EA and international fisheries in the context of this volume, and consider the reasons for the limited EA practice in areas beyond national jurisdiction (ABNJ), making suggestions as to the future.

2. EA OBLIGATIONS IN THE LOS CONVENTION AND GLOBAL FISHERIES INSTRUMENTS

The LOS Convention prescribes the main obligations to conduct EA in the marine environment. States are required to "observe, measure, evaluate and analyze, by recognized scientific methods, the risks or effects of pollution of the marine environment".[20] However, of direct relevance to international fisheries law – where pollution does not necessarily result from fishing activities – is the more typically worded EA obligation triggered not only by the likelihood of pollution, but also by potentially significant harm resulting from proposed actions:

> When States have reasonable grounds for believing that planned activities under their jurisdiction or control may cause substantial pollution of or significant and harmful changes to the marine environment, they shall, as far as practicable, assess the potential effects of such activities on the marine environment and shall communicate reports of the results of such assessments.[21]

Together with the other matters included, the limited nature of this provision was an important consideration for the UNGA in developing the new ILBI.[22]

[18] See *Certain Activities Carried out by Nicaragua in the Border Area (Costa Rica v. Nicaragua)*; joined case with *Construction of a Road in Costa Rica along the San Juan River (Nicaragua v. Costa Rica)* ICJ Reports, 16 December 2015, para. 104. (*'Certain Activities/Construction of a Road'*).

[19] Note 3.

[20] LOS Convention, Art. 204.

[21] Ibid., Art. 206, which refers also to Art. 205 entitled 'Publication of reports'.

[22] Agenda 21, the soft-law international programme of action for the environment, is also referred to in two of the recitals in the Preamble to the Compliance Agreement, note 14.

The LOS Convention's EA provisions were considered at length in the *Deep-Sea Mining* Advisory Opinion by the International Tribunal for the Law of Sea (ITLOS) in 2011,[23] which focused on the seabed (part of the 'Area') regulated by the International Seabed Authority (ISA).[24] It noted that:

> While article 206 of the Convention gives only a few indications of [...] scope and content, the indications in the [Sulphides] Regulations, and especially in the [Polymetallic Nodules] Recommendations [...] add precision and specificity to the obligation as it applied in the context of activities in the Area.[25]

This emphasizes that the EA requirements in the LOS Convention are essentially reliant upon further guidance from other sources in order for them to be implemented effectively. This chapter is intended to examine whether there is sufficient guidance for this in a fisheries context, and if not, how this can be rectified. The framework nature of the LOS Convention obligations also applies to ABNJ and needs to be detailed in connection with international fisheries, as Subsection 6.4 below will indicate.

There are no specific EA obligations in the Compliance Agreement, although EA is referred to in emphasizing its importance. The first two recitals therefore refer to the 'limiting articles' of the LOS Convention (Articles 205 and 206), which are designed to mitigate the effects of fishing on ABNJ; these are 'limiting' since the purpose of the Compliance Agreement is "to promote compliance with international conservation and management measures" in accordance with the title.[26]

In contrast, the Fish Stocks Agreement explicitly notes "the need to avoid adverse impacts on the marine environment, preserve biodiversity, [and] maintain the integrity of marine ecosystems".[27] Article 5(d), in giving effect to the duty to cooperate, requires States to "assess the impacts of fishing, other human activities and environmental factors on target stocks and species belonging to the same ecosystem or associated with or dependent upon the target stocks". This recognizes not only effects upon the marine environment from fishing, but

---

[23] *Responsibilities and obligations of States sponsoring persons and entities with respect to activities in the Area (Request for Advisory Opinion submitted to the Seabed Disputes Chamber)*, Advisory Opinion of 1 February 2011. See D French "From the Depths: Rich Pickings of Principles of Sustainable Development and General International Law on the Ocean Floor – the Seabed Disputes Chamber's 2011 Advisory Opinion" (2011) 26 *International Journal of Marine and Coastal Law* 525–568.

[24] G Le Gurun "Environmental Impact Assessment and the International Seabed Authority" in Bastmeijer and Koivurova, note 1.

[25] *Deep-Sea Mining* Advisory Opinion, note 23 at para. 149.

[26] Art. III.1(b) of the Compliance Agreement defines these as "measures to conserve or manage one or more species of living marine resources that are adopted and applied in accordance with the relevant rules of international law as reflected in [the LOS Convention]". Given the inclusion of EA provisions in Arts. 205–206, it can be anticipated that, if interpreted by the International Court of the Justice (ICJ) or ITLOS, these would need to reflect customary international legal developments.

[27] Fish Stocks Agreement, Recital 7.

in specifying "other human activities", effects upon fish stocks from, for example, major infrastructure development.

The Code of Conduct, while not binding, provides global context for the growing environmental focus of Parties to these agreements and other relevant international law. The 'overriding' management objective is "long-term sustainable use";[28] one of the measures required for this is EA, as "adverse environmental impacts on the resources from human activities are [to be] assessed, and, where appropriate, corrected".[29] It is significant however that, like the LOS Convention provisions, none of these instruments detail the scope or extent of the requirements or objectives of an EA. This is a key reason why the prospective ILBI must provide clarity on these and other matters, and that customary international law must recognize the growth in EA state practice more generally; these matters are considered in Section 6, the latter particularly with reference to the Espoo Convention.

3. TYPES OF ASSESSMENT

EA processes typically consider impacts both *from* the fishery, and *upon* the fishery. The focus of this chapter is upon the former. It is however important to understand the latter, for while impacts from both domestic and international fisheries may be bycatch,[30] negative impacts upon biodiversity[31] or effects upon the seabed,[32] impacts upon the fishery may come from offshore infrastructure projects (including oil and gas exploration and exploitation, land reclamation and windfarms[33]) and climate change.[34] Specific examples of projects which may impact upon an international marine fishery are pipelines (e.g. Nordstream Baltic Sea),[35] offshore oil and gas development (e.g. Timor Sea),[36] rig blowouts

---

[28] Code of Conduct, Art. 7.2

[29] Ibid, Art. 7.2.2(f).

[30] See Chapter 8 of this volume (Scott).

[31] M Kienzlea et al. "Environmental and Fishing Effects on the Dynamics of Brown Tiger Prawn (Penaeus Esculentus) in Moreton Bay (Australia)" (2014) 155 *Fisheries Research* 138.

[32] S Agbayani et al. "Cumulative Impact of Bottom Fisheries on Benthic Habitats: A Quantitative Spatial Assessment in British Columbia, Canada" (2015) 116 *Ocean and Coastal Management* 423.

[33] J Berkenhagen et al. "Decision Bias in Marine Spatial Planning of Offshore Wind Farms: Problems of Singular Versus Cumulative Assessments of Economic Impacts on Fisheries" (2010) 34 *Marine Policy* 733–736.

[34] JS Christiansen et al. "Arctic Marine Fishes and their Fisheries in Light of Global Change" (2014) 20 *Global Change Biology* 352–359.

[35] T Koivurova and I Pölönen "Transboundary Environmental Impact Assessment in the Case of the Baltic Sea Gas Pipeline" (2010) 25 *International Journal of Marine and Coastal Law* 151–181.

[36] S Marsden "Strategic Environmental Assessment of Australian Offshore Oil and Gas Development: Ecologically Sustainable Development or Deregulation?" (2016) 33 *Environmental and Planning Law Journal* 21–30.

(e.g. Gulf of Mexico or Timor Sea),[37] the creation of artificial islands (e.g. South China Sea)[38] or geoengineering activities (e.g. ocean fertilization).[39]

The different types of assessment must contend with the broad range of environmental effects and how best to avoid, limit and manage them. An important unifying feature, however, is that EA is an *ex ante* process, which must be applied *before* action is taken.[40] EA comprises a range of tools: notably EIA as applied to individual projects; strategic environmental assessment (SEA) to policies, plans and programmes that set the framework for projects,[41] which can help avoid cumulative effects; and social impact assessment (SIA), as applied to projects that affect individuals and communities.[42]

Transboundary EIA can be used to evaluate effects from projects proposed in the maritime zone of one coastal State, which may impact negatively upon the maritime zones of others or ABNJ; or from ABNJ (by flag States) on the maritime zones of one or more coastal States.[43] Although content obligations are not prescribed by international law,[44] the Espoo Convention specifies established steps with public and expert input: screening a proposal for significant effects, scoping the terms of reference and deciding on content, reporting on significant effects, and decision-making on whether to proceed and, if so, under what conditions.

Cumulative impact assessment (CIA) is particularly useful, recognizing that the total impact from projects in combination may be greater than the sum

---

[37] S Marsden "Regulatory Reform of Australia's Offshore Oil and Gas Sector after the Montara Commission of Inquiry: What about Transboundary Environmental Impact Assessment?" (2013) 15(1) *Flinders Law Journal* 41–53.

[38] See PCA Case No. 2013–19 *in the Matter of an Arbitration before An Arbitral Tribunal Constituted under Annex VII to the 1982 United Nations Convention on the Law of the Sea between the Republic of the Philippines and the People's Republic of China' (South China Sea* case), Award on Merits, 12 July 2016. The Tribunal found that China had failed to protect the marine environment and violated Art. 206 of the LOS Convention, by tolerating harmful harvesting activities by Chinese fishing vessels and through its island-building activities. In connection with the harvesting, see para. 950: "the Tribunal is satisfied that Chinese fishing vessels have been involved in harvesting of threatened or endangered species". In connection with island-building, see para 983 "the Tribunal has no doubt that China's artificial island-building activities on the seven reefs in the Spratly Islands have caused devastating and long-lasting damage to the marine environment".

[39] KN Scott "Geoengineering and the Law of the Sea" in R Rayfuse (ed.) *Research Handbook on International Marine Environmental Law* (Edward Elgar, Cheltenham: 2015) 451–472.

[40] *Certain Activities*, ICJ, note 18 at para. 104.

[41] Marsden, notes 36 and 50; Caddell, note 46.

[42] RB Pollnac et al. "Toward a Model for Fisheries Social Impact Assessment" (2006) 68 *Marine Fisheries Review* 1–4. Note Secretariat of the Convention on Biological Diversity, *Akwé: Kon Voluntary Guidelines for the Conduct of Cultural, Environmental and Social Impact Assessment regarding Developments Proposed to Take Place on, or which are Likely to Impact on, Sacred Sites and on Lands and Waters Traditionally Occupied or Used by Indigenous and Local Communities* (CBD, Montreal: 2004).

[43] W Gullett "Transboundary Environmental Impact Assessment in Marine Areas" in R Warner and S Marsden (eds.) *Transboundary Environmental Governance: Inland, Coastal and Marine Perspectives* (Ashgate, Farnham: 2012) 269–296.

[44] *Certain Activities*, ICJ, note 18, para. 104.

of each.[45] However, applying SEA to higher level proposals can also avoid later cumulative effects from individual projects, because such effects may already have been evaluated as part of the strategic assessment process. CIA can also be used to evaluate the range of environmental effects from different project proposals, and if SEA is not applied, it is an essential means of potentially avoiding such effects. The difficulties of both CIA and SEA in offshore settings are however acknowledged, as issues of ocean noise often illustrate.[46]

Although EIA has been recognized as an obligation of general international law,[47] it has been said that "the evidence to support the duty to conduct SEAs as a binding legal obligation is 'sparse'".[48] Caddell notes "there has been little consideration of the application of the principles [of SEA] within the marine environment worldwide".[49] Yet SEA is useful to examine what the effects of a fishery programme upon the environment can be.[50] It may also be useful in relation to impacts from offshore oil and gas development,[51] carbon capture and storage,[52] deep-seabed mining and hydraulic fracturing,[53] with its relevance in the sensitive Arctic[54] and Antarctic[55] environments noted.

Although the LOS Convention requires assessment, no specific form of this is required, leading to potentially different opinions and the need for legal clarification. While at the time of adoption in 1982, EIA was more prevalent than SEA,[56] the considerations of the drafters may also have been influenced by the obligations of NEPA which required both.[57] The implications of the extent of

---

[45] See SC King and R Pushchak "Incorporating Cumulative Effects into Environmental Assessments of Mariculture: Limitations and Failures of Current Siting Methods" (2008) 28 *Environmental Impact Assessment Review* 572–586.

[46] See R Caddell "Unchartered Waters: SEA in the UK Offshore Area" in G Jones and E Scotford (eds.) *The Strategic Environmental Assessment Directive: A Plan for Success?* (Hart, Oxford: 2017) 283–309, at 299–308.

[47] *Case Concerning Pulp Mills on the River Uruguay (Argentina v. Uruguay)* (20 April 2010, Judgment), ICJ Reports 2010 (I), para. 204.

[48] RL Johnstone *Offshore Oil and Gas Development in the Arctic under International Law: Risk and Responsibility* (Brill, Leiden: 2015) 172.

[49] Caddell note 46 at 283.

[50] S Marsden "Strategic Environmental Assessment and Fisheries Management in Australia: How Effective is the Commonwealth Legal Framework?" in S Marsden and S Dovers (eds.) *Strategic Environmental Assessment in Australasia* (Federation Press, Sydney: 2002) 47–70.

[51] L Lamorgese et al. "Reviewing Strategic Environmental Assessment Practice in the Oil and Gas Sector" (2015) 17(2) *Journal of Environmental Assessment Policy and Management* 1550017-1.

[52] A Gao "The Application of the European SEA Directive to Carbon Capture and Storage Activities: The Issue of Screening" (2008) 17 *European Energy and Environmental Law Review* 341–371.

[53] Caddell note 46 at 289.

[54] G Sander "International Legal Obligations for Environmental Impact Assessment and Strategic Environmental Assessment in the Arctic Ocean" (2016) 31 *International Journal of Marine and Coastal Law* 88–119.

[55] S Marsden "Introducing Strategic Environmental Assessment to the Madrid Protocol: Lessons from International Experience" (2011) 1 *The Polar Journal* 33–47.

[56] Caddell note 46 at 287.

[57] Sander note 54 at 109; Clark note 2.

the obligation are significant because first, EIA does not address cumulative effects either at all or very well in most places, and second EIA is often a simpler process to follow, meaning that the advantages of a potentially more challenging SEA process are overlooked.

4. PRECAUTIONARY AND ECOSYSTEM APPROACHES TO FISHERIES MANAGEMENT

The precautionary approach (or principle), is acknowledged in international jurisprudence as underpinning the obligation to conduct an EIA for environmentally significant activities. Although not mentioned by the International Court of Justice (ICJ) in *Certain Activities/Construction of a Road*, its relevance to risk and significance thresholds is clear. Judge Bhandari, although recognizing that "its status in international law is still evolving", comments also that it "aims to provide guidance in development and application of international environmental law where there is scientific uncertainty".[58] Bhandari cites the reference to the principle by New Zealand in the *Nuclear Tests II* case, although "in that Order the Court did not make any finding as to the applicability of the precautionary principle".[59] In the *Antarctic Whaling* case,[60] again despite advocacy by New Zealand, it was not taken into account by the Court. Ad Hoc Judge Charlesworth, however, commented on relevance of the precautionary approach to the use of lethal capture methods of cetaceans, noting its role in connection with fish stocks:

> The essence of the precautionary approach has informed the development of international environmental law and is recognized implicitly or explicitly in instruments dealing with a wide range of subject-matter, from the regulation of the oceans and international watercourses to the conservation and management of fish stocks, the conservation of endangered species and biosafety.[61]

The Fish Stocks Agreement makes specific reference to the precautionary approach, both as a general principle,[62] and in detailing that it is to be applied "widely ... in order to protect the living marine resources and preserve the marine environment".[63] Moreover, "the absence of adequate scientific

---

[58] Separate Opinion of Judge Bhandari, in *Certain Activities/Construction of a Road*, note 18, para. 17, p.4, available at www.icj-cij.org/files/case-related/150/18860.pdf.

[59] Ibid, para. 18, p. 5; see *Request for an Examination of the Situation in Accordance with Paragraph 63 of the Court's Judgment of 20 December 1974 in the Nuclear Tests (New Zealand v. France) Case (New Zealand v. France)*, Judgment, ICJ Reports 1995, p. 288.

[60] *Whaling in the Antarctic (Australia v. Japan)* (31 March 2014), ICJ Reports 2014, p. 226.

[61] Separate Opinion, ICJ, *Whaling in the Antarctic (Australia v. Japan)* (31 March 2014), para. 6, p. 455.

[62] Fish Stocks Agreement, Arts, 5.1 and 6. See also Annex II Guidelines.

[63] Ibid., Art. 6.1.

information shall not be used as a reason for postponing or failing to take" measures, and the obligation is enhanced by specifying further the need to "be more cautious when information is uncertain, unreliable or inadequate".[64] The relationship between the precautionary approach and EA emphasizes the need to consider "the impact of fishing activities on non-target and associated or dependent species",[65] and "to assess the impact of fishing on non-target and associated or dependent species and their environment".[66]

Under the Code of Conduct, States "should apply a precautionary approach widely". The Code also explains the significance of the precautionary approach to fisheries. Uncertainties as to "size and productivity of the stocks, reference points, stock condition in relation to such reference points, levels and distribution of fishing mortality and the impact of fishing activities"[67] are all relevant in implementing the approach. Furthermore, in the case of new or exploratory fisheries, "States should adopt as soon as possible cautious conservation and management measures".[68]

The Fish Stocks Agreement also refers indirectly to the ecosystem approach to fisheries management, ensuring the compatibility of the measures States are required to "take into account the biological unity and other biological characteristics of the stocks",[69] and "ensure that such measures do not result in harmful impact on the living marine resources as a whole".[70] In emphasizing the need for ecosystem approaches, it has furthermore been noted that RFMOs:

> [T]end to apply a sector-based, fragmented approach, leaving unregulated a number of activities with a potential impact on the same area ... do not give adequate weight to scientific knowledge ... [and] establish very poor, if any, linkages with other regimes – either regional or global – concerned with other activities having an impact on the marine environment.[71]

Such concerns have resulted in advocacy for both ecosystem and precautionary approaches to fisheries management, and are relevant in connection with the development of EA globally because effective EA is arguably a key element of both approaches. The SPRFMO Convention includes both approaches in its objective,[72] and the UNGA Sustainable Fisheries Resolutions (2006–2017) refer

---

[64] Ibid., Art. 6.2.
[65] Ibid., Art. 6.3(c).
[66] Ibid., Art. 6.3(d).
[67] Code of Conduct, Art. 7.5.2.
[68] Ibid., Art. 7.5.4. See also Art. 6(6) Fish Stocks Agreement.
[69] Fish Stocks Agreement, Art. 7.2(d).
[70] Ibid., Art. 7.2(f).
[71] A Fabra and V Gascón "The Convention on the Conservation of Antarctic Marine Living Resources (CCAMLR) and the Ecosystem Approach" (2008) 23 *International Journal of Marine and Coastal Law* 567.
[72] Note 191, Arts. 2 and 3(2)(a).

to both approaches regularly.[73] In general terms it can be said that EA is based upon the precautionary approach and is the underlying rationale for the process; it can also help tackle new issues impacting the environment.[74] Similarly however, EA relates clearly and closely to the ecosystem approach,[75] especially where higher level decisions (policies, plans and programmes) and broader areas are considered as potential targets. Both approaches have been developed with reference to the CBD in particular, which is relevant in the light of the BBNJ discourse.[76]

5. FISHERIES RESEARCH AND DATA-GATHERING

It must be emphasized that there is a clear difference between what is often referred to as an 'assessment' and an EA. In the case of an EA this must be carried out *before* any works are carried out. The evaluation must therefore be *ex ante*, rather than *ex post*. The ICJ in the *Certain Activities/Construction of a Road* case, distinguishes between Costa Rica's 'Environmental Diagnostic Assessment' and an EIA for example. The former was an assessment of the "environmental impact of the stretches of the road that had already been built",[77] and was "carried out approximately three years into the road's construction".[78] It was therefore *ex post*, and not an EA, with the Court confirming that "the obligation to conduct an environmental impact assessment requires an *ex ante* evaluation of the risk of significant transboundary harm".[79] In support, it notes the previous conclusion in the *Pulp Mills* case, that "an environmental impact assessment must be conducted prior to the implementation of a project".[80]

Ex post assessments are generally used for data collection,[81] and fish stock assessments are the main example, although they do not necessarily assess the

---

[73] See e.g. UNGA Resolution 61/105, para. 6.

[74] M Pan and HP Huntington "A Precautionary Approach to Fisheries in the Central Arctic Ocean: Policy, Science and China" (2016) 63 *Marine Policy* 153–157.

[75] SM Garcia et al. "The Ecosystem Approach to Fisheries: Issues, Terminology" (2003) 443 (*FAO Technical Paper* No. 443) and EA Kirk "The Ecosystem Approach and the Search for an Objective and Content for the Concept of Holistic Ocean Governance" (2015) 46 *Ocean Development and International Law* 33–49. On ecosystem approaches under the CBD, see www.cbd.int/ecosystem/default.shtml.

[76] See www.cbd.int/ecosystem/default.shtml, and RD Smith and E Maltby *Using the Ecosystem Approach to implement the CBD: A Global Synthesis Report Drawing Lessons from Three Regional Pathfinder Workshops* 32 (available at www.cbd.int/programmes/cross-cutting/ecosystem/cs.aspx).

[77] Note 18, para. 161, p. 60.

[78] Ibid.

[79] Ibid.

[80] Note 47, para. 205, at 83.

[81] EJ Simmonds et al. "The Role of Fisheries Data in the Development Evaluation and Impact Assessment in Support of European Fisheries Plans" (2011) 68 *ICES Journal of Marine Science* 1689–1698.

impact of human activities on the stock, rather its general condition in terms of distribution, abundance and composition.[82] Life cycle assessment (LCA) is another example of a non-EA approach, which considers resource use and environmental impacts of a product from a cradle-to-grave perspective.[83] While risk assessments may also be used by resource managers responsible for individual target stocks to consider forward projections of natural hazards and accidents, they are also not EAs. Although there is a relationship with EIA as ecological risk assessment considers anthropogenic changes to the environment, again these are not typical EAs because they do not evaluate the effects of human activities. In relation to SEA – which like EIA should also be an *ex ante* process –, some 'SEAs' – given the flexibility of language usage like EA/EIAs – may confusingly not be what they appear.[84] With regard to the relationship between EIAs and SEAs, it should also be emphasized that information generated in relation to one process may benefit the other, with less need for detailed information for EIAs if a previous SEA has been carried out.[85]

Fisheries research and data-gathering requirements are clearly indicated in the Fish Stocks Agreement, with a general principle to "collect and share, in a timely manner, complete and accurate data concerning fishing activities ... as well as information from national and international research programmes";[86] and to "promote and conduct scientific research ... in support of fishery conservation and management".[87] Specific functions of RFMOs include the need to "agree on standards" for data collection and "promote and conduct scientific assessments of the stocks".[88] The link between these requirements and EA is furthermore clearly indicated as, in elaborating the application of the precautionary approach, the obligation is to "develop data collection and research programmes to assess the impact of fishing".[89] This is important to ensure that baseline information is available to input any EA process after a new

[82] K Lorenzen "Toward a New Paradigm for Growth Modelling in Fisheries Stock Assessments: Embracing Plasticity and its Consequences" (2016) 180 *Fisheries Research* 4–22; and A Winter and A Arkhipkin "Environmental Impacts on Recruitment Migrations of Patagonian Longfin Squid (Doryteuthis gahi) in the Falkland Islands with Reference to Stock Assessment" (2015) 172 *Fisheries Research* 185–195.

[83] S Hornborg et al. "Integrated Environmental Assessment of Fisheries Management: Swedish Nephrops Trawl Fisheries Evaluated Using a Life Cycle Approach" (2012) 36 *Marine Policy* 1193–1201.

[84] See A Stępień, T Koivurova and P Kankaanpää (eds.) *Strategic Impact Assessment of Development in the Arctic* (Arctic Centre/European Union: Rovaniemi: 2014) (available at www.arcticinfo. eu/en/sada).

[85] Caddell cites SEA information being used in relation to the designation of a UK protected area. See note 46, 301. He also notes (at 303) "considerable practical challenges incumbent in gathering effective baseline data". In addition, see Simmonds et al., note 81.

[86] Fish Stocks Agreement, Art. 5(j).

[87] Ibid., Art. 5(k).

[88] Ibid., Art. 10(e) and (g).

[89] Ibid., Art. 6.3(d).

international fishery has begun.[90] It is also important where proposals in the marine context which are unrelated to a fishery (as highlighted in Section 2) may impact upon it.

Further to Annex I of the Fish Stocks Agreement,[91] States are obliged to "collect and exchange scientific, technical and statistical data",[92] "ensure that data are collected in sufficient detail to facilitate effective stock assessment",[93] and "take appropriate measures to verify the accuracy of such data".[94] Other measures require cooperation on data specification and format, developing and sharing techniques and methodologies,[95] and strengthening scientific research capacity.[96] The Compliance Agreement requires records of fishing vessels to be maintained and international cooperation to exchange information.[97]

The Code of Conduct details provisions for fisheries research[98] requiring "an appropriate institutional framework",[99] "support and strengthen[ing of] national research capabilities",[100] studies on "the environmental impact of fishing gear on target species"[101] and that activities should be collaborative,[102] including the provision of support to developing countries and small island States.[103] The Code also requires that

> States should assess the impacts of environmental factors on target stocks and species belonging to the same ecosystem or associated ecosystem or associated with or dependent upon the target stocks, and assess the relationship among the populations in the ecosystem.[104]

This clearly illustrates the difference between *ex ante* EA and assessment used as a means of data collection. In respect of all of the provisions in the agreements considered above therefore, it is very important to distinguish between assessments of the significant negative effects of human activity carried out in advance of that activity, and assessments carried out to determine environmental baselines, which may change following human activity in the marine environment such as detrimental fishing activity.

---

[90] See ibid., Arts. 3(1)(v) and 23, SPRFMO Convention, note 190.
[91] Entitled 'standard requirements for the collection and sharing of data'.
[92] Ibid., Art. 14.1(a).
[93] Ibid., Art. 14.1(b).
[94] Ibid., Art. 14.1(c).
[95] Ibid., Art. 14.2.
[96] Ibid., Art. 14.3. With reference to the Part XIII, LOS Convention.
[97] Compliance Agreement, Arts. IV, V and VI.
[98] Code of Conduct, Arts. 12 and 7.4.
[99] Ibid., Art. 12.2.
[100] Ibid., Art. 12.6.
[101] Ibid., Art. 12.10.
[102] Ibid., Art. 12.17.
[103] Ibid., Arts. 12.18, and 12.20.
[104] Ibid., Art. 7.2.3.

6. OTHER RELEVANT INTERNATIONAL INSTRUMENTS AND OBLIGATIONS

6.1. Customary International Law

In the *Gabčíkovo-Nagymaros* case, a separate judicial opinion supported the view that EIA had assumed the status of a principle of customary international law. Judge Weeramantry referred to the need for "continuing EIA", acknowledging the significance of ongoing assessment and monitoring of a project while in operation.[105] His Opinion helped form a clearer view of EIA as an international obligation, stating that a duty of EIA is to be read into treaties whose subject can reasonably be considered to have a significant impact on the environment. In the *MOX Plant* case,[106] and especially *Pulp Mills*,[107] EIA again was emphasized, in the latter to the extent that "the Court clearly perceives that EIA and other procedural duties form part and parcel of the principles of no-harm and due diligence".[108] The Court also considered that "a precautionary approach may be relevant in the interpretation and application of the provisions of [the 1975 Statute of the River Uruguay]"[109] and

> [T]he obligation to protect and preserve, [under the Statute] [...], has to be interpreted in accordance with a practice, which in recent years has gained so much acceptance among States that it may now be considered a requirement under general international law to undertake an environmental impact assessment where there is a risk that the proposed industrial activity may have a significant adverse impact in a transboundary context, in particular, on a shared resource.

In the 2011 ITLOS Advisory Opinion the status of EIA as a "general obligation under customary international law"[110] was emphasized in relation to monitoring and evaluating impacts of deep-seabed mining upon the marine environment. Importantly, expanding the scope beyond industrial activities, the application to international areas was also considered applicable,[111] with the Tribunal stating

---

[105] Separate Opinion, *Gabčíkovo-Nagymaros Project* (*Hungary v. Slovakia*) [1997] ICJ Reports 7.

[106] *MOX Plant* (*Ireland v. United Kingdom*) (provisional measures) [1997] ICJ Reports; *MOX Plant* (*Ireland v. United Kingdom*) (suspension of proceedings on jurisdiction and merits and request for further provisional measures) (order 3, of 24 June 2003) (2003) 42 ILM 1187 (order 4, of 14 November 2003) (order 5, of 22 January 2007).

[107] *Pulp Mills* note 47; see A Boyle "Developments in the International Law of Environmental Impact Assessments and their Relation to the Espoo Convention" (2011) 20 *Review of European Community and International Environmental Law* 227–231.

[108] See T Koivurova "Transboundary Environmental Impact Assessment in International Law" in S Marsden and T Koivurova (eds.) *Transboundary Environmental Impact Assessment in the European Union: The Espoo Convention and its Kiev Protocol on Strategic Environmental Assessment* (Earthscan, London: 2011) 23–25.

[109] *Pulp Mills* note 47, para. 164.

[110] Note 23, para. 145, p. 44.

[111] See French, note 23.

of the *Pulp Mills* ruling "The Court's reasoning in a transboundary context may also apply to activities with an impact on the environment in an area beyond the limit of national jurisdiction".[112]

ITLOS had previously considered the risk of harm to the marine environment in *Land Reclamation*[113] – where risks and effects of works had to be assessed – and *Southern Bluefin Tuna*[114] – where catch quotas could only be increased by agreement once further studies of the stock had been completed. Boyle comments:

> The outcome in these cases shows that an EIA must be undertaken if there is some evidence of a risk of significant harm to the human or natural environment – even if the risk is uncertain and the potential harm not necessarily irreparable.[115]

While the 2011 ITLOS Advisory Opinion considered that *Pulp Mills* may oblige States to conduct EA in ABNJ, general international law has yet to conclusively decide this.[116]

In 2015 ITLOS also considered a number of questions from the Sub-Regional Fisheries Commission (SRFC),[117] in relation to the definition of the minimum access conditions and exploitation of fisheries resources within the maritime zones under the jurisdiction of SRFC Member States (MAC Convention).[118] These included the obligations of the flag State in cases where IUU fishing activities are conducted within the exclusive economic zones (EEZs) of third-party States. In relation to this it emphasized the role of due diligence and the obligation to cooperate as outlined by *Pulp Mills*, the *Seabed Disputes Chamber* and *MOX Plant*.[119] While also considering the rights and obligations of the coastal State in ensuring the sustainable management of shared stocks and

---

[112] Note 23, para. 148.

[113] *Case Concerning Land Reclamation by Singapore in and around the Straits of Johor* (*Malaysia v. Singapore*), Request for Provisional Measures, 126 ILR (2003) 487, para. 96.

[114] *Southern Bluefin Tuna Cases* (*New Zealand v. Japan; Australia v. Japan*), Request for Provisional Measures, 117 ILR (1999), 148, para. 79.

[115] See Boyle, note 107 at 228.

[116] Judge Bhandari in his Separate Opinion in *Certain Activities/Construction of a Road*, "draw[s] inspiration from the words of Judge Weeramantry in his dissenting opinion" in the *Nuclear Tests II* Order, where the significance of environmental law in the global commons is emphasized, note 58, para. 7. This aspect has yet to be highlighted by academics; for other reviews, see JK Cogan "Certain Activities Carried out by Nicaragua in the Border Area (Costa Rica v. Nicaragua); Construction of a Road in Costa Rica along the San Juan River (Nicaragua v. Costa Rica)" in DP Stewart (ed.) "International Decisions" (2016) 110 *American Journal of International Law* 320; and R Yotova "The Principles of Due Diligence and Prevention in International Environmental Law" (2016) 75 *Cambridge Law Journal* 445.

[117] Request for Advisory Opinion submitted by the Sub-Regional Fisheries Commission, Advisory Opinion of 2 April 2015.

[118] Convention on the Determination of the Minimal Conditions for Access and Exploitation of Marine Resources within the Maritime Areas Under Jurisdiction of the Member States of the Sub-Regional Fisheries Commission (SRFC) (Dakar, 8 June 2012).

[119] Note 117, paras. 131–132 and 140.

stocks of common interest, and considering at length the meaning of "sustainable management", it did not, however, take the opportunity to consider further the position of EA.[120]

Also in 2015, in *Certain Activities/Construction of a Road*, the customary international law status of EIA was confirmed by the Court, which like ITLOS, expanded the application to other types of activities. It noted

> [a]lthough the Court's statement in the Pulp Mills case refers to industrial activities, the underlying principle applies generally to proposed activities which may have a significant adverse impact in a transboundary context.[121]

Resistance to accepting anything other than the principle of EIA as part of customary international law was, however, maintained, with the content – alongside the triggering process of significance – left for proponent States to decide.[122] As with the view of the Court in *Pulp Mills*,[123] the Court in *Certain Activities/Construction of a Road* took essentially the same line that "determination of the content of the environmental impact assessment should be made in light of the specific circumstances of each case".[124]

Because of the concerns of allowing a proponent State to determine whether the threshold for significant environmental effects has been reached, the strength of this obligation has been contested. Desierto states

> the Court was utterly silent on whether such an EIA was to be judged solely from the *lens of the State determining the scope and content of an EIA and conducting the said EIA*, or whether there are objective, empirical, or scientific criteria under international law for determining the existence of such significant risk of transboundary harm.[125]

The Separate Opinion of Judge Bhandari in *Certain Activities/Construction of a Road* highlights the subjective nature of implementation of the significance threshold, as "[a] country proposing a project might argue that any impact is neither significant nor adverse".[126]

---

[120] Ibid., paras 189–218.

[121] Note 18, para. 104, p. 45.

[122] See Y Tanaka "Costa Rica v. Nicaragua and Nicaragua v. Costa Rica: Some Reflections on the Obligation to Conduct an Environmental Impact Assessment" (2017) *Review of European, Comparative and International Environmental Law* 91, 94; and J Bendel and J Harrison "Determining the Legal Nature and Content of EIAs in International Environmental Law: What Does the ICJ Decision in the Joined Costa Rica v Nicaragua/Nicaragua v Costa Rica Cases Tell Us?" (2017) 42 *Questions of International Law* 13.

[123] *Pulp Mills*, note 47, para. 205. See Boyle note 107 at 229–230.

[124] *Certain Activities*, note 18, para. 104.

[125] D Desierto "Evidence but not Empiricism: Environmental Impact Assessments at the International Court of Justice etc", 26 February 2017 (available at www.ejiltalk.org/evidence-but-not-empiricism-environmental-impact-assessments-at-the-international-court-of-justice-in-certain-activities-carried-out-by-nicaragua-in-the-border-area-costa-rica-v-nicaragua-and-con/).

[126] Separate Opinion of Judge Bhandari, note 58, para. 36.

State practice may additionally support the customary status of EIA through growing compliance with the Espoo Convention.[127] Judge Bhandari comments:

> [This] contains novel and progressive guidelines that the community of nations would be well served to treat as persuasive authority in creating a more comprehensive global regime regarding the required content of transboundary EIAs under public international law.[128]

The future recognition of SEA requirements in general international law will, however, likely take much longer.[129]

The specific treaty law relevant to transboundary EIA, notably the Espoo Convention, must be examined further because it contains the detailed content and triggering processes that the ICJ has yet to confirm meet the test for customary international law. Limitations in a marine context are a specific concern; also notable is the scholarly debate about its global application, and the potential application to ABNJ. Because the Espoo regime is largely concerned with evaluating significant environmental effects of proposals upon terrestrial and coastal environments, its potential application in a marine context must hence be treated with some caution.[130] However, as its content is well used and it has relevance for State relationships in a marine setting, it is important to consider fully.

6.2. The Espoo Convention

The Espoo Convention built upon other international and European law with transboundary procedures, particularly the 1974 Nordic Convention[131] and the 1985 EIA Directive.[132] There are currently 45 Parties, and since the entry into force of an amendment, the treaty is now potentially open to all Members of the

---

[127] In a non-European context, see S Marsden and E Brandon *Transboundary Environmental Governance in Asia: Practice and Prospects with the UNECE Agreements* (Edward Elgar, Cheltenham: 2015) 268–275.

[128] Separate Opinion of Judge Bhandari, note 58, para. 33.

[129] In *Antarctic Whaling*, Ad Hoc Judge Charlesworth indirectly referenced the potential of SEA when commenting on the Japanese 'programme' for whaling in the Southern Ocean; note 60.

[130] T Koivurova "Could the Espoo Convention Become a Global Regime for Environmental Impact Assessment and Strategic Environmental Assessment?" in R Warner and S Marsden (eds.) *Transboundary Environmental Governance: Island, Coastal and Marine Perspective* (Ashgate, Farnham: 2012) 323–342.

[131] Nordic Environmental Protection Convention of 19 February 1974; UNE EPL, Vol. 1, 1975–1976 p. 44. This was the first international agreement on transboundary EIA.

[132] Council Directive 85/337/EEC of 27 June 1985 on the assessment of the effects of certain public and private projects on the environment [1985] OJ L175/40; note J Ebbesson "Innovative Elements and Expected Effectiveness of the 1991 EIA Convention" (1999) 19 *Environmental Impact Assessment Review* 47–55.

UN beyond the United Nations Economic Commission for Europe (UNECE) region.[133] The related SEA Protocol is also in force with 30 Parties.[134] Although mainly applicable in a domestic context, it also contains a provision for trans-boundary application;[135] similarly, the Espoo Convention encourages Parties to apply its principles to policies, plans and programmes.[136] The main substantive provision in the Espoo Convention is the requirement for the 'party of origin' to take 'due account' of the EIA and the comments received from the public and the 'affected party'. There are, however, no requirements to prohibit proposed activities or minimize adverse transboundary effects, which have caused some to question its validity.[137]

EIA is defined as a national procedure to evaluate likely environmental impacts,[138] and 'transboundary impact' refers to the impacts within the current jurisdiction when the source originates from another jurisdiction.[139] Parties must "take all appropriate and effective measures to prevent, reduce and control significant adverse transboundary environmental impact from proposed activities".[140] Appendix I lists the proposed activities that are likely to cause impacts, and for which an EIA procedure is to be established,[141] including public participation and with the documentation required by Appendix II). The EIA must be undertaken by the party of origin prior to any authorizing decision being taken,[142] and the party of origin must also provide an opportunity for the public to participate.[143]

The detailed specific provisions of the Convention then follow: notification,[144] documentation,[145] consultation,[146] the final decision,[147] post project analysis[148]

---

[133] "UNECE Espoo Convention on Environmental Impact Assessment becomes a global instrument", press release 27 August 2014 (available at www.unece.org/index.php?id=36354).

[134] Protocol on Strategic Environmental Assessment to the Convention on Environmental Impact Assessment in a Transboundary Context of 21 May 2003 (2685 UNTS 140).

[135] J de Mulder "The Protocol on Strategic Environmental Assessment: A Matter of Good Governance" (2011) 20 *Review of European Community and International Environmental Law* 232–247; and S Marsden "The Espoo Convention and Kiev Protocol in the European Union: Implementation, Compliance, Enforcement and Reform" (2011) 20 *Review of European Community and International Environmental Law* 267–276.

[136] Espoo Convention, Art. 2(7).

[137] J Knox "The Myth and Reality of Transboundary Environmental Impact Assessment" (2002) 96 *American Journal of International Law* 291, at 304.

[138] Espoo Convention, Art. 1(vi).

[139] Ibid., Art. 1(viii).

[140] Ibid., Art. 2(1).

[141] Ibid., Art. 2(2).

[142] Ibid., Art. 2(3).

[143] Ibid., Art. 2(6).

[144] Ibid., Art. 3.

[145] Ibid., Art. 4.

[146] Ibid., Art. 5.

[147] Ibid., Art. 6.

[148] Ibid., Art. 7.

and bilateral and multilateral cooperation.[149] The party of origin must give notification of proposals to any affected party or parties as soon as possible, consistent with notifying its own public.[150] Specific content requirements are set out concerning the proposed activity and potential transboundary impacts, the decision and response times.[151] The Implementation Committee (responsible for the compliance procedure) has confirmed that even a low likelihood of such impact should trigger the obligation to notify affected parties, which "means that notification is necessary unless a significant adverse transboundary impact can be excluded".[152]

If the affected party wishes to participate, the party of origin must provide relevant information.[153] The affected party is also obliged to provide information on the potentially affected environment to enable the party of origin to prepare the EIA documentation.[154] This must be provided promptly through a joint body if one exists.[155] If notification has not been given to a potentially affected party which considers itself such, discussions should commence with the party of origin which must be based on the exchange of sufficient information between the parties.[156] Failing a successful outcome, the Appendix IV inquiry procedure may be triggered to determine whether there are likely to be significant adverse environmental effects.[157] This has been used only once to date, in relation to the Danube-Black Sea Deep Water Navigation Canal in the Ukrainian Sector of the Danube Delta.[158]

The concerned parties are to inform the public of the proposed activity, and of the right of the public to make comments in relation to this, to the competent authority of the party of origin.[159] EIA documentation must comprise the

---

[149] Ibid., Art. 8.

[150] Ibid., Art. 3(1).

[151] Ibid., Art. 3(2).

[152] Economic Commission for Europe, Convention on Environmental Impact Assessment in a Transboundary Context, *Opinions of the Implementation Committee (2001–2010)* (United Nations: 2011), para. 17 (Committee Opinions).

[153] Espoo Convention., Art. 3(5).

[154] Ibid., Art. 3(6).

[155] There is no definition of 'joint body', reference to which is also made in other requirements such as Arts. 4(2) and 5 below. App. VI concerning elements for bilateral and multilateral cooperation also does not refer to the establishment of such bodies, although para. 2(g) suggests joint EIA and joint monitoring programmes.

[156] Espoo Convention, Art. 3(7).

[157] In relation to significance determinations, see: www.unece.org/env/eia/pubs/cepwg3r6.html.

[158] Espoo Inquiry Commission, *Report on the Likely Significant Adverse Transboundary Impacts of the Danube-Black Sea Navigation Route at the Border of Romania and the Ukraine*, July 2006 (available at www.unece.org/fileadmin/DAM/env/eia/documents/inquiry/Final%20Report%2010%20July%202006.pdf).

[159] Espoo Convention, Art. 3(8). The importance of public participation has been confirmed by several decisions of the Implementation Committee, see *Committee Opinions*, note 152, paras. 13 (domestic regulatory framework needed), 11 (to be included in primary rather than secondary legislation) and 12 (for the competent authority not the proponent unless the proponent is also the State).

minimum information specified in Appendix II, which must be submitted to the competent authority of the party of origin.[160] This information must be forwarded to the affected party via a joint body, again if one exists,[161] and the concerned parties must then distribute documentation to the public and competent authorities of affected parties in areas likely to be affected. Any comments must also be submitted within a reasonable time before any final decision is taken.

After the EIA documentation is complete, the party of origin must enter into consultations with the affected party without delay.[162] These must include the potential transboundary impact of the proposed activity and measures to reduce or eliminate it. Alternatives, monitoring and other measures should also be included in the consultations. Reasonable timeframes must be agreed on and consultations held via a joint body if one exists. Detailed obligations concern the final decision taken;[163] due account must be taken of the EIA,[164] including the documentation, comments received and consultation outcomes; the final decision must also be transmitted to the affected party together with the reasons and considerations on which it is based.[165] If additional information on the significant adverse transboundary impact comes to light before the project commences – and which would have affected the decision to allow it – consultations must begin immediately between the concerned parties with a view to changing the decision if one of them requests it.[166]

The concerned parties must decide if monitoring is required of the impacts of an approved activity, with a view to achieving the objectives listed in Appendix V.[167] If, following the post-project analysis, a party has reasons to believe there are significant adverse transboundary impacts, the other party must be informed. Consultations with the objective of reducing or eliminating the impact must then begin between the concerned parties.[168] Appendix VI provides further information in relation to such cooperation, and Article 9 provides for the establishment or intensification of research programmes to aid further cooperation in relation to the procedures and science of EIA.[169]

---

[160] Ibid., Art. 4(1).
[161] Ibid., Art. 4(2).
[162] Ibid., Art. 5.
[163] Ibid., Art. 6.
[164] Ibid., Art. 6(1). 'Due account' is not defined, but as with the information and public participation provisions (such as timeframes), reference can be made to the Aarhus Convention (note 221) and its *Implementation Guide*, (available at www.unece.org/fileadmin/DAM/env/pp/Publications/Aarhus_Implementation_Guide_interactive_eng.pdf). Art. 6(8) elaborates on 'due account' to include the reasons and considerations on which the decision was taken.
[165] Ibid., Art. 6(2).
[166] Ibid., Art. 6(3).
[167] Ibid., Art. 7(1).
[168] Ibid., Art. 8.
[169] See *Committee Opinions*, note 152, paras. 80–83.

Although global application of the treaty is important,[170] the practical application of the Espoo Convention to ABNJ is far from straightforward. The list of activities considered significant in Appendix I does not include impacts from international fisheries;[171] it has, however, been applied in marine areas, and impacts upon fisheries have been considered alongside the seabed.[172] Appendix III does enable other activities to be assessed where size, location and effects are particularly important, and this may be useful, although the language of the Convention is limited to impacts from one State or States upon others. While amendments are possible,[173] and the global application of the Convention may assist in overcoming the historical UNECE focus upon European, Caucasian and Central Asian States, there is, however, much to be done to expand the application terrestrially, regardless of in maritime contexts. In the context of international fisheries law, one of the main issues would be deciding on who to consult and allow participation with; presumably the affected parties (relevant coastal and ABNJ fishing States) whether directly or through the RFMO.

It has long been considered that the Espoo Convention regime could be expanded, or a specific protocol appended to the LOS Convention in a manner now envisaged by the nascent ILBI, to introduce EIA as a more direct component of maritime regulation.[174] Koivurova considers the "much more challenging question for the Espoo regime [is] whether it could cover EIA/SEA over impacts to ABNJ".[175] There is little question that the Espoo Convention in itself "is not a natural 'nesting' place for EIA/SEA rules for activities having a likely impact on the environment in ABNJ".[176] This is notwithstanding the 'persuasive authority' of this regime as noted by Judge Bhandari,[177] the relevant experience gained by the Parties in marine contexts, the detailed procedural rules which could be adapted to some extent, and discussion of the potential for a subsidiary instrument underneath it.[178] In any event, questions over the pursuit of EA in ABNJ have since been taken up by wider BBNJ process, as considered further below.

---

[170] See Information on the workshop on the globalization of the Espoo Convention and the Protocol on SEA, and the role of international financial institutions, 9 November 2016, ECE/MP.EIA/WG.2/2016/INF.11.

[171] Note, however, the inclusion of "deforestation of large areas" as one of these activities, which could be interpreted of relevance to the seabed. See JB Jones "Environmental Impact of Trawling on the Seabed: A Review" (1992) 26 *New Zealand Journal of Marine and Freshwater Research* 59–67.

[172] See Koivurova and Pölönen, note 35 at 157.

[173] Espoo Convention, Art. 14.

[174] M Tanaka, "Lessons from the Protracted MOX Plant Dispute: A Proposed Protocol on Marine Environmental Impact Assessment to the United Nations Convention on the Law of the Sea" (2003–2004) 25 *Michigan Journal of International Law* 337.

[175] Koivurova, note 130.

[176] Ibid., 340.

[177] Separate Opinion of Judge Bhandari note 58.

[178] Koivurova, note 130 at 341–342.

6.3. Bottom Fishing and EA

Bottom fishing is implicated in significant environmental impacts, with bottom trawling the most destructive method as heavy fishing gear dragged across the seabed.[179] In accordance with UNGA Resolution 61/105,[180] specific fisheries may be closed to protect marine biodiversity.[181] The Resolution specifically calls for EA

> to assess … whether individual bottom fishing activities would have significant adverse impacts on vulnerable marine ecosystems, and to ensure that … [activities are either managed] to prevent these impacts, or are not authorised to proceed.[182]

Unlike the list-approach of Appendix I of the Espoo Convention, Currie emphasizes that the provision is triggered for all individual bottom fishing activities where they impact adversely upon vulnerable marine ecosystems (VMEs).[183] Closure of such areas is one of the key options available where it is not possible to prevent such impacts.[184] As outlined earlier in Chapters 7 (Caddell) and 9 (Dunn, Ortuño Crespo and Caddell) of this volume, in 2011 a Resolution was adopted making further specific reference to EA. Para 129 of the Resolution notes that

> the urgent actions called for in the relevant paragraphs of resolutions 61/105 and 64/72[185] have not been fully implemented in all cases, and in this regard further actions in accordance with the precautionary approach, ecosystem approaches and international law and consistent with the Guidelines are needed.[186]

In accordance with this, it calls on States "to take the following urgent actions":

> (*a*) To strengthen procedures for carrying out assessments to take into account individual, collective and cumulative impacts, and for making the assessments publicly available, recognizing that doing so can support transparency and capacity-building globally;
>
> (*b*) To establish and improve procedures to ensure that assessments are updated when new conditions or information so require;

---

[179] See Jones, note 171.

[180] Note 73.

[181] G Wright et al. "Advancing Marine Biodiversity Protection through Regional Fisheries Management: A Review of Bottom Fisheries Closures in Areas Beyond National Jurisdiction" (2015) 61 *Marine Policy* 134–148.

[182] Note 73, para. 83(a).

[183] D Currie "Key Components and Best Practices for Environmental Impact Assessments and Strategic Environmental Assessments" 24 August 2016 at 3 (available at http://highseasalliance.org/sites/highseasalliance.org/files/eia%20key%20components.pdf).

[184] Note 73, para. 83(c).

[185] UNGA Resolution 64/72 of 4 December 2009.

[186] UNGA Resolution 66/68 of 28 March 2012.

(c) To establish and improve procedures for evaluating, reviewing and revising, on a regular basis, assessments based on best available science and management measures ...[187]

It is notable, however, that despite the availability of EA and its link with closures, there is little reported evidence of the application of EA by RFMOs in any of the closure areas surveyed.[188] In 2016, the UNGA called *inter alia* for impact assessments to be reviewed "periodically" and revised whenever "a substantial change in the fishery has occurred or there is relevant new information, and that, where such impact assessments have not been undertaken, they are carried out as a priority before authorizing bottom fishing activities".[189]

Concerns have nevertheless been raised that practice has been weak in general, while attention to cumulative impacts has been especially limited.[190] Motivated at least in part by the UNGA commitments, a number of RFMOs have established requirements for prior assessment as part of their broader regulatory frameworks on bottom fishing. A prominent example is the South Pacific Regional Fisheries Management Organization (SPRFMO),[191] which requires Benthic Impact Assessments,[192] following the adoption of an agreed process in February 2012. The Convention's framework process is concise and does not detail arrangements for consultation and with whom, although the intention is to elaborate on other matters at a later stage.[193] The process now includes provision for public comment following posting of the assessments on the SPRFMO website, subsequent flag State assessments and comments, with the Science Working Group of the Convention preparing comments on the assessment and public views thereafter.[194]

Australia, New Zealand and the European Union have each prepared EAs for fisheries under the SPRFMO Convention. In respect of the Australian EA, the impact of Australian vessels is the primary concern, with trawl, demersal lines and gillnets respectively evaluated.[195] Significant adverse impacts from these methods upon VMEs are a particular focus, with the assessment carried out in accordance with the Bottom Fishery Impact Assessment Standard. Issues of concern are outlined in the scoping stage, with the likelihood of significant impact determined to be low based on low fishing effort and few

---

[187] Ibid., para. 129.

[188] Wright et al, note 181.

[189] UNGA Resolution 71/123 of 7 December 2016, para. 180.

[190] Report of the Secretary-General, UN Doc. A/66/307, para. 158.

[191] Convention on the Conservation and Management of High Seas Fishery Resources in the South Pacific Ocean of 14 November 2009 ([2012] ATS 28).

[192] www.southpacificrfmo.org/benthic-impact-assessments/.

[193] www.southpacificrfmo.org/assets/SPRFMO4%20Report%20Annex%20C.pdf.

[194] www.southpacificrfmo.org/assets/SPRFMO4%20Report%20Annex%20D.pdf.

[195] A Williams et al. *Bottom Fishery Impact Assessment – Australian Report for the South Pacific Regional Fisheries Management Organisation* (CSIRO, July 2011) ix.

areas of high fishing intensity, together with restrictions upon fishing areas and the management arrangements in place to monitor and mitigate impacts and risks.

6.4. The BBNJ Process

The 2015 UNGA BBNJ Resolution establishes a clear link with EA.[196] However, unlike the earlier suggestion for a specific protocol for marine EIA to the LOS Convention,[197] the Resolution includes EA as just one of the issues of focus.[198] This is significant, because the extent to which States will accept the EA component of the BBNJ Process remains to be seen, given the emphasis that existing legal instruments must not be undermined by the Process.[199] The role of other international EA law in a marine context, particularly the CBD, must therefore also be emphasized. The CBD requires Parties to introduce procedures for EIA and SEA for proposals "that are likely to have significant adverse effects on biological diversity".[200] Public participation is also necessary for procedures for "notification, exchange of information and consultation".[201]

During the first Session of the Preparatory Committee ('PrepCom1'), an overview of the main issues was organized around clusters. In one cluster, different types of EAs were distinguished and it was suggested that existing instruments could help clarify and guide their application to ABNJ.[202] International jurisprudence was suggested as one source of potential guidance.[203] The chair noted "the need to further elaborate and strengthen the relevant provisions of UNCLOS, in particular articles 204–206".[204] Other matters emphasized were the need to provide common/minimum standards, clarify the definition, scope and content of EIAs, and to align with best practice. Guiding principles and approaches were to inform the new agreement, including the precautionary and

---

[196] UNGA BBNJ Resolution, note 11 at para. 2.

[197] Tanaka, note 174.

[198] Annex I, Preparatory Committee established by General Assembly Resolution 69/292, Chair's Overview of the first session of the Preparatory Committee.

[199] UNGA BBNJ Resolution, note 11 at para. 3.

[200] CBD, Art. 14.1(a) and (b).

[201] Ibid., Art. 14.1(c).

[202] Examples included the UNEP Goals and Principles, CBD Art.14 and Voluntary Guidelines on Biodiversity-Inclusive Impact Assessment and Voluntary Guidelines for the Consideration of biodiversity in EIAs and SEAs in marine and coastal areas, ISA Regulations on prospecting and exploration of mineral resources in the Area, the Espoo Convention and SEA Protocol, the Antarctic Environmental Protocol and the EA guideline of the Secretariat of the Pacific Regional Environment Programme.

[203] See notes 18 (ICJ, *Certain Activities/Construction of a Road*); 23 (ITLOS, *Activities in the Area*), and 47 (ICJ, *Pulp Mills*) in particular.

[204] Annex II, Preparatory Committee established by General Assembly Resolution 69/292, Chair's Overview of the first session of the Preparatory Committee, para. 7.

ecosystem approaches, public participation, cooperation and coordination with existing bodies and organizations, assessment of cumulative impacts, avoiding duplication of assessments, and carrying out EAs prior to activity or authorization in ABNJ.

Other principles included that sectoral bodies, such as RFMOs and the ISA, would continue to decide their own EA processes alongside coastal States in ABNJ; the ISA is considering the potential for SEA as well as EIA.[205] The special circumstances of developing States were recognized, and assessments could be carried out jointly to reduce the burdens, with preferential treatment given. Threshold issues were examined at length, with one or more thresholds triggering an EA, and either a full or partial approach taken.[206] Consistency with Article 206 of the LOS Convention was maintained,[207] although other international legal obligations were also recognized.[208] Lists of activities that should always be subject to prior EIAs before being authorized, including Appendix I of the Espoo Convention, were furthermore emphasized, which should be reviewed on a regular basis to include new and emerging activities.[209] Warner and Gjerde consider

> An indicative list of such activities for ABNJ could include fishing, aquaculture, dumping of waste, marine geo-engineering, offshore hydrocarbon production, marine scientific research, laying of submarine cables and pipelines, ballast water exchange, deep sea tourism expeditions and ocean energy operations.[210]

Finally, assessment reports, procedural elements (including monitoring, review and compliance) and institutional arrangements, were all examined in some detail. For reports, specifying the type and information needs was considered important: cumulative impacts over time and across sectors, impacts caused by activities outside ABNJ, socio-economic impacts, the risks of impacts and alternatives were all highlighted; the area where the activity or activities take place and the vulnerability of that area to impacts, and adverse effects on other

---

[205] See Co-Chair's report, Griffith Law School and the International Seabed Authority Workshop on Environmental Assessment and Management for Exploitation of Minerals in the Area, Surfers Paradise, Queensland, Australia. 2016, para. 37 (available at www.isa.org.jm/files/documents/EN/Pubs/2016/GLS-ISA-Rep.pdf).

[206] E.g. under the Protocol on Environmental Protection to the Antarctic Treaty of 4 October 1991 (30 ILM 1455 (1991)); see Marsden, note 55 at 38–39, and Currie, note 183 at 3–4.

[207] Other sources of thresholds in the LOS Convention – such as Arts. 145, 192, 194, 198, 207 and 208 – were also noted.

[208] Principle 17 of the Rio Declaration, Art. 7 of the International Law Commission's Draft Articles on Prevention of Transboundary Harm from Hazardous Activities, and the Antarctic Protocol.

[209] Examples of activities requiring prior EAs included those in sensitive areas, such as VMEs and Particularly Sensitive Sea Areas (PSSAs).

[210] R Warner (with comments from K Gjerde), "An International Instrument on Conservation and Sustainable Use of Biodiversity in Marine Areas beyond National Jurisdiction: Exploring Different Elements to Consider" IUCN, undated at 3 (available at http://docplayer.net/13443483-An-international-instrument-on-conservation-and-sustainable-use-of-biodiversity-in-marine-areas-beyond-national-jurisdiction.html).

activities were also significant. States with jurisdiction or control over an activity were to be responsible for conducting EIAs and SEAs, although a framework could be set up under which the public or private entities could carry out such assessments; however, proponents of an activity would bear the costs. As to the role of the public and other stakeholders, Warner and Gjerde recommend that

> In the ABNJ context, potential stakeholders could include States, members of the public, international and regional organizations, inter-governmental and nongovernmental organizations, industry representatives and corporate entities, as well as research communities.[211]

It was decided that decision-making would be by the State responsible for taking the decision. However a scientific body with equitable geographical representation could decide on the admissibility of an activity, or provide advice to a governing body adopting such a decision. Activities would not be permitted if they had significant adverse effects and, where such effects were possible, preventative measures needed to be in place. It is not clear from this whether States could be prevented from proceeding with activities if the scientific or governing body decided otherwise. Warner and Gjerde also recommend that a

> Meeting of the Parties to the international instrument advised by a subsidiary scientific and technical body could function as the decision-making body for EIAs. Its functions could include setting standards for best practice EIA and reviewing EIAs undertaken by sectoral bodies for activities in ABNJ.[212]

This is in accord with the PrepCom view that an international governing body with equitable geographical representation be established to commission and conduct EAs and oversee monitoring and reporting. Furthermore, a scientific and technical committee/advisory body would have the power to conduct EAs, review reports, define activities subject to EAs, evaluate cumulative impacts, define specific guidelines for activities, accredit independent experts, manage a public database and review state practice. Other bodies identified were a compliance committee, a clearing-house mechanism for information, a capacity-building mechanism to assist developing countries, and a fund to finance efforts to repair harmful effects.

Following PrepCom1 three further sessions were convened, culminating in PrepCom4 in July 2017. Emphasizing the difficulties ahead, the chair concluded that "the elements of the draft text of an international legally binding instrument do not reflect consensus between those involved",[213] although

---

[211] Ibid., 5.
[212] Ibid., 6.
[213] E Morgera "PrepCom4Final: Earth Negotiations Bulletin" http://enb.iisd.org/download/pdf/enb25141e.pdf.

a conference to elaborate the ILBI will open in September 2018.[214] In relation to EIA – and to emphasize these difficulties – one of the final recommendations was that the instrument "set out the relationship to (other) EIA processes under relevant legal instruments and frameworks and relevant global, regional and sectoral bodies".[215] Although many issues were supported,[216] there were particular divergences of views on "whether the instrument should address SEAs, and the degree to which the EIA process should be conducted by states or be 'internationalized'".[217]

As an example of one aspect of these EA processes, public participation and expert input are fundamental elements generally, as evidenced by both domestic practice and internationally by the Espoo Convention,[218] and this will have to be reflected in the terms of any resulting ILBI. Public participation is also a key part of international marine governance.[219] Decision-makers must take account of feedback received and explain how and why this has influenced the final decision. It depends upon adequate information, which must be made available at an early time. Particular groups will require information to be provided in a format that is readily accessible to them, and Indigenous communities have particular needs under international law.[220] Fisheries strategic assessments in Australia have followed a process of consultation,[221] and domestic practice must be determined in the next and final stage of the negotiations.

Internationally, the Aarhus Convention has been the guide for best practice in public participation approaches,[222] and it has also been applied in fisheries contexts.[223] The approach to participation under the Espoo Convention follows

---

[214] UNGA Resolution 72/249 of 24 December 2017.

[215] Ibid., 14; for the recommendations for EIA (also SEA) as viewed from the perspectives of different States and groups, see 12–14.

[216] Ibid., 14 ('Section A').

[217] Ibid, 14 ('Section B').

[218] S Marsden "Public Participation in Transboundary Environmental Impact Assessment – Closing the Gap between International and Public Law?" in B Jessup and K Rubenstein (eds.) *Environmental Discourses in Public and International Law* (Cambridge University Press, Cambridge: 2012) 238–259.

[219] EM de Santo "Assessing Public 'Participation' in Environmental Decision-making: Lessons Learned from the UK Marine Conservation Zone (MCZ) Site Selection Process" (2016) 64 *Marine Policy* 91–101; M Voyer et al. "Methods of Social Assessment in Marine Protected Area Planning: Is Public Participation Enough?" (2012) 36 *Marine Policy* 432–439; and for related efforts, see M Portman "Involving the Public in the Impact Assessment of Offshore Renewable Energy Facilities" (2009) 33 *Marine Policy* 332–338. See also Caddell note 46 at 306 in relation to practical difficulties.

[220] *United Nations Declaration on the Rights of Indigenous Peoples*, GA Res 61/295, UN GAOR, 61st Sess, Supp No 49, UN Doc. A/RES/61/295 (2007) 4, 32.

[221] Marsden, note 50.

[222] Convention on Access to Information, Public Participation in Decision-Making and Access to Justice in Environmental Matters of 25 June 1998 (2161 UNTS 447).

[223] See generally M Pallemaerts (ed.) *The Aarhus Convention at Ten – Interactions and Tensions between Conventional International Law and EU Environmental Law* (Europa Law Publishing, Amsterdam: 2011); and also in a European context, ClientEarth *Transparency in the*

this closely. The Compliance Agreement contains measures for the exchange of information which, as indicated by both the Aarhus and Espoo Conventions, is needed to ensure meaningful participation.

7. CONCLUSIONS

EA is a significant tool for the ecosystem approach to fisheries management; it is also informed fundamentally by the precautionary approach. While important EA obligations are found in the LOS Convention and the Fish Stocks Agreement, further elaboration and guidance are needed to ensure both approaches are implemented as effectively as possible. This is important because detailed content requirements are absent, leading to confusion about how matters such as triggering the EA process is to be initiated, what procedures are to be followed, and in both cases when. While international courts and tribunals – notably the ICJ and ITLOS – have decided recent cases with an EA element, the position on important matters such as these remains unclear. Misconceptions continue for example as to what constitutes an EA, with this specific tool often conflated with general exercises in research and data collection. Similarly, the involvement of the public and the role of experts is yet to be clearly established in many cases.

The significance of EA in international law was however confirmed by the ICJ in 2015 in *Certain Activities/Construction of a Road*, whether in the context of customary international law in general or international fisheries law specifically. Yet the application of the EA instrument and its detailed content remains with individual States unless they have obligations under specific treaties, such as the Espoo Convention. While this treaty has a growing reach geographically and in connection with the different sectors to which it applies, it crucially excludes international fisheries. It is also not best placed to apply to ABNJ because its focus is on the actions of a State affecting another State or States, particularly in a terrestrial context. It has furthermore largely been overtaken by the momentum in the BBNJ Process to include EA as an important aspect.

The prospective establishment of a BBNJ ILBI provides an extremely valuable opportunity to extend the current customary obligation for EA in international law to international fisheries, in addition to other activities significantly impacting ABNJ. This is important because other than as noted – for example in the specific context of the seabed and benthic assessments – there is very limited practice of EA being applied to the significant negative environmental effects of international fisheries upon the marine environment. The rudimentary nature of the obligations in the LOS Convention and the Fish Stocks Agreement – whether as a result of the triggering mechanism or content requirements – suggests there is potential for considerable improvement if there is a wish to expand application and strengthen the protective obligations contained within. The difficulties facing the BBNJ Process however cannot be underestimated. EA remains just one aspect of the Process and there are fundamental differences of opinion which must still be reconciled.

Overall, it can be considered that there is no single repository of international legal obligations for EA of marine fisheries. Whether found in customary international law, the LOS Convention, Fish Stocks Agreement (and related Compliance Agreement and Code), UNGA Resolutions, the Espoo Convention, or prospectively the new ILBI, there is a need to analyze each of these EA arrangements to distill the nature and full extent of the obligations. This is less than satisfactory, but is unlikely to change given that the BBNJ Process is guided by the dual wish for the LOS Convention to be the principal instrument, while at the same time respecting the role of existing international instruments. Despite its primarily terrestrial focus, the procedures and practices of the Espoo Convention may inform the development of the ILBI, and if so, protection of international fisheries may be enhanced.

11

Addressing Climate Change Impacts in Regional Fisheries Management Organizations

ROSEMARY RAYFUSE*

1. INTRODUCTION

T HE OCEANS WERE once described as the "Cinderella of the UN climate negotiations".[1] Despite constituting the largest sink of carbon dioxide (CO_2) and representing more than 30 per cent of the global carbon cycle "no one ha[d] asked them to the Ball".[2] References to the oceans were also few and far between in the first four Assessment Reports of the Intergovernmental Panel on Climate Change (IPCC). Indeed, it was not until its Fifth Assessment Report (AR5) – published in 2013 – that the IPCC called for the "international community to progress rapidly to a 'whole of ocean' strategy for responding to the risks and challenges posed by anthropogenic ocean warming and acidification".[3] In the two chapters of AR5 devoted to the oceans and ocean systems, the IPCC noted the need for the development of international, regional and national policy responses to the challenges posed by the changing ocean.[4]

* The author acknowledges the support of the Swedish Research Council and Lund University in the writing of this chapter during her tenure as the Swedish Research Council's Kerstin Hesselgren Visiting Professor. Grateful thanks are also due to Ms Tempe McMinn for her exceptional research assistance, and to the editors, in particular Erik Molenaar, for their extremely helpful comments on earlier drafts of this chapter.

[1] D Freestone "Climate Change and the Oceans" (2009) 4 *Carbon and Climate Law Review* 383–386, at 383.

[2] Ibid.

[3] O Hoegh-Guldberg et al. "The Ocean" in V Barros et al. (eds.) *Climate Change 2014: Impacts, Adaptation and Vulnerability. Part B: Regional Aspects. Contribution of Working Group II of the Fifth Assessment Report of the Intergovernmental Panel on Climate Change* (Cambridge University Press, UK and NY USA: 2014) 1655–1731, at 1661.

[4] Ibid., 1711.

In December 2015, the 21st Conference of the Parties to the UNFCCC[5] adopted the Paris Agreement[6] whose Preamble recognized, for the first time, the importance of ensuring the integrity of all ecosystems (which by definition must include ocean ecosystems) and the protection of biodiversity when taking action to address climate change, as well as the fundamental priority of safeguarding global food security.

Fish represent a major portion of marine biodiversity and constitute a vital contribution to global food security, providing about 20 per cent of global animal intake.[7] In its AR5, the IPCC warned that by 2055 global redistribution of fish yields, coupled with decreases in open ocean net primary production and fish habitat caused by ocean warming, anoxia and acidification, will have profound implications for fish stocks and thus for global food security.[8] Indeed, as Cheung et al. make clear in Chapter 2 of this volume, it is now beyond question that a warming and changing ocean has implications for international fisheries.

Of course, fish and the marine ecosystems in which they occur, are naturally subject to climate-related variability that drives fluctuations in abundance and distribution of fish stocks. However, climate change-related changes in water temperature, oxygenation, ocean acidity and ocean currents are predicted to amplify these natural variations leading to greater changes in abundance and distribution.[9] Indeed, evidence exists that ocean warming is already displacing species towards the poles and causing changes in their size and abundance.[10] Climate change-related ocean acidification poses even greater challenges,[11] associated with destruction of prey and habitat, which are predicted to have profoundly detrimental impacts on fisheries, broader ecosystem services and livelihoods.[12]

When combined with ocean warming, the effects of ocean acidification are amplified.[13] When combined with other existing stressors such as overfishing

[5] United Nations Framework Convention on Climate Change of 9 May 1992 (1771 UNTS 107).

[6] Paris Agreement of 12 December 2015 (available at unfccc.int/2860.php).

[7] HO Pörtner et al. "Ocean Systems" in CB Field et al. (eds.) *Climate Change 2014: Impacts, Adaptation, and Vulnerability, Part A: Global and Sectoral Aspects. Contribution of Working Group II to the Fifth Assessment Report of the Intergovernmental Panel on Climate Change* (Cambridge University Press, UK and NY USA: 2014) 411–484, at 417.

[8] Ibid. See also Q Ding, X Chen, R Hilborn and Y Chen, "Vulnerability to Impacts of Climate Change on Marine Fisheries and Food Security" (2017) 83 *Marine Policy* 55–61.

[9] See Chapter 2 of this volume (Cheung, Lam, Ota and Swartz).

[10] WWL Cheung, JL Sarmiento, J Dunne, TL Fröelicher, VWY Lam, MLD Palomares, R Watson and D Pauly "Shrinking of Fishes Exacerbates Impacts of Global Ocean Changes on Marine Ecosystems" (2013) 3(3) *Nature Climate Change* 254–258.

[11] IPCC "Ocean Systems", note 7 at 465. See also K Kroeker et al. "Impacts of Ocean Acidification on Marine Organisms: Quantifying Sensitivities and Interaction with Warming" (2013) 19 *Global Change Biology* 1884–1896; C Turley et al. "Future Biological Impacts of Ocean Acidification and their Socioeconomic-policy Implications" (2010) 4 *Current Opinion in Environmental Sustainability* 278–286; and JP Gattuso and L Hanson (eds.) *Ocean Acidification* (Oxford University Press, Oxford: 2011).

[12] Pörtner et al., note 7 at 434; Hoegh-Guldberg et al., note 3 at 1701–1702.

[13] Hoegh-Guldberg et al., note 3 at 1708–1710.

and pollution, the accumulated negative effects of rapid climatic shifts will not only further complicate the sustainable management of fish stocks but may well threaten the continued viability of many species.[14] Of particular concern is the possibility of exceeding 'tipping points' beyond which fundamental changes in ecosystem structure and function will occur, causing major impacts on oceanic food-webs and thus on human food security. In the Arctic, for example, evidence exists that the Arctic Ocean and its ecosystems are moving towards a new state dominated by seasonally open water and younger, thinner ice.[15] In the Antarctic, concern is mounting over the possibility of a shift from the current stable state based on krill to a different stable state based on salps, a gelatinous planktonic invertebrate that resembles a jelly fish.[16] However, as salps are 95 per cent water, they are not considered to be a link to higher trophic levels such as pelagic fish, seabirds and whales, and cannot replace krill in the foodweb.[17] Climate change- or ocean acidification-induced reductions in krill productivity and abundance therefore represent a major threat to the Antarctic ecosystem.

In short, climate change-induced changes in species composition, distribution and abundance pose significant threats to global fish stocks. Yet, despite this growing body of evidence, one question that neither the IPCC nor the Paris negotiators addressed is how to ensure the sustainability of global fish stocks in a climate change-challenged world. At the international level, this task falls to the regimes that have been established for the conservation and management of international fisheries. However, the transformation of ocean ecosystems as a result of climate change and associated ocean acidification also poses significant challenges for these international fisheries regimes; challenges which are both jurisdictional and managerial in nature. The challenge of climate change can thus be viewed not just as a question of ecosystem resilience, but also of the institutional robustness and resilience of the regimes charged with the conservation and management of international fisheries.[18]

---

[14] IPCC, "Summary for Policy Makers" in *Climate Change 2014: Impacts, Adaptation and Vulnerability. Part A: Global and Sectoral Aspects. Contribution of Working Group II of the Fifth Assessment Report of the Intergovernmental Panel on Climate Change* (IPCC, WGII Summary for Policy Makers: 2014) 17.

[15] AMAP, 2017. *Snow, Water, Ice and Permafrost in the Arctic (SWIPA 2017)*, Arctic Monitoring and Assessment Programme (AMAP) Oslo, Norway (2017) (available at www.amap.no/documents/doc/Snow-Water-Ice-and-Permarost-in-the-Arctic-SWIPA-2017/1610).

[16] H Flores et al. "Impact of Climate Change on Antarctic Krill" (2012) 458 *Marine Ecology Progress Series* 1–19.

[17] MM McBride et al. "Krill, Climate and Contrasting Future Scenarios for Arctic and Antarctic Fisheries" (2014) 71 *ICES Journal of Marine Science* 1934–1955, at 1944–1945; PN Trathan and D Agnew "Climate Change and the Antarctic Marine Ecosystem: An Essay on Management Implications" (2010) 22 *Antarctic Science* 387–398; A Constable "Climate Change and Southern Ocean Ecosystems: How Changes in Physical Habitats Directly Affect Marine Biota" (2014) 20 *Global Change Biology* 3004–3025.

[18] R Rayfuse "Climate Change and the Law of the Sea" in R Rayfuse and S Scott (eds.) *International Law in the Era of Climate Change* (Edward Elgar, Cheltenham: 2012) 147–174.

The purpose of this chapter is to examine the legal implications of climate change for international fisheries regimes and their robustness and resilience in addressing the impacts of climate change on the stocks they manage. The chapter focuses exclusively on high seas fisheries and regional fisheries management organizations (RFMOs), defined here as encompassing the self-standing international organizations that have been established for the purpose of adopting legally binding conservation and management measures in respect of the high seas fish stocks under their jurisdiction.[19] This includes five 'tuna' RFMOs[20] and seven 'non-tuna' RFMOs.[21] Not included are the two anadromous fish organizations,[22] other high seas arrangements that "fall short of establishing a formal international organisation"[23] and whose Parties are not currently engaged in the regulation of a high seas fishery, either because the fishery is under a moratorium or because no regulatory measures have yet been adopted,[24] bilateral arrangements[25] and other bi- or multilateral arrangements that do not manage high seas fisheries.[26]

The chapter begins with a discussion of the challenges posed by climate change to RFMOs focusing first on the 'jurisdictional challenges' resulting from changes in the distributional ranges of the fish stocks they manage. It then turns to an examination of the 'managerial challenges', focusing on the practice within RFMOs relating to the incorporation of climate change into their management processes. In particular, this chapter examines the extent to which RFMOs are (1) actively anticipating climate stressors in their scientific research; (2) absorbing the importance of these stressors into their decision-making; and (3) reshaping their management measures to address climate-driven changes.

[19] For more extensive discussion of the role of RFMOs and other regional fisheries bodies, see Chapter 5 of this volume (Harrison).

[20] The Commission on the Conservation of Southern Bluefin Tuna (CCSBT); the Indian Ocean Tuna Commission (IOTC); the International Commission for the Conservation of Atlantic Tunas (ICCAT); the Inter-American Tropical Tuna Commission (IATTC); and the Western and Central Pacific Fisheries Commission (WCPFC).

[21] The Commission on the Conservation of Antarctic Marine Living Resources (CCAMLR); the General Fisheries Commission for the Mediterranean (GFCM); the North-East Atlantic Fisheries Commission (NEAFC); the Northwest Atlantic Fisheries Organization (NAFO); the North Pacific Fisheries Commission (NPFC); the South-East Atlantic Fisheries Organization (SEAFO); and the South Pacific Regional Fisheries Management Organization (SPRFMO).

[22] The North Pacific Anadromous Fish Commission and the North Atlantic Salmon Conservation Organization. Since all high seas fishing for anadromous stocks is prohibited by virtue of Art. 64 of the LOS Convention (United Nations Convention on the Law of the Sea of 10 December 1982 (1833 UNTS 3)), these commissions do not actually manage any high seas fisheries. Nevertheless, both are alive to the scientific issues relating to the effects of climate change on salmon stocks.

[23] Chapter 5 of this volume (Harrison).

[24] Such as the Convention on the Conservation and Management of Pollock Resources in the Central Bering Sea and the Southern Indian Ocean Fisheries Agreement. Also excluded is the recently concluded Agreement to Prevent Unregulated High Seas Fisheries in the Central Arctic Ocean, which, after considerable delay, was opened for signature on 3 October 2018 but is not yet in force.

[25] Such as the Joint Norwegian-Russian Fisheries Commission. For discussion of this Commission see Chapter 6 of this volume (Molenaar).

[26] Such as the International Pacific Halibut Commission or the Pacific Salmon Commission.

It is acknowledged at the outset that the solution to climate change lies not with RFMOs but rather with the climate regime. Nevertheless, as Trathan and Agnew put it: "exacerbation of climate impacts should not be allowed to occur through inappropriate management practices".[27] As this chapter will demonstrate, RFMOs still have a long way to go in integrating climate change impacts into their institutional frameworks and management decisions.

2. CLIMATE CHANGE AND RFMOS: THE JURISDICTIONAL CHALLENGE

RFMOs are the international community's mechanism of choice through which the duty to cooperate in the conservation and management of high seas fisheries resources is to be implemented. However, while on paper RFMO management frameworks appear to have the potential to respond to climate-related challenges,[28] in practice these regimes are often considered to be deficient in the essential capacities for adaptive, integrated governance and management required to effectively support the resilience of marine ecosystems in an increasingly dynamic, climate change-challenged environment.[29] The reasons for these shortcomings are rooted in limitations to their competences, in particular those limitations resulting from the principle of *pacta tertiis* and the primacy of flag State jurisdiction.[30]

Beyond the complications arising from these general limitations, however, climate change poses specific jurisdictional challenges for RFMOs as a result of their geographical and managerial competences. RFMOs generally manage stocks on either a species-specific or a geographic basis. The former approach is largely pursued by the tuna RFMOs, while the latter is largely pursued by the non-tuna RFMOs. Stock- or species management boundaries therefore often do not align with ecological boundaries. One significant exception is the Southern Ocean where the CAMLR Convention[31] applies to the Antarctic marine living resources found south of the Antarctic Convergence;[32] the natural biogeographic

---

[27] Trathan and Agnew, note 17 at 388.

[28] B Pentz, N Klenk, S Ogle and JAD Fisher "Can Regional Fisheries Management Organisations (RFMOs) Manage Resources Effectively during Climate Change?" (2018) 92 *Marine Policy* 13–20.

[29] C Folke "Social-ecological Systems and Adaptive Governance of the Commons" (2007) 22 *Ecological Research* 14–15; M Lockwood et al. "Marine Biodiversity Conservation Governance and Management: Regime Requirements for Global Environmental Change" (2012) 69 *Ocean and Coastal Management* 160–172.

[30] These issues are canvassed in other Chapters of this volume. See, in particular, Chapters 5 (Harrison), 6 (Molenaar), 13 (van der Marel) and 15 (Klein) of this volume. See also R Rayfuse "Regional Fisheries Management Organisations" in DR Rothwell, AG Oude Elferink, K Scott and T Stephens (eds.) *Oxford Handbook of the Law of the Sea* (Oxford University Press, Oxford: 2015) 439–462.

[31] Convention on the Conservation of Antarctic Marine Living Resources of 20 May 1980 (1329 UNTS 47).

[32] Ibid., Art. I.

boundary where cold waters of the Antarctic circumpolar current meet and sink beneath the relatively warmer waters to the north. Although the precise location of the Convergence changes seasonally, the Convention deems its location to be defined by a line joining precise geographical points.[33] The Convention boundary is thus, at best, an approximation of the ecological boundary with some differences existing between the location of the two at the time of the adoption of the Convention. More importantly, however, recent evidence suggests that there has been a marked (and not merely seasonal) southward shift in the position of the Convergence in some regions.[34] If this trend continues, the Convention boundary and the ecological boundary will increasingly diverge.

Indeed, the effects of this divergence have already been seen in the CAMLR Convention Area, providing a useful illustration of one of the climate change-related jurisdictional challenges faced by RFMOs. Species such as Southern Bluefin tuna (*Thunnus maccoyii*; hereafter SBT), which occur in areas to the north of the Convergence are unable to survive in the lower temperatures to its south. The potential for invasion south of the Antarctic Convergence of "large and highly productive pelagic finfish species" (including SBT) is therefore considered low.[35] However, as the Convergence moves southward these species have begun to enter the CAMLR Convention Area. In 2005 it was discovered that SBT – and vessels fishing for them – were migrating southwards into the CAMLR Convention Area. The concern for the Commission for the Conservation of Antarctic Marine Living Resources (CCAMLR) was that vessels ostensibly fishing for SBT might either take fish and non-fish species, in particular sea-birds, as bycatch in their long-line fisheries or, perhaps, engage surreptitiously in unregulated or unreported fishing for stocks managed by CCAMLR.[36] While CCAMLR possesses managerial and enforcement competence in relation to all living marine resources within the CAMLR Convention Area, the Commission for the Conservation of Southern Bluefin Tuna (CCSBT) possesses overlapping jurisdiction over SBT throughout their migratory range. The question for the two RFMOs was, therefore, whose conservation and management measures were to apply to vessels fishing for SBT within the CAMLR Convention Area. CCAMLR took the position that the issue would best be resolved by the adoption of an agreement defining the respective responsibilities of each RFMO.[37] CCSBT eventually agreed, and the issue was resolved, in 2015, on the basis of an agreement between CCAMLR and CCSBT which provides, *inter alia*, for reciprocal exchange of data and information on fisheries and fishing activities

---

[33] Ibid., Art. I(4). A map of the Convention Area is available at www.ccamlr.org/en/organisation/convention-area.

[34] McBride et al, note 17 at 1949.

[35] Ibid.

[36] Report of the 24th (2005) Annual CCAMLR Meeting, paras. 15.20–15.23.

[37] Ibid., para. 5.21. See also D Leary "Developments in International Environmental Law – Fisheries and Marine Mammals: The Year in Review" (2005) 16 *Yearbook of International Environmental Law* 470–487, at 475.

relevant to each organization.[38] Similar arrangements have also been adopted between CCAMLR and other RFMOs whose geographical competence borders the CAMLR Convention Area.[39]

As the CCAMLR example demonstrates, where species or stocks migrate outside the area of competence of one RFMO they may move into an area regulated by another RFMO leading to possible conflict between the two RFMOs as to the proper locus of managerial competence. The situation has also arisen in the North Atlantic where it was discovered in the 1980s and 1990s that Oceanic redfish (*Sebastes mantella*) were migrating from the regulatory area of the North-East Atlantic Fisheries Commission (NEAFC) into the regulatory area of the Northwest Atlantic Fisheries Organization (NAFO). Although reasons for the migration of the stock were unknown at the time, climate factors and the general increase in sea temperature were suspected as the main drivers.[40] Assessment and management of the stock had hitherto been the responsibility of NEAFC. However, NAFO Members now sought to exploit the stock leading to "great controversy and potential antagonism"[41] between the two organizations, and potentially serious implications for the stock as Members of both RFMOs sought to maximize their catches. It was not until 2001 that agreement was finally reached on a mechanism whereby the total allowable catch (TAC) would continue to be set by NEAFC for the entire stock but an agreed specific percentage would be set aside for treatment by NAFO.[42] The two organizations continue to share management of the stock.

RFMO boundaries, themselves, may also overlap leading to conflict over managerial competence. For example, while the 1949 IATTC Convention,[43] which established the Inter-American Tropical Tuna Commission (IATTC), did not describe its boundaries, in practice IATTC scientists and managers had used 50° N and 50° S as the northern and southern boundaries respectively, and 150° W as the western boundary of the IATTC fishery since at least 1972.[44]

---

[38] Arrangement between The Commission for the Conservation of Southern Bluefin Tuna and The Commission for the Conservation of Antarctic Marine Living Resources of 30 October 2015 (available at www.ccamlr.org/en/system/files/CCSBT.pdf).

[39] For information, see www.ccamlr.org/en/organisation/cooperation-others.

[40] A Thomson "The Management of Redfish (*Sebastes Mentella*) in The North Atlantic Ocean – A Stock in Movement" in *Papers presented at the Norway-FAO Expert Consultation on the Management of Shared Fish Stocks, Bergen, Norway, 7–10 October 2002* (FAO Fisheries Report No. 695, Supplement: 2003) 192–199.

[41] Ibid., 196.

[42] Ibid.,197–198. See also Report of the NAFO/NEAFC Joint Working Group on Oceanic Redfish, 13–14 February 2001, NAFO/FC Doc. 01/3; and the Report of the Special Fisheries Commission Meeting 28–30 March 2001, NAFO/FC Doc. 01/7 in NAFO Meeting Proceedings of the General Council and Fisheries Commission, 2001, 23–35 and 55–72.

[43] Convention for the Establishment of an Inter-American Tropical Tuna Commission of 31 May 1949 (80 UNTS 4).

[44] For discussion, see "WCPFC-IATTC Overlap Area", doc. WCPFC-2011-41 Rev 1 of 18 November 2011 (available at www.wcpfc.int/node/3021).

The revised 2003 IATTC Convention[45] – which came into force in 2010 – formally adopted these boundaries, including 150° W as the western boundary of the Commission's competence. However, this created a significant area of overlap with the regulatory area of the Western and Central Pacific Fisheries Commission (WCPFC), which is defined in the WCPF Convention as extending, in the area between 4° S and 50° S, as far east as 130° W.[46] Negotiations at the time of adoption of the WCPF Convention and again at the time of the adoption of the 2003 IATTC Convention failed to resolve the boundary issue.[47] In the event, it was resolved in 2009 with the adoption of a memorandum of understanding (MOU) providing for consultation, cooperation and collaboration in the exchange of data and information, in research efforts relating to stocks and species of mutual interest, and in the adoption of harmonized and compatible conservation and management measures.[48] Further MOUs on the exchange and release of data[49] and the cross-endorsement of observers[50] were adopted in 2009 and 2011 respectively.

Moreover, it must be remembered that some high seas areas remain unregulated and many stocks and species are therefore unmanaged. This is true, for example, for non-tuna species in the Central and Southwest Atlantic Ocean. Where an unregulated stock or species migrates *into* an RFMO area of competence, the ability of the RFMO to exert managerial competence will depend on its mandate and decision-making processes as well as the will of the Members to regulate a new fishery. In this respect, several RFMOs have adopted measures regulating 'exploratory' or 'new' fisheries aimed at ensuring a fishery is not depleted or exhausted before acquisition of the relevant data on which sound stock assessments can be made.[51] These measures may equally be applied where the new fishery involves stocks or species that have migrated as a result of climate drivers. However, this will not stop unreported and unregulated exploitation in the waters beyond the RFMO, thereby potentially undermining its measures. Similarly, where a stock or species migrates *out of* an RFMO area into an unregulated area of ocean, this may render the existing management regime either inadequate or wholly obsolete and leave the species or stock vulnerable

---

[45] Convention for the Strengthening of the Inter-American Tropical Tuna Commission Established by the 1949 Convention Between the United States of America and the Republic of Costa Rica of 14 November 2003 (also known as the "Antigua Convention"; available at www.iattc.org).

[46] Convention on the Conservation and Management of Highly Migratory Fish Stocks in the Western and Central Pacific Ocean of 5 September 2000 (2275 UNTS 43), Art. 3.

[47] "WCPFC-IATTC Overlap Area", note 44.

[48] WCPFC-IATTC Memorandum of Understanding (available at www.wcpfc.int/doc/wcpfc-iattc-memorandum-understanding).

[49] Available at www.wcpfc.int/doc/wcpfc-iattc-memorandum-cooperation-exchange-and-release-data.

[50] Available at www.wcpfc.int/doc/memorandum-cooperation-cross-endorsement-iattc-and-wcpfc.

[51] For fuller discussion, see Rayfuse, note 30.

to unregulated and potentially unstoppable over-exploitation in the area beyond the RFMO boundaries.

Similar challenges arise where a stock or species migrates from coastal State maritime zones into an RFMO area and *vice versa*. Article 7 of the Fish Stocks Agreement[52] requires coastal States and high seas fishing States to adopt 'compatible' conservation and management measures in respect of straddling and highly migratory fish stocks. However, a range shift to a coastal State's maritime zones will aggravate the management and conservation status if it leads to increased fishing pressure within those maritime zones and no corresponding reduction in the high seas or in the maritime zones of other coastal States. The potential ramifications of such a range shift can be discerned from the experience in the North-East Atlantic where climate-related changes have led to a northwest expansion of North-East Atlantic mackerel, from Norwegian and European Union (EU) maritime zones into Faeroese, Icelandic and Greenlandic maritime zones. Increasing catches in the Faeroese and Icelandic maritime zones and an unwillingness by the EU and Norway to decrease their catches have led to overfishing of mackerel and to conflict between these coastal States and other NEAFC Members over quota allocations. NEAFC has been forced to leave the assessment of the TAC and the total distribution of the quota shares unresolved pending prior agreement amongst the coastal States, the reaching of which is not in their interest.[53]

Dramatic shifts in migration will be particularly problematic in the case of highly migratory species – such as tuna – in areas where pockets of high seas are interspersed with coastal State maritime zones, such as in the Western and Central Pacific.[54] In a preview of debates that have been occurring in WCPFC, Axelrod has hypothesized that coastal States most vulnerable to these anticipated changes will be more likely to push for greater control over the resources that straddle their exclusive economic zones (EEZs) through more stringent RFMO measures including reduction of quota for distant water fishing fleets. The latter, however, will be more likely to insist on maintaining their quota and less restrictive measures while shifting the organizational goals away from catch limits to enable them to maintain their presence in the fishery even in the face of increasing catches in coastal State maritime zones.[55] Arguably, a range shift

[52] Agreement for the Implementation of the Provisions of the United Nations Convention on the Law of the Sea of 10 December 1982 relating to the Conservation and management of Straddling Fish Stocks and Highly Migratory Fish Stocks of 4 August 1995 (2167 UNTS 3).

[53] Report of the 36th (2017) Annual NEAFC Meeting, para. 11.5. For discussion, see J Spijkers and WJ Boonstra "Environmental Change and Social Conflict: the Northeast Atlantic Mackerel Dispute" (2017) 17 *Regional Environmental Change* 1835–1851; KM Hughes, L Dransfeld and MP Johnson "Climate and Stock Influences on the Spread and Locations of Catches in the Northeast Atlantic Mackerel Fishery" (2015) 24 *Fisheries Oceanography* 540–552; and R Hannesson "Sharing the Northeast Atlantic Mackerel" (2013) 70 *ICES Journal of Marine Science* 259–269.

[54] Hoegh-Guldberg et al., note 3 at 1710–1715.

[55] M Axelrod "Climate Change and Global Fisheries Management: Linking Issues to Protect Ecosystems or to Save Political Interests?" (2011) 11(3) *Global Environmental Politics* 64–84, at 71–73.

away from the coastal State will weaken that State's conservation incentives and aggravate management as between that State and the relevant RFMO as both the coastal State and the other RFMO Members seek to maintain their share of the catch. A range shift away from a coastal State to an unregulated area of the high seas will pose an even more significant threat of over-exploitation. In a worst-case scenario, continued take by a coastal State losing the stocks coupled with increased unregulated take on the high seas may lead to the stock being fished to commercial, if not biological, extinction.

It was the concern with a shift from coastal State maritime zones to an unregulated high seas area that led the five central Arctic Ocean coastal States, in 2015, to adopt the Oslo Declaration,[56] in which they agreed to refrain from commercial fishing in the high seas of the central Arctic Ocean unless and until appropriate science-based management measures are in place. Following adoption of the Oslo Declaration, discussions evolved into a 'Broader Process' involving China, the EU, Iceland, Japan and South Korea, in which all delegations agreed, initially, to interim measures to prevent unregulated commercial fishing in the high seas of the central Arctic Ocean, to promote the conservation and sustainable use of the living marine resources there, and to safeguard a healthy ecosystem in the central Arctic Ocean.[57] In November 2017, after six negotiating sessions, outstanding differences over decision-making procedures and the trigger for commencement of negotiations for the establishment of a formal RFMO were overcome, and a new agreement to prevent unregulated fishing in the high seas portion of the central Arctic Ocean was adopted.[58] The agreement will have an initial duration of 16 years from the date of its entry into force, during which time, should the science indicate that some commercial fishing could be undertaken on a sustainable basis, any decision to authorize such fishing or to initiate negotiations to a broader management agreement, will require a consensus. Without such a consensus, the status quo will prevail. The agreement may be extended, unless any Party objects, for successive

---

[56] Declaration Concerning the Prevention of Unregulated High Seas Fishing in the Central Arctic Ocean of 16 July 2015 (available at www.regjeringen.no/globalassets/departementene/ud/vedlegg/folkerett/declaration-on-arctic-fisheries-16-july-2015.pdf).

[57] The Chairman's Statements, issued at the close of each meeting, are available at www.afsc.noaa.gov/Arctic_fish_stocks_fourth_meeting/default.htm; www.afsc.noaa.gov/Arctic_fish_stocks_fifth_meeting/ and www.state.gov/e/oes/ocns/opa/rls/269126.htm.
See also EJ Molenaar "International Regulation of Central Arctic Ocean Fisheries" in MH Nordquist, JN Moore and R Long (eds.) *Challenges of the Changing Arctic* (Brill/Nijhoff, Leiden/Boston: 2016) 429–463; and R Rayfuse "Regulating Fisheries in the Central Arctic Ocean: Much Ado About Nothing?" in N Vestergaard, B Kaiser, L Fernandez and J Nymand Larsen (eds.) *Arctic Resource Governance and Development* (Springer, Berlin: 2018) 35–51.

[58] Chairman's Statement on the Meeting on High Seas Fisheries in the Central Arctic Ocean, Washington, D.C., 28–30 November 2017, available at https://www.state.gov/e/oes/ocns/fish/regionalorganizations/arctic/statements/index.htm. The text of the CAOF Agreement is included in the Annex to doc. COM(2018) 453 final, of 12 June 2018. See also C Welch, "9 Countries and the EU Are Protecting the Arctic Ocean Before the Ice Melts" (*National Geographic*, 8 December 2017) (available at https://news.nationalgeographic.com/2017/12/arctic-ocean-protected-from-fishing-before-ice-melts-climate-change/).

five-year periods, however, should it lapse, there is no requirement to commence negotiations towards a broader management regime.

Clearly, the expectation is that by the end of the initial 16-year period adequate scientific information will be available to allow the Parties to the central Arctic Ocean agreement to make informed decisions about the state of the resources and the potential to initiate any commercial fishing on a sustainable basis. Whether this proves to be correct remains to be seen. In the meantime, the central Arctic Ocean experience serves as an indication that the adoption and implementation of both interim and permanent measures to prevent unregulated commercial high seas fishing in climate-changed ocean areas will continue to test the mettle of the international community into the future. As the following section discusses, the challenge is no less great in areas already subject to regulation by existing RFMOs.

3. CLIMATE CHANGE AND RFMOS: THE MANAGEMENT CHALLENGE

3.1. Introduction

From the foregoing, it will be immediately apparent that the difficulties of managing stocks and species which cross biologically arbitrary geopolitical and legal jurisdictional lines will only increase as species distributions change. Thus, climate change-induced biological regime shifts will necessitate more than ever cooperation and coordination between (extant and future) RFMOs, both within and across jurisdictional and geographic boundaries.[59] However, climate change also poses significant challenges to the managerial competences of, and practices within, RFMOs.

At its heart, the challenge for RFMOs relates to their ability to manage under conditions of uncertainty relating both to the fish under their management and to the associated broader marine ecosystem. Although initially designed for managing under more biologically stable conditions, in a climate-changed world RFMOs will need to ensure that their conservation and management measures are aimed at enhancing the climate resilience of the fisheries they are managing. As Trathan and Agnew put it: "as climate change potentially introduces a greater level of ecosystem uncertainty, successful ecosystem outcomes potentially mean that management practices need to be more conservative".[60] In addition, as others contend, these management practices must also "be flexible enough to account for changes in stock distribution and abundance".[61]

---

[59] Lockwood et al, note 29 at 167.

[60] Trathan and Agnew, note 17 at 338.

[61] T Daw, WN Adger, K Brown and M-C Badjeck "Climate Change and Capture Fisheries: Potential Impacts, Adaptation and Mitigation" in FAO "Climate Change Implications for Fisheries and Aquaculture: Overview of Current Scientific Knowledge" (*FAO Fisheries and Aquaculture Technical Paper* No. 530: 2009) 107–150, at 108.

Precautionary and ecosystem approaches to fisheries management are now generally considered to be the approaches most highly-equipped for climate change adaptation.[62] As Ogier et al. put it, the ecosystem approach

> can help increase the adaptability and resilience of fisheries resources, associated ecosystems, and dependent communities and industries; consider multiple sectors and policies; address cumulative impacts; consider scientific and technical information; and embrace ecosystem services.[63]

While neither the precautionary nor the ecosystem approach are specifically articulated in the LOS Convention, they are both implicit in the Convention's requirements that States adopt measures on the basis of the best scientific evidence available, consider effects on associated and dependent species, and maintain or restore populations of harvested species at levels that ensure Maximum Sustainable Yield.[64] Both approaches are also incorporated in the Fish Stocks Agreement; the precautionary approach specifically[65] and the ecosystem approach by implication.[66] These approaches are also now incorporated into either the constitutive treaty or management frameworks of virtually all RFMOs.

Nevertheless, despite the appeal of the precautionary and ecosystem approaches to fisheries management, experience shows that their actual application is a complicated and difficult task. Grafting climate change impacts – such as changes in species distribution and abundance – onto the range of factors already to be considered in implementing these approaches presents even more significant challenges, particularly given that many of the fisheries concerned are already over-exploited.[67] Since current climate change-induced effects are unlikely to be reversed by ecosystem management alone, fisheries management needs to continually adapt to new ecological realities arising as a result of changing climatic conditions. Fisheries management must therefore be fully integrated with an understanding of the ecological consequences of climate change.[68] This, in turn, requires the mainstreaming of adaptive capacity in order for RFMOs to adequately address climate-driven changes on an ongoing basis.[69]

[62] Ibid.

[63] EM Ogier et al. "Fisheries Management Approaches as Platforms for Climate Change Adaptation: Comparing Theory and Practice in Australian Fisheries" (2016) 71 *Marine Policy* 82–93, at 90.

[64] Arts. 117–119 of the LOS Convention. These requirements are also set out in Art. 61 relating to the conservation and management of the living resources of the EEZ.

[65] Ibid., Arts. 5(c) and (d) and 6 and Annex II.

[66] Ibid., Arts. 5, 6 and 10.

[67] *The State of World Fisheries and Aquaculture 2016* (FAO, Rome: 2016), 5–6. See also TJ Pitcher and WWL Cheung "Fisheries: Hope or Despair" (2013) 74 *Marine Pollution Bulletin* 506–516.

[68] For discussion, see K Miller et al., "Climate Change, Uncertainty, and Resilient Fisheries: Institutional Responses through Integrative Science" (2010) 87 *Progress in Oceanography* 338–346.

[69] According to Pentz and Klenk, "adaptive management has assumed a central role in contemporary fisheries management theory for its potential to mitigate the effects of climate change" (B Pentz and N Klenk "The 'Responsiveness Gap' in RFMOs: The Critical Role of Decision-making Policies in the Fisheries Management Response to Climate Change" (2017) 145 *Ocean and Coastal Management* 44–51, at 47).

Of course, differentiating between climate change and other non-climate-related impacts on fisheries is a difficult task. In this respect, a preliminary question must be whether RFMOs have adequate mechanisms in place to deal with ecosystem concerns and uncertainty in general. Only then can the incorporation by RFMOs of climate change considerations into those mechanisms be fully studied. A comprehensive examination of current mechanisms for ecosystem management in RFMOs is, however, beyond the scope of this chapter. Rather, the following subsections focus on the extent to which RFMOs are taking action specifically with respect to climate change in order to actively anticipate climate stressors in their scientific research, to absorb the importance of these stressors into their decision-making, and to reshape their management measures to address climate-driven changes.

3.2. Anticipating Climate Stressors in their Science

As noted above, the central challenge posed by climate change for RFMOs relates to their ability to manage under conditions of uncertainty. However, this uncertainty is not merely "associated with 'status quo' environmental effects"[70] but, more specifically, with climate change effects which, in addition to changes in species composition, abundance and location, may push marine ecosystems beyond certain tipping points and cause fundamental changes in ecosystem structure and function.[71] This begs the question as to what RFMOs are doing to anticipate climate stressors. In other words, in what manner and to what extent are RFMOs engaging with climate science of relevance to their managerial objectives.

In a study conducted in 2010, Axelrod identified only CCAMLR, the Indian Ocean Tuna Commission (IOTC), NAFO and WCPFC as having taken 'action' related to climate change either by deciding "to undertake climate adaptation or mitigation activities or to allocate funds towards climate change research".[72] A current review of RFMO reports and documents by the author of this Chapter suggests that little has changed. While the term 'climate change' and related terms such as 'environmentally-induced variability', 'climate-induced variability', 'environmental variability' and 'climate shift' are often used in RFMOs, they are generally invoked in the context of referring to more general climatic variance rather than to climate change as a specific environmental phenomenon. Indeed, a number of RFMOs treat climate change simply as a sub-category of general climate fluctuations and not as its own distinct environmental challenge. While multiple references to the importance of ecosystems are

---

[70] Trathan and Agnew, note 17 at 393.
[71] AJ Constable et al., "Climate Change and Southern Ocean Ecosystems I: How Changes in Physical Habitats Directly Affect Marine Biota" (2014) 20 *Global Change Biology* 3004–3025, at 3018.
[72] Axelrod, note 55, 68.

common, these references are not necessarily made in the context of considering climate change but rather in the context of considering the interactions of various species. In general, there appears to be considerable commonality between the annual reports of the various RFMOs containing a general statement that climate change is recognized in a general way as possibly affecting the oceans and the fisheries under their management, but little by way of explicit engagement with climate change-relevant science or substantive suggestions to remedy or address the issue.

Looking at individual RFMOs, within the tuna RFMOs positive indications of climate change-relevant science appear in three of the organizations. The work of IATTC stands out as focusing specifically on understanding the impacts of climate change and ocean acidification on the population status and dynamics of managed species. Scientific reports have linked climate change to community structures in the Eastern Tropical Pacific and to major changes in mid-trophic level prey communities.[73] IATTC staff have developed a model of the pelagic ecosystem in the tropical Eastern Pacific Ocean (EPO) to explore how fishing and climate variation might affect the animals at middle and upper trophic levels.[74] Within IOTC, the focus has been on monitoring ocean climate conditions to depict the inter-annual trend and to track major changes that may affect the large pelagic ecosystem.[75] In WCPFC, the effects of climate variability on species under its management figure primarily in relation to the development of stock assessments and harvest control rules.[76]

In contrast, ICCAT has done little to date by way of climate change specific research, and ecosystem, environmental and climate approaches do not feature heavily in its reports. Admittedly, ICCAT's Science Strategic Plan for 2015–2020 calls for enhanced participation by researchers from different disciplines – including climate scientists – in the Standing Committee on Research and Statistics (SCRS) and its Subcommittee on Ecosystems and Bycatch, as well as improved dialogue both within the SCRS and between the SCRS and other tuna RFMOs.[77] The Subcommittee has even developed a draft template for an ecosystem report card, the purpose of which will be to assist the Commission to advance the implementation of the ecosystem approach to fisheries management by monitoring the state of the ecosystem components supporting ICCAT fisheries. However, reference to climate change or associated ecosystem

---

[73] See e.g. M Hinton "Oceanographic Conditions in the EPO and Their Effects on Tuna Fisheries", Report for the 6th Meeting of the IATTC Scientific Advisory Committee, 2015 (available at www.researchgate.net/publication/307924749_Oceanographic_conditions_in_the_EPO_and_their_effects_on_tuna_fisheries).

[74] IATTC Doc. SAC-07-07b of 9–13 May 2016 (available at https://www.iattc.org/Meetings/Meetings2016/SAC-07/7thMeetingScientificAdvisoryCommitteeENG.htm).

[75] See e.g. Doc. IOTC-2016-WPTT18-09 of 26 October 2016.

[76] See e.g. P Lehodey et al. "Modelling the impact of climate change including ocean acidification on Pacific yellowfin tuna" Doc. WCPFC-SC13-2017/EB-WP-01 of 23 July 2017.

[77] Available at www.iccat.int/en/StrategicPlan.html.

impacts is noticeably absent from the template and from the reports of both the Subcommittee and the SCRS.[78]

For its part, the CCSBT Strategic Plan for 2015–2020 stipulates the need to improve knowledge of the effects of climate change on reproduction and recruitment of SBT by 2018.[79] However, at its 2017 meeting the Commission decided to defer discussion on the promotion of research aimed at improving knowledge of the effect of climate change on the ecosystem conditions that may affect reproduction and recruitment of SBT, pending completion of work on a revised Management Procedure, which is expected by 2020.[80]

In the non-tuna RFMOs the importance given to climate science is equally mixed. NAFO's Standing Committee on Fisheries Environment produces an annual climate status report describing environmental conditions in the convention area in the previous year.[81] For its part, NEAFC conducts no scientific work of its own but rather relies on the International Council for the Exploration of the Sea (ICES) for scientific advice. The Report of the Second NEAFC Performance Review Panel specifically recommended that climate effects be considered more explicitly by NEAFC in developing its management programme and that the scientific basis for such considerations be improved.[82] In response, in 2015 NEAFC agreed that cooperation with ICES should be improved to provide a mechanism through which possible climate effects and other ecosystem considerations can be better discussed.[83] As regards the South-East Atlantic Fisheries Organization (SEAFO), while its Commission has taken important steps to collect data, prepare stock status reports and establish harvest control rules, the Report of the Second SEAFO Performance Review Panel suggests that it should now move to more holistically develop its ecosystem approach, including considering wider ecosystem effects on fisheries.[84] There is, however, no specific mention of climate change. Similar considerations are evident in the South Pacific Regional Fisheries Management Organization (SPRFMO), where environmental variability is mentioned only in the context of discussions of seasonal cycles (i.e. *el niño*/*la niña* events) and uncertainty in regime shifts/oceanographic conditions is considered to be dealt with through the existing range of scenarios used in stock projections.[85]

---

[78] Docs. SCRS/2017/009 "Report of the 2017 intersessional meeting of the sub-committee on ecosystems (Madrid, Spain, 10–14 July 2017)" (2018) 74(7) *Collected Volumes of Scientific Papers of ICCAT*, 3565–3638 and SCRS/2017/140 "A template for an indicator-based ecosystem report card for ICCAT" (2018) 74(7) *Collected Volumes of Scientific Papers of ICCAT* 3639–3670 (available at www.iccat.int/Documents/CVSP/CV074_2017/colvol74.html#1).

[79] Available at www.ccsbt.org/en/file/ccsbtstrategicplanpdf.

[80] Report of the 24th (2017) Annual CCSBT Meeting, paras. 117–118.

[81] See e.g. The 2016 NAFO Annual Ocean Climate Status Summary for the Northwest Atlantic, available at www.nafo.int/Science/Ecosystem/Ocean-Climate/PgrID/1251/PageID/1.

[82] Report of the 2015 Extraordinary NEAFC Meeting, Annex J, 39–40.

[83] Report of the 2015 Extraordinary NEAFC Meeting, 4.

[84] SEAFO, Report of the Second Performance Review Panel, October 2016, 26.

[85] Report of the 1st (2013) Annual Scientific Committee Meeting, 4.

Perhaps not surprisingly, given its express ecosystem mandate, which provides for conservation and management of all marine living resources and not just fish,[86] CCAMLR is the only RFMO that explicitly and repeatedly takes climate change into consideration in its research and research questions.[87] Indeed, the potential impacts of climate change on the Antarctic marine ecosystem have been under general discussion in the Commission – or, more appropriately, the Scientific Committee (SC) – since 2002. In 2006 the Commission acknowledged "the need to address climate effects and to monitor such effects in relation to future potential changes in, and influences on, the species and area for which CCAMLR is responsible",[88] and in 2008 the topic of climate change became a regular reporting item on the agendas of both the Commission and the SC, indicating recognition of climate change as a problem in its own right and not just another aspect of environmental variability. Since then the SC has identified the consequences of climate change that could carry significant risks to Antarctic marine ecosystems and has singled out four major areas of impact for consideration: potential effects on invertebrates; potential effects on higher-trophic levels; potential effects on CCAMLR managed fisheries; and the special effects of increased accessibility associated with the increase in ice-free areas. Work has revolved around three key areas the SC considers necessary to enable it to provide advice to the Commission on appropriate management responses to climate change: the robustness of SC advice and stock assessments in light of increasing uncertainty accompanying climate change; the need to improve monitoring programmes to provide robust and timely indicators of climate change impacts; and the determination of whether management objectives and performance indicators require modification to remain appropriate in face of climate change uncertainty.[89] Nevertheless, despite this activity, the Report of the Second CCAMLR Performance Review Panel considered that "environmental and climate change impacts are not being systematically considered in the context of the activities undertaken in the Convention Area".[90]

3.3. Absorbing Climate Change in their Decision-Making

Even assuming RFMOs recognize the critical importance of climate change and climate change relevant science to their work, application of the precautionary and ecosystem approaches to fisheries management requires more than just

---

[86] Art. II of the CAMLR Convention.

[87] See R Rayfuse "Climate Change and Antarctic Fisheries: Ecosystem Management in CCAMLR" (2018) 45 *Ecology Law Quarterly* 53–81.

[88] Report of the 25th (2006) Annual CCAMLR Meeting, paras. 17.4–17.5.

[89] Report of the 27th (2008) Annual SC Meeting, paras. 7.10–7.14.

[90] Report of the Second CCAMLR Performance Review Panel, August 2017 (CCAMLR PR2 Report).

encouragement of consideration of climate impacts. It also requires the actual integration of these considerations into RFMO decision-making and, ultimately, into actual decisions. In particular, decision-making rules and processes, such as predetermined harvest control rules, must be robust enough to ensure climate change impacts are accounted for in stock assessments and allocation decisions. Unfortunately, the consensus model of decision-making pursued in most RFMOs can severely undermine such efforts.[91]

While RFMOs are now working to implement precautionary and ecosystem approaches in general, they are doing so with varying degrees of alacrity and with varying degrees of success.[92] The challenges lie in breaking down traditional – often single-species – management structures, in connecting multiple disciplines and establishing realistic ecosystem reference point indicators, and, more fundamentally, in overcoming the perception that the ecosystem approach is just too complicated and that it requires endless highly detailed information.[93] To the extent that ecosystem considerations are explored during decision-making, they generally relate only to the impact of a fishery on the broader marine ecosystem and not the other way round.[94] Indeed, there is little evidence at the moment to suggest that RFMOs are explicitly absorbing climate change into their decision rules for stock assessment and harvest rules, or into their catch allocations.

By way of example, in 2014 the second performance review of CCSBT called for CCSBT to undertake to test the robustness of its Management Plan to climate change,[95] but the Scientific Committee responded that it considered this a low priority on the basis that existing robustness tests broadly covered the area.[96] A slightly more positive response to similar concerns in ICCAT at least saw a proposal to the SCRS to initiate a study on the Design of Best Practices when Including Environmental Information into ICCAT Indices of Abundance, the objective of which would ultimately be the generation of data sets for use in accounting for responses of tuna to environmental change in ICCAT management decisions.[97] In a similar vein, the 2013 WCPFC performance review noted

---

[91] Pentz and Klenk, note 69 at 49.

[92] See e.g. PD Szigeti and G Lugten "The Implementation of Performance Review Reports by Regional Fishery Bodies, 2004–2014" (*FAO Fisheries and Aquaculture Circular* No. 1108 (FAO, Rome: 2015); FAO, *Report of the Joint Meeting of TUNA RFMOs on the Implementation of the Ecosystem Approach to Fisheries Management, 12–14 December 2016* (FAO, Rome: 2016) (Report of Tuna RFMOs).

[93] H Tallis et al. "The Many Faces of Ecosystem-based Management: Making the Process Work Today in Real Places" (2010) 34 *Marine Policy* 340–348, at 340.

[94] Report of Tuna RFMOs, note 92 at 4.

[95] SM Garcia and HR Koehler *Performance of the CCSBT 2009–2013: Independent Review* (2014).

[96] Report of the 20th (2015) Meeting of the Scientific Committee, Attachment 10, 2.

[97] MJ Schirripa and CP Goodyear "Proposed Study Design for Best Practices When Including Environmental Information into ICCAT Indices of Abundance" (2016) 72(8) *Collected Volume of the Scientific Papers of ICCAT* (Doc. SCRS/2015/031), 2313–2317.

the need to take the ecosystem into account in taking management decisions, although climate change and its impacts were not specifically mentioned.[98]

Within NAFO, there is no clear indication of whether, or to what extent, its climate status report is integrated into stock or other assessments, although its Ecosystem Approach to Fisheries Management ostensibly provides a mechanism through which climate impacts may be considered implicitly, even if not explicitly, by the Scientific Council in providing its advice on assessment, allocation and other management decisions.[99] For its part, in response to the recommendations of its second performance review, in 2015 NEAFC established biennial meetings with ICES for the purpose of discussing long-term developments including possible multispecies advice, possible climate effects and other ecosystem considerations, with a view to better informing both NEAFC's advice requests and its management decisions.[100] According to the submission provided by NEAFC to the 2017 Annual Report of the United Nations Secretary General (UNSG) on Oceans and Law of the Sea, "the NEAFC Contracting Parties have thereby demonstrated that they are concerned about the future effects that climate change may have" and that they will be able "to address the possible effects of climate change in a timely manner".[101]

Needless to say, in the absence of express statements that climate change and ocean acidification impacts on managed species have been included in stock assessment projections or in other aspects of their ecosystem management, it is difficult to assess the extent to which RFMOs are absorbing climate change into their decision-making processes. This is true even in CCAMLR, despite its explicit recognition of the critical importance of climate change to its work. CCAMLR Resolution 30/XXVIII on 'Climate change', adopted in 2009, recognizes climate change as one of the greatest challenges facing the Southern Ocean and urges increased consideration of climate change impacts in the Southern Ocean to better inform CCAMLR's management decisions. To date, however, a formal mechanism for doing so is lacking and verifiable progress in this respect has been slow. A 2014 proposal aimed at formalizing the integration of climate change considerations into its decision-making through a requirement to include a climate change implications statement in all Commission and SC working papers and fisheries reports was met with objection.[102] Instead, in 2015, the Commission agreed to establish an Intersessional Correspondence Group (ICG) to provide both itself and the SC with information, advice and

---

[98] WCPFC Performance Review, Doc. WCPFC8-2011/12 of 28 February 2012.

[99] NAFO Performance Assessment Review 2011, at 91, paras. 193–195.

[100] Report of the 2015 Extraordinary NEAFC Meeting, 4.

[101] "Submission by the North East Atlantic Fisheries Commission regarding Part I of the report of the Secretary-General of the United Nations on oceans and the law of the sea, pursuant to General Assembly resolution 71/257 (provisionally available as A/RES/71/L.26)" (available at www.un.org/depts/los/general_assembly/contributions_2017/NEAFC.pdf).

[102] Report of the 33rd (2014) Annual CCAMLR Meeting, paras 5.93–5.97. See also Doc. CCAMLR-XXXIII/BG/21 of 22 September 2014.

recommendations as to how they might more appropriately integrate climate change impacts into their work.[103] The ICG again suggested the idea of climate change implications statements and also proposed that work proceed on assessing the status and trends of habitats, key species and ecosystems, for the express purpose of assessing the effects of climate change. It also recommended that climate change response work programmes be developed for both the SC and the Commission.[104] However, despite extensive discussion about processes for the better integration of climate change considerations into decision-making, the Commission has yet to reach agreement on the adoption of these proposals.[105] Similar suggestions within NAFO have also languished.[106]

3.4. Addressing Climate-Driven Changes in their Management Regimes

As noted at the outset, RFMOs cannot stop climate change. Nevertheless, appropriate science-based management decisions can mitigate some of the negative effects of climate change on both the specific fisheries they manage and on the broader marine ecosystem. In short, since climate change impacts can be moderated by reducing stresses from existing human activities, the effective and transparent implementation by RFMOs of precautionary and ecosystem approaches to fisheries management should, in general, go some way towards alleviating the climate change threat and ensuring that RFMOs meet their conservation and sustainable management objectives into the future. On paper, at least, recent studies suggest that RFMO management frameworks are already generally adequate to manage resources effectively in a climate-changed world.[107] The question examined here is whether they are explicitly doing so.

As with the absorption of climate change into decision-making rules and processes, assessing the extent to which climate change is driving changes in management regimes and the adoption of actual decisions is difficult given that RFMO conservation and management measures generally make no mention of climate change or other environmental change terminology.

---

[103] Report of the 34th (2015) Annual CCAMLR Meeting, para. 7.12. See also CCAMLR, "Establishing an Intersessional Correspondence Group (ICG) to Consider Approaches for Appropriately Integrating Climate Change into the Work of the Commission for the Conservation of Antarctic Marine Living Resources" Doc. CCAMLR-XXXIV/31 of 4 September 2015 (submitted by the Delegations of Australia and Norway (copy on file with the author).

[104] Report of the 35th (2016) Annual CCAMLR Meeting, paras. 7.1–7.14.

[105] Report of the 36th (2017) Annual CCAMLR Meeting, para. 7.8. See also paras. 7.1–7.20.

[106] WWF (World Wildlife Fund), Ecology Action Centre (EAC) and DeepSea Conservation Coalition, 'Recommendation to NAFO for the 37th Annual Meeting' (available at www.savethehighseas.org/2015/09/18/recommendations-nafo-37th-annual-meeting/). See also the Joint Opening Statement by EAC and in the Report of the 37th (2015) Annual General Council Meeting, Annex 14 and the Opening Statement by EAC in the Report of the 38th (2016) Annual General Council Meeting, Annex 11.

[107] Pentz et al., note 28 at 16.

Here, again, CCAMLR is the exception. Although no existing CCAMLR conservation measures (CMs) have been amended with the obvious intent of incorporating climate change and ocean acidification effects, two new CMs which expressly relate to climate change have been adopted.

The first, and most, obvious is CM 24-04 (2016) on 'Establishing time-limited Special Areas for Scientific Study in newly exposed marine areas following ice-shelf retreat or collapse in Statistical Subareas 48.1, 48.5 and 88.3'.[108] CM 24-04 establishes a two-stage process for the protection of these newly exposed areas. During the first stage, the area will be granted a provisional designation as a Special Area for Scientific Study (SASS) for a period of up to two years in order to allow detailed review of available data, including relevant fishery research proposals. The second stage of protection – to be accorded by the Commission on advice from the SC – will allow for SASS designation for up to 10 years to enable research to be conducted to provide an understanding of ecosystem processes in relation to climate change.

The second measure that has been adopted by CCAMLR and which relates to climate change – albeit in a less direct manner – is CM 91-05 (2016) on the 'Ross Sea region marine protected area' (RSRMPA). The potential contribution of marine protected areas (MPAs) as a management tool for enhancing resilience and adapting to the impacts of climate change is well recognized.[109] It can come as no surprise, then, that one of the explicitly stated objectives of the RSRMPA is the protection of areas which can serve as control or reference areas for monitoring both natural variability and long-term change as well as the ecosystem effects of climate change and fishing and thereby help to maintain resilience or the ability to adapt to the effects of climate change.[110] Disappointingly, however, this objective is rather undermined by the limitation of the MPA to a period of 35 years,[111] "which is shorter than the life histories of many birds, mammals and fish that the MPA sets out to protect".[112]

Assuming MPAs and other area closures can be considered either direct or indirect climate change measures,[113] then CCAMLR is not the only RFMO to have acted to date. Closures aimed at the protection of vulnerable marine ecosystems (VMEs) have been adopted in a number of RFMOs, including NAFO,

---

[108] Now listed as CM 24-04 (2017), see paras. 3, 10 and 13. For discussion of its adoption, see the Report of the 35th (2016) Annual CCAMLR Meeting, paras. 5.86–5.90 and 8.35–8.36.

[109] 2017 Annual UNSG Report on Oceans and the Law of the Sea, Doc. A/72/70 of 6 March 2017, para. 68. See also AL Green et al. "Designing Marine Reserves for Fisheries Management, Biodiversity Conservation and Climate Change Adaptation" (2014) 42 *Coastal Management* 143–159; E McLeod et al., "Designing Marine Protected Area Networks to Address the Impacts of Climate Change" (2009) 7 *Frontiers in Ecology and the Environment* 362–370.

[110] CM 91-05 (2016), para. 3.

[111] Ibid., para. 20. For discussion, see the Report of the 35th (2016) Annual CCAMLR Meeting, para. 8.39.

[112] CCAMLR PR2 Report, note 90 at 17.

[113] Pentz et al., note 28 at 17–18.

NEAFC and SEAFO.[114] While their primary focus is the protection of benthic communities, these closures also have potential benefits for fisheries productivity and hence, potentially, for climate-related resilience. In other RFMOs, such as WCPFC, different types of fisheries closures have been adopted to promote sustainable resource exploitation.[115] Again, since sustainable exploitation is another key component in ensuring the resilience of fish stocks to environmental impacts such as climate change, these measures might also be considered as addressing, at least implicitly, some aspects of climate-driven changes.

Ultimately, however, the utility and efficacy of RFMO measures in addressing climate change impacts is circumscribed by the political and scientific compromises that are necessary to secure their adoption, be it either by way of consensus or by way of majority vote. Such compromises are evident, for example, in the controversial time limitations in the CCAMLR measures referred to above, and in the raft of compromises, necessitated by years of acrimonious debate within CCAMLR that preceded adoption of the much watered-down RSRMPA.[116] Indeed, CCAMLR has come under considerable criticism for both the slow rate at which it completed work on the MPA designation and the extent to which that designation is sufficiently enduring and conservation focused.[117] Similar compromises also affect catch and quota allocation decisions in many RFMOs, as is evident from the ubiquitous practice of ignoring scientific advice regarding sustainable catch limits in favour of socio-economic and political factors.[118] As NEAFC's experience with the mackerel fishery demonstrates, arguments over such compromises will become increasingly fraught as climate change drives changes in stock/species distribution and abundance, rendering the adoption of *any* measures less, rather than more certain.

4. CONCLUSION

As noted at the outset, climate change poses significant threats and challenges, not only to global fish stocks but also to the international regimes charged with their conservation and management. In the high seas context, the science being conducted in a number of RFMOs appears, at least, to be talking about climate change and to be investigating climate-related impacts on the stocks they manage, even if the precise terminology is not always used. However, in the absence of express statements it is difficult to gauge the extent to which climate impacts are being taken into consideration in management decisions, if at all.

---

[114] For discussion see Rayfuse, note 30 at 457–459.

[115] Pentz et al., note 28 at 18.

[116] Report of the 35th (2016) Annual CCAMLR Meeting, para. 8.39.

[117] See e.g. CM Brooks et al. "Science-based Management in Decline in the Southern Ocean" (2016) 354 *Science* 185–187, at 186. See also CCAMLR PR2 Report, note 90 at 17–18.

[118] Pentz et al., note 28 at 18.

Certainly, there is little explicit evidence of specific management responses to date. Thus, it appears that much remains to be done to ensure that the climate impacts on the stocks they manage are comprehensively researched and assessed by RFMOs, and that consideration of these impacts is fully integrated into their management decisions and reflected in their management measures.

Moving forward, where they have not already done so, RFMOs will need to meet the managerial challenges posed by climate change; initially by promoting, and then by utilizing scientific research that focuses on understanding the impacts of climate change and the broader environmental and climate-related stresses on the fish stocks they manage. Stock assessments, catch limits and quota allocations will all need to be reviewed periodically and adjusted to take account of climate-induced changes in stock abundance and distribution. Indeed, RFMOs will need to reframe and adapt their precautionary and ecosystem approaches to fisheries management in light of climate change, and they will need to develop robust strategies and measures for responding to climate change-induced ecosystem changes. How all of this will be achieved in the context of existing decision-making rules and processes remains unclear, although the introduction of explicit climate change implications statements, such as those suggested in CCAMLR and NAFO, may go some way towards identifying where action is required, thereby assisting RFMOs to meet these challenges.

As for the jurisdictional challenges, it is clear that mechanisms for cooperation and coordination between RFMOs will need to be strengthened to ensure holistic ecosystem management of stocks that are 'shared' by two or more RFMOs. In the end, changes in stock distribution may result in some RFMOs losing some – or even all – of their *raison d'être*, and wholly new regulatory regimes may be needed to ensure the sustainable conservation and use of fisheries resources in a climate-changed ocean.

While it may be true that the solution to climate change lies not with RFMOs but with the international climate regime, it is RFMOs who are charged with conserving and sustainably managing high seas fisheries resources. If they fail to do so, they will fail to meet their responsibility to the international community. Unfortunately, if the past record of managing fisheries in the face of anthropogenic impacts is prologue, then the climate-changed future for high seas fisheries is not particularly bright.

Part IV

Compliance and Enforcement

12

An International Relations Perspective on Compliance and Enforcement

ÁSLAUG ÁSGEIRSDÓTTIR

1. INTRODUCTION

S UCCESSFUL MANAGEMENT OF straddling and highly migratory fish stocks
requires cooperation among coastal and flag States whose vessels engage
in high seas fisheries.[1] Cooperation is difficult to negotiate in a competitive
arena such as fisheries, where management measures often entail distributing
reduced fishing quotas among participating States. The management measures
impose costs on the many vessel owners engaged in these fisheries in the form
of smaller catches; costs which they are often unwilling or unable to shoulder.
Achieving cooperation is only half the battle though, as problems of compliance and enforcement of international agreements governing straddling and
highly migratory fish stocks are ubiquitous, a task made more difficult by the
fact that Parties to those agreements are responsible for ensuring compliance of
often numerous fishing vessels fishing far from shore. Because many States are
unable, or unwilling, to enforce agreed-upon rules, combined with the potential
economic costs imposed on vessel owners by diminished quotas, the temptation
to evade management measures through illegal, unreported and unregulated
(IUU) fishing is increased. As a result, agreements that seem, on paper, to make
good progress in sustaining fish stocks on the high seas, are in reality often not
achieving their goals. The cost of operating a fishing vessel is high, which pushes
vessels to fish as much as they can. In addition, the incentives to be the only
trawler following the rules when enforcement is lacking, is low. In the long run,
this threatens the sustainability of straddling and highly migratory fish stocks.

---

[1] This chapter does not discuss discrete fish stocks found solely on the high seas. While the author
agrees that such stocks should be cooperatively managed, given the poverty of existing management measures for these stocks, the discussion about compliance and enforcement is moot. But were
States to agree on management measures, most of the compliance and enforcement challenges will
apply.

Unregulated fisheries are the classic common pool resource, defined as non-excludable and rival.[2] As a result of the long-standing, open-access nature of global fisheries, overfishing is a persistent problem. Globally, the Food and Agriculture Organization of the United Nations (FAO) estimates that biologically sustainable fisheries have declined from 90 per cent in 1974 to 68.8 per cent in 2013.[3] In a study extending to about half of global commercial fish stocks between the years 2000 and 2003, estimated overfishing ranged from 4 per cent in the South-West Pacific to 37 per cent in the South-West Atlantic, with the global rate of overfishing averaging 18 per cent.[4] The extent of overfishing in the high seas cannot be deduced from these numbers, but, given the distance from shore and the lack of incentives for coastal States to take on the increased cost of enforcement beyond their exclusive economic zones (EEZs), the extent of overfishing is likely to be much higher on the high seas than in EEZs.

The high seas cover about 40 per cent of the oceans. They lie outside the EEZs or other 200-nautical miles maritime zones of coastal States recognized by the LOS Convention.[5] Within the EEZ, States have sovereign rights and jurisdiction over living resources found in the water column, and on or under the seabed. Many stocks straddle boundaries though, migrating either between EEZs or between EEZs and the high seas. In those instances, Articles 63 and 64 of the LOS Convention require States to cooperate on the conservation and management of these transboundary fish stocks. This requirement is reinforced by the Fish Stocks Agreement,[6] which encourages the use of regional fisheries management organizations (RFMOs) in this regard. Given that the high seas are beyond coastal State jurisdiction, combined with an increasing number of vessels able to fish there, efforts to manage migrating fish stocks have been fraught with difficulties of achieving agreements that help keep stocks sustainable.

Since World War II, the size and capacity of fishing vessels has increased significantly, often helped by State subsidies. This has expanded State capacity to fish beyond what is sustainable. The global number of fishing vessels was estimated to be about 4.6 million in 2014, 75 per cent of which are found in Asia, and 64 per cent of which are motorized.[7] The growth in capacity has been especially noticeable in wealthy States. Once capacity increases, it becomes domestically

---

[2] Non-excludable means the fishery is open access. Therefore vessels with the appropriate capacity can partake in the fishery, increasing fishing effort sometimes beyond the capacity of the stock. A fishery is also a rival good, which means that anyone who fishes a stock reduces the amount left for other fishermen. This increases the competition for a share of the stock, which also threatens sustainability.

[3] Food and Agriculture Organization of the United Nations (FAO) *The State of World Fisheries and Aquaculture 2016* (FAO, Rome: 2016).

[4] D Agnew et al. "Estimating the Worldwide Extent of Illegal Fishing" (2009) 4 *PloS one* 1–8.

[5] United Nations Convention on the Law of the Sea of 10 December 1982 (1833 UNTS 3).

[6] Agreement for the Implementation of the Provisions of the United Nations Convention on the Law of the Sea of 10 December 1982 relating to the Conservation and Management of Straddling Fish Stocks and Highly Migratory Fish Stocks of 4 August 1995 (2167 UNTS 3).

[7] SOFIA 2016, note 3 at 1.

difficult to reduce it as that has economic ramifications for vessel owners and their employees.[8] Recent studies have shown that there has been some success in reducing fishing capacity, especially in developed States.[9] When States have been successful in cutting down capacity and ensuring effective regulations in their own maritime zones, the vessels impacted have often gone elsewhere to fish. This movement of excess capacity elsewhere has been labelled the "balloon problem"; similar to when you squeeze a balloon, it expands elsewhere.[10] There are two ways in which excess capacity moves elsewhere. Either vessels are sold and/or reflagged and then begin to fish on the high seas or, alternatively, developed States have negotiated fisheries agreements with developing States that do not have sufficient capacity for fishing in their own maritime zones, allowing the vessels of the former access to the maritime zones of the latter. One area where the balloon problem has had adverse effects on fisheries is along the west coast of Africa, where the European Union (EU) fleet has negotiated access to other nations' EEZs, as EU quotas have been cut.[11]

Sovereign States are reluctant to subject themselves to third-party enforcement and therefore intergovernmental agreements need to be self-enforcing, allowing Parties to ensure and enforce compliance among their nationally flagged vessels.[12] The self-enforcement nature of international cooperation results in agreements that either reflect the least change each State is willing to commit to, or States only commit to agreements whose provisions require little or no change in State behaviour. Self-enforcement can involve deep commitment to an agreement, though, as States are often reluctant to defect even when there is evidence that other Parties are shirking.[13]

States often become Parties to agreements after years of negotiation, and this is also the case with agreements relating to straddling and highly migratory fish stocks. Once initial fisheries agreements are reached, they are usually revisited on either an annual or biannual basis. In cases where the key management measure is a total allowable catch (TAC), the initial discussion of the TAC is based on scientific knowledge of stocks. The final TAC is, however, often higher than the scientific advice warrants, due to political factors when negotiators try to appease domestic fishermen.[14]

---

[8] JS Barkin and ER DeSombre *Saving Global Fisheries: Reducing Fishing Capacity to Promote Sustainability* (MIT Press, Boston: 2013).

[9] Ibid., 578–585.

[10] Ibid., 2.

[11] VM Kaczynski and DL Fluharty "European Policies in West Africa: Who Benefits from Fisheries Agreements?" (2002) 26 *Marine Policy* 75–93.

[12] BA Simmons "Treaty Compliance and Violation" (2010) 13 *Annual Review of Political Science* 273–296.

[13] J Goldstein, M Kahler, RO Keohane and AM Slaughter "Introduction: Legalization and World Politics" (2000) 54 *International Organization* 385–399; B Koremenos "Loosening the Ties That Bind: A Learning Model of Agreement Flexibility" (2001) 55 *Internaitonal Organization* 289–325.

[14] T Polacheck "Politics and Independent Scientific Advice in RFMO Processes: A Case Study of Crossing Boundaries" (2012) 36 *Marine Policy* 132–141.

On the high seas, fisheries management measures are primarily enforced by flag States, an arrangement that poses several challenges to them. First, the system of annual or biannual revision of management measures is inflexible to changes in stock size and geographical distribution of stocks, especially if they are sudden. Second, States are often unable or unwilling to punish non-complying Parties to intergovernmental agreements. Finally, ensuring compliance of many privately-owned vessels is difficult. Let me elaborate a bit on each of these.

First, while States are engaged in negotiations to establish initial management measures, vessel owners often have a great deal of leeway to continue fishing as much as they want. For example, in the mid-1990s it took three years in the North-East Atlantic to reach an agreement on the allocation of fishing quotas for the Atlanto-Scandian herring stock. During this time, coastal States continued fishing it, sometimes with self-imposed limits, which collectively were higher than the TAC that existed at the time. In addition, once fisheries have established management measures, enforcement rarely happens quickly. Over-fishing is frequently identified only one or two years after the fact, which delays enforcement measures.

Second, many States lack the ability or willingness to enforce management rules they have agreed to. Enforcement of fishing regulations is expensive, and States often lack resources to create the infrastructure to effectively monitor landings. Monitoring of at-sea fishing operations is expensive as it requires either employing independent observers, or using navy or coastguard vessels, airplanes or helicopters, if the State in fact has them. Combined with the challenge of identifying and punishing those who violate rules, compliance suffers.[15] The cost of fisheries enforcement increases with the distance from the coast. Whereas States have an incentive to manage their EEZs, the incentives to police fishing efforts on the high seas are limited as States lack exclusive jurisdiction over those waters. Without exclusive jurisdiction, the ability of non-flag States to unilaterally punish violators when their flag States do not, also disappears. Owners and operators of fishing vessels know this and thus have high incentives to violate fisheries management measures on the high seas. There may also be domestic challenges to ensuring compliance, either because of the economic or political importance of the fishing industry, allowing vessel owners to skirt rules without the fear of punishment.

Finally, international agreements differ in whether it is the State and/or its agents who are required to change their behaviour, or if it is a private entity. Privately owned fishing vessels have an incentive to fish as much as they possibly can to recoup high fixed costs.[16] This distinction is relevant for a State's capacity to enforce an agreement and therefore influences compliance rates as well.

---

[15] DM McEvoy and JK Stranlund "Self-Enforcing International Environmental Agreements with Costly Monitoring for Compliance" (2008) 42 *Environmental and Resource Economics* 491–508.
[16] Á Ásgeirsdóttir *Who Gets What? Domestic Influences on International Negotiations Allocating Shared Resources* (State University of New York Press, Albany, NY: 2008).

In some cases, however, the State is actually the actor who needs to change its behaviour, for example to produce fewer nuclear weapons, and thus it should be easier to comply with agreed-upon rules. In other cases, the State is agreeing to enforce the behaviour of privately-owned enterprises, which are maximizing profits. This is the case with fisheries, most of which are privately owned and operated by a diverse set of individuals and groups. Adding to this, ownership of fishing vessels is often unclear, due to extensive use of complex shell companies to mask ownership. Ensuring compliance by a multitude of private actors operating far from shore, where monitoring and enforcement is difficult and expensive has proven to be a challenge.

This chapter discusses how political scientists study compliance and enforcement as it pertains to the difficulties of ensuring effective international agreements. It will first discuss the challenge of compliance (Section 2), and then discuss how political scientists think of enforcement problems (Section 3). The chapter will then examine the role of regional fisheries management organizations (RFMOs) in the management of straddling fish stocks (Section 4) as well as several new and emerging compliance and enforcement measures (Section 5). Finally, the chapter discusses how changes in stock size and distribution of the fishery can easily derail effective management of high fish fisheries (Section 6). This is an especially important issue given how climate change is expected to impact migratory stocks. The chapter ends with Section 7, "Conclusion".

2. THE CHALLENGE OF COMPLIANCE

Political scientists distinguish between implementation, compliance and effectiveness of international agreements. Oran Young argues that "[c]ompliance can be said to occur when the actual behavior of a given subject conforms to prescribed behavior, and non-compliance or violation occurs when actual behavior departs significantly from prescribed behavior",[17] thus distinguishing compliance from enforcement and effectiveness. Other scholars have defined compliance as conformity between actors, behaviours and a specified rule.[18] Implementation refers to the actions of States to change laws and regulations to bring about compliance with an agreement, whereas effectiveness measures to what extent agreements solve the problems they set out to solve.[19] Compliance is

---

[17] OR Young *Compliance and Public Authority: A Theory with International Applications* (Johns Hopkins University Press, Baltimore, MD: 1979).

[18] K Raustiala and AM Slaughter "International Law, International Relations and Compliance" in W Carlsnaes, T Risse and BA Simmons (eds.) *Handbook of International Relations* (Sage Press, London England: 2002) 508–529.

[19] See H Breitmeier, A Underdal and O Young "The Effectiveness of International Environmental Regimes: Comparing and Contrasting Findings from Quantitative Research" (2011) 13 *International Studies Review* 579–605; BA Simmons "Compliance with International Agreements" (1998) 1 *Annual Review of Political Science* 75–93; OR Young *The Effectiveness of International*

thus concerned with the conformity of behaviour to rules, but not necessarily the active outcome of adhering to agreements.[20] Applied to international fisheries agreements, compliance means to what extent vessels adhere to rules covering the fishery they are engaged in, including by using approved gear, adhering to fishing seasons, observing area restrictions, keeping within quota limits for the stocks they fish, and keeping accurate records of their fishing activities, to name a few.

While compliance is a paramount issue when it comes to ensuring the effectiveness of international fisheries agreements, its study has been hampered by two issues. First, measuring compliance is difficult. Therefore, how compliance measures are identified changes from study to study, making generalizations about successful compliance measures impossible. Second, it can be difficult to determine whether or not the agreement is improving compliance. That is, can we say for certain that a State would have acted differently in the absence of an agreement? Alternatively, did a State join an agreement because it thinks it can ensure compliance or did it join because it knows the agreement cannot really be enforced?[21]

Scholars also disagree to what extent international agreements – or regimes – can and do influence State behaviour, with three perspectives prominent. First, international agreements successfully change State behaviour. Second, they negatively influence the willingness to cooperate. Third, they have no influence on State behaviour as States only cooperate when it is in their interest.[22] This chapter takes the position that agreements can, and do, influence State behaviour.

Scholars also disagree about how to explain State compliance with internationally agreed-upon rules, with two main camps distinguished: the managerial school and the enforcement school.[23] The managerial school argues that most States comply with most of the rules they agree to most of the time. But what defines an acceptable level of compliance is left unresolved.[24] Others argue that States comply because treaties are shallow,[25] and because non-compliance arises from ambiguities in treaties, insufficient State capacity or changing strategic

---

Environmental Regimes: Causal Connections and Behavioral Mechanisms (MIT Press, Boston, MA: 1999); OR Young "Effectiveness of International Environmental Regimes: Existing Knowledge, Cutting-Edge Themes, and Research Strategies" (2011) 50 *Proceedings of the National Academy of Sciences of the United States of America* 19853–19860.

[20] Simmons, note 19.

[21] EM Hafner-Burton, DG Victor and Y Lupu "Political Science Research on International Law: The State of the Field" (2012) 106 *American Journal of International Law* 47–97.

[22] S McLaughlin Mitchell and PR Hensel "International Institutions and Compliance with Agreements" (2007) 51 *American Journal of Political Science* 721–737.

[23] HH Koh "Why Do Nations Obey International Law? Review Essay" (1997) 106 *Yale Law Journal* 2599–2659; J von Stein "The Engines of Compliance" in JL Dunoff and MA Pollack (eds.) *Interdisciplinary Perspectives on International Law and International Relations. The State of the Art* (Cambridge University Press, New York: 2012) 477–501.

[24] A Chayes and A Handler Chayes "On Compliance" (1993) 47 *International Organization* 175–205.

[25] J von Stein "Do Treaties Constrain or Screen? Selection Bias and Treaty Compliance" (2005) 99 *American Political Science Review* 611–622.

environments, either domestically or internationally.[26] The managerial school therefore argues that non-compliance can be addressed by drafting better and more precise international agreements, thereby weakening the ability of States to avoid non-compliance by liberal interpretations of rules, and facilitating the identification of non-compliance.

The enforcement school, on the other hand, argues that States will only comply if someone actually enforces the agreement, dismissing the notion that compliance can be improved by better drafting of international agreements.[27] They distinguish between first- and second-order compliance. First-order compliance relies on the actors engaged in fishing to comply directly with rules or management measures. Second-order compliance discusses how States comply with rulings of third-party enforcement mechanisms, such as international courts or private efforts (e.g. certification schemes). Whereas enforcement of high seas fisheries agreements relies primarily on first-order compliance, rather than second-order compliance, in view of the growth of certification schemes this may be changing.

International relations scholars trace compliance to three mechanisms: reciprocity, retaliation and reputation.[28] As regards the first, States comply because they think other States will comply; i.e. there is a reciprocal nature to international affairs. So if there is general shirking from cooperation, agreements are rendered less effective. The second mechanism – retaliation – motivates States to comply in order to avoid sanctions. But retaliation is rare, and on balance States are reluctant to use third-party enforcement to settle disputes, preferring instead to either ignore shirking or directly negotiate solutions. Finally, scholars focusing on reputation argue that if reciprocity and retaliation do not work to ensure compliance, States can be pushed to comply if they think their reputation will suffer from non-compliance with agreements.[29] This issue of the role of reputation is contested though, as scholars have pointed out that it is not clear whose reputation is at stake – the State's or the government's – and this issue is fundamental to the role of reputation. In addition, States can have different reputations in different issue areas.[30]

3. THE PROBLEM OF ENFORCEMENT

Enforcement is secondary to compliance. If everyone willingly complied with rules, enforcement and monitoring would not be needed. Responsible States

---

[26] K Raustiala "Compliance and Effectiveness in International Regulatory Cooperation" (2000) 32 *Case Western Reserve Journal of International Law* 387–440; Raustiala and Slaughter, note 18.

[27] Von Stein, note 23 at 477–501.

[28] AT Guzman *How International Law Works: A Rational Choice Theory* (Oxford University Press, Oxford: 2008); M Tomz *Reputation and International Cooperation: Sovereign Debt across Three Centuries* (Princeton University Press, Princeton: 2012).

[29] Guzman, note 28 at 7.

[30] R Brewster "The Limits of Reputation on Compliance" (2009) 1 *International Theory* 323–333.

can ensure compliance in a variety of ways. They can use force, which is costly and thus rare, or they can use either positive (rewards) or negative (punishment) incentives to increase compliance. The monitoring of fisheries to detect violation of rules takes various forms, with the monitoring of landings and the tracking of vessels by satellites being the most common. In addition, some fisheries are observed directly, either through having observers on board, by using coastguard vessels or by using planes and helicopters to monitor activities. These monitoring efforts are very costly, and the cost increases the further out to sea that the authorities are forced to venture. Coastal States have full authority to enforce compliance in their own maritime zones, but not on the high seas. In the absence of the ability to effectively monitor fisheries, States rely on self-reporting from ships, which is in itself problematic as the vessel operators can often simply evade rules by misreporting catches, leave out bycatch and change logbooks to hide questionable activity. States that provide flags of convenience to vessels often have a poor record in enforcing international rules applicable to their fleet. There are also some instances of third-party reporting of violations, which get reported to either the flag State or the relevant RFMO. These are expected to investigate violations and punish those found guilty.

The problem of enforcing fishing regulations on the high seas can be divided into two challenges based on the cost of enforcement, which influence the incentive to enforce rules. First, governments can face both political and economic costs in seeking the strict enforcement of rules. Second, when the cost of enforcement increases for the vessels, vessel operators can sometimes evade regulations by engaging in IUU fishing. Where enforcement is contentious, there can be a political cost involved in pursuing those who violate the rules. For instance, fishermen need to accept monitoring as part of the right to fish. If not, they have the ability to evade rules and they do.[31]

Enforcement costs the State money and enforcement is more expensive the further away from shore it is conducted. The States with the resources to actively monitor their domestic fisheries have an infrastructure that relies on careful monitoring of landings. As a result, wealthy States with long histories of fishing tend to have lower levels of illegal fishing.[32] But the cost of enforcement goes beyond just money. The ability of States to enforce rules relies on the State's relationship to its fishing fleet as well and to what extent the vessel owners and operators can exert political costs onto the government if the government seeks to enforce rules that the operators oppose.[33] The operators have two choices: where permitted they can fight the rules, or they can displace their activities to

---

[31] Agnew, note 4 at 1; OS Stokke "Managing Fisheries in the Barents Sea Loophole: Interplay with the UN Fish Stocks Agreement" (2001) 32 *Ocean Development & International Law* 241–262.

[32] Agnew, note 4 at 1.

[33] Ásgeirsdóttir, note 16 at 4.

the high seas, although States like Norway have begun to restrict this behaviour by tying fishing rights in its own maritime zones to compliance with Norwegian rules on high seas fishing.[34]

The challenge of ensuring compliance by having States enforce the behaviour of their own fleet is ingrained in the international instruments and organizations charged with ensuring the sustainability of fisheries, specifically RFMOs with a mandate relating to high seas fisheries; as discussed in the next section.

4. RFMOs, COMPLIANCE AND ENFORCEMENT

RFMOs are the principal intergovernmental mechanism to manage high seas fisheries. At present, there are around 15 RFMOs that manage high seas fisheries. As such, these organizations manage most of the fisheries in most of the world's oceans, but gaps still exist which undermine management efforts.[35]

The Fish Stocks Agreement further constrains flag State jurisdiction over fishing vessels, among other things by requiring more cooperation with other States and RFMOs. This is a central weakness, as States have often not been willing to live up to their duties when their ships are on the high seas. The Agreement requires flag States to monitor all fishing activities of their ships to ensure they follow established management measures, and it requires flag States to ensure their vessels comply with RFMO regulations.[36] RFMOs, however, do not have the authority to enforce agreements; that authority rests with States which make up the RFMOs. Fishing vessels are required to submit data to their flag States, which allows States to monitor the fishing efforts of their vessels. Compliance is then measured by the data submitted by Members to the relevant RFMOs. The organizations also have the right to request information from Members. Submissions are subsequently verified and evaluated by States and/or RFMOs.[37] States have explicit permission to enforce RFMO rules in areas of the high seas that are covered by the RFMO,[38] but in reality they have little incentive to do so.

Regulation of high seas fishing through RFMOs has been ongoing as the issue is faced with several challenges, most notably States' lack of enforcement of rules and ability to evade rules, especially by flag of convenience States.[39]

---

[34] Law No. 37 of 6 June 2008 "About the Utilization of Wild Marine Resources" (*Lov om forvaltning av viltlevande marine ressursar*).

[35] See Chapter 6 of this volume (Molenaar).

[36] Fish Stocks Agreement, Art. 18.

[37] Ibid, Art. 6 of Annex I.

[38] D Englender, J Kirschley, A Stöfen and A Zink "Cooperation and Compliance Control in Areas Beyond National Jurisdiction" (2014) 49 *Marine Policy* 186–194.

[39] ER DeSombre and JS Barkin *Fish* (Wiley and Sons, Cambridge, UK: 2011); DG Webster *Beyond the Tragedy in Global Fisheries* (MIT Press, Boston: 2015) 468.

Some States that are non-Members of RFMOs but still cooperate – so-called 'cooperating non-members' (CNMs) – agree to follow the fisheries management rules set by RFMOs.[40] If they do not, they risk trade sanctions against their fisheries. But despite the expectation created by the Fish Stocks Agreement, there are still States who remain outside key RFMOs, which means vessels which fly their flags are not formally bound by the rules of these RFMOs.

Each RFMO negotiates its own management measures. Once Members reach an agreement, RFMOs have three main compliance mechanisms. First, they gather information, usually on an annual basis. Second, they review or assess the information and, finally, they provide feedback to Members and CNMs as well as suggesting corrective measures.[41] But their effectiveness varies a great deal, depending primarily on the political will of States to commit to management measures. In States where there is neither the ability nor the willingness to enforce these rules, vessel owners have plenty of incentives not to comply fully, or at all.[42] For example, a comprehensive review of compliance mechanisms of the five tuna RFMOs details how States shirk their commitments by not providing catch and effort data or bycatch data, while States also fail to submit annual reports and, on occasion, fail to pay their financial contributions, leaving RFMOs strapped for funds with obvious implications for their effectiveness.[43]

In addition, there are reports of exceeding quotas, non-compliance with area and time closures, or shortfalls in on-board observers that further undermine compliance.[44] Members that exceed their quota are supposed to get reduced quota the following year, but if overfishing continues, some RFMOs can impose bans on fish imports for these Members. However, because decisions are often made by consensus – including decisions on sanctions for non-compliance with an RFMO's conservation and management measures – these sanctions have been primarily imposed on non-Members.[45] This issue is difficult to solve because of the politics involved. States are less inclined to join RFMOs if they are effective and able to impose serious penalties for non-compliance.[46] Hence, in order to strengthen compliance, ideally it needs to be negotiated alongside membership.

A review of 18 RFMOs suggests that Members are more concerned with exploitation of marine resources, rather than their conservation.[47] So while these

---

[40] KM Gjerde, D Currie, K Wowk and K Sack "Ocean in Peril: Reforming the Management of Global Ocean Living Resources in Areas Beyond National Jurisdiction" (2013) 74 *Marine Pollution Bulletin* 540–551. See also Chapter 6 of this volume (Molenaar).

[41] HR Koehler *Promoting Compliance in Tuna RFMOS: A Comprehensive Baseline Survey of the Current Mechanics of Reviewing, Assessing and Addressing Compliance with RFMO Obligations and Measures* (International Seafood Sustainability Foundation, McLean: 2013) 15.

[42] Gjerde et al., note 40 at 542.

[43] Koehler, note 41 at 32.

[44] Ibid., 29.

[45] DeSombre and Barkin, note 39 at 12.

[46] Ibid.

[47] S Cullis-Suzuki and D Pauly "Failing the High Seas: A Global Evaluation of Regional Fisheries Management Organizations" (2010) 34 *Marine Policy* 1036–1042.

scholars take the view that the Commission for the Conservation of Antarctic Marine Living Resources (CCALMR) is an effective management organization – by measuring behaviour against what it says it will do – they also argue that the International Commission on the Conservation of Atlantic Tunas (ICCAT) is considered to have failed in its effort to protect its stocks from overfishing.[48] A historical examination of the size of the biomass of Atlantic tuna showed that it has declined every year after ICCAT introduced management measures.[49] But while the failure of ICCAT is clear, there is also evidence to support that some States can become more willing to impose management measures when they are vulnerable to declines in catches due to lower stock sizes.[50] That is, when States face the potential of significant economic losses because of stock declines, that sometimes results in the ability to agree on stricter management measures.

Scholars have argued that RFMOs are perhaps no longer suited to manage high seas fisheries in a globalized world as they are only as effective as their Members want them to be. Moreover, given that RFMOs commonly operate on consensus, they will only agree on minimal management.[51] Because RFMOs face no consequences for poor performance, the default position is also that States can fish as much as they want until they reach an agreement to lower quotas.[52]

First, beyond the inability of RFMOs to ensure compliance by their Members, their challenge is even larger due to the fact that not all fishing States are Members or CNMs with the appropriate RFMOs, which means they are not bound by any rules set by the RFMO.

Second, enforcing violations of management rules takes a long time, given that each RFMO evaluates the information it receives on an annual basis. For example, the timeline from non-compliance to perhaps being allocated a lower fishing quotum can be two to three years.[53] This is due to the fact that a flag State first has to collect its data, usually on an annual basis, then submit it to the RFMO, which then takes time to assess and evaluate the data to assess the need to impose a penalty for the following year. That non-compliance has already done damage to the stock, as an RFMO's review of fishing data is timed to annual meetings.[54]

Third, the consequences of overfishing – e.g. perhaps receiving a lower fishing quota at a later date – are not always dire. For example, the Commission for the Conservation of Southern Bluefin Tuna (CCSBT) instituted a corrective

---

[48] Cullis-Suzuki and Pauly, note 47 at 12; Gjerde et al., note 40 at 12.
[49] Cullis-Suzuki and Pauly, note 47 at 12.
[50] DG Webster *Adaptive Governance: The Dynamics of Atlantic Fisheries Management* (MIT Press, Boston: 2008).
[51] Barkin and DeSombre, note 39 at 12.
[52] Gjerde et al., note 40 at 12.
[53] Koehler, note 41 at 12.
[54] Ibid.

action policy in 2011, which led to Australia – a Member – to get a lower quota allocation in 2012 because of overfishing in the years between 2009 and 2011. But in 2013, South Africa – which was then still a CNM – refused to repay its excess catch during the 2011–2012 fishing season, and suffered no consequences.[55]

There is correlation between the extent to which States can and do enforce domestic rules on the one hand, and the ability of RFMOs to expect compliance from their Members on the other hand. Hence, the North-East Atlantic Fisheries Commission (NEAFC) and the Northwest Atlantic Fisheries Organization (NAFO) – whose membership is primarily composed of developed coastal States around the North Atlantic – both have a comprehensive infrastructure to monitor catches, and can afford to finance compliance committees, enforcement measures, and to instigate punishment.

Because of the inability of RFMOs to ensure sufficient compliance, non-governmental organizations (NGOs) have increased their efforts to develop more market-based mechanisms to ensure compliance.

5. NEW AND EMERGING COMPLIANCE AND ENFORCEMENT MECHANISMS

Because of the inherent weaknesses in requiring States to ensure compliance of all vessels flying their flag, and the legal ambiguity and high cost of enforcing agreements on the high seas, NGOs such as Greenpeace have been working with the fishing industry and groups of vessel owners to develop mechanisms aimed at enhancing compliance with rules. These mechanisms can be broadly regarded as market-based, and include using certification of fisheries to generate compliance, imposition of trade sanctions by preventing repeat violators from landing their catch, and better technology to remotely monitor fishing activities in conjunction with marine protected areas (MPAs).[56] These are examined in the three subsections below.

5.1. Certification

Scholars have argued that private authorities that use schemes to certify fisheries as sustainable face significant obstacles to do work as intended. That said, they do have the potential to improve compliance with fisheries management rules.[57] The largest and best-known certifier of fisheries is the Marine Stewardship Council (MSC), established by Unilever and the World Wildlife Fund in 1997

---

[55] Ibid.

[56] See also Chapter 16 of this volume (Massarella).

[57] J Ellis *Network Governance for High Seas Fisheries: The Role of the Marine Stewardship Council* (available at SSRN 1905493: 2011), 1. See also Chapter 4 of this volume (Stokke).

and headquartered in the United Kingdom. The idea behind certification schemes is that, by being certified, a fishery becomes more commercially valuable as consumers reward more environmentally responsible practices through their willingness to pay a higher price for products harvested sustainably.[58] While other certifying bodies exist, the focus here will be on the MSC as it is the largest, and best-known organization involved in certification.

The MSC certifies fisheries either at the behest of a particular fishery or some collective of fishing companies. The organization does not carry out the certification itself, but instead uses third-party certifiers. MSC certifies fisheries based on three key principles aimed at determining the sustainability of fisheries. The first principle states that the fishery activity must be at a level that sustains the fishery indefinitely. The second principle is that fisheries must ensure that their operations maintain the diversity of the ecosystem, and the third and final principle requires the fishery to comply with relevant laws.[59]

Critics contend, however, that certification is too costly. In 2011, the certification cost ranged between USD 15,000 and USD 120,000; borne by the applicant(s). Those who object to the certification of particular fisheries can lodge formal objections, which cost around USD 8,000.[60] This high cost of MSC certification favours larger fishing companies seeking certification of established fisheries, and thereby encourages increased industrialization of fishing. Because the MSC derives a proportion of its budget from certifications, critics argue that the organization has a financial incentive to certify fisheries that are unsustainable.[61] Hence, scholars have identified evidence of MSC certifiers violating all of the MSC's three key principles in certifying some fisheries.[62] For example, the certification of the Antarctic toothfish fishery in 2009, certified a fishery in which there is still a significant lack of data about the stock, despite the requirement of certification being done on the basis of adequate scientific information.[63]

The ability of certification to make a big difference in enhancing compliance in high seas fisheries is questionable for two additional reasons. First, many fisheries that are certified already have high compliance rates as operators or organizations will not seek certification unless the fishery is decently managed. Second, certification schemes face a unique challenge were they to be applied to high seas fishing as certifying a fishery would require operators of fishing

---

[58] C Christian et al. "A Review of Formal Objections to Marine Stewardship Council Fisheries Certifications" (2013) 161 *Biological Conservation* 10–17.
[59] See the item "MSC Fisheries Standard" (available at www.msc.org/about-us/standards/fisheries-standard).
[60] Christian et al., note 58 at 15.
[61] D Zwerdling and M Williams "Conditions Allow for More Sustainable-Labeled Seafood" (*National Public Radio*, 12 February 2013) (available at www.npr.org/2013/02/12/171376617/conditions-allow-for-more-sustainable-labeled-seafood).
[62] Christian et al., note 58 at 15.
[63] J Jacquet et al. "Seafood Stewardship in Crisis" (2010) 467 *Nature* 28–29.

vessels from different States to cooperate in providing information and coordinating activities, which is difficult. But it is not impossible, as the example of the Mackerel Industry Northern Sustainability Alliance (MINSA) showed in 2012, when industry actors representing 700 vessels banded together to seek MSC re-certification of the North-East Atlantic mackerel fisheries, which had been lost because of increased fishing by new actors and the unwillingness of States who had management agreements to include new States in their annual quota allocation.[64] It is worth noting, though, that the group does not include any Icelandic or Faroese vessels, which are both newcomers to this North-East Atlantic fishery. This will be discussed in further detail in Section 6.

5.2. Landing and Trade Sanctions

Trade sanctions are thought to be the punishment of last resort, only levied after all other means have been exhausted.[65] Imposition of trade sanctions – either by preventing landings by ships from States violating management rules, or barring selling of fish from States who have registered vessels engaged in IUU fishing – is rare though, as States have shown great reluctance in punishing fellow Members of RFMOs for breaking the rules. In addition, traceability of fish is often a problem. Because most RFMOs require consensus among Members to impose trade sanctions, a Member facing such sanctions is highly likely to block consensus. There are exceptions to decision-making by consensus or unanimity though; for instance NEAFC, which uses qualified majority voting.

The threat of trade sanctions forced several States to join RFMOs in the early 2000s, as the organizations were most likely to punish non-Members for non-compliance with those RFMOs' conservation and management measures. There is no indication that this increased compliance with these measures RFMOs, however. The threat of sanctioning vessels of non-Members of RFMOs by refusing them landing rights for their catches worked especially well for ICCAT, which increased its membership in the early 2000s. NAFO and NEAFC – whose Members primarily include wealthy States with extensive networks to monitor landings – have both implemented strict port inspection regimes in order to facilitate compliance. Vessels of non-Members and non-CNMs are denied landing rights, and thus the ability to trade fish.[66]

---

[64] "North-East Atlantic Mackerel Wins Back Sustainable Status" (*The Guardian*, 11 May 2016) (available at www.theguardian.com/environment/2016/may/11/north-east-atlantic-mackerel-wins-back-sustainable-status).

[65] OS Stokke "Trade Measures and the Combat of IUU Fishing: Institutional Interplay and Effective Governance in the Northeast Atlantic" (2009) 33 *Marine Policy* 339–349. See also Chapters 13 (van der Marel) and 14 (Churchill) of this volume.

[66] ER DeSombre "Fishing under Flags of Convenience: Using Market Power to Increase Participation in International Regulation" (2005) 5 *Global Environmental Politics* 73–94.

A second economic incentive to comply might be worth mentioning here. The membership of tuna RFMOs may in the future have a bigger incentive to comply. In 2014, the Members of the International Seafood Sustainability Foundation (ISSF) – which include canners – decided to only buy seafood for processing from purse seine vessels that fly the flag of States that are in substantial compliance with their RFMO obligations. This decision applies both to Members and CNMs of the relevant RFMO.[67] In addition, the ISSF encourages certain actions from individual purse seine vessels, for example mitigation of bycatch, retaining the entire catch, submission of logbooks and 100 per cent on-board observer coverage.[68] It is too soon to say to what extent these efforts will increase compliance, but if these companies are effective in preventing vessels who flaunt the rules from selling their fish, this might increase compliance in the future. Additionally, the ISSF has entered into an agreement with major retailers in Canada and the United States, to sell only seafood that has been certified by the MSC. These retailers include Walmart and Loblaws, two major food sellers in North America.

States are also seeking to use trade related measures to overcome the weakness of the international instruments governing high seas fisheries, taking a cue from NGOs such as Greenpeace, which has been identifying individual ships engaged in illegal fishing and publishing their names and nationalities. The EU's IUU Regulation[69] focuses on pressuring States to clean up their act by establishing a catch documentation system for imports, exports and re-exports to and from EU Member States. States whose vessels are suspected of not adhering to international fisheries rules enter into discussions with the EU. If States improve compliance, negotiations continue until the EU is satisfied. If a State does not improve its compliance measures, its fisheries products will not be able to access EU markets, a move that can be significantly costly to States.[70] As of 2017, six States have been blacklisted (Belize, Cambodia, Comoros, Republic of Guinea, Sri Lanka and St. Vincent and Grenadines), with three of these reversed later (Belize, Republic of Guinea and Sri Lanka).[71] By focusing on States, the EU is trying to incentivize States to enforce the fisheries management measures in effect, by rewarding those who comply with access to the largest market for fish in the world. Similarly, Norway has been somewhat successful with these kinds of measures in relation to fishing in the Barents Sea.[72]

---

[67] Koehler, note 41 at 12.

[68] Ibid.

[69] Council Regulation (EC) No. 1005/2008 of 29 September 2008 "establishing a Community system to prevent, deter and eliminate illegal, unreported and unregulated fishing", as amended.

[70] C Elvestad and I Kvalvik "Implementing the EU-IUU Regulation: Enhancing Flag State Performance through Trade Measures" (2015) 46 *Ocean Development & International Law* 241–255.

[71] See the overview at https://ec.europa.eu/fisheries/sites/fisheries/files/illegal-fishing-overview-of-existing-procedures-third-countries_en.pdf.

[72] See Stokke, note 65.

5.3. Marine Protected Areas as a Fisheries Management Tool

While not a trade measure, MPAs can protect fish stocks from overharvesting. The CBD[73] set the goal of setting aside 10 per cent of global oceans as MPAs by 2010, which was later changed to 2020 because of slow progress. As of 2013, experts estimated that only 3.27 per cent of global oceans were protected.[74] Protection has though been shown to be weak, especially when it comes to limiting fisheries in MPAs, with only 12 per cent of all MPAs designated as no-take zones.[75]

One of the advantages of MPAs from the point of view of compliance and enforcement, is that modern technology makes it fairly easy to see what type of vessel is found within an MPA, and in some cases it is also possible to know what they are doing. An automatic identification system (AIS) is required by the International Maritime Organization for all vessels above 300 tonnes and all passenger ships. AISs transmit location and speed of vessels, but it has the drawback that it can be turned on and off. Satellite-based vessel monitoring systems (VMSs) are specifically designed to allow fisheries authorities to track conduct of fishing vessels, but it is limited by the lack of full coverage among all fishing vessels, especially among vessels fishing the high seas, as costs are high. One of the challenges of using VMS for research of fishing activity is the large amount of data that gets collected, which can be difficult to handle, and time-consuming to analyze.

NGOs are now calling for the creation of MPAs in the high seas, which environmental and conservation groups argue will help protect biodiversity and ensure sustainability. But, over all, this tool has proved to be less effective than expected. As local involvement and a strong legal framework have been especially critical to influence compliance with MPAs,[76] compliance with MPAs on the high seas could be troublesome due to the absence of local involvement.[77]

6. LEARNING FROM SUCCESSFUL AND FAILED ATTEMPTS TO REGULATE HIGH SEAS FISHING

Even when States have managed to negotiate an agreement and ensure its compliance, changes in the distribution of straddling and highly migratory fish stocks repeatedly challenge support for such agreements. This often results in higher

---

[73] Convention on Biological Diversity of 22 May 1992 (1760 UNTS 143).

[74] L Boonzaier and D Pauly "Marine Protection Targets: An Updated Assessment of Global Progress" (2016) 50 *Oryx* 27–35.

[75] Ibid.

[76] B McCay and P Jones "Marine Protected Areas and the Governance of Marine Ecosystems and Fisheries" (2011) 25 *Conservation Biology* 1130–1133.

[77] A more detailed discussion on MPAs can be found in Chapter 9 of this volume (Dunn, Ortuño Crespo and Caddell).

catches than existed when the original States Party to the management measures were able to enforce their agreement. Two examples from the North-East Atlantic adequately illustrate this point, namely the attempts at multilateral management of Atlanto-Scandian herring[78] in the 1990s and Atlantic mackerel in the past ten years. In the North-East Atlantic, the herring and mackerel stocks were both well managed through multilateral cooperation for many years, or until these agreements were challenged by changing stock sizes and distribution patterns. These cases illustrate two things: how changing migration patterns can render decades-long effective management measures moot and how challenging it can be to add new entrants to existing international agreements, as doing so requires renegotiating quota allocation agreements, resulting in less quota for those who have engaged in the fisheries for a while.

The herring stock was one of the largest and most valuable fish stocks of the North Atlantic in the 1950s and 60s, but collapsed in the late 1960s. Following the collapse, the stock was only found in the maritime zones of Norway and Russia. Over the next 25 years, the stock was managed through international cooperation between Russia and Norway, where Russia agreed not to fish juvenile herring in its waters, in exchange for herring quotas in Norwegian waters, where the herring was more valuable because of a higher fat content. By the early 1990s, the herring stock had grown substantially and began to change its migration patterns from primarily residing in Norwegian and Russian waters, to migrating into the 'Loop Hole'; the high seas pocket in the Barents Sea. Subsequently, its distribution changed further, to also include the EEZs of Iceland and the Faroe Islands.[79]

These shifts in abundance and distributional range increased the number of coastal States in whose maritime zones herring occurred. The wider distribution into the EEZs of Iceland and the Faroe Islands meant that these States had full rights to fish the stock in their waters. In addition, the Loop Hole was subject to the freedom of high seas fishing, and thereby in principle open to all States. More specifically, the aforementioned shifts introduced three new actors into the fishery: Iceland, the Faroe Islands and the EU. These new actors challenged the established management order by increasing their catches in the high seas and within the Faroese and Icelandic maritime zones. This rendered the existing arrangement between Russia and Norway moot, and it took several years to negotiate a new quota allocation arrangement that adequately reflected the stock's new distributional range. During these years, despite States setting unilateral quota to signal responsible fishing, the stock was fished at a higher level than before. This cumulative increase in the total catch threatened to set

---

[78] This stock is also referred to as the Norwegian Spring Spawning Herring stock.
[79] Ásgeirsdóttir, note 16 at 4. See also EH Sissener and T Bjørndal "Climate Change and the Migratory Pattern for Norwegian Spring-Spawning Herring – Implications for Management" (2005) 29 *Marine Policy* 299–309.

back the successful bilateral management of the stock that had contributed to its growth.[80] The five coastal States – Faroe Islands, EU, Iceland, Norway and Russia – eventually managed to reach a quota allocation agreement on herring in 1997. It only lasted until 2003, when it broke down. It was not until 2007 that the five coastal States were able to renegotiate a quota allocation agreement.[81] In the intervening years, the stock was managed through States setting unilateral quota for the stock. But the 2007 quota allocation agreement was challenged by the Faroe Islands, which argued that, because of increasing quantities of herring in its waters, its allocation of 5.16 per cent of the quota – which amounted to 31,000 tonnes in 2012 – was inadequate. The four other coastal States refused the Faroese request to renegotiate the allocation. As a result, the Faroese increased the catch in their waters and set a unilateral catch limit in 2013 of 105,230 tonnes, or about 17 per cent of the TAC. This action led to the EU to issue trade restrictions on bans of the landing of herring and mackerel from Faroese fisheries in EU ports. Denmark, then, on behalf of the Faroe Islands, filed two cases against the EU, one with the WTO and the other under the LOS Convention.[82] Both cases were eventually settled out of court.

The case of the Atlantic mackerel stock illustrates how disputes that arise because of changing distribution of fish stocks can be intractable. Until the mid-2000s, mackerel was found primarily in Norwegian and EU waters, where it was managed by 10-year quota agreements between Norway and the EU. When mackerel began to occur in significant numbers in the EEZs of Iceland and the Faroe Islands, these States began fishing it, which they had not traditionally done. As a result, the total catch increased significantly.[83] What followed has been a testy dispute that has not yet been fully resolved.[84] In order to pressure Iceland and the Faroe Islands into negotiations, Norway banned all landings of Icelandic-caught mackerel in its ports and the EU threatened trade sanctions against both Iceland and the Faroe Islands. The Faroe Islands and Norway reached an agreement in late 2014, which expanded the Norwegian-EU quota agreement.[85] Iceland, however, still remains outside the annual multilateral

[80] Ásgeirsdóttir, note 16 at 4.

[81] Á Ásgeirsdóttir "Á Hafi Úti: Áhrif Hagsmunahópa Á Samninga Íslendinga Og Norðmanna Vegna Veiða Úr Flökkustofnum Frá Árinu 1980" [Out at Sea: Interest Group Influence on Negotiations between Iceland and Norway Sharing Straddling Fish Stocks Since 1980] in V Ingimundarson (ed.) *Uppbrot Hugmyndakerfis: Endurmótun Íslenskrar Utanríkisstefnu 1991–2007* [*Ripping up of Ideologies: Reform of Icelandic Foreign Policy 1991–2007*]. (Hið íslenska bókmenntafélag, Reykjavik: 2008); T Bjørndal and NA Ekerhovd "Management of Pelagic Fisheries in the North East Atlantic: Norwegian Spring Spawning Herring, Mackerel, and Blue Whiting" (2014) 29 *Marine Resource Economics* 69–83.

[82] N Matz-Lück "The Faroe Islands' Response to EU Trade Restrictions on Atlanto-Scandian Herring" post of 3 May 2014 (available at http://site.uit.no/jclos/2014/03/05/the-faroe-islands-response-to-eu-trade-restrictions-on-atlanto-scandian-herring/).

[83] Bjørndal and Ekerhovd, note 82 at 69–83.

[84] NA Ekerhovd and SI Steinshamn "Economic Benefits of Multi-Species Management: The Pelagic Fisheries in the Northeast Atlantic" (2016) 31 *Marine Resource Economics* 193–210.

[85] "Faroe Islands, Norway Mackerel Quota Agreement Reached" (*SeafoodSource*, 24 November 2014).

quota negotiations, meaning the total mackerel catch continues to exceed scientific advice.

These two cases show that even in areas of high compliance with international fisheries agreements, changes in distribution of stocks can undermine those agreements, resulting in higher levels of fishing for years or decades.

7. CONCLUSION

State sovereignty, combined with the expectation that States enforce compliance of sometimes large fleets fishing around the globe, makes ensuring compliance a difficult affair. As a result, States and NGOs continue to experiment with new ways to improve compliance, but it is yet unclear to what extent this will ensure sustainability of valuable straddling and highly migratory fish stocks in the future. To seek to overcome these challenges, two prominent international relations scholars have called for the creation of a global fisheries organization that would address overfishing by setting TACs for all stocks and then allocate quota to individual States.[86] This is unlikely to happen, given the lack of capacity many States have to ensure compliance. In addition, willingness of States to subject themselves to third-party enforcement is low. Hence, any future management measures on the high seas will in all likelihood continue to evolve so as to put pressure on States to improve compliance, primarily by using more market-based measures and improved monitoring technology.

---

[86] Barkin and DeSombre, note 8 at 3.

13

Problems and Progress in Combating IUU Fishing

EVA R VAN DER MAREL

1. INTRODUCTION

THE 'SCOURGE' OF illegal, unreported and unregulated fishing (IUU) has been considered an obstacle to achieving sustainable fisheries by, *inter alia*, causing economic damage, affecting local biodiversity, and threatening food security in many countries.[1] IUU fishing is difficult to define, as explained in this chapter, but accounts for approximately one-third of global catches.[2] It concerns different types of disregard for international fisheries law, notably the obligations of the LOS Convention,[3] Fish Stocks Agreement,[4] the Compliance Agreement[5] and conservation and management measures (CMMs) adopted through regional fisheries management organizations (RFMOs).

This chapter examines the progress made in combating IUU fishing, and the obstacles yet to be overcome. First, this chapter analyses the problem that is 'IUU fishing' (Section 2). Section 3 then considers progress made at the multilateral level, outlining the international and regional instruments that have been developed to prevent, deter and eliminate IUU fishing and the toolkit they create, which has facilitated a growing trend towards deploying trade restrictions to obstruct the market for products of IUU fishing. The legality of such

---

[1] FAO, *The State of World Fisheries and Aquaculture* (FAO, Rome: 2016) iii and 184.

[2] D Agnew et al. "Estimating the Worldwide Extent of Illegal Fishing" (2009) 4(2) *PLoS ONE*; note that these data are currently outdated: see G Macfadyen, B Caillart and D Agnew *Review of Studies Estimating Levels of IUU Fishing and the Methodologies Utilized*, available at www.fao.org/3/a-bl765e.pdf.

[3] United Nations Convention on the Law of the Sea of 10 December 1982 (1833 UNTS 3).

[4] Agreement for the Implementation of the Provisions of the United Nations Convention on the Law of the Sea of 10 December 1982 relating to the Conservation and Management of Straddling Fish Stocks and Highly Migratory Fish Stocks of 4 August 1995 (2167 UNTS 3).

[5] Agreement to Promote Compliance with International Conservation and Management Measures by Fishing Vessels on the High Seas of 24 November 1993 (2221 UNTS 91).

measures is discussed in further detail by Churchill in Chapter 14 of this volume. Section 4 considers the use of unilateral measures, with particular reference to the approach of the European Union (EU). Section 5 considers whether these initiatives measures support or undermine multilateral efforts to combat IUU fishing. Section 6 concludes.

2. THE CONCEPT OF IUU FISHING

The term 'IUU fishing' is widely used by RFMOs and States. Its origins are usually traced back to a 1997 meeting of the Commission for the Conservation of Antarctic Marine Living Resources (CCAMLR),[6] although the problems associated with IUU fishing existed well before this terminology became fashionable.[7] The notion of IUU fishing quickly gained traction in other RFMOs and at the international level, culminating in the adoption of an International Plan of Action on IUU Fishing (IPOA-IUU) in 2001.[8] The IPOA-IUU is one of four IPOAs adopted under the framework of the United Nations Food and Agricultural Organization (FAO)'s Code of Conduct.[9]

The IPOA-IUU provides a lengthy description of what IUU fishing 'refers to' rather than advancing a precise, clearly drafted definition.[10] It is therefore still somewhat uncertain what is – and what is not and *should* not – be captured by the concept of IUU fishing.[11] Spatial constraints preclude reproducing this 'definition' here, but it can be broadly summarized and explained as follows.

---

[6] CCAMLR-XVI Report of the Sixteenth Meeting of the Commission, para. 2.1 and Annex V paras. 1.2 and 1.28.

[7] W Edeson "Closing the Gap: The Role of 'Soft' International Instruments to Control Fishing" (1999) 83 *Australian Yearbook of International Law* 83–104, 97; M Tsamenyi et al. *Promoting Sustainable Fisheries: The International Legal and Policy Framework to Combat Illegal, Unreported and Unregulated Fishing* (Martinus Nijhoff, Leiden: 2010) 26.

[8] 2001 International Plan of Action to Prevent, Deter and Eliminate Illegal, Unreported and Unregulated Fishing.

[9] 1995 FAO Code of Conduct on Responsible Fisheries.

[10] W Edeson "The International Plan of Action on Illegal, Unreported and Unregulated Fishing: The Legal Context of a Non-Legally Binding Instrument" (2001) 16 *International Journal of Marine and Coastal Law* 603–623, at 609 and 617–620.

[11] J Theilen "What's in a Name? The Illegality of Illegal, Unreported and Unregulated Fishing" (2013) 28 *International Journal of Marine and Coastal Law* 533–550; A Serdy "Simplistic or Surreptitious? Beyond the Flawed Concept(s) of IUU Fishing" in WW Taylor, AJ Lynch and MG Schechter (eds.) *Sustainable Fisheries: Multi-Level Approaches to a Global Problem* (American Fisheries Society, Bethesda, Maryland: 2011) 253–279; ER van der Marel "An Opaque Blacklist: the Lack of Transparency in Identifying Non Cooperating Countries under the EU IUU Regulation" in L Martin, C Salonidis and C Hioueras (eds.) *Natural Resources and the Law of the Sea* (Juris, Huntington, NY: 2017) 237–256.

2.1. I, U and U

Illegal fishing 'refers to' fishing in violation of (foreign) national, regional (RFMO), or international laws.[12] This could mean, for instance, not complying with the laws and regulations of a coastal State when fishing in its exclusive economic zone (EEZ). Unreported fishing 'refers to' failing to report or misreporting catches in contravention of national or regional (RFMO) rules.[13] It is therefore widely understood that both 'illegal' and 'unreported' fishing are essentially concerned with illegal behaviour – namely fishing and related activities that do not comply with the rules. 'Unregulated' fishing is more complex and has generated considerable scholarly attention.[14] The IPOA-IUU describes two types of unregulated fishing, which will be discussed in turn.

2.1.1. Fishing that is Inconsistent with a State's Responsibilities in Respect of the Conservation of Marine Living Resources

The IPOA-IUU refers to fishing in an unregulated area or on an unregulated stock, which is inconsistent with States' responsibilities for the conservation of living resources under international law. The geographical scope of this provision likely addresses areas of the high seas that are unregulated, rather than areas under national jurisdiction for which the coastal State has failed to adopt the necessary measures.[15]

Responsibilities to conserve living marine resources outside areas that are (or should be) regulated are set out in various provisions of the LOS Convention. Of particular relevance are Articles 119, which requires a total allowable catch (TAC) for fishing on the high seas that achieves Maximum Sustainable Yield, as qualified by environmental and economic factors; and indirectly Article 192, which establishes the general duty to protect and preserve the marine environment. These obligations are loosely phrased and allow for considerable discretion, but some guidance was forthcoming in the *Advisory Opinion to the SRFC*[16] and the *South China Sea* award.[17] In these cases, the International Tribunal for the Law of the Sea (ITLOS) and the Arbitral Tribunal respectively considered the nature of States' responsibilities and the actions required to

---

[12] IPOA-IUU, para. 3.1.

[13] Ibid., para. 3.2.

[14] E.g. Theilen; Serdy; van der Marel, note 11.

[15] FAO Fisheries Department "Implementation of the International Plan of Action to Prevent, Deter and Eliminate Illegal, Unreported and Unregulated Fishing" (*FAO Technical Guidelines for Responsible Fisheries* No. 9: 2002) 122, 5–6.

[16] *Request for an Advisory Opinion Submitted by the Sub-Regional Fisheries Commission*, ITLOS Reports 2015, 2 April 2015.

[17] *Republic of the Philippines v. the Peoples' Republic of China (Award)*, PCA Case No. 2013–19, 12 July 2016.

ensure that nationally-registered fishing vessels do not undermine them. Both cases emphasized that States have a clear duty to protect and preserve the marine environment pursuant to Article 192 of the LOS Convention,[18] of which marine living resources form an integral part.[19] This duty applies to all maritime zones, including any unregulated areas of the high seas.[20] The obligation to protect and preserve marine living resources must be interpreted widely. It is informed by the corpus of international law relating to the environment, the other provisions of Part XII and specific obligations set out in other international agreements, as envisaged in Article 237 of the LOS Convention.[21]

Fishing in unregulated waters, or the use of particular fishing methods, may or may not regulated by the flag State and therefore may or may not be legal from a *national* perspective. But, from an *international* perspective, 'unsustainable' fishing undermines a flag State's obligations to conserve marine living resources and may trigger that State's international responsibility. We are thus once again concerned with illegality.

Even so, unlawful (and unregulated) fishing is often "carried out covertly, far from any official presence, and it will be far from obvious what the flag State could realistically have done to prevent it".[22] It should thus not always and not necessarily be equated with irresponsible flag State behaviour. The standard of flag State responsibility was determined in *SRFC* and *South China Sea* as one of 'due diligence', which the International Court of Justice (ICJ) had previously described as "an obligation which entails not only the adoption of appropriate rules and measures, but also a certain level of vigilance in their enforcement".[23] In *SRFC*, the ITLOS specified that this includes adopting the necessary laws and administrative measures (including properly marking vessels) and instituting enforcement mechanisms to monitor and secure compliance (including sufficient sanctions to deter violations and to deprive offenders of the benefits accruing from their illegal fishing activities).[24]

---

[18] Ibid., para, 941; *SRFC*, note 16 at para. 120.

[19] *SRFC*, note 16 at para. 216; reinforcing a similar view in *Southern Bluefin Tuna (New Zealand v. Japan; Australia v. Japan), Provisional Measures*, ITLOS Reports 1999, Order of 27 August 1999, para. 70.

[20] *SRFC*, note 16, at paras. 111, 120 and 129. This situation concerned illegal fishing in the EEZ of another coastal State, which the coastal State is obliged to regulate and therefore falls outside the scope of 'unregulated fishing'. Given this geographical limitation, the ITLOS considered the general provision of Art. 192 but also the requirement to show "due regard" to the rights and duties of other States (Art. 56(2) and 58(3)) and the obligation on foreign nationals to respect the coastal State's rules and regulations (Art. 62(4)).

[21] *South China Sea Award*, note 17 at paras. 941 and 956.

[22] Ibid,. para. 754.

[23] Ibid,. para. 944, approving *SRFC*, note 16; *Responsibilities and obligations of States with respect to activities in the Area*, Advisory Opinion, ITLOS Reports 2011, 1 February 2011; and *Pulp Mills on the River Uruguay (Argentina v. Uruguay)*, Judgment, ICJ Reports 2010.

[24] *SRFC*, note 16, at paras. 129, 137, 138.

2.1.2. *Fishing not in Compliance with an RFMO's CMMs by Non-Members*

The IPOA-IUU also refers to fishing that is not in compliance with an RFMO's CMMs by stateless vessels or those flagged to a *non-Member* of that RFMO. From the outset, it should be noted the most important type of CMM is "obviously that which generally constitutes the very basis of prevention of over-fishing", namely the TAC and its allocation.[25] Any non-Member catch will thus not be in compliance with an RFMO's CMMs.[26]

Fishing by a non-Member not in compliance with a CMM (e.g. fishing without a quota, provided quotas are set) only undermines a flag State's respon-sibilities under international law – i.e. is 'illegal' – where that flag State is bound to observe those CMMs. This is clearly the case where a State has ratified the Fish Stocks Agreement, which provides that States fishing for stocks on the high seas and relevant coastal States shall give effect to their duty to cooper-ate by becoming Members of an existing RFMO or by agreeing to apply its CMMs.[27] However, the Fish Stocks Agreement lacks universal ratification and it is doubtful that its provisions on membership and compliance with RFMO CMMs have reached the status of customary law.[28] Or, if such a customary duty does exist, Serdy argues that the same could then be said of Article 11, from which it would follow that a universal standard now exists that regulates the right to join RFMOs and receive an allocated quota.[29]

Arguably, fishing by a non-Member not in compliance with a CMM is also in breach of Article III(1)(a) of the Compliance Agreement, which obliges its Parties to take the necessary measures to ensure that their fishing vessels do not undermine the "effectiveness" of international CMMs. However, the concept of 'undermining' is vague and unqualified and the instrument still lacks certain important ratifications, notably China.

As for the LOS Convention, it remains uncertain whether, or more likely when, fishing by a non-Member of an RFMO without or exceeding a quota would undermine that State's responsibilities. On the one hand, the LOS Convention lays down general obligations to cooperate (which can be effec-tuated bilaterally) and to conserve the living resources on the high seas and protect and preserve the marine environment, as aforementioned.[30] This duty

---

[25] EJ Molenaar "The Concept of 'Real Interest' and Other Aspects of Co-operation through Regional Fisheries Management Mechanisms" (2000) 15 *International Journal of Marine and Coastal Law* 475–531, at 491.

[26] A Serdy *The New Entrants Problem in International Fisheries Law* (Cambridge University Press, Cambridge: 2016) 149.

[27] Fish Stocks Agreement, Art. 8(3).

[28] A Serdy "*Pacta Tertiis* and Regional Fisheries Management Mechanisms: The IUU Fishing Concept as an Illegitimate Short-Cut to a Legitimate Goal" (2017) 48 *Ocean Development and International Law* 345–364, at 349.

[29] Ibid.

[30] Particularly Arts. 64 and 116–119.

to cooperate is one of conduct, not of result, which is unlikely to infer a duty to comply with an RFMO's CMMs.[31] Indeed

> an obligation on the third States to accept the conservation and management measures adopted by an RFMO would probably be overstretching the duty to cooperate and the obligation of negotiation in the LOS Convention.[32]

A reluctance to hold non-Member States to CMMs adopted by RFMOs is moreover evident from the PSM Agreement,[33] discussed further below. The PSM Agreement stipulates that a party does not "become bound by measures or decisions of, or recognize, any regional fisheries management organization of which it is not a member".[34]

On the other hand, Rayfuse argues that

> State practice indicates both the assertion and the acceptance of a customary duty to cooperate through the medium of (RFMOs) and that an essential element of that duty is the requirement for both member and non-member flag States alike to respect (its measures) either by compliance or through restraint from fishing. This duty is not limited to straddling and highly migratory stocks fisheries but arguably applies to discrete high seas stocks as well.[35]

This would result in an effective prohibition on fishing for a species regulated by an RFMO, depending on how generous the RFMO is in allocating quotas to non-Members. If this is the correct interpretation of the LOS Convention's obligations to conserve and to cooperate, and/or if this represents the current status of customary international law, then both prongs of unregulated fishing – and indeed all elements of IUU fishing as defined in the IPOA-IUU – effectively concern illegal activities.

Recent practice does little to help resolve the debate. RFMOs widely assimilate unregulated fishing with illegal fishing, and indeed adopt sanctions against vessels of non-Members fishing in RFMO regulated areas, as discussed below. This could indicate a new customary duty and de facto *mare clausum*. But acceptance of this practice is not uniform and more likely the result of political compromise than a sense of legal obligation.[36] Such an obligation would ignore issues of equity unless RFMOs operated a fair and accessible quota allocation system. This is not yet the case. Rather, Serdy observes the

---

[31] T Henriksen "Revisiting the Freedom of Fishing and Legal Obligations on States Not Party to Regional Fisheries Management Organizations" (2009) 40 *Ocean Development and International Law* 80–96, 88.

[32] Ibid., 91.

[33] Agreement on Port State Measures to Prevent, Deter and Eliminate Illegal, Unreported and Unregulated Fishing of 22 November 2009, www.fao.org/documents/card/en/c/915655b8-e31c-479c-bf07-30cba21ea4b0.

[34] PSM Agreement, Art. 4(2).

[35] R Rayfuse "Countermeasures and High Seas Fisheries Enforcement" (2004) 51 *Netherlands International Law Review* 41–76, 59.

[36] Serdy, note 26 at 157.

"regrettable propensity in international fisheries for States to favour imposing disciplines on others that they are not prepared to accept for themselves".[37]

That unregulated fishing is not always illegal is seemingly confirmed by paragraph 3.4 of the IPOA-IUU, stating that "notwithstanding paragraph 3.3, certain unregulated fishing may take place in a manner which is not in violation of applicable international law, and may not require the application of measures envisaged under the (IPOA-IUU)". Moreover, the FAO Technical Guidelines on the Implementation of the IPOA-IUU note that "'IUU fishing' is a broad term that captures a wide variety of fishing activity, *most of which is illicit*".[38] The IUU fishing definition thus represents an amalgam of both legal and illegal activities, and gives no indication of the degree of responsibility required (in ICJ-speak, the level of 'vigilance' expected) of a State under international law.

2.2. The Definition of IUU Fishing: More Problems than Progress?

A key difficulty with the IPOA-IUU definition is that by conflating a set of distinct behaviours as a single phenomenon, it obscures more than it reveals. The legality of a particular specific fishing or fishing-related activity must be clarified by reference to the nature of that conduct and the obligations of the flag State in question.[39] Yet the IUU concept is often used as a synonym for 'illegality', both in popular discourse and official documentation.

The IUU definition is too broad to give sufficient insight into the particular activities in question. For example, in Pacific tuna fisheries, the lion's share of highlighted IUU fishing constitutes misreporting and non-compliance with other licence conditions; unlicensed fishing only represents a marginal 4 per cent of the overall volume.[40] Conversely, other regions grapple predominantly with the latter.[41] Simply terming both instances as 'IUU fishing' is insufficiently nuanced to accurately reflect the true nature of these respective problems.[42] The definition is moreover too narrow, as it neglects the many *legal* fishing activities that may be as environmentally problematic, for instance due to the gear used or their volume and intensity.[43] Nor does it accommodate

---

[37] Ibid, 154.

[38] FAO, note 15 at 5.

[39] High Seas Task Force *Closing the Net: Stopping Illegal Fishing on the High Seas* (DEFRA, London: 2006) 16.

[40] MRAG Asia Pacific *Towards the Quantification of Illegal, Unreported and Unregulated (IUU) Fishing in the Pacific Islands Region* (MRAG, Toowong, QLD: 2016) 101.

[41] E.g. on fishing by non-CCAMLR Members, see DJ Agnew "The Illegal and Unregulated Fishery for Toothfish in the Southern Ocean, and the CCAMLR Catch Documentation Scheme" (2000) 24 *Marine Policy* 361–374; on *inter alia* foreign vessels fishing without coastal State consent off West-Africa, see A Daniels et al. "Western Africa's Missing Fish", available at: www.odi.org/sites/odi.org.uk/files/resource-documents/10665.pdf.

[42] See also Macfadyen et al., note 2 at 6–7.

[43] In SPRFMO, e.g., this problem is mitigated because IUU fishing also refers to "other activities as may be decided by the Commission" (Art. 1(j) of the Convention).

additional concerns associated with IUU vessels – such as slavery or other criminality (considered by Caddell, Leloudas and Soyer in Chapter 17 of this volume).

The different uses and interpretations of this concept render it virtually impossible to legitimately and consistently quantify IUU fishing globally.[44] It has therefore been suggested that any future technical guidelines on a common methodology to quantify IUU fishing could revisit the definitions of the IPOA-IUU, identifying separate categories "that are more attuned to current experience and practices".[45]

3. MULTILATERAL ACTION TO COMBAT IUU FISHING

This section examines the instruments and measures that have been specifically designed to prevent, deter and eliminate IUU fishing, notably the tools they propose and their operative requirements. They complement other relevant initiatives, such as the development of a Global Record of Fishing Vessels[46] and the FAO Guidelines on Flag State Performance,[47] considered by Klein in Chapter 15 of this volume.

3.1. IPOA-IUU

The IPOA-IUU is credited with initiating the global movement to combat IUU fishing. While it was the first instrument to use the IUU terminology, it should be reiterated that the many activities that constitute IUU fishing were already, and continue to be, regulated by numerous international fisheries laws and policy instruments. It is their perceived lack of effectiveness that spurred the creation of the IPOA-IUU, which itself recognizes a "lack of political will, priority, capacity and resources to ratify, accede to and implement them".[48]

The IPOA-IUU is a voluntary instrument and therefore utilizes 'soft' language (States "should", "are encouraged", "to the greatest extent possible").[49] It provides a toolkit of measures to prevent, deter and eliminate IUU fishing, while acknowledging that nothing in the instrument affects States' existing obligations under international law.[50] Although the IPOA-IUU is voluntary, it has been adopted by consensus and is widely referenced in international fora. The annual UN General Assembly (UNGA) Resolutions on Oceans and Law of the Sea call

---

[44] Macfadyen et al., note 2 at 23.
[45] Ibid.
[46] Available at /www.fao.org/cofi/33133-01d7de5488a77180759efacea7c39dbb7.pdf.
[47] Available at /www.fao.org/3/a-i4577t.pdf.
[48] IPOA-IUU, para. 1.
[49] Ibid, paras. 4 and 13.
[50] Ibid, paras. 8 and 13.

upon States to implement the IPOA-IUU, and the instrument has found wide traction with RFMOs.[51] The IPOA-IUU has influenced legal developments at a regional[52] and global level (adoption of the PSM Agreement); has spurred the development of IUU-oriented CMMs in RFMOs; has led to the development of the FAO Guidelines on Catch Documentation Schemes (CDS); and influenced the adoption of the EU IUU Regulation,[53] as discussed further below.

The IPOA-IUU has a broad scope, requiring States to use "all available jurisdiction in accordance with international law" and to cooperate so as to apply measures in an "integrated manner".[54] The IPOA-IUU encourages all States to ratify and implement the Fish Stocks Agreement and the Compliance Agreement;[55] to encourage scientific research on fish identification;[56] to apply CMMs adopted by RFMOs which have a bearing on IUU fishing, even where they are not a Member, in the spirit of cooperation;[57] to develop innovative ways to combat IUU fishing within RFMOs;[58] and to cooperate to provide support to developing countries.[59] Institutionally, the IPOA-IUU calls for the strengthening of RFMOs,[60] while also establishing a clear role for the FAO, namely to collect data; support the development and implementation of national action plans; convene an expert consultation on CDS; and carry out research on IUU fishing (in collaboration with the International Maritime Organization).[61]

More specifically, the IPOA-IUU lists the following measures that States should adopt in their different capacities. It identifies the primary responsibility of the *flag State* to exercise jurisdiction over vessels flying its flag to ensure that they do not engage in, or support, IUU fishing.[62] It stipulates *inter alia* that the flag State should ensure that it is capable of doing so before it registers a vessel; avoid flagging vessels with a history of IUU fishing; disincentivize flag-hopping

---

[51] See e.g. the Resolution Relating to IUU Fishing and Limits on Fishing Capacity, WCPFC/PrepCon/22, 22 November 2002, which urges "all States and other entities concerned to take every appropriate measure, in accordance with their international obligations and with the IPOA-IUU and other relevant international instruments, to prevent, deter and eliminate IUU fishing in the (WCPFC) Area"; and more generally the standard references to the IPOA-IUU in RFMO CMMs establishing IUU vessel lists, such as IOTTC Resolution 11/03; WCPFC CMM 2010-06; SPRFMO CMM 04-2017.

[52] Indeed, the Parties to the SRFC revised their Convention on Access Conditions specifically in light of the IPOA-IUU and PSM Agreement, see *SRFC*, note 16 at para. 91.

[53] Council Regulation (EC) No. 1005/2008 of 29 September 2008 establishing a Community system to prevent, deter and eliminate illegal, unreported and unregulated fishing, amending Regulations (EEC) No. 2847/93, (EC) No. 1936/2001 and EC No. 601/2004 and repealing Regulations (EC) No. 1093/94 and (EC) No. 1447/1999, OJ 2008 L266/1.

[54] IPOA-IUU, para. 9.3.

[55] Ibid., paras. 11–12.

[56] Ibid., para. 77.

[57] Ibid., paras. 78–79.

[58] Ibid, para. 80.

[59] Ibid., paras. 85–86.

[60] Ibid., para. 80(1).

[61] Ibid., paras. 88–93.

[62] Ibid., paras. 9.3 and 34.

through refusing fishing permits; maintain a record of its fishing vessels; and make catch and transshipment data available to other States, RFMOs and the FAO.[63] Priorities for the *coastal State* include undertaking effective monitoring, control and surveillance of fishing activities in its EEZ; cooperation with other States; and only issuing fishing licences to vessels with no history of IUU fishing.[64] For the *port State*, the IPOA-IUU calls for port access to be restricted to certain ports and requested prior to entry, and be subject to the provision of catch data. Access should be denied (except in cases of *force majeure* or distress) where there is evidence of IUU fishing, while in-port inspections should be conducted and the flag State notified of any IUU fishing.[65]

The IPOA-IUU also encourages States to utilize their *market power* to incentivize other actors, over which they have no direct control, to comply with their obligations. States are to take all steps necessary, consistent with international law, to prevent fish caught by vessels identified by RFMOs to have been engaged in IUU fishing from being traded or imported into their territories.[66] States should cooperate to adopt appropriate multilaterally agreed trade-related measures that are necessary to combat IUU fishing for specific stocks or species, such as multilateral CDS and import and export prohibitions.[67] Moreover, States are encouraged to improve the transparency of their own markets, allowing for better traceability of fish or related products.[68]

3.2. PSM Agreement

In 2005, to reinforce the implementation of the IPOA-IUU, the FAO adopted a voluntary 'Model Scheme' on port State measures to combat IUU fishing.[69] Within months of its adoption, moves were underway towards more binding measures, culminating in the PSM Agreement. The PSM Agreement was approved at the 36th Session of the FAO Conference in November 2009 and entered into force on 5 June 2016, and is the first and only legally binding global instrument directly concerned with IUU fishing.

The PSM Agreement aims to prevent, deter and eliminate IUU fishing, as defined in the IPOA-IUU, by implementing effective port State measures.[70] Its adoption marks a high point in the evolution of port State jurisdiction in the law of the sea, a process that arguably started with Article 23 of the Fish Stocks

---

[63] Ibid., paras. 35–50.
[64] Ibid., para. 51.
[65] Ibid., paras. 52–64.
[66] Ibid., para. 66.
[67] Ibid., paras. 68–69.
[68] Ibid., para. 71.
[69] Available at www.fao.org/3/a-a0985t.pdf.
[70] PSM Agreement, Art. 2.

Agreement[71] and which provided a 'springboard' for the development of global standards for port State measures.[72] The PSM Agreement harmonizes minimum standards for exercising port State jurisdiction in the context of IUU fishing. A key provision is the denial of access to ports (and thereby to national and international markets) to vessels upon proof that they have engaged in IUU fishing, exemplified by inclusion on an IUU vessel list operated by an RFMO.[73] The PSM Agreement thus continues the trend of leveraging market access to combat IUU fishing, although it does not *expressly* include trade-related measures "because it was not intended as a trade instrument".[74]

The PSM Agreement builds upon the generally accepted presumption that vessels have no right under international law to access to port;[75] thus, access to ports may be denied also to vessels flagged to non-Parties to the Agreement.[76] Accordingly, the PSM Agreement constitutes an obligation rather than a right for parties to exercise port State jurisdiction to deny access to vessels having engaged in IUU fishing. The PSM Agreement further establishes minimum requirements for port inspections and requires the denial of port services to vessels once they have entered the port under certain conditions or if, upon inspection, it transpires they have engaged in IUU fishing or related activities, or where the port State has "reasonable grounds" to believe this is the case.[77]

3.3. CMMs Developed within RFMOs

Given the broad nature of IUU fishing, essentially all CMMs adopted by RFMOs are of (in)direct relevance to IUU fishing. Some CMMs more directly address the concept, and these will now be discussed in turn. Such measures are often born out of a concern for fishing by non-Member vessels that do not comply with the RFMO's CMMs ('unregulated fishing').

---

[71] Stipulating that the port State has the "right and the duty" to take measures in its ports to promote the effectiveness of RFMO conservation and management measures.

[72] J Swan "Port State Measures – From Residual Port State Jurisdiction to Global Standards" (2016) 31 *International Journal of Marine and Coastal Law* 395–421, at 399.

[73] PSM Agreement, Art. 9.

[74] D Doulman and J Swan "A Guide to the Background and Implementation of the 2009 FAO Agreement on Port State Measures to Prevent, Deter, and Eliminate Illegal, Unreported and Unregulated Fishing" (2012) *FAO Fisheries and Aquaculture Circular 1074*, 68.

[75] Though subject to general principles of good faith and abuse of right, and of course trade obligations; see S Kopela "Port-State Jurisdiction, Extraterritoriality, and the Protection of Global Commons Global Commons" (2017) 47 *Ocean Development & International Law* 89–130, at 94, who also discusses the question whether entry requirements should be restricted by a jurisdictional basis.

[76] On whether the PSM Agreement could override other obligations established under bilateral or multilateral agreements (such as the WTO) to ensure access to ports (and thereby markets), see A Serdy "The Shaky Foundations of the FAO Port State Measures Agreement: How Watertight Is the Legal Seal against Access for Foreign Fishing Vessels?" (2016) 31 *International Journal of Marine and Coastal Law* 422–441.

[77] PSM Agreement, Arts. 11 and 18.

3.3.1. Positive and Negative Vessel Lists

Many RFMOs operate positive and/or negative lists specifying those vessels that are authorized to operate in the management area of the RFMO or, conversely, those precluded from fishing due to IUU activities.[78] This allows Members of the RFMO (and other States) to adopt targeted restrictions in their ports against these vessels, disincentivizing IUU fishing through the loss of market access.

The process of listing and de-listing vessels can be highly politicized and decision-making processes in many RFMOs often lacks transparency. The problem that unregulated fishing may not be in contravention of that flag State's responsibilities has already been discussed above. Fishing allocations are not always fairly distributed or may be difficult to obtain for new entrants,[79] which encourages unregulated fishing, while dispute settlement mechanisms often leave much to be desired.[80] Although the IPOA-IUU urges that the identification of IUU fishing vessels by RFMOs should be made "through agreed procedures in a fair, transparent and non-discriminatory manner",[81] this is clearly not always the case. In a damning critique, the EU has observed that

> in some cases, lists are drawn up on the basis of information from a few States and are not verified before being adopted (by RFMOs), thus undermining their legitimacy. The management procedures (enrolment, striking off) are not transparent. In addition, the consequences associated with listing are not spelled out. It is crucial therefore to clarify the procedures and criteria for identifying IUU activities in order to achieve standardization within (RFMOs).[82]

Another factor undermining IUU lists as a legitimate CMM and the increasingly common practice of exchanging them between RFMOs is the lack of uniform criteria or a common process for listing vessels, as considered by Harrison in Chapter 5 of this volume. This was highlighted by the Regional Fishery Body Secretariats Network's third meeting in 2011, which revealed scepticism between some tuna RFMOs over a joint IUU list. It was noted that their respective listing criteria are variable, often because of the different geographical scope of RFMOs (high seas only or also EEZs).[83] Procedure and due process are clearly issues to be improved, as discussed below in comparing RFMO lists with the EU IUU vessel negative list.

---

[78] DS Calley *Market Denial and International Fisheries Regulation* (Martinus Nijhoff, Leiden: 2012) 285, at 114–123. The nine RFMOs that currently operate IUU vessel negative lists are CCAMLR, IATTC, ICCAT, IOTC, NAFO, NEAFC, SEAFO, WCPFC and SPRFMO.

[79] Serdy, note 26 at 76–78.

[80] M Ceo et al. "Performance Reviews by Regional Fishery Bodies: Introduction, Summaries, Synthesis and Best Practices, Volume I: CCAMLR, CCSBT, ICCAT, IOTC, NAFO, NASCO, NEAFC" (2012) *FAO Fisheries and Aquaculture Circular* No. 1072.

[81] IPOA-IUU, paras. 63 and 66.

[82] European Commission, Community action plan for the eradication of illegal, unreported and unregulated fishing, COM(2002)180 Final (Brussels, 28 May 2002) para. 3.3.

[83] Report of the Third Meeting of Regional Fishery Body Secretariats Network, *FAO Fisheries and Aquaculture Report* No. 980 (FAO, Rome: 2011) 61.

3.3.2. Port Measures

Many RFMOs recommend the use of port measures in some form or another. Common provisions include the designation of ports; requirements for advance notice of port entry and authorization to enter; general procedures for carrying out port inspections; requirements for follow-up action in case an infringement is found; and provisions related to cooperation and contact points.[84] RFMOs like the Indian Ocean Tuna Commission (IOTC), South-East Atlantic Fisheries Organization (SEAFO), and North-East Atlantic Fisheries Commission (NEAFC) furthermore encourage the denial of access to port and port services in case of suspected IUU fishing, through schemes based on or similar to the PSM Agreement, thereby de facto blocking market access to IUU fishing.

The entry into force of the PSM Agreement in 2016 has provided further impetus for developing port State measures. It has also revealed obstacles, in particular for developing coastal States and in RFMOs where not all Members have ratified the PSM Agreement. This is exemplified by the development of port State measures in the Western and Central Pacific Fisheries Commission (WCPFC). Here, the EU drove the adoption of port measures to combat IUU fishing long before the entry into force of the PSM Agreement, proposing in 2010 and 2011 a 'fully fledged' PSM Agreement-model approach.[85] This was met with limited enthusiasm by Pacific Small Island Developing Nations (SIDS), who *inter alia* feared this might result in a disproportionately heavy burden on their ports, unless sufficient assistance would be made available to help with implementation.[86] These and other concerns finally led to the adoption of a more modest scheme establishing minimum requirements for the inspection of vessels suspected of IUU fishing, including a detailed provision on developing a funding support mechanism for SIDS and the obligation to mitigate any disproportionate burden that may result from implementation.[87]

3.3.3. Identification of Non-cooperating Countries

Aside from port measures, which target individual vessels, nine RFMOs currently allow their Members to adopt trade restrictive measures against identified countries.[88] For example, as early as 1994 and 1995, ICCAT adopted its Bluefin Tuna Action Plan and Swordfish Action Plan,[89] wherein ICCAT would identify

---

[84] On the different port State measures adopted by IATTC, ICCAT, CCSBT, IOTC, SEAFO, NAFO, NEAFC, and CAMMLR see WCPFC-TCC12-2016-22 of 24 August 2016.

[85] WCPFC8-2011-DP/26 of 31 January 2012.

[86] WCPFC8- 2011- DP/07 of 7 November 2011, and Summary Report of the Ninth Regular Session of the WCPFC of 2–6 December 2012, para. 83(h).

[87] CMM 2017-2 of 7 December 2017.

[88] G Hosch *Trade Measures to Combat IUU Fishing: Comparative Analysis of Unilateral and Multilateral Approaches* (International Centre for Trade and Sustainable Development, Geneva: 2016) 9.

[89] Resolution 94-3 on Bluefin Tuna, and Resolution 95-13 on Atlantic Swordfish (entered into force 22 June 1996).

non-Members whose vessels had fished in a way that "diminished the effectiveness" of its CMMs (i.e. 'unregulated fishing'). If further cooperation with the third country in question proved unsuccessful, ICCAT would require its Members to prohibit the importation of those particular species where they were caught by a vessel registered to that country. This was the first occasion that multilaterally-endorsed trade measures were adopted in the context of fishing, with Panama, Honduras and Belize identified in this manner.[90] A similar scheme was adopted in 1996, extending this time to ICCAT Members.[91] This led to its identification of Equatorial New Guinea in 1999, which had exported significant numbers of Atlantic bluefin tuna despite having a zero catch limit at the time, and which had neither responded to ICCAT's inquiries nor reported any catch data.[92]

The EU has previously driven the development of similar competences for CCAMLR. CCAMLR allows its Members to "cooperate to adopt appropriate multilaterally agreed trade-related measures" to combat IUU fishing[93] but lacks a mandate to identify countries or adopt such measures. From 2006–2014, the EU has repeatedly submitted a Proposal that would allow CCAMLR to recommend trade-related measures concerning *Dissostichus spp*, including suggestions for procedures and criteria for doing so.[94] The EU's Proposal received mixed reviews however, with Argentina, Brazil and Namibia in particular opposed to the adoption of trade-related measures.[95] In light of this, deliberations now appear to have moved towards alternative mechanisms to combat IUU fishing. These include ensuring that insurers and other providers of financial services do not enable IUU fishing[96] and improving transparency in the investigation of vessels engaged in IUU.[97]

3.3.4. Catch Documentation Schemes (CDS)

Many RFMOs also adopt CDS, which can be considered modern generation Trade Documentation/Information Schemes (TDSs).[98] TDSs have operated since the 1990s and are still applied by particular RFMOs.[99] Whereas TDSs

---

[90] Recommendations 96-11 and 96-12 (entered into force 4 August 1997); see also the summary of trade-related measures used to combat IUU fishing submitted in CCAMLR-XXVI/BG/26 of 28 September 2006.

[91] Recommendation 96-14 (entered into force 4 August 1997).

[92] Recommendation 99-10 (entered into force 15 June 2000).

[93] Conservation Measures 10-06 and 10-07, paras. 25 and 30 respectively.

[94] First tabled at CCAMLR-XXV of 23 October–3 November 2006, para. 3.55.

[95] CCAMLR-XXXII of 23 October–1 November 2013, Annex 4, paras. 141–143; CCAMLR-XXXIII of 20–31 October 2014, paras. 3.72. 3.74, 3.7; also Serdy, note 26 at 161–171.

[96] Amendment to Conservation Measure 10-08 at CCAMLR-XXXVI, 16–27 October 2017. See further Chapter 17 of this volume (Caddell, Leloudas and Soyer).

[97] Amendment to Conservation Measures 10-06 and 10-07 to allow for proper investigation timeframes and increased transparency at CAMLR-XXXV, 17–28 October 2016.

[98] Hosch, note 88 at 7.

[99] Ibid.

predominantly aim to gather information about trade flows, CDS certify the legality of a unit of catch (individual fish) at the point of capture by issuing a catch certificate to the legal owner, subsequently allowing the product to be traced throughout the supply chain by linking the catch certificate to an associated trade certificate.[100]

It should be observed that current CDS only track the *international* movement of fish, not domestic landings. CDS are highly complex and rely on close cooperation between different authorities responsible for the various stages from the point of harvest to the point of sale. This is both their strength and their weakness, since the schemes are only ever as reliable as the weakest link in the chain.[101] While many RFMOs apply some type of scheme to require the inspection of catch before it is landed or transshipped, only three RFMOs currently operate a CDS that covers the full supply chain.[102] Although these three CDS are a valuable tool in the fight against IUU fishing, Hosch notes that their effectiveness is compromised by various practical shortcomings, and that cumulatively they cover less than 0.1 per cent of global catches.[103] The development of other CDS is underway,[104] potentially along the lines of the guidelines on CDS that have been negotiated by the FAO, discussed next.

3.4. CDS Guidelines

The CDS developed by RFMOs differ not only from one another, but also in their modus operandi from the CDS operated by the EU (discussed below). The variations between these schemes prompted FAO consultations towards a set of best practice guidelines on developing CDS, which were finally adopted in July 2017.[105] They represent a "cautious first step" in the development of benchmarks for CDS, including their scope, objectives, principles and design.[106]

---

[100] Ibid.

[101] High Seas Task Force, note 39, p. 31.

[102] Hosch, note 88 at 10.

[103] Ibid., 11–12.

[104] See the recommendations at the 87th Meeting of IATTC (resumed Session) to establish a CDS for Bluefin tuna as a matter of priority, although no agreement has been reached so far; see also the proposals by the EU between 2009 and 2013 to the IOTC to develop a CDS, but which were rejected by the Commission; and the work of the intersessional working group on CDS of the WCPFC to develop a CDS for big-eye tuna, which last met in September 2016.

[105] See UNGA Resolution 68/71 of 9 December 2013 on Sustainable Fisheries, which called upon States to initiate work through the FAO to "develop guidelines and other relevant criteria relating to catch documentation schemes, including possible formats" (at para. 68); FAO Committee on Fisheries, *The Voluntary Guidelines for Catch Documentation Schemes*, paper from the 32nd Session in Rome, 11–15 July 2016.

[106] G Hosch "The 2017 FAO Voluntary Guidelines on Catch Documentation Schemes" (2017) 6 *INFOFISH International Magazine*, 27–30.

Two main points of contention hampered the completion of the CDS Guidelines.[107] Firstly, it was disputed whether regional or multilateral CDS should be *preferred* over unilateral measures such as those adopted by the EU; whether they should have *precedence*; or whether criteria should be established to establish a test of *equivalence*. Secondly, concerns arose whether responsibility for validating the catch certificate should be vested in the flag State, or port or coastal States. Indeed, under the EU's catch certification scheme, the flag State may question the validity of documents issued by port and coastal States concerning fishing activities carried out within their jurisdiction, which many port and coastal States consider an encroachment on their sovereignty.

Both issues were finally resolved in the following way. The Guidelines clearly state that "multilateral or regional CDS are preferred".[108] Yet, they do not entirely dismiss unilateral CDS, since they refer to the "basic principle" of recognizing equivalence[109] and specifically note that "[d]ifferent CDS could be recognised as equivalent for the purpose of achieving the objectives of the guidelines if they result in equivalent outcomes. In addition, existing schemes should be taken into account".[110] As for sharing responsibilities between flag and coastal States, the Guidelines provide that "CDS are most effective when all States involved cooperate in the schemes" and that "all States involved in events in the supply chain in the CDS should designate a competent authority to ensure availability of accurate and verifiable information along the supply chain", thus allowing all relevant States to participate in the verification of catch documentation information.[111]

4. UNILATERAL TRADE-RELATED MEASURES TO COMBAT IUU FISHING

There is a growing trend towards deploying trade-related measures and their corresponding acceptance by the international community as a "powerful tool" to combat IUU fishing.[112] The EU, considered here in more detail, has unilaterally instituted a far-reaching strategy to combat IUU fishing, both within and beyond its jurisdiction. The EU is a powerhouse of fish trade,[113] and is currently the most prominent example of the use of market strength to deter IUU fishing. The basis for the EU's approach is intriguing. In its Proposal for the EU IUU

---

[107] "RFMO Catch Documentation Schemes: A Summary", para. 42, available at www.wcpfc.int/node/27883.

[108] Guidelines, para. 5.1.

[109] Ibid., para. 3.3.

[110] Ibid., para. 4.3.

[111] Ibid., paras. 5.1 and 5.3; Hosch, note 106 at 29–30.

[112] Doulman and Swan, note 74 at 94; on RFMO trade-related measures to combat IUU generally, see Calley, note 78 at 114–123 and 147–152. Note however the need for more hard evidence on the effectiveness of restrictive trade measures as a solution to IUU; see High Seas Task Force, note 39 at 31.

[113] The EU Fish Market, available at www.eumofa.eu/documents/20178/77960/The+EU+fish+market+-+2016+Edition.pdf.

Regulation, the Commission stated that the EU, in line with its international commitments, had a "specific responsibility in leading international efforts on the fight against IUU fishing" and the "specific responsibility in making sure that fisheries products imported into its territory do not originate from IUU fishing".[114] In this respect, the EU appears to be acting out of a sense of moral duty to exercise market leadership in a similar manner to aspects of its climate change policies.[115]

The IUU Regulation is merely one element in the EU's arsenal of measures to manage and control fisheries. Other important provisions include the Control Regulation,[116] which ensures compliance with the EU's Common Fisheries Policy,[117] and, as far as third countries are concerned, the Non-Sustainable Fishing Regulation.[118] The latter allows for the adoption of trade-restrictions vis-à-vis countries that facilitate unsustainable fishing on a stock of common interest, although to date this has been invoked only once.[119] The EU IUU Regulation is the sole instrument dedicated specifically to ensuring that only fish products caught in compliance with relevant conservation and management measures enter the EU market. Accordingly, its geographical scope extends well beyond the EU's boundaries.

Its main components are: prior notification of and authorization to enter EU ports for third country fishing vessels;[120] increased inspections in EU ports;[121] an EU-wide alert system;[122] an obligation for fishery products entering the EU to be accompanied by a validated catch certificate;[123] increased control over

---

[114] COM(2007) 602 final, Proposal for a Council Regulation establishing a Community system to prevent, deter and eliminate illegal, unreported and unregulated fishing.

[115] This may be referred to as a "second order responsibility", where a State is motivated not by a legal requirement, but from a moral duty to enforce, enable or otherwise encourage others to meet their obligations: S Caney "Two Kinds of Climate Justice: Avoiding Harm and Sharing Burdens" (2015) 9 *Political Theory Without Borders: Philosophy, Politics and Society* 125–149, at 142; see also J Scott "The Geographical Scope of the EU's Climate Responsibilities" (2015) 17 *Cambridge Yearbook of European Legal Studies* 92–120.

[116] Council Regulation (EC) No. 1224/2009 of 20 November 2009 establishing a Community control system for ensuring compliance with the rules of the common fisheries policy, amending Regulations (EC) No. 847/96, (EC) No. 2371/2002, (EC) No. 811/2004, (EC) No. 768/2005, (EC) No. 2115/2005, (EC) No. 2166/2005, (EC) No. 388/2006, (EC) No. 509/2007, (EC) No. 676/2007, (EC) No. 1098/2007, (EC) No. 1300/2008, (EC) No. 1342/2008 and repealing Regulations (EEC) No. 2847/93, (EC) No. 1627/94 and (EC) No. 1966/2006, 22 December 2009, OJ J343/1.

[117] Regulation (EU) No. 1380/2013 of the European Parliament and of the Council of 11 December 2013 on the Common Fisheries Policy, amending Council Regulations (EC) No. 1954/2003 and (EC) No. 1224/2009 and repealing Council Regulations (EC) No. 2371/2002 and (EC) No. 639/2004 and Council Decision 2004/585/EC, 28 December 2013, OJ L354/22.

[118] Regulation (EU) No. 1026/2012 of the European Parliament and of the Council of 25 October 2012 on certain measures for the purpose of the conservation of fish stocks in relation to countries allowing non-sustainable fishing, 14 November 2012, OJ L 316/4.

[119] See M Vatsov "Changes in the Geographical Distribution of Shared Fish Stocks and the Mackerel War: Confronting the Cooperation Maze" (2016) Working Paper No. 13, Scottish Centre for International Law, Edinburgh.

[120] EU IUU Regulation, note 53, Arts. 6 and 7.

[121] Ibid., Arts. 9–11.

[122] Ibid., Art. 23.

[123] Ibid., Art. 12.

EU nationals' support for and engagement in IUU fishing;[124] the listing of fishing vessels known to have engaged in IUU fishing and a prohibition on listed vessels entering EU ports;[125] and the possibility of listing third countries.[126] This section considers the most important and far-reaching of these measures, namely the CDS and third country 'negative list'. The IUU vessel 'negative list' is considered further below.

4.1. The EU CDS

All imports and re-exports of fish and fish products[127] must be accompanied by a catch certificate as evidence that catches have occurred in accordance with applicable laws, regulations and international conservation and management measures.[128] While broadly similar to the CDS operated by RFMOs, the EU system is unilateral and only applies to exports to the EU. Catch certificates are validated by the competent authorities of the flag State,[129] which as discussed above was a contested issue in the context of the adoption of the CDS Guidelines. Moreover, the EU CDS is in need of some modernization, and many advocate the replacement of the current paper-based scheme with a centralized electronic database to facilitate a more coordinated approach and the real-time exchange of information.[130]

To meet the EU criteria, a third country must notify the Commission beforehand that it has established national arrangements for the implementation, control and enforcement of laws, regulations and conservation and management measures which must be complied with by its fishing vessels, and that its public authorities are empowered to attest to the veracity of the information contained in the certificates and able to verify this upon the request of the importing EU Member State.[131] This includes details of the competent validating authorities, which are retained and disseminated to authorities in the Member States and published in the Official Journal.[132] The Commission can only highlight missing elements from the notification and is not explicitly empowered to evaluate the competence of a third country's authorities.[133] However, the EU conducts overseas missions to these countries to expressly verify the arrangements. This may

---

[124] Ibid., Art. 39.
[125] Ibid., Arts. 27 and 37.
[126] Ibid., Arts. 31 and 38.
[127] Exceptions to this provision are listed in Art. 12(5) and Annex I.
[128] Ibid., Art. 12(3).
[129] Ibid., Art. 12(4).
[130] *Opinion: Improving Implementation of the EU Regulation to Fight IUU Fishing* (2016), available at http://ldac.chil.me/download-doc/125741.
[131] EU IUU Regulation, Art. 20(1) and Annex III, EU IUU Regulation.
[132] Ibid., Art. 22.
[133] Ibid., Art. 20(3).

cause a third country to be put on the 'negative list' if these systems are ultimately deficient, to which this chapter now turns.

4.2. The Country 'Negative List' and 'Carding System'

The Regulation stipulates that the Commission "shall identify third countries that it considers as non-cooperating third countries in fighting IUU fishing".[134] A third country may be identified as such "if it fails to discharge the duties incumbent upon it under international law as flag, port, coastal or market State, to take action to prevent, deter and eliminate IUU fishing".[135] These non-cooperating third countries are then listed upon what may be termed the 'negative list'. A listed country faces a number of consequences, the most severe of which are trade restrictions – or, indeed, an outright ban – on fish and fishery products caught by its nationally-registered vessels.[136] The negative list operates in distinct stages of information-gathering and dialogue, known colloquially as a 'carding system', and proceeds as follows.

The Regulation provides a non-exhaustive list of sources to assist the Commission in determining whether a country has complied with what can be termed its 'international anti-IUU obligations'.[137] The process of information-gathering commonly starts when a non-EU flag State notifies the Commission that it has instituted the necessary arrangements to validate catch certificates.[138] Following this, the Commission may conduct a mission to verify these arrangements and to consider the measures taken by that State "to implement its obligations in the fight against IUU fishing and to fulfil its requirements", as well as its implementation of the EU CDS.[139] The Commission subsequently sends a report to that State. In most cases, comments on the report are exchanged, and the Commission may conduct further missions to review actions arising from the first mission, alongside various videoconferences, technical meetings and capacity-building workshops.[140] On the basis of the information thus obtained,

---

[134] Ibid., Art. 31(1).

[135] Ibid., Art. 31(3).

[136] Ibid., Art. 38. An import ban may be restricted to certain stocks or species if the justification for listing was a lack of appropriate measures for a given stock or species.

[137] Ibid., Art. 31(2).

[138] Although the Commission has also undertaken missions in the absence of such a notification: Commission Decision of 1 October 2015 on notifying a Third Country of the possibility of being identified as non-cooperating third country in fighting illegal, unreported and unregulated fishing, [2015] OJ C324/7.

[139] See e.g. the case of Thailand: Commission Decision of 21 April 2015 on notifying a third country of the possibility of being identified as a non-cooperating third country in fighting illegal, unreported and unregulated fishing [2015] OJ C142/7.

[140] Commission Decision of 10 June 2014 on notifying a Third Country that the Commission considers as possible of being identified as non-cooperating Third Countries pursuant to Council Regulation (EC) No. 1005/2008 establishing a Community system to prevent, deter and eliminate illegal, unreported and unregulated fishing, 17 June 2014, OJ C 185/17.

as well as from other sources considered in the Regulation,[141] the Commission makes a preliminary assessment of the fisheries sector of that country. If it is considered not to be complying with its international obligations, it is notified of the possibility of being identified as a non-cooperating third country (often referred to as a 'yellow card').[142]

The IUU Regulation contains no formal requirements for this pre-identification stage. Indeed, the extent of these exchanges varies markedly. Following the yellow card, the Commission engages in a more formalized dialogue with national representatives concerning that country's fisheries sector. The notification is accompanied by an official request to take measures to cease IUU fishing activities, to prevent any future such activities, and to rectify any act or omission that may have diminished the effectiveness of applicable laws, regulations, or international conservation and management measures.[143] Although a yellow card does not entail formal sanctions, the (reputational) costs of avoiding a red card are significant and high.[144] To provide a meaningful opportunity to respond to and rectify the situation, the Commission's notification must be reasoned and accompanied by supporting evidence. The recipient may respond by providing contrary evidence, a plan of action to improve the situation, or by requesting further information.[145] While there is no fixed compliance period, the national authorities must be afforded adequate time to answer the notification and reasonable time to remedy the situation.[146]

If the national authorities make the necessary improvements and cooperate with the Commission, the threat of listing recedes. If the situation has not been rectified within a reasonable period of time, the Commission will propose to the Council that the country is placed on the negative list. The Council will take the ultimate decision on a qualified majority basis.[147] The same process is followed in removing a country from the list. The burden of proof lies on that country to demonstrate that the situation has changed, and the Commission will consider whether the adopted measures are capable of facilitating a "lasting improvement of the situation".[148] So far, 25 countries have received a yellow card, of which ten have been rescinded; six countries have been formally listed, and three countries have been subsequently de-listed.[149]

---

[141] EU IUU Regulation, Art. 31(2).

[142] Ibid., Art. 32(1).

[143] Ibid., Art. 32(2).

[144] The yellow card made it "virtually impossible" for the Solomon Islands to develop alternative markets: www.abc.net.au/news/2015-02-03/tuna-industries-in-solomon-islands2c-png-and-tuvalu-warned-to-/6066732. Moreover, some countries (Spain) have operated an effective embargo on yellow-carded countries: see Hosch, note 88 at 47.

[145] EU IUU Regulation, Art. 32(1).

[146] Ibid., Art. 32(4).

[147] Ibid., Art. 33(1).

[148] Ibid., Art. 34(1).

[149] Information available at: https://ec.europa.eu/fisheries/cfp/illegal_fishing/info.

5. DO UNILATERAL MEASURES UNDERMINE
OR SUPPORT GLOBAL EFFORTS?

Insofar as they are not based on an international obligation, measures such as those adopted by the EU are unilateral in character. This does not *necessarily* make them problematic: sovereign States are not obliged to trade with one another and States have long been entitled to attach conditions in granting trade rights.[150] Market access can therefore be lawfully withheld by a State, typically to protect its own market or society or to influence other States to (not) act in a particular way. This right was confirmed in the *Nicaragua* case, where the ICJ declared that, absent a treaty commitment or other specific legal obligation, "a State is not bound to continue particular trade relations longer than it sees fit".[151] Where a State *is* bound to do so, for instance through its membership of the WTO, this situation is different and negative vessel- or country lists such as those unilaterally operated by the EU may run the gauntlet of WTO law, as considered by Churchill in Chapter 14 of this volume.

Notwithstanding their possible (il)legality, the coercive nature of unilateral trade-related measures is widely seen as undesirable. The UNGA has adopted several Resolutions strongly discouraging the use of economic measures – such as trade restrictions – by developed countries in order to induce economic, political, commercial or social change abroad.[152] Specifically concerning environmental matters, Principle 12 of the Rio Declaration declares that "unilateral actions to deal with environmental challenges outside the jurisdiction of the importing country should be avoided".[153] The IPOA-IUU and CDS Guidelines mirror this approach. The CDS clearly states that "multilateral or regional CDS are preferred",[154] while the IPOA-IUU observes the utility of multilaterally-agreed instruments such as CDS or multilaterally-agreed import prohibitions.[155] Such measures should comply with WTO law and it is explicitly stated that "unilateral trade measures should be avoided".[156]

Even the EU itself is much aware of this, as illustrated by its proposal for CCAMLR to be able to adopt trade-related measures to combat IUU fishing. Unlike other models, such as the ICCAT measures or the similar IOTC

---

[150] S Cleveland "Norm Internalization and U. S. Economic Sanctions" (2001) 26 *Yale Journal of International Law* 1–103, at 53.

[151] *Nicaragua v. United States*, Jurisdiction and Admissibility, Judgment, ICJ Reports 1984, para. 276.

[152] E.g. UNGA Resolutions 44/215 (22 December 1989), 46/210 (20 December 1991), 64/189 (9 February 2010).

[153] Report of the United Nations Conference on Environment and Development (Rio de Janeiro, Brazil, 3 to 14 June 1992) Annex I 'Rio Declaration on Environment and Development', Principle 12, 12 August 1992.

[154] CDS Guidelines, para. 5.

[155] IPOA-IUU Guidelines, paras. 68, 69.

[156] Ibid., para. 66.

scheme,[157] CCAMLR recommendations to adopt trade-related measures would not be binding on CCAMLR's Members. Nevertheless, the EU attached great importance to the identification coming *from* CCAMLR, emphasizing the legitimizing effect of multilateralism, whereby "the more it looks as if a single country is trying to use its economic clout to influence the policies of another country, the more difficult it might be to justify".[158]

This begs the question whether unilateral efforts to combat IUU fishing through trade-related measures strengthen or undermine global efforts. For reasons of space, the following sections only consider selected examples.

5.1. The Dangers of Unilateralism

Measures such as those adopted by the EU effectively exercise a self-appointed moral responsibility to ensure that other States comply with their obligations. A logical concern is therefore the risk of creating an unfair distribution of responsibilities.[159] When has a State 'done enough' and at what point is a powerful market State justified in intervening? The EU IUU Regulation amply exemplifies these challenges. The EU adopts a very broad interpretation of the nature of pertinent international obligations, and arguably goes beyond ensuring conformity with international (as opposed to EU) standards.

For instance, the Commission has habitually considered that compliance with RFMO CMMs is required by *all* States, regardless of the treaties they have ratified. This offends against the notion of *pacta tertiis* and reignites the question of whether unregulated fishing is always unlawful – which, as discussed above, is not automatically the case. The experience of Cambodia is particularly enlightening in this respect. Cambodia has not ratified either the Fish Stocks Agreement or the LOS Convention, nor is it a Member of any RFMO. Nevertheless, the Commission considered that Cambodia's failure to ensure compliance by its vessels with the conservation and management measures adopted by ICCAT and CCAMLR, which it could have done by deterring its vessels from fishing in their management area, constituted proof of a failure to fulfil its international obligations as a flag State.[160] In so doing, the Commission considered that flag States are obliged, as a matter of customary law, to ensure compliance by their vessels with RFMO CMMs, where these exist.[161] Cambodia

---

[157] IOTC Resolution 10/10.

[158] CCAMLR-XXXIII/25, Rev. 1 Annex A of 9 September 2014.

[159] Scott, note 115 at 100.

[160] Commission Decision of 15 November 2012 on notifying the Third Countries that the Commission considers as possible of being identified as non-cooperating Third Countries pursuant to Council Regulation (EC) 1005/2008 establishing a Community system to prevent, deter and eliminate illegal, unreported and unregulated fishing, [2012] OJ C354/1, 9–10.

[161] Ibid., 9.

was placed on the country negative list in March 2014 (precluding all trade in fishery products), where it still remains.[162]

The Commission has repeatedly adopted this line of reasoning. Another example is Togo, which received a yellow card in 2012,[163] which was only lifted two years later.[164] At the time of the Commission's decision, Togo was not a party to the Fish Stocks Agreement (although it has ratified the LOSC) nor a Member or a cooperative non-Member of any RFMO. Yet, as with Cambodia, Togo's reluctance to prevent its vessels from fishing in the Convention areas of various RFMOs, and its non-compliance with CCAMLR CMMs, led to the conclusion that it had failed in its flag State obligations under international law.[165]

The Commission furthermore requires compliance with 'soft' obligations such as paragraph 71 of the IPOA-IUU and Article 11 of the Code of Conduct, which advise States to improve the transparency of their markets and ensure traceability, which set good practices for responsible international trade. This was the case for Trinidad and Tobago. The Commission decided, *inter alia* on those grounds, that the country had failed to discharge its duties under international law as a flag and market State to prevent the presence of products stemming from IUU fishing to its market.[166] It received a yellow card in April 2016 that has not yet been lifted to date.[167] Though the need for market transparency and traceability may reflect shared social understandings, they are not (yet) legally binding obligations.

Concerns over power politics are prevalent when comparing those countries that have been sanctioned so far. Imports of fish and fish products from China, for example, are valued at over EUR 1.5 billion, and China's compliance with its international obligations regarding fishing are highly questionable.[168] Yet the EU's measures primarily identify developing third countries – including those that do not actually export to the EU, such as Tuvalu.[169]

---

[162] COM(2013) 819 final of 26 November 2013.

[163] Commission Decision, note 160 at 37.

[164] Notice of information of the termination of the demarches with third countries notified on 15 November 2012 of the possibility of being identified as non-cooperating third countries pursuant to Council Regulation (EC) No. 1005/2008 establishing a Community system to prevent, deter and eliminate illegal, unreported and unregulated fishing, [2014] OJ C364/2.

[165] Commission Decision, note 160.

[166] Commission Decision of 21 April 2016 on notifying a third country of the possibility of being identified as a non-cooperating third country in fighting illegal, unreported and unregulated fishing, 23 April 2016, OJ C144/14.

[167] Ibid.

[168] Note 113.

[169] Commission Decision of 12 December 2014 on notifying a third country of the possibility of being identified as a non-cooperating third country in fighting illegal, unreported and unregulated fishing, 13 December 2014, OJ C 447/23. In 2018, some 44% of these countries (11 out of 25) did not trade in fish with the EU.

The difficulty for any State in fairly distributing responsibilities and coming to the 'right' conclusion as to which States have acted sufficiently is also evident when comparing the IUU Regulation to measures adopted by the US. In a somewhat similar manner to the EU, the US prohibits the import of fish products from countries whose vessels have engaged in IUU fishing.[170] The Secretary of Commerce first notifies States of the possibility of being identified, triggering consultations with the relevant authorities on improving their fisheries management and enforcement practices, which that State must address within two years. The proceedings are documented in Biennial Reports to Congress which (1) identify countries for failing their international obligations, predominantly for violations of RFMO conservation measures by their vessels; (2) list (but not identify) countries 'of interest', for instance those whose vessels are also committing violations but which are being sanctioned for doing so; and (3) give a positive (or negative) certification of those countries that were identified in the previous report. A positive certification means that a country has documented corrective action to address the issues identified; a negative certification means that this is lacking and will lead to the denial of port privileges or import prohibitions. The US is moreover developing a Seafood Import Monitoring Program.[171]

Despite attempts to coordinate US and EU efforts through "voluntary cooperation and sharing of information on IUU fishing", according to a Joint Statement on IUU fishing signed in 2011,[172] the methodologies for identification and the countries identified by each market State continue to differ. It is clear that the US focuses on the identification of flag States, whereas this chapter has shown that the EU also considers (the lack of) actions by coastal-, port- and market States. Over the last decade, the US has identified various EU countries for failing in their flag State obligations, including France, Italy, Portugal and Spain – some of which have been identified multiple times for continuous violations and an enduring lack of corrective action.[173] This highlights the subjectivity of the listing exercise, and moreover shows that the EU *itself* has perhaps not 'done enough', despite purporting to take a strong lead in ensuring that others do. It must, however, be acknowledged that the EU continues to work on getting its own house in order.[174] This perceived lack of impartiality risks

---

[170] High Seas Driftnet Fishing Moratorium Protection Act, as amended by the Magnuson-Stevens Fishery Conservation and Management Act. See also the Illegal, Unreported, and Unregulated Fisheries Enforcement Act of 2015 (IUU Fisheries Enforcement Act), P.L. 114–81.

[171] 2017 Report to Congress, available at www.nmfs.noaa.gov/ia/slider_stories/2017/01/2017bienni alreport.pdf.

[172] Available at http://ec.europa.eu/archives/commission_2010-2014/damanaki/headlines/press-releases/2011/09/20110907_jointstatement_eu-us_iuu_en.pdf.

[173] All biennial reports are available at www.fisheries.noaa.gov/national/international-affairs/ identification-iuu-fishing-activities.

[174] The relevant measure for controlling compliance with the Common Fisheries Policy, the Control Regulation (No. 1224/2009) is currently under review.

undermining the legitimacy of its actions and harms the EU's self-proclaimed image as a global leader in combating IUU fishing.[175]

Moreover, the variable approaches emerging from different jurisdictions risks creating an excessive burden on exporters, particularly those from developing countries. The divergent approaches adopted by the EU and the US (and future strategies that may be considered by other major market powers) and the associated risk of fragmentation thus further call into question the merits of unilateral trade measures to combat IUU fishing.

5.2. A Role for Unilateralism?

By using their economic might, market States can provide the teeth that are arguably needed for strengthening multilaterally efforts, though care should be taken not to overestimate their bite. In 2006, the High Seas Task Force stated that

> there is very little hard evidence to date that restrictive trade measures are an effective solution to the IUU problem, although it may well be said that the threat that trade measures might be imposed is sufficient. In any event, restrictive trade measures are a blunt instrument, and best viewed as simply another potential weapon in the armory, for use when other measures have been exhausted.[176]

That said, the EU IUU Regulation could be a useful weapon in supporting the policies and procedures of RFMOs. For example, the EU operates an IUU vessel negative list that automatically incorporates vessels so listed by RFMOs[177] while one of the grounds on which a vessel shall be presumed to have engaged in IUU fishing includes fishing activities in the area of an RFMO in a manner inconsistent with its CMMs[178] and catch documents validated in conformity with CDS adopted by an RFMO may be accepted by the EU as if they were catch certificates for the purpose of the EU IUU Regulation.[179] At the same time, unilateral measures such as those adopted by the EU are not subject to political compromise between RFMO Members. This allows them to go further and allows them to be more specific. Moreover, the EU aims to ensure that demands of due process are met – though much remains to be improved – precisely *because* its unilateral character makes the Regulation more vulnerable to international scrutiny.[180]

---

[175] The EU is often cited as leading the fight against IUU fishing, not least by the EU itself. See e.g. Karmenu Vella's speech on the opening day of the Seafood Expo Global in Brussels, available at https://ec.europa.eu/dgs/maritimeaffairs_fisheries/magazine/en/policy/eu-markets-driving-good-governance-fisheries.

[176] High Seas Task Force, note 39.

[177] EU IUU Regulation, Art. 30.

[178] Ibid., Art. 3(1)(k).

[179] Ibid., Art. 13.

[180] European Commission Staff Working Document, SEC(2007) 1336, 17 October 2007, 68–69.

A good example is the vessel negative list. Unlike the heavily politicized RFMO IUU vessel lists, the process adopted by the EU IUU Regulation for placing a vessel on the EU IUU vessel blacklist (where this does not emulate that of an RFMO) is established in detail in the Regulation and provides for procedural safeguards that protect the owner or operator of the fishing vessel concerned. This may provide a welcome impetus for updating procedures within RFMOs. The EU IUU Regulation already provides a framework for exchanging information about IUU lists between the EU and RFMOs, which could be used as an avenue for discussing procedural rights. The EU IUU vessel blacklist is updated every three months, and the Regulation stipulates that the Commission shall provide for a system to automatically notify updates to EU Member States, RFMOs and any member of the civil society that requests this.[181] Both the EU IUU vessel negative list and the EU country negative list are then transmitted to RFMOs and the FAO "for the purposes of enhancing cooperation".[182]

Through their powerful interactions with existing international legal norms, unilateral trade-related measures may moreover help to maintain the relevance of these norms, and even contribute to their development.[183] Unilateralism can serve a useful function where multilateral action stagnates and can thus play a 'catalytic role' in the promotion and development of international regimes, particularly when it is "aimed at developing multilateral standards that are impartial and advances shared objectives, rather than parochial national interests".[184] In the past, unilateral actions have successfully shaped the law of the sea on numerous occasions, for example by facilitating the emergence of new customary norms.[185] It is indeed the EU's intention to fill the gaps left by multilateral efforts, possibly even with the formation of new norms in mind. In its Proposal for the IUU Regulation, the Commission considered that the EU would ultimately play a supporting role, because it would rely in the first place on multilateral action (in particular through RFMOs) and unilateral action would "only be used in case multilateral solutions prove insufficient to address serious manifestations of IUU fishing".[186]

The EU's actions are indeed provocative, but in so doing they may not only give effect to multilateral decisions but can instigate further decisions.[187]

---

[181] EU IUU Regulation, Art. 29(3).

[182] Ibid., Arts. 29(3) and 35.

[183] Forming part of a 'practice of legality', as considered by J Brunnée and S Toope *Legitimacy and Legality in International Law: An Interactional Account* (Cambridge University Press, Cambridge: 2010).

[184] D Bodansky "What's So Bad about Unilateral Action to Protect the Environment ?" (2000) 11 *European Journal of International Law* 339–347, at 345.

[185] A Boyle "EU Unilateralism and the Law of the Sea" (2006) 21 *International Journal of Marine and Coastal Law* 15–32.

[186] European Commission, note 180 at 69.

[187] See M Hakimi "Unfriendly Unilateralism" (2014) 55 *Harvard Journal of International Law* 106–150 (arguing that unilateral, and even unlawful, exercises of state power can buttress the rule of law); and M Rosello "Cooperation and Unregulated Fishing: Interactions between Customary

Even the aforementioned enforcement by the EU of what appear to be non-binding norms, such as the need for market transparency and full compliance with RFMO rules, can be seen in this light. They not only give effect to existing legal norms but aim to shape new ones, in the interests of the shared objective of combating IUU fishing. As such, they can be a valuable component of the global effort to combat IUU fishing.

However, in order to improve the perceived legitimacy of trade-related measures and enhance their potential to shape existing norms, it is important to further foster due process rights and other principles that will allow for a (greater) degree of accountability. This applies both to multilateral as well as unilateral efforts. Of particular importance is increased transparency and a clear duty to give reasons, which would strengthen the acceptability of these measures to those affected.[188] Without a duty to give reasons, a market State's decision that a country has failed in its international obligations remains opaque, potentially partisan, and susceptible to legal challenge. The CDS Guidelines show an awareness of this rationale for reasoned decisions. They state that adopted measures should be made available on relevant websites, and that "such notice should include an explanation of how domestic and imported products are treated to ensure even-handedness".[189]

A broad duty of transparency and reasoning that would extend beyond affected parties to external agents as well, such as NGOs, would further allow for critical reflection and discussion on the role of both unilateral and multilateral measures in combating IUU fishing.[190] It would provide a forum to debate the distribution of responsibilities amongst States, potentially reduce fragmentation through better insights into why certain measures are taken and what is expected and ultimately ensure that unilateral trade-related efforts find their place in the global fight against IUU fishing. The EU's yellow card process and practice of publishing its reasons in the EU's Official Journal is a step in this direction, albeit with considerable room for improvement.

6. CONCLUSION

This chapter has considered the recent progress made at the regional and global levels to combat IUU fishing. Notwithstanding laudable efforts, IUU fishing remains a highly complex problem encompassing a suite of different

---

International Law and the European Union IUU Fishing Regulation" (2017) 84 *Marine Policy* 306–312, at 308 (noting that the IUU Regulation provides an opportunity to contribute to the development of international law through consistent interpretive practice).

[188] B Kingsbury, N Krisch and RB Stewart "The Emergence of Global Administrative Law" (2005) 68 *Law and Contemporary Problems* 15–61, 39.

[189] CDS Guidelines, Art. 4(5)(b).

[190] A Buchanan and RO Keohane "The Legitimacy of Global Governance Institutions" (2006) 20 *Ethics and International Affairs* 405–436, at 428.

fishing activities, and therefore requires an array of different, and coordinated, responses. In the light of continuing problems such as the non-ratification of the Fish Stocks Agreement by key States and deficient enforcement of fisheries obligations, market States such as the EU are increasingly deploying their market power as both a carrot and stick against IUU fishing. This chapter has shown that such a tactic can strengthen and contribute to global efforts to combat IUU fishing by imposing an intimidating practical sanction for non-compliance, but can also generate additional problems in the process – including risks of fragmentation, obstacles to trade, and the unfair distribution of responsibilities.

In developing strategies against IUU fishing, the international community has demonstrated a strong preference for multilateral action. In this respect, the FAO has noted that RFMOs serve as the primary international bodies for the development of trade-related measures to combat IUU fishing.[191] Balancing the competing considerations of unilateral versus multilateral measures in the fight against IUU fishing, this chapter concludes that while the former have the *potential* to agitate for significant change, greater care should be taken that they follow a fair and non-discriminatory process; take into account the rights and interests of those affected; and ensure the greatest degree of transparency, including a broad duty to give reasons. Such standards can to some extent already be found in the law and jurisprudence of the WTO.[192] There is, however, merit in reflecting on these and similar standards *outside* the trade regime, specific to the context of the law of the sea and fisheries, for instance by building on the general obligations that can be found in the LOS Convention to cooperate, and to have due regard to the interests of other States. Without such standards, it is possible that any normative change achieved by unilateral activity to combat IUU fishing would be short-lived, and that such measures would "smack more of the nastiness of power politics than of the order and stability of law".[193]

---

[191] FAO, note 15 at 48.
[192] RB Stewart and MRS Badin "The World Trade Organization and Global Administrative Law" (2009) *IILJ Working Paper 2009/7 (Global Administrative Law Series)*, 12.
[193] Hakimi, note 187 at 111.

14

International Trade Law Aspects of Measures to Combat IUU and Unsustainable Fishing

ROBIN CHURCHILL

1. INTRODUCTION

O
VER THE PAST 20 years or so trade measures have been increasingly used to combat illegal, unreported and unregulated (IUU) fishing, as well as unsustainable fishing.[1] Such measures, defined in the following section, are called for by the IPOA-IUU, adopted by the UN Food and Agriculture Organization in 2001,[2] although, according to the Plan, they are only to be used in 'exceptional circumstances', where other measures have proved unsuccessful.[3] In practice, however, trade measures have not been used as sparingly as the IPOA-IUU might suggest. They have become recognized as a valuable tool in the fight against IUU and unsustainable fishing because they act as an economic disincentive to engage in such fishing by making it more difficult to find a market for the catch.[4] A recent study suggests that trade measures, at least where applied multilaterally, have been effective in combating IUU fishing and recommends that they should be continued

---

[1] The concepts of IUU fishing and unsustainable fishing, and the distinction between them, are discussed in Section 2 below.

[2] International Plan of Action to Prevent, Deter and Eliminate Illegal, Unreported and Unregulated Fishing, adopted by the FAO in 2001, paras. 65–76, available at www.fao.org/publications/card/en/c/71be21c9-8406-5f66-ac68-1e74604464e7.

[3] Ibid., para. 66.

[4] See further M Lack *Catching On? Trade-related Measures as a Fisheries Management Tool* (TRAFFIC International, Cambridge: 2007); MW Lodge et al. *Recommended Best Practices for Regional Fisheries Management Organizations* (Chatham House, London: 2007); OECD *Fish Piracy: Combating Illegal, Unreported and Unregulated Fishing* (OCED, Paris: 2004); and CA Roheim and J Sutinen *Trade and Marketplace Measures to Promote Sustainable Fishing Practices* (International Centre for Trade and Sustainable Development (ICTSD), Geneva: 2006).

and strengthened,[5] a recommendation also made by others.[6] Nevertheless, the utility of trade measures is limited by the fact that they can, of course, only be used in relation to that part of the marine fish catch that is internationally traded. This is estimated to be around 37 per cent of the total world catch.[7]

The previous chapter looked at measures to combat IUU fishing from the perspective of international fisheries law. This chapter examines such measures through the prism of international trade law. It begins by addressing some necessary, if perhaps rather obvious, questions of definition (Section 2), before outlining the various types of trade measure that have been used to combat both IUU and unsustainable fishing (Section 3). A constant refrain of the IPOA-IUU is that such measures should be compatible with international trade law.[8] The last, and major, part of the chapter is therefore concerned with this question. Section 4 outlines the relevant trade law, while Section 5 assesses how far the various types of trade measure outlined in Section 3 are compatible with the law discussed in Section 4. The focus of this chapter is thus on the compatibility of trade measures used to combat IUU and unsustainable fishing with international trade law. The question of the effectiveness of such measures lies beyond the scope of this chapter.[9] The chapter ends with some brief conclusions (Section 6).

2. SOME DEFINITIONAL ISSUES

So far reference has been made to 'trade measures' without attempting to define this term. For the purposes of this chapter a trade measure is any measure that prohibits, restricts or imposes conditions on the import or export of fish[10] with the aim of combating IUU or unsustainable fishing, regardless of how a measure is characterized by its author. This last point is important because some

---

[5] G Hosch *Trade Measures to Combat IUU Fishing* (ICTSD, Geneva: 2016), especially 58–60.
[6] See e.g. UR Sumaila *Trade Policy Options for Sustainable Oceans and Fisheries* (ICTSD, Geneva: 2016); Northwest Atlantic Fisheries Organization NAFO *Performance Assessment Review 2011*, 32–33 and 126, www.nafo.int/Portals/0/PDFs/gc/PAR-2011.pdf?ver=2016-02-24-141015-577; (US) *Presidential Task Force on Combating IUU Fishing and Seafood Fraud Action Plan for Implementing the Task Force Recommendations* (2015) www.iuufishing.noaa.gov/Portals/33/noaa_taskforce_report_final.pdf; and UN General Assembly Resolutions on sustainable fishing, e.g. A/Res/71/123 of 7 December 2016, paras. 87, 103 and 104.
[7] Hosch, note 5, at 3. Whether the proportion of IUU and unsustainably caught fish that is traded is at the same level is probably impossible to discover. It is estimated that about 18 per cent of the total world marine fish catch is the product of illegal fishing: see DJ Agnew et al. "Estimating the Worldwide Extent of Illegal Fishing" (2009) 4(2) *PLoS ONE* available at http://journals.plos.org/plosone/article?id=10.1371/journal.pone.0004570.
[8] IPOA-IUU, note 2 at paras. 65–68.
[9] See further Hosch, note 5; and MA Young *Trade-Related Measures to Address Illegal, Unreported and Unregulated Fishing* (ICTSD, Geneva: 2015).
[10] 'Fish' in this chapter refers both to unprocessed fish (e.g. fresh, chilled and frozen fish) and to processed fishery products.

measures that are in reality trade measures are characterized by their authors in other terms, notably as port State measures.[11] One trade measure of potential relevance is action against subsidies for fishing operations, a major problem in world fisheries because such subsidies often lead to over-capacity.[12] This type of trade measure will not be discussed in this chapter for the reasons that such subsidies are not directly a cause of IUU fishing; there is uncertainty as to how far the Agreement on Subsidies and Countervailing Measures of the World Trade Organization (WTO) applies to such subsidies;[13] and no action has ever been taken against WTO Members employing such subsidies, either by applying countervailing measures under the Agreement or by challenging such subsidies as a breach of the Agreement in proceedings under the WTO's Dispute Settlement Understanding (DSU).[14] Since 2001, Members of the WTO have been engaged in negotiations on a regime to control fisheries subsidies as part of the Doha Development Agenda, but no agreement has yet been forthcoming.[15]

This chapter is concerned with trade measures that target IUU and unsustainable fishing, and it is therefore necessary to say something about the meaning of each of these two terms. As regards IUU fishing, there is a tendency to use the term as though it refers to a monolithic concept, when in fact it refers to a variety of undesirable fishing activities.[16] Certainly, for the purposes of this chapter, the various elements that make up IUU fishing, as set out in the widely accepted definition of that term in Article 3 of the IPOA-IUU, need to be disaggregated.[17] 'Illegal' fishing refers either to fishing within the limits of national jurisdiction contrary to the laws of the relevant coastal State or to fishing within the regulatory area of a regional fisheries management organization (RFMO) by vessels

---

[11] Cf. the IPOA-IUU, which distinguishes between port State measures (paras. 52–64), some (but not all) of which are clearly trade measures (e.g. paras. 56 and 63), and 'internationally agreed market-related measures' (paras. 65–76). Virtually all of the latter are trade measures. A number of writers make a distinction between 'port States' and 'market States', the latter meaning States that deny access to their markets: see e.g. C Elvestad and I Kvalvik "Implementing the EU-IUU Regulation: Enhancing Flag State Performance through Regulatory Measures" (2015) 46 *Ocean Development and International Law* 241, at 241–242 and 243. However, as will become evident, these categories are not mutually exclusive. A State that prohibits a foreign fishing vessel from landing its catch in that State's ports for the purpose of sale is both a port State and a market State.

[12] See further UR Sumaila et al. "A Bottom-up Re-estimation of Global Fisheries Subsidies" (2010) 12 *Journal of Bioeconomics* 201–225; and World Bank *The Sunken Billions Revisited: Progress and Challenges in Global Marine Fisheries* (World Bank, Washington DC: 2017).

[13] Agreement on Subsidies and Countervailing Measures, of 15 April 1994 (1869 UNTS 14).

[14] Agreement establishing the World Trade Organization, Annex 2 Understanding on Rules and Procedures governing the Settlement of Disputes (1867 UNTS 3).

[15] Further on the application of international trade law to fisheries subsidies, see C-J Chen *Fisheries Subsidies under International Law* (Springer, Berlin: 2010); MA Young *Trading Fish, Saving Fish* (Cambridge University Press, Cambridge: 2011) 85–133; and R Barnes and C Massarella "High Seas Fisheries" in E Morgera and K Kulovesi (eds.) *Research Handbook on International Law and Natural Resources* (Edward Elgar, Cheltenham: 2016) 369–89, at 381–383.

[16] See further A Serdy *The New Entrants Problem in International Fisheries Law* (Cambridge University Press, Cambridge: 2016) 141–76.

[17] See also Chapter 13 of this volume (Van der Marel).

registered in a Member of that RFMO contrary to the latter's binding conservation and management measures. Trade measures have frequently been used against the latter type of illegal fishing, but only incidentally against the former type. For that reason the term 'illegal fishing' in this chapter will refer only to the latter type of unlawful fishing unless otherwise clearly indicated. The second element of IUU fishing, unreported fishing, refers to fishing activities that that have not been reported or have been misreported to the relevant coastal State or RFMO, contrary to a legal obligation to do so. It is therefore a form of illegal fishing. Thus, for the sake of simplicity, unreported fishing will not be distinguished in this chapter from other kinds of unlawful fishing but will be included in the term 'illegal fishing' as used above. The third element of IUU fishing, unregulated fishing, is defined in the IPOA-IUU as fishing in the regulatory area of an RFMO by stateless vessels or by vessels registered in a non-Member of that RFMO contrary to the latter's conservation and management measures, as well as fishing activities (whether within or beyond the limits of national jurisdiction) where there are no applicable conservation and management measures and where such activities "are conducted in a manner inconsistent with State responsibilities for the conservation of living resources under international law".[18] Trade measures have rarely, if ever, been used against the latter type of unregulated fishing, and so the term 'unregulated fishing' is used in this chapter to refer only to the former type of unregulated fishing unless otherwise clearly indicated.

Unlike the term 'IUU fishing', the term 'unsustainable fishing' has not been officially defined. In a narrow sense it refers to fishing for one or more fish stocks at a level that is not sustainable over a period of time, in other words at a level that will cause the size of the stock(s) concerned to decline. Unsustainable fishing in this sense is not synonymous with IUU fishing. It is true that illegal and/or unregulated fishing will often be at or lead to a level of fishing that is unsustainable, but it need not necessarily do so. Conversely, it is possible for lawful fishing to be unsustainable, for example if total allowable catches or total effort limits are set at excessive levels by the relevant management body. Apart from the definition just given, unsustainable fishing can also be given a broader meaning, where fishing activities are conducted in a way that is unsustainable for the marine environment as a whole. This includes activities that result in non-target species (not only fish but also fauna such as marine mammals or marine amphibians) being caught at levels where the long-term wellbeing of those species is threatened,[19] and fishing activities that damage habitats such as seamounts and coral reefs through trawling and dynamite fishing, respectively.[20] Unsustainable fishing in this broad sense may occur in

---

[18] IPOA-IUU, note 2 at para. 3.3.2.
[19] See further Chapter 8 of this volume (Scott).
[20] See further Chapter 9 of this volume (Dunn, Ortuño Crespo and Caddell).

both legal and illegal fishing. This chapter will deal with unsustainable fishing in both the narrow and broad senses just described, although trade measures against unsustainable fishing in the narrow sense have been used relatively infrequently.

Trade measures against illegal, unregulated or unsustainable fishing can only be used, of course, where fish is internationally traded.[21] That raises the question of when fish is traded. The answer to this question is not as straightforward as might be initially supposed. In broad terms, trade in goods occurs where goods originating in one State are transported to another State and sold there. But where do goods originate when they are taken from the sea? The answer to this question depends on rules of origin. Rules relating to the origin of marine fish have not (yet) been harmonized by the WTO,[22] so national rules of origin or the rules of origin contained in preferential trade agreements apply to determine whence fish originate.[23] Since it is clearly impossible to examine all or even a majority of such rules, a brief review of the rules of origin of the European Union (EU) will be given as an exemplar, as the EU is by far the world's largest importer and trader of fish.[24] EU law provides that where fish are caught in the territorial sea or internal waters of a particular State, they originate in that State. Where fish are caught beyond such waters, i.e. in the exclusive economic zone (EEZ) and on the high seas, the flag State of the vessel catching the fish is the State of origin.[25] Fish obtained or produced from factory ships is considered to originate from the flag State of the factory ship where the fish is supplied by a vessel having the same nationality and caught in the EEZ or on the high seas.[26] EU law does not specify what the position is where a factory ship and its supplying vessel have different nationalities or where fish is transhipped to a vessel other than a factory ship. In both cases it would seem likely that the State of origin will be the flag State of the vessel that caught the fish. Where fish has

[21] For simplicity's sake the terms 'trade' and 'traded' will be used henceforth in this chapter rather than 'international trade' and 'internationally traded'.

[22] See further A Serdy "Law of the Sea Aspects of the Negotiations in the World Trade Organization to Harmonise Rules of Origin" (2007) 22 *International Journal of Marine and Coastal Law* 235–56.

[23] The concept of preferential trade agreements is explained below: see text at note 64. On the origin of fish, see also the discussion below concerning the term 'introduced from the sea': see text at note 51. In general terms, fish become potentially subject to international trade law from the time that they are caught: see K Kulovesi "International Trade: Natural Resources and the World Trade Organization" in Morgera and Kulovesi, note 15, 46–65, at 48–53.

[24] FAO, *The State of World Fisheries and Aquaculture 2016*, 53–54, available at www.fao.org/3/a-i5555e.pdf.

[25] Commission Delegated Regulation (EU) No. 2015/2446 of 28 July 2015 supplementing Regulation (EU) No. 952/2013 of the European Parliament and of the Council as regards detailed rules concerning certain provisions of the Union Customs Code, *Official Journal of the European Union* (OJ) 2015 L343/1, Arts. 31(e) and (f), 44(f) and (h) and 60(f) and (g). In the case of the preferential rules of origin, there are also certain conditions to be fulfilled that are aimed at ensuring that there is a close link between a fishing vessel and its flag State.

[26] Ibid., Arts. 31(g), 44(i) and 60(h).

been processed, the State of origin will be the State on whose territory or on one of whose vessels the fish underwent its last, substantial, economically-justified processing or working resulting in the manufacture of a new product or representing an important stage of manufacture.[27] One consequence of the EU's rules of origin is that where a fishing vessel registered in State A lands a catch of fish at a port in State B, and the catch has been taken from outside B's territorial sea, this will constitute trade, with A being the exporting State and B the importing State. This is particularly significant where port States regulate the landing of catches from foreign vessels.

3. A SURVEY OF TRADE MEASURES USED TO COMBAT ILLEGAL, UNREGULATED AND UNSUSTAINABLE FISHING

3.1. Introduction

This section surveys the different types of trade measures that have been used against illegal, unregulated and unsustainable fishing. Such measures have been adopted multilaterally by international organizations (notably RFMOs), the Meetings of Parties to various treaties, and directly in the provisions of certain treaties. Measures have also been adopted unilaterally (in other words, a national measure adopted not in implementation of a multilateral measure) by a variety of States (notably the United States (US)) and the EU, even though the IPOA-IUU states that unilateral trade measures "should be avoided".[28] Some measures have been directed at States, others at individual fishing vessels.[29] These distinctions are important because, as will be seen, they bear upon the question of whether trade measures to combat illegal, unregulated and unsustainable fishing are compatible with international trade law.

As well as measures adopted at the multilateral level or by individual States, there are also measures adopted by non-governmental organizations (NGOs) relating to sustainable fishing that are capable of affecting trade. Of those, the best known is probably the certification scheme operated by the Marine Stewardship Council (MSC), which encourages sellers of fish products to attach appropriate labelling to products that have been derived from stocks that the MSC has certified as being sustainably fished.[30] The scheme is designed to influence consumer choice and may therefore indirectly affect the volume of trade.

---

[27] Regulation (EU) No. 952/2013 of the European Parliament and of the Council of 9 October 2013 laying down the Union Customs Code, OJ 2013 L269/1, Art. 60(2); and Reg. 2015/2446, note 25, Arts. 41(b) and 59(1)(b).

[28] IPOA-IUU, note 2 at para. 66.

[29] On the application of international fisheries measures to private actors, see Chapter 16 of this volume (Massarella).

[30] On the MSC and its certification scheme, see its website at www.msc.org/ and Chapter 4 of this volume (Stokke).

NGO measures will not be discussed in this chapter because international trade law does not apply to non-State actors.

In roughly descending order of severity (as well as frequency of use), the following types of trade measure to combat illegal, unregulated or unsustainable fishing have been used: bans on imports; restrictions on transhipments; landing requirements; catch documentation and similar schemes; and labelling requirements. Each will now be examined in turn.

3.2. Bans on Imports

Bans on the import of fish that is the product of IUU or unsustainable fishing have been used quite widely, both at the multilateral level and unilaterally. As pointed out in Section 2 above, where a fishing vessel lands its catch in the port of a State other than the State of its own nationality, that landing constitutes an import. Thus, a ban on landing amounts to a ban on imports,[31] as well as to a ban on the transit of the fish onwards to a third State if such transit had been intended. Bans on imports can also be applied to more conventional forms of trading, such as where fish is transported by road, rail or air.

At the multilateral level many RFMOs use import bans as a means of combating illegal or unregulated fishing in their regulatory areas.[32] Import bans for the same purpose are also to be imposed under the FAO's PSM Agreement.[33]

Import bans have also been imposed unilaterally (i.e. not in the implementation of the above multilateral measures) by a number of States (notably the US)[34] and the EU. Perhaps the best-known example is the EU's IUU Regulation.[35]

---

[31] See note 11 above on the relationship between port State measures and trade measures.

[32] For further details, see DS Calley *Market Denial and International Fisheries Regulation* (Martinus Nijhoff, Leiden: 2012) 103–159; Hosch, note 5 at 9–18; Lodge et al., note 4 at 54–65; R Rayfuse "Regional Fisheries Management Organizations" in DR Rothwell, AG Oude Elferink, KN Scott and T Stephens (eds.) *The Oxford Handbook of the Law of the Sea* (Oxford University Press, Oxford: 2015) 439–62, at 453–7; and J Swan *Implementation of Port State Measures: Legislative Template, Framework for Procedures, Role of Regional Fisheries Management Organizations* (FAO, Rome: 2016) 143–72, available at www.fao.org/3/a-i5801e.pdf.

[33] Agreement on Port State Measures to Prevent, Deter and Eliminate Illegal, Unreported and Unregulated Fishing of 22 November 2009, www.fao.org/documents/card/en/c/915655b8-e31c-479c-bf07-30cba21ea4b0, Arts. 9(4)-(6), 11(1) and 18(1). For comment on the Agreement, especially in relation to its provisions relevant to international trade law, see A Serdy "The Shaky Foundations of the Port State Measures Agreement: How Watertight is the Legal Seal against Access for Foreign Fishing Vessels?" (2016) 31 *International Journal of Marine and Coastal Law* 421, at 432–441.

[34] The US has a raft of legislation that authorizes the prohibition of imports of the products of IUU and unsustainable fishing. See National Oceanic and Atmospheric Administration, US Department of Commerce, *Improving International Fisheries Management. January 2017 Report to Congress* www.nmfs.noaa.gov/ia/slider_stories/2017/01/2017biennialreport.pdf. Annex II lists the legislation, while the main body of the report gives examples of its application.

[35] Council Regulation (EC) No. 1005/2008 of 29 September 2008 establishing a Community system to prevent, deter and eliminate illegal, unreported and unregulated fishing, amending Regulations (EEC) No. 2847/93, (EC) No. 1936/2001 and EC No. 601/2004 and repealing Regulations

The Regulation, *inter alia*, prohibits the landing of catches in the ports of EU Member States by foreign fishing vessels unless the catch is accompanied by a catch certificate and the vessel has provided specified information in advance. Landings by vessels on the EU's IUU vessel list or otherwise suspected of having engaged in IUU fishing are automatically prohibited.[36] There is also a prohibition on importing by means other than direct landings products obtained from IUU fishing and from non-cooperating States. Since the entry into force of the PSM Agreement in 2016, the prohibition on landings in the IUU Regulation should no longer be regarded as a unilateral measure, but rather as a means of implementing the Agreement. There is also a less well-known EU measure aimed at combating unsustainable fishing. Regulation 1026/2012 authorizes the imposition of quantitative restrictions on imports from third States that allow unsustainable fishing for stocks of common interest to the EU and that third State.[37] The Regulation was used for the first, and so far only, time against the Faroe Islands in 2013, giving rise to litigation in the WTO, discussed in Subsection 5.1 below.

3.3. Restrictions on Transhipments

It is not uncommon for fishing vessels to tranship their catches at sea. Quite often this is done to try to avoid detection for having engaged in IUU or unsustainable fishing.[38] Where a fish and the vessel to which the catch is transhipped both have the same nationality, no trade occurs. Where, however, the two vessels have different nationalities, and transhipment takes place outside the territorial sea of any State, there is a trading relationship, with the fishing vessel being the exporter and the vessel to which the catch is transhipped being the importer. Where such transhipment is made subject to conditions or is prohibited, it amounts to a restriction or ban on exports for the fishing vessel, and a restriction or ban on imports for the vessel to which the catch is transhipped. Where transhipment takes place in the territorial sea or internal waters (including ports) of a State other than the State of the nationality of the fishing vessel, there is also a trading relationship, with the coastal/port State being the importer. Any restriction on such transhipment will again amount to a restriction or ban on exports for the transhipping vessel and a restriction or ban on imports for the port State.

(EC) No. 1093/94 and (EC) No. 1447/1999, OJ 2008 L266/1. The Regulation is discussed in detail in the previous chapter; see also Hosch, note 5 at 27–38; and Elvested and Kvalvik, note 11.

[36] Ibid., Arts. 4(2), 6–8, 11(2) and 37(5).

[37] Regulation (EU) No. 1026/2012 of the European Parliament and of the Council of 25 October 2012 on certain measures for the purpose of the conservation of fish stocks in relation to countries allowing non-sustainable fishing, OJ 2012 L316/34.

[38] See further Lodge et al., note 4 at 52.

Transhipment in order to discourage IUU fishing has been regulated both at the multilateral level, by RFMOs[39] and the PSM Agreement,[40] and unilaterally by individual States and the EU.[41]

3.4. Landing Requirements

It is not uncommon for a coastal State to require foreign vessels permitted to fish in its EEZ to land all or part of their catches in its ports. Such a requirement is expressly included in the type of measures that the LOS Convention permits a coastal State to adopt in respect of foreign vessels fishing in its EEZ.[42] The reasons for laying down a landing requirement vary. In some cases the reason may be to provide raw material for fish processing plants in the coastal State or to provide food for direct consumption by the coastal State's population. In other cases the purpose of a landing requirement is to ensure that a foreign vessel is observing the coastal State's legislation and the conditions of its licence to fish.

It follows from what was said in Section 2 about the origin of fish that where a foreign vessel fishing in the EEZ lands its catch in the coastal State, it is exporting to that State, and conversely the coastal State is importing the catch. Thus, a landing requirement is a trade measure in the sense used in this chapter, albeit of a very unusual kind, since it requires a foreign vessel to export its catch to the coastal State and prohibits that vessel from re-exporting its catch to other States. Where a landing requirement is for the purpose of combating illegal fishing, it will be a trade measure of the kind relevant to this chapter.

3.5. Catch Documentation and Similar Schemes

The FAO defines a catch documentation scheme (CDS) as

> a system with the primary purpose of helping determine throughout the supply chain whether fish originate from catches taken consistent with applicable national, regional and international conservation and management measures, established in accordance with relevant international obligations.[43]

---

[39] For details, see ibid., at 53; Rayfuse, note 32, at 454–455.
[40] Agreement, note 33, Arts. 9(6), 11(1) and 18(1).
[41] See e.g. EU Reg. No. 1005/2008, note 35, Art. 4(3) and (4) and 5.
[42] United Nations Convention on the Law of the Sea of 10 December 1982 (1833 UNTS 3); Art. 62(4)(h).
[43] FAO, *Voluntary Guidelines for Catch Documentation Schemes* (2017; CDS Guidelines), para. 2.1, available at www.fao.org/fi/static-media/MeetingDocuments/CDS/TC2016/wpAnnex.pdf. The CDS Guidelines are discussed below, at notes 59 and following.

'The supply chain' referred to is defined as "a sequence of processes involved in the production and distribution of fish from catch to the point of import in the end market, including events such as landing, transhipment, re-export, processing, and transport".[44] Thus, a CDS requires fish throughout the supply chain (as just defined) to be accompanied by documentation showing whether it was caught lawfully or whether it is the product of IUU fishing. Where the documentation reveals the latter to be the case, or a consignment of fish lacks the relevant documentation, import should be refused. The aim of CDS, therefore, is to deny market access to illegally caught fish at all levels of the supply chain.[45] In trade law terms, CDS amount to a condition of import; and where import is refused, a ban on imports.

CDS and similar schemes have been adopted both at the multilateral level and unilaterally. At the multilateral level CDS have been adopted by some RFMOs and directly by treaty. As far as action by RFMOs is concerned, at the present time only three RFMOs (the Commission for the Conservation of Antarctic Marine Living Resources (CCAMLR), the Commission for the Conservation of Southern Bluefin Tuna (CCSBT) and the International Commission for the Conservation of Atlantic Tunas (ICCAT)) operate fully-fledged CDS, while three other RFMOs are in the process of developing CDS.[46] Some RFMOs have a more limited form of CDS, known as a catch certificate, which requires catches taken in the regulatory area of the RFMO concerned to be certified by the flag State as being within the set quota, properly reported, derived from authorized fishing operations and originating in an area confirmed through vessel monitoring systems data. A catch without such a certificate may not be landed or transhipped in the port of a Member of the RFMO concerned.[47] Unlike a CDS proper, a catch certificate does not accompany a catch for onward trade after landing.

A rather different form of trade documentation is provided for in CITES.[48] The Convention seeks to protect endangered species "against over-exploitation through international trade" by tightly controlling trade in such species.[49] It provides that trade in species threatened with extinction, listed in Appendix I, may only be authorized in exceptional circumstances, such authorization being evidenced by the grant of both an export permit and an import permit by the States concerned.[50] Where a listed species is "introduced from the sea", i.e. taken

[44] Ibid., para. 2.9.
[45] Hosch, note 5, at 7 and 10. See also 11–13 and 18–22, and Lodge, note 4 at 58–60 for detailed discussion of how CDS operate.
[46] Hosch, ibid., at 10–11. For a detailed study of CCAMLR's CDS, see Calley, note 32, at 150–159.
[47] Elvestad and Kvalvik, note 11 at 243.
[48] Convention on International Trade in Endangered Species of Wild Fauna and Flora of 3 March 1973 (993 UNTS 243).
[49] CITES, fourth preambular para.
[50] Arts. II(1) and III.

in the marine environment beyond the limits of national jurisdiction,[51] a certificate is required from the State of introduction. The latter is the flag State of the vessel that took the species concerned and is equivalent to the State of export.[52] Trade in species that are not immediately threatened with extinction but may become so unless trade is strictly regulated, which are listed in Appendix II, may only be authorized where trade will not be detrimental to the survival of the species concerned, such authorization being evidenced by the grant of an export permit or a certificate from the State of introduction, as the case may be.[53] In the case of both Appendix I and II species, where authorization is not forthcoming, trade is not permitted. Thus, in practice CITES either imposes a complete ban on trade or requires traded species to be accompanied by the documentation referred to. Fish of commercial interest were not originally included in the CITES Appendices. However, since 2002 the CITES Conference of the Parties (COP), which has the power to add and remove species from the Appendices, has added a number of fish species of commercial interest to the Appendices, including several species of shark.[54] The addition of marine fish to the CITES Appendices has proved extremely controversial, and attempts to add some species, such as toothfish and bluefin tuna, have been unsuccessful.[55] It is evident from the provisions of CITES that the object of listing marine fish is primarily to prevent unsustainable fishing. However, a Resolution of the CITES COP recommends that prior to issuing permits or certificates for listed species introduced from the sea, the States of introduction and of import shall take into account whether the species concerned is the product of IUU fishing.[56]

CDS and similar schemes have also been applied unilaterally. The best-known example is probably that set out in the EU's IUU Regulation, which establishes a catch certification scheme to be used where there is no applicable RFMO CDS. The scheme requires imports of fishery products into the EU from non-EU Member States to be accompanied by a catch certificate issued by the flag State of the vessel that caught the fish, certifying that the exported fish came from a catch made "in accordance with applicable laws, regulations and international conservation and management measures", or broadly speaking, was not the product of IUU fishing.[57] If the fish was processed in a State other than the

---

[51] See Art. 1(e), as read with a Resolution of the CITES Conference of the Parties, Resolution Conf. 14.6 (Rev. CoP16) (2013), 'Introduction from the Sea', available at https://cites.org/eng/res/14/14-06R16.php.

[52] Resolution Conf. 14.6 (Rev. CoP16).

[53] Arts. F II(2) and IV of CITES.

[54] Young, note 15 at 140–141.

[55] For the operation of CITES in relation to marine fish species, see Calley, note 32, 161–205; Young, note 15, 134–188, especially 141–154; and S Guggisberg *The Use of CITES for Commercially-Exploited Fish Species: A Solution to Illegal, Unreported and Unregulated Fishing?* (Springer, Heidelberg: 2016), especially 215–316.

[56] Resolution Conf. 14.6 (Rev. CoP16), note 52.

[57] Reg. No. 1005/2008, note 35, Arts. 12 and 13. For discussion of the scheme, see the literature listed in note 35. Hosch is particularly critical of the IUU Regulation: see Hosch, note 5 at 29–52.

flag State, there must also be a processing statement issued by that other State. Imports of fish without the required documentation are prohibited.[58]

In 2017 the FAO Conference adopted the CDS Guidelines.[59] The aim of the Guidelines is to provide assistance to States, RFMOs and others when developing and implementing new CDS, which are seen as "a valuable supplement" to port State and other measures.[60] The Guidelines emphasize that a CDS should be in conformity with relevant provisions of international law, including WTO agreements, and should "not create unnecessary barriers to trade," i.e. "be the least-trade restrictive measure to achieve its objective".[61] As will be seen in Section 4 below, this echoes wording in relevant WTO law.

3.6. Labelling Requirements

A requirement to label a fishery product to show that it is not the product of IUU or unsustainable fishing is designed to influence consumer choice, and is thereby potentially restrictive of trade.[62] There appear to be no requirements for mandatory labelling relating to IUU and unsustainable fishing that have been laid down at the multilateral level. The best-known proponent of unilateral mandatory labelling requirements is the US, exemplified by the Dolphin Protection Consumer Information Act, which lays down the conditions under which tuna products may be labelled as 'dolphin-safe'. Such a label signifies that the tuna has been caught by methods that minimized any bycatch of dolphins. Such bycatch has been considerable in certain tuna fisheries, particularly those in the Eastern Tropical Pacific.[63] This labelling measure is therefore designed to promote sustainable fishing in the broad sense.

4. AN OVERVIEW OF RELEVANT INTERNATIONAL TRADE LAW

As mentioned earlier, the main aim of this chapter is to assess the compatibility of the trade measures outlined in the previous section with international trade law. This section gives an overview of that law, while the following section assesses the compatibility of the various types of trade measures outlined in

---

[58] Ibid., Arts. 12(2) and 15.
[59] See note 43.
[60] Ibid., at paras. 1.2 and 1.3.
[61] Ibid., paras. 3 and 4.
[62] The European Court of Justice, e.g., has consistently held that a measure of an EU Member State designed to influence consumer choice in favour of products from that State is contrary to EU law on free movement of goods: see Case 249/81, *Commission v. Ireland* [1982] ECR 4005; and Case 102/86, *Apple and Pear Development Council v. Commissioners for Customs and Excise* [1988] ECR 1443.
[63] See further Chapter 8 of this volume (Scott).

the preceding section with that law. When the question of such compatibility is raised, it is common to think primarily or even exclusively about compatibility with WTO law. However, goods are increasingly being traded, not under the most-favoured-nation regime of the WTO, but under preferential trade agreements (PTAs) (often called regional trade agreements, including by the WTO, even though their application is frequently not regional in any geographical sense),[64] albeit that many of the provisions of such PTAs are frequently similar to those of WTO law. As of January 2018 there were 284 PTAs in force.[65] It follows that in order to ascertain whether a particular trade measure is compatible with international trade law, it is necessary to consider not only WTO law but also any relevant PTA. Clearly, in a chapter of this length it is impossible to consider the compatibility of the trade measures outlined in the previous section with PTAs, and so this section will be limited to considering only WTO law. Two of the WTO's so-called 'covered agreements' are relevant in this context, the GATT[66] and the TBT Agreement.[67] Each will be considered in turn.

4.1. General Agreement on Tariffs and Trade

There are four provisions of the GATT with which the measures outlined in Section 3 may be incompatible, namely Articles I.1, III, V and XI. However, even if a measure is incompatible with one or more of those provisions, it may not necessarily be unlawful as Article XX permits trade measures that would otherwise be inconsistent with the GATT if necessary to protect certain societal interests.

Article I.1 contains the most-favoured-nation principle, which prohibits a WTO Member[68] from discriminating between other WTO Members in relation to customs duties, other charges and all rules and formalities on imports or exports of 'like products'.[69] Article III sets out the principle of national treatment.

---

[64] PTAs may take one of two forms, a free trade agreement or a customs union: see Art. XXIV of the General Agreement on Tariffs and Trade (note 66 below).

[65] Information at www.wto.org/english/tratop_e/region_e/region_e.htm.

[66] General Agreement on Tariffs and Trade of 15 April 1994 (1867 UNTS 187). The 1994 GATT is the successor, and very similar, to the General Agreement on Tariffs and Trade of 30 October 1947 (55 UNTS 308).

[67] Agreement on Technical Barriers to Trade of 14 April 1994 (1868 UNTS 120).

[68] The term 'WTO Member' is used rather than 'Party to the GATT' as all WTO Members are automatically Parties to the GATT. The same applies to the TBT Agreement, discussed below.

[69] For a useful exposition by the Appellate Body as to its approach in determining whether a measure breaches Art. I.1, see its ruling in *European Communities – Measures prohibiting the Importation and Marketing of Seal Products* (hereafter *Seal Products* case), Report of the Appellate Body, WT/DS400/AB/R (2014), paras. 5.86–5.93. All the reports of WTO Panels and the Appellate Body referred to in this chapter can be found on the website of the WTO, www.wto.org/english/tratop_e/dispu_e/distabase_wto_members1_e.htm.

This principle requires an importing State not to discriminate between 'like' imported products and domestic products so as to afford protection to domestic production, either as regards internal taxation (Article III.2) or laws and regulations affecting the internal sale, transportation, distribution or use of goods (Article III.4).[70]

Article V provides for freedom of transit, stipulating that any WTO Member may transport goods across the territory of another WTO Member for export to any third Member. In this regard it prohibits discrimination "based on the flag of vessels, the place of origin, departure, entry, exit or destination, or on any circumstances relating to the ownership of goods, of vessels or of other means of transport". Lastly, Article XI.1, headed "General Elimination of Quantitative Restrictions", prohibits quantitative restrictions on imports and exports by providing that "[n]o prohibitions or restrictions other than duties, taxes or other charges ... shall be instituted or maintained by" any WTO Member on the import or export of any product from or to any other WTO Member. It therefore follows, as was confirmed by the report of the WTO Panel in *Colombia – Indicative Prices and Restrictions on Ports of Entry*,[71] that a WTO Member that refuses access to a ship registered in another Member to its ports for the purpose of unloading or loading goods for import or export to or from the first WTO Member, or for transit to or from a third State, would be acting contrary to Articles XI and/or V, and therefore would violate the GATT unless its action could be justified under Article XX.

As mentioned earlier, Article XX permits measures that would otherwise be inconsistent with the provisions of the GATT just outlined in order to protect certain listed societal interests. Three of those interests are potentially relevant in the present context. First, paragraph (b) permits GATT-inconsistent measures if they are "necessary to protect human, animal or plant life or health". The Appellate Body has held that if measures are to be justified under paragraph (b), they must be designed (i.e. have the policy objective) to protect human, animal or plant life or health.[72] Measures directed at unsustainable fishing fulfil that requirement as they are clearly designed to protect animal life. Insofar as alleged illegal or unregulated fishing leads to overfishing, as it frequently, but not automatically, does, measures to combat such fishing are also designed to protect animal life. Paragraph (b) stipulates that measures to protect animal life must be "necessary" if they are to be justified under Article XX. According to the Appellate Body, necessity relates to the necessity of the measure taken to achieve the policy objective, not the necessity of the policy objective itself. For a measure

---

[70] For a useful exposition by the Appellate Body as to its approach in determining whether a measure breaches Art. III.4, see its ruling in the *Seal Products* case, paras. 5.99–5.117.

[71] *Colombia – Indicative Prices and Restrictions on Ports of Entry*, Report of the Panel, WT/DS366/R (2009).

[72] P Van den Bossche and W Zdouc *The Law and Policy of the World Trade Organization* (Cambridge University Press, Cambridge: 2013) 554.

to be necessary, there must be no alternative measure reasonably available that would achieve the same objective but be less restrictive of trade.[73]

Second, paragraph (d) permits GATT-inconsistent measures if they are "necessary to ensure compliance with laws or regulations which are not inconsistent with the provisions [of the GATT]". 'Necessary' here has much the same meaning as in paragraph (b), in other words a measure is necessary if there is no alternative less trade-restrictive measure reasonably available.[74] In theory paragraph (d) is relevant to measures that target illegal fishing. However, in practice its relevance is rather limited as the Appellate Body has held that a WTO Member may not use paragraph (d) to ensure compliance with another WTO Member's obligations under an international agreement (which would include RFMO measures and the PSM Agreement), only compliance with its own national laws.[75]

The third societal interest relevant in the present context is set out in paragraph (g). This permits GATT-inconsistent measures "relating to the conservation of exhaustible natural resources if such measures are made effective in conjunction with restrictions on domestic production or consumption". The Appellate Body has held that 'exhaustible natural resources' include renewable marine living resources.[76] To be justifiable under paragraph (g), a measure must "relat[e] to" the conservation of such resources. That means that there must be a reasonable relationship between the measure and the conservation objective, i.e. the measure must not be disproportionately wide in its scope or reach in relation to the policy objective pursued.[77] Measures to combat unsustainable fishing and unregulated fishing, as in the second sense used in Section 2 above,[78] will clearly 'relate' to the conservation of exhaustible natural resources. However, it may not be so straightforward to show that measures targeted at illegal fishing and unregulated fishing, as used in the first sense, relate to the conservation of exhaustible natural resources since illegal and such unregulated fishing do not necessarily lead to overfishing, as explained in Section 2 above. In order for a measure to be justified under paragraph (g) of Article XX, it is also necessary that a measure is "made effective in conjunction with restrictions on domestic production or consumption". That means that there must be some restrictions on domestic products, although not necessarily identical to those on imports. The Appellate Body has characterized that requirement as "even-handedness in the imposition of restrictions, in the name

---

[73] Ibid., 556–560.

[74] *Korea – Various Measures on Beef*, Report of the Appellate Body, WS/DS161/AB/R (2001), paras. 157 and 166.

[75] *Mexico – Taxes on Soft Drinks*, Report of the Appellate Body, WS/DS308/AB/R (2006), paras. 69–78.

[76] *United States – Import Prohibition of Certain Shrimp and Shrimp Products* (hereafter *Shrimp/Turtle* case), Report of the Appellate Body, WT/DS58/AB/R (1998), paras. 128–134.

[77] Ibid., paras. 135–141.

[78] See text at note 19.

of conservation, upon the production or consumption of exhaustible natural resources".[79]

In order to be justified under Article XX, a measure must not only be for one of the societal interests listed in Article XX, it must also satisfy the requirements of that Article's introductory provision, the so-called '*chapeau*'. The latter requires that the measure that a WTO Member is seeking to justify under one of those interests must not be "applied in a manner which would constitute a means of arbitrary or unjustifiable discrimination between countries where the same conditions prevail, or a disguised restriction on international trade". Discrimination will be arbitrary or unjustifiable where the reasons for the discrimination bear no rational connection to the policy objective under which the measure was provisionally justified under Article XX or would go against it.[80] A measure will constitute a disguised restriction on trade if the design, architecture or structure of the measure does not pursue the legitimate policy objective on which the measure was provisionally justified, but in fact pursues trade-restrictive objectives.[81] The *Shrimp/Turtle* litigation suggests that the requirements of the *chapeau* of Article XX will be more easily satisfied if a measure implements an international agreement or there has been an attempt to engage in meaningful negotiations to conclude an international agreement to give effect to the desired policy objective.[82]

4.2. Agreement on Technical Barriers to Trade

The TBT Agreement deals with restrictions on trade that may result from 'technical regulations'. Only measures that are 'technical regulations' fall within the scope of the Agreement. A technical regulation is defined in Annex I.1 of the Agreement as:

> [A] document which lays down product characteristics or their related processes and production methods, including the applicable administrative provisions, with which compliance is mandatory. It may also include or deal exclusively with terminology, symbols, packaging, marking and labelling requirements as they apply to a product, process or production method.

---

[79] *United States – Standards for Reformulated and Conventional Gasoline*, Report of the Appellate Body, WT/DS2/AB/R (1996) 19–21.

[80] *United States – Measures concerning the Importation, Marketing and Sale of Tuna and Tuna Products*, Recourse to Art. 21.5 of the DSU by Mexico, Report of the Appellate Body, WT/DS381/AB/RX (2015), paras. 7.316, 7.329 and 7.343. Further on how to determine whether there is discrimination, see para. 7.301 and the *Seal Products* case, note 69, paras. 5.299–5.302.

[81] *United States – Import Prohibition of Certain Shrimp and Shrimp Products*, Recourse to Art. 21.5 of the DSU by Malaysia, Report of the Appellate Body, WT/DS58/AB/RW (2001), paras. 5.138–5.144.

[82] Ibid., and *Shrimp/Turtle* case, note 76 at paras. 166–172. See further the discussion of the case in Subsection 5.1 below.

In the *Seal Products* case the Appellate Body summed up and developed its existing jurisprudence on the meaning of this provision, stating that the scope of Annex I.1 "appears to be limited to those documents that establish or prescribe something and thus have a certain normative content".[83] As for the term 'product characteristics' that are the subject of such documents, these are "features and qualities intrinsic to the product itself" and include "objectively definable 'features', 'qualities', 'attributes' or other 'distinguishing mark[s]'", and may relate, for example, to a product's "composition, size, shape, colour, texture, hardness, tensile strength, flammability, conductivity or viscosity".[84] The terms 'related processes and production methods' have not yet featured in WTO litigation, but the Appellate Body considers that each individual term (process, production, method) has its ordinary dictionary meaning. The process or production method must be 'related' to the characteristics of the product in question, which means that it must be "connected or ha[ve] a relation to the characteristics of the product".[85] As for the second sentence of Annex I.1, the Appellate Body states that it "includes elements that are additional to, or may be distinct from, those covered by the first sentence".[86] There is no clear-cut distinction between technical regulations dealt with by the TBT Agreement and measures that are the subject of the GATT. Thus, in the *US – Tuna II (Mexico)* case (see Subsection 5.5 below) the Appellate Body assessed US labelling requirements for their compatibility with both the TBT Agreement and the GATT.

Article 2.1 of the TBT Agreement is similar to Articles I and III of the GATT. It requires WTO Members to ensure that in respect of technical regulations, products imported from other WTO Members are accorded 'treatment no less favourable' than that accorded to 'like' products of national origin and products originating in another country. In the *Tuna/Dolphin III* case the Appellate Body ruled that for a technical regulation to breach Article 2.1, it was not sufficient that the regulation modified conditions of competition in the market to the detriment of imported products; that detrimental impact must stem not from a legitimate regulatory distinction, but rather reflect discrimination against a group of imported products.[87] In short, there must be a lack of even-handedness in the treatment of imported products, amounting to arbitrary and unjustified discrimination.[88]

---

[83] *Seal Products* case, note 69 at para. 5.10. 'Documents' covers "a broad range of instruments or apply to a variety of measures" (ibid.).

[84] Ibid., para. 5.11.

[85] Ibid., para. 5.12. See also paras. 5.67 and 5.69.

[86] Ibid., para. 5.14.

[87] *United States – Measures concerning the Importation, Marketing and Sale of Tuna and Tuna Products* (hereafter *US – Tuna II (Mexico)*, Report of the Appellate Body, WT/DS381/AB/R (2012), para. 215.

[88] Ibid., paras. 213 and 216.

Article 2.2 of the TBT Agreement has parallels with Article XX of the GATT. It provides that technical regulations must not create

> unnecessary obstacles to international trade. For this purpose, technical regulations must not be more trade-restrictive than necessary to fulfil a legitimate objective, taking account of the risks non-fulfilment would create.

Such legitimate objectives include, "*inter alia*", protection of animal or plant life or health and the environment. The use of '*inter alia*' indicates that the list of objectives is not closed. According to the Appellate Body, the objectives listed provide a reference point from which other objectives may be considered legitimate. Objectives recognized in other WTO covered agreements "may provide guidance for, or may inform, analysis of what might be considered a legitimate objective under Art 2.2".[89] As for the requirement in Article 2.2 that technical regulations must not create "unnecessary obstacles to international trade" or be "more trade-restrictive than necessary", that provision is aimed at ensuring that restrictions on trade do not exceed what is necessary to achieve the legitimate objective concerned. In determining that question, it is necessary to consider what other less trade-restrictive measures may be reasonably available and the risks that would result from not fulfilling the objective concerned.[90]

Article 2.4 stipulates that where international standards exist, WTO Members must use them "as a basis for their technical regulations except when such international standards ... would be an ineffective or inappropriate means for the fulfilment of the legitimate objectives pursued". According to the Appellate Body, an international standard is one adopted by a body that has recognized activities in standardization and whose membership is open to all WTO Members.[91] Article 2.5 provides that there is a rebuttable presumption that a technical regulation adopted for the one of the legitimate objectives mentioned in Article 2.2 and that is "in accordance with" relevant international standards does not create an unnecessary obstacle to international trade.

5. AN ASSESSMENT OF THE COMPATIBILITY OF TRADE MEASURES TO COMBAT ILLEGAL, UNREGULATED AND UNSUSTAINABLE FISHING WITH INTERNATIONAL TRADE LAW

An assessment will now be made of the compatibility of each of the five types of trade measures reviewed in Section 3 with the provisions of WTO law outlined in Section 4. For reasons of space it will not be possible to try to determine definitively whether every particular measure referred to in Section 3 is compatible. Rather what will be done will be to indicate the questions that will need to

---

[89] Ibid., para. 313.
[90] Ibid., paras. 318–22.
[91] Ibid., para. 359.

be considered for such a determination to be made. In doing so, reference will be made to those cases where trade measures identified in Section 3 have been challenged for their compatibility with WTO law under the WTO's DSU. An important, if rather obvious, preliminary point (but one overlooked by some writers) is that multilateral measures in the form of RFMO decisions and treaties cannot be challenged directly under the DSU as RFMOs and treaty COPs are not Members of the WTO. Rather it is the implementation of an RFMO measure by an RFMO Member or the implementation of a treaty by a State Party to the treaty that can be challenged where that RFMO Member or State Party is a Member of the WTO.

5.1. Bans on Imports

It is widely accepted that a ban on imports, whether in the form of a prohibition on the direct landing of catches in port or on the import of fishery products by other means, is a quantitative restriction and therefore contrary to Article XI of the GATT.[92] That proposition has, however, has been challenged by Serdy. He argues that because Article XI refers to "the importation of any product *of the territory* of any other contracting party" (emphasis added), it cannot apply to fish directly landed at a foreign port as the fish is not the product of any 'territory' but of the sea.[93] It must be doubted whether this literal reading of Article XI is correct. Article XI was drafted in the late 1940s, when most fishing vessels landed their catches in their home port, so no trade occurred. In view of this, it may be doubted whether the drafters of the GATT gave much thought to fish trade in the form of direct landings. In the *Shrimp/Turtle* case the Appellate Body employed an intertemporal approach to interpretation, as well as making reference to other international instruments to interpret the GATT.[94]

Employing a similar approach, and noting that both the rules of origin and CITES treat the flag State as equivalent to the State of export, one could, and arguably should, interpret 'territory' in Article XI to include vessels of the flag State in the case of marine fish caught outside the territorial sea. Article III.4 uses the same phrase as Article XI (apart from the plural), "products of the territory". Thus, if Serdy was correct, direct landings of fish in a foreign port would fall outside the scope of two of the central provisions of the GATT. It must be doubted whether that was really the intention of the drafters of the GATT. Furthermore, a very literal construction could consider that fish products landed in one State and transported in an unprocessed form to another State were also not products of the territory of the first State, thus creating an even bigger loophole in the GATT.

---

[92] See e.g. the literature listed in note 95 below.
[93] Serdy, note 33 at 433.
[94] *Shrimp/Turtle* case, note 76 at paras. 129–131.

If the would-be exporter intended that its fish should simply transit the territory of the State imposing the landing ban for onward transport to a third State, there would also be a breach of Article V on the right of transit. Furthermore, import bans that target individual named States, as a few RFMO measures have done, raise questions as to their compatibility with Article I.1 of the GATT as they appear to discriminate between imports from different States.

Import bans that are incompatible with Articles I.1, V and XI.1 of the GATT may nevertheless be lawful if they can be justified under Article XX. It follows from the discussion of Article XX in Subsection 4.1 above that an import ban to combat illegal, unregulated and unsustainable fishing may be justified under paragraph (b) if its purpose is to protect animal life and if it is "necessary", i.e. there is no alternative measure reasonably available that is less restrictive of trade. Import bans for the purpose of combating unsustainable fishing will generally have no difficulty in fulfilling the first requirement. The position with bans aimed at illegal and unregulated fishing is not quite so straightforward, as explained below. Whether import bans fulfil the second requirement (the unavailability of less trade-restrictive measures) will depend on the circumstances of each case. Where an import ban is a sanction for non-compliance with a CDS or similar scheme, it would seem easier to show that this requirement is satisfied. An import ban may, additionally or alternatively, be justifiable under paragraph (g) as being a measure "relating to the conservation of exhaustible natural resources". Since illegal or unregulated fishing does not necessarily lead to overfishing, an import ban aimed at combating such fishing may be easier to justify under paragraph (g) than paragraph (b), since it may be more straightforward to show that it 'relat[es] to' fisheries conservation, rather than having to show that it is designed for conservation, as is necessary under paragraph (b). A State seeking to justify an import ban under paragraph (g) also has to show that the ban had been made effective in conjunction with restrictions on its domestic fishing industry. So, for example, in the case of a ban on imports from unregulated fishing, the importing State would have to show that its own vessels were prevented from fishing in the area concerned in a manner contrary to its international responsibilities.

If an import ban can be provisionally justified under paragraphs (b) and/or (g), it must still satisfy the requirements of the *chapeau* of Article XX in order to be lawful. It follows from the *Shrimp/Turtle* case that it is easier to show that an import ban does not constitute arbitrary or unjustifiable discrimination or a disguised restriction on trade if it has been imposed pursuant to an international agreement. Thus import bans that are imposed to implement RFMO measures, the PSM Agreement or CITES are likely to satisfy the *chapeau*.[95] An important question is whether that is also the case where action is taken against a WTO Member that is not a Member of the RFMO concerned or a Party to the

---

[95] This is a widely held view: see Calley, note 32 at 219; Roheim and Sutinen, note 4; RG Tarasofsky *Regional Fisheries Organizations and the World Trade Organization: Compatibility or Conflict?* (TRAFFIC International, Cambridge: 2003) 18–29; and Young, note 15 at 77 and literature cited there.

treaties mentioned. In the case of CITES there should be no problem, as virtually all Members of the WTO are Parties to CITES. While there is an argument that action cannot be taken against non RFMO Members or non-Parties to a treaty,[96] an alternative (and preferable) view is that given the general hostility of the international community to IUU fishing, as reflected in numerous international instruments, the treaties and RFMO measures mentioned should be seen as reflecting the interests of the international community and therefore on that basis should not be regarded as arbitrary or unjustifiable discrimination or a disguised restriction on trade. After all, the Appellate Body in the *Shrimp/Turtle* case did not suggest that it was a necessary condition that the defendant WTO Member had to have concluded a treaty or entered into negotiations with the complainant WTO Member in order for a measure not to be adjudged arbitrary or unjustifiable discrimination or a disguised restriction on trade. It may also be significant that the import bans imposed by RFMO Members against non-Members have so far never been challenged under the DSU as being contrary to the GATT.

It follows from discussion above that it will be more difficult for a WTO Member to show that an import ban that it has imposed unilaterally, i.e. not in implementation of an international measure, satisfies the requirements of the *chapeau* of Article XX. The position is complicated by the fact that it is still unclear whether or how far a WTO Member may seek to protect a societal value outside its own territorial jurisdiction and still be in conformity with Article XX.[97] That it is more difficult to justify unilateral measures is shown by the fact that such measures have to date been challenged in five cases, each of which will now be discussed briefly.

The first two cases were brought, not under the DSU, but under the pre-WTO dispute settlement procedures of the 1947 GATT. In *Tuna/Dolphin I*, Mexico challenged a US ban on imports of tuna that had been imposed because Mexico did not have in place a regulatory regime for avoiding the incidental catch of dolphins in tuna fisheries that was comparable to the US regime. The US ban was thus a trade measure to combat unsustainable fishing in the broad sense. The Panel found that the import ban was a breach of Article XI of the GATT and could not be justified under either paragraphs (b) or (g) of Article XX because, in seeking to change the policies of other States towards the tuna/dolphin bycatch issue, the ban failed to satisfy the tests of necessity in paragraph (b) and relatedness in paragraph (g).[98] Three years later, in *Tuna/Dolphin II*, another Panel reached the same conclusion in relation to a US ban on

---

[96] This argument is made by Serdy, note 33 at 435.

[97] In the *Shrimp/Turtle* and *Seal Products* cases the Appellate Body explicitly left this point open: see note 76 at para. 133 and note 69 at 5.173, respectively. See further B Cooreman "Addressing Environmental Concerns through Trade: A Case for Extraterritoriality" (2016) 65 *International and Comparative Law Quarterly* 229.

[98] *United States – Restrictions on Imports of Tuna*, GATT document DS21/R (Mexico) (1991), reproduced in (1991) 30 *International Legal Materials* 1594. The Panel's report was not adopted by the Parties to the GATT and therefore was not legally binding.

imports of processed tuna where the raw material came from fisheries that failed to meet the US regulatory standard on dolphin bycatch.[99]

Some years later, after the establishment of the WTO, there was another, not dissimilar, case involving the US. Concerned by the high level of turtle bycatch in some shrimp fisheries, the US banned the import of shrimps that were caught with gear that had not been fitted with a turtle excluder device (TED). Thus, the ban was directed at unsustainable fishing in the broad sense. The ban was challenged by a number of Asian States in the *Shrimp/Turtle* case. The Appellate Body (reversing the Panel on many points) found that that the ban was a breach of Article XI of the GATT, but was provisionally justified under paragraph (g) of Article XX as turtles were an exhaustible natural resource, the ban was reasonably related to the legitimate policy objective of conserving turtles, and it had been made effective in conjunction with domestic producers, as US shrimp fishermen were also required to use TEDs. However, the US ban did not meet the requirements of the *chapeau* of Article XX because it constituted arbitrary and unjustifiable discrimination. Discrimination was arbitrary because there was a lack of due process in dealing with applications for import licences. The discrimination was also unjustifiable because the US had applied the same standard to all shrimp fisheries without taking into account the different conditions prevailing in the complainant WTO Members and because the US had failed to engage in negotiations with the complainants to address a problem that could only be sufficiently addressed through multilateral cooperation.[100]

Following the Appellate Body's ruling, the US amended its legislation. Malaysia challenged that amendment under Article 21.5 of the DSU (dealing with compliance with rulings), arguing that the US had failed to implement the ruling correctly. However, the Appellate Body rejected that challenge. The US measure no longer amounted to arbitrary or unjustifiable discrimination as the same standard (the use of TEDs) was no longer applied: instead, exporting States were required to have a programme of comparable effectiveness. Furthermore, the US had engaged in negotiations with Indian and Pacific Ocean States (including the original complainants) and had concluded a Memorandum of Understanding on turtle conservation; it was not necessary that a legally binding agreement should have been adopted.[101]

In the two other cases where a unilateral import ban was challenged under the DSU, the parties reached a settlement of the dispute before a WTO Panel was called on to give a ruling. The first case concerned a ban by Chile on the landing in its ports of swordfish caught by EU vessels on the high seas of the

---

[99] *United States – Restrictions on Imports of Tuna*, GATT document DS29/R (Netherlands and the European Community) (1994), reproduced in (1994) 33 *International Legal Materials* 839. The Panel's report was not legally binding for the same reason as in the previous case.

[100] *Shrimp/Turtle* case, note 76 at paras. 161–176.

[101] *Shrimp/Turtle case Recourse to Art. 21.5*, note 81.

South-east Pacific. This could be characterized as a measure directed at alleged unregulated and/or unsustainable fishing. The EU commenced proceedings against Chile in 2000, arguing that the ban breached Articles V and XI of the GATT.[102] At the same time Chile instituted proceedings against the EU before the International Tribunal for the Law of the Sea, arguing that the EU was in breach of its obligations under the LOS Convention to cooperate over fisheries conservation. Both sets of proceedings were suspended in 2001, when the parties reached a provisional settlement, and terminated in 2009, when the parties reached a definitive settlement.[103]

In the second case the EU was the respondent rather than the complainant. In 2013, it imposed a ban on imports of herring and mackerel from the Faroe Islands under its Regulation on unsustainable fishing.[104] Denmark (on behalf of the Faroes) challenged the ban as a breach of Articles I, V and XI of the GATT. It also brought proceedings against the EU before an arbitral tribunal constituted under Annex VII of the LOS Convention, arguing that the EU had breached obligations of cooperation under the Convention. Both proceedings were terminated in 2014, when the parties reached a settlement of the dispute.[105]

5.2. Restrictions on Transhipments

It was concluded in Subsection 3.3 above that restrictions on transhipment constitute, in trade law terms, a prohibition on imports and exports where transhipment takes place outside the territorial sea of any State and is between vessels of different nationalities, or where transhipment takes place in the territorial sea or port of a State other than the flag State of the fishing vessel. In those situations it follows from what was said in Subsections 4.1 and 5.1 above that the resulting restrictions on imports and exports are contrary to Article XI of the GATT and will only be lawful if they can be justified under Article XX of the GATT. What was said in Subsection 5.1 about Article XX will apply equally here.

5.3. Landing Requirements

As observed in Subsection 3.4 above, a coastal State that requires foreign vessels fishing in its EEZ to land their catches in its ports is effectively compelling such

---

[102] *Chile – Measures affecting the Transit and Importation of Swordfish*, WT/DS193.

[103] See further R Churchill "Dispute Settlement under the UN Convention on the Law of the Sea: Survey for 2009" (2010) 25 *International Journal of Marine and Coastal Law* 457–482, at 463–464.

[104] See text at note 37.

[105] *European Union – Measures on Atlanto-Scandian Herring*, WT/DS469.

vessels to export to it, and thereby preventing them from re-exporting to other States. In other words, it is a restriction on exports. It will therefore be contrary to Article XI of the GATT. The question then is whether a landing requirement may nevertheless be permissible under Article XX of the GATT. If the purpose of the landing requirement is to ensure that foreign vessels fish lawfully in the coastal State's EEZ, the measure may be provisionally justified under paragraph (d) of Article XX as being "necessary to ensure compliance" with its laws or regulations, provided that there were no less trade-restrictive alternative measure available to ensure compliance with the coastal State's legislation, such as at-sea enforcement or some form of collaborative enforcement between the coastal State and the flag State. Whether such an alternative was readily available and was as effective as a landing requirement would depend on the circumstances of each case. If the landing requirement could be provisionally justified under paragraph (d) of Article XX, it would then have to meet the requirements of the *chapeau*. Provided that a coastal State applied equally strict measures to ensure that its own vessels fishing in its EEZ complied with its legislation, there should be no question of arbitrary or unjustifiable discrimination. Nor would a landing requirement appear to be a disguised restriction on trade as the LOS Convention specifically authorizes coastal States to prescribe landing requirements for foreign vessels.[106] The position would probably be different, however, if foreign vessels were prohibited from re-exporting their catches but the coastal State's vessels were allowed to export their catches, as that would constitute unjustified discrimination.

A landing requirement designed to ensure compliance with the coastal State's laws could possibly also be justified under paragraph (g) of Article XX as being reasonably related to the need to conserve fish. The compatibility with the GATT of a landing requirement for the purposes of conservation was considered by a Panel established under the Canada-US free trade agreement in a case that concerned a Canadian measure requiring vessels fishing in Canadian waters to land their catches of herring and salmon in Canada.[107] Although established under the Canada-US free trade agreement, the Panel was required to consider the relevant provisions of the GATT. It found that Canada's measure was a restriction on exports and therefore contrary to Article XI.1 of the GATT. The measure could not be justified under paragraph (g) of Article XX of the GATT because a landing requirement that applied to 100 per cent of catches was not primarily aimed at conservation and therefore was not a measure "relating to the conservation of exhaustible natural resources" within the meaning of paragraph (g) of Article XX. However, the Panel suggested that a landing requirement would be justified under paragraph (g) "if provision were

---

[106] See text at note 42 above.
[107] *Canada's Landing Requirement for Pacific Coast Salmon and Herring*, Report of the Panel, 16 October 1989, http://publications.gc.ca/collections/collection_2016/alena-sec-nafta/E100-2-1-89-1807-01-eng.pdf.

made to exempt from landing that proportion of the catch whose exportation without landing would not impede the data collection process" used for conservation and management purposes.[108] Since that decision was given (in 1989), the case law on Article XX has developed significantly and the LOS Convention, which authorizes a landing requirement, has come into force. It may well be, therefore, that a less strict approach would be taken today.

5.4. Catch Documentation and Similar Schemes

A CDS may fall within the scope of both the GATT and the TBT Agreement and be potentially incompatible with either or both. In practice, no CDS has yet been challenged under the WTO's DSU for its compatibility with either agreement.

In the case of the TBT Agreement, the first question is whether a CDS is a 'technical regulation' as defined in Annex I.1 of the Agreement and therefore falls within the scope of the Agreement. Applying the various elements in Article I.1 outlined in Subsection 4.2, a CDS obviously requires the mandatory use of a 'document'. However, the documentation required in a CDS would not seem to lay down 'product characteristics'. Such documentation is concerned with where fish is caught and whether the vessel that caught it complied with RFMO or other applicable conservation and management measures. It is not concerned with the 'characteristics' of the fish within the meaning of Annex I.1 – an illegally caught fish has exactly the same product characteristics as a legally caught fish. A CDS may be concerned with 'production methods' if, for example, an RFMO prohibits the use of a particular type of fishing method (such as longlining) and the documentation is required to show the method of fishing employed. The question then is whether the production method specified is 'related to', i.e. connected or having a relation to the product characteristics of the fish. It seems very unlikely that this will be the case, since fish will have the same characteristics howsoever caught. The second sentence of Annex I.1 is plainly not relevant in the present context. It thus seems very unlikely that a CDS is a technical regulation. This conclusion is supported by the *Seal Products* case where the Appellate Body found the measure at issue was not a technical regulation, primarily because it was concerned with the identity of the hunter and the type or purpose of the hunt from which the product was derived: those were not product characteristics.[109]

However, determining whether a measure is or is not a technical regulation within the meaning of Annex 1.1 of the TBT Agreement is clearly not an

---

[108] Ibid., at para. 7.40.
[109] *Seal Products* case, note 69 at paras. 5.41, 5.45 and 5.55. The Appellate Body decided that it did not have the information to consider whether the measure might relate to processes or production methods: see para. 5.69.

exact science. In the *Seal Products* case, for example, the Panel and the Appellate Body reached diametrically opposed conclusions as to whether the measure at issue in that case was a technical regulation. It would be wise, therefore, to consider the position in the (unlikely) situation that a CDS was considered to be a technical regulation, and specifically its compatibility with Article 2 of the TBT Agreement. As long as a WTO Member applies a CDS equally to all foreign vessels, and the CDS or a measure of equivalent effectiveness to catches landed by its own vessels, there should be no question of a breach of Article 2.1. That leads on to a consideration of Article 2.2, in particular the question of whether a CDS is more trade-restrictive than necessary to fulfil a legitimate objective. It may be argued that combating IUU fishing is a legitimate objective even though, as suggested earlier, it does not directly relate to the "protection of ... animal ... life or health" or protection of the environment, the only two potentially relevant objectives explicitly mentioned in Article 2.2. However, the list of 'legitimate objectives' in Article 2.2 is not closed. Given the extensive opposition to IUU fishing expressed by the international community over many years in, for example, the IPOA-IUU, PSM Agreement, the actions of RFMOs and numerous UN General Assembly Resolutions, it would seem reasonable to regard action to combat IUU fishing as a legitimate objective for the purposes of Article 2.2. The question then is whether a CDS is more trade-restrictive than necessary to fulfil that objective. Having to compile and show the necessary documentation would not seem to be excessively burdensome, and there does not appear to be any obvious alternative to a CDS that would be less trade-restrictive.

Article 2.4 of the TBT Agreement, it will be recalled, requires technical regulations to be based on international standards unless the latter are ineffective or inappropriate for the fulfilment of the legitimate objective pursued by the technical regulation in question. That raises the question of whether RFMO CDS may be regarded as international standards. The answer would appear to be that they are not. RFMOs are not recognized as having standardizing functions, nor is their membership open to all WTO Members. The position with the FAO is arguably different. It does have standardizing functions (for example, in relation to fish hygiene) and its membership is open to all WTO Members (with the possible exceptions of Chinese Taipei, Hong Kong and Macau). Thus, the CDS Guidelines (discussed in Subsection 3.5 above) would seem to be an international standard. As those Guidelines appear to be neither ineffective nor inappropriate, a CDS must be based on them. Those CDS that are so based and whose objective is to combat IUU fishing will be presumed not to create an unnecessary obstacle to international trade and will therefore be lawful under the TBT Agreement.

Turning now to the compatibility of a CDS with the GATT, the two provisions of the latter with which there may be potential incompatibility are Articles I.1 and III.4. As regards Article I.1, a CDS comes within the 'rules and formalities' of import and export referred to in that provision. It is thus necessary that a WTO Member, when implementing an RFMO scheme or CITES, or applying its own unilateral scheme, does not discriminate between the imports of fish from other WTO Members. As for Article III.4, a measure of a WTO Member that implements an international CDS or applies its own scheme is a law, regulation or requirement affecting the internal sale of fish and thus comes within the scope of Article III.4. That means that the CDS must not lead to less favourable treatment for imported fish than fish caught by that State's own vessels. As long as the latter are subject to the CDS or some other catch certification requirement that is equivalent in effect, there should be no question of a breach of Article III.4. It should therefore be a straight-forward matter to ensure that a CDS is compatible with Articles I.1 and III.4 of the GATT.

Those CDS that stipulate that non-compliance with their provisions requires imports of the products concerned to be prohibited, would seem to breach Article XI of the GATT. They may, however, be saved by Article XX. What was said in Section 5.1 about Article XX will apply equally here.

5.5. Labelling requirements

A measure requiring fishery products to be labelled in order to show whether or not they are the product of IUU or unsustainable fishing may fall within the scope of both the GATT and the TBT Agreement and be potentially incompatible with either or both. In the case of the TBT Agreement, the first question is whether a labelling scheme is a 'technical regulation' as defined in Annex I.1 of the Agreement and therefore falls within the scope of the Agreement. It may be recalled from the discussion of the meaning of Annex I.1 in Section 4.2 above that a technical regulation may include a measure requiring the use of certain labels, whether supplementary to or unconnected with measures relating to the characteristics, processes and production methods of a particular product. Thus, a mandatory labellling scheme is a technical regulation, as confirmed by WTO jurisprudence.[110] The question then is whether a labelling scheme is compatible with Article 2 of the TBT Agreement. As long as a WTO Member applies a labelling scheme equally to all foreign vessels and to its own vessels, there should be no question of a breach of Article 2.1. As regards Article 2.2, the same points may be made as were made above in relation to CDS.

Article 2.4 of the TBT Agreement, it will be recalled, requires technical regulations to be based on international standards unless the latter are ineffective or inappropriate for the fulfilment of the legitimate objective pursued by the technical regulation in question. Bearing in mind what was said about the

---

[110] See Van den Bossche and Zdouc, note 72 at 857–858.

FAO as a standardizing body in Section 5.4, the FAO's Ecolabelling Guidelines would appear to be effective and appropriate international standards.[111] A labelilng scheme must therefore be based on those Guidelines. A scheme that is so based and which is designed to fulfil a legitimate objective will be presumed not to create an unnecessary obstacle to international trade and will therefore be lawful under Article 2.2.

Turning now to the compatibility of a labelling scheme with the GATT, the two provisions of the latter which may be potentially incompatible are Article I.1 and Article III.4. As regards Article I.1, a labelling scheme comes within the 'rules and formalities' of import and export referred to in that provision. It is thus necessary that a WTO Member, when implementing a labelling scheme, does not discriminate between the imports of fish from other WTO Members. Turning to Article III.4, a labelling scheme is a law, regulation or requirement affecting the internal sale of the fish concerned and thus falls within the scope of that provision. That means that a labelling scheme must not lead to less favourable treatment for imported fish than fish caught by that State's own vessels. As long as the latter are subject to the same labelling scheme, there should no question of a breach of Article III.4. It should, therefore, be a relatively straightforward matter to design a labelling scheme that is compatible with Articles I.1 and III.4 of the GATT. Any scheme that is not so compatible would only be lawful if it could be saved by Article XX. What was said about Article XX in Sections 4.1 and 5.1 above will apply equally here.

In practice, there have been two challenges to labelling schemes, the first under the pre-WTO GATT dispute settlement machinery, the second under the WTO's DSU. Both cases were brought by Mexico. Both concern US schemes relating to the labelling of tuna products as 'dolphin-safe' and their application to the Eastern Tropical Pacific (ETP), where, as explained in Subsection 3.6 above, there has traditionally been a high bycatch of dolphins in tuna fisheries. In *Tuna/Dolphin I* a GATT Panel found that the then US scheme, permitting tuna products to be labelled as 'dolphin safe' if they did not contain tuna from fisheries with a significant dolphin bycatch but not prohibiting their sale if not so labelled, did not breach Article I.1 of the GATT, as alleged by Mexico, because there was no discrimination in its application.[112]

The second case was *US – Tuna II (Mexico)*, brought more than 20 years later. The Appellate Body found that the labelling scheme in use by that time was a technical regulation within the meaning of the TBT Agreement and was in breach of Article 2.1 of the Agreement because it was not even-handed in the manner in which it addressed the risks to dolphins from tuna fishing. The scheme took a much stricter approach to the method of tuna fishing in the

---

[111] Guidelines for the Ecolabelling of Fish and Fishery Products from Marine Capture Fisheries. Available at www.fao.org/docrep/012/i1119t/i1119t.pdf. The Guidelines were adopted in 2005 and amended in 2009.

[112] See note 98 above.

ETP than it did in relation to methods of tuna fishing in other parts of the world, which was not justified on the basis of the risks to dolphin mortality.[113] On the other hand, the Appellate Body found that there was no breach of Article 2.2 as the US scheme had a legitimate objective (the protection of animal life – that of dolphins) and there were no alternative means available for achieving that objective that were less trade-restrictive. The Appellate Body also found that there was no breach of Article 2.4 of the TBT Agreement because there was no 'relevant international standard' in existence. The dolphin-safe definition and certification developed within the framework of the AIDCP was no such standard, as the Agreement was not a standardizing body and was not open to participation by all WTO Members.[114] The Appellate Body did not refer to the FAO's Guidelines on Ecolabelling.

Following the Appellate Body's ruling, the US amended its legislation. Mexico brought further proceedings under Article 21.5 of the DSU, arguing that the amendments did not comply with the Appellate Body's ruling and that the US labelling scheme was still contrary to the TBT Agreement and the GATT. The Appellate Body, overruling the Panel on most points, found that the US scheme continued to violate Article 2.1 of the TBT Agreement because there were stricter observer certification requirements in the ETP tuna fishery than in tuna fisheries in other parts of the world that presented a comparably high risk of dolphin mortality.[115] The Appellate Body also dealt with the GATT, which had not been considered in the original proceedings for reasons of judicial economy. It held that there were breaches of Articles I.1 and III.4 of the GATT for broadly the same reasons that there was a breach of Article 2.1 of the TBT Agreement.[116] Those breaches were not saved by Article XX of the GATT because the US scheme did not fulfil the requirements of the *chapeau* of Article XX, as the differences in the observer certification requirements between the ETP tuna fishery and tuna fisheries elsewhere amounted to arbitrary and unjustifiable discrimination.

In the light of the Appellate Body's ruling (which was given in 2015), Mexico sought permission to take retaliatory action against the US under Article 22 of

---

[113] *United States – Tuna II (Mexico)*, note 87. For comment on the case, see M Crowley and R Howse "Tuna-Dolphin II: A Legal and Economic Analysis of the Appellate Body's Report" (2014) 13 *World Trade Review* 321–55.

[114] Agreement on the International Dolphin Conservation Program of 15 May 1998. The text of the Agreement, as amended in 2014, is available at www.iattc.org/PDFFiles/AIDCP/_English/AIDCP-amended-Oct-2017.pdf.

[115] *US – Tuna II (Mexico)* (Art. 21.5 proceedings), note 80. For comment on the decision, see C Coglianese and A Sapir "Risk and Regulatory Calibration: WTO Compliance Review of the US Dolphin-Safe Tuna Labeling Regime" (2017) 16 *World Trade Review* 327–48.

[116] But the test for discrimination is not identical as between Art. 2 of the TBT Agreement and Arts. I.1 and III.4 of the GATT: see ibid. at paras. 7.277–7.278. See also *US – Tuna II (Mexico)* note 87 at para. 215 and the *Seal Products* case, note 69 at paras. 5.122–5.129. On the relationship between discrimination in Art. 2 of the TBT Agreement and Art. XX of the GATT, see *US – Tuna II (Mexico)* (Art. 21.5 proceedings), note 80 at para. 7.345.

the DSU. That was challenged by the US and referred to arbitration. Following the arbitral tribunal's ruling,[117] the WTO's Dispute Settlement Body in 2017 authorized Mexico to suspend the application of certain tariff concessions and related obligations to the US in the amount of USD 163 million per annum.[118] While the arbitration proceedings were ongoing, the US made yet further amendments to its tuna labelling scheme in order to try to bring it into compliance with the Appellate Body's ruling. Those amendments were again challenged by Mexico for non-compliance with the Appellate Body's ruling. However, the Panel rejected that challenge.[119] Mexico has appealed the Panel's finding. As of March 2018 the Appellate Body had not given its ruling.

Mexico brought its original complaint that the US labelling scheme violated the TBT Agreement and the GATT in 2008. A decade later, that dispute had still not been resolved. The case offers a cautionary tale to any other WTO Member contemplating the unilateral introduction of a labelling scheme. At least the various rulings have clarified what a WTO Member needs to do to try to ensure that any labelling scheme aimed at discouraging illegal, unregulated or unsustainable fishing is compliant with WTO law. What is also clear is that WTO law does not prevent WTO Members from introducing such schemes; what it does require, above all, is that there is no discrimination, in the sense of differences of treatment that cannot be justified on the basis of factual differences, in the operation of such schemes.

6. CONCLUSIONS

States and international organizations have used a variety of trade measures to combat illegal, unregulated and unsustainable fishing. They include import bans, restrictions on transhipment, landing requirements, catch documentation and similar schemes, and labelling schemes. All these types of measures raise questions about their compatibility with WTO law. Import bans and restrictions on transhipment breach Article XI of the GATT, but may nevertheless be lawful if they can be justified under Article XX of the GATT. It will usually be fairly straightforward to show that they have been imposed to protect one of the societal interests listed in Article XX (protection of animal life and health and/or conservation of exhaustible natural resources), but less easy to show that they meet the requirements of the *chapeau* of Article XX of not amounting to arbitrary or unjustifiable discrimination or a disguised restriction on trade. Practice shows that bans that implement international instruments are

---

[117] *US – Tuna II (Mexico)*, Recourse to Art. 22.6, Decision of the Arbitrator, WT/DS381/ARB (2017).

[118] See www.wto.org/english/tratop_e/dispu_e/cases_e/ds381_e.htm.

[119] *US – Tuna II (Mexico)*, Second Recourse to Art. 21.5, Panel Report, WT/DS381/RW2 (2017).

far less likely to be challenged in judicial proceedings under the WTO's dispute settlement procedures than purely unilateral measures.

A requirement by a coastal State that a foreign vessel fishing in its EEZ land the catch in one of its ports in order to enable it to determine whether the vessel has been fishing lawfully will also be contrary to Article XI of the GATT as a restriction upon the vessel's ability to export. However, it is likely to be saved by Article XX as the latter allows WTO Members to adopt otherwise inconsistent WTO measures in order to secure compliance with their national laws and because the LOS Convention authorizes coastal States to impose landing requirements on foreign vessels fishing in their EEZs, which means that there should be no question of the requirements of the *chapeau* of Article XX not being fulfilled.

Catch documentation schemes may possibly be technical regulations within the meaning of the Agreement on Technical Barriers to Trade and therefore fall within its purview, but that is unlikely. As long as they are not discriminatory, such schemes should not breach the GATT, specifically Articles I.1 and III.4. Unlike catch documentation schemes, a measure requiring the labelling of fishery products to show that it is not the product of IUU or unsustainable fishing will be a technical regulation within the meaning of the TBT agreement. That means that it must be applied without discrimination and should probably be based on the Ecolabelling Guidelines. The GATT also requires that a labelling scheme is not discriminatory. The decade-long saga before the WTO dispute settlement bodies concerning the legality of the 'dolphin-safe' labelling of tuna products required by the US shows vividly how a labelling scheme may be discriminatory.

15

Strengthening Flag State Performance in Compliance and Enforcement

NATALIE KLEIN

1. INTRODUCTION

THE FOUNDATIONS OF the law of the sea ascribe primary importance to the role of the flag State in the regulation of maritime activities. As a result, the pursuit of particular goals within ocean governance necessitates both recognition of the status of flag States and their participation. Flag States have played, and will continue to play, a critical role in any legal developments seeking to improve the conservation and management of international fisheries. Central in this regard are the contributions of and expectations placed on flag States for the purposes of ensuring compliance with and enforcing international laws and standards.

Diverse actors regulate and influence control over fishing activities, including coastal States, regional fisheries management organizations (RFMOs), other intergovernmental organizations, conservation advocates, scientists, criminals, transnational business and – most relevant for present purposes – flag States. Each of these actors will have varying degrees of influence, particularly depending on where the fishing activity might be occurring. Emphasis is placed on the role of the flag State because it has the legal authority not only to determine which vessels may fly its flag,[1] but it must also effectively exercise jurisdiction and control over those particular ships.[2] How well the flag State has performed in this regard has been an ongoing concern and precipitated the diverse initiatives discussed in this chapter as part of global efforts to improve international

---

[1] United Nations Convention on the Law of the Sea of 10 December 1982 (LOS Convention; 1833 UNTS 396), Art. 91(1). RA Barnes "Flag States" in DR Rothwell et al. (eds.) *The Oxford Handbook of the Law of the Sea* (Oxford University Press, Oxford: 2015) 304–331, at 305 notes: "Since ancient times, ships have been identified with particular communities through the use of flags and other insignia".

[2] LOS Convention, Art. 94.

fisheries law. I argue that there is scope for additional steps to be considered to continue strengthening flag State performance.

To this end, Section 2 of this chapter lays out the existing legal framework that underlines flag State authority and grants important responsibilities to flag States in the conservation and management of marine living resources. Section 3 examines recent developments that build on this framework in (1) the United Nations General Assembly (UNGA); (2) the Food and Agriculture Organization of the United Nations (FAO); (3) the International Tribunal for the Law of the Sea (ITLOS); and (4) within RFMOs. Each of these developments has emphasized in different ways the assessment of flag State performance. Notably, they have incrementally advanced the legal regulations for ensuring better flag State performance and thereby improved the benchmarks against which it can be measured. Section 4 considers what further steps could be taken, particularly considering how the improved articulation of international regulations could better hold flag States to account in the future.

2. EXISTING LEGAL FRAMEWORK

The flag State has prescriptive and enforcement jurisdiction over vessels flying its flag. A vessel flies the flag of a State where it has concluded the domestic formalities and requirements necessary for the registration or granting of nationality to the vessel.[3] A requirement of a genuine link under Article 91(1) of the LOS Convention between the flag State and the ship exists so as to ensure that the flag State secures the effective implementation of its duties.[4] In the *Virginia G* case, the ITLOS stated:

> In the view of the Tribunal, once a ship is registered, the flag State is required, under article 94 of the Convention, to exercise effective jurisdiction and control over that ship in order to ensure that it operates in accordance with generally accepted international regulations, procedures and practices. This is the meaning of 'genuine link'.[5]

States have a discretion in determining whether to grant nationality to a fishing vessel through registration and may determine what conditions must be met for this purpose.[6]

A key challenge is that fishing companies may register or flag their vessels with 'flag of convenience', 'flag of non-compliance', or 'open registry' States. These States allow "the registration of foreign-owned and foreign-controlled

---

[3] Nationality is usually granted through a process of registration (Barnes, note 1 at 306).

[4] *M/V Saiga (No. 2) (Saint Vincent and the Grenadines v. Guinea)* (Admissibility and Merits) (1999) 120 ILR 143, para. 83.

[5] *M/V "Virginia G" (Panama v. Guinea-Bissau)* (2014) 53 ILM 1164, para. 113.

[6] D Warner-Kramer "Control Begins at Home: Tackling Flags of Convenience and IUU Fishing" (2004) 34 *Golden Gate University Law Review* 497–530, at 507.

vessels under conditions which, for whatever the reasons, are convenient and opportune for the persons who are registering the vessels".[7] It would not typically be anticipated that these vessels fish in the exclusive economic zone (EEZ) of the State in which they register, as a motivation to register with the particular State is to avoid relevant management regimes and/or to fish illegally.[8] In some instances, there may be a tactical advantage for a vessel to register with a particular State, thereby gaining additional access to fish stocks from which it may otherwise be barred.

While our starting point is that the flag State has primary authority over its vessels, it holds concurrent jurisdiction or otherwise has limits on the exercise of its jurisdiction depending on the maritime zone in which the vessel is located.[9] Notably, the LOS Convention provides that a coastal State has sovereign rights to conserve and manage the natural resources of its EEZ.[10] Pursuant to these rights, the coastal State is entitled to prescribe laws and regulations for fishing activities in its EEZ, as well as exerting authority to enforce those laws.[11] Nonetheless, when coastal States exercise their rights and duties in the EEZ, due regard must still be accorded to the rights and duties of other States.[12] The flag State may potentially institute proceedings at the ITLOS under Article 292 of the LOS Convention in the event that the coastal State fails to promptly release an arrested vessel and its crew upon the posting of a reasonable bond or other security.[13] It is, however, indispensable that flag States cooperate to ensure support for coastal State efforts in fisheries conservation and management.[14]

For straddling and highly migratory fish stocks, the coastal State must cooperate with the flag State and coordinate through international organizations in the conservation and management of these species.[15] The Fish Stocks Agreement[16] provides further detail as to the responsibility of flag States in

---

[7] BA Boczek *Flags of Convenience: An International Legal Study* (Harvard University Press, Harvard: 1962) 2.

[8] Warner-Kramer, note 6 at 500.

[9] Barnes, note 1 at 311.

[10] LOS Convention, Art. 56(1).

[11] MA Palma-Robles "Fisheries Enforcement and the Concepts of Compliance and Monitoring, Control and Surveillance" in R Warner and SB Kaye (eds.), *Routledge Handbook of Maritime Regulation and Enforcement* (Routledge, Abingdon: 2015) 139–160, at 143–145 highlights that Art. 73 of the LOS Convention encapsulates which vessels can be boarded, what offences justify boarding and who can board. The role of private actors in enforcement is discussed in Chapter 16 of this volume (Massarella).

[12] LOS Convention, Art. 56(2).

[13] The requirement to release the fishing vessel being set out in Art. 73(2) of the LOS Convention.

[14] G Handl "Flag State Responsibility for Illegal, Unreported and Unregulated Fishing in Foreign EEZs" (2014) 44 *Environmental Policy and Law* 158–167, at 160.

[15] LOS Convention, Arts. 63(2) and 64.

[16] Agreement for the Implementation of the Provisions of the United Nations Convention on the Law of the Sea of 10 December 1982 relating to the Conservation and Management of Straddling Fish Stocks and Highly Migratory Fish Stocks of 4 August 1995 (2167 UNTS 3).

relation to straddling and highly migratory fish stocks.[17] Article 19 of the Fish Stocks Agreement requires flag States to enforce any regional conservation and management measures irrespective of where the violation may occur. In this situation, the Fish Stocks Agreement obliges the flag State to investigate immediately and fully any alleged violations of conservation and management measures, as well as cooperate with other States in providing information required for the investigation of possible violations.[18]

In addition to responsibilities associated with straddling and highly migratory fish stocks on the high seas, flag States must also ensure that the freedom to fish on the high seas is conducted in a manner consistent with their duty to take, or to cooperate with other States in taking, measures necessary for the conservation of high seas fisheries resources.[19] Among other things, flag States are to determine the total allowable catch as well as other conservation measures,[20] and have obligations to contribute to and exchange information relevant to the conservation of fish stocks.[21]

The responsibilities of flag States have not only been elaborated in the LOS Convention and the Fish Stocks Agreement, but also through the Code of Conduct.[22] The Code also spurred the adoption of various International Plans of Action (IPOAs), including the IPOA-IUU.[23] The Code builds on the Fish Stocks Agreement and the Compliance Agreement,[24] and further articulates flag State duties in relation to administrative, technical and social matters for fishing and support vessels as well as requirements to ensure implementation of conservation and management measures.[25] The Code may be seen as recommended international minimum standards for flag States in relation to fisheries conservation and management.[26]

---

[17] Art. 18 sets out the duties of the flag State, which include ensuring compliance of its vessels with international and regional obligations; establishing regulations to authorize and control fishing activities; recording vessels authorized to fish on the high seas; reporting obligations; verifying catch; monitoring, control and surveillance of vessels; and ensuring compatibility of measures with those of international or regional organizations.

[18] Fish Stocks Agreement, Art. 19(1)(d).

[19] LOS Convention, Art. 117. See also Art. 118.

[20] Ibid., Art. 119(1).

[21] Ibid., Art. 119(2).

[22] Code of Conduct for Responsible Fisheries of 31 October 1995; available at www.fao.org/3/a-v9878e.pdf.

[23] International Plan of Action to Prevent, Deter and Eliminate Illegal, Unreported and Unregulated Fishing of 2 March 2001; available at www.fao.org/iuu-fishing/en/.

[24] Agreement to Promote Compliance with International Conservation and Management Measures by Fishing Vessels on the High Seas of 24 November 1993 (33 ILM 969 (1994): the Compliance Agreement forms an integral part of the Code of Conduct in accordance with Art. 1.1 of the Code of Conduct.

[25] For discussion, see Y Takei "Assessing Flag State Performance in Legal Terms: Clarifications of the Margin of Discretion" (2013) 28 *International Journal of Marine and Coastal Law* 97–133, at 109.

[26] Ibid., 120.

The exercise of enforcement jurisdiction on the high seas is an important responsibility of the flag State because of the limited instances by which other States may be able to exercise enforcement jurisdiction over fishing vessels. In the absence of specific treaty authorization, no State may board, inspect or take other enforcement actions against a vessel flagged to another State on the high seas unless it has obtained the consent of the flag State.[27] This basic position is enshrined in the LOS Convention,[28] but has been elaborated further in the Fish Stocks Agreement. Article 21(1) of the Fish Stocks Agreement provides the authority to board and inspect the vessels of Parties to that Agreement to ensure compliance with applicable conservation and management measures established by an RFMO.[29] If the boarding and inspection reveal that the vessel has engaged in fishing activity inconsistent with such measures, the inspecting State is to gather evidence and promptly notify the flag State of the alleged violation.[30] The flag State must then investigate, or allow the inspecting State to do so.[31] If warranted, the flag State is to take enforcement action against the vessel or may authorize the inspecting State to undertake such action in its stead.[32]

Both the Fish Stocks Agreement and the Compliance Agreement provide indications as to penalties that flag States must or may impose in the event of fisheries violations.[33] Penalties shall be "adequate in severity to be effective in securing compliance and to discourage violations wherever they occur and shall deprive offenders of the benefits accruing from their illegal activities".[34] These sanctions may include withdrawing, suspending or cancelling authorizations to fish.[35]

A strong international legal framework derived from treaties such as the LOS Convention, the Fish Stocks Agreement and the Compliance Agreement thus regulates the responsibilities of flag States in relation to the management of fisheries. This legal structure has been supplemented through additional international obligations derived from international environmental law,

---

[27] The key exception to this requirement being the exercise of universal jurisdiction, which accrues in relation to pirates.

[28] LOS Convention, Art. 110. The right of hot pursuit provides another basis for boarding a fishing vessel on the high seas, provided the conditions of Art. 111 of the LOS Convention are met.

[29] The RFMO's procedures for conducting such boarding and inspection are to be set out and duly notified, consistent with the requirements in Art. 21(2) of the Fish Stocks Agreement. There is otherwise an inspection and boarding procedure to be followed consistent with Art. 22 of the Fish Stocks Agreement.

[30] Fish Stocks Agreement, Art. 21(5).

[31] Ibid., Art. 21(6).

[32] Ibid., Art. 21(7).

[33] The Compliance Agreement was a multilateral endeavour to address the reflagging of vessels for the purpose of avoiding compliance with an increasing array of conservation and management measures. See Palma-Robles, note 11 at 140.

[34] Fish Stocks Agreement, Art. 19(2). See further Palma-Robles, note 11 at 148.

[35] Fish Stocks Agreement, Art. 19(2); Compliance Agreement, Art. III(8).

including the precautionary approach and ecosystem-based management, as well as other treaties moderating flag State conduct over fishing. The latter treaties include the PSM Agreement,[36] CITES,[37] the CBD[38] and the CMS.[39] Soft law has been developed through the Code of Conduct and its related IPOAs, as well as other instruments adopted under the auspices of the FAO. Further requirements are stipulated through RFMOs or bilateral arrangements drawn from fisheries access agreements between States.[40] This dense legal matrix has gradually increased the international regulatory regime associated with flag State conduct over its fishing vessels. Nonetheless, as the status of the world's fish stocks continues to decline, efforts have carried on to improve flag State performance. The most recent initiatives are examined in the next section.

3. RECENT DEVELOPMENTS

Several key institutions have been at the forefront in developing further international rules and guidance on flag State responsibilities for the conservation and management of international fish stocks. This section addresses in particular the efforts of the UNGA in relation to bottom fisheries on the high seas as well as the 2016 Resumed Fish Stocks Agreement Review Conference. It then considers important steps within the FAO, including in relation to enhanced identification of fishing vessels to improve monitoring, compliance and enforcement, and the adoption of the Flag State Performance Guidelines in 2014.[41] A 2015 Advisory Opinion from the ITLOS, provided pursuant to a request from the Sub-Regional Fisheries Commission (SRFC), also engaged with vital questions on assessing flag State performance in response to illegal, unregulated or unreported (IUU) fishing. Finally, RFMOs continue to improve their responses to poor flag State performance through novel monitoring and sanctions regimes. These developments all reflect increased international scrutiny on flag State performance in connection with international fisheries law.

---

[36] Agreement on Port State Measures to Prevent, Deter and Eliminate Illegal, Unreported and Unregulated Fishing of 22 November 2009; available at www.fao.org/fileadmin/user_upload/legal/docs/037t-e.pdf.

[37] Convention on International Trade in Endangered Species of Wild Fauna and Flora of 3 March 1973 (993 UNTS 243).

[38] Convention on Biological Diversity of 5 June 1992 (1760 UNTS 143).

[39] Convention on the Conservation of Migratory Species of Wild Animals of 23 June 1979 (1651 UNTS 333).

[40] See VJ Schatz "The Contribution of Fisheries Access Agreements to Flag State Responsibility" (2017) 84 *Marine Policy* 313–319.

[41] Voluntary Guidelines for Flag State Performance, endorsed by the Committee on Fisheries in June 2014; available at www.fao.org/3/a-i4577t.pdf.

3.1. UNGA

Each year the UNGA adopts a resolution on Sustainable Fisheries, which addresses critical fisheries issues for the attention of UN Members, including flag States.[42] The resolutions affirm flag State responsibilities to exercise effective control over their fishing vessels, and ensure that these vessels do not prejudice efforts at conservation and management of fisheries resources.[43] Flag State efforts are not limited to their fishing vessels, but extend to their support vessels, especially in terms of taking all measures necessary to ensure that these vessels do not engage in transshipment of fish caught by vessels engaged in IUU fishing.[44] Flag States are further called upon

> not to permit vessels flying their flag to engage in fishing on the high seas or in areas under the national jurisdiction of other States, unless duly authorized by the authorities of the States concerned and in accordance with the conditions set out in the authorization.[45]

Where an area is regulated by an RFMO, flag States are to ensure their vessels comply with that RFMO's conservation and management measures even where they are not Members of that RFMO.[46]

The UNGA has particularly heeded the importance of flag State performance in ocean areas that are not governed by any RFMO. In this regard, flag States are to collect and disseminate fishing data from their fishing vessels on the high seas,[47] and to take action in relation to fishing vessels engaged in bottom fisheries.[48] Bottom fishing has been of particular concern because of its negative impacts on vulnerable marine ecosystems and the long-term sustainability of deep-sea fish stocks.[49] While views have been mixed as to flag State performance in this regard to date,[50] there remains a need for flag States to undertake assessments and implement measures based on the best scientific information available.[51] Measures adopted by flag States thus far include prohibition of bottom fishing, granting licences only after impact assessments are completed, closing certain areas to bottom fishing and limiting the use of fishing gear.[52]

---

[42] The most recent resolution at time of writing was Resolution 72/73 of 4 January 2018.

[43] See e.g. ibid., at Preamble and paras. 8, 66 and 68–69.

[44] Ibid., para. 86.

[45] Ibid., para. 72.

[46] Ibid., para. 138.

[47] Ibid., para. 54.

[48] Ibid., paras. 119–124, and Resolution 66/68 of 6 December 2011, paras. 129–130 and 132–134.

[49] See UN doc. A/71/377 of 9 September 2016.

[50] See ibid., para. 11. See further UN doc. A/71/351 of 22 August 2016, which reports on State and RFMO actions addressing the impact of bottom fishing. Only a small number of flag States had responded to requests for information, however (see ibid., fn. 117).

[51] UN doc. A/71/377, note 48 at para. 21.

[52] See UN doc. A/71/351, note 49 at paras. 107 and 158–159.

Further technical work on this issue now continues at the FAO, further to its International Deep-sea Fisheries Guidelines.[53]

Consistent with UNGA Resolutions,[54] the 2016 Resumed Fish Stocks Agreement Review Conference was convened as a follow-up to earlier conferences in 2010 and 2006. The 2016 Resumed Fish Stocks Agreement Review Conference provided an opportunity for States Parties to consider further the role of the flag State, as it was noted that "ineffective flag State enforcement remained a major challenge for high-seas fisheries and required further efforts".[55] In this context, some brief attention was paid to the genuine link requirement,[56] and a proposal made that the licensing of vessels should be tied to flag States implementing their obligations.[57] A recommendation adopted at the end of the Review Conference took the position that flag States should ensure they "have the ability to fulfill their responsibilities [...] before they grant the right to fly their flag to fishing vessels or issue authorization for fishing to such vessels".[58] Discussions are ongoing as to the development of criteria to clarify what constitutes a genuine link.[59] States consider this task to be another means of strengthening flag State responsibility in relation to monitoring, control and surveillance, and compliance and enforcement.[60]

Connected to the issue of registration of vessels is the de-registration of fishing vessels that have engaged in IUU fishing. At the 2016 Resumed Fish Stocks Agreement Review Conference, participants recommended that flag States should augment the penalties imposed or otherwise devise adequate sanctions rather than de-registering vessels.[61] The rationale for such an approach would be to limit the number of stateless vessels that may then subsequently engage in IUU fishing outside the purview of any State. A further recommendation relating to the assessment of flag State performance provided:

> Develop regional or global guidelines for fisheries sanctions to be applied by flag States so that those States may evaluate their sanctions systems with a view to ensuring that they are effective in securing compliance and deterring violations.[62]

It must therefore be anticipated that flag State sanctions and penalty regimes will come under increased scrutiny in the future, especially as States consider how to respond to the problems posed by stateless vessels in the conservation and management of fish stocks.

---

[53] International Guidelines for the Management of Deep-sea Fisheries in the High Seas of 29 August 2008; text available at www.fao.org/docrep/011/i0816t/i0816t00.htm.
[54] Resolution 63/112 of 5 December 2008 and Resolution 64/72 of 4 December 2009.
[55] UN doc. A/CONF.210/2016/5 of 1 August 2016, para. 112.
[56] Ibid., para. 119.
[57] Ibid., para. 112.
[58] Ibid., Recommendation B(7)(c), p. 43.
[59] See, e.g. ibid., para. 119.
[60] Ibid., Recommendation C(1)(a), p. 43.
[61] Ibid., Recommendation C(1)(c), p. 43.
[62] Ibid., Recommendation C(2)(b), p. 44.

3.2. FAO

The FAO was created to improve efficiency in the production and distribution of food, which includes fisheries and marine products.[63] While the FAO has competence to address a range of fisheries-related issues, it is not directly involved in the management of fisheries, which is above all left to individual States and RFMOs. The important work of the FAO in relation to fisheries resources, and the role of the flag State in particular, tends to relate to the development of international rules and standards, as well as providing technical support and services to actors with direct competence for fisheries management.[64] Two significant developments at the FAO that are particularly relevant to flag State performance are the development of a Unique Vessel Identifier for fishing vessels and the adoption of the Flag State Performance Guidelines. These are assessed in the following subsections.

3.2.1. Unique Vessel Identifier

Within the FAO, a coordinated effort to improve identification of fishing vessels is currently underway. In this regard, the FAO has looked to the use of the International Maritime Organization's Ship Identification Number as a prerequisite to participating in the FAO's programme of Unique Vessel Identifier (UVI).[65] The UVI is a "global unique number" assigned to a vessel to "ensure traceability through reliable, verified and permanent identification of the vessel" throughout its life irrespective of flag, name or ownership changes.[66] The UVI is part of the FAO's Global Record of Fishing Vessels, Refrigerated Transport Vessels and Supply Vessels (Global Record), which is intended to become a global repository of data identifying vessels engaged in fishing and fishing-related activities.

The key aim of the Global Record is to assist in preventing and deterring IUU fishing by making the illegal or unregulated activity more obvious and allowing rapid responses.[67] RFMOs have embraced this development with nearly all now mandating that larger vessels obtain and report their UVI. The European Union (EU) has also made the UVI mandatory for all vessels over 24 metres in length fishing in EU waters and for EU vessels over 15 metres fishing overseas.[68]

---

[63] Constitution of the Food and Agriculture Organization of 16 October 1945 (40 AJIL Supp. 76), Preamble and Art. 1(1).

[64] See Y Takei "Institutional Reactions to the Flag State that has Failed to Discharge Flag State Responsibilities" (2012) LIX *Netherlands International Law Review* 65–90, at 68.

[65] Although there has been a long-standing exemption for fishing vessels, this initiative was supported by several delegations at the 2016 Resumed Fish Stocks Agreement Review Conference as a means of combating IUU fishing. See UN doc. A/CONF.210/2016/5, note 55 at para. 157.

[66] Based on information available at www.fao.org/in-action/global-record/background/unique-vessel-identifier/en/.

[67] Ibid.

[68] "Improving performance in the fight against illegal, unreported and unregulated (IUU) fishing, The EU IUU Regulation carding process: A review of European Commission carding decisions", *Issue Brief*, April 2016; text available at www.issuelab.org/resources/25908/25908.pdf.

As this system develops, it will be critical for flag States not only to ensure their vessels obtain such a number but also to react to information obtained through the Global Record as part of their responsibilities.[69] Alternatively, it remains to be seen what role will be accorded to other actors in responding to the information garnered through the Global Record.

3.2.2. Flag State Performance Guidelines

In 2007, the FAO engaged in a process to consider criteria for assessing flag State performance and possible actions that could be taken against vessels that do not meet those criteria.[70] The criteria for assessment had to be developed based on an understanding of flag State responsibilities, namely the duty to cooperate and to effectively control fishing vessels.[71] Moreover, any actions that could be taken had to distinguish between sanctions against the vessel itself and the international responsibility of the flag State.[72] These efforts culminated in the Flag State Performance Guidelines,[73] which provide criteria to clarify the varied obligations imposed on flag States for fishing and fishing-related activities in maritime areas beyond national jurisdiction.[74]

One important issue addressed in the Guidelines concerns flagging practices of States, including obligations to prevent the abuse of re-flagging. Under the LOS Convention, ships are to sail only under one flag and may not change flag during a voyage unless there is "a real transfer of ownership or change of registry".[75] As noted in the Preambles to the Compliance Agreement and the Code of Conduct, Agenda 21 called upon States to "take effective action, consistent with international law, to deter re-flagging of vessels as a means of avoiding compliance with applicable conservation and management rules for fishing activities on the high seas". Under the Compliance Agreement, flag States

---

[69] In 2016, a pilot project was launched (see information available at www.fao.org/global-record/background/global-record-pilot-project/en/). The FAO also anticipates undertaking a feasibility study to determine if UVI could be used for smaller fishing vessels (see information available at http://www.fao.org/global-record/background/way-forward/en/).

[70] Report of the 27th Session of the Committee on Fisheries (*FAO Fisheries Report* No. 830: 2007), para. 71. See further "Expert Workshop on Flag State Responsibilities: Assessing Performance and Taking Action, 25–28 March 2008, Vancouver, Canada", available at http://publications.gc.ca/site/eng/435182/publication.html; further: Expert Workshop Report; Report of the Expert Consultation on Flag State Performance, Rome, 23-26 June 2009 (*FAO Fisheries and Aquaculture Report* No. 918: 2009; further: Expert Consultation Report).

[71] Expert Workshop Report, note 70 at 10. See also Expert Consultation Report, note 70 at 29, para. 8.

[72] Expert Workshop Report, note 70 at 10.

[73] For further background on the drafting history of the Flag State Performance Guidelines, see K Erikstein and J Swan "Voluntary Guidelines for Flag State Performance: A New Tool to Conquer IUU Fishing" (2014) 29 *International Journal of Marine and Coastal Law* 116–147, at 131–134.

[74] See discussion in VAMF Ventura "Tackling Illegal, Unregulated and Unreported Fishing: the ITLOS Advisory Opinion on Flag State Responsibility for IUU Fishing and the Principle of Due Diligence" (2015) 12 *Brazilian Journal of International Law* 50–67, at 58.

[75] LOS Convention, Art. 92(1).

must assess their ability to exercise effective control over their vessels before providing authorizations to fish on the high seas.[76] RFMOs have documented how vessels have moved their registration to different States when their original State of registration was sanctioned by an RFMO.[77] Flagging of fishing vessels therefore becomes particularly problematic if a flag State is not Party to the relevant fisheries regime, or where it is not exercising the effective control expected by virtue of being the flag State.

The Guidelines detail the information a flag State should consider in registering a vessel, such as the vessel's history and its possible listing as a vessel conducting IUU fishing,[78] and refer to the need to ensure that the registration process is accessible and transparent, with publicly available registry information.[79] The flag State is to maintain a record of its registered vessels, consistent with requirements found in Article VI of the Compliance Agreement.[80] The record may also include details about the registered owner, beneficial owner, the manager of the vessel and previous names of the vessel.[81] If these record obligations were binding on all flag States, or the suggestion in the Guidelines was adhered to by all flag States, greater monitoring of re-flagging practice to detect IUU fishing vessels would be possible.

Notable in the Guidelines are the 'performance assessment criteria', which set out minimum benchmarks for flag States. There is a suite of general standards in the Guidelines that largely encapsulate existing international obligations:

6. The flag State has incorporated the flag State principles and rules that are binding on it in accordance with international law into its domestic laws, regulations, policies and practices.

7. The flag State has taken such measures as may be necessary to ensure that vessels flying its flag do not engage in any activity that undermines the effectiveness of international conservation and management measures or the flag State accepts and implements the conservation and management measures adopted by a relevant regional fisheries management organization or arrangement (RFMO/As).

8. The flag State effectively contributes to the functioning of the RFMO/A in which it participates (i.e. the flag State implements its duties as a contracting party or as a cooperating non-party, including reporting requirements for fishing and fishing related activities and ensuring compliance by its vessels).

9. The flag State ensures that vessels flying its flag do not conduct unauthorized fishing and fishing related activities within areas under the national jurisdiction of other States.

---

[76] Compliance Agreement, Art. III. See also Warner-Kramer, note 6 at 510.

[77] See Warner-Kramer, note 6 at 515 (referring to the experience of the International Commission on the Conservation of Atlantic Tunas (ICCAT) in this regard).

[78] Flag State Performance Guidelines, para. 16.

[79] Ibid., paras. 17, 21 and 22.

[80] Ibid., para. 25.

[81] Ibid., para. 25.

10. The flag State supports cooperation among flag States on managing capacity and fishing effort, catch limits and output controls.

The Guidelines further incorporate minimum standards for flag States in creating national laws and regulations, as well as the necessary institutional structures to ensure compliance with international obligations.[82] Flag State performance is also assessed by reference to the regime it has in place for authorizing fishing and fishing-related activity,[83] as well as the monitoring, control, surveillance and enforcement regimes that are needed as a minimum.[84] A flag State's willingness to undertake performance assessment may be seen as a measure of cooperation.[85]

The implementation of the Guidelines remains a work in progress at present. Beyond the FAO, the UNGA has underlined the importance of assessing flag State performance.[86] In Resolution 71/123 of 2016, the Assembly called upon flag States to implement the Guidelines "as soon as possible, including, as a first step, by carrying out a voluntary assessment".[87] Delegates to the 2016 Review Conference also supported flag States conducting self-assessments, and potentially RFMOs using the Guidelines to assess their Members' compliance.[88]

3.3. ITLOS

In its *SRFC Advisory Opinion*,[89] the ITLOS considered that flag States had a responsibility to ensure that their vessels were not violating international fisheries requirements within the EEZs of the SRFC Members. In doing so, the ITLOS limited its views to the Members of the SRFC and the rights and duties being exercised in the EEZ of those Members. Yet, the standards set forth may be indicative of relevant benchmarks for all flag States in controlling fisheries operations of their vessels.

The Tribunal was of the view that flag States have responsibilities to implement conservation and management measures both on the high seas and within the EEZ of coastal States.[90] While the coastal State has the primary responsibility for taking any measures that are necessary to prevent, deter and eliminate IUU fishing in its EEZ,[91] responsibility also falls to flag States to ensure that their vessels act consistently with conservation and management requirements.[92]

---

[82] Ibid., paras. 11–13.
[83] Ibid., para. 29.
[84] Ibid., paras. 31–32.
[85] Expert Consultation Report, note 70 at p. 21, para. 12.
[86] See e.g. Resolution 71/123 of 7 December 2016, para. 73.
[87] Ibid., para. 96. See also doc. A/CONF.210/2016/5, note 55, Recommendation C(2)(a), p. 44.
[88] UN doc. A/CONF.210/2016/5, note 55 at para. 114.
[89] *Request for an Advisory Opinion Submitted by the Sub-Regional Fisheries Commission (SRFC)*, Advisory Opinion, Order of 2 April 2015, ITLOS Reports 2015, 31.
[90] Ibid., para. 111.
[91] Ibid., para. 106.
[92] Ibid., para. 109.

If a vessel violates the coastal State's fisheries laws and regulations, the flag State is not immediately held internationally responsible for the actions of its vessel.[93] Rather, the Tribunal stated: "The flag State is under the 'due diligence obligation' to take all necessary measures to ensure compliance and to prevent IUU fishing by fishing vessels flying its flag".[94] This view reflects the core position set out in Article III of the Compliance Agreement, and Article 18(1) of the Fish Stocks Agreement. It may therefore be the case that a flag State that is a Party to the Fish Stocks Agreement, but not a Member of a relevant RFMO, must still take steps to ensure its vessels are adhering to the requirements of that organization or arrangement.[95] This obligation will obviously function well only if conservation and management measures have been adopted by the organization in question.[96]

The due diligence requirement has been described in the International Court of Justice's decision on *Pulp Mills* as:

> [...] entail[ing] not only the adoption of appropriate rules and measures, but also a certain level of vigilance in their enforcement and the exercise of administrative control applicable to public and private operators, such as the monitoring of activities undertaken by such operators, to safeguard the rights of the other party.[97]

The due diligence obligation is not one of result on this basis, but one of conduct.[98]

In terms of what conduct should be expected of flag States to meet the due diligence standard, the Fish Stocks Agreement provides some level of detail as to the obligations imposed on flag States, including the use of the precautionary approach,[99] cooperation in scientific research and cooperation with coastal States in developing conservation and management measures.[100] Based on the *SRFC Advisory Opinion*, van der Marel has identified measures for flag States drawn from Articles 58(3) and 62(4) of the LOS Convention with regard to ensuring compliance with coastal State laws and regulations as well as prohibiting their vessels from fishing in a coastal State's EEZ unless authorized

---

[93] Ibid., para. 146.

[94] Ibid., para. 129.

[95] Warner-Kramer, note 6 at 506.

[96] See E Hey "Global Fisheries Regulations in the First Half of the 1990s" (1996) 11 *International Journal of Marine and Coastal Law* 459–490, at 470.

[97] *Pulp Mills on the River Uruguay (Argentina v. Uruguay)*, Judgment, ICJ Reports, 2010, 18 (Apr. 20), 197.

[98] *Responsibilities and obligations of States with respect to activities in the Area,* Advisory Opinion, 1 February 2011, ITLOS Reports 2011, 41. This approach was applied in the *South China Sea* arbitration (*The Republic of Philippines v. The People's Republic of China (Philippines v. China)*, Award on the Merits of 12 July 2016 available at www.pcacases.com/web/view/7, at paras. 744 and 755–757, where it was found that China failed to exercise due diligence to prevent fishing by its vessels and was aware of and tolerated Chinese fishing at Mischief Reef and Second Thomas Shoal.

[99] Fish Stocks Agreement, Art. 6.

[100] Barnes, note 1, at 318, referring to Fish Stocks Agreement, Arts. 7, 8 and 14.

to do so.[101] Further, flag States would need to adopt measures to ensure that their vessels comply with requirements on the protection and preservation of the marine environment adopted pursuant to Articles 192 and 193 of the LOS Convention.[102] The requirements regarding flag State duties articulated in Article 94 would additionally be relevant in this regard.[103]

Although the Tribunal did not articulate precise means for flag States to use in combating IUU fishing, Ventura has suggested that the Flag State Performance Guidelines may provide a useful reference point for determining if the requirements of due diligence have been met in assessing flag State responsibility.[104] An FAO representative has commented, however, that the Guidelines do "not refer to the discharge by flag States of their responsibilities under international law, but rather to the undertaking of voluntary assessments of their performance".[105] As such, it is possible that the Guidelines will predominantly be utilized as a tool for flag States themselves and/or within the frame of RFMO decision-making. The extent that they are used to hold flag States responsible is discussed further in Section 4 below.

3.4. RFMOs

As discussed throughout this volume, RFMOs play diverse and important roles in international fisheries law.[106] Commonly, all RFMOs require flag States to control their vessels through licensing or other authorization and through the adoption of regulations that incorporate the permitted terms and conditions for fishing associated with the authorization. This subsection focuses on some recent initiatives in RFMOs relating to flag State compliance and enforcement efforts.

Monitoring and inspection regimes are now common tools to ensure that fishing vessels are complying with the conservation and management measures established in RFMOs. Observers are used on board vessels in different regional schemes, which can support the use of proper gear and adherence to fishing regulations. Flag State consent is critical for participation in such observer regimes. Drawbacks to the use of observers include the cost and the risk of improper

---

[101] ER van der Marel "ITLOS Issues its Advisory Opinion on IUU Fishing", *The JCLOS Blog*, 21 April 2015 available at http://site.uit.no/jclos/2015/04/21/itlos-issues-its-advisory-opinion-on-iuu-fishing/.

[102] Ibid.

[103] Ibid.

[104] Ventura, note 74 at 58. However, Handl, note 14 at 161, has observed that the Guidelines are criticized as too deferential to the coastal State's sovereign rights in the EEZ.

[105] UN doc. A/CONF.210/2016/5, note 55 at para. 121.

[106] See *inter alia* Chapters 5 (Harrison) and 6 (Molenaar) of this volume.

influence or inability to observe everything that occurs on a large fishing vessel.[107] When a flag State Member of an RFMO is considered non-compliant with the conservation and management measures of the organization, this may lead to an adjustment of its allocation,[108] as well as restrictions on participation in the RFMO, including limiting access to the resources managed by it.[109]

RFMOs have increasingly utilized a variety of enforcement measures to prejudice the operation of non-Members. For example, there is a presumption that a vessel flagged to a non-Member fishing in the RFMO's region is undermining the conservation and management measures of the organization. Consequently, the vessel must be inspected by a Member when it comes into port, or a Member must or could refuse to allow landings or transshipments of fish on board those vessels.[110]

Members of RFMOs have also taken steps to identify vessels that are considered as potential violators of international requirements for fishing.[111] These lists include the names of vessels flagged to non-Members that have been identified as unlawfully exploiting fish resources. RFMOs have also shared IUU Vessel Lists to facilitate enforcement mechanisms across the different regions covered by the organizations.[112]

Within RFMOs, steps have further been taken so that coastal States may exert more control over foreign-flagged vessels through the use of catch documentation schemes.[113] Typically, flag States have responsibilities within such a scheme to certify that a fish catch has been harvested consistently with international or regional regulations. Such certified catches may then be imported and re-exported or on-sold.

RFMOs have also introduced sanction regimes as a response to overharvesting, failures to report catch data or other acts of non-compliance. For example, ICCAT[114] has adopted a schedule of actions to improve compliance.[115]

---

[107] JR Wigginton "Governing a Global Commons: Sharks in the High Seas" (2014) 25 *Villanova Environmental Law Journal* 431–463, at 454.

[108] As has occurred in the Commission for the Conservation of Southern Bluefin Tuna (see Takei, note 64 at 69).

[109] Expert Consultation Report, note 70 at 35, para. 31.

[110] Warner-Kramer, note 6 at 521 (referring to the experience of the Commission for the Conservation of Antarctic Marine Living Resources (CCAMLR) and the Northwest Atlantic Fisheries Organization (NAFO) in this regard).

[111] See further Chapter 13 of this volume (van der Marel).

[112] See S van Osch "Save our Sharks: Using International Fisheries Law within Regional Fisheries Management Organizations to Improve Shark Conservation" (2012) 33 *Michigan Journal of International Law* 383–431, at 427. See also Chapter 5 of this volume (Harrison).

[113] These schemes are discussed in more detail in Chapters 13 (van der Marel) and 14 (Churchill) of this volume.

[114] See note 77.

[115] ICCAT Resolution 16-17 (2016) Establishing an ICCAT Schedule of Actions to Improve Compliance and Cooperation with ICCAT Measures.

It initially requires a determination of non-compliance across conservation and management measures, reporting requirements, monitoring, control and surveillance measures, and an assessment of the severity of non-compliance.[116] For minor non-compliance, ICCAT's Compliance Committee would request the flag State to rectify the situation and report to the Committee on actions taken. For significant non-compliance, the Committee would further consider if there were mitigating or aggravating considerations to determine whether or not the following actions should be taken: enhanced reporting requirements, fishing restrictions, additional monitoring, control and surveillance measures, "and/or, as a last resort, trade restrictive measures".[117]

4. FURTHER STEPS NEEDED?

The international governance framework directed at international fisheries is unquestionably becoming denser with increased regulation and higher engagement of varied institutions and diverse actors. Yet, flag State performance still has scope to improve when regard is had to the continued decline in the world's fish stocks and in this regard, additional legal tools may be brought to bear. Three such possibilities are considered in this section. First, improved technology may not only enhance coastal State efforts in monitoring activities in their maritime areas, but could also be engaged more fully by flag States so as to demonstrate sufficient efforts to comply with their international obligations. Second, more rigorous effort is needed in holding flag States accountable if they fail to meet due diligence standards. Finally, there has been some political willingness evinced to challenge flag State fishing activity under the compulsory dispute settlement mechanism of the LOS Convention and it is therefore important to emphasize further potential for this mechanism in assessing flag State performance and holding flag States to account where necessary for improved compliance and enforcement.

4.1. Vessel Monitoring Systems

States have recognized that new and emerging technologies could be better used to strengthen effective control over fishing vessels.[118] The need for active flag State engagement in relation to the use of a vessel monitoring system (VMS) is critical. In Resolution 63/112 of 2008, the UNGA had urged that large-scale

---

[116] Ibid.

[117] Ibid. Trade-restrictive measures are addressed in Chapter 14 of this volume (Churchill).

[118] See UN doc. A/CONF.210/2016/5, note 55 at para. 115 and Recommendation C(1)(f), pp. 43–44.

fishing vessels be required to carry VMS.[119] VMS provide information as to the movement of fishing vessels, including where they might be fishing or transshipping fish catch, or when they are on approach to port or moving into a closed or restricted fishing area within a coastal State's jurisdiction.

RFMOs are increasingly requiring the use of VMS as a means of enhancing compliance, but the VMS must be fully centralized for data to be automatically transmitted to the RFMO.[120] Koehler has noted that despite most fishing vessels operating under the jurisdiction of two or more RFMOs, core elements of the VMS may differ between each regional body making compatibility an issue.[121] The FAO has observed that:

> The major stumbling block facing effective global deployment of VMS is not technology or cost, it is mainly the will to deploy the systems and the imperative to reach global agreement on system standards and data sharing arrangements.[122]

There are in any event weaknesses with VMS as, for instance, not all fishing vessels will have VMS equipment installed, the equipment may not be switched on, or may be tampered with, and it may not allow for near-real time submission of data and two-way communication.[123] An additional issue may arise in relation to the storage of data. Flag State partnership, if not leadership, in this area will be critical.

4.2. Responding to Flag State Non-Performance

In the development of the Flag State Performance Guidelines, the initial discussions had canvassed the process for ascertaining flag State performance as well as the legal implications for flag States if they failed to meet the identified performance requirements.[124] The latter dimension was ultimately not

---

[119] This position was reiterated in Resolution 71/123 of 7 December 2016, para. 98 and hence remains an issue requiring flag State response.

[120] R Rayfuse and E Meltzer "The MCS and Enforcement Regime" in E Meltzer et al. (ed.) *The Quest for Sustainable International Fisheries: Regional Efforts to Implement the 1995 United Nations Fish Stocks Agreement: An Overview for the May 2006 Review Conference* (National Research Council of Canada Research Press, Ottawa: 2009) 219–260, at 232. Further efforts are nevertheless being made to share data more broadly: see "Tracking Fishing Vessels Around the Globe" available at www.pewtrusts.org/~/media/assets/2016/05/tracking-fishing-vessels.

[121] H Koehler "A Survey of RFMO Vessel Monitoring Systems and Set of Best Practices" (IOTC, 2016) available at www.iotc.org/documents/issf-technical-report-2016-02.

[122] JM Davis "Monitoring Control Surveillance and Vessel Monitoring System Requirements to Combat IUU Fishing" (FAO, Rome: 2000) available at www.fao.org/docrep/005/y3274e/y3274e0g.htm, 70.

[123] See T Long "Tracking Fishing Vessels Around the Globe: Vessel Monitoring Systems Play a Critical Role" (Pew Charitable Trusts: 2016) available at www.pewtrusts.org/en/research-and-analysis/fact-sheets/2016/05/tracking-fishing-vessels-around-the-globe).

[124] See in particular the paper prepared by R Rayfuse (Expert Consultation Report, note 70, App. E.2, at 28).

comprehensively addressed in the Guidelines, although some measures, such as corrective or cooperative actions, are suggested as possible responses following an assessment process.[125] This approach enables the Guidelines to be facilitative but leaves open legal questions about assessing due diligence and international responsibility. One question that emerges is whether a vessel's single infraction would be sufficient to trigger the international responsibility of the flag State, or whether a pattern of conduct is required to demonstrate that the flag State has not exerted reasonable efforts.[126]

The act(s) of non-compliance may be determinative of the responses by diverse actors: whether a coastal State may arrest a fishing vessel, a port State denies access, or an RFMO introduces trade restrictive measures against that vessel.[127] These responses are predominantly directed at the vessel concerned rather than the flag State. Further consequences may result where the flag State manifests a consistent pattern of failure of performance, as indicated by Rayfuse:

> Where a flag State fails in this regard [...], although it will retain its right to grant its flag to vessels, this grant of flag will be non-opposable to other States whose rights and interests have been affected. In other words, the vessels of [those flag] States may be assimilated to Stateless and subject to the full jurisdiction of other States in situations where they are found to be engaged in IUU fishing or other activities that undermine international conservation and management measures.[128]

While this position is arguable and may prove advantageous for States wishing to take action against non-performing flag States' non-compliance, there remains strong political resistance to challenging flag State primacy. The ITLOS has commented that

> [t]here is nothing in article 94 [of the LOS Convention] to permit a State which discovers evidence indicating the absence of proper jurisdiction and control by a flag State over a ship to refuse to recognize the right of the ship to fly the flag of the flag State.[129]

The right to fly the flag encapsulates the right to have the flag State's protection, including responding to claims from other States.[130] Rayfuse has offered an alternative whereby States negatively affected by flag State non-performance could take counter-measures against the flag State as a means of inducing that State to comply with its international obligations.[131]

---

[125] Flag State Performance Guidelines, para. 47.
[126] See Takei, note 25 at 131. See also Expert Consultation Report, note 70 at 22, para. 21.
[127] Rayfuse, note 124, at paras. 27–31.
[128] Ibid., para. 35.
[129] *M/V Saiga (No. 2)*, note 4 at para. 82. See also *Virginia G*, note 5 at para. 111 (reiterating the statement made in the *M/V Saiga (No. 2)*).
[130] So much is reflected in e.g. Draft Article 18 of the International Law Commission's Articles on Diplomatic Protection (available at http://legal.un.org/ilc/texts/instruments/english/draft_articles/9_8_2006.pdf).
[131] Rayfuse, note 124, at paras. 38–40. See further R Rayfuse "Countermeasures and High Seas Fisheries Enforcement" (2004) 51 *Netherlands International Law Quarterly* 41–76; D Guilfoyle

The Guidelines further contemplate that developing States have special requirements for assistance in improving their performance as flag States.[132] Recognition of the position of developing States, especially the least-developed and small island developing States, raises the question of whether any particular allowance is required in assessing flag State performance by these States. In particular, does the due diligence standard account for the position of developing States in assessing State responsibility for non-compliance with international conservation and management measures for fisheries resources? The Seabed Disputes Chamber of the ITLOS considered the position of developing States in relation to due diligence standards associated with deep seabed exploitation in its 2011 *Seabed Advisory Opinion*.[133] The Chamber considered that the principle of equality had to apply to prevent a situation comparable to 'flags of convenience' occurring in relation to State sponsorship of mining activities.[134] On this basis, it would seem that while assistance to developing States is essential as a practical matter, the status as a developing State would not necessarily preclude findings of international responsibility in a due diligence assessment. Ultimately, much would depend on the facts of any particular case for a proper determination.

4.3. International Dispute Settlement

There is increasing scope to challenge flag State action in relation to fishing under the LOS Convention's dispute settlement regime, which allows for the possibility of compulsory arbitration or adjudication among Parties.[135] Disputes concerning fishing in the territorial sea would fall within the scope of compulsory dispute settlement, including where there might be separate fishing agreements concerning fishing in the territorial sea by a foreign State,[136] or where there is a traditional fishing regime in place.[137]

While disputes concerning coastal State decision-making over fisheries in the EEZ are excluded from mandatory arbitration or adjudication, a flag State may still have its actions challenged under compulsory jurisdiction for its actions within the EEZ of another State. For example, in the *South China Sea*

"Interdicting Vessels to Enforce the Common Interest: Maritime Countermeasures and the Use of Force" (2007) 56 *International and Comparative Law Quarterly* 69–82.

[132] Flag State Performance Guidelines, para. 49.

[133] *Responsibilities and Obligations of States Sponsoring Persons and Entities with Respect to Activities in the Area*, Advisory Opinion, ITLOS Case No 17, 1 February 2011 (2011) ITLOS Rep 10.

[134] *Seabed Advisory Opinion*, para. 159.

[135] The LOS Convention dispute settlement regime applies *mutatis mutandis* to the Fish Stocks Agreement (Fish Stocks Agreement, Art. 30(1)). There is, however, no such comparable compulsory regime for the Compliance Agreement.

[136] Consistent with Art. 2(3) of the LOS Convention.

[137] See note 98 at paras. 794–804.

arbitration, the Philippines successfully challenged China's failure to prevent or deter its fishing vessels from harvesting fish, including endangered species, from waters adjudicated to be subject to the sovereign rights of the Philippines in the course of the arbitration.[138] China was also found to have unlawfully asserted law enforcement jurisdiction over fishing vessels in the Philippines' EEZ.[139] These claims could be resolved in arbitration, even though the coastal State's fishing activity in the EEZ would be insulated from such review.

With regard to fishing activities on the high seas, States may seek to challenge a flag State's failure to adhere to its conservation and cooperation obligations set out in Articles 116 to 119 of the LOS Convention. Australia and New Zealand sought arbitration against Japan, arguing that Japan's experimental fishing programme in relation to southern bluefin tuna was conducted without regard to Japan's obligations under the LOS Convention.[140] Although the Tribunal ultimately concluded that it lacked jurisdiction,[141] the case still demonstrates the possibility of using the high seas fishing provisions in the LOS Convention as a basis for making claims against flag States that are not adhering to their international obligations in the conservation and management of fisheries.

States may continue to resist the use of binding third-party settlement as a means of addressing flag State non-performance, as has already been evident in China's non-appearance in the *South China Sea* arbitration and Japan's recent declaration under Article 36(2) of the International Court of Justice's Statute excluding from review disputes relating to living marine resources. However, there is an increasing trend in cases brought under the LOS Convention's dispute settlement mechanism to expand the scope of jurisdiction available under that treaty regime,[142] and it must therefore be anticipated that fisheries disputes may well find their way before a court or tribunal constituted under the LOS Convention.

5. CONCLUDING REMARKS

In sum, when considering how we might strengthen flag State performance, it is critical to acknowledge that we are starting from a position where the flag State

---

[138] See ibid., paras. 682 and 695.

[139] Ibid., para. 695.

[140] *Southern Bluefin Tuna* case *(Australia and New Zealand v. Japan)* (Jurisdiction and Admissibility) (Arbitral Tribunal constituted under annex VII of the United Nations Convention on the Law of the Sea) (Award of 4 August 2000), XXIII UNRIAA 1, available at http://legal.un.org/riaa/cases/vol_XXIII/1-57.pdf.

[141] The reasoning of the *Southern Bluefin Tuna* to deny jurisdiction was in any event rejected in the *South China Sea* arbitration (note 98), Award on Jurisdiction and Admissibility of 25 October 2015, at para. 286.

[142] See discussion in N Klein "The Vicissitudes of Dispute Settlement under the Law of the Sea Convention" (2017) 32 *International Journal of Marine and Coastal Law* 332–363; K Parlett "Beyond the Four Corners of the Convention: Expanding the Scope of Jurisdiction of Law of the Sea Tribunals" (2017) 48 *Ocean Development and International Law* 284–299.

has a fundamental position of importance in the order of the oceans. The flag State has distinct responsibilities in bestowing nationality on fishing vessels and then in exercising prescriptive and enforcement jurisdiction over those vessels. The key failing when assessing flag State performance is in relation to the effective implementation of the existing international fisheries regimes. As a factual matter, not every flag State is meeting its core legal obligation in fisheries conservation and management. Political will, economic incentive, social structures and expectations, food security, as well as human, financial and technological resources all play a part in understanding why this core obligation is not being met. Tackling these dimensions are vital components to strengthening flag State performance overall.

A radical legal change would require a direct confrontation with the concept of the flag State and the rights and duties that flow from that status. Such change could entail operationalizing the genuine link in a meaningful way so as to allow international scrutiny of the link, setting international standards for registration and potentially eliminating flags of convenience. The steps already taken in relation to the Global Record could progress to an international registry of fishing vessels so as to completely internationalize fishing vessel ownership,[143] permitting enforcement by any State authority. The flag State's primary position for law enforcement could be reversed so that other States affected by the illegal conduct of a fishing vessel could act and the flag State has residual responsibility to enforce laws against its vessels if no other State has taken action. An alternative step in this direction could be modelled on the complementarity principle in international criminal law where the flag State might have primary responsibility to enforce but its failure to do so would entitle other States (or even an international organization) to act in its stead. Should universal jurisdiction apply to IUU fishing? We are only limited by imagination in terms of ideas that deviate from the current norms in place. Ultimately, though, radical change is politically and economically unlikely.

Given that scenario, it is then incumbent on all actors to work better with what we have but to do so more cleverly.[144] In doing so, we should consider how to engage better with a diversity of State and non-State actors, as well as drawing on other legal regimes, seeking better integration across legal regimes and engaging further with technology. For example, Erikstein and Swan have noted that States have taken steps to implement international instruments upon which the Flag State Performance Guidelines are based and consequently "implementation of the Guidelines will be synergistic and enhance the processes

---

[143] Could this be conceived of as rendering every fishing vessel stateless? Does it lead to the chaos in the oceans that prompted the need for flag State primacy or does it enable us to subsume the increasing problem of stateless vessels in fisheries regulations and other law enforcement efforts?

[144] This idea is explored in relation to shark conservation and management in EJ Techera and N Klein, *International Law of Sharks: Obstacles, Options and Opportunities* (Brill Nijhoff, Leiden: 2017) 239–243.

already initiated".[145] Agreeing on the consequences for non-compliance should be another priority task in this process. Otherwise, the threat of relying on sources of authority other than the flag State may be enough to spur flag States into greater action to ensure that they maintain their paramount role within the law of the sea framework. However, if that motivation does not emerge, at least there is the opportunity to consider viable alternatives to flag State implementation so the key responsibilities are met, even if not by the flag States concerned.

[145] Erikstein and Swan, note 73 at 145.

16

Ensuring Compliance with Fisheries Regulations by Private Actors

CARMINO MASSARELLA

1. INTRODUCTION

THE CHALLENGE OF effectively regulating fisheries is often a problem of implementation and enforcement rather than the lack of rules themselves. This could be for a number of reasons, including political reluctance or lack of financial resources. For example, a number of reports by the non-governmental organization (NGO) ClientEarth have argued that fisheries regulations under the European Union (EU)'s Common Fisheries Policy are not implemented effectively,[1] something acknowledged by the European Commission itself[2] and in academic literature.[3] The problem is also evident more generally in different geographical regions.[4] One way in which this problem can be addressed is by intervention in various ways by private actors. This chapter examines whether, and to what extent, private actors, with or without governmental authority, are able to take practical action to ensure compliance with fisheries regulations. It will not address the role of private actors in influencing the legislative process, or the private sector role in fisheries management, including co-management.

---

[1] Client Earth "Slipping Through the Net – The Control and Enforcement of Fisheries in France, Ireland, the Netherlands, Poland, Spain and the UK (England)" (29 September 2017) (available at www.documents.clientearth.org/library/download-info/slipping-through-the-net-the-control-and-enforcement-of-fisheries-in-france-ireland-the-netherlands-poland-spain-and-the-uk-england).

[2] European Commission "Evaluation of the impact of Council Regulation (EC) No. 1224/2009 of 20 November 2009 'establishing a Community control system for ensuring compliance with rules of the common fisheries policy' Synthesis report of the first five years report of Member States according to Art 118" (available at https://publications.europa.eu/en/publication-detail/-/publication/0edfa926-d328-11e6-ad7c-01aa75ed71a1).

[3] JM Da Rocha, S Cerviño and S Villasante "The Common Fisheries Policy: An Enforcement Problem" (2012) 36 *Marine Policy* 1309–1314.

[4] MO Haughton "Compliance and Enforcement of Fisheries Regulations in the Caribbean" (2003) 54 *Proceedings of the Fifty Fourth Annual Gulf and Caribbean Fisheries Institute* 188–201.

The chapter first examines questions of authority and legitimacy surrounding the activities of private actors seeking to ensure compliance with fisheries regulations (Section 2). It then considers the relevant rules of international law to acts of enforcement at sea (Section 3). Subsequently, the chapter goes on to survey the three main ways in which private actors are able to play a role in the enforcement of fisheries regulations, specifically: evidence-gathering (Section 4); unilateral protest and direct action (Section 5); enforcement by private actors working together in partnership with public authorities (Section 6); and the conduct of litigation (Section 7). Some of the more prominent recent cases in which the role of private actors has come under scrutiny will be surveyed in these sections. Finally, the chapter will draw conclusions from this analysis, including the potential legal ramifications of private actors playing a role in the enforcement of fisheries regulations, and consider the options for the potential future development of this field (Section 8). It will be suggested that evaluation of recent developments points to a developing number of ways in which private actors are able to play a role in ensuring compliance with fisheries regulations, in particular in relation to monitoring and bringing litigation. At the same time, it is possible that, as direct action by environmental NGOs faces ever more robust responses from States, other less confrontational activities, including partnering with governments, may increasingly take their place.

2. QUESTIONS OF AUTHORITY AND LEGITIMACY

The participation of private actors in what would normally be thought of as a public role, is not a novel one. Historically speaking, private actors played a significant role on the international stage, as mercenaries, filibusters, mercantile companies such as the Dutch and British East India Companies, and, of particular relevance in the present context, as privateers. Privateers were private actors who were authorized by States to perform belligerent acts at sea, and specifically to seize enemy vessels, or vessels trading with the enemy, as prize.[5] The role of private actors was important to States at the time because it enabled them to project military force without the corresponding financial investment in regular naval forces. Privateering, however, posed a risk both to those who practised it, and to the State system itself. Privateers who exceeded their commissions potentially imperilled the freedom of navigation, commercial interests, and even the very authority of the State.[6] Such individuals were pirates, subject to the severest punishment. Some of these controversies have

---

[5] DJ Bederman "Privateering" in *Max Planck Encyclopedia of Public International Law On-line Edition* (Oxford University Press, Oxford: 2008).
[6] On the history of non-State actors in international affairs, see generally J Thomson *Mercenaries, Pirates, and Sovereigns* (Princeton University Press, Princeton: 1994).

returned today, in particular with concerns over the regulation of private maritime security companies (PMSCs) and the now widespread use of armed guards aboard commercial vessels.[7]

In the context of the role of private actors in tackling illegal fishing, the most significant actors are activist NGOs such as the Sea Shepherd Conservation Society (hereafter: Sea Shepherd) and Greenpeace. Just as questions of authority played an important role in the activities of private actors historically, so too do they remain a significant factor today. Sea Shepherd famously claims that the authority for its direct action campaigns derives from international agreements protecting wildlife and the environment. In more than one interview Paul Watson,[8] the founder of Sea Shepherd, has claimed that the organization is empowered to intervene by the United Nations (UN) World Charter for Nature,[9] even going as far as claiming that the organization's "primary mandate is to assume a law enforcement role as provided by" that document.[10] Sea Shepherd also claims that this was successfully used in its defence in criminal proceedings in Canada.[11] In reality, however, the Charter is merely a UN General Assembly resolution, and is not in itself a source of legal authority. Furthermore, although it urges all persons, including NGOs, to "safeguard and conserve nature in areas beyond national jurisdiction",[12] it does not set out specific rights or powers to do so. Sea Shepherd's claim that their direct action activities were authorized by the Charter was specifically rejected by a District Court in the United States (US).[13]

Greenpeace on the other hand frames its rights to take action within human rights law, in particular the right to freedom of expression[14] and peaceful assembly.[15] Private actors are also able to rely on general freedoms protected by the law of the sea, such as the freedom of navigation on the high seas, protected by Articles 87 and 91 of the LOS Convention.[16] Private actors are also increasingly recognized as having standing to bring proceedings for the protection of

---

[7] A Priddy and S Casey-Maslen "Counter-piracy Operations by Private Maritime Security Contractors: Key Legal Issues and Challenges" (2012) 10 *Journal of International Criminal Justice* 839–856, at 839–843.

[8] The Maritime Executive "Top Ten Misconceptions about Sea Shepherd" (14 April 2017) (available at http://maritime-executive.com/editorials/top-ten-misconceptions-about-sea-shepherd).

[9] United Nations General Assembly (UNGA) Res. 37/7 of 28 October 1982.

[10] Sea Shepherd Conservation Society 'Mandate', https://seashepherd.org/mandate/.

[11] Ibid.

[12] Charter for Nature, note 9 at para. 21(e).

[13] *Institute of Cetacean Research et al. v. Sea Shepherd Conservation Society et al.* 860 F. Supp 2d 1216 (W.D. Wash 2012) at 1236.

[14] E.g. under Art. 19 of the ICCPR (International Covenant on Civil and Political Rights of 19 December 1966 (999 UNTS 171)).

[15] E.g. under Art. 21 of the ICCPR, note 14. See J Teulings "Peaceful Protests against Whaling on the High Seas – A Human Rights Based Approach" in CR Symons (ed.) *Selected Contemporary Issues in the Law of the Sea* (Martinus Nijhoff, Leiden: 2011) 221–250, at 235–236.

[16] United Nations Convention on the Law of the Sea of 10 December 1982 (1833 UNTS 3).

the environment generally by virtue of the public interest in such issues. These possibilities are examined below.

3. PRIVATE ACTORS AND THE LAW OF SEA

The extent to which private actors are able to play a role in ensuring compliance with fisheries regulations depends on a number of factors. Private actors can engage in a range of activities, which differ in the extent to which they pose a challenge to State authority. On the one hand, there is protest activity which can range from passive protest to direct action. Direct action can include forcible actions, including boarding, ramming and attempting to otherwise damage target vessels.[17] On the other hand, activities such as evidence-gathering, and enforcement action in cooperation with public authorities, pose less risk of putting private actors on the wrong side of the law.

These activities are regulated by several different areas of law, including the rules governing the different maritime zones in the law of the sea, human rights protections, questions of flag State jurisdiction, immunities and public authority (if any), and the effect of certain international instruments on conduct at sea.

Of the different maritime zones, the one in which the enforcement of fisheries regulations is the most difficult is the high seas, which lies outside of the jurisdiction of coastal States. It is also within this maritime zone that private actors potentially have the greatest freedom of action, since they are able to rely on the freedom of navigation afforded to all States under Article 87 of the LOS Convention and customary international law. This allows them to engage in a range of activities including observation and monitoring as well as more direct activities. Jurisdiction on the high seas is generally reserved to the flag State, subject to the narrow exceptions set out in Article 110, and in particular jurisdiction over piracy and Stateless vessels. Statelessness presents a risk to vessels conducting protests or direct action, since such vessels often have multinational crews, and have been known to fly their organizations' flags rather than the flag of the State in which they are registered.[18] At the same time, flag States have often come under pressure to de-register vessels that are engaged in these activities.[19] Consequently, NGOs involved in protest and direct action take care to ensure that they have adequate support from their flag State, in particular

---

[17] G Plant "International Law and Direct Action Protests at Sea: Twenty Years On" (2002) 33 *Netherlands Yearbook of International Law* 75–117, at 80–81; R Caddell "Regulating the Whale Wars: Freedom of Protest, Navigational Safety and the Law of the Sea in the Polar Regions" (2014) 6 *Yearbook of Polar Law* 497–544, at 500.

[18] Art. 92 of the LOS Convention. On this point, see Plant, note 17 at 80.

[19] See e.g. the news-item "Anti-Whaling Ships Say They Have Been Made 'Pirates'" (2 February 2007) available at www.reuters.com/article/idUSSYD91724.

its willingness to take diplomatic and legal action to ensure protection of the rights of the private actors.[20]

Activities closer to land become subject to greater control by the coastal State. Within the exclusive economic zone (EEZ), the coastal State has sovereign rights over living and non-living natural resources, and has jurisdiction over artificial islands and structures, marine scientific research, and the protection and preservation of the marine environment.[21] Beyond this coastal State authority, the EEZ can be said to have a residual high seas nature, being otherwise subject to the same rules as the high seas.[22] This includes the freedom of navigation, but also, for example, the rules relating to piracy.[23]

Although this provides a substantial measure of freedom to private vessels in this maritime zone, jurisprudence suggests that the level of control granted to the coastal State under Article 56 of the LOS Convention is nevertheless broad. For example, in the *M/V Virginia G* case,[24] the ITLOS[25] held that activities relatively loosely related to fishing – specifically in that case the bunkering of fishing vessels – fell within the jurisdiction of the coastal State.[26] Since Article 56 grants the coastal State sovereign rights over fishing within its EEZ, the coastal State arguably would also have jurisdiction over activities that interfere with those rights, for example interfering with fishing vessels or their fishing gear. This issue was also considered in the *Arctic Sunrise* arbitration[27] (see Section 5).

In addition to the EEZ, other potentially significant maritime areas and zones include international straits and archipelagic waters, within which the ability to engage in activities is even more constrained. Within international straits vessels are permitted to exercise 'transit passage' pursuant to Article 38 of the LOS Convention, which is defined as "the freedom of navigation and overflight solely for the purpose of continuous and expeditious transit of the strait" and in compliance with the rules of international law. Within archipelagic waters, a not dissimilar regime exists in the form of "archipelagic sea lanes passage" under Article 53 of the LOS Convention, which also limits navigation to continuous and expeditious transit.

---

[20] E.g. the initiation of proceedings by the Netherlands against the Russian Federation in the *Arctic Sunrise* case (*Netherlands v. Russian Federation*), Order on Provisional Measures of 22 November 2013) before the International Tribunal for the Law of the Sea (ITLOS) discussed in Section 5.

[21] Art. 56 of the LOS Convention.

[22] Ibid., Art. 58.

[23] Although the LOS Convention's definition of piracy appears in the high seas part (Part VII) of the Convention, the general view is that the piracy rules nevertheless also apply in the EEZ by virtue of Art. 58(2). For a discussion of this point, see D Guilfoyle *Shipping Interdiction and the Law of the Sea* (Cambridge University Press, Cambridge: 2009) 44.

[24] *The M/V "Virginia G"* case (*Panama v. Guinea Bissau*), Judgment of 14 April 2014.

[25] See note 20.

[26] Ibid., para. 217. See also DR Rothwell and T Stephens *The International Law of the Sea* (Hart Publishing, Oxford & Portland: 2016) 324.

[27] *In the Matter of the Arctic Sunrise Arbitration* (*Netherlands v. Russian Federation*), Award on the Merits of 14 August 2015 (PCA Case No. 2014-02; available at www.pcacases.com/web/).

Within the territorial sea and internal waters the ability of private actors to perform acts of protest or monitoring are much more restrictive. Within the territorial sea, vessels are subject to the constraints of the regime of innocent passage.[28] This would present substantial limits to monitoring and observation of fishing activities by vessels not flying the flag of the coastal State, without the permission of that State, since loitering in the territorial sea would not constitute 'passage' under Article 18 of the LOS Convention. Additionally, Article 19(2) of the LOS Convention lists a number of particular activities that, if undertaken, would render passage non-innocent, including research and survey activities, and the launching, landing or taking on board of any aircraft, which would preclude the use of vessel-launched aerial and sea drones. Additional coastal State jurisdiction is provided by the rules relating to hot pursuit,[29] the contiguous zone[30] and constructive presence.

Where vessels enter into port or internal waters, vessels and their crew fall within the plenary prescriptive and enforcement jurisdiction of the port or coastal State. In practice, this means that such vessels could be subject to proceedings for breaches of regulations themselves, such as failure to comply with the COLREGs,[31] during protest or monitoring activities. They can also be subject to inspection and delay by the port State in order to frustrate activities at sea.[32] At the same time, observation and monitoring activities by private actors are comparatively straightforward in port. As noted below, private individuals are able to make observations of which vessels enter port and when, and are able to observe fishing gear and landing of catches. Although fishing vessels are not necessarily engaged in illegal fishing activity while in port, it is possible for such information-gathering activities to build a general picture of movements and activities of fishing vessels. Vessels may be engaged in other illegal activity including breach of labour standards, landing of illegal catch and taking on board or possession of illegal fishing gear. Where protest activities are concerned, private actors would fall squarely within the jurisdiction of the port or coastal State. To the extent that those activities contravene the domestic law of the State, then, subject to the protections afforded by international human rights law, they are susceptible to sanction accordingly.

Turning to the question of human rights as a basis for the activities of private actors – as noted above – some measure of protection is provided by the right to freedom of expression, and the right to freedom of assembly, and is explicitly relied upon by Greenpeace as the basis for their activities. The extent to which international human rights law defends the right of protest at sea is illustrated

---

[28] LOS Convention, Arts. 17–19.

[29] Ibid., Art. 111.

[30] Ibid., Art. 33.

[31] Convention on the International Regulations for Preventing Collisions at Sea of 20 October 1972 (1050 UNTS 16; as regularly amended), discussed further below.

[32] See G Plant "Civilian Protest Vessels and the Law of the Sea" (1983) 14 *Netherlands Yearbook of International Law* 133–163, at 143–144.

by case law from the European Court of Human Rights (ECtHR) concerning Articles 10 and 11 of the ECHR.[33] In the conjoined cases of *Steel and Others v. UK*, the Court considered several cases that had involved a range of activities from peaceful protest by means of placards and leaflets, to cases involving physical interference with activities. The Court observed that States were entitled to a margin of appreciation regarding the question of whether it was legitimate to interfere with the right of protest, and in particular whether the interference was prescribed by law, and necessary in a democratic society. The Court considered that 'physically impeding' activities was in general not a protected form of freedom of expression.[34]

The Court's approach to protest activities at sea is illustrated by the cases of *Women on Waves and Others v. Portugal* and *Drieman and Others v. Norway*. In the first of these cases, the closure of the territorial sea to a vessel belonging to abortion activists was held to be excessively restrictive. The Court considered that the respondent government had a range of other means at its disposal to regulate the activities at issue, and that completely preventing passage through the territorial sea was not a proportionate response.[35] The *Drieman* case concerned Greenpeace activists who obstructed whaling activities in the Norwegian EEZ. The Court took the view that the Norwegian authorities had provided Greenpeace with adequate opportunity to demonstrate peacefully, and had acted lawfully in bringing proceedings against the activists for their physical interference with Norwegian whaling vessels.[36]

In reality therefore, notwithstanding the fact that much reliance is placed on the right to freedom of expression to support the right of protest and to carry out direct action at sea, the extent of those rights is limited. On the one hand by a wide margin of appreciation on the part of public authorities, and on the other by limiting the rights to passive demonstration and excluding direct action and interference.

An entirely different approach to the role of private actors in enforcing fisheries regulations is that of partnering with public authorities. Where private actors are commissioned by public authorities, it is possible for them to benefit from enhanced rights. However, these rights are also limited to the extent that they could be exercised by the States themselves. Examples of rights that can be claimed by publicly authorized vessels are the rights of visit and hot pursuit. Under Article 110 of the LOS Convention, vessels that are duly authorized and clearly marked and identifiable as being on government service may

---

[33] Convention for the Protection of Human Rights and Fundamental Freedoms of 4 November 1950 (213 UNTS 221), as amended.

[34] *Steel and Others v. UK* (1999) 28 E.H.R.R. 603.

[35] *Women on Waves and Others v. Portugal* (App no. 31276/05 ECtHR, 3 February 2009).

[36] *Drieman and Others v. Norway* (App no. 33678/969 ECtHR, 4 May 2000). See further Caddell, note 17; and J Kraska "The Laws of Civil Obedience in the Maritime Domain" in C Espósito, J Kraska, HN Scheiber and MS Kwon (eds.) *Ocean Law and Policy Twenty Years of Development Under the UNCLOS Regime* (Brill/Nijhoff, Leiden: 2016) 161–202.

exercise the right of visit. Article 111 provides that vessels acting on behalf of the coastal State may engage in hot pursuit and interdict vessels that have committed relevant offences within the coastal State's internal waters, territorial sea, archipelagic waters, contiguous zone or EEZ. The condition for this is provided in Article 111(5), which specifies that the vessel must be "clearly marked and identifiable as being on government service and authorized to that effect".

Another example is the authority contemplated under the Fish Stocks Agreement.[37] Under the regime of regional fisheries management organizations (RFMOs), Members can grant one another the right to board and inspect each other's vessels. The Fish Stocks Agreement makes explicit provision for private actors to participate in fisheries enforcement, provided that they are duly authorized by a State Party. Under Article 21(1) of the Agreement, a Party "may through its duly authorized inspectors, board and inspect [...] fishing vessels flying the flag of another State" which is Party to the Agreement. Article 21(4) provides that:

> Prior to taking action under this article, inspecting States shall, either directly or through the relevant subregional or regional fisheries management organization or arrangement, inform all States whose vessels fish on the high seas in the subregion or region of the form of identification issued to their duly authorized inspectors. The vessels used for boarding and inspection shall be clearly marked and identifiable as being on government service.

Thus, provided that the inspecting fisheries management vessel is duly authorized and marked and identifiable as being on government service, then it is possible for fisheries inspections to be contracted out to private actors. Within coastal State maritime zones – including the EEZ, archipelagic waters and the territorial sea – where coastal States have jurisdiction over fisheries, there is also in principle nothing stopping the coastal State from authorizing private actors to play a role in the enforcement of fisheries regulations, essentially privatizing that function.

An aspect of States authorizing private individuals to exercise public functions that is not well theorized is the question of immunities. Some illustration of the complexity of this issue is offered by the United Kingdom (UK) case of *Fogg v. Secretary of State for Defence*, which concerns the slightly different issue of the status of underwater shipwrecks.[38] In that case, an issue had arisen over the purchase of the wreck of a merchant navy vessel that had been sunk as a result of enemy action during World War II. The vessel had been heavily armed and partly crewed by military personnel. Family members of servicemen who

---

[37] Agreement for the Implementation of the Provisions of the United Nations Convention on the Law of the Sea of 10 December 1982 relating to the Conservation and Management of Straddling Fish Stocks and Highly Migratory Fish Stocks of 4 August 1995 (2167 UNTS 3).

[38] R. *(on the application of Fogg) v. Secretary of State for Defence* [2005] EWHC 2888 Admin (13 December 2005), [2006] EWCA Civ 1270 (5 October 2006).

had perished aboard the vessel argued that the wreck should not be interfered with since it was entitled to immunity under UK domestic law through the Protection of Military Remains Act 1986. The High Court and then the Court of Appeal found that the vessel had been in the service of the armed forces at the time of its sinking, and agreed that it should be considered by the Secretary of State for the granting of immunity under the Act.

Certainly, vessels "owned or operated by a State and used only on government non-commercial service shall, on the high seas, have complete immunity" from States other than their flag State under Article 96 of the LOS Convention. Furthermore, individuals who could be said to be 'State officials' would be entitled to functional immunity for actions that they undertake in the course of their duties. In practice, there appears to be an increasing number of instances where private actors are partnering with States by providing vessels and crew who, together with public official ship-riders, operate under public authority and supervision. These activities blur the public-private distinction, and it could be argued that such individuals are no longer private actors, strictly speaking. Recent developments in this regard are examined in Section 6 below.

Although international law offers a number of protections and rights for private actors when undertaking activities at sea, it also regulates conduct at sea, raising the possibility of private actors incurring liability. The first of these is the regulation of safe navigation by the COLREGs, which are generally implemented in flag States' domestic law. These regulations could, for example, give rise to liability in instances where direct action involves navigating in such a way as to risk causing collision between vessels.[39] Following a collision between the Greenpeace ship *Arctic Sunrise* and the Japanese whaling vessel *Nisshin Maru* in January 2016, Japan put forward a draft Code of Conduct which sought to more closely regulate the specific activities of NGOs carrying out acts of protest and direct action.[40] The draft Code was specifically concerned with requiring that such activities be conducted in a non-violent manner, and in a way that did not endanger the safety of persons or vessels at sea. The Code also sought to place more responsibility on the flag States of protest vessels. These proposals were opposed by Greenpeace in particular, who argued that the Code was an unnecessary duplication of existing measures including the COLREGs. In the event, the Code was not adopted, but the International Maritime Organization (IMO) instead passed a Resolution expressing its concern at the potential dangers to navigation posed by direct action protests, and urged States to ensure that existing legal measures are enforced.[41]

Finally, carrying out direct action at sea without any form of public authority also carries the risk of liability under the piracy provisions of the

---

[39] Plant, note 17 at 88.
[40] IMO Doc. NAV 54/10/1 of 25 April 2008, Annex.
[41] Res. MSC.303(87) of 17 May 2010. See Kraska, note 36 at 196–200.

LOS Convention, and potentially also under the SUA Convention.[42] So far as piracy is concerned, any illegal acts of violence or detention conducted by one vessel against another on the high seas or outside the jurisdiction of any State 'for private ends', falls within the definition of piracy under Article 101 of the LOS Convention. This allows any State to exercise prescriptive and enforcement jurisdiction over the vessel and its crew under Article 105. It is generally accepted that the 'private ends' requirement encompasses all activities performed without public authority.[43]

It is also possible for protesters at sea to find themselves in danger of prosecution under the provisions of the SUA Convention. This little used counter-terrorism convention was adopted in the aftermath of the 1985 *Achille Lauro* hijacking, and requires Parties to establish criminal offences and jurisdiction over activities endangering the safety of maritime navigation. Although it would not immediately seem applicable to issues of protest at sea, its provisions are so broad that they pose a risk to actors performing unauthorized direct action at sea, and is specifically referred to in the above-mentioned IMO Resolution.

4. MONITORING AND EVIDENCE-GATHERING

One of the most important ways in which private actors are involved in ensuring compliance with fisheries regulations is by performing monitoring and evidence-gathering, whether remotely, at sea, or in port. This information can serve two main purposes. The first is to raise awareness, investigate and – potentially – to put pressure on authorities to take action against infringements of fisheries regulations. The second is where sufficient evidence is gathered to allow legal proceedings to be brought, or for other measures to be taken, such as blacklisting. These activities can themselves be divided into three main categories depending on whether the monitoring and evidence-gathering takes place remotely, within port, or at sea.

The first method of gathering evidence is that undertaken remotely. Although satellite-based vessel monitoring systems, the use of radar monitoring, and other methods of tracking fishing vessels are all available to developed States, the same is not necessarily true for developing States. In these circumstances, private actors are able to play a potentially significant role in supporting those States with the technology to allow them to monitor fishing activities. One such initiative is that of the Pew Charitable Trusts, which is able to provide fisheries monitoring information to allow coastal States to observe fishing activities in their maritime zones.[44] Another similar initiative is that of Global Fishing

---

[42] Convention for the Suppression of Unlawful Acts Against the Safety of Maritime Navigation of 10 March 1988 (1678 UNTS 201).

[43] Guilfoyle, note 23 at 32–42.

[44] See T Long "Satellite Tracking Can Unmask Illegal Fishing Vessels" (*The Pew Charitable Trusts*, 20 November 2015) (available at www.pewtrusts.org/en/research-and-analysis/analysis/2015/11/20/

Watch, which also provides tracking information to identify illegal, unreported and unregulated (IUU) fishing.[45]

A second significant way in which private actors can undertake information-gathering is in port. One example is the work undertaken by the 'Black Fish' initiative, which involves training citizen-activists to monitor fishing vessel movements and look out for illegal fishing gear.[46] An initiative that has attracted attention recently is that of the Environmental Justice Foundation, which has been active in uncovering and investigating slavery in the fishing industry in Thailand.[47] One result of their investigation was that the European Commission imposed a 'yellow card' warning to the Thai fishing industry, requiring action to be taken to remedy these issues. The foundation is also active in tackling IUU fishing.[48]

Monitoring can also take place at sea, including by 'shadowing' suspected IUU vessels. Evidence-gathering can identify illegal fishing, illegal fishing techniques and gear, and can also identify illegal at-sea transhipments. Sea Shepherd in particular has had a number of successes in gathering sufficient evidence to allow prosecutions to proceed against illegal fishing. One example was the success of their 'Operation Driftnet' launched in February 2016. That action targeted a fleet of Chinese fishing vessels using driftnets in the Indian Ocean. The evidence gathered was subsequently submitted to the Chinese Government, who reportedly prosecuted the masters of the vessels concerned, and imposed fines on the company operating them.[49] In another widely publicised action, the Sea Shepherd vessels *Bob Barker* and *Sam Simon* shadowed the fishing vessel *Thunder*, one of six vessels suspected of illegal toothfish fishing in the Southern Ocean. After pursuing the vessel for 110 days over 10,000 miles, the *Thunder* sank in the Gulf of Guinea, apparently having been scuttled by

satellite-tracking-can-unmask-illegal-fishing-vessels); and J Amos "Satellite Watchroom Targets Illegal Fishing" (*BBC News*, 22 January 2015) (available at www.bbc.co.uk/news/science-environment-30929047).

[45] See the item "About the Project" at http://globalfishingwatch.org/the-project. See also G Lubin "Satellite Watchers Busted and Illegal Fishing Vessel, and They're Coming for Others Around the World" (*Business Insider UK*, 1 November 2016) (available at http://uk.businessinsider.com/global-fishing-watch-catches-illegal-fishing-vessel-2016-11).

[46] See the item "About" at https://theblackfish.org. See also M Green "The Black Fish: Undercover with Vigilantes Fighting Organised Crime at Sea" (*The Guardian*, 24 February 2016) (available at www.theguardian.com/environment/2016/feb/24/black-fish-undercover-with-vigilantes-fighting-organised-crime-at-sea).

[47] See the item "Combating Seafood Slavery" at http://ejfoundation.org/campaigns/oceans/item/seafood-not-slavefood. See also K Hodal "Slavery and Trafficking Continue in Thai Fishing Industry, Claim Activists" (*The Guardian*, 25 February 2016) (available at www.theguardian.com/global-development/2016/feb/25/slavery-trafficking-thai-fishing-industry-environmental-justice-foundation).

[48] See the item "Ending Pirate Fishing" at http://ejfoundation.org/campaigns/oceans/item/ending-pirate-fishing. See also Chapters 13 (van der Marel), 14 (Churchill) and 17 (Caddell, Leloudas and Soyer) of this volume.

[49] See the item "Operation Driftnet a Resounding Success; Sea Shepherd Shuts Down Entire Illegal Driftnet Fleet" (29 June 2016) (available at www.seashepherdglobal.org/news-and-commentary/news/operation-driftnet-a-resounding-success-sea-shepherd-shuts-down-entire-illegal-driftnet-fleet.html).

the crew. The Sea Shepherd vessels rescued the 40 crew members, but were also able to salvage evidence from the vessel before it sank, including computers and documents.[50] The captain and two other crew members were put on trial in São Tomé and Príncipe and fined and sentenced to prison for a range of offences including "pollution, reckless driving, forgery, and negligence".[51]

5. PROTEST AND DIRECT ACTION

Direct action can take different forms, ranging from peaceful protest to more forcible action. Protest action has taken place against a variety of environmentally damaging activities, including nuclear testing, dumping of nuclear and chemical waste, as well as controversial marine activities such as whaling.[52] Whilst Greenpeace states that their activities are limited to peaceful protest, methods have included boarding vessels and damaging them. Sea Shepherd has historically been even more prepared to use forcible measures, including the ramming of other vessels, attempting to disable propeller blades with reinforced ropes, and scuttling and even mining vessels in port.[53] These kinds of activities often push the limits of what is legally permissible, and have resulted in legal action against the activists on a number of occasions, even to the extent of arrest and imprisonment. The reaction of States to protest activities of NGOs has also resulted in a number of high-profile cases, which illustrate the legal issues that affect protest activities.

Greenpeace has been the subject of litigation on a number of occasions over the years.[54] One of the most significant cases for the purposes of the present discussion was the case of *Castle John* in 1985. That case involved a protest by Greenpeace activists against the dumping of titanium oxide waste in the North Sea. Greenpeace took action using their own vessel – the Dutch-flagged ship *Sirius* – against two vessels operating out of the port of Antwerp, the *M.S. Falco* and the *Wadsy Tanker*. Proceedings were brought in Belgium against Greenpeace for an injunction and damages. In examining the claim, the Belgian Court

---

[50] T Hume "110-day Ocean Hunt Ends with Sea Shepherd Rescuing Alleged Poachers" (*CNN*, 8 April 2015) (available at: http://edition.cnn.com/2015/04/07/africa/sea-shepherd-rescue-fishing-ship/index.html); I Urbina "A Renegade Trawler, Hunted for 10,000 Miles by Vigilantes" (*New York Times*, 28 July 2015) (available at: www.nytimes.com/2015/07/28/world/a-renegade-trawler-hunted-for-10000-miles-by-vigilantes.html).

[51] I Urbina "African Court Convicts Captain of Renegade Ship in Illegal Fishing Case" (*New York Times*, 12 October 2015) (available at www.nytimes.com/2015/10/13/world/africa/african-court-convicts-captain-of-renegade-ship-in-illegal-fishing-case.html).

[52] Plant, note 17 at 137.

[53] SP Menefee "The Case of the *Castle John*, Or Greenbeard the Pirate?: Environmentalism, Piracy and Development of International Law" (1993) 24(1) *California Western International Law Journal* 1–16, at 7–9; JE Roeschke "Eco-Terrorism and Piracy on the High Seas: Japanese Whaling and the Rights of Private Groups to Enforce International Conservation Law in Neutral Waters (2009) 20 *Villanova Environmental Law Journal* 99–136, at 107–108.

[54] Many of these historical cases are surveyed in Plant, notes 17 and 32.

of First Instance recognized that Greenpeace was able to claim a right to protest, but that this right was limited, and could not be allowed to interfere with the freedom of navigation, or to justify damage to the vessels concerned.[55] The case was appealed to the Belgian Court of Cassation, in particular concerning the argument over jurisdiction over the activities. The Court held that it had jurisdiction on the basis that the activities amounted to piracy, and that the Court had jurisdiction to impose measures on Greenpeace, notwithstanding arguments about the definition of 'private ends'.[56]

Perhaps one of the most high-profile cases of recent times involving direct action at sea is that involving the Greenpeace vessel *Arctic Sunrise*. The case arose out of an incident in September 2013 when the *Arctic Sunrise* and its crew were engaged in a protest against the *Prirazlomnaya* oil platform within the EEZ of the Russian Federation in the Pechora Sea. The vessel was seized by the Russian authorities, and the crew arrested. Although all of those on board were charged with offences in relation to the protest, they were later released and pardoned, but not before the Netherlands – as flag State of the *Arctic Sunrise* – had brought proceedings under the LOS Convention against the Russian Federation: first for provisional measures before the ITLOS (hereafter: *Arctic Sunrise* case),[57] and then subsequently proceedings for wrongful interference with the vessel before an Annex VII Arbitral Tribunal (hereafter: *Arctic Sunrise* arbitration).[58]

The question of Russia's jurisdiction over the *Arctic Sunrise* is complex, since it is not only concerned with the question of jurisdiction in the EEZ, but also jurisdiction relating to fixed platforms, the safety zones around them, and the right of hot pursuit from them under Article 111 of the LOS Convention. The Dutch and Russian authorities took differing views on the legality of the action of the Greenpeace vessel. The Russian Government also took the position that neither the ITLOS nor the Annex VII Arbitral Tribunal had jurisdiction over the dispute, and declined to take part in the proceedings.

In assessing the lawfulness of Russia's seizure of the *Arctic Sunrise*, the arbitral tribunal accepted the Netherlands' assertion that it should apply a threefold test, namely whether:

> (i) the measures had a basis in international law; and (ii) the measures were carried out in accordance with international law, including with the principle of

---

[55] *M.S. Wady Tanker, M.S. Sirius N.V. Mabeco, N.V. Parfin v. 1 J. Castle, 2 Nederlandse Stichting Sirius*, 20 European Transport Law 536 (Summary hearing of Court of First Instance, 12 June 1985).
[56] *Castle John and Nederlandse Stichting Sirius v. Nv Marjlo and Nv Parfin* 77 *International Law Reports* 537. Also see generally Menefee, note 53.
[57] See note 20.
[58] See note 27. See generally AG Oude Elferink "The Arctic Sunrise Incident: A Multi-faceted Law of the Sea Case with a Human Rights Dimension" (2014) 29 *International Journal of Marine and Coastal Law* 244–289; J Mossop "Protests against Oil Exploration at Sea: Lessons from the Arctic Sunrise Arbitration (2016) 31 *International Journal of Marine and Coastal Law* 60–87; and R Caddell "Platforms, Protestors and Provisional Measures: The *Arctic Sunrise* Dispute and Environmental Activism at Sea" (2014) 45 *Netherlands Yearbook of International Law* 359–384.

reasonableness. Where such measures involve enforcement measures they are subject to the general principles of necessity and proportionality.[59]

The Tribunal acknowledged that there is a right of protest at sea, and that the exercise of this right is "an internationally lawful use of the sea related to the freedom of navigation". It observed that the right to protest at sea is "necessarily exercised in conjunction with the freedom of navigation" and that the right to protest "derives from the freedom of expression and the freedom of assembly", derived from international human rights instruments. It also noted, however, that the right of protest is subject to limitations, including those defined by the law of the sea.[60]

The Tribunal examined a number of possible bases upon which Russia might lawfully have exercised jurisdiction over the *Arctic Sunrise*. In the case of piracy, the Tribunal discounted this on the basis that the *Prirazlomnaya* platform was not a ship, and that the definition of piracy in Article 101 of the LOS Convention consequently did not apply. It did not consider the question of piracy any further for that reason.[61] The Tribunal also rejected the idea that the Russian authorities may have suspected the protestors of being engaged in terrorism, since they were aware of the nature of the activities of the *Arctic Sunrise*.

Of particular interest was the Tribunal's discussion of the coastal State's rights to regulate activities related to its sovereign rights over natural resources in the EEZ. The Tribunal stated that in its view the protection of the coastal State's sovereign rights "is a legitimate aim that allows it to take appropriate measures for that purpose", again noting that those measures "must fulfil the tests of reasonableness, necessity, and proportionality".[62] The Tribunal stated that in its opinion the right of the coastal State to intervene to protect its sovereign rights in the EEZ would extend to "(i) violations of its laws adopted in conformity with the Convention; (ii) dangerous situations that can result in injuries to persons and damage to equipment and installations; (iii) negative environmental consequences [...]; and (iv) delay or interruption in essential operations" on the oil platform.[63]

Ultimately the Tribunal took the view that the measures taken against the *Arctic Sunrise* "did not constitute a lawful exercise of Russia's law enforcement powers concerning the exploration and exploitation of its non-living resources in the EEZ"[64] under Article 77 of the LOS Convention. Neither did it consider that Russia's actions could be justified under Articles 220 and 234 of the LOS Convention relating to pollution.[65] Finally, the Tribunal also held that at least

---

[59] *Arctic Sunrise* arbitration, note 27 at para. 222.
[60] Ibid., para. 227.
[61] Ibid., paras. 238–240.
[62] Ibid., para. 222.
[63] Ibid., para. 327.
[64] Ibid., para. 285.
[65] Ibid., para. 297.

one of the conditions for the lawful exercise of the right of hot pursuit was not met.[66]

Greenpeace is of course not alone in its involvement in cases of this type. Sea Shepherd – established by Paul Watson, who left Greenpeace in 1977 – soon became famous for its direct action efforts. Initially called the Earthforce Environmental Society, the organization was later formally incorporated under its current name in the US in 1981.[67] From the outset Watson and his organization became known for their confrontational tactics and brushes with the law. Tactics have included ramming vessels at sea and scuttling them in port, as well as accusations of using mines against vessels. Watson himself has been arrested on several occasions in connection with direct action activities, starting with the seizure of his original vessel *Sea Shepherd* by the Portuguese authorities in 1979.[68]

An important case in the present context is that of the *Institute of Cetacean Research v. Sea Shepherd Conservation Society* litigation in the US under the Alien Tort Statute.[69] In that case the Institute of Cetacean Research – a Japanese government organization – had sought and been granted an injunction against Sea Shepherd preventing it from taking action to obstruct whaling activities in the Southern Pacific. Once again, the decision of the Court turned on the question of the definition of piracy, and 'for private ends' in particular. The Court held that direct action environmental protest at sea could meet the definition in Article 101 of the LOS Convention.[70]

When Sea Shepherd did breach the injunction in 2014, the Institute brought proceedings again, and Sea Shepherd was found in contempt of court, despite its arguments that the activities were taken by the Australian branch rather than the US organization. Sea Shepherd had more success with this defence in another case brought in the UK, *Fish & Fish*. In that case the UK Supreme Court found that proceedings against the UK branch of Sea Shepherd for direct action involving the cutting of fishing nets could not succeed because the activities of the branch did not constitute assistance in the commission of a tort.[71]

6. ENFORCEMENT THROUGH PUBLIC-PRIVATE PARTNERSHIPS

In the summer of 2017, Sea Shepherd announced that it would not be seeking to oppose the Japanese whaling fleet in the coming whaling season, citing the

---

[66] Ibid., para. 275.

[67] Information obtained from https://seashepherd.org/our-history/.

[68] On the activities and history of Sea Shepherd generally, see G Nagtzaam *From Environmental Action to Ecoterrorism?* (Edward Elgar, Cheltenham: 2017) 203–217.

[69] *Institute of Cetacean Research and ors v. Sea Shepherd Conservation Society and Watson*, Appeal judgment, 725 F3d 940 (9th Cir).

[70] Ibid., at 4–5.

[71] *Sea Shepherd UK v. Fish & Fish Limited* [2015] UKSC 10.

increased use of technology by the Japanese Government to track Sea Shepherd vessels, but also the introduction of controversial new counter-terrorism legislation that potentially criminalizes protest activities.[72] Sea Shepherd has in the meantime been developing another approach to its direct action activities, specifically partnering with governments to assist them with law enforcement activities. Sea Shepherd has been involved in the protection of marine wildlife around the Galapagos Islands for a number of years, partnering with Colombia, Costa Rica and Ecuador, in particular. Joint projects include providing patrol vessels and crew who operate under the supervision of Costa Rican officials.[73] The arrangements with Costa Rica have, however, suffered from ongoing controversies.

In an incident in April 2002, the then Canadian-flagged Sea Shepherd vessel *Farley Mowat* collided with a Costa Rican vessel – the *Varadero I* – whilst trying to prevent it from illegally hunting sharks. When the *Farley Mowat* returned to port in Costa Rica, Paul Watson – who had been captain of the vessel – was accused of various offences including attempted murder. When Watson did not appear for trial, the Costa Rican authorities issued a 'red notice' through Interpol, which resulted in him being detained while visiting Germany.[74] Although he subsequently left Germany, and proceedings have not been able to progress against him, at the time of writing the notice remains outstanding.[75]

The practice of deploying ship-riders first developed in the inter-State context primarily in the context of the suppression of narcotics smuggling. A ship-rider is a law enforcement official who is embarked on a law enforcement vessel of another nationality than that of the official. Such a law enforcement vessel is able to interdict vessels flagged to either State and also – depending on the extent of the ship-rider agreement – to perform acts of enforcement in waters under the jurisdiction of either State vis-à-vis vessels of third States.[76] These have also been used in the context of maritime security and fisheries enforcement, notably between the US and China in the context of tackling the use of large-scale driftnets in the Pacific,[77] and between Australia and France

---

[72] See L Sieg "Japan Ruling Bloc Pushes Through Anti-Conspiracy Bill Despite Privacy Concerns" (*Reuters*, 15 June 2017) (available at www.reuters.com/article/us-japan-politics-conspiracy/japan-ruling-bloc-pushes-through-anti-conspiracy-bill-despite-privacy-concerns-idUSKBN1953BZ); and the news item "Japan Passes Controversial Anti-Terror Conspiracy Law" (*BBC News*, 15 June 2017) (available at www.bbc.co.uk/news/world-asia-40283730).

[73] See news item "Sea Shepherd Arrives in Costa Rica with Offer to Help Curb Illegal Fishing Activities in Cocos Island" (20 May 2017) (available at https://seashepherd.org/news/sea-shepherd-arrives-in-costa-rica-with-offer-to-help-curb-illegal-fishing-activities-in-cocos-island/).

[74] A Sanchez "Sea Shepherd In Latin America" (*The Maritime Executive*, 21 September 2016) (available at www.maritime-executive.com/editorials/sea-shepherd-in-latin-america).

[75] See www.interpol.int/notice/search/wanted/2013-60414.

[76] Guilfoyle, note 23 at 72.

[77] Memorandum of Understanding between the Government of the United States of America and the Government of the People's Republic of China on Effective Cooperation and Implementation of United Nations General Assembly Resolution 46/215 of December 20, 1991 (available at www.nmfs.noaa.gov/ia/agreements/LMR%20report/us_china_46_215_agreement.pdf). See further Guilfoyle, note 23 at 119.

in the Southern Ocean.[78] This concept has recently been adapted by PMSCs and NGOs – in particular Sea Shepherd – in public-private partnerships.[79] Such arrangements have the benefit of providing the State concerned with equipment (including vessels), manpower and knowhow, while the embarkation of officials aboard such vessels ensures authority to perform acts of law enforcement, and provide public oversight, potentially reducing friction with public authorities.

Sea Shepherd has successfully worked with a number of governments to provide technical and material support to their law enforcement agencies to take action against illegal fishing. These have included: São Tomé and Príncipe (October 2017), East Timor, (September 2017), Gabon (July 2017), Mexico (December 2016) and Senegal in 2014.[80]

7. LITIGATION BY PRIVATE ACTORS

The last of the ways private actors are able to take action to ensure compliance with fisheries regulations considered here is the conduct of litigation. There are four main ways that this can be done: civil proceedings against illegal activities in domestic courts; private prosecutions in respect of such activities; claims against public authorities (e.g. by way of judicial review); and claims before international courts or tribunals (e.g. applications to human rights courts).

One area that was thought to have considerable potential was litigation under the Alien Tort Statute in the US.[81] This type of case focused on the possibility of bringing claims for human rights abuses, including damage to the environment and livelihoods (and consequently potentially for activities relevant in the present context), by subsidiary companies whose parent companies are based in locations in which they are susceptible to litigation (particularly Europe and North America). Those hopes were dashed in the US with the *Kiobel* case, where

---

[78] Ibid., at 144.

[79] V Schatz "Marine Fisheries Law Enforcement Partnerships in Waters under National Jurisdiction: The Legal Framework for Inter-State Cooperation and Public-Private Partnerships with Non-Governmental Organizations and Private Security Companies" (2018) 32 *Ocean Yearbook* 329–375.

[80] See the news items "Fishing Fleet Caught Red-Handed in a Dawn Raid by Sea Shepherd and East Timor Police" (12 September 2017) (available at www.seashepherdglobal.org/latest-news/dawn-raid-east-timor); "Sea Shepherd Assists Gabonese Navy and Fisheries Enforcement in the Arrest of Two Illegal Fishing Trawlers" (13 July 2017) (available at www.seashepherdglobal.org/latest-news/sea-shepherd-assists-gabonese-navy-and-fisheries-e); "Our Return to Gabon to Help Combat Illegal Fishing in Africa's Largest Marine Protected Area" (5 July 2017) (available at www.seashepherd global.org/latest-news/sea-shepherd-returns-to-gabon-to-help-combat-illeg); "Sea Shepherd and the Mexican Navy Team Up to Catch Illegal Poachers; Fishermen Arrested" (29 December 2016) (available at https://seashepherd.org/news/sea-shepherd-and-the-mexican-navy-team-up-to-catch-illegal-poachers-fishermen-arrested/); and "Sea Shepherd Launches West Africa Anti-Poaching Campaign" (27 March 2014) (available at https://seashepherd.org/news/sea-shepherd-launches-west-africa-anti-poaching-campaign/).

[81] 28 U.S.C. § 1350 (2006).

it was decided that extraterritorial wrongs committed by subsidiary companies did not come within US jurisdiction.[82] Ironically, this was precisely the opposite of the decision made against Sea Shepherd in the *Institute of Cetacean Research* case.[83] However, although the possibility of bringing this kind of case has been closed off in the US, it has continued to develop in other jurisdictions, in particular in the UK.[84] This has potentially expanded in the recent *Lungowe* case, decided by the UK Court of Appeal.[85]

When it comes to considering proceedings brought by private actors against States for the enforcement of environmental legislation, the coverage is equally uneven. Here one of the main problems is the question of standing, particularly for NGOs. Whereas some jurisdictions such as the UK have adopted a permissive approach to the problem,[86] others have taken a much more restrictive view.[87] Public interest litigation brought by NGOs in environmental cases is in theory facilitated by the Aarhus Convention.[88]

In the US, the 1992 High Seas Driftnet Fisheries Enforcement Act requires the Secretary of Commerce to determine whether other States are taking sufficient steps to prevent fishing with driftnets and, if not, requires the President to first ask the other State to take steps to prevent their use.[89] If the State concerned fails to do so, the US Government must then ban the import of their fish and fish products. The Act has also provision for NGOs to intervene to require the Secretary of Commerce to take action. In a series of cases, NGOs succeeded in establishing standing to challenge the lack of action by the government in specific instances. The most important of these cases in the present context was a case brought by the US Humane Society before the US Court of International Trade. In that case the Court held that the US should take action to demand that Italy (and the EU) take steps to prevent the use of driftnets by Italian fishermen in the Mediterranean.[90] Also in the US, there has been a substantial amount of

---

[82] *Kiobel v. Royal Dutch Petroleum Co.*, 621 F.3d 11 (2d Cir. 2010), cert. granted, 80 U.S.L.W. 3237 (Oct. 17, 2011) (No. 10-1491).

[83] See note 69 and accompanying text.

[84] For an overview, see MD Goldhaber "Corporate Human Rights Litigation in Non-US Courts: A Comparative Scorecard" (2013) 3 *UC Irvine Law Review* 127–149.

[85] *Lungowe and others v. Vedanta Resources Plc and Konkola Copper Mines Plc* [2017] EWCA Civ 1528. See also G Holly "Access to Remedy under the UNGPs: Vedanta and the Expansion of Parent Company Liability" (*EJIL: Talk!*, 31 October 2017) (available at: www.ejiltalk.org/if-the-pleading-represents-the-actuality-vedanta-access-to-remedy-and-the-prospect-of-a-duty-of-care-owed-by-a-parent-company-to-those-affected-by-acts-of-subsidiaries/).

[86] *R. v. Inspectorate of Pollution, ex parte Greenpeace Ltd (No. 2)* [1994] 4 All ER 328.

[87] C Schall "Public Interest Litigation Concerning Environmental Matters Before Human Rights Courts: A Promising Future Concept?" (2008) 20 *Journal of Environmental Law* 417–453.

[88] Convention on Access to Information, Public Participation in Decision-making and Access to Justice in Environmental Matters of 25 June 1998 (2161 UNTS 450).

[89] 16 U.S.C. § 1826a (1994).

[90] *Humane Society of the United States v. Brown* 920 F. Supp. 178 (Court of International Trade 1996). See further A Blackwell "The Humane Society and Italian Driftnetters: Environmental Activists and Unilateral Action in International Environmental Law" (1997) 23 *North Carolina Journal*

litigation under the Magnuson-Stevens Fishery Conservation and Management Reauthorization Act of 2006,[91] in particular by the ocean conservation organization Oceana, who has challenged aspects of the Act relating to measures for the minimization of bycatch.[92]

Another example of domestic legislation permitting the intervention of private actors for the protection of marine wildlife was the litigation brought in Australia against Japanese whaling in the Australian Antarctic EEZ, by the Humane Society International (HSI).[93] In that case, HSI successfully brought proceedings under the Environment Protection and Biodiversity Conservation Act 1999, which permits private individuals and organizations to seek an injunction restraining activities contravening the Act.[94] Although the Australian Government has not taken any action to enforce the decision of the Federal Court prohibiting whaling in Australia's Antarctic EEZ, HSI nevertheless hailed the legal decision as progress in establishing a role for the Act.

Lastly, a potential role for private actors exists in the initiation of private prosecutions. These are a way of triggering criminal proceedings where the public authorities fail to do so. This procedure is available in a number of different jurisdictions, and has been used to tackle breaches of environmental regulation in Canada,[95] including in relation to fisheries.[96]

8. CONCLUSIONS

It can be seen from the foregoing that private actors are able to play a significant role in ensuring compliance with fisheries regulations. First of all in relation to evidence-gathering, private actors often have considerable expertise as well as motivation to investigate and monitor IUU fishing, unconstrained by

---

of *International Law and Commercial Regulation* 313–340; DR Rothwell "The General Assembly Ban on Driftnet Fishing" in D Shelton (ed.) *Commitment and Compliance: The Role of Non-Binding Norms in the International Legal System* (Oxford University Press, Oxford: 2000) 121–145 and Chapter 7 of this volume (Caddell).

[91] Magnuson-Stevens Fishery Conservation and Management Reauthorization Act of 2006, Pub. L. No. 109–479, 120 Stat. 3575 (2007).

[92] *Oceana, Inc. v. Locke*, 831 F. Supp. 2d 95, 107 (D.D.C. 2011). For discussion, see SM Gehan and M Hallowell "Battle to Determine the Meaning of the Magnuson-Stevens Fishery Conservation and Management Reauthorization Act of 2006: A Survey of Recent Judicial Decisions" (2012–2013) 18 *Ocean & Coastal Law Journal* 1.

[93] *Humane Society International v. Kyodo Senpaku Kaisha Ltd*. (2006) 154 FCR 425.

[94] See R Davis "Enforcing Australian Law in Antarctica: The HSI Litigation" (2007) 8 *Melbourne Journal of International Law* 142–158.

[95] J Swaigen, A Koehl and C Hatt "Private Prosecutions Revisited: The Continuing Importance of Private Prosecutions in Protecting the Environment" (2013) 26 *Journal of Environmental Law and Practice* 31–57.

[96] M Hume "Ottawa Takes Over Prosecution of Salmon Farm" (*The Globe and Mail*, 21 April 2010) (available at https://beta.theglobeandmail.com/news/british-columbia/ottawa-takes-over-prosecution-of-salmon-farm/article4315761).

considerations of diplomacy and political or commercial interests. Furthermore, their expertise and resources can play an important role in supporting States with little investigatory capacity of their own, in particular in respect of at-sea patrols and monitoring, and the deployment of new methods such as remote monitoring and tracking technology.

With regard to direct action on the other hand, it may be that there is the beginning of a shift in the way that this is perceived. In particular, increasing concerns about maritime security and unsympathetic reactions from some States – individually and through the IMO – mean that responses – unwelcoming at the best of times – appear to be increasingly hostile, and attended by more robust legal measures against direct action at sea. From a legal standpoint, the protections that human rights law and the law of the sea offer to private actors performing acts of protest and direct action are modest. Human rights protections do not generally permit direct action as such, and States are permitted a broad margin of appreciation in regulating protest generally. At the same time, although the law of the sea provides rights of navigation in principle, those rights are also limited in many respects, in particular in coastal State maritime zones including the EEZ. As a result, the recent experience and practice of Sea Shepherd suggests that direct action by private actors – certainly against States' interests – may become less frequent. Instead, that practice suggests that efforts in the future may concentrate on partnering with States who wish to protect their fisheries, but lack the means and expertise to do so without external assistance.

Finally, it also seems not only that private actors are increasingly playing a role in litigation to secure compliance with fisheries regulation, but that legal mechanisms continue to develop to facilitate this. Although there is not yet consistency or predictability in the field of litigation against environmental damage, there have been a number of important developments. These include increasing recognition of human rights protections extending to the environment, the role of access to justice under the Aarhus Convention, the recognition of standing of NGOs to bring cases in the public interest, and the potential effects of the drive to hold multinational corporations responsible for overseas human rights violations.

In conclusion, it seems clear that not only are there a number of ways private actors are able to play a role in ensuring compliance with fisheries regulations, but that the ways in which they are able to do so are currently potentially in a state of rapid change and development. On the one hand, more opportunities are potentially opening up as legal mechanisms become more accessible and sophisticated, whilst on the other, there appears to be a shift away from direct action, towards taking action within the law, in particular in partnership with government authorities.

17

Emerging Regulatory Responses to IUU Fishing

RICHARD CADDELL, GEORGE LELOUDAS AND BARIŞ SOYER*

1. INTRODUCTION

ILLEGAL, UNREPORTED AND unregulated (IUU) fishing remains the most insidious regulatory problem currently facing the global fishing industry. Although the clandestine nature of such practices militates against a full accounting of the global scale of IUU fishing, it has been estimated that illegal and unreported catches amounting to between 11 and 16 million tonnes (valued at between USD 10 and 23.5 billion) are landed worldwide each year.[1] Illegally-caught fish often penetrate legitimate global seafood markets, including those featuring high levels of vigilance towards criminality, with recent investigations indicating that illegal and unreported catches represented between 20 and 32 per cent of wild-caught seafood imports (worth approximately USD 1.3 to 2.1 billion) into the United States alone.[2] Compounding these concerns, IUU fishing may represent merely the tip of an iceberg of associated criminality, encompassing not only unauthorized fishing practices, but also wholesale human rights violations and sophisticated financial offences, as well as a means of funding the pursuit of even more serious transnational crimes.

The continued proliferation of IUU fishing activities globally is not attributable to political indifference or a dearth of legislation. Indeed, myriad policy

* Richard Caddell gratefully acknowledges the support of the Nereus Program (www.nereusprogram.org) and George Leloudas and Baris Soyer gratefully acknowledge the support of the Waterloo Foundation (www.waterloofoundation.org.uk) in facilitating the writing of this chapter. This chapter is dedicated to the memory of our originally-intended co-author and long-standing colleague Dr Theodora Nikaki.

[1] DJ Agnew et al. "Estimating the Worldwide Extent of Illegal Fishing" (2009) 4 *PLoS ONE*, 1–8, at 4.

[2] G Pramod et al. "Estimates of Illegal and Unreported Fish in Seafood Imports to the USA" (2014) 48 *Marine Policy* 102–113, at 105.

responses have been adopted at the national, regional and international levels in order to combat such practices.[3] Notably, these have tended to involve the introduction of monitoring, control and surveillance (MCS) systems to identify potential instances of fisheries violations, or the denial of port services to vessels engaged in IUU fishing. The physical inspection of catch, gear and documentation may also help to ensure that fishing vessels are continuing to abide by all applicable laws and thus further impede the access of IUU catches to markets.[4] Regional fisheries management organizations (RFMOs) have established collaborative measures to maintain lists of vessels conducting IUU fishing and to share information to facilitate enforcement activities.[5] Initiatives within the private sector have also emerged, aiming to discourage IUU fishing through the use of traceability and labelling schemes.[6] Moreover, through the efforts of several non-governmental organizations (NGOs), valuable information has been uncovered and provided both to the authorities and to the public, lending evidential assistance towards arrests and raising general awareness about IUU fishing and related issues. In some instances, the role of private actors has extended even further to include direct action against IUU fishing vessels to enforce legal standards, acting on either an unsolicited basis or in (quasi-) official conjunction with the appropriate authorities.[7]

Yet despite these combined efforts, IUU fishing remains prevalent. There is accordingly a pressing need to consider novel approaches, including commercial disincentives and mechanisms designed to combat ancillary criminal activities, which have been under-examined in a fisheries context. To this end, this chapter first considers the scope for bolstering measures against IUU fishing by promoting stronger obligations upon those sectors that provide valuable support services to fishing vessels. Section 2 therefore considers a contextual example of this approach, evaluating the prospective role of denying insurance cover to vessels as a means of curtailing the operative capacity of individual vessels and increasing the financial risks for companies contemplating activities that lie at the margins of the law. Section 3 evaluates the application of legal provisions to combat transnational organized crime against operators that have embraced IUU fishing as a convenient and lucrative enterprise within a wider portfolio of criminal activities, while Section 4 concludes.

---

[3] See Chapter 13 of this volume (van der Marel).

[4] J Swan "Port State Measures to Combat IUU Fishing: International and Regional Developments" (2006) 7 *Sustainable Development Law & Policy* 38–43.

[5] See Chapter 5 of this volume (Harrison).

[6] See further J Jacquet et al. "Conserving Wild Fish in a Sea of Market-Based Efforts" (2010) 44 *Oryx* 45–56; M Karavias "Interactions between International Law and Private Fisheries Certification" (2017) 7 *Transnational Environmental Law* 165–184; and Chapter 4 of this volume (Stokke).

[7] See Chapter 16 of this volume (Massarella).

2. THE EMERGING ROLE OF MARINE INSURANCE IN COMBATING IUU FISHING

As with many instances of proscribed behaviour, illegal fishing[8] is attractive to its exponents as it offers high financial rewards in exchange for a modest degree of attendant risk. Moreover, IUU fishing is undertaken almost exclusively for economic reasons, hence there is little natural disincentive to desist until the costs of such activities begin to noticeably outweigh the benefits. It has therefore long been mooted that measures that serve to undermine the profitability of such activities could play a significant role in global efforts to curtail IUU fishing.[9] Thus far, consideration of economic disincentives to IUU fishing has primarily focused on reducing the profitability of such activities by expanding the operative capacity of MCS systems and in levying effective fines and other financial sanctions upon those vessels caught in the act.[10] This remains a central element of international fisheries law. Indeed, the Fish Stocks Agreement[11] mandates that

> [s]anctions applicable in respect of violations shall be adequate in severity to be effective in securing compliance and to discourage violations wherever they occur and shall deprive offenders of the benefits accruing from their illegal activities.[12]

This language and approach has been reinforced by numerous States and RFMOs in their policies against IUU fishing. Depriving IUU fishers of the benefits of their activities has also included the mandatory discarding of catches, disbarring such vessels from claiming potentially lucrative exploratory fishing privileges,[13] confiscating property and, rather more dramatically, destroying vessels found to have violated national fisheries law in particular jurisdictions.

---

[8] This chapter predominantly focuses on illegal activities. As van der Marel observes (note 3), treating the individual components of IUU fishing as a homogenous whole has continued to raise policy complications. Indeed, fishing activities that are unregulated and unreported are not necessarily illegal in nature, whereas an express finding of illegality is highly significant for the successful application of insurance and organized crime provisions against undesirable fishing activities.

[9] UR Sumalia, J Alder and H Keith "Global Scope and Economics of Illegal Fishing" (2006) 30 *Marine Policy* 696–703, at 697.

[10] See C-C Schmidt "Economic Drivers of Illegal, Unreported and Unregulated (IUU) Fishing" (2005) 20 *International Journal of Marine and Coastal Law* 479–507.

[11] Agreement for the Implementation of the Provisions of the United Nations Convention on the Law of the Sea of 10 December 1982 relating to the Conservation and Management of Straddling Fish Stocks and Highly Migratory Fish Stocks of 4 August 1995 (2167 UNTS 3). The wording of this provision is nonetheless intriguing from the perspective of the IUU concept, expressly focusing on *illegal* activities.

[12] Ibid., Art. 19(2).

[13] Most notably within the Commission for the Conservation of Antarctic Marine Living Resources (CCAMLR): see further R Caddell "Precautionary Management and the Development of Future Fishing Opportunities: The International Regulation of New and Exploratory Fisheries" (2018) 33 *International Journal of Marine and Coastal Law* 199–262, at 227–228.

To date, there has been little consideration of the responsibilities of those providing ancillary and financial services to fishing vessels in curtailing IUU activities. As a case in point, the insurance industry has been sporadically identified as a potentially useful ally in combating IUU fishing. Denying insurance cover to delinquent fishing vessels may indeed constitute a helpful means of increasing the costs and risks associated with IUU fishing. In particular instances, valid insurance cover is a formal legal obligation for vessels, although these requirements are not globally uniform and not all forms of marine insurance are compulsory in nature for fishing vessels.[14] More practically, the true value of marine insurance arguably lies in the event of the loss of or damage to the vessel, or in incurring third-party liabilities, which would be ruinously expensive to an operator that is uninsured or whose policy has been annulled due to unauthorized fishing practices. For those operators that value such coverage, a 'zero tolerance' stance against IUU fishing by the insurance industry could therefore provide a powerful disincentive against illicit activities. Moreover, a proactive approach by insurers in precluding insurance cover to vessels with a record of IUU fishing could further inhibit the financial attraction of such conduct.

Worryingly, however, recent studies have found that vessels with previous involvement in IUU fishing have experienced little difficulty obtaining liability insurance cover from the market.[15] One study reveals that some 47.9 per cent of 94 fishing vessels monitored (1,000 gross tonnes or over) known for their ongoing involvement in IUU fishing had successfully secured liability insurance.[16] This is strikingly exemplified by the *Thunder*, a trawler globally notorious for IUU fishing that sank in 2015, which held hull insurance from a Spanish insurer at the time of the casualty, from whom her owner subsequently (and unsuccessfully) attempted to seek indemnity.[17] Accordingly, this section proceeds to outline the insurance considerations raised by IUU fishing and the next steps required in order to fully realize the potential role of this sector in discouraging such activities.

2.1. Liability Insurance

Liability insurance for large fishing and support vessels (e.g. reefers) is often provided by Protection and Indemnity (P&I) Clubs, which are mutual insurance organizations that offer cover to their members to protect them against liability

---

[14] DD Miller et al. "Cutting a Lifeline to Maritime Crime: Marine Insurance and IUU Fishing" (2016) 14 *Frontiers in Ecology and the Environment* 357–362, at 360.

[15] Ibid.

[16] See B Soyer, G Leloudas and D Miller "Tackling Illegal Fishing – Developing A Holistic Legal Response" (2018) 7 *Transnational Environmental Law* 139–163, at 143–145.

[17] E Endal and K Sæter *Catching Thunder: The True Story of the World's Longest Sea Chase* (Zed Books, London: 2018) 343–348.

claims arising from the crew and third parties.[18] Liability claims covered under this category of insurance typically involve collisions, property damage, pollution, environmental damage and the removal of wrecks. Although numerous jurisdictions have enacted specific legislation concerning liability insurance, the vast majority of vessels worldwide are entered into UK-based P&I Clubs, and are thus subject to English law. Accordingly, the discussion below is conducted essentially from the perspective of English law, although a similar position will also apply within a host of other common law jurisdictions, as the English provisions were used as a basis for marine insurance legislation across the Commonwealth.

If a vessel entered into a Club incurs liability when involved in IUU fishing, it is likely that the law would preclude recovery in most instances. This is because the rules of most, if not all, P&I Clubs expressly exclude liability if a loss or fine is incurred as a result of illegal activities. For example, Rule 14 of the London P&I Club stipulates that "[t]here shall be no recovery in respect of any liability, costs or expenses arising out of or in consequence of an entered Ship carrying contraband, blockade running or being employed in an unlawful trade".[19] Interestingly, the Club Rules do not expressly stipulate under which law this illegality should arise, but it is very likely that an act contrary to international law or a national law to which that vessel was closely connected would suffice for the purposes of this exclusion. Moreover, the Rules of most Clubs extend this exception so as to avoid liability in cases where the directors of the Club consider that the adventure is 'improper'. On that basis, a voyage that involves fishing activities that are illegal under international law or the national law of a foreign State is likely to be treated as 'improper' by the directors.

The position is unlikely to differ in the context of commercial liability policies, even though few would typically contain an express exclusion of this nature. The claim of the assured is still likely to fail under such policies, on the basis that engaging in IUU fishing would almost certainly amount to a breach of the implied warranty of legality contained in section 41 of the Marine Insurance Act 1906.[20] This provision stipulates that "[t]here is an implied warranty that the adventure insured is a lawful one, and that, so far as the assured can control the matter, the adventure shall be carried out in a lawful manner". An insured vessel involved in IUU fishing activities with the knowledge and consent of the assured would therefore evidently breach this warranty. It is clear that illegality under this section includes illegality under the law that applies to the contract,

---

[18] Liability cover for fishing vessels can also be obtained from the commercial market, although this is likely to be more restricted and more expensive for the assured.

[19] The London P&I Club Rules 2018/19; available at www.londonpandi.com/documents/the-london-club-pi-rules-class-5/.

[20] Although the remedy for breach of a warranty has been altered by s. 10 of the Insurance Act 2015, it is submitted that this will not affect this analysis. The cover will be suspended if the warranty is breached, meaning that the assured will not be able to recover under the policy.

namely English law[21] (including EU Regulations and provisions of international law that have been incorporated into English law). It is tenable to suggest that it would also include illegality under the law of the flag State and of any State in whose exclusive economic zone (EEZ) the vessel was fishing, by analogy with the rule that English law will not enforce any contract involving the commission in a given jurisdiction of an act illegal in that jurisdiction.[22]

The prospects of recovery under a liability policy or P&I cover are bleak if a vessel with prior involvement in IUU fishing activities incurs a liability even when she is not involved in IUU fishing at the material time. Assuming that the liability insurance is subject to English law, the assured is expected to disclose all material circumstances relating to the risk when applying for P&I membership or seeking commercial insurance. Under section 7(3) of the Insurance Act 2015 "a circumstance or representation is material if it would influence the judgement of a prudent insurer in determining whether to take the risk and, if so, on what terms".[23] If the vessel in question has previously been detained or fined for IUU fishing infractions, or indeed identified on the IUU vessel lists maintained by RFMOs, this would appear to be a 'material circumstance' requiring disclosure to a Club or commercial insurer at the time of making an application to obtain insurance cover.[24]

In case of non-disclosure, it is possible that the insurer could avoid the policy later upon discovery of the failure of the assured to make a fair presentation, as long it can be demonstrated that either that the insurer would not have entered into the contract on any terms were the true state of affairs known, or that the assured had acted deliberately or recklessly.[25] One lifeline for the assured

---

[21] *Royal Boskalis Westminster v. Trevor Rex Mountain* [1997] LRLR 523, *per* Rix J., at 589. On appeal, Phillips LJ indicated that a section 41 warranty "probably refers to English law, not foreign law", but did not express a final view: see [1999] QB 674, at 736. See also *Sea Glory Maritime Co v. Al Sagr National Insurance Co (The Nancy)* [2013] EWHC 2116 (Comm); [2013] 2 All ER 913, *per* Blair J., at [295]. It is not thought that the submission made here is affected by the recent decision of the Supreme Court on the illegality principle in general in *Patel v. Mirza* [2016] UKSC 42; [2016] 3 WLR 399.

[22] See e.g. *Foster v. Driscoll* [1929] 1 KB 470 and *Regazzoni v. KC Sethia (1944) Ltd* [1956] 2 QB 490; also more recently *Beijing Jianlong Heavy Industry Group v. Golden Ocean Group Ltd* [2013] EWHC 1063 (Comm); [2013] 1 CLC 906, at [17]-[20]. See also *Euro Diam Ltd v. Bathurst* [1987] 2 WLR 1368, which indicates that English law would bar a claim if the insurance contract is sufficiently connected with the illegal acts arising under the foreign law.

[23] Eight P&I Clubs whose Rules are subject to English law have agreed to contract out of various provisions of the Insurance Act 2015, although they apply the duty of 'fair presentation' stipulated in the Act. Accordingly, any breach of the duty of fair presentation shall entitle the Club to avoid the policy, regardless of whether the breach of the duty of fair presentation is innocent, deliberate or reckless.

[24] See *March Cabaret Club & Casino Ltd v. The London Assurance* [1975] 1 Lloyd's Rep 169 (QB); *James v. CGU Insurance Co plc* [2002] Lloyd's Rep IR 206 (Com Ct) and *North Star Shipping v. Sphere Drake Insurance plc* [2006] EWCA Civ 378; [2006] 2 All ER 65.

[25] Insurance Act 2015, Sch. 1. Where the P&I Club has contracted out of this provision, avoidance will be available as the sole remedy regardless of whether non-disclosure is fraudulent, negligent or innocent.

in that case would be to argue there was no obligation on them to disclose the detention, fine or listing on the basis that such facts were presumed to be known by the insurer.[26] Such a position would incentivize vigilance on the part of the insurer as to the prior conduct of a fishing vessel seeking insurance cover. This is especially so where a record of the detention, fine or listing was in the public domain or could be readily found by a search of the relevant databases (which are easily available to insurers[27]) or IUU fishing vessel lists maintained and shared by RFMOs. Another possible argument in favour of coverage under these circumstances is that there is no duty under the Act to disclose matters covered by a warranty. Therefore, given the implied warranty of illegality in the policy, it would be superfluous to disclose the matters concerning any IUU fishing activities engaged in by that vessel prior to the fixing of the contract.[28] Nevertheless, neither possibility appears likely to succeed because concealing previous fines and/or convictions associated with IUU fishing would, in all likelihood, constitute a material fact that relates to the moral hazard of the assured.[29]

A P&I Club could also cancel the cover if it becomes aware of the vessel being involved in illegal activities, even though at that stage no liability has yet been incurred. Under the Rules of some Clubs, cancellation is automatic if the vessel is involved in illegal activity. For instance, Rule 25(2)(j) of Gard (2016) indicates that "[t]he Member shall (...) cease to be covered by the Association in respect of any Ship entered by him (...) if the Ship, with the consent or knowledge of the Member, is being used for the furtherance of illegal purposes".[30] A similar stance may well be taken by a commercial liability insurance provider.

Given that liability insurance is unlikely to provide any practical assistance to the assured in the case of an incident, it remains an intriguing question why so many of those involved in IUU fishing diligently solicit such cover. It may be speculated that the primary motivation of those obtaining this form

---

[26] Under s. 5(3) of the Insurance Act 2015, the insurer is presumed to know "(a) things which are common knowledge, and (b) things which an insurer offering insurance of the class in question to insureds in the field of activity in question would reasonably be expected to know in the ordinary course of business".

[27] It was deliberated in *The Nancy* (note 21) whether the underwriter was deemed to possess information that appears on databases, such as Lloyd's MIU and Sea-web. Blair J. was convinced that the mere fact that the information is available online does not trigger a presumption of knowledge on the part of underwriters. However, it is clear from the judgment that an underwriter is presumed to know information that he has access to as long as he has an interest in such information when it is received.

[28] *Inversiones Manria SA v. Sphere Drake Insurance Co (The Dora)* [1989] 1 Lloyd's Rep 69.

[29] The English courts are receptive to the notion that the assured's running of its business affairs in a dishonest and criminal fashion could amount to a moral hazard. See *Insurance Corporation of Channel Islands v. Royal Hotel Ltd* [1998] Lloyd's Rep IR 151; *James v. CGU Insurance Co plc* [2002] Lloyd's Rep IR 206; and *Sharon's Bakery (Europe) Ltd v. AXA Insurance UK plc* [2011] EWHC 210 (Comm); [2012] Lloyd's Rep IR 164.

[30] Gard, *Rules for Ships (2016)* available at www.gard.no/web/publications/document/chapter?p_subdoc_id=781872&p_document_id=781871.

of insurance is not to guard against the incurrence of potential liabilities per se, but rather to hold the requisite certification in order to satisfy documentary obligations under international liability regimes such as the Bunkers Convention.[31] This documentation – even if essentially cosmetic in nature – thus enables the owners of vessels involved in IUU fishing to continue to ply their trade, since an uncertified vessel may be vulnerable to detention by the relevant port authority,[32] albeit for administrative violations if not proscribed fisheries conduct. If this is indeed the motivation, the fact that a significant number of vessels with documented or credibly suspected prior involvement in IUU fishing are able to secure liability cover with ease, and in most instances without any qualification in cover,[33] confirms the suspicion that liability insurers may be inadvertently contributing to the continuing problem of IUU fishing.

2.2. Hull Insurance

Hull insurance covers damage sustained by a vessel and its machinery and equipment. There is no international regime currently requiring the compulsory acquisition of hull insurance on the part of a vessel owner. However, it has been documented that a number of vessels that had a notorious record of IUU fishing were in full possession of such cover at the time at which they were lost. Although commercial confidentiality renders it impossible to ascertain whether the owners of such vessels were ultimately indemnified for these losses, recovery in English law under these circumstances would nevertheless also seem unlikely.

Even assuming that such a vessel was not deliberately sunk by her owner to conceal evidence of illegal activity, as seemingly the case with the *Thunder*, the assured will probably not recover under the policy if a vessel is lost while involved in IUU fishing. Under such circumstances section 41 of the Marine Insurance Act 1906 (discussed above) will not apply, as the scope of the warranty of legality expressed in this section has been qualified by the term 'adventure insured', hence the illegal conduct of the vessel is not part of the insured adventure. However, English law could still bar recovery where an illegal act unrelated to the insured adventure arises during the performance of the contract. In *Royal Boskalis Westminster NV v. Mountain*,[34] a claim was considered unenforceable in circumstances involving "the commission of a crime (and this, in most, albeit

---

[31] International Convention on Civil Liability for Bunker Oil Pollution Damage of 23 March 2001 (402 UNTS 71).

[32] As is the position in the UK, under s. 163A(5) of the Merchant Shipping Act 1995.

[33] The current system could be enhanced by offering liability cover to vessels with a history of IUU fishing only on the condition that they maintain an operational GPS system at all times or that they undergo regular spot checks to reduce the possibility of IUU catches.

[34] [1997] LRLR 523.

not all, cases involves the existence of *mens rea*) and a (direct) causative connection between the crime and claim under the policy".[35] On that premise, recovery would be barred under an insurance contract if: (1) the illegality is sufficiently serious in nature to bring notions of public policy into play;[36] (2) the assured is relying upon their own illegality in order to found his claim;[37] and (3) there is sufficient connection between the assured's illegal conduct and the resultant loss.[38] If the loss is caused as a result of the vessel being involved in IUU fishing, it will be a relatively straightforward task for the insurer to establish a causal link with the illegal conduct and thus disbar the claim.

2.3. Strengthening Insurance Practices to Address IUU Fishing

Notwithstanding these considerations, it is clear that vessels with a record of IUU fishing have generally encountered relatively few difficulties in obtaining insurance cover from the market.[39] This indicates that investigating prior conduct has generally been a low priority in underwriting practices involving fishing vessels. An alternative – and perhaps unfairly cynical – interpretation is that such practices have allowed insurers to avail themselves of regular payments from vessel owners engaged in IUU practices, whose conduct will render indemnification a remote prospect in the event of a nautical accident. Ultimately, it is clear that the law and practice relating to insurance ought to be strengthened markedly if it is to provide a meaningful tool by which to combat IUU fishing activities.

To this end, three key strategies could be considered further. Firstly, there is a need to strengthen or amend current legal provisions addressing IUU fishing to expressly include insurance considerations. Secondly, the role of insurance should more explicitly permeate the agenda of global bodies, RFMOs and other fora established for the review of policies against IUU fishing. Thirdly, IUU fishing needs to be given greater prominence as a particular concern within the insurance industry itself, facilitating an appropriate adjustment of underwriting practices to ensure enhanced scrutiny of the prior (mis)conduct of vessels seeking insurance coverage.

---

[35] Ibid., at 589–590 (*per* Rix J.).

[36] The public policy rule applies to both criminal conduct and quasi-criminal conduct, such as a contravention of administrative rules by reason of corruption or infringement of competition rules.

[37] As stated by Staughton J. in *Euro-Diam Ltd v. Bathurst* [1987] 2 WLR 1368, "a claim may be said to be tainted with illegality in English law... if the plaintiff needs to plead or prove illegal conduct in order to establish his claim; or... if the claim is so closely connected with the proceeds of crime as to offend the conscience of the court" (at 1380).

[38] *Safeway Stores Ltd v. Twigger* [2010] EWHC 11 (Comm); [2010] 2 Lloyd's Rep. 39, at [26] *per* Flaux J.

[39] Miller et al., note 14 at 360–361.

2.3.1. *Recognizing the Role of Insurance within IUU Fishing Provisions*

The recognition of insurance considerations occupies something of a grey area in current legislation adopted to combat IUU fishing, or indeed has been discounted completely. Although such instruments routinely prescribe obligations upon a variety of actors, it remains questionable whether insurers are expressly caught by these provisions. Indeed, the application of the relevant European Union (EU) legislation against IUU fishing provides an illuminating practical example of these difficulties. As outlined by van der Marel,[40] the EU has a strong regulatory role to play against IUU fishing due to its global significance as a market State for fish products and its prominence within a number of RFMOs. To this end, the EU has adopted a sophisticated system to regulate the fisheries supply chain "from the net to the plate",[41] concentrated around Regulation 1005/2008 (the EU IUU Regulation).[42]

Central to the EU IUU Regulation is the creation and regular updating of two blacklists, the first identifying Community and third country fishing vessels that engage in IUU fishing,[43] and the second listing countries that fail to act over IUU fishing.[44] Once a vessel is designated to either list, Articles 37 and 38 prescribe a wide range of restrictions against it. Non-EU IUU fishing vessels are prohibited from entering EU ports (unless in distress and/or upon agreement that the catches and/or the fishing gear on board are confiscated),[45] being supplied in ports with provisions, fuel or a change of crew (unless in distress),[46] fishing in EU waters and being chartered,[47] and/or being granted the flag of an EU Member State.[48] EU IUU fishing vessels are permitted access only to their home ports and are prohibited from participating in or assisting any fish processing operations or any transhipment or joint fishing operations with IUU fishing vessels.[49] Furthermore, the Regulation prohibits the import and export

---

[40] See Chapter 13 of this volume (van der Marel).

[41] Commission, "Communication from the Commission to the European Parliament, the Council, the European Economic and Social Committee and the Committee of the Regions on a new strategy for the Community to prevent, deter and eliminate illegal, unreported and unregulated fishing" COM(2007) 601, at 7.

[42] Regulation (EC) No. 1005/2008 establishing a Community system to prevent, deter and eliminate illegal, unreported and unregulated fishing [2008] OJ L286/1. This is complemented by Commission Regulation (EC) No. 1010/2009 of 22 October 2009 laying down detailed rules for the implementation of Council Regulation (EC) No. 1005/2008 establishing a Community system to prevent, deter and eliminate illegal, unreported and unregulated fishing [2009] OJ L280/5. These two Regulations are supplemented by a number of implementing Regulations and Decisions of the Commission that deal, *inter alia*, with the IUU vessel/NCTCs lists and the arrangements with third countries regarding the catch certificates: van der Marel, ibid.

[43] EU IUU Regulation, Art. 27(1).

[44] Ibid., Art. 33.

[45] Ibid., Art. 37(5)

[46] Ibid., Art. 37(6)

[47] Ibid., Art. 37(3)

[48] Ibid., Art. 37(8)

[49] Ibid., Art. 37(4).

(including re-export for processing) of fishery products caught by IUU fishing vessels.[50] An even broader set of restrictions are imposed upon blacklisted countries: no fishery products caught by fishing vessels flying the flag of such countries are permitted into the EU;[51] the purchase, charter or reflagging of such vessels is prohibited, as is the export of EU vessels to such countries;[52] and joint fishing operations with such vessels are also prohibited, as well as private trade agreements with nationals of such countries.[53]

The inherent value of these requirements notwithstanding, the drafters of the Regulation opted for more generic (and thereby less committed) language in restricting the wider commercial interests that may support IUU fishing. Article 39(1) prohibits "nationals that are subject to the jurisdiction of Member States" from being operators or beneficial owners of blacklisted IUU vessels. Alongside this prohibition, Article 40(1) advises Member States to encourage persons and entities under their jurisdiction to "notify any information pertaining to legal, beneficial or financial interests in, or control of, fishing vessels flagged to a third country which they hold and the names of the vessels concerned". Furthermore Article 40(2), mirroring Article 37, prohibits the "[sale] or export [of] any fishing vessel to operators involved in the operation, management or ownership of fishing vessels included in the Community IUU vessel list". This prohibition is supplemented by a restriction on granting Community funds to these operators.[54]

However, the IUU Regulation does not explicitly prohibit the provision of insurance to IUU vessels. There is no reference to insurance within the text of the Regulation, an omission that leaves its scope of application open to debate. Although the EU Commission has previously stated that insurers should not provide support to IUU fishing vessels,[55] these concerns failed to translate into further oversight within either the IUU Regulation itself or the Commission's evaluation of its application.[56] Nor do the measures imposed against blacklisted vessels and non-compliant third countries under Articles 37 and 38 directly target insurers. Even the reference to "other services" in Article 37(6) must be read in conjunction with the remainder of this provision, which prohibits the supply of these vessels "with provisions, fuel" in EU ports. Moreover, while these measures could serve to deter future investment in IUU fishing vessels and cut off the existing supply of finance to the actual perpetrators, they do not provide a comprehensive set of checks that would oblige a wide range of financial interests, such as insurers and banks, to modify their practices towards IUU fishing.

---

[50] Ibid., Art. 37(10).
[51] Ibid., Art. 38(1).
[52] Ibid., Art. 37 (2)–(4).
[53] Ibid., Art. 37 (6)–(7).
[54] Ibid., Art. 40(3).
[55] Commission Communication, "Action Plan to Eradicate Illegal, Unreported and Unregulated Fishing" COM(2002) 180.
[56] Soyer, Leloudas and Miller, note 16 at 158.

Confronted with these limitations, there would appear to be two options in seeking to interpret the IUU Regulation as applying to insurers. The first, and arguably more speculative, possibility is through Article 42(1)(b), which stipulates that it is a serious infringement of the IUU Regulation to "conduct (...) business directly connected to IUU fishing, including the trade in/or the importation of fishery products". The practice of the UK is illuminating in this regard, in its capacity (pre-Brexit, at least[57]) as the EU Member State most closely associated with the provision of insurance services. In November 2015, the UK Marine Management Organisation and Foreign and Commonwealth Office stated that insurance provision would constitute an activity directly connected to the operation of IUU vessels and is thereby prohibited under Article 42(1)(b).[58] However, the legal position may not be as clear-cut as this statement would imply. Indeed, the use of the term 'directly' may be considered to refer to the primary objective of the Regulation to regulate the supply chain and its ancillary activities. The two examples cited in Article 42(1)(b), namely "the trade in/or the importations of fishery products", are core activities within the supply chain. Admittedly, the reference to these two activities is not exhaustive, yet it inevitably influences the interpretation of this provision. Liability insurance covers the liability exposure of the vessel's owners, thus providing indirect support to IUU fishing. It is conceivable that cargo insurance for IUU fishery products *could* be caught by this prohibition as it relates more 'directly' to the transit of the prohibited goods. Nevertheless, it remains contentious whether the provision of any type of insurance is sufficiently 'directly connected' to IUU fishing within the current wording of the Regulation as to be clearly subject to Article 42(1)(b).

The second approach is via Article 39(1), which provides that

> [n]ationals subject to the jurisdiction of Member States (...) shall neither support nor engage in IUU fishing, including by engagement on board or as operators or beneficial owners of fishing vessels included in the Community IUU vessel list.

The expression 'support (...) IUU fishing' has a broader meaning than the term 'directly connected to' cited in Article 42(1)(b). It covers the beneficial owners of blacklisted vessels, who have a direct legal relationship to the vessel in question and thus have the capacity to control its operations. Insurers do not have the same capacity, yet the word 'support' has a wider meaning than the term 'control'. As such, it is arguable that insurers could be treated as beneficial owners for the purposes of Article 39(1) – even if they have little, if any, control over the actual activities of the vessel – although this too remains an ambitious approach. Nevertheless, if this interpretation is indeed correct, it

---

[57] Many elements of fisheries regulation post-Brexit remain highly uncertain, although given the market prominence of the UK in the provision of insurance services, there remains a strong opportunity to address supporting industries more centrally in future domestic fisheries legislation.

[58] See   www.gov.uk/government/news/mmo-and-fco-host-joint-iuu-workshop-with-the-uk-insurance-industry.

raises the tantalizing prospect that financial institutions could also be caught by the prohibitions advanced by the IUU Regulation. Even so, however, the penalties imposed by the IUU Regulation[59] are evidently not designed to deal with insurance-related infringements. They target the fishing activities themselves (concerning the vessel and any unlawfully-generated proceeds) rather than ancillary matters. Moreover, the fines for serious infringements are calculated by reference to the value of the fishery products in question, which may constitute a significant penalty for individual fishers, but is hardly an intimidating financial prospect for globally-prominent insurers.[60]

A purposive interpretation of Article 39(1) thus offers some scope to bring insurance within the ambit of the Regulation. However, it remains abundantly clear that the Regulation was not drafted with insurance in mind, which complicates its potential application to this sector. Accordingly, the optimal approach would be to revise the Regulation to expressly include an insurance prohibition. This would require the various Member States to contemplate this issue rather more directly than has thus far proved to be the case. Moreover, a more central consideration of insurance requirements within domestic legislation against IUU fishing could eventually serve to influence the practice of jurisdictions outside the EU, wherein a number of States with significant interests in both fisheries and the provision of insurance services have yet to adopt such measures under their respective national laws.[61]

2.3.2. *Incorporating Insurance Considerations within the Global IUU Fishing Agenda*

Mirroring these difficulties, insurance issues have thus far occupied a peripheral position upon the agenda of RFMOs and other global bodies with an interest in regulating IUU fishing. Accordingly, there has been little regulatory inspiration or injunction to actively consider the insurance industry as an avenue through which to strengthen the suite of measures against IUU fishing activities. Indeed, notwithstanding regular statements within the annual Sustainable Fisheries Resolution of the UN General Assembly (UNGA) calling upon States to ensure that "chartering arrangements and practices relating to fishing vessels" do not undermine efforts to combat IUU fishing,[62] the insurance sector has not been expressly identified as component in the global system against such activities and the wording of the Resolution appears to be insufficient to directly inspire further legislation to this effect.

---

[59] See EU IUU Regulation, Arts. 37–38 and Arts. 43–45.

[60] Ibid., Art. 44(2).

[61] A review of the legislation of ten countries, including Australia, Canada, Chile and the US, revealed no such measures in domestic anti-IUU fishing legislation: Soyer, Leloudas and Miller, note 16 at 158.

[62] See most recently UNGA Resolution 72/72 of 19 January 2018, para. 84.

Nevertheless, insurers have been sporadically identified as actors of allied significance in addressing the economic drivers of IUU fishing. Notably, in 2005 the Organization for Economic Cooperation and Development (OECD) considered that further engagement with the insurance industry should be included in the suite of trade measures to be pursued against IUU fishing, as "[r]ecent examples suggest that such measures may be efficient in some situations, at a relatively limited cost".[63] The marine insurance sector was further identified as an industry that comprises a sufficiently small number of individual actors (albeit large multinational enterprises) for an effective embargo on the provision of services to be a feasible prospect.[64] Similarly, alongside other financial operators, insurers were identified in the non-binding 2001 International Plan of Action to Prevent, Deter and Eliminate Illegal, Unreported and Unregulated Fishing (IPOA-IUU), whereby States were requested to take measures to ensure that such actors were "aware of the detrimental effects of doing business with vessels identified as engaged in IUU fishing", which could include domestic legislation to discourage the provision of commercial services.[65] However, this element of the IPOA-IUU has done little to inspire any such legislative activity by States. It may be speculated that insurance-related measures have been generally viewed as ineffective, secondary policies under the IPOA-IUU. As such, priority has been given to sharp-end measures, the practical application of which is arguably more politically visible.

To date, the potential contribution of insurers to policies against IUU fishing has been directly recognized by one lone fisheries actor. In 2017 CCAMLR amended its Conservation Measure 10–08 – which concerns its scheme to promote compliance by Party nationals with the various CCAMLR CMs – to acknowledge that "international corporate structures, insurance providers and other financial arrangements are often employed by IUU operators to limit their liability and avoid legitimate acceptable codes of behaviour". Parties are obliged to verify whether insurance providers subject to their jurisdiction are responsible for, benefit from or support IUU fishing. Furthermore, it requires them to take appropriate action to "effectively deprive any of the participants in such activities of the benefits obtained and effectively dissuade the actors of further illegal activities".[66]

Somewhat ironically, perhaps, given that insurers were largely airbrushed from the final version of the IUU Regulation, these proposals were advanced

---

[63] OECD, *Why Fish Piracy Persists: The Economics of Illegal, Unreported and Unregulated Fishing* (OECD, Paris: 2005) 98; available at www.oecd-ilibrary.org/agriculture-and-food/why-fish-piracy-persists_9789264010888-en.

[64] Ibid., 91.

[65] Para. 73 of the International Plan of Action to Prevent, Deter and Eliminate Illegal, Unreported and Unregulated Fishing 2001; available at www.fao.org/publications/card/en/c/71be21c9-8406-5f66-ac68-1e74604464e7.

[66] CM 10-08 (2017), para. 1(ii) and (iii).

by the EU in order to clarify that CM 10-08 directly applies to those offering financial services to the fishing industry.[67] In endorsing these amendments the various CCAMLR Members collectively acknowledged the importance of "the insurance and financial sectors in closing the links between these services and IUU fishing operators".[68] Nevertheless it remains to be seen how assiduously the Members apply these requirements to their domestic sectors and whether they in turn serve to inspire similar policies and pronouncements within other RFMOs.

2.3.3. *Adjusting Underwriting Practices*

Although the development of formal obligations to promote a greater degree of vigilance and accountability within the insurance sector towards IUU fishing remains nascent, there have been recent indications that the industry itself is open to improving its underwriting practices in this respect. In October 2017, in partnership with the prominent NGO Oceana, a number of leading marine insurers adopted a Statement on Assisting Ocean Stewardship through Marine Insurance.[69] Recognizing the need to facilitate "better maritime industry practices that could contribute to conserving and improving the health of our oceans", the signatories pledged to transact future policies in line with two key principles. Firstly, and with particular reference to education and awareness-building, these respective companies aim to encourage the adoption of measures to help reduce and eliminate IUU fishing. Secondly, and arguably of greater practical value, the signatories also committed themselves to

> the use of appropriate risk management protocols and effective due diligence procedures to help reduce the risk of insuring vessels or companies that are acting contrary to agreed international governance frameworks and international law covering IUU fishing.

Most specifically, and with direct reference to the IUU vessel lists maintained by RFMOs and the EU, they undertook to refrain from "knowingly insur[ing] or facilitat[ing] the insuring of vessels that have been officially blacklisted for their involvement in IUU fishing".[70]

If diligently applied, these commitments to improving underwriting practices could ultimately constitute a significant development, as the previous safeguards imposed by insurers and insurance law more generally have proved insufficient to deter the provision of cover and assistance – however inadvertent – to IUU fishing vessels. At a minimum, this ought to ensure that no vessel currently designated upon an RFMO blacklist benefits from insurance services

---

[67] Report of the Standing Committee on Implementation and Compliance, 2017, para. 107.
[68] Ibid., para. 108.
[69] See   http://eu.oceana.org/sites/default/files/oceana-psi_marine_insurance_statement_with_signaries_and_supporting_institutions_23.05.2018.pdf.
[70] Ibid.

in the future, unless there has been a meaningful change in conduct. Nevertheless, this proposition is not entirely unproblematic – indeed, concerns have arisen over procedural transparency in the listing and de-listing of vessels on IUU lists[71] and, given commercial confidentiality considerations, it is currently difficult to monitor whether these commitments are being rigorously observed in practice. More optimistically, perhaps, if these principles gain evident traction within the insurance industry, there is clear scope for other providers of financial services to follow suit, notably the banking sector. Moreover, the public recognition of the problems associated with IUU fishing (or, at least, the commercial benefits associated with visibly supporting an issue that has steadily attracted greater popular concern) on the part of leading companies may also exert a transformative effect upon corporate behaviour more widely, as has been identified by the conduct of other 'keystone actors' in driving improvements in fishing-related practices.[72] In this manner, international fisheries law could be considerably strengthened by the operational practices of key ancillary industries, even in the absence of express and unambiguous legal obligations upon the commercial sector from the current suite of fisheries-related instruments.

3. IUU FISHING AND THE TOOLKIT OF CRIMINAL LAW

A further basis for strengthening legal responses towards IUU fishing lies in the potential application of criminal and administrative sanctions that are more commonly associated with the pursuit of organized crime syndicates and elaborate financial misconduct. As Telesetsky observes, IUU fishing has been traditionally regarded "as a fisheries resource management problem rather than an egregious criminal act".[73] Increasingly, however, it is suggested that resource-based misconduct such as IUU fishing could be more effectively addressed by either coupling it more directly to the sanctions of criminal law or reformulating it as a distinct form of criminal activity.[74] This is attractive for a number of reasons. A closer alignment with criminal law facilitates the deterrent effect of more weighty sanctions, including financial restitution and incarceration, which are not commonly applied to IUU fishing. Moreover, current responses to IUU fishing can be markedly strengthened by the application of a separate and well-resourced toolkit, including the pursuit of the proceeds of illicit activity and sanctions against the organizational entities behind IUU fishing rather than

---

[71] van der Marel, note 3.

[72] H Österblom et al. "Transnational Corporations as 'Keystone Actors' in Marine Ecosystems" (2015) 10 *PLoS One* e0127533 1–15, at 7–11.

[73] A Telesetsky, "Laundering Fish in the Global Undercurrents: Illegal, Unreported and Unregulated Fishing and Transnational Organized Crime" (2015) 41 *Ecology Law Quarterly* 939, at 943.

[74] See further MA Palma-Robles, "Tightening the Net: The Link between Illegal, Unreported and Unregulated Fishing and Transnational Crime under International Law" (2015) 29 *Ocean Yearbook* 144–165, at 154–158.

individual (and often impecunious) fishers. Similarly, it allows for the mobilization of political pressure and financial resources to address this problem more effectively.[75] Additionally, IUU fishing is often merely one clandestine activity masterminded by organized syndicates, hence investigative efforts in this regard could ultimately assist in inhibiting a wider suite of more serious criminality.

These conceptual merits notwithstanding, the IUU construct does not assimilate easily into the terminology deployed by the legal and institutional framework of transnational criminal law. As a preliminary point, and mirroring the problems associated with the conglomeration of multiple examples of distinct fisheries misconduct within the IUU formulation, international bodies and treaties concerned with law enforcement recognize a far broader notion of 'fisheries crime'.[76] Like the IUU paradigm this is also an amorphous concept, encompassing all elements of criminality associated with fishing vessels and personnel, including the trafficking and smuggling of drugs and human beings, piracy, environmental crime (which may include, but is by no means restricted to, IUU fishing) and financial offences facilitated by the fishing industry such as fraud, corruption and money laundering. Accordingly, international instruments respectively governing fisheries and law enforcement understand fisheries-based offences in markedly different ways.

Two further complicating factors are also apparent, which are examined in this section. Firstly, IUU fishing has struggled to gain widespread recognition as a distinct form of internationally significant crime, which undermines the potential application of key instruments to such activities. Secondly, where the strengthening of fisheries laws through associated criminal procedures and provisions has been contemplated, these regimes have not always been fully interconnected. Accordingly, while criminal law offers an intriguing basis to strengthen international fisheries law in the context of IUU fishing, a degree of caution is appropriate and the results have proved to be a decidedly qualified success.

3.1. Transnational Organized Crime Law and IUU Fishing

The primary multilateral mechanism through which IUU fishing could be recalibrated as misconduct that merits the closer attention of criminal investigators – and the application of penalties commensurate with an internationally significant offence – is the UNTOC.[77] The UNTOC is the pre-eminent international instrument addressing the activities of organized criminal syndicates.

---

[75] H Österblom, A Constable and S Fukumi, "Illegal Fishing and the Organized Crime Analogy" (2011) 26 *Trends in Ecology and Evolution* 261–262.

[76] See further Palma-Robles, note 74 at 146–158.

[77] United Nations Convention against Transnational Organized Crime of 12 December 2000 (2225 UNTS 209).

It was adopted by the UNGA in 2000, entering into force in 2003, and is supplemented by three further Protocols respectively addressing human trafficking, migrant smuggling and the illicit manufacturing of and trafficking in firearms, their components and ammunition. These specific issues, as well as the enduring links between crime and terrorism, largely dominated the development and focus of the UNTOC.[78] Its prospective utility in the context of IUU fishing is therefore as a blueprint for States to frame their responses to transnational organized crime in its myriad forms and motivations, as opposed to offering clear provisions addressing fisheries-based offences. In this manner, the UNTOC seeks to improve cooperation and coordination between national investigative authorities, streamline extradition practices and promote capacity-building and mutual assistance, as well as harmonizing sanctions and requiring the universal criminalization of particular activities, all of which can serve to inhibit the conditions under which IUU fishing activities may flourish. These aspirations are bolstered by its near-universal participation with 189 current Parties, which stands in marked contrast to a number of international instruments purporting to improve cooperation in the enforcement of fisheries standards. Accordingly, if fully and effectively implemented, the UNTOC provides a platform to strengthen domestic responses and multi-jurisdictional collaboration against a number of activities that underpin criminal interests in fishing and thus "create the needed global momentum to nationally prosecute transnational IUU criminal networks".[79]

The fundamental objective of the UNTOC is expressed in a concise statement of purpose as being "to promote cooperation to prevent and combat transnational organized crime more effectively".[80] Due to enduring definitional difficulties,[81] the precise notion of transnational organized crime is not articulated within the Convention. As observed further below, this raises interpretive questions as to the extent to which IUU fishing may be recognized as an issue of direct concern to the UNTOC. However the UNTOC concerns the prevention, investigation and prosecution of two broad streams of criminal activities,[82] both of which are relevant to addressing the illegal intent behind many of the more organized and pervasive interests in IUU fishing.

In the first instance, the UNTOC requires the Parties to criminalize a distinct suite of activities, namely participation in an organized criminal group,[83] laundering the proceeds of crime,[84] corruption[85] and obstruction of justice,[86]

---

[78] Preamble to the Convention.
[79] Telesetsky, note 73 at 966.
[80] UNTOC, Art. 1.
[81] See T Obokata, *Transnational Organised Crime in International Law* (Hart, Oxford: 2010) 24–36.
[82] UNTOC, Art. 3.
[83] Ibid., Art. 5.
[84] Ibid., Art. 6.
[85] Ibid., Art. 8.
[86] Ibid., Art. 23.

which are each commonly engaged to at least some extent in the conduct of IUU fishing. In this regard, an 'organized criminal group' is defined in Article 2(a) as a

> structured group of three or more persons, existing for a period of time and acting in concert with the aim of committing one or more serious crimes or offences established in accordance with this Convention, in order to obtain, directly or indirectly, a financial or other material benefit.[87]

This definition would correspond to the broad modus operandi of many IUU fishing operations, which are "typified by loosely organised networks of individuals with specialist knowledge of the area in which they work".[88] Significantly, the notion of laundering the proceeds of crime includes "[t]he concealment or disguise of the true nature, source, location, disposition, movement or ownership of or rights with respect to property, knowing that such property is the proceeds of crime".[89] Such actions are essential to ensuring that the products of IUU fishing are able to enter legitimate markets.[90] Similarly, the establishment of clearer anti-corruption legislation could also bolster attempts to combat IUU fishing, given the clear links between these practices experienced in particular regions. Meanwhile, the criminalization of interference in the production of evidence as mandated under Article 23(a) could also bolster domestic sanctions regarding a particularly pernicious problem in prosecuting fisheries infractions, as considered further below.

The second stream of organized criminal activity contemplated by the UNTOC involves the commission of a 'serious crime', inelegantly defined as "conduct constituting an offence punishable by a maximum deprivation of liberty of at least four years or a more serious penalty".[91] This awkward formulation is attributed to negotiating disagreements over the most appropriate forms of criminal sanctions and the extent to which probation and financial penalties fell within its ambit.[92] In an IUU context, however, this is likely to pertain to the more extreme abuses that may befall fishers on vessels owned by particularly unscrupulous operators, as well as other forms of criminality that may be practised by fishing vessels operating in remote areas with little oversight. For fishing vessels in which the crew are held in conditions of near-slavery, or who are trafficked into forced labour or debt bondage, the provisions of the

---

[87] A 'structured group' is defined as "a group that is not randomly formed for the immediate commission of an offence and that does not need to have formally defined roles for its members, continuity of its membership or a developed structure": ibid., Art. 2(c).

[88] High Seas Task Force, *Closing the Net: Stopping Illegal Fishing on the High Seas* (DEFRA, London: 2006) 22.

[89] UNTOC, Art. 6(1)(a)(ii).

[90] See further A Couper, HD Smith and B Ciceri, *Fishers and Plunderers: Theft, Slavery and Violence at Sea* (Pluto Press, London: 2015) 95–103.

[91] UNTOC, Art. 2(b).

[92] Telesetsky, note 73 at 968.

associated Trafficking Protocol also provide a broad framework to strengthen national law to curtail such abuses and to assist in the rehabilitation of the victims.

Where transnational organized crime is committed, Parties to the UNTOC undertake to confiscate and seize assets and proceeds of crime derived from such offences.[93] Moreover, as part of the suite of commitments towards preventing transnational organized crime, Parties are required to reduce existing or future opportunities for organized criminals to participate in lawful markets through the proceeds of crime, with particular focus upon strengthening cooperation with relevant private entities and formulating standards and procedures to safeguard the integrity of private entities, including codes of conduct for relevant professions.[94] If IUU fishing is expressly recognized as an area of priority activity under the ambit of the Convention, this provision could therefore provide a clear basis to promote increased scrutiny of the provision of commercial services to fishing vessels, as advocated above in the context of marine insurance.

Ultimately, however, the current value of the UNTOC in the context of IUU fishing appears to be largely residual. As with the prospective denial of insurance services, the Convention aims to eliminate safe havens for criminality and inhibit lucrative misconduct more generally by reducing the scope for organized criminals to operate effectively and increasing the risks and costs associated with particular activities. Accordingly, impeding IUU fishing is a more tangential concern and progress attained in this respect may be largely an opportune by-product of wider measures taken against organized criminal syndicates that has the effect of curtailing an array of illegal activities, which includes interests in the illicit catch of and trade in fish.

Nevertheless, in recent years, individual Parties have sought to increase the prominence of IUU fishing upon the agenda of the UNTOC and thus link combating such activities more directly to the central commitments established under the Convention. Indeed, the precise application of the UNTOC to IUU fishing remains an intriguing question. Notwithstanding its stated focus on particular crimes, the scope of the Convention is deliberately non-exhaustive, hence is not confined to the crimes that inspired its development. Crimes against natural resources fall within the express contemplation of the UNTOC, which is intended to provide "the necessary legal framework for international cooperation in combating such criminal activities as, *inter alia* … illicit trafficking in endangered species of wild flora and fauna".[95] Even so, IUU fishing does not fit comfortably within this formulation: not all illegally-caught fish are endangered, nor are they necessarily trafficked. The scope and implementation of the Convention is reviewed through the Conference of the Parties (COP), wherein the Parties have long recognized an array of (non-exhaustive) "emerging issues"

---

[93] UNTOC, Arts. 12–14.
[94] Ibid., Art. 31(2)(a) and (b).
[95] Preamble to the UNTOC.

requiring further consideration. Although IUU fishing lies outside the substantive issues regularly discussed under this item, concerted efforts have been made within the COPs to explicitly recognize IUU fishing as an example of transnational organized crime – or, at the very least, as misconduct meriting regular consideration within the framework of the Convention.

The threat posed by IUU fishing was first contemplated at the fourth COP, convened in 2008, wherein particular delegations considered that these activities shared "the elements of crimes that fall within the definitions provided in articles 2 and 3 of the Convention", for which existing approaches to such activities "had to be supplemented by using the criminalization provisions of the Convention".[96] Similarly, certain Parties have made the case that IUU fishing is "not only an environmental threat but also an organized criminal activity, as it diverted revenue from Governments, which regulated the legal fishing industry".[97] This is not a unanimous viewpoint, however, and other Parties have voiced reservations that the express designation of IUU fishing as a transnational organized crime "needed to be considered carefully because of the legal and practical impact that such criminalization might have".[98] In the absence of a wider groundswell of agreement, individual States have included information on steps taken against IUU fishing in their official reports on the national implementation of the UNTOC, denoting that in some quarters at least, such activities are considered to clearly fall within the obligations advanced by the Convention.[99]

At present, however, there is little external support for recognizing IUU fishing as a distinct form of transnational organized crime. Successive UNGA Sustainable Fisheries Resolutions have stopped studiously short of acknowledging IUU fishing in such a manner, noting instead "concerns about *possible* connections between transnational organised crime and illegal fishing in certain regions of the world".[100] Instead, the Resolution 'encourages' States to study the causes and methods of illegal fishing to further understand "these possible connections ... bearing in mind the distinct legal regimes and remedies under international law applicable to illegal fishing and transnational organised crime".[101] Similar reticence has been encountered within the UN Open-Ended Informal Consultative

---

[96] Report of the Conference of the Parties to the United Nations Convention against Transnational Organized Crime on its Fourth Session (doc. CTOC/COP/2008/19), para. 210. The COP to the UNTOC exercises the same reporting convention as other key UN fora, in which interlocutors are individually identified only at their direct insistence.

[97] Report of the Conference of the Parties to the United Nations Convention against Transnational Organized Crime on its Fifth Session (doc. CTOC/COP/2010/17), para. 130.

[98] Ibid.

[99] Report of the Conference of the Parties to the United Nations Convention against Transnational Organized Crime on its Seventh Session (doc. CTOC/COP/2015/13), para. 30; and Report of the Conference of the Parties to the United Nations Convention against Transnational Organized Crime on its Eighth Session (doc. CTOC/COP/2016/15), para. 82.

[100] See most recently Resolution 72/72, note 62, para. 98 (emphasis added).

[101] Ibid.

Process on Oceans and the Law of the Sea (UNICPOLOS),[102] and the Review Conference of the Fish Stocks Agreement, which recently observed that strengthening law enforcement mechanisms may also "includ[e] working on the relationship between IUU fishing and transnational organized crime".[103]

Crucially, the UN Office on Drugs and Crime (UNODC) has considered the notion of IUU fishing to be "difficult to apply" in the context of transnational organized crime.[104] In an extensive report published in 2011, which was "welcomed" by the Parties to the UNTOC,[105] the UNODC instead focused on the notion of fisheries crime more broadly, in the sense of the prospective involvement of fishers in transnational organized crime, rather than in combating IUU fishing under the auspices of the Convention. Indeed, in the view of the UNODC, the long-standing problem of conflating a variety of discrete issues within the IUU paradigm appears to most seriously undermine the potential recognition of IUU fishing as an example of transnational organized crime, not least since it incorporates activities that are not necessarily illegal in nature, while its narrow application to fishing vessels precludes consideration of criminal involvement in related spheres of activity, such as aquaculture.[106] Moreover, the IUU concept is not considered to recognize the 'downstream' elements of illegal fishing, such as laundering products and proceeds, corruption, fraud and trafficking,[107] which fall within the wider concern of the UNTOC. These sentiments notwithstanding, particular States still have strong aspirations to promote a more forceful pronouncement within the Sustainable Fisheries Resolution to recognize IUU fishing as a distinct category of transnational organized crime,[108] although this appears to be a distant prospect at this stage.

Even if IUU fishing does not presently benefit from universal recognition under the UNTOC, it has nonetheless received considerable attention within INTERPOL, the pre-eminent global institution associated with international law enforcement, where a series of valuable initiatives have been launched to assist in combating IUU fishing on the ground.[109] In February 2013, in conjunction with the Norwegian Government and Pew Charitable Trusts, INTERPOL launched 'Project Scale', a global initiative to detect, suppress and combat

---

[102] See further Palma-Robles, note 74 at 144–145.

[103] Report of the Resumed Review Conference of UNFSA 2016 (doc. A/CONF.210.2016/5), para. 120.

[104] UNODC, *Transnational Organized Crime in the Fishing Industry* (UNODC, Geneva: 2011), 96. In keeping with the thematic priorities of the UNTOC, the report focused predominantly on human trafficking, migrant smuggling and the transportation of illicit drugs.

[105] Report of the Conference of the Parties to the United Nations Convention against Transnational Organized Crime on its Sixth Session (doc. CTOC/COP/2012/15), para. 92.

[106] UNODC, note 104 at 96.

[107] Ibid.

[108] See e.g. Ocean Action 18271 pledged by Indonesia at the 2017 UN Ocean Conference to secure the recognition of IUU fishing as a form of transnational organized crime. Indonesia is currently lobbying for this to be included within an appropriate UNGA resolution.

[109] See further Chapter 4 of this volume (Stokke).

fisheries crime, supported by a Fisheries Crime Working Group to facilitate the exchange of information, intelligence and technical expertise. Although framed in the context of fisheries crime, Project Scale represents a central repository for information on all aspects of fishing-related infractions, including those that may be of less direct concern to the UNTOC. Moreover, INTERPOL also provides an important information-sharing tool through its Purple Notices, which are issued to seek or provide details on the modus operandi, objects, devices and concealment methods used by criminals. An increasing number of Purple Notices have been issued against individual vessels considered to have committed IUU infractions, which facilitates the tracking of individual craft that frequently modify their name, flag and companies of supposed incorporation to continually evade the authorities. Indeed, the Purple Notice issued against the *Thunder* proved instrumental in coordinating the extensive efforts between a number of interested States, as well as the NGO Sea Shepherd which pursued the vessel to São Tomé and Príncipe, where three senior crewmembers were eventually convicted and imprisoned for having conducted widespread illegal fishing in the Southern Ocean.

3.2. Enduring Challenges of IUU Fishing and the Limits of Alternative Criminal Provisions

Although the UNTOC does not prescribe a clear and unambiguous requirement to address IUU fishing through the broader suite of offences associated with transnational organized crime, elements of this approach have nevertheless been apparent within the actions of a number of individual States. These experiences provide further insights into the role that allied criminal legislation may play in addressing problems commonly experienced in prosecuting IUU fishing.

A primary concern remains the evidential challenges inherent in securing convictions for fisheries infractions. Incriminating items, such as logbooks, navigational equipment, netting and the catch, are frequently jettisoned prior to arrest – and in extreme cases such as the *Thunder*, the vessel itself may be scuttled – thereby stymying effective investigation of the wider interests involved in IUU fishing.[110] Self-evidently, the destruction of evidence has considerable implications for the prospects of a meaningful prosecution. This is abundantly illustrated by the saga of the *Viarsa I*, a vessel with a long record of IUU longlining for Patagonian toothfish within the CCAMLR area. In August 2003, the *Viarsa I* was eventually arrested following a 21-day pursuit through the dangerous waters of the Southern Ocean, which remains the most extensive – and expensive – fisheries enforcement operation ever conducted by the Australian navy. The crew seemingly made numerous attempts to conceal

---

[110] High Seas Task Force, note 88 at 32.

incriminating documentation,[111] and were eventually acquitted by a jury on the basis that the evidence that was ultimately retrieved proved to be largely circumstantial.[112] Notwithstanding legitimate judicial sensitivity towards the correct application of due process at sea, the limited prospects for securing a conviction appears to have engendered a chilling effect upon the willingness of naval commanders to consider similar operations against individual vessels in highly remote waters.[113]

With these difficulties in mind, legislation more commonly associated with combating other sub-species of serious crime presents an intriguing scope to inhibit tampering with or destroying the evidence of IUU fishing. A striking example of this approach was recently considered by the US Supreme Court, albeit with mixed results. In *Yates v. United States*,[114] the appellant had been convicted of discarding 72 fractionally undersized specimens of red grouper that had been discovered during a routine at-sea inspection, and replacing them with individuals of full legal length upon his return to shore. Although this would appear to be a relatively minor infraction, albeit one causing great frustration to the local authorities, the magnitude of the offence was dramatically amplified by a decision to indict the appellant under 18 USC§1519, which had originated from the 2002 Sarbanes-Oxley Act. Having been introduced in the wake of a series of corporate scandals, this provision establishes an intimidating raft of federal sanctions to curtail interference with any "record, document, or tangible object" with an intent to impede a lawful investigation, carrying a maximum sentence of 20 years' imprisonment. In throwing overboard these specimens of fish, the appellant was thus convicted of impeding a lawful investigation by destroying a 'tangible object'. Yates sought to vacate this conviction on the basis that the documentary analogy was excessively removed from its original legislative intent. By an extremely narrow margin, the Supreme Court concurred that such an expansive interpretation would serve to "cut §1519 loose from its financial-fraud mooring" and that a 'tangible object' in this context is restricted to an item used to restore or record information.[115] This arguably leaves the spectacular deterrent effect of §1519 intact where federal charges are brought against a fisherman[116] and documentary evidence such as a logbook is falsified,

[111] GB Knecht, *Hooked: A True Story of Pirates, Poaching and the Perfect Fish* (Allen & Unwin, Sydney: 2006) 205–241.

[112] *Ribot-Cabrera and Others v. The Queen* [2004] WASCA 101.

[113] Knecht, note 111 at 238.

[114] 574 US (2015). See further R Caddell, "So Long, and Thanks for All the Tangible Objects: Defining 'Fish' in the US Supreme Court" (2015) 21 *Journal of International Maritime Law* 175–177.

[115] Ibid., 2 *per* Ginsberg J.

[116] This is a significant limitation, however. Indeed the initial prosecution owes much to a quirk of administrative fate, since Yates had the personal misfortune to be boarded by an enforcement officer who had been previously deputized as a Federal Marshall, thereby raising the prospect of federal charges. It nonetheless appears unlikely that a full sentence would be imposed under §1519 unless there were especially aggravated circumstances: Yates ultimately served 30 days in prison upon conviction.

amended or destroyed. Nevertheless, the tenor of the Supreme Court judgment suggests that innovative transplants between such legislation have clear thematic limitations in addressing the nuances of IUU fishing, and could even risk diluting their application in their intended context.

Both the *Ribot-Cabrera* and *Yates* cases exemplify what is arguably the predominant frustration in fisheries-related prosecutions: they are most frequently brought against essentially subsistence fishers that have cut regulatory corners or involve the lowest-ranked operatives within a far lengthier chain of culpability. Such achievements are thus often Pyrrhic, given the outlay in financial and human resources, since the defendants are often in straitened economic circumstances and unable to provide adequate recompense for these offences.[117] Moreover, they are frequently abandoned to their fate by unscrupulous operators, who will often also sacrifice a vessel of dubious seaworthiness to satisfy forfeiture laws.[118] Perhaps the greatest attraction of associated criminal provisions is therefore the potential use of financial legislation to track the beneficial owners of vessels and to pursue those with the deepest pockets.

This has been the purported approach of certain States in which IUU fishing is an endemic problem. In 2012, the Philippines was seemingly the first jurisdiction to consider linking domestic money laundering law to illegal fishing, followed swiftly by Indonesia.[119] This has not been unproblematic, however, and in the absence of stronger legislative reform the application of money laundering provisions to IUU fishing remains a theoretical prospect at best. Neither jurisdiction has yet formally established illegal fishing as a predicate offence that would meet the threshold for investigation under its money laundering or anti-corruption legislation.[120] Moreover, in Indonesia, despite the change in legislation, corresponding instruments have not been adjusted to take these new approaches into account, hence the domestic fisheries authorities ultimately lack the legal competence to pursue money laundering investigations, which remain the sole preserve of other law-enforcement agencies.[121]

Less problematic alternatives to the uneasy union of fisheries and serious crime provisions do exist, which can provide a useful avenue to pursue steep penalties against the economic backers of vessels engaged in IUU fishing. The most notable example is the US Lacey Act,[122] enacted in 1900, under which it

---

[117] Exemplified by the bleak accounting of the defendants' personal assets in *Ribot-Cabrera* (note 112).

[118] High Seas Task Force, note 88 at 25.

[119] See further MA Palma-Robles, "Integrating Monitoring, Control and Surveillance and Anti-Money Laundering Tools to Address Illegal Fishing in the Philippines and Indonesia" in G Rose (ed.), *Following the Proceeds of Environmental Crime: Forests, Fishing and Filthy Lucre* (Routledge, Abingdon: 2014) 100–115, at 107–109.

[120] Ibid., 110.

[121] "Indonesia Seeks to Slap Money Laundering Label on Illegal Fishing", available at https://news.mongabay.com/2017/12/indonesia-seeks-to-slap-money-laundering-label-on-illegal-fishing/.

[122] 16 USC §§3371–3378.

is illegal to import, export, transport, sell, receive, acquire or purchase any fish possessed, transported or sold in violation of any law, treaty or regulation of the United States. Significantly, the Lacey Act also has an extraterritorial application and can be an effective means of addressing instances wherein the legal provisions of the jurisdiction in which the infractions have occurred prove to be inadequate. A prominent example is *United States v. Bengis*,[123] involving the prosecution of a South African company that had undertaken wholesale over-fishing of rock lobster, which had subsequently been imported into the lucrative US seafood market.[124] Having been fined USD 1.2 million in South Africa, a comparatively modest sanction considering the vast profits accrued from years of illicit activities, the defendants were finally ordered to pay over USD 29 million in restitutionary damages. While prosecutions under the Lacey Act have been criticized in a fisheries context for a general trend of eschewing incarceration as a penalty,[125] these provisions nonetheless represent a powerful deterrent and can also serve to by-pass deficiencies in local fisheries provisions. Such successes also promote the merits of improved international cooperation[126] and incentivize the adequate resourcing of national agencies charged with addressing IUU fishing that are often competing for funds from the wider government budget.

Ultimately, however, it would appear that sanctions against IUU fishing are most likely to take the form of financial penalties under administrative law, even where such actions are egregious in nature and have been conducted over an extensive period of time. Domestic fisheries legislation continues to view fisheries infractions primarily as a resource-based problem and direct connections between IUU fishing and the criminal law remain the exception rather than the rule. Indeed, this was strikingly exemplified in the 2016 judgment of the Supreme Court of Spain in a criminal action brought against Vidal Armadores SA, a Galician conglomerate globally notorious for its association with IUU fishing vessels, including the *Viarsa I* and allegedly the *Thunder*. Despite the imposition of extensive civil penalties, attempts to impose criminal liability foundered when the Supreme Court ruled that IUU fishing on the high seas lay outside the closed series of offences considered as exceptions to the principle of personality established under the *Ley Orgánica del Poder Judicial*, which would have thus allowed for the prosecution of actions undertaken outside Spanish jurisdiction.[127] This finding also negated the possibility of domestic money laundering provisions being brought to bear against the defendant. Accordingly, it appears that in

---

[123] (2012) WL 3518477.
[124] See J Glazewski, "*United States v Bengis*: A Victory for Wildlife Law and Lessons for International Fisheries Crime" (2014) 29 *International Journal of Marine and Coastal Law* 173–183.
[125] Telesetsky, note 73 at 978.
[126] On the domestic impact of *Bengis*, see E de Coning and E Witbooi, "Towards a New 'Fisheries Crime' Paradigm: South Africa as an Illustrative Example" (2015) 60 *Marine Policy* 208–215, at 209.
[127] Sentencia Número 974/2016 of 23 December 2016.

many jurisdictions, criminality is largely absent from provisions on IUU fishing or, where it is recognized, the cumbersome process of linking it to the full suite of domestic criminal laws and procedures, so as to allow for the imposition of a wider array of penalties, remains nascent.

4. CONCLUSIONS

The continued proliferation of IUU fishing indicates that international fisheries law requires further strengthening in order to more effectively combat such activities. Intriguing possibilities are presented by more closely considering the role and obligations of those providing assistance to fishing vessels (and support vessels such as transhipment and provisioning services) and in facilitating a more targeted alignment between IUU fishing and criminal law. Both avenues provide differing opportunities to achieve essentially the same goal: namely undermining the attraction of IUU fishing by increasing its associated risks and costs. However, as this chapter illustrates, neither approach as yet offers an uncomplicated pathway to attaining this objective.

A considerable array of actors are involved – whether wittingly or inadvertently – in facilitating IUU fishing. To date, international fisheries law has accorded little attention to those who provide ancillary services to vessels. This oversight means that few clear and unambiguous obligations are readily discernible with respect to these sectors. As this chapter demonstrates in the specific context of insurance providers, this represents a missed opportunity to strengthen international fisheries law, albeit in a rather indirect manner. Although it appears highly unlikely that a vessel involved in IUU fishing would be able to successfully claim indemnification, the mere possession of insurance certification offers operational advantages far beyond the obvious merits of coverage in the case of a maritime incident. Thus far, no State with a meaningful presence in the marine insurance market appears to have enacted legislation to prohibit the provision of insurance to vessels with a record of IUU fishing, while the EU IUU Regulation remains highly ambiguous in this respect. Likewise, clear requirements for the providers of commercial and supporting services have not yet been established in leading fisheries instruments, the pronouncements of influential international bodies or the general practice of RFMOs. While encouraging developments in this regard have recently emerged within the insurance industry itself, wherein the greatest practical benefit is likely to be forthcoming, there remains a strong case for legislative intervention to buttress current obligations upon these hitherto under-scrutinized industries to further inhibit IUU fishing opportunities.

Likewise, a closer alignment with (transnational) criminal law has been advocated as a means of bolstering the rather limited deterrents currently established against IUU fishing. Such approaches offer the enforcement advantages of an enhanced toolkit of procedures and penalties, as well as access to the greater political and financial capital associated with the fight against transnational organized crime. Nevertheless, considerable difficulties have been encountered in facilitating this approach. International instruments respectively addressing fisheries and law enforcement lack a common understanding of illicit fishing activities, with a strong degree of mutual exclusivity evident between the equally unwieldy concepts of IUU fishing and fisheries crime. This has undermined initiatives to recognize IUU fishing as a distinct form of transnational organized crime and thus directly connect such activities to the suite of obligations established under the UNTOC. Moreover, attempts to establish IUU fishing as a serious crime under domestic law have also proved ineffective. Fatally, such initiatives have not been accompanied by the highly technical task of exhaustively adapting criminal laws and processes to incorporate IUU fishing and to empower the relevant agencies accordingly. Consequently, such policies tend to be high in political impact but often transpire to be largely symbolic in practice.

Ultimately, this chapter reveals that current legal instruments do not readily facilitate alternative approaches to combating IUU fishing, either because regulatory regimes that lie beyond the traditional nexus of IUU fishing are not expressly addressed within IUU fishing provisions, or because the IUU concept is not easily accommodated within these alternative systems. Indeed, it is the element of illegality recognized in the IUU paradigm that most directly transcends international fisheries law and potentially engages the assistance of alternative regulatory regimes. Nevertheless, merely equating IUU fishing with illegal conduct undermines its original intent to facilitate a holistic response to the mismanagement of natural resources.[128] In this manner, there would appear to be a strong case for expectation management in assessing the scope for responses to IUU fishing to be rapidly strengthened through alternative regulatory principles.

---

[128] JT Theilen, "What's in a Name? The Illegality of Illegal, Unreported and Unregulated Fishing" (2013) 28 *International Journal of Marine and Coastal Law* 533–550, at 550.

Part V

Options and Pathways to Strengthen International Fisheries Law in an Era of Changing Oceans

18

Options and Pathways to Strengthen International Fisheries Law in an Era of Changing Oceans

ERIK J MOLENAAR AND RICHARD CADDELL

1. INTRODUCTION

A S ADVANCED IN Chapter 1 of this volume, the domain of international fisheries law has made significant progress since the 1990s, in particular through the adoption and establishment of international instruments and bodies at the global and regional levels. While this has unquestionably strengthened international fisheries law, global fish stocks remain in a troubling state. Fisheries management authorities face a wide array of internal and external challenges, as well as the critical limitations associated with States that are unable or unwilling to comply with their international obligations.

A multitude of options and pathways to address these challenges and limitations has been identified over the years. Some are laid down in legally binding or non-legally binding fisheries instruments or acts of regional fisheries management organizations or arrangements (RFMO/As). Others have the form of recommendations and were adopted by a diverse number of bodies and fora, including the United Nations General Assembly (UNGA) through its annual 'Sustainable Fisheries' Resolutions, the (Resumed) Fish Stocks Agreement Review Conferences – whose next resumption is provisionally scheduled for 2021[1] – the ICSP,[2] panels established to review the performance of RFMO/As, fishing industry associations,[3] the ministerially-led Task Force

---

[1] See the Report of the 13th (2018) round of informal consultations of States Parties to the Fish Stocks Agreement (ICSP), para. 87.

[2] See note 1.

[3] E.g. the best practices advocated by the International Seafood Sustainability Foundation (ISSF) available at iss-foundation.org/.

on IUU Fishing on the High Seas (High Seas Task Force),[4] the Organization for Economic Co-operation and Development (OECD)[5] and independent associations.[6] In light of these myriad recommendations and the significant repetition and overlap among them, it may even be opportune to create order and overview by means of a consolidation effort.

In view of the recent commencement of negotiations towards the third implementation agreement of the LOS Convention[7] – the BBNJ Implementation Agreement[8] – the question logically arises as to whether this represents an option and pathway to strengthen international fisheries law. Unquestionably, fishing in areas beyond national jurisdiction (ABNJ) – the high seas and the international sea-bed beyond (outer) continental shelves (the 'Area') – is among the main threats, if not the main threat, to the conservation and sustainable use of marine biodiversity in ABNJ. The negotiation-mandate is nevertheless subject to the constraint that the negotiations "and its result should not undermine existing relevant legal instruments and frameworks and relevant global, regional and sectoral bodies".[9] As regards the impacts of fishing in ABNJ, the rationale of this constraint is that these impacts must be addressed in the existing domain of international fisheries law. However, even if it is indeed true that delegations primarily had the domain of international fisheries law in mind when they negotiated the constraint, this is by no means clear from its wording. Accordingly, the constraint may be invoked for numerous other domains and bodies, both within and outside the domain of the international law of the sea, for instance international intellectual property law. On the other hand, the words "should not undermine" still give delegations a considerable margin of appreciation to ensure at least some impact on the domain of international fisheries law.[10] The authors of Chapters 9 (Dunn, Ortuño Crespo and Caddell) and 10 (Marsden) are hopeful that delegations will do exactly that in relation to area-based management tools and environmental assessment.

---

[4] See Closing the Net: Stopping Illegal Fishing on the High Seas (High Seas Task Force: 2006).

[5] E.g. Strengthening Regional Fisheries Management Organisations (OECD: 2009).

[6] E.g. Recommended Best Practices for Regional Fisheries Management Organizations (Chatham House: 2007).

[7] United Nations Convention on the Law of the Sea of 10 December 1982 (1833 UNTS 3).

[8] The implementation agreement to the LOS Convention on "the conservation and sustainable use of marine biological diversity of areas beyond national jurisdiction" is envisaged by UNGA Res 72/249 of 24 December 2017.

[9] Ibid., para. 7.

[10] See also R Barnes "The Proposed LOSC Implementation Agreement on Areas Beyond National Jurisdiction and Its Impact on International Fisheries Law" (2016) 31 *International Journal of Marine and Coastal Law* 583–619; and Z Scanlon "The Art of 'Not Undermining': Possibilities within Existing Architecture to Improve Environmental Protections in Areas beyond National Jurisdiction" (2018) 75 *ICES Journal of Marine Science* 405–416.

2. INTERCONNECTEDNESS AND INTERNATIONAL FISHERIES LAW

While the interconnectedness of international fisheries instruments and bodies has advanced significantly over the years, the effectiveness or problem-solving capacity of the domain of international fisheries law can be enhanced further by steadily broadening the set of relevant institutions and other actors. Increasing efforts in cooperation and coordination between these institutions and other actors will nevertheless be required to ensure internal coherence. This will constitute a significant element of a broader strategy to respond to climate change-induced impacts upon fish and their associated ecosystems, including projected changes in species productivity, composition, distribution and abundance. Cooperation and coordination in relation to the scientific research that is necessary to predict such changes will be crucial, among other things for reasons of cost-efficiency and the limited expertise that is available.

While some regional fisheries bodies have been established under an over-arching body or system – such as the United Nations Food and Agriculture Organization (FAO) or the Antarctic Treaty System – most are entirely separate, autonomous bodies. Thus Molenaar (Chapter 6) highlights that the uniqueness of individual RFMO/As is reflected, *inter alia*, in the number and composition of their participants as well as their rules and practices concerning participation. As concluded by Harrison (Chapter 5), however, a growing ethos towards interconnectedness between regional fisheries bodies has led to the emergence of a system of regional fisheries governance. This has provided a pathway to improved fisheries management through the exchange of data and enhanced enforcement capacity, through the sharing of lists of illegal, unreported and unregulated (IUU) fishing vessels and information about their whereabouts and practices. Cross-fertilization between regional fisheries bodies should thus be encouraged further. This may ultimately prove to be a particularly important pathway to improved fisheries governance, especially as the productivity, composition, distribution and abundance of important fish stocks are increasingly impacted by climate change and associated processes. As highlighted by Rayfuse (Chapter 11), closer cooperation and coordination between RFMO/As will become increasingly significant as stocks begin to straddle regulatory boundaries. While this could be facilitated through bilateral or multilateral arrangements, Stokke (Chapter 4) also highlights that diffusion of best practices among regional fisheries bodies is enhanced by overlaps in participation.

While RFMO/As are increasingly interacting with each other to positive effect, the scope for strengthening international fisheries law through its interconnections with alternative domains of international law has generally been little explored. Many chapters in this volume therefore canvas the potential role and contribution of such other specialized domains – such as international trade law, international environmental law and the international law on merchant shipping, maritime labour standards, human rights and transnational organized crime – in addressing the manifold challenges and limitations faced by international fisheries law. Here too, the solution lies largely in an acknowledgement of the autonomy of these domains and the need for cooperation and coordination to ensure a mutually satisfactory outcome of the different balances of interests represented within them.

Interactions with alternative domains of international law could represent a further pathway to strengthening current fisheries provisions, as advocated further in Chapters 7 (Caddell), 8 (Scott) and 9 (Dunn, Ortuño Crespo and Caddell). Particular advantages are apparent in promoting strategic alignments with institutions more closely associated with international environmental law. This has particular merit in the context of data-sharing initiatives, where RFMO/As often lack fisheries-independent data concerning their areas of operation, while multilateral environmental agreements (MEAs) frequently lack data from fisheries which, as noted above, constitute arguably the most significant anthropogenic activity impacting upon these ecosystems. With both sets of institutions holding complementary information that has not always been freely available to the other, access to such information may enable more holistic management in support of the respective objectives of these sectoral regulators. This has also enabled the development of further synergies, most notably a closer alignment between the protected areas established by MEAs and fisheries restrictions adopted by particular RFMO/As, strikingly exemplified by the cooperation between the North-East Atlantic Fisheries Commission (NEAFC) and the OSPAR Commission. Interactions of this nature have also been identified as a pathway for strengthening international fisheries law in other influential fora, such as the BBNJ Process and the UNGA Sustainable Fisheries Resolutions. While such synergies remain dependent upon the unique regulatory conditions that vary markedly between individual regions, it is apparent that considerable operational advantages can be forthcoming in pursuing this particular pathway.

3. THE ECOSYSTEM APPROACH TO FISHERIES MANAGEMENT

The ecosystem approach to fisheries management is generally accepted by the international community and has been integrated explicitly or implicitly into most international fisheries instruments adopted since the 1990s and adopted by most RFMO/As, especially those established in the wake of the Fish Stocks Agreement.[11] Operationalizing this approach is nevertheless fraught with problems. A prominent example in this regard are the persistent problems posed by bycatch and discards. In view of the disappointing progress towards addressing these issues in many parts of the world, Scott (Chapter 8) proposes the development of a global legally binding instrument that would contain minimum

---

[11] Agreement for the Implementation of the Provisions of the United Nations Convention on the Law of the Sea of 10 December 1982 relating to the Conservation and Management of Straddling Fish Stocks and Highly Migratory Fish Stocks of 4 August 1995 (2167 UNTS 3).

standards for parties, a global oversight mechanism and clear guidance for RFMO/As.

Rayfuse (Chapter 11) calls for the reframing and adaptation of precautionary and ecosystem approaches to fisheries management in light of climate change. As a first step, RFMO/As will need to promote and then utilize scientific research that focuses on understanding the impacts of climate change and the broader environmental and climate-related stresses on the fish stocks they manage. This call is echoed by Cheung, Lam, Ota and Swartz (Chapter 2), who also argue that greater consideration of local fishing conditions is required, given that the impacts of climate change on stocks is highly likely to create and perpetuate inherent inequalities between individual fishers and States. This re-oriented scientific basis will then have to be reflected in strategies, stock assessments and key fisheries measures such as total allowable catches (TACs) and allocations of fishing opportunities. A considerable degree of operational flexibility to respond to changing conditions will be increasingly required not only for RFMO/As, but other multilateral bodies regulating marine resources. This is particularly apparent in the context of area-based management tools (ABMTs), which remain largely static designations, for which Dunn, Ortuño Crespo and Caddell (Chapter 9) advocate a greater use of emerging management approaches to promote further dynamism in spatial regulation.

Improving the available panorama of scientific information evidently contributes to more informed decision-making and improved fisheries management. Thus Dunn, Ortuño Crespo and Caddell (Chapter 9) further highlight the need to acquire significant data concerning not only the status of fish stocks, but also to achieve as full an inventory as possible of associated species and their habitat preferences in order to minimize conflicts and thus establish more effective ABMTs. Similarly, Marsden (Chapter 10) argues that current participatory and decision-making tools can be strengthened considerably by adopting clearer obligations towards the more widespread use of environmental assessment. At present, it is unclear when such assessments ought to be conducted and what form they should take – both for marine-based projects more generally and for fisheries specifically – resulting in highly variable practices between individual States concerned with the management of common stocks. Similar problems are encountered in the purported establishment of protected areas in ABNJ. A further pathway to strengthening the implementation of the ecosystem approach to fisheries management is therefore through the identification of standardized methodologies and explicit guidance on the appropriate conditions under which environmental assessment and spatial management should proceed.

4. COMPLIANCE AND ENFORCEMENT

As argued in Chapter 1, the challenges related to compliance and enforcement in international fisheries law are rooted in the sovereign equality of States, the consensual nature of international law and the principle of *pacta tertiis*. As part of the "comprehensive and integrated approach" advocated by the IPOA-IUU,[12] States are encouraged to invoke an array of jurisdictional grounds in order to exert pressure on unwilling or non-complying States. As argued by van der Marel (Chapter 13), the use of market power has considerable potential to enhance the effectiveness of international fisheries law. Care should nevertheless be taken to ensure fairness, non-discrimination, transparency and meaningful consideration of the rights and interests of those affected, as counselled by Churchill (Chapter 14).

Klein (Chapter 15) sees particular opportunities in relation to technological developments, holding flag States accountable – whether through dispute settlement mechanisms or direct intervention – and further efforts to agree on consequences for non-compliance. Prospects also exist for an enhanced role for private actors, such as environmental non-governmental organizations. As detailed by Massarella (Chapter 16), there appears to be shift away from unsolicited direct action, towards undertaking compliance-related activities within the general framework of the law – for instance through evidence-gathering – notably in partnership with national and international authorities. However, the role of private actors in enforcement activities remains more ambiguous and contentious, although as amply demonstrated by the unlamented demise of the notorious *Thunder*, these interventions are not without great practical utility. There is accordingly considerable scope for developing this pathway further, and establishing clearer principles and procedures underpinning the prospective involvement of (quasi-) private actors, given that enforcement actions by orthodox maritime authorities have been unable to prevent IUU fishing fleets operating with relative impunity.

In a similar vein, there is also a strong case for expanding the traditional nexus of instruments combating IUU fishing to establish clearer obligations upon those providing ancillary services to fishing vessels. This remains an intriguing but under-utilized approach. As argued by Caddell, Leloudas and Soyer (Chapter 17), further scrutiny of the industries that operate concentrically around the fishing sector, such as financial and insurance services, transhipment and other forms of material support, could be subject to additional scrutiny so as to increase the risks and costs associated with IUU fishing and to inhibit the opportunity for and attraction of such activities. Improving labour standards also has an under-appreciated role to play in this respect, although as Caddell advocates (Chapter 7), this should be pursued as a distinct objective in its own right for which a number of regulatory pathways could be further advanced, rather than (as current practices indicate) merely aggregating responses to this problem within the already congested umbrella conglomeration of 'IUU fishing'.

---

[12] International Plan of Action to Prevent, Deter and Eliminate Illegal, Unreported and Unregulated Fishing of 2 March 2001 (available at www.fao.org/fi), para. 9.3.

Likewise, the toolkit provided by alternative regimes presents intriguing possibilities for strengthening fisheries provisions, as are being tentatively explored on a global, regional and domestic basis. Thus as Stokke (Chapter 4) and Caddell, Leloudas and Soyer (Chapter 17) argue, a greater use of extraterritorial enforcement opportunities, such as the United States Lacey Act,[13] provides a pathway for the imposition of intimidating sanctions against fisheries infractions where domestic provisions in other jurisdictions have proved ineffective. Moreover, these authors also point to the increased focus upon IUU fishing within INTERPOL, whose procedures and operational tools provide a helpful pathway towards vital intelligence-gathering and information-sharing. These in turn facilitate the pursuit of IUU fishing vessels and actions against the ports used by them, diminishing the safe havens available for such vessels to ply their illicit trade. Moreover, the toolkit of transnational organized crime prevention provides a further and under-utilized pathway to pursue the ultimate profiteers from IUU fishing. While this route faces considerable challenges – not least a lack of connectivity between the concepts of illegal fishing and fisheries-based illegality – a growing number of States are increasingly seeking to facilitate this approach domestically.

Finally, a number of chapters highlight the under-utilized potential of international dispute resolution mechanisms as an option and pathway to strengthen international fisheries law. This could for instance be pursued to ensure enhanced flag State accountability or to obtain clarification on particular aspects of the flag State's obligation to exercise effective jurisdiction and control over vessels flying its flag and the implications of non-compliance with these aspects, the rules and practices of RFMO/As concerning participation and allocation, and their competence to impose to trade measures against non-Members in light of these rules and practices.

---

[13] 16 U.S.C. §§3371–3378.

Bibliography

Abrams, PA et al., "Necessary Elements of Precautionary Management: Implications for Antarctic Toothfish" (2016) 17 *Fish and Fisheries* 1152–1174.

Agbayani, S et al., "Cumulative Impact of Bottom Fisheries on Benthic Habitats: A Quantitative Spatial Assessment in British Columbia, Canada" (2015) 116 *Ocean and Coastal Management* 423–434.

Agnew, DJ, "The Illegal and Unregulated Fishery for Toothfish in the Southern Ocean, and the CCAMLR Catch Documentation Scheme" (2000) 24 *Marine Policy* 361–374.

—— et al., "Estimating the Worldwide Extent of Illegal Fishing" (2009) 4 *PLoS ONE* 1–8.

Aldrich, H, *Organizations Evolving* (Sage, London: 1999).

Allison, EH et al., "Vulnerability of National Economies to the Impacts of Climate Change on Fisheries" (2009) 10 *Fish and Fisheries* 173–196.

Alvarez, J, *International Organizations as Law-Makers* (Oxford University Press, Oxford: 2005).

Álvarez de Quevedo, I et al., "Sources of Bycatch of Loggerhead Sea Turtles in the Western Mediterranean other than Drifting Longlines" (2010) 67 *ICES Journal of Marine Science* 677–685.

Ardron, JA et al., "The Sustainable Use and Conservation of Biodiversity in ABNJ: What can be Achieved using Existing International Agreements?" (2014) 49 *Marine Policy* 98–10.

Árnadóttir, S, "Ecological Changes Justifying Termination or Revision of EEZ and EFZ Boundaries" (2017) 84 *Marine Policy* 287–292.

Ásgeirsdóttir, Á, *Who Gets What? Domestic Influences on International Negotiations Allocating Shared Resources* (State University of New York Press, Albany, NY: 2008).

——, "Á Hafi Úti: Áhrif Hagsmunahópa Á Samninga Íslendinga Og Norðmanna Vegna Veiða Úr Flökkustofnum Frá Árinu 1980" [Out at Sea: Interest Group Influence on Negotiations between Iceland and Norway Sharing Straddling Fish Stocks Since 1980] in V Ingimundarson (ed.), *Uppbrot Hugmyndakerfis: Endurmótun Íslenskrar Utanríkisstefnu 1991–2007* [*Ripping up of Ideologies: Reform of Icelandic Foreign Policy 1991–2007*]. (Hið íslenska bókmenntafélag, Reykjavik: 2008).

Asmundsson, S and Corcoran, E, "The Process of Forming a Cooperative Mechanism between NEAFC and OSPAR" (*UNEP Regional Seas Reports and Studies* No. 196: 2015).

Axelrod, M, "Climate Change and Global Fisheries Management: Linking Issues to Protect Ecosystems or to Save Political Interests?" (2011) 11 *Global Environmental Politics* 64–84.

Auld, G, Gulbrandsen, LH and McDermott, CL, "Certification Schemes and the Impacts on Forests and Forestry" (2008) 33 *Annual Review of Environment and Resources* 187–211.

Auster, PJ et al., "Definition and Detection of Vulnerable Marine Ecosystems on the High Seas: Problems with the 'Move-On' Rule" (2011) 68 *ICES Journal of Marine Science* 254–264.

Balton, DA, "Strengthening the Law of the Sea: The New Agreement on Straddling Fish Stocks and Highly Migratory Fish Stocks" (1996) 27 *Ocean Development and International Law* 125–151.

——, "The Bering Sea Doughnut Hole Convention: Regional Solution, Global Implications" in OS Stokke (ed.), *Governing High Seas Fisheries* (Oxford University Press, Oxford: 2001) 143–178.

Ban, NC et al., "Better Integration of Sectoral Planning and Management Approaches for the Interlinked Ecology of the Open Oceans" (2014) 49 *Marine Policy* 127–136.

Bangert, K, "The Effective Enforcement of High Seas Fishing Regimes: The Case of the Convention for the Regulation of the Policing of the North Sea Fisheries of 6 May 1882" in G Goodwin Gill and S Talmon (eds.), *The Reality of International Law: Essays in Honour of Ian Brownlie* (Oxford University Press, Oxford: 1999) 1–20.

Bangert, K, "Fisheries Agreements" in *Max Planck Encyclopedia of Public International Law On-line Edition* (Oxford University Press, Oxford: 2008).

Barange, M et al., "Impacts of Climate Change on Marine Ecosystem Production in Societies Dependent on Fisheries" (2014) 4 *Nature Climate Change* 211–216.

Barkin, JS and DeSombre, ER, *Saving Global Fisheries: Reducing Fishing Capacity to Promote Sustainability* (Boston, MIT Press: 2013).

Barnes, JN, "The Emerging Convention on the Conservation of Antarctic Marine Living Resources: An Attempt to Meet the New Realities of Resource Exploitation in the Southern Ocean" in JI Charney (ed.), *The New Nationalism and the Use of Common Spaces* (Osmun Publishers, Allenheld: 1982) 239–286.

Barnes, R, "Fisheries and Biodiversity" in M Fitzmaurice, D Ong and P Merkouris (eds.), *Research Handbook on International Environmental Law* (Edward Elgar, Cheltenham: 2010) 542–563.

——, "The Law of the Sea Convention and the Integrated Regulation of the Oceans" (2012) 27 *International Journal of Marine and Coastal Law* 859–866.

——, "Flag States" in DR Rothwell, AG Oude Elferink, KN Scott and T Stephens (eds.), *The Oxford Handbook of the Law of the Sea* (Oxford University Press, Oxford: 2015) 304–331.

——, "The Proposed LOSC Implementation Agreement on Areas beyond National Jurisdiction and its Impact on International Fisheries Law" (2016) 31 *International Journal of Marine and Coastal Law* 583–616.

—— and Massarella, C, "High Seas Fisheries" in E Morgera and K Kulovesi (eds.), *Research Handbook on International Law and Natural Resources* (Edward Elgar, Cheltenham: 2016) 369–389.

Bastmeijer, K and Koivurova, T (eds.), *Theory and Practice of Transboundary Environmental Impact Assessment* (Martinus Nijhoff, Leiden: 2008).

Bax, NJ et al., "Results and Implications of the First Global Effort to Identify Ecologically or Biologically Significant Marine Areas" (2016) 30 *Conservation Biology* 571–581.

Beaugrand, G et al., "Synchronous Marine Pelagic Regime Shifts in the Northern Hemisphere" (2014) 370 *Philosophical Transactions of the Royal Society B: Biological Sciences* 20130272.

Bederman, DJ, "Privateering" in *Max Planck Encyclopedia of Public International Law On-line Edition* (Oxford University Press, Oxford: 2008).

Bell, J, et al., "Impacts and Effects of Ocean Warming on the Contributions of Fisheries and Aquaculture to Food Security" in "Explaining Ocean Warming: Causes, Scale, Effects and Consequences" (IUCN, Gland: 2016).

Bendel, J and Harrison, J, "Determining the Legal Nature and Content of EIAs in International Environmental Law: What Does the ICJ Decision in the Joined Costa Rica v Nicaragua/Nicaragua v Costa Rica Cases Tell Us?" (2017) 42 *Questions of International Law* 13–21.

Bensch, A et al., "Worldwide Review of Bottom Fisheries in the High Seas" (FAO, Rome: 2009).

Bergin, A, "Albatross and Longlining – Managing Seabird Bycatch" (1997) 21 *Marine Policy* 63–72.

Berkenhagen, J et al., "Decision Bias in Marine Spatial Planning of Offshore Wind Farms: Problems of Singular Versus Cumulative Assessments of Economic Impacts on Fisheries" (2010) 34 *Marine Policy* 733–736.

Billé, R, Chabason, L, Drankier, P, Molenaar, EJ and Rochette, J, "Regional Oceans Governance. Making Regional Seas Programmes, Regional Fishery Bodies and Large Marine Ecosystem Mechanisms Work Better Together" *UNEP Regional Seas Reports and Studies* No. 197.

Birnie, P, Boyle, A and Redgwell, C, *International Law and the Environment* (Oxford University Press, Oxford: 2009).

Bjørndal, T and Ekerhovd, NA, "Management of Pelagic Fisheries in the North East Atlantic: Norwegian Spring Spawning Herring, Mackerel, and Blue Whiting" (2014) 29 *Marine Resource Economics* 69–83.

Blackwell, A, "The Humane Society and Italian Driftnetters: Environmental Activists and Unilateral Action in International Environmental Law" (1997) 23 *North Carolina Journal of International Law and Commercial Regulation* 313–340.

Blanchard, C, "Could 'Not Undermining' Undermine the BBNJ Process? Possible Interpretations of the Relationship between the "Not Undermining" Clause and the Upcoming Legally Binding Instrument" (2019) 34 *International Journal of Marine and Coastal Law* (in press).

Block, BA et al., "Tracking Apex Marine Predator Movements in a Dynamic Ocean" (2011) 475 *Nature* 86–90.

Boczek, BA, *Flags of Convenience: An International Legal Study* (Harvard University Press, Cambridge, Massachusetts: 1962).

Bodansky, D, "What's So Bad about Unilateral Action to Protect the Environment?" (2000) 11 *European Journal of International Law* 339–347.

——, *The Art and Craft of International Environmental Law* (Harvard University Press, Cambridge, Massachusetts: 2010).

Boonzaier, L and Pauly, D, "Marine Protection Targets: An Updated Assessment of Global Progress" (2016) 50 *Oryx* 27–35.

Boyle, AE, "Problems of Compulsory Jurisdiction and the Settlement of Disputes relating to Straddling Fish Stocks" in OS Stokke (ed.), *Governing High Seas Fisheries* (Oxford University Press, Oxford: 2001) 91–120.

——, "Further Development of the Law of the Sea Convention: Mechanisms for Change" (2005) 54 *International and Comparative Law Quarterly* 563–584.

——, "EU Unilateralism and the Law of the Sea" (2006) 21 *International Journal of Marine and Coastal Law* 15–32.

——, "Developments in the International Law of Environmental Impact Assessments and their Relation to the Espoo Convention" (2011) 20 *Review of European Community and International Environmental Law* 227–231.

Brady, HE, "Causation and Explanation in Social Science" in RE Goodwin (ed.), *The Oxford Handbook of Political Science* (Oxford University Press, Oxford: 2011) 1054–1107.

Breitmeier, H, Underdal, A and Young, O, "The Effectiveness of International Environmental Regimes: Comparing and Contrasting Findings from Quantitative Research" (2011) 13 *International Studies Review* 579–605.

Brewer, D et al., "The Impact of Turtle Excluder Devices and Bycatch Reduction Devices on Diverse Tropical Marine Communities in Australia's Northern Prawn Trawl Fishery" (2006) 83 *Fisheries Research* 176–188.

Brewster, R, "The Limits of Reputation on Compliance" (2009) 1 *International Theory* 323–333.

Britten, GL, Dowd, M and Worm, B, "Changing Recruitment Capacity in Global Fish Stocks" (2016) 113 *Proceedings of the National Academy of Sciences* 134–139.

Brodziak, J and Link, J, "Ecosystem-based Fisheries Management: What is it and How Can We Do It?" (2002) 70 *Bulletin of Marine Science* 589–611.

Brooks, CM, "Competing Values on the Antarctic High Seas: CCAMLR and the Challenge of Marine Protected Areas" (2013) 3 *Polar Journal* 277–300.

—— et al., "Science-based Management in Decline in the Southern Ocean" (2016) 354 *Science* 185–187.

Brown, SL, Reid, D and Rogan, E, "Spatial and Temporal Assessment of Potential Risk to Cetaceans from Static Fishing Gears" (2015) 51 *Marine Policy* 267–280.

Brunnée, J and Toope, S, *Legitimacy and Legality in International Law: An Interactional Account* (Cambridge University Press, Cambridge: 2010).

Buchanan, A and Keohane, RO, "The Legitimacy of Global Governance Institutions" (2006) 20 *Ethics and International Affairs* 405–436.

Bull, LS, "Reducing Seabird Bycatch in Longline, Trawl and Gillnet Fisheries" (2007) 8 *Fish and Fisheries* 31–56.

Burke, WT, Freeberg, M and Miles, EL, "United Nations Resolutions on Driftnet Fishing: An Unsustainable Precedent for High Seas and Coastal Fisheries Management" (1994) 25 *Ocean Development and International Law* 127–186.

Caddell, R, "The Prohibition of Driftnet Fishing in European Community Waters: Problems, Progress and Prospects" (2007) 13 *Journal of International Maritime Law* 265–288.

——, "Caught in the Net: Driftnet Fishing Restrictions and the European Court of Justice" (2010) 22 *Journal of Environmental Law* 301–314.

——, "The Integration of Multilateral Environmental Agreements: Lessons from the Biodiversity-Related Conventions" (2012) 22 *Yearbook of International Environmental Law* 37–75.

——, "Regulating the Whale Wars: Freedom of Protest, Navigational Safety and the Law of the Sea in the Polar Regions" (2014) 6 *Yearbook of Polar Law* 497–544.

——, "Platforms, Protestors and Provisional Measures: The *Arctic Sunrise* Dispute and Environmental Activism at Sea" (2014) 45 *Netherlands Yearbook of International Law* 359–384.

——, "So Long, and Thanks for All the Tangible Objects: Defining 'Fish' in the US Supreme Court" (2015) 21 *Journal of International Maritime Law* 175–177.

——, "'Only Connect'? Regime Interaction and Global Biodiversity Conservation" in M Bowman, P Davies and E Goodwin (eds.), *Research Handbook on Biodiversity and Law* (Edward Elgar, Cheltenham: 2016) 437–471.

——, "Uncharted Waters: SEA in the UK Offshore Area" in G Jones and E Scotford (eds.), *The Strategic Environmental Assessment Directive: A Plan for Success?* (Hart, Oxford: 2017) 283–309.

——, "Precautionary Management and the Development of Future Fishing Opportunities: The International Regulation of New and Exploratory Fisheries" (2018) 33 *International Journal of Marine and Coastal Law* 199–260.

——, "International Environmental Governance and the Final Frontier: The Protection of Vulnerable Marine Ecosystems in Deep-Sea Areas beyond National Jurisdiction" (2018) 29 *Yearbook of International Environmental Law* 1–36.

Calley, DS, *Market Denial and International Fisheries Regulation* (Martinus Nijhoff, Leiden/Boston: 2012).

Cameron, P and Abouchar, J, "The Status of the Precautionary Principle" in D Freestone and E Hey (eds.), *The Precautionary Principle and International Law: The Challenge of Implementation* (Kluwer, The Hague: 1996) 29–52.

Caney, S, "Two Kinds of Climate Justice: Avoiding Harm and Sharing Burdens" (2015) 9 *Political Theory Without Borders: Philosophy, Politics and Society* 125–149.

Carlisle, AB et al., "Influence of Temperature and Oxygen on the Distribution of Blue Marlin (Makaira Nigricans) in the Central Pacific" (2017) 26 *Fisheries Oceanography* 34–48.

Carr, EH, *What is History?* (Macmillan, London: 1961).

Catchpole, TL and Revill, AS, "Gear Technology in *Nephrops* Trawl Fisheries" (2008) 18 *Reviews in Fish Biology and Fisheries* 17–31.

Ceo, M et al., "Performance Reviews by Regional Fishery Bodies: Introduction, Summaries, Synthesis and Best Practices, Volume I: CCAMLR, CCSBT, ICCAT, IOTC, NAFO, NASCO, NEAFC" (*FAO Fisheries and Aquaculture Circular* No. 1072: 2012).

Chassot, E et al., "Satellite Remote Sensing for an Ecosystem Approach to Fisheries Management" (2011) 68 *ICES Journal of Marine Science* 651–666.

Chayes, A and Handler Chayes, A, "On Compliance" (1993) 47 *International Organization* 175–205.

Chen, C-J, *Fisheries Subsidies under International Law* (Springer, Berlin: 2010).

Cheung, WWL et al., "Application of Macroecological Theory to Predict Effects of Climate Change on Global Fisheries Potential" (2008) 365 *Marine Ecology Progress Series* 187–197.

—— et al., "Projecting Global Marine Biodiversity Impacts under Climate Change Scenarios" (2009) 10 *Fish and Fisheries* 235–251.

—— et al., "Large-Scale Redistribution of Maximum Fisheries Catch Potential in the Global Ocean under Climate Change" (2010) 16 *Global Change Biology* 24–35.

—— et al. "Shrinking of Fishes Exacerbates Impacts of Global Ocean Changes on Marine Ecosystems" (2013) 3 *Nature Climate Change* 254–258.

—— et al., "Transform High Seas Management to Build Climate Resilience in Marine Seafood Supply" (2017) *Fish and Fisheries* 254–263.

—— and Pauly, D, "Impacts and Effects of Ocean Warming on Marine Fishes" in D Laffoley and JM Baxter (eds) *Explaining Ocean Warming: Causes, Scale, Effects and Consequences* (IUCN, Gland: 2016) 239–253.

——, Watson, R and Pauly, D, "Signature of Ocean Warming in Global Fisheries Catch" (2013) 497 *Nature* 365–368.

——, Reygondeau, G and Frölicher, TL, "Large Benefits to Marine Fisheries of Meeting the 1.5 C Global Warming Target" (2016) 354 *Science* 1591–1594.

Christian, C et al., "A Review of Formal Objections to Marine Stewardship Council Fisheries Certifications" (2013) 161 *Biological Conservation* 10–17.

Christiansen, JS et al., "Arctic Marine Fishes and their Fisheries in Light of Global Change" (2014) 20 *Global Change Biology* 352–359.

Churchill, RR, "The Barents Sea Loophole Agreement: A 'Coastal State' Solution to a Straddling Stock Problem" (1999) 14 *International Journal of Marine and Coastal Law* 467–483.

——, "Dispute Settlement under the UN Convention on the Law of the Sea: Survey for 2009" (2010) 25 *International Journal of Marine and Coastal Law* 457–482.

——, "The Growing Establishment of High Seas Marine Protected Areas: Implications for Shipping" in R Caddell and R Thomas (eds.), *Shipping, Law and the Marine Environment in the Twenty-First Century* (Lawtext, Witney: 2013) 53–88.

——, "The 1982 United Nations Convention on the Law of the Sea" in DR Rothwell, AG Oude Elferink, KN Scott and T Stephens (eds.), *The Oxford Handbook of the Law of the Sea* (Oxford University Press, Oxford: 2015) 24–45.

—— and Lowe, AV, *The Law of the Sea* (Manchester University Press, Manchester: 1999).

—— and Ulfstein, G, "Autonomous Institutional Arrangements in Multilateral Environmental Agreements" (2000) 94 *American Journal of International Law* 623–659.

—— and Owen, D, *The EC Common Fisheries Policy* (Oxford University Press, Oxford: 2010).

Clark, MR et al., "Effects of Fishing on the Benthic Biodiversity of Seamounts of the "Graveyard" Complex, Northern Chatham Rise" (2010) 46 *New Zealand Aquatic Environment and Biodiversity Report* 1–40.

—— et al., "The Impacts of Deep-sea Fisheries on Benthic Communities: A Review" (2016) 73 *ICES Journal of Marine Science* i51–i69.

Clark, R et al., "SEA in the USA" in B Sadler et al. (eds.), *Handbook of Strategic Environmental Assessment* (Earthscan, London: 2011) 74–88.

Clark, WC, Mitchell, RB and Cash, DW, "Evaluating the Influence of Global Environmental Assessments" in WC Clark, RB Mitchell, DW Cash and NM Dickson (eds.), *Global Environmental Assessments: Information and Influence* (MIT Press, Cambridge, Massachusetts: 2006) 1–28.

Cleveland, S, "Norm Internalization and U. S. Economic Sanctions" (2001) 26 *Yale Journal of International Law* 1–103.

Cogan, JK, "Certain Activities Carried out by Nicaragua in the Border Area (Costa Rica v. Nicaragua); Construction of a Road in Costa Rica along the San Juan River (Nicaragua v. Costa Rica)" (2016) 110 *American Journal of International Law* 320–323.

Coglianese, C and Sapir, A, "Risk and Regulatory Calibration: WTO Compliance Review of the US Dolphin-Safe Tuna Labelling Regime" (2017) 16 *World Trade Review* 327–348.

Collie, J et al., "Indirect Effects of Bottom Fishing on the Productivity of Marine Fish" (2017) 18 *Fish and Fisheries* 619–637.

Constable, A, "Climate Change and Southern Ocean Ecosystems: How Changes in Physical Habitats Directly Affect Marine Biota" (2014) 20 *Global Change Biology* 3004–3025.

Constable, AJ et al., "Climate Change and Sothern Ocean Ecosystems I: How Changes in Physical Habitats Directly Affect Marine Biota" (2014) 20 *Global Change Biology* 3004–3025.

Cooreman, B, "Addressing Environmental Concerns through Trade: A Case for Extraterritoriality" (2016) 65 *International and Comparative Law Quarterly* 229–248.

Copello, S, et al., "Exporting the Problem: Issues with Fishing Closures in Seabird Conservation" (2016) 74 *Marine Policy* 120–127.

Costello, C et al., "Status and Solutions for the World's Unassessed Fisheries" (2012) 338 *Science* 517–520.

Couper, A, Smith, HD and Ciceri, B, *Fishers and Plunderers: Theft, Slavery and Violence at Sea* (Pluto Press, London: 2015).

Cox, TM et al., "Comparing Effectiveness of Experimental and Implemented Bycatch Reduction Measures: The Ideal and the Real" (2007) 21 *Conservation Biology* 1155–1164.

Craik, N, *The International Law of Environmental Impact Assessment: Process, Substance and Integration* (Cambridge University Press, Cambridge: 2008).

Crespo, GO et al., "The Environmental Niche of the Global High Seas Pelagic Longline Fleet" (2018) 4 *Science Advances* eaat3681.

—— and Dunn, DC, "A Review of the Impacts of Fisheries on Open-Ocean Ecosystems" (2017) 74 *ICES Journal of Marine Science* 2283–2297.

Crowley, M and Howse, R, "Tuna-Dolphin II: A Legal and Economic Analysis of the Appellate Body's Report" (2014) 13 *World Trade Review* 321–355.

Cullis-Suzuki, S and Pauly, D, "Failing the High Seas: A Global Evaluation of Regional Fisheries Management Organizations" (2010) 34 *Marine Policy* 1036–1042.

Dagorn, L, Holland, KN and Restrepo, V, "Is it Good or Bad to Fish with FADs? What are the Real Impacts of the Use of Drifting FADs on Pelagic Marine Ecosystems?" (2013) 14 *Fish and Fisheries* 391–415.

Da Rocha, JM, Cerviño, S and Villasante, S, "The Common Fisheries Policy: An Enforcement Problem" (2012) 36 *Marine Policy* 1309–1314.

Davies, PGG, "The EC/Canadian Fisheries Dispute in the Northwest Atlantic" (1995) 44 *International and Comparative Law Quarterly* 927–939.

Davies, RWD et al., "Defining and Estimating Global Marine Fisheries Bycatch" (2009) 33 *Marine Policy* 661–672.

Davies, TK, Mees, CC and Milner-Gulland, EJ, "Use of a Counterfactual Approach to Evaluate the Effect of Area Closures on Fishing Location in a Tropical Tuna Fishery" (2017) 12 *PLoS One* e0174758.

Davis, B and Worm, B, "The International Plan of Action for Sharks: How Does National Implementation Measure Up?" (2013) 38 *Marine Policy* 312–320.

Davis, R, "Enforcing Australian Law in Antarctica: The HSI Litigation" (2007) 8 *Melbourne Journal of International Law* 142–158.

Dayton, PK et al., "Environmental Effects of Marine Fishing" (1995) 5 *Aquatic Conservation: Marine and Freshwater Ecosystems* 205–232.

de Coning, E and Witbooi, E, "Towards a New 'Fisheries Crime' Paradigm: South Africa as an Illustrative Example" (2015) 60 *Marine Policy* 208–215.

de la Fayette, L, "The Role of the United Nations in International Oceans Governance" in D Freestone, R Barnes and D Ong (eds.), *The Law of the Sea: Progress and Prospects* (Oxford University Press, Oxford: 2006) 63–74.

de Mulder, J, "The Protocol on Strategic Environmental Assessment: A Matter of Good Governance" (2011) 20 *Review of European Community and International Environmental Law* 232–247.

de Santo, EM, "Assessing Public 'Participation' in Environmental Decision-making: Lessons Learned from the UK Marine Conservation Zone (MCZ) Site Selection Process" (2016) 64 *Marine Policy* 91–101.

DeSombre, ER, "Fishing under Flags of Convenience: Using Market Power to Increase Participation in International Regulation" (2005) 5 *Global Environmental Politics* 73–94.

DeSombre, E, *Global Environmental Institutions* (Routledge, London: 2006).

—— and Barkin, JS, *Fish* (Wiley and Sons, Cambridge: 2011).

Ding, Q, et al., "Vulnerability to Impacts of Climate Change on Marine Fisheries and Food Security" (2017) 83 *Marine Policy* 55–61.

Diz Pereira Pinto, D, *Fisheries Management in Areas Beyond National Jurisdiction: The Impact of Ecosystem-Based Law-Making* (Martinus Nijhoff, Leiden/Boston: 2013).

Druel, E and Gjerde, KM, "Sustaining Marine Life Beyond Boundaries: Options for an Implementing Agreement for Marine Biodiversity Beyond National Jurisdiction under the United Nations Convention on the Law of the Sea" (2014) 49 *Marine Policy* 90–97.

Dulvy, NK et al., "Climate Change and Deepening of the North Sea Fish Assemblage: A Biotic Indicator of Warming Seas" (2008) 45 *Journal of Applied Ecology* 1029–1039.

—— et al., "Extinction Risk and Conservation of the World's Sharks and Rays" (2014) *eLife3*: e00590.

Dunlop, CA and Radaelli, CM (eds.), *Research Handbook of Regulatory Impact Assessment* (Edward Elgar, Cheltenham: 2016).

Dunn, DC et al., "The Convention on Biological Diversity's Ecologically or Biologically Significant Areas: Origins, Development, and Current Status" (2014) 49 *Marine Policy* 137–145.

—— et al., "Empirical Move-on Rules to Inform Fishing Strategies: A New England Case Study" (2014) 15 *Fish and Fisheries* 359–375.

—— et al., "Dynamic Ocean Management Increases the Efficiency and Efficacy of Fisheries Management" (2016) 113 *PNAS* 668–676.

—— et al., "A Strategy for the Conservation of Biodiversity on Mid-Ocean Ridges from Deep-Sea Mining" (2018) 4 *Science Advances* eaar4313.

—— et al., "Empowering High Seas Governance with Satellite Vessel Tracking Data" (2018) 19 *Fish and Fisheries* 729–739.

Dutton, PH and Squires, D, "Reconciling Biodiversity with Fishing: A Holistic Strategy for Pacific Sea Turtle Recovery" (2008) 39 *Ocean Development and International Law* 200–222.

Ebbesson, J, "Innovative Elements and Expected Effectiveness of the 1991 EIA Convention" (1999) 19 *Environmental Impact Assessment Review* 47–55.

Eckersley, R, "The Big Chill: The WTO and Multilateral Environmental Agreements" (2004) 4 *Global Environmental Politics* 24–50.

Edeson, W, "Closing the Gap: The Role of 'Soft' International Instruments to Control Fishing" (1999) 83 *Australian Yearbook of International Law* 83–104.

——, "The International Plan of Action on Illegal, Unreported and Unregulated Fishing: The Legal Context of a Non-Legally Binding Instrument" (2001) 16 *International Journal of Marine and Coastal Law* 603–623.

Edwards, M and Richardson, AJ, "Impact of Climate Change on Marine Pelagic Phenology and Trophic Mismatch" (2004) 430 *Nature* 881–884.

Ekerhovd, NA and Steinshamn, SI, "Economic Benefits of Multi-Species Management: The Pelagic Fisheries in the Northeast Atlantic" (2016) 31 *Marine Resource Economics* 193–210.

Ellis, J, *Network Governance for High Seas Fisheries: The Role of the Marine Stewardship Council* (available at SSRN 1905493: 2011).

Elvestad, C and Kvalvik, I, "Implementing the EU-IUU Regulation: Enhancing Flag State Performance through Regulatory Measures" (2015) 46 *Ocean Development and International Law* 241–255.

Endal, E and Sæter, K, *Catching Thunder: The True Story of the World's Longest Sea Chase* (Zed Books, London: 2018).

Englender, D et al., "Cooperation and Compliance Control in Areas Beyond National Jurisdiction" (2014) 49 *Marine Policy* 186–194.

Erikstein, K and Swan, J, "Voluntary Guidelines for Flag State Performance: A New Tool to Conquer IUU Fishing" (2014) 29 *International Journal of Marine and Coastal Law* 116–147.

Esty, DC, "Beyond Rio: Trade and the Environment" (1993) 23 *Environmental Law* 387–396.

Evans, RJ, *Altered Pasts: Counterfactuals in History* (Brandeis University Press, Lebanon, NE: 2014).

Fabra, A and Gascón, V, "The Convention on the Conservation of Antarctic Marine Living Resources (CCAMLR) and the Ecosystem Approach" (2008) 23 *International Journal of Marine and Coastal Law* 567–598.

Fallon, LD and Kriwoken, LK, "International Influence of an Australian Nongovernment Organization in the Protection of Patagonian Toothfish" (2004) 35 *Ocean Development & International Law* 221–266.

Fearon, JD, "Counterfactuals and Hypothesis Testing in Political Science" (1991) 43 *World Politics* 169–195.

Ferri, N, *Conflicts over the Conservation of Marine Living Resources. Third States, Governance, Fragmentation and Other Recurring Issues in International Law* (G. Giappichelli Editore, Turin: 2015).

Fitzmaurice, M, *Whaling and International Law* (Cambridge University Press, Cambridge: 2015).

Fitzpatrick, D and Anderson, M, *Seafarers' Rights* (Oxford University Press, Oxford: 2005).

Flores, H et al., "Impact of Climate Change on Antarctic Krill" (2012) 458 *Marine Ecology Progress Series* 1–19.

Folke, C, "Social-ecological Systems and Adaptive Governance of the Commons" (2007) 22 *Ecological Research* 14–15.

Freestone, D, "International Fisheries Law since Rio: The Continued Rise of the Precautionary Principle" in A Boyle and D Freestone (eds.), *International Law and Sustainable Development: Past Achievements and Future Challenges* (Oxford University Press, Oxford: 1999) 135–164.

——, "Climate Change and the Oceans" (2009) 4 *Carbon and Climate Law Review* 383–386.

——, et al. "Can Existing Institutions Protect Biodiversity in Areas beyond National Jurisdiction? Experiences from Two On-Going Processes" (2014) 49 *Marine Policy* 167–175.

——, "Governance of Areas beyond National Jurisdiction: An Unfinished Agenda?" in J Barrett and R Barnes (eds.), *Law of the Sea: UNCLOS as a Living Instrument* (BIICL, London: 2016) 231–265.

—— and Hey, E, 'Origins and Development of the Precautionary Principle' in D Freestone and E Hey (eds.) *The Precautionary Principle and International Law: The Challenge of Implementation* (Kluwer, The Hague: 1996) 3–15.

French, D, "From the Depths: Rich Pickings of Principles of Sustainable Development and General International Law on the Ocean Floor – the Seabed Disputes Chamber's 2011 Advisory Opinion" (2011) 26 *International Journal of Marine and Coastal Law* 525–568.

Froese, R et al., "What Catch Data Can Tell us about the Status of Global Fisheries?" (2012) 159 *Marine Biology* 1283–1292.

Game, ET et al., "Pelagic Protected Areas: The Missing Dimension in Ocean Conservation" (2009) 24 *Trends in Ecology and Evolution* 360–369.

—— et al., "Pelagic MPAs: The Devil You Know" (2010) 25 *Trends in Ecology and Evolution* 63–64.

Gao, A, "The Application of the European SEA Directive to Carbon Capture and Storage Activities: The Issue of Screening" (2008) 17 *European Energy and Environmental Law Review* 341–371.

Garcia, SM et al., *The Ecosystem Approach to Fisheries. Issues, Terminology, Principles, Institutional Foundations, Implementation and Outlook* (FAO Fisheries Technical Paper No. 443).

Gattuso, JP and Hanson, L (eds.), *Ocean Acidification* (Oxford University Press, Oxford: 2011).

Gehan, SM and Hallowell, M, "Battle to Determine the Meaning of the Magnuson-Stevens Fishery Conservation and Management Reauthorization Act of 2006: A Survey of Recent Judicial Decisions" (2012–2013) 18 *Ocean and Coastal Law Journal* 1–35.

Geijer, CKA and Read, AJ, "Mitigation of Marine Mammal Bycatch in US Fisheries since 1994" (2013) 159 *Biological Conservation* 54–60.

Genner, MJ et al., "Temperature-Driven Phenological Changes within a Marine Larval Fish Assemblage" (2009) 32 *Journal of Plankton Research* 699–708.

Gill, DA et al., "Capacity Shortfalls Hinder the Performance of Marine Protected Areas Globally" (2017) 543 *Nature* 665–669.

Gillespie, A, "Wasting the Oceans: Searching for Principles to Control Bycatch in International Law" (2002) 17 *International Journal of Marine and Coastal Law* 161–193.

Gilman, EL, "Bycatch Governance and Best Practice Mitigation Technology in Global Tuna Fisheries" (2011) 35 *Marine Policy* 590–609.

Gilman, E, "Status of International Monitoring and Management of Abandoned, Lost and Discarded Fishing Gear and Ghost Fishing" (2015) 60 *Marine Policy* 225–239.

——, Passfield, K and Nakamura, K, "Performance of Regional Fisheries Management Organizations: Ecosystem-Based Governance of Bycatch and Discards" (2014) 15 *Fish and Fisheries* 327–351.

Gjerde, KM, "High Seas Fisheries Management under the Convention on the Law of the Sea" in D Freestone, R Barnes and D Ong (eds.), *The Law of the Sea: Progress and Prospects* (Oxford University Press, Oxford: 2006) 281–307.

—— et al., "Ocean in Peril: Reforming the Management of Global Ocean Living Resources in Areas Beyond National Jurisdiction" (2013) 74 *Marine Pollution Bulletin* 540–551.

——, "Protecting Earth's Last Conservation Frontier: Scientific, Management and Legal Priorities for MPAs beyond National Boundaries" (2016) 26 *Aquatic Conservation: Marine and Freshwater Ecosystems* 45–60.

Glazewski, J, "*United States v Bengis*: A Victory for Wildlife Law and Lessons for International Fisheries Crime" (2014) 29 *International Journal of Marine and Coastal Law* 173–183.

Glennon, M, "Remarks. Does International Law Matter?" (2004) 98 *ASIL Proceedings* 311–317.

Golden, CD et al., "Fall in Fish Catch Threatens Human Health" (2016) 534 *Nature* 317–320.

Goldhaber, MD, "Corporate Human Rights Litigation in Non-US Courts: A Comparative Scorecard" (2013) 3 *UC Irvine Law Review* 127–149.

Goldstein, J, Kahler, M, Keohane, RO and Slaughter, AM, "Introduction: Legalization and World Politics" (2000) 54 *International Organization* 385–399.

Grantham, H, Petersen, S and Possingham, H, "Reducing Bycatch in the South African Pelagic Longline Fishery: The Utility of Different Approaches to Fisheries Closures" (2008) 5 *Endangered Species Research* 291–299.

Green, AL et al., "Designing Marine Reserves for Fisheries Management, Biodiversity Conservation and Climate Change Adaptation" (2014) 42 *Coastal Management* 143–159.

Guerra, F et al., "Environmental Impact Assessment in the Marine Environment: A Comparison of Legal Frameworks" (2015) 55 *Environmental Impact Assessment Review* 182–194.

Guggisberg, S, *The Use of CITES for Commercially-Exploited Fish Species: A Solution to Illegal, Unreported and Unregulated Fishing?* (Springer, Heidelberg: 2016).

Guilfoyle, D, "Interdicting Vessels to Enforce the Common Interest: Maritime Countermeasures and the Use of Force" (2007) 56 *International and Comparative Law Quarterly* 69–82.

——, *Shipping Interdiction and the Law of the Sea* (Cambridge University Press, Cambridge: 2009).

Gulbrandsen, LH, "The Emergence and Effectiveness of the Marine Stewardship Council" (2009) 33 *Marine Policy* 654–660.

—— and Auld, G, "Contested Accountability Logics in Evolving Nonstate Certification for Fisheries Sustainability" (2016) 16 *Global Environmental Politics* 42–60.

—— and Hønneland, G, "Fisheries Certification in Russia: The Emergence of Non-state Authority in a Post-communist Economy" (2014) 45 *Ocean Development & International Law* 341–359.

Gullestad, P, "The Scope for Research in Practical Fishery Management" (1998) 37 *Fisheries Research* 251–258.

Gullett, W, "Transboundary Environmental Impact Assessment in Marine Areas" in R Warner and S Marsden (eds.), *Transboundary Environmental Governance: Inland, Coastal and Marine Perspectives* (Ashgate, Farnham: 2012) 269–296.

Guzman, AT, *How International Law Works: A Rational Choice Theory* (Oxford University Press, Oxford: 2008).

Haddon, M, *Modelling and Quantitative Methods in Fisheries* (CRC Press, Boca Raton: 2011).

Hafner-Burton, EM, Victor DG and Lupu, Y, "Political Science Research on International Law: The State of the Field" (2012) 106 *American Journal of International Law* 47–97.

Hakimi, M, "Unfriendly Unilateralism" (2014) 55 *Harvard Journal of International Law* 106–150.

Halpern, BS et al., "A Global Map of Human Impact on Marine Ecosystems" (2008) 319 *Science* 948–952.

——, "Spatial and Temporal Changes in Cumulative Human Impacts on the World's Ocean" (2015) 6 *Nature Communications* 6:7615.

—— and Warner, RR, "Marine Reserves have Rapid and Lasting Effects" (2002) 5 *Ecology Letters* 361–366.

——, Lester, SE and McLeod, KL, "Placing Marine Protected Areas onto the Ecosystem-based Management Seascape" (2010) 107 *PNAS* 18312–18317.

Handl, G, "Flag State Responsibility for Illegal, Unreported and Unregulated Fishing in Foreign EEZs" (2014) 44 *Environmental Policy and Law* 158–167.

Hanich, Q and Ota, Y, "Moving beyond Rights-Based Management: A Transparent Approach to Distributing the Conservation Burden and Benefit in Tuna Fisheries" (2013) 28 *International Journal of Marine and Coastal Law* 135–170.

Hannesson, R, "Sharing the Northeast Atlantic Mackerel" (2013) 70 *ICES Journal of Marine Science* 259–269.

Hardin, G, "The Tragedy of the Commons" (1968) 162 *Science* 1243–1248.

Hart, HLA and Honoré, T, *Causation in the Law* (Clarendon Press, Oxford: 2002).

Harrison, J, *Making the Law of the Sea: A Study in the Development of International Law* (Cambridge University Press, Cambridge: 2013).

——, "The Law of the Sea Convention Institutions" in DR Rothwell, AG Oude Elferink, KN Scott and T Stephens (eds.), *The Oxford Handbook of the Law of the Sea* (Oxford University Press, Oxford: 2015) 373–393.

Hatchard, J and Gray, T, "Stakeholders and the Reform of the European Unions' Common Fisheries Policy" (2003) 2 *Maritime Studies (MAST)* 5–20.

Haughton, MO, "Compliance and Enforcement of Fisheries Regulations in the Caribbean" (2003) 54 *Proceedings of the Fifty Fourth Annual Gulf and Caribbean Fisheries Institute* 188–201.

Hedley, C, "The 1998 Agreement on the International Dolphin Conservation Program: Recent Developments in the Tuna-Dolphin Controversy in the Eastern Pacific Ocean" (2001) 32 *Ocean Development and International Law* 71–92.

Henriksen, T, "Revisiting the Freedom of Fishing and Legal Obligations on States Not Party to Regional Fisheries Management Organizations" (2009) 40 *Ocean Development and International Law* 80–96.

Hewison, GJ, "High Seas Driftnet Fishing in the South Pacific and the Law of the Sea" (1993) 5 *Georgetown International Environmental Law Review* 313–374.

——, "The Legally Binding Nature of the Moratorium on Large-Scale High Seas Driftnet Fishing" (1994) 25 *Journal of Maritime Law and Commerce* 557–580.

——, 'The Precautionary Approach to Fisheries Management: An Environmental Perspective' (1996) 11 *International Journal of Marine and Coastal Law* 301–332.

Hey, E, "Global Fisheries Regulations in the First Half of the 1990s" (1996) 11 *International Journal of Marine and Coastal Law* 459–490.

Hilborn, R et al., "When Can Marine Reserves Improve Fisheries Management?" (2004) 47 *Ocean and Coastal Management* 197–205.

Hobday, AJ and Hartmann, K, "Near Real-Time Spatial Management Based on Habitat Predictions for a Longline Bycatch Species" (2006) 13 *Fisheries Management and Ecology* 365–380.

—— et al., "Dynamic Spatial Zoning to Manage Southern Bluefin Tuna (Thunnus Maccoyii) Capture in a Multi-Species Longline Fishery" (2010) 19 *Fisheries Oceanography* 243–253.

—— et al., "Seasonal Forecasting of Tuna Habitat for Dynamic Spatial Management" (2011) 68 *Canadian Journal of Fisheries and Aquatic Sciences* 898–911.

—— et al., "Dynamic Ocean Management: Integrating Scientific and Technological Capacity with Law, Policy and Management" (2014) 33 *Stanford Environmental Law Journal* 125–165.

Hoegh-Guldberg, O et al. "The Ocean" in V Barros et al. (eds.), *Climate Change 2014: Impacts, Adaptation and Vulnerability. Part B: Regional Aspects. Contribution of Working Group II of the Fifth Assessment Report of the Intergovernmental Panel on Climate Change* (Cambridge University Press, UK and NY USA: 2014) 1655–1731.

Hønneland, G, "Fisheries Certification in the Southern Ocean", paper presented at the international workshop *Law and Governance: Emerging Issues of the Polar Regions*, 20–21 June 2017, Shanghai Jiao Tong University, Shanghai, China.

Hornborg, S et al., "Integrated Environmental Assessment of Fisheries Management: Swedish Nephrops Trawl Fisheries Evaluated Using a Life Cycle Approach" (2012) 36 *Marine Policy* 1193–1201.

Horodysky, AZ et al., "Fisheries Conservation on the High Seas: Linking Conservation Physiology and Fisheries Ecology for the Management of Large Pelagic Fishes" (2016) 4 *Conservation Physiology* cov059.

Hosch, G, *Trade Measures to Combat IUU Fishing: Comparative Analysis of Unilateral and Multilateral Approaches* (International Centre for Trade and Sustainable Development, Geneva: 2016).

——, "The 2017 FAO Voluntary Guidelines on Catch Documentation Schemes" (2017) 6 *INFOFISH International Magazine* 27–30.

Hoydal, K, "Findings of the Independent Cost-Benefit Assessment of the Options for Strategic Re-Orientation of WECAFC" (*FAO Fisheries and Aquaculture Circular* No. 1117: 2016).

Howell, EA et al., "TurtleWatch: A Tool to Aid in the Bycatch Reduction of Loggerhead Turtles Caretta Caretta in the Hawaii-Based Pelagic Longline Fishery" (2008) 5 *Endangered Species Research* 267–278.

Huang, H et al., "Influence of Hook Type on Catch of Commercial and Bycatch Species in an Atlantic Tuna Fishery" (2016) 65 *Marine Policy* 68–75.

Hughes, KM, Dransfeld, L and Johnson, MP, "Climate and Stock Influences on the Spread and Locations of Catches in the Northeast Atlantic Mackerel Fishery" (2015) 24 *Fisheries Oceanography* 540–552.

Ishimura, G, Herrick, S and Sumaila, UR, "Stability of Cooperative Management of the Pacific Sardine Fishery under Climate Variability" (2013) 39 *Marine Policy* 333–340.

Islam, MR, 'The Proposed 'Driftnet-Free' Zone in the South Pacific and the Law of the Sea Convention' (1991) 40 *International and Comparative Law Quarterly* 184–198.

Jacquet, J et al., "Conserving Wild Fish in a Sea of Market-Based Efforts" (2010) 44 *Oryx* 45–56.

—— et al., "Seafood Stewardship in Crisis" (2010) 467 *Nature* 28–29.

Jaeckel, A, "An Environmental Management Strategy for the International Seabed Authority? The Legal Basis" (2015) 30 *International Journal of Marine and Coastal Law* 93–119.

——, Gjerde, KM and Ardron, JA, "Conserving the Common Heritage of Humankind – Options for the Deep-seabed Mining Regime" (2017) 78 *Marine Policy* 150–157.

Jaleel, A and Grewal, D, "A Perspective on Safety and Governance Issues of Fishing Vessels" (2017) 31 *Ocean Yearbook* 472–501.

James, KC, et al. "Drivers of Retention and Discards of Elasmobranch Non-target Catch" (2016) 43 *Environmental Conservation* 3–12.

Jennings, S and Kaiser, MJ, "The Effects of Fishing on Marine Ecosystems" (1998) 34 *Advances in Marine Biology* 201–352.

Johnson, D, "Can Competent Authorities Cooperate for the Common Good: Towards a Collective Arrangement for the North-East Atlantic" in PA Beckman and AN Vylegzhanin (eds.), *Environmental Security in the Arctic Ocean* (Springer, New York: 2013) 333–343.

——, Ferreira, ME and Kenchington, M, "Climate Change Is Likely to Severely Limit the Effectiveness of Deep-Sea ABMTs in the North Atlantic" (2018) 87 *Marine Policy* 111–122.

—— et al., "Reviewing the EBSA Process: Improving on Success" (2018) 88 *Marine Policy* 75–85.

Johnstone, RL, *Offshore Oil and Gas Development in the Arctic under International Law: Risk and Responsibility* (Brill, Leiden/Boston: 2015).

Jones, JB, "Environmental Impact of Trawling on the Seabed: A Review" (1992) 26 *New Zealand Journal of Marine and Freshwater Research* 59–67.

Jones, MC and Cheung, WWL, "Multi-Model Ensemble Projections of Climate Change Effects on Global Marine Biodiversity" (2015) 72 *ICES Journal of Marine Science* 741–752.

Kacev, D and Lewison, RL, "Satellite Remote Sensing in Support of Fisheries Management in Global Oceans" in F Hossein (ed.), *Earth Science Satellite Applications: Current and Future Prospects* (Springer, Heidelberg: 2016) 207–222.

Kaczynski, VM and Fluharty, DL "European Policies in West Africa: Who Benefits from Fisheries Agreements?" (2002) 26 *Marine Policy* 75–93.

Kaplan, DM et al., "Pelagic MPAs: The Devil Is in the Details" (2010) 25 *Trends in Ecology and Evolution* 62–63.

Karavias, M, "Interactions between International Law and Private Fisheries Certification" (2017) 7 *Transnational Environmental Law* 165–184.

Keohane, RO, "Neoliberal Institutionalism: A Perspective on World Politics" in RO Keohane (ed.) *International Institutions and State Power. Essays in International Relations Theory* (Westview Press, Boulder, CO: 1989) 1–12.

Khaliq, U, "Jurisdiction, Ships and Human Rights Treaties" in H Ringbom (ed.), *Jurisdiction over Ships: Post-UNCLOS Developments in the Law of the Sea* (Martinus Nijhoff, Leiden/Boston: 2015) 324–361.

Kienzlea, M et al., "Environmental and Fishing Effects on the Dynamics of Brown Tiger Prawn (Penaeus Esculentus) in Moreton Bay (Australia)" (2014) 155 *Fisheries Research* 138–148.

Kimball, LA, "Deep-Sea Fisheries of the High Seas: The Management Impasse" (2004) 19 *International Journal of Marine and Coastal Law* 259–287.

King, SC and Pushchak, R, "Incorporating Cumulative Effects into Environmental Assessments of Mariculture: Limitations and Failures of Current Siting Methods" (2008) 28 *Environmental Impact Assessment Review* 572–586.

Kingsbury, B, Krisch, N and Stewart, RB, "The Emergence of Global Administrative Law" (2005) 68 *Law and Contemporary Problems* 15–61.

Kirk, EA, "The Ecosystem Approach and the Search for an Objective and Content for the Concept of Holistic Ocean Governance" (2015) 46 *Ocean Development and International Law* 33–49.

Kittinger, JN et al., "Committing to Socially Responsible Seafood" (2017) 356 *Science* 912–913.

Klein, N, "The Vicissitudes of Dispute Settlement under the Law of the Sea Convention" (2017) 32 *International Journal of Marine and Coastal Law* 332–363.

Knecht, GB, *Hooked: A True Story of Pirates, Poaching and the Perfect Fish* (Allen & Unwin, Sydney: 2006).

Knox, J, "The Myth and Reality of Transboundary Environmental Impact Assessment" (2002) 96 *American Journal of International Law* 291–319.

Koehler, HR, *Promoting Compliance in Tuna RFMOS: A Comprehensive Baseline Survey of the Current Mechanics of Reviewing, Assessing and Addressing Compliance with RFMO Obligations and Measures* (International Seafood Sustainability Foundation, McLean: 2013).

Koh, HH, "Why Do Nations Obey International Law?" (1997) 106 *Yale Law Journal* 2599–2659.

Koivurova, T and Pölönen, I, "Transboundary Environmental Impact Assessment in the Case of the Baltic Sea Gas Pipeline" (2010) 25 *International Journal of Marine and Coastal Law* 151–181.

Koivurova, T, "Transboundary Environmental Impact Assessment in International Law" in S Marsden and T Koivurova (eds.), *Transboundary Environmental Impact Assessment in the European Union: The Espoo Convention and its Kiev Protocol on Strategic Environmental Assessment* (Earthscan, London: 2011) 23–25.

Koivurova, T, "Could the Espoo Convention Become a Global Regime for Environmental Impact Assessment and Strategic Environmental Assessment?" in R Warner and S Marsden (eds.), *Transboundary Environmental Governance: Island, Coastal and Marine Perspective* (Ashgate, Farnham: 2012) 323–342.

Kopela, S, "Port-State Jurisdiction, Extraterritoriality, and the Protection of Global Commons Global Commons" (2017) 47 *Ocean Development and International Law* 89–130.

Koremenos, B, "Loosening the Ties That Bind: A Learning Model of Agreement Flexibility" (2001) 55 *International Organization* 289–325.

Kraska, J, "The Laws of Civil Obedience in the Maritime Domain" in C Espósito, J Kraska, HN Scheiber and MS Kwon (eds.), *Ocean Law and Policy Twenty Years of Development Under the UNCLOS Regime* (Brill, Leiden/Boston: 2016) 161–202.

—— and Gaskins, L, 'Can Sharks be Saved? A Global Plan of Action for Shark Conservation in the Regime of the Convention on Migratory Species' (2015) 5 *Seattle Journal of Environmental Law* 415–439.

Kroeker, K et al., "Impacts of Ocean Acidification on Marine Organisms: Quantifying Sensitivities and Interaction with Warming" (2013) 19 *Global Change Biology* 1884–1896.

Kroodsma, DA et al., "Tracking the Global Footprint of Fisheries" (2018) 359 *Science* 904–908.

Kulovesi, K, "International Trade: Natural Resources and the World Trade Organization" in E Morgera and K Kulovesi (eds.), *Research Handbook on International Law and Natural Resources* (Edward Elgar, Cheltenham: 2016) 46–65.

Kvalvik, I, "Managing Institutional Overlap in the Protection of Marine Ecosystems on the High Seas. The Case of the North East Atlantic" (2012) 56 *Ocean & Coastal Management* 35–43.

Kynoch, RJ, Freyer, RJ and Neat, FC, "A Simple Technical Measure to Reduce Bycatch and Discard of Skates and Sharks in Missed-species Bottom-trawl fisheries" (2015) 72 *ICES Journal of Marine Science* 1861–1868.

Lack, M, *Catching On? Trade-related Measures as a Fisheries Management Tool* (TRAFFIC International, Cambridge: 2007).

Laffoley, D and Freestone, D, "A World of Difference – Opportunities for Applying the 1972 World Heritage Convention to the High Seas" (2017) 27 *Aquatic Conservation: Marine and Freshwater Ecosystems* 78–88.

Lam, VWY et al., "Climate Change Impacts on Fisheries in West Africa: Implications for Economic, Food and Nutritional Security" (2012) 34 *African Journal of Marine Science* 103–117.

—— et al., "Projected Change in Global Fisheries Revenues under Climate Change" (2016) 6 *Scientific Reports* 32607.

——, Cheung, WWL and Sumaila, UR, "Marine Capture Fisheries in the Arctic: Winners or Losers under Climate Change and Ocean Acidification?" (2016) 17 *Fish and Fisheries* 335–357.

Lamorgese, L et al., "Reviewing Strategic Environmental Assessment Practice in the Oil and Gas Sector" (2015) 17 *Journal of Environmental Assessment Policy and Management* 1550017-1.

Leary, D, "Developments in International Environmental Law – Fisheries and Marine Mammals: The Year in Review" (2005) 16 *Yearbook of International Environmental Law* 470–487.

Lewis, D, "Causation as Influence" in J Collins, E Hall and L Paul (eds.), *Causation and Counterfactuals* (MIT Press, Cambridge, Massachusetts: 2004) 75–106.

Link, JS, "What Does Ecosystem-Based Fisheries Management Mean?" (2002) 27 *Fisheries* 18–21.

Little, SA et al., "Real-Time Spatial Management Approaches to Reduce Bycatch and Discards: Experiences from Europe and the United States" (2015) 16 *Fish and Fisheries* 576–602.

Lluch-Belda, D et al., "Sardine and Anchovy Regime Fluctuations of Abundance in Four Regions of the World Oceans: A Workshop Report" (1992) 1 *Fisheries Oceanography* 339–347.

Lockwood, M et al., "Marine Biodiversity Conservation Governance and Management: Regime Requirements for Global Environmental Change" (2012) 69 *Ocean and Coastal Management* 160–172.

Lodge, MW et al., *Recommended Best Practices for Regional Fisheries Management Organizations* (Chatham House, London: 2007).

Long, RD, Charles, A and Stephenson, RL, "Key Principles of Marine Ecosystem-based Management" (2015) 57 *Marine Policy* 53–60.

Lorenzen, K, "Toward a New Paradigm for Growth Modelling in Fisheries Stock Assessments: Embracing Plasticity and its Consequences" (2016) 180 *Fisheries Research* 4–22.

Marciniak, KJ, "New Implementing Agreement under UNCLOS: A Threat or an Opportunity for Fisheries Governance?" (2017) 84 *Marine Policy* 320–326.

Marks, S, "False Contingency" (2009) 62 *Current Legal Problems* 1–21.

Marschke, M and Vandergeest, P, "Slavery Scandals: Unpacking Labour Challenges and Policy Responses within the Off-shore Fisheries Sector" (2016) 68 *Marine Policy* 39–46.

Marsden, S, "Strategic Environmental Assessment and Fisheries Management in Australia: How Effective is the Commonwealth Legal Framework?" in S Marsden and S Dovers (eds.), *Strategic Environmental Assessment in Australasia* (Federation Press, Sydney: 2002) 47–70.

——, "Introducing Strategic Environmental Assessment to the Madrid Protocol: Lessons from International Experience" (2011) 1 *The Polar Journal* 33–47.

——, "The Espoo Convention and Kiev Protocol in the European Union: Implementation, Compliance, Enforcement and Reform" (2011) 20 *Review of European Community and International Environmental Law* 267–276.

——, "Public Participation in Transboundary Environmental Impact Assessment – Closing the Gap between International and Public Law?" in B Jessup and K Rubenstein (eds.), *Environmental Discourses in Public and International Law* (Cambridge University Press, Cambridge: 2012) 238–259.

——, "Regulatory Reform of Australia's Offshore Oil and Gas Sector after the Montara Commission of Inquiry: What about Transboundary Environmental Impact Assessment?" (2013) 15 *Flinders Law Journal* 41–53.

——, "Strategic Environmental Assessment of Australian Offshore Oil and Gas Development: Ecologically Sustainable Development or Deregulation?" (2016) 33 *Environmental and Planning Law Journal* 21–30.

—— and Brandon, E, *Transboundary Environmental Governance in Asia: Practice and Prospects with the UNECE Agreements* (Edward Elgar, Cheltenham: 2015).

Mathis, K, "Consequentialism in Law" in K Mathis (ed.), *Efficiency, Sustainability, and Justice to Future Generations* (Springer, Dordrecht: 2012) 3–29.

Maxwell, SM et al., "Dynamic Ocean Management: Defining and Conceptualizing Real-Time Management of the Ocean" (2015) 58 *Marine Policy* 42–50.

Mazor, TK et al., "Trawl Exposure and Protection of Seabed Fauna at Large Spatial Scales" (2017) 23 *Diversity and Distributions* 1280–1291.

McBride, MM et al., "Krill, Climate and Contrasting Future Scenarios for Arctic and Antarctic Fisheries" (2014) 71 *ICES Journal of Marine Science* 1934–1955.

McCauley, DJ et al., "Ending Hide and Seek at Sea" (2016) 351 *Science* 1148–1150.

McCay, B and Jones, P, 'Marine Protected Areas and the Governance of Marine Ecosystems and Fisheries' (2011) 25 *Conservation Biology* 1130–113.

McDorman, TL, "Stateless Fishing Vessels, International Law and the UN High Seas Fisheries Conference" (1994) 25 *Journal of Maritime Law and Commerce* 531–555.

——, "Implementing Existing Tools: Turning Words into Actions – Decision-making processes of Regional Fisheries Management Organizations (RFMOs)" (2005) 20 *International Journal of Marine and Coastal Law* 423–457.

McEvoy, DM and Stranlund, JK "Self-Enforcing International Environmental Agreements with Costly Monitoring for Compliance" (2008) 42 *Environmental and Resource Economics* 491–508.

McLachlan, C, "The Principle of Systemic Integration and Article 31(3)(c) of the Vienna Convention" (2005) 54 *International and Comparative Law Quarterly* 279–319.

McLaughlin-Mitchell, S and Hensel, PR, "International Institutions and Compliance with Agreements" (2007) 51 *American Journal of Political Science* 721–737.

McLeod, E et al., "Designing Marine Protected Area Networks to Address the Impacts of Climate Change" (2009) 7 *Frontiers in Ecology and the Environment* 362–370.

Menefee, SP, "The Case of the *Castle John*, Or Greenbeard the Pirate? Environmentalism, Piracy and Development of International Law" (1993) 24 *California Western International Law Journal* 1–16.

Merrie, A et al. "An Ocean of Surprises – Trends in Human Use, Unexpected Dynamics and Governance Challenges in Areas beyond National Jurisdiction" (2014) 27 *Global Environmental Change* 19–31.

Miller, B, "Combating Drift-Net Fishing in the Pacific" in J Crawford and DR Rothwell (eds.), *The Law of the Sea in the Asian Pacific Region: Developments and Prospects* (Martinus Nijhoff, Leiden/Boston: 1995) 155–170.

Miller, DD et al., "Cutting a Lifeline to Maritime Crime: Marine Insurance and IUU Fishing" (2016) 14 *Frontiers in Ecology and the Environment* 357–362.

—— and Sumaila, UR, "Flag Use Behavior and IUU Activity within the International Fishing Fleet: Refining Definitions and Identifying Areas of Concern" (2014) 44 *Marine Policy* 204–211.

Miller, K et al., "Climate Change, Uncertainty, and Resilient Fisheries: Institutional Responses through Integrative Science" (2010) 87 *Progress in Oceanography* 338–346.

—— et al., "Governing Marine Fisheries in a Changing Climate: A Game-Theoretic Perspective" (2013) 61 *Canadian Journal of Agricultural Economics* 309–334.

Mitchell, G, "Case Studies, Counterfactuals, and Causal Explanations" (2004) 152 *University of Pennsylvania Law Review* 1517–1608.

Mitchell, RB, "Evaluating the Performance of Environmental Institutions: What to Evaluate and How to Evaluate It?" in OR Young, LA King and H Schroeder (eds.), *Institutions and Environmental Change: Principal Findings, Applications and Research Frontiers* (MIT Press, Cambridge Massachusetts: 2008) 79–114.

Miyaoka, I, *Legitimacy in International Society: Japan's Response to Global Wildlife Preservation* (Palgrave, Basingstoke: 2004).

Molenaar, EJ, "The Concept of 'Real Interest' and Other Aspects of Co-operation through Regional Fisheries Management Mechanisms" (2000) 15 *International Journal of Marine and Coastal Law* 475–531.

——, "CCAMLR and Southern Ocean Fisheries" (2001) 16 *International Journal of Marine and Coastal Law* 465–499.

——, "Participation, Allocation and Unregulated Fishing: The Practice of Regional Fisheries Management Organizations" (2003) 18 *International Journal of Marine and Coastal Law* 457–480.

——, "Addressing Regulatory Gaps in High Seas Fisheries" (2005) 20 *International Journal of Marine and Coastal Law* 533–570.

——, "Non-Participation in the Fish Stocks Agreement: Status and Reasons" (2011) 26 *International Journal of Marine and Coastal Law* 195–234.

——, "International Regulation of Central Arctic Ocean Fisheries" in MH Nordquist, J Moore and R Long (eds.), *Challenges of the Changing Arctic. Continental Shelf, Navigation, and Fisheries* (Brill, Leiden/Boston: 2016) 429–463.

——, "Participation in the Central Arctic Ocean Fisheries Agreement" in A Shibata et al. (eds.), *Emerging Legal Orders in the Arctic: The Role of Non-Arctic Actors* (Routledge, Abingdon: 2019) in press.

—— and Oude Elferink, AG, "Marine Protected Areas in Areas beyond National Jurisdiction: The Pioneering Efforts under the OSPAR Convention" (2009) 5 *Utrecht Law Review* 5–20.

Morandeau, G et al., "Why Do Fisherman Discard? Distribution and Quantification of the Causes of Discards in the Southern Bay of Biscay Passive Gear Fisheries" (2014) 48 *Marine Policy* 30–38.

Morato, T et al., "Fishing Down The Deep" (2006) 7 *Fish and Fisheries* 24–34.

Mossop, J, "Protests against Oil Exploration at Sea: Lessons from the *Arctic Sunrise* Arbitration" (2016) 31 *International Journal of Marine and Coastal Law* 60–87.

——, *The Continental Shelf Beyond 200 Nautical Miles: Rights and Responsibilities* (Oxford University Press, Oxford: 2016).

Mushkat, R, "Counterfactual Reasoning: An Effective Component of the International Law Methodological Armor?" (2017) 18 *German Law Journal* 59–98.

Musyl, MK et al., "Postrelease Survival, Vertical and Horizontal Movements, and Thermal Habitats of Five Species of Pelagic Sharks in the Central Pacific Ocean" (2011) 109 *Fishery Bulletin* 341–368.

Nagtzaam, G, *From Environmental Action to Ecoterrorism?* (Edward Elgar, Cheltenham: 2017).

Natale, F et al., "Mapping Fishing Effort through AIS Data" (2015) 10 *PLoS One* e0130746.

Needle, CL and Catarino, R, "Evaluating the Effect of Real-Time Closures on Cod Targeting" (2011) 68 *ICES Journal of Marine Science* 1647–1655.

Norse, EA et al., "Sustainability of Deep-Sea Fisheries" (2012) 36 *Marine Policy* 307–320.

Notarbatolo-di-Sciarra, G, "The Pelagos Sanctuary for Mediterranean Marine Mammals" (2008) 18 *Aquatic Conservation: Marine and Freshwater Ecosystems* 367–391.

Oanta, GA, "International Organizations and Deep-Sea Fisheries: Current Status and Future Prospects" (2018) 87 *Marine Policy* 51–59.

Oberthür, S, "Interplay Management: Enhancing Environmental Policy Integration among International Institutions" (2009) 9 *International Environmental Agreements* 371–391.

Obokata, T, *Transnational Organised Crime in International Law* (Hart, Oxford: 2010).

Ogier, EM et al., "Fisheries Management Approaches as Platforms for Climate Change Adaptation: Comparing Theory and Practice in Australian Fisheries" (2016) 71 *Marine Policy* 82–93.

Okemwa, GM et al. "Managing Coastal Pelagic Fisheries: A Case Study of the Small-scale Purse Seine Fishery in Kenya" (2017) *Ocean and Coastal Management* 31–39.

O'Keefe, CE and DeCelles, GR, "Forming a Partnership to Avoid Bycatch" (2013) 38 *Fisheries* 434–444.

——, Cadrin, SX and Stokesbury, KDE, "Evaluating the Effectiveness of Time/Area Closures, Quotas/Caps, and Fleet Communications to Reduce Fisheries Bycatch" (2015) 71 *ICES Journal of Marine Science* 1286–1297.

O'Leary, B et al., "The First Network of Marine Protected Areas (MPAs) in the High Seas: The Process, the Challenges and Where Next" (2012) 36 *Marine Policy* 598–605.

Oliver, S et al., "Global Patterns in the Bycatch of Sharks and Rays" (2015) 54 *Marine Policy* 86–97.

O'Neill, FG and Ivanović, A, "The Physical Impact of Towed Demersal Fishing Gears on Soft Sediments" (2016) 73 *ICES Journal of Marine Science* i5–i14.

Orford, A, "The Past as Law or History? The Relevance of Imperialism for Modern International Law" *Institute for International Law and Justice (IILJ)* Working Paper 2012/2.

Österblom, H et al., "Transnational Corporations as 'Keystone Actors' in Marine Ecosystems" (2015) 10 *PLoS One* e0127533.

——, Constable, A and Fukumi, S, "Illegal Fishing and the Organized Crime Analogy" (2011) 26 *Trends in Ecology and Evolution* 261–262.

—— and Sumaila, UR, "Toothfish Crises, Actor Diversity and the Emergence of Compliance Mechanisms in the Southern Ocean" (2011) 21 *Global Environmental Change* 972–982.

Oude Elferink AG, "Reviewing the Implementation of the LOS Convention: The Role of the United Nations General Assembly and the Meeting of States Parties" in AG Oude Elferink and DR Rothwell (eds.), *Oceans Management in the 21st Century: Institutional Frameworks and Responses* (Martinus Nijhoff, Leiden/Boston: 2004) 295–312.

——, "The *Arctic Sunrise* Incident: A Multi-faceted Law of the Sea Case with a Human Rights Dimension" (2014) 29 *International Journal of Marine and Coastal Law* 244–289.

Ouellette, W and Getinet, W, "Remote Sensing for Marine Spatial Planning and Integrated Coastal Areas Management: Achievements, Challenges, Opportunities and Future Prospects" (2016) 4 *Remote Sensing Applications: Society and Environment* 138–157.

Pace, ML et al., "Trophic Cascades Revealed in Diverse Ecosystems" (1999) 14 *Trends in Ecology and Evolution* 483–488.

Pallemaerts, M (ed.), *The Aarhus Convention at Ten – Interactions and Tensions between Conventional International Law and EU Environmental Law* (Europa Law Publishing, Amsterdam: 2011).

Palma-Robles, MA, "Integrating Monitoring, Control and Surveillance and Anti-Money Laundering Tools to Address Illegal Fishing in the Philippines and Indonesia" in G Rose (ed.), *Following the Proceeds of Environmental Crime: Forests, Fishing and Filthy Lucre* (Routledge, Abingdon: 2014) 100–115.

——, "Tightening the Net: The Link between Illegal, Unreported and Unregulated Fishing and Transnational Crime under International Law" (2015) 29 *Ocean Yearbook* 144–165.

——, "Fisheries Enforcement and the Concepts of Compliance and Monitoring, Control and Surveillance" in R Warner and SB Kaye (eds.), *Routledge Handbook of Maritime Regulation and Enforcement* (Routledge, Abingdon: 2015) 139–160.

Pan, M and Huntington, HP, "A Precautionary Approach to Fisheries in the Central Arctic Ocean: Policy, Science and China" (2016) 63 *Marine Policy* 153–157.

Papanicolopoulou, I, *International Law and the Protection of People at Sea* (Oxford University Press, Oxford: 2018).

Parlett, K, "Beyond the Four Corners of the Convention: Expanding the Scope of Jurisdiction of Law of the Sea Tribunals" (2017) 48 *Ocean Development and International Law* 284–299.

Pauly, D and Zeller, D, "Catch Reconstructions Reveal That Global Marine Fisheries Catches Are Higher than Reported and Declining" (2016) 7 *Nature Communications* 7:10244.

Pentz, B, Klenk, N, Ogle, S and Fisher, JAD, "Can Regional Fisheries Management Organisations (RFMOs) Manage Resources Effectively During Climate Change?" (2018) 92 *Marine Policy* 13–20.

—— and Klenk, N, "The 'Responsiveness Gap' in RFMOs: The Critical Role of Decision-making Policies in the Fisheries Management Response to Climate Change" (2017) 145 *Ocean and Coastal Management* 44–51.

Perry, AL et al., "Climate Change and Distribution Shifts in Marine Fishes" (2005) 308 *Science* 1912–1915.

Pershing, AJ et al. "Slow Adaptation in the Face of Rapid Warming Leads to Collapse of the Gulf of Maine Cod Fishery" (2015) 350 *Science* 809–812.

Pikitch, E et al., "Ecosystem-based Fishery Management" (2004) 305 *Science* 346–347.

Pinsky, ML et al., "Marine Taxa Track Local Climate Velocities" (2013) 341 *Science* 1239–1242.

Pinsky, ML et al., "Preparing Ocean Governance for Species on the Move" (2018) 360 *Science* 1189–1191.

Pita, C, Pierce, GJ and Theodossiou, I, "Stakeholders' Participation in the Fisheries Management Decision-making Process: Fishers' Perceptions of Participation" (2010) 34 *Marine Policy* 1093–1102.

Pitcher TJ and Cheung, WWL, "Fisheries: Hope or Despair?" (2013) 74 *Marine Pollution Bulletin* 506–516.

Plant, G, "Civilian Protest Vessels and the Law of the Sea" (1983) 14 *Netherlands Yearbook of International Law* 133–163.

——, "International Law and Direct Action Protests at Sea: Twenty Years On" (2002) 33 *Netherlands Yearbook of International Law* 75–117.

Polacheck, T, "Politics and Independent Scientific Advice in RFMO Processes: A Case Study of Crossing Boundaries" (2012) 36 *Marine Policy* 132–141.

Politakis, GP, "From Tankers to Trawlers: The International Labour Organization's New Work in Fishing Convention" (2008) 39 *Ocean Development and International Law* 119–128.

Pollnac, RB et al., "Toward a Model for Fisheries Social Impact Assessment" (2006) 68 *Marine Fisheries Review* 1–4.

Poloczanska, ES, "Responses of Marine Organisms to Climate Change across Oceans" (2016) 3 *Frontiers in Marine Science* 62–83.

Polovina, JJ and Woodworth-Jefcoats, P, "Fishery-Induced Changes in the Subtropical Pacific Pelagic Ecosystem Size Structure: Observations and Theory" (2013) 8 *PLoS ONE* e62341.

Portman, M, "Involving the Public in the Impact Assessment of Offshore Renewable Energy Facilities" (2009) 33 *Marine Policy* 332–338.

Pörtner, HO et al., "Ocean Systems" in CB Field et al. (eds.), *Climate Change 2014: Impacts, Adaptation, and Vulnerability, Part A: Global and Sectoral Aspects. Contribution of Working Group II to the Fifth Assessment Report of the Intergovernmental Panel on Climate Change* (Cambridge University Press, UK and NY USA: 2014) 411–484.

——, *IPCC Fifth Assessment Report Working Group II: Ocean Systems* (IPCC, 2014).

Pramod, G, et al., "Estimates of Illegal and Unreported Fish in Seafood Imports to the USA" (2014) 48 *Marine Policy* 102–113.

Priddy, A and Casey-Maslen, S, "Counter-piracy Operations by Private Maritime Security Contractors: Key Legal Issues and Challenges" (2012) 10 *Journal of International Criminal Justice* 839–856.

Proelss, A et al., "Protection of Cetaceans in European Waters – A Case Study on Bottom-Set Gillnet Fisheries within Marine Protected Areas" (2011) 26 *International Journal of Marine and Coastal Law* 5–46.

—— (ed.), *United Nations Convention on the Law of the Sea. A Commentary* (C.H. Beck/Hart/Nomos: 2017).

Raustiala, K, "Compliance and Effectiveness in International Regulatory Cooperation" (2000) 32 *Case Western Reserve Journal of International Law* 387–440.

—— and Slaughter, AM, "International Law, International Relations and Compliance" in W Carlsnaes, T Risse and BA Simmons (eds.), *Handbook of International Relations* (Sage Press, London: 2002) 508–529.

—— and Victor, DG, "The Regime Complex for Plant Genetic Resources" (2004) 58 *International Organization* 277–309.

Rawls, J, *A Theory of Justice* (Oxford University Press, Oxford: 1973).

Rayfuse, R, "Countermeasures and High Seas Fisheries Enforcement" (2004) 51 *Netherlands International Law Quarterly* 41–76.

——, "Climate Change and the Law of the Sea" in R Rayfuse and S Scott (eds.) *International Law in the Era of Climate Change* (Edward Elgar, Cheltenham: 2012) 147–174.

——, "Regional Fisheries Management Organizations" in DR Rothwell, AG Oude Elferink, KN Scott and T Stephens (eds.) *The Oxford Handbook of the Law of the Sea* (Oxford University Press, Oxford: 2015) 439–462.

——, "Climate Change and Antarctic Fisheries: Ecosystem Management in CCAMLR" (2018) 45 *Ecology Law Quarterly* 53–81.

——, "Regulating Fisheries in the Central Arctic Ocean: Much Ado About Nothing?" in N Vestergaard, B Kaiser, L Fernandez and J Nymand Larsen (eds.), *Arctic Resource Governance and Development* (Springer, Berlin: 2018) 35–51.

—— and Meltzer, E, 'The MCS and Enforcement Regime' in E Meltzer et al. (ed.), *The Quest for Sustainable International Fisheries: Regional Efforts to Implement the 1995 United Nations Fish Stocks Agreement: An Overview for the May 2006 Review Conference* (National Research Council of Canada Research Press, Ottowa: 2009) 219–260.

Ribeiro, MC, "The 'Rainbow': The First National Marine Protected Area Proposed Under the High Seas" (2010) 25 *International Journal of Marine and Coastal Law* 183–207.

Riser, SC et al., "Fifteen Years of Ocean Observations with the Global Argo Array" (2016) 6 *Nature Climate Change* 145–153.

Roberts, J, Chircop, A and Prior, S, "Area-Based Management on the High Seas: The Application of the IMO's Particularly Sensitive Sea Area Concept" (2010) 25 *International Journal of Marine and Coastal Law* 483–522.

Rochette, J et al., "Regional Oceans Governance Mechanisms: A Review" (2015) 60 *Marine Policy* 9–19.

Roeschke, JE, "Eco-Terrorism and Piracy on the High Seas: Japanese Whaling and the Rights of Private Groups to Enforce International Conservation Law in Neutral Waters" (2009) 20 *Villanova Environmental Law Journal* 99–136.

Roese, NJ and Vohs, KD "Hindsight Bias" (2012) 7 *Perspectives on Psychological Science* 411–426.

Roheim, CA and Sutinen, J, *Trade and Marketplace Measures to Promote Sustainable Fishing Practices* (International Centre for Trade and Sustainable Development, Geneva: 2006).

Rosello, M, "Cooperation and Unregulated Fishing: Interactions between Customary International Law and the European Union IUU Fishing Regulation" (2017) 84 *Marine Policy* 306–312.

Rosenne, S and Sohn, LB (eds.), *United Nations Convention on the Law of the Sea 1982, A Commentary, Volume V* (Martinus Nijhoff Publishers, Dordrecht/Boston/London: 1989).

Rothwell, DR, "The General Assembly Ban on Driftnet Fishing" in D Shelton (ed.), *Commitment and Compliance: The Role of Non-Binding Norms in the International Legal System* (Oxford University Press, Oxford: 2003) 121–146.

—— and Stephens, T, *The International Law of the Sea* (Hart Publishing, Oxford/Portland: 2016).

Rudden, B, "Consequences" (1979) 24 *Juridical Review* 193–201.

Sage-Fuller, B, *The Precautionary Principle in Marine Environmental Law with Special Reference to High Risk Vessels* (Routledge, Abingdon: 2013).

Sander, G, "International Legal Obligations for Environmental Impact Assessment and Strategic Environmental Assessment in the Arctic Ocean" (2016) 31 *International Journal of Marine and Coastal Law* 88–119.

Scanlon, Z, "The Art of 'Not Undermining': Possibilities within Existing Architecture to Improve Environmental Protections in Areas beyond National Jurisdiction" (2018) 75 *ICES Journal of Marine Science* 405–416.

Schall, C, "Public Interest Litigation Concerning Environmental Matters Before Human Rights Courts: A Promising Future Concept?" (2008) 20 *Journal of Environmental Law* 417–453.

Schatz, VJ, "The Contribution of Fisheries Access Agreements to Flag State Responsibility" (2017) 84 *Marine Policy* 313–319.

——, "Marine Fisheries Law Enforcement Partnerships in Waters under National Jurisdiction: The Legal Framework for Inter-State Cooperation and Public-Private Partnerships with Non-Governmental Organizations and Private Security Companies" (2018) 32 *Ocean Yearbook* 329–375.

Scheiber, H, "Origins of the Abstention Doctrine in Ocean Law: Japanese-US Relations and Pacific Fisheries 1937–1958" (1989) 16 *Ecology Law Quarterly* 23–99.

Schermers, HG and Blokkers, NM, *International Institutional Law* 3rd ed. (Brill, Leiden: 1995).

Schiffman, HS, *Marine Conservation Agreements: The Law and Policy of Reservations and Vetoes* (Martinus Nijhoff, Leiden: 2008).

Schirripa, MJ and Goodyear, CP, "Proposed Study Design for Best Practices When Including Environmental Information into ICCAT Indices of Abundance" (2016) 72(8) *Collected Volume of the Scientific Papers of ICCAT* (Doc. SCRS/2015/031), 2313–2317.

Schmidt, C-C, "Economic Drivers of Illegal, Unreported and Unregulated (IUU) Fishing" (2005) 20 *International Journal of Marine and Coastal Law* 479–507.

Schoenbaum, TJ, "International Trade and Protection of the Environment: The Continuing Search for Reconciliation" (1997) 91 *American Journal of International Law* 268–313.

Scott, J, "The Geographical Scope of the EU's Climate Responsibilities" (2015) 17 *Cambridge Yearbook of European Legal Studies* 1–29.

Scott, KN, "International Environmental Governance: Managing Fragmentation through Institutional Connection" (2011) 12 *Melbourne Journal of International Law* 177–207.

——, "Geoengineering and the Law of the Sea" in R Rayfuse (ed.), *Research Handbook on International Marine Environmental Law* (Edward Elgar, Cheltenham: 2015) 451–472.

Serdy, A, "Law of the Sea Aspects of the Negotiations in the World Trade Organization to Harmonise Rules of Origin" (2007) 22 *International Journal of Marine and Coastal Law* 235–256.

——, "Simplistic or Surreptitious? Beyond the Flawed Concept(s) of IUU Fishing" in WW Taylor, AJ Lynch, and MG Schechter (eds.) *Sustainable Fisheries: Multi-Level Approaches to a Global Problem* (American Fisheries Society, Bethesda, Maryland: 2011) 253–279.

——, *The New Entrants Problem in International Fisheries Law* (Cambridge University Press, Cambridge: 2015).

——, "The Shaky Foundations of the FAO Port State Measures Agreement: How Watertight Is the Legal Seal against Access for Foreign Fishing Vessels?" (2016) 31 *International Journal of Marine and Coastal Law* 422–441.

——, "Implementing Article 28 of the UN Fish Stocks Agreement: The First Review of a Conservation Measure in the South Pacific Regional Fisheries Management Organisation" (2016) 47 *Ocean Development and International Law* 1–28.

——, "*Pacta Tertiis* and Regional Fisheries Management Mechanisms: The IUU Fishing Concept as an Illegitimate Short-Cut to a Legitimate Goal" (2017) 48 *Ocean Development and International Law* 345–364.

Simmonds, EJ et al., "The Role of Fisheries Data in the Development Evaluation and Impact Assessment in Support of European Fisheries Plans" (2011) 68 *ICES Journal of Marine Science* 1689–1698.

Simmons, BA, "Compliance with International Agreements" (1998) 1 *Annual Review of Political Science* 75–93.

——, "Treaty Compliance and Violation" (2010) 13 *Annual Review of Political Science* 273–296.

Sissener, EH and Bjørndal, T, "Climate Change and the Migratory Pattern for Norwegian Spring-Spawning Herring – Implications for Management" (2005) 29 *Marine Policy* 299–309.

Smith, D and Jabour, J, "MPAs in ABNJ: Lessons from Two High Seas Regimes" (2017) 75 *ICES Journal of Marine Science* 417–425.

Smith, T, *Scaling Fisheries: The Science of Measuring the Effects* (Cambridge University Press, Cambridge: 1994).

Soyer, B, Leloudas G and Miller, D, "Tackling Illegal Fishing – Developing A Holistic Legal Response" (2018) 7 *Transnational Environmental Law* 139–163.

Spijkers, J and Boonstra, WJ, "Environmental Change and Social Conflict: The Northeast Atlantic Mackerel Dispute" (2017) 17 *Regional Environmental Change* 1835–1851.

Srinivasan, UT et al., "Food Security Implications of Global Marine Catch Losses due to Overfishing" (2010) 12 *Journal of Bioeconomics* 183–200.

Stępień, A, Koivurova, T and Kankaanpää, P (eds.,) *Strategic Impact Assessment of Development in the Arctic* (Arctic Centre/European Union: Rovaniemi: 2014).

Stewart, RB and Badin, MRS, "The World Trade Organization and Global Administrative Law" (2009) *IILJ Working Paper 2009/7 Global Administrative Law Series*.

Stock, CA et al., "Reconciling Fisheries Catch and Ocean Productivity" (2017) 114 *PNAS* E1441–E1449.

Stokke, OS, "Managing Fisheries in the Barents Sea Loophole: Interplay with the UN Fish Stocks Agreement" (2001) 32 *Ocean Development and International Law* 241–262.

——, *The Interplay of International Regimes: Putting Effectiveness Theory to Work*, FNI Report 10/2001 (The Fridtjof Nansen Institute, Lysaker: 2001).

——, "Trade Measures and Climate Compliance: Interplay between WTO and the Marrakesh Accords" (2004) 4 *International Environmental Agreements* 339–357.

——, "Trade Measures and the Combat of IUU Fishing: Institutional Interplay and Effective Governance in the Northeast Atlantic" (2009) 33 *Marine Policy* 339–349.

——, "Barents Sea Fisheries: The IUU Struggle" (2010) 1 *Arctic Review on Law and Politics* 207–224.

——, *Disaggregating International Regimes: A New Approach to Evaluation and Comparison* (MIT Press, Cambridge, Massachusetts: 2012).

——, "International Fisheries Politics: From Sustainability to Precaution" in EL Boasson, G Hønneland and S Andresen (eds.), *International Environmental Agreements: An Introduction* (Routledge, London: 2012) 97–116.

——, "Actor Configurations and Compliance Tasks in International Environmental Governance" in N Kanie, S Andresen and PM Haas (eds.), *Improving Global Environmental Governance. Best Practices for Architecture and Agency* (Routledge, London: 2014) 83–107.

——, "Fisheries and Whaling" in PH Pattbery and F Zelli (eds.), *Encyclopedia of Global Environmental Governance and Politics* (Edward Elgar, Cheltenham: 2015) 364–373.

—— and Coffey, C, "Precaution, ICES and the Common Fisheries Policy: A Study of Regime Interplay" (2004) 28 *Marine Policy* 117–126.

—— and Oberthür, S, "Introduction: Institutional Interaction in Global Environmental Change" in S Oberthür and OS Stokke (eds.), *Managing Institutional Complexity: Regime Interplay and Global Environmental Change* (MIT Press, Cambridge, Massachusetts: 2011) 1–24.

—— and Young, OR, "Integrating Earth Observation Systems and International Environmental Regimes" in M Onoda and OR Young (eds.), *Satellite Earth Observations and Their Impact on Society and Policy* (Springer, Singapore: 2017) 179–203.

—— (ed.), *Governing High Seas Fisheries: The Interplay of Global and Regional Regimes* (Oxford University Press, Oxford: 2001).

Stramma, L et al., "Ocean Oxygen Minima Expansions and Their Biological Impacts" (2010) 57 *Deep Sea Research Part I: Oceanographic Research Papers* 587–595.

Strassfield, RN, "Counterfactuals in the Law" (1992) 60 *George Washington Law Review* 339–416.

Szigeti, PD and Lugten, G, "The Implementation of Performance Reviews Reports by Regional Fisheries Bodies, 2004–2014" (*FAO Fisheries and Aquaculture Circular* No. 1108: 2013).

Sumalia, UR, Alder, J and Keith, H, "Global Scope and Economics of Illegal Fishing" (2006) 30 *Marine Policy* 696–703.

—— et al., "A Bottom-up Re-estimation of Global Fisheries Subsidies" (2010) 12 *Journal of Bioeconomics* 201–225.

—— et al. "Benefits of Rebuilding Global Marine Fisheries Outweigh Costs" (2012) 7 *PloS One* e40542.

——, *Trade Policy Options for Sustainable Oceans and Fisheries* (International Centre for Trade and Sustainable Development, Geneva: 2016).

Swaigen, J, Koehl, A and Hatt, C, "Private Prosecutions Revisited: The Continuing Importance of Private Prosecutions in Protecting the Environment" (2013) 26 *Journal of Environmental Law and Practice* 31–57.

Swan, J, "Decision-Making in Regional Fisheries Bodies or Arrangements: The Evolving Role of RFBs and International Agreement on Decision-Making Processes" (*FAO Fisheries Circular* No. 995: 2004).

——, "Port State Measures to Combat IUU Fishing: International and Regional Developments" (2006) 7 *Sustainable Development Law and Policy* 38–43.

——, "Port State Measures – From Residual Port State Jurisdiction to Global Standards" (2016) 31 *International Journal of Marine and Coastal Law* 395–421.

Swartz, W et al., "The Spatial Expansion and Ecological Footprint of Fisheries (1950 to Present)" (2010) 5 *PLoS ONE* e15143.

Takei, Y, "Institutional Reactions to the Flag State that has Failed to Discharge Flag State Responsibilities" (2012) LIX *Netherlands International Law Review* 65–90.

——, "Assessing Flag State Performance in Legal Terms: Clarifications of the Margin of Discretion" (2013) 28 *International Journal of Marine and Coastal Law* 97–13.

——, *Filling Regulatory Gaps in High Seas Fisheries: Discrete High Seas Fish Stocks, Deep-Sea Fisheries and Vulnerable Marine Ecosystems* (Martinus Nijhoff, Leiden/Boston: 2013).

Tallis, H et al., "The Many Faces of Ecosystem-based Management: Making the Process Work Today in Real Places" (2010) 34 *Marine Policy* 340–348.

Tanaka, M, "Lessons from the Protracted MOX Plant Dispute: A Proposed Protocol on Marine Environmental Impact Assessment to the United Nations Convention on the Law of the Sea" (2003–2004) 25 *Michigan Journal of International Law* 337–428.

Tanaka, Y, "Costa Rica v. Nicaragua and Nicaragua v. Costa Rica: Some Reflections on the Obligation to Conduct an Environmental Impact Assessment" (2017) *Review of European, Comparative and International Environmental Law* 91–97.

Tarasofsky, RG, *Regional Fisheries Organizations and the World Trade Organization: Compatibility or Conflict?* (TRAFFIC International, Cambridge: 2003).

Techera, EJ, "Fishing, Finning and Tourism: Trends in Pacific Shark Conservation and Management" (2012) 27 *International Journal of Marine and Coastal Law* 597–621.

—— and Klein, N, "Fragmented Governance: Reconciling Legal Strategies for Shark Conservation and Management" (2011) 35 *Marine Policy* 73–78.

—— and Klein, N, *International Law of Sharks: Obstacles, Options and Opportunities* (Brill Nijhoff, Leiden/Boston: 2017).

Teh, LCL and Sumaila, UR, "Contribution of Marine Fisheries to Worldwide Employment" (2013) 14 *Fish and Fisheries* 77–88.

Telesetsky, A, "Laundering Fish in the Global Undercurrents: Illegal, Unreported and Unregulated Fishing and Transnational Organized Crime" (2015) 41 *Ecology Law Quarterly* 939–997.

Tetlock, PE, "Theory-Driven Reasoning about Plausible Pasts and Probable Futures in World Politics: Are We Prisoners of Our Preconceptions?" (1999) 43 *American Journal of Political Science* 335–336.

Teulings, J, "Peaceful Protests against Whaling on the High Seas – A Human Rights Based Approach" in CR Symons (ed.) *Selected Contemporary Issues in the Law of the Sea* (Martinus Nijhoff, Leiden/Boston: 2011) 221–250.

Theilen, JH, "What's in a Name? The Illegality of Illegal, Unreported and Unregulated Fishing" (2013) 28 *International Journal of Marine and Coastal Law* 533–550.

Thomson, A, "The Management of Redfish *(Sebastes Mentella)* in the North Atlantic: A Stock in Movement" in *Papers Presented at the Norway-FAO Expert Consultation on the Management of Shared Fish Stocks (FAO Fisheries Report* No. 695, Supplement: 2003)

Thompson, EP, *The Poverty of Theory: or an Orrery of Errors* (Merlin Press, London: 1995).

Thomson, J, *Mercenaries, Pirates, and Sovereigns* (Princeton University Press, Princeton: 1994).

Thrush, SF, Ellingsen, KE and Davis, K, "Implications of Fisheries Impacts to Seabed Biodiversity and Ecosystem-Based Management" (2016) 73 *ICES Journal of Marine Science* i44–i50.

Tolotti, MT et al., 'Banning is Not Enough: The Complexities of Oceanic Shark Management by Tuna Regional Fisheries Management Organizations' (2015) 4 *Global Ecology and Conservation* 1–7.

Tomz, M, *Reputation and International Cooperation: Sovereign Debt across Three Centuries* (Princeton University Press, Princeton: 2012).

Torres-Irineo, E et al., "Effects of Time-Area Closure on Tropical Tuna Purse-Seine Fleet Dynamics through Some Fishery Indicators" (2011) 24 *Aquatic Living Resources* 337–350.

Trathan, PN and Agnew, D, "Climate Change and the Antarctic Marine Ecosystem: An Essay on Management Implications" (2010) 22 *Antarctic Science* 387–398.

Treves, T, "The General Assembly and the Meeting of the States Parties in the Implementation of the LOS Convention" in AG Oude Elferink (ed.), *Stability and Change in the Law of the Sea: The Role of the LOS Convention* (Martinus Nijhoff, Leiden/Boston: 2005) 55–74.

Trouwborst, A, "Seabird Bycatch – Deathbed Conservation or a Precautionary and Holistic Approach" (2009) 11 *Journal of International Wildlife Law and Policy* 293–333.

Tsamenyi, M et al., *Promoting Sustainable Fisheries: The International Legal and Policy Framework to Combat Illegal, Unreported and Unregulated Fishing* (Martinus Nijhoff, Leiden: 2010).

Turley, C et al. "Future Biological Impacts of Ocean Acidification and their Socioeconomic-policy Implications" (2010) 4 *Current Opinion in Environmental Sustainability* 278–286.

Underdal, A, "International Cooperation: Transforming 'Needs' into 'Deeds'" (1987) 24 *Journal of Peace Research* 167–183.

——, "The Concept of Regime 'Effectiveness'" (1992) 27 *Cooperation and Conflict* 227–240.

——, "One Question, Two Answers" in A Underdal, EL Miles, S Andresen, J Wettestad, JB Skjærseth and EM Carlin (eds) *Environmental Regime Effectiveness: Confronting Theory with Evidence* (MIT Press, Cambridge, Massachusetts: 2002) 3–45.

Unger, RM, *False Necessity* (Verso, London: 2001).

van den Bossche, P and Zdouc, W, *The Law and Policy of the World Trade Organization* (Cambridge University Press, Cambridge: 2013).

van der Marel, ER, "An Opaque Blacklist: the Lack of Transparency in Identifying Non Cooperating Countries under the EU IUU Regulation" in L Martin, C Salonidis and C Hioueras (eds.), *Natural Resources and the Law of the Sea* (Juris, Huntington, NY: 2017) 237–256.

van Osch, S, "Save our Sharks: Using International Fisheries Law within Regional Fisheries Management Organizations to Improve Shark Conservation" (2012) 33 *Michigan Journal of International Law* 383–431.

Vatsov, M, "Changes in the Geographical Distribution of Shared Fish Stocks and the Mackerel War: Confronting the Cooperation Maze" (2016) Working Paper No. 13, Scottish Centre for International Law, Edinburgh.

Ventura, VAMF, "Tackling Illegal, Unregulated and Unreported Fishing: the ITLOS Advisory Opinion on Flag State Responsibility for IUU Fishing and the Principle of Due Diligence" (2015) 12 *Brazilian Journal of International Law* 50–67.

Venzke, I, "What If? Counterfactual (Hi)stories of International Law" *Amsterdam Law School Research Paper* No. 2016–66; available at https://papers.ssrn.com/sol3/papers.cfm?abstract_id=2881226.

Viñuales, JE (ed.), *The Rio Declaration on Environment and Development: A Commentary* (Oxford University Press, Oxford: 2015).

von Stein, J, "Do Treaties Constrain or Screen? Selection Bias and Treaty Compliance" (2005) 99 *American Political Science Review* 611–622.

——, "The Engines of Compliance" in JL Dunoff and MA Pollack (eds.), *Interdisciplinary Perspectives on International Law and International Relations. The State of the Art* (Cambridge University Press, New York: 2012) 477–501.

Voyer, M et al., "Methods of Social Assessment in Marine Protected Area Planning: Is Public Participation Enough?" (2012) 36 *Marine Policy* 432–439.

Vukas, B and Vidas, D, "Flags of Convenience and High Seas Fishing: The Emergence of a Legal Framework" in OS Stokke (ed.), *Governing High Seas Fisheries: The Interplay of Global and Regional Regimes* (Oxford University Press, Oxford: 2001) 53–90.

Walsh, MR et al., "Maladaptive Changes in Multiple Traits Caused by Fishing: Impediments to Population Recovery" (2006) 9 *Ecology Letters* 142–148.

Ward, P and Myers, RA, "Shifts in Open-Ocean Fish Communities Coinciding with the Commencement of Commercial Fishing" (2005) 86 *Ecology* 835–847.

Warner, R, "Assessing Environmental Impacts of Activities in Areas Beyond National Jurisdiction" in R Rayfuse (ed.), *Research Handbook on International Marine Environmental Law* (Edward Elgar, Cheltenham: 2015).

Warner-Kramer, D, "Control Begins at Home: Tackling Flags of Convenience and IUU Fishing" (2004) 34 *Golden Gate University Law Review* 497–530.

Watson, RA et al., "Global Marine Yield Halved as Fishing Intensity Redoubles" (2013) 14 *Fish and Fisheries* 493–503.

Webb, TJ, Vanden Berghe, E and O'Dor, R, "Biodiversity's Big Wet Secret: The Global Distribution of Marine Biological Records Reveals Chronic Under-Exploration of the Deep Pelagic Ocean" (2010) 5 *PloS One* e10223.

Weber, M, *Kritische Studien auf dem Gebiet kulturwissenschaftlicher Logik* (Archiv für Sozialwissenschaft und Sozialpolitik: 1904; reprinted as "Critical Studies in the Logic of the Cultural Sciences" in *The Methodology of the Social Sciences* (transl and ed, EA Shils and HA Finch; Free Press, New York: 1949)) 113–188

Webster, DG, *Adaptive Governance: The Dynamics of Atlantic Fisheries Management* (MIT Press, Boston: 2008).

——, *Beyond the Tragedy in Global Fisheries* (MIT Press, Boston: 2015).

Wenzel, L, *Framework for the National System of Marine Protected Areas of the United States of America* (NOAA, Silver Spring, MD: 2015).

Wigginton, JR, "Governing a Global Commons: Sharks in the High Seas" (2014) 25 *Villanova Environmental Law Journal* 431–463.

Willis, AJ, "The Ecosystem: An Evolving Concept Viewed Historically" (1997) 11 *Functional Ecology* 268–271.

Winter, A and Arkhipkin, A, "Environmental Impacts on Recruitment Migrations of Patagonian Longfin Squid (Doryteuthis gahi) in the Falkland Islands with Reference to Stock Assessment" (2015) 172 *Fisheries Research* 185–195.

Worm, B and Tittensor, DP, "Range Contraction in Large Pelagic Predators" (2011) 108 *PNAS* 11942–11947.

Wright, A and Doulman, DJ, "Driftnet Fishing in the South Pacific: From Controversy to Management" (1991) 15 *Marine Policy* 303–329.

Wright, G et al., "Advancing Marine Biodiversity Protection through Regional Fisheries Management: A Review of Bottom Fisheries Closures in Areas beyond National Jurisdiction" (2015) 61 *Marine Policy* 134–148.

Wright, G and Rochette, J, "Regional Management of Areas beyond National Jurisdiction in the Western Indian Ocean: State of Play and Possible Ways Forward" (2017) 32 *International Journal of Marine and Coastal Law* 765–796.

Yankov, A, "The Law of the Sea and Agenda 21: Marine Environmental Implications" in A Boyle and D Freestone (eds.), *International Law and Sustainable Development: Past Achievements and Future Challenges* (Oxford University Press, Oxford: 1999) 271–296.

Yotova, R, "The Principles of Due Diligence and Prevention in International Environmental Law" (2016) 75 *Cambridge Law Journal* 445–448.

Young, MA, *Trading Fish, Saving Fish: The Interaction between Regimes in International Law* (Cambridge University Press, Cambridge: 2011).

——, *Trade-Related Measures to Address Illegal, Unreported and Unregulated Fishing* (International Centre for Trade and Sustainable Development, Geneva: 2015).

Young, OR, *Compliance and Public Authority: A Theory with International Applications* (Johns Hopkins University Press, Baltimore, MD: 1979).

——, *The Effectiveness of International Environmental Regimes: Causal Connections and Behavioral Mechanisms* (MIT Press, Boston: 1999).

——, "Effectiveness of International Environmental Regimes: Existing Knowledge, Cutting-Edge Themes, and Research Strategies" (2011) 50 *PNAS* 19853–19860.

Index